Scientology Symbol
The S and double triangle.

There are two triangles, over which the S is imposed. The S simply stands for Scientology which is derived from the Latin *scio* (knowing in the fullest sense) and the Greek *logos* (study).

The lower triangle is the ARC triangle—its points being affinity, reality and communication. These are the three elements which combined give understanding.

The upper triangle is the KRC triangle. The points are K for knowledge, R for responsibility and C for control.

TO THE READER

Scientology is a religious philosophy containing pastoral counseling procedures intended to assist an individual to gain greater knowledge of self. The mission of the Church of Scientology is a simple one: to help the individual achieve greater self-confidence and personal integrity, thereby enabling him to really trust and respect himself and his fellow man. The attainment of the benefits and goals of Scientology requires each individual's dedicated participation as only through his own efforts can he achieve these.

This book is based on the religious literature and works of the Founder of Scientology, L. Ron Hubbard. It is presented to the reader as part of the record of his personal research into life, and the application of same by others, and should be construed only as a written report of such research and not as a statement of claims made by the Church or the Founder.

Scientology and its forerunner, Dianetics, as practiced by the Church, address only the "Thetan" (Spirit). Although the Church, as are all churches, is free to engage in spiritual healing, it does not, as its primary goal is increased *spiritual awareness* for all. For this reason, the Church does not wish to accept individuals who desire treatment of physical or mental illness but prefers to refer these to qualified specialists of other organizations who deal in these matters.

The Hubbard Electrometer is a religious artifact used in the Church confessional. It in itself does nothing, and is used by ministers only, to assist parishioners in locating areas of spiritual distress or travail.

We hope the reading of this book is only the first stage of a personal voyage of discovery into the new and vital world religion of Scientology.

This book belongs to_____

Date_____

THE BOARD OF DIRECTORS
Church of Scientology

YOU CAN ALWAYS WRITE TO RON

All mail addressed to me
shall be received by me.
I am always willing to help.
By my own creed,
a being is only as valuable
as he can serve others.

Any message addressed to me
and sent to the address
of the nearest Scientology Church
listed in this book,
will be forwarded to me directly.

What is Scientology?

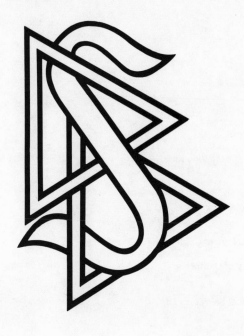

Based on the works of

L. Ron Hubbard
Founder of Dianetics and Scientology

Published in
the United States of America
by
CHURCH OF SCIENTOLOGY OF CALIFORNIA
Publications Organization United States
4833 Fountain Avenue
East Annex
Los Angeles, California 90029

and in all other countries
by
AOSH DK Publications Department A/S
Jernbanegade 6
1608 Copenhagen V
Denmark

*The Church of Scientology of
California is a nonprofit organization.*

*Scientology is an Applied Religious Philosophy.
Dianetics® and Scientology® are registered names.*

First Printing 1978
Second Printing 1979
Copyright © 1950, 1951. 1952,
1953, 1954, 1955, 1956, 1957,
1958, 1959, 1960, 1961, 1962,
1963, 1964, 1965, 1966, 1967,
1968, 1969, 1970, 1971, 1972,
1973, 1974, 1975, 1976, 1977, 1978
by L. Ron Hubbard
ALL RIGHTS RESERVED

*The E-Meter is not intended or effective for the diagnosis,
treatment or prevention of any disease.*

*A Dianetics Publication.
Dianetics is the trademark of L. Ron Hubbard
in respect of his published works.*

Compiled by staff of the Church of Scientology of California,
based on the works of L. Ron Hubbard,
and Archives of the Church of Scientology of California
Worldwide.

Assembled and edited by the LRH Personal Secretary Office,
LRH Personal Compilations Bureau.
LRH Personal Secretary: Alethiea C. Taylor
Editors: Pat Brice/Barbara de Celle
Assembly staff: Maggie Sibersky/Ernie Ryan

Associate Editors: Julia Watson/Harvey Haber

Color photography by L. Ron Hubbard
Cover paintings by Arthur Hubbard
Paintings: Arthur Hubbard/André Clavel
Designer: André Clavel

Library of Congress Catalog Card No. 78-71006
ISBN 0-88404-061-5 (United States of America)
ISBN 87-7336-028-7 (Denmark)

Printed in the United States by Kingsport Press, Inc.
Typeset by Freedmen's Organization, Los Angeles

Acknowledgments

We wish to thank the following staff of the Church of Scientology for their contributions to the writing of this volume:

David Gaiman
Charles Parselle
Sheila Gaiman
Kenneth Urquhart
Caroline Charbonneau
Peter Ginever
Carol Andrews
Alan Graham
Rory Boulding
Jeremy Heath
Larry Brennan
Jan Logan
Nancy Hochman
Harvey Haber

Don Arnow
Ann Roberts
Hans Diebschlag
Lin Field
Sheila Aldrich
David Mayo
Julie Gillespie
John Eastment
W. B. Robertson
Pat Marcus
Carleen Colon
John Mustard
Nancy Foster
Sheila Chaleff

We would also like to thank these staff members for their assistance in the composition of the book:

Nancy Reitze
Richard Sheehy
Diana Hubbard Horwich
Laurel Rock
Carol Titus
Laura Marlowe
Jeff Hawkins
Mary Ziff
Roy McMurray
Ken Delderfield
Edy Lundeen

Steve Boyd
Chip Deichman
Kathy Jarvis
Lynn Risi
Karl Whitcher
Harriet Foster
Raymond Peck
Vince Barbarick
Lynn Visk
Curt Hahn

The Editors

Important Note

One of the biggest barriers to learning a new subject is its nomenclature, meaning the set of terms used to describe the things it deals with. A subject must have accurate labels which have exact meanings before it can be understood and communicated.

If I were to describe parts of the body as "thingamabobs" and "whatsernames," we would all be in a confusion, so the accurate naming of something is a very important part of any field.

A student comes along and starts to study something and has a terrible time of it. Why? Because he or she not only has a lot of new principles and methods to learn, but a whole new language as well. Unless the student understands this, unless he or she realizes that one has to "know the words before one can sing the tune," he or she is not going to get very far in any field of study or endeavor.

Now I am going to give you an important datum:

The only reason a person gives up a study or becomes confused or unable to learn is because he or she has gone past a word that was not understood.

The confusion or inability to grasp or learn comes AFTER a word that the person did not have defined and understood.

Have you ever had the experience of coming to the end of a page and realizing you didn't know what you had read? Well, somewhere earlier on that page you went past a word that you had no definition for.

Here's an example. "It was found that when the crepuscule arrived the children were quieter and when it was not present, they were much livelier." You see what happens. You think you don't understand the whole idea, but the inability to understand came entirely from the one word you could not define, *crepuscule* which means twilight or darkness.

This datum about not going past an undefined word is the most important fact in the whole subject of study. Every subject you have taken up and abandoned had its words which you failed to get defined.

Therefore, in studying Dianetics and Scientology be very, very certain you never go past a word you do not fully understand. If the material becomes confusing or you can't seem to grasp it, there will be a word just earlier that you have not understood. Don't go any further, but go back to BEFORE you got into trouble, find the misunderstood word and get it defined.

Many of the Dianetics and Scientology terms in this book are defined in the text when they are used. Where the definitions were too lengthy, these have been included in a large glossary at the end of the text. You are urged to make good use of the glossary while reading this book.

Some non-Dianetics and Scientology terms used in the text, which cannot be found in a regular English language dictionary, have also been defined in the glossary.

You will encounter a number of abbreviations throughout the text. With the exception of those usually found in English language dictionaries, a complete list of these spelled out is provided, and appears just before the glossary.

It will not only be the new and unusual words that you will have to look up. Some commonly used words can be misdefined and so cause confusion. So don't depend on our glossary alone. Use a general English language dictionary as well for any nonspecialized word you do not understand when you are reading or studying.

Dianetics and Scientology words and their definitions are the gateway to a new look and understanding of life. Understanding them will help you live better.

Contents

Introduction

In envisioning this present work, the Founder, L. Ron Hubbard, has filled not one but *many* needs that were originally brought about by the questions of people concerning Scientology. The book has been designed on the premise that Scientologists and those interested in Scientology have only to ask and here in *What is Scientology?* will be the answers for them.

This long awaited book is a "first" in Scientology publications in that it contains much specialized knowledge and information not heretofore published.

It is in effect a data book, the entire motif of which is *giving information about Scientology.* Thus it is of enormous use and value to both Scientologists and public persons in that it holds pertinent information about Scientology history, its classifications of thought and technology and applications, and its wide and varied achievements. Readers now have recourse to this book whenever they want to know about a date or an event important to Scientology or the answer to a question somebody was asking.

For example, the chapters—"Date Chronology of Scientology," "Holidays of Scientology," "Victories of Scientology"—together make up a date/event calendar that is comprehensive and detailed, assembled for easy reference. Evident in the "Victories of Scientology" portion is a long long parade of wins for Scientology over attacks upon it—documented on all points, exactly as these events have happened.

Let us suppose that a new person asks about Scientology and its accomplishments. Nowhere is there such an extensive description of Scientology's accomplishments as is given in the first chapter of this book. It expresses fully the true religious and philosophical nature of Scientology and its value to life and societies.

As one progresses, he most certainly would need to be informed on the overall services of Scientology. A chapter consisting of a compilation of everything the Church of Scientology offers to its public is now available here, and included are realistic estimations of the availability of each service. In "The Effectiveness of Scientology" chapter can be found a roster of success stories written by persons who have received training and processing services —the very real rewards they have obtained from being effectively processed or after having successfully completed a course.

The Dianetics and Scientology organizations all over the world that deliver these services are listed in a separate chapter with addresses and telephone numbers so that any of them can be reached or contacted at any given time. It should be noted that addresses may change, and as new Scientology organizations come into being, they will be added in future editions.

The chapter "Statistics of Scientology" shows the steady and very often spectacular expansion that has occurred in Scientology, and gives considerable information to anybody wanting further statistical data on the subject.

At this moment there are many people in Scientology who are deciding what will be their next steps to take in training and processing. The chapters, "An Advised Course of Action for Training" and "An Advised Course of Action for Processing," are included to help them make correct choices, with references to a basic model training program and a realistic processing program based on the Hubbard Classification Gradation and Awareness Chart. Thus the student may continue on his way being trained on the proper gradient, or the preclear receiving auditing may be assured his route to Clear and beyond is accurately laid out.

A unique addition to Scientology literature is a complete catechism, Chapter 15. Put in question-and-answer format, this catechism focuses on specific areas that have been brought up by people's questions concerning Scientology's activities, attitudes and its viewpoints and beliefs on a great number of subjects.

In two chapters devoted to the social services of Scientology and the effectiveness of such programs, the reader has a full description of all the Scientology social services now operating, including data as to how to form units of the various types of social reform groups. As well, the dynamic wins of individuals participating in these groups have been included.

The popular and successful Volunteer Minister Program is described in Chapter 12 from its inception several years ago with the publication of the best-selling *Volunteer Minister's Handbook* to the present. In this period thousands of people have helped themselves and their fellow man on a volunteer basis after having been trained to provide fundamental counseling to the public by the use of Scientology technology.

The development of Scientology's advanced ethics system and the Creeds and Codes of Scientology which Scientologists abide by in their work is traced in detail in Chapters 7 and 14, respectively.

The most extensive list of all Scientology books ever published, tape recordings ever made and the variety of Scientology insignia are tabulated in the book's final chapter. There exist enormous amounts of material which are available on the subject of Scientology.

We have provided over one hundred brilliant color photographs many of which were taken by L. Ron Hubbard, and 36 full-color paintings. These remarkable illustrations which begin on the following pages are in three parts: 1) an historical progression of Man's spiritual, philosophical and scientific searchings through time, 2) the highlights of the Founder's life and 3) pictorial story examples showing the accomplishments of Scientology technology when applied to everyday life situations.

What is Scientology? is a very valuable and needed book. We think you will agree.

The Editors

What is Scientology?

Illustrations

Throughout his long history, Man has sought wisdom and knowledge. He has tried to understand himself and the world around him so that he could live a better life. "Who am I?", "Why am I here?" are questions which have plagued Man since the beginning of time.

Since precious little could be learned in one life span, Man has always tried to pass on what wisdom he had to those who came after him, hoping that someday someone would come up with some answers to the myriad problems of mankind.

Many, many attempts have been made to fathom the mysteries of life and understand the world and one's fellow man. One such attempt at understanding was the Persian religion of Zoroastrianism, which sought to define the concepts of "good" and "evil".

In Persia, as in much of the ancient world, a study of the earth and the heavens went hand in hand with a study of Man and the spirit. Religious men were the men of learning, and were the "scientists" of their day. They studied the movements of the stars and tried to predict their movements.

With the conquest of Persia by Alexander's troops, however, Zoroastrianism was heavily suppressed, and the bulk of the scriptures burned. While they might have been able to predict the movements of stars, Man still had no knowledge with which to predict the movements of his fellow man, or avoid wars, intolerance and suppression.

The Egyptians made great strides in what we would call the "physical sciences". They learned some physiology and surgery, developed a practical system of geometry and a system of mathematics. They studied the stars, named the constellations and even developed a calendar.

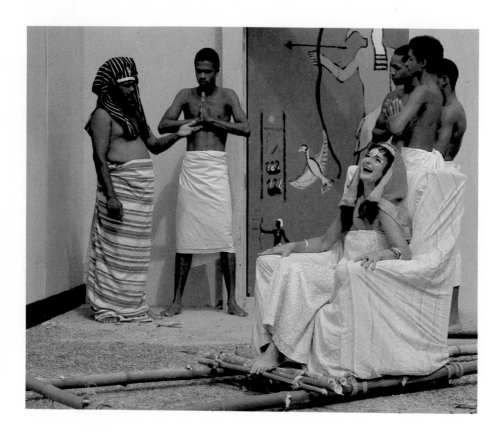

Yet despite all their developments in the physical sciences, the civilization which thrived in Egypt crumbled and weakened. After a painful 1000-year decline, it became too feeble and too corrupted to resist the Roman centurions. Again, real wisdom was lacking. They did not know enough about themselves and their fellow man to solve the problems which beset them.

The religion of Taoism began with a legendary monk named Lao Tsu (which literally means "Old Philosopher"). According to the Chinese historian Ssu-ma Ch'ien, Lao Tsu decided to leave the city after seeing the decay of the dynasty. But the gatekeeper beseeched him to write a book before he left.

The book thus produced was the *Tao Te Ching*, which became the basis for the religion of Taoism. Taoism held out the hope for Man that there might be a higher state that Man could aspire to; a state where he could be happier, could understand himself better and could have greater ability. But paradoxically, although *Tao* literally means "The Way", Taoism did not provide a workable way to reach a higher state of existence.

One of the brightest chapters in Man's long search for wisdom was the work of Siddhartha Gautama, who became known as the Buddha. He was the founder of the world's first international religion, Buddhism, which brought civilization to three-quarters of Asia.

He also gave to Man the hope of a higher spiritual state, which he called *Bodhi*. Unfortunately, he left no technology behind him for people to attain a higher state.

The Greeks continued the search for knowledge, about the world *and* the nature of Man. When Socrates heard that the Delphic Oracle had proclaimed him "the wisest man in the world", he realized that he was wise only in that he knew that he did not know. He tried to get his followers to cast aside their preconceptions about the world and really observe and study things around them.

Socrates held that neither he nor anyone else had the right to force opinions on others. Rather, he sought to lead his followers to new opinions through systematic questioning. He felt that through increased understanding, Man would become happier and more tolerant.

Yet there were those who did not want the established beliefs questioned by the young people or by anyone. In 399 B.C., Socrates was tried and found guilty of "denying the Gods" and "corrupting the young". Although urged by his followers to escape and save his skin, Socrates refused to compromise the stand he had taken against tyranny and suppression, and drank the cup of hemlock, a bitter poison, instead.

Two thousand years ago, a new beacon of hope was brought to Man by Jesus of Nazareth. He taught that this life was not all that there was, that Man was more than just his body and would continue to exist after death. This hope, that there was a way out of the sufferings and problems of mankind, brought civilization to Europe.

But there are always those who do not want to see Man become enlightened and more able. The Roman authorities feared Christ because they thought his teachings would undermine their power and authority.

The hope that Christ brought to Man did not die, however, despite what the Roman authorities may have hoped. On the contrary, his death became a symbol to Man of the triumph of the spirit over death itself.

At about the same time that Christ was teaching in the Middle East, the first Buddhist monks were arriving in China and spreading the word of Buddha. They met with resistance from the Taoists, and often suppression by the state.

In the 6th century, Mohammed began to spread his message in the city of Mecca. He taught that spiritual goals are more important than material goals, and that Man should look to his own salvation. But his message was seen as a threat to the revenues which were pouring into Mecca — then the center of Arabian Polytheism. He was driven out of the city, thus beginning the *Hegira*, or flight, which marks the beginning of the Moslem calendar.

But within eight years, he returned and took Mecca by force, and within 100 years, his "holy war" reached from Spain to the borders of China.

The subsequent wars which embroiled Europe for hundreds of years "in the name of religion" were a severe drain on the economy. Heavy taxation brought protest, and the first glimmerings of democracy. In 1216, the barons of England forced King John to sign the Magna Carta, the first document which limited the absolute power of a monarch and forced him to recognize the rights of others.

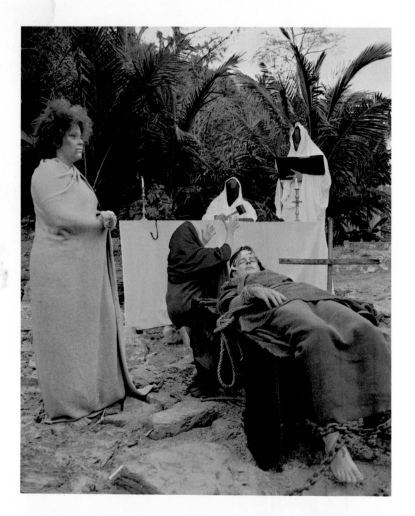

In the 13th century, the church itself became the vehicle for those who would suppress knowledge and wisdom. Under the Inquisition, anyone holding beliefs or ideas different from those of the church could be brought to trial and tortured until they denied their "heretical beliefs."

The Inquisition seized anyone who was thought to be "strange" or "different" and labelled them "heretic" or even "witch". Death at the stake awaited anyone who insisted on questioning the established beliefs.

But even the extremes of the Inquisition could not stop Man's search for knowledge. Leonardo da Vinci enthusiastically studied many different subjects in order to understand and deal with the world around him. As well as being one of the most brilliant artists of the Renaissance, he was an inventor, engineer, geologist, astronomer and botanist. But even these studies had to be undertaken with discretion, as the watchful eye of the Inquisition was ever-present. Leonardo, in fact, wrote his notes out so that they could only be read in a mirror.

Many scholars did run afoul of the Inquisition. Galileo, for one, was arrested after he wrote a paper publicly supporting the theory of Copernicus: that the earth revolved around the sun. This was contrary to church doctrine and was therefore heresy. Thus was real knowledge suppressed.

Galileo was sentenced to an indefinite prison term for his heresy. When he publicly denied that there was any truth to the Copernican theory, he was allowed to return to his villa, where he spent the rest of his life under the watchful eye of the Inquisition.

With the opening of the New World for settlers, Man dreamed of a new freedom from the suppression and intolerance of the church and state. Perhaps Jefferson best summed up this dream when he wrote, in the Declaration of Independence, ". . . that all men are created equal, that they are endowed by their Creator with certain inalienable rights, that among these are Life, Liberty and the pursuit of Happiness."

Man *does* have a right to his own happiness. He does have the right to search for knowledge and understanding which he can use to live better and get along better with his fellows.

But suppression of wisdom did not end with the Inquisition. Even today, in the 20th century, new ideas are fought by totalitarian states, and wisdom and learning are suppressed by those who would keep Man ignorant. Even in our own time we have seen book burnings.

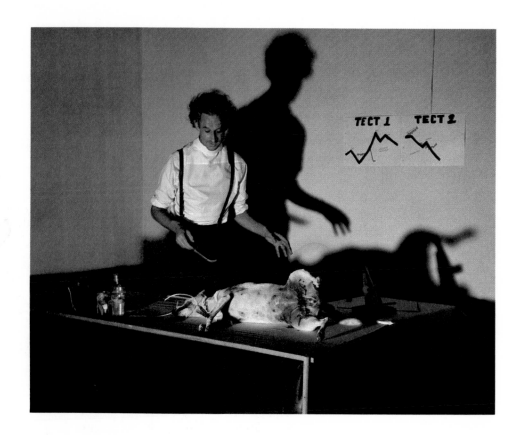

Even the search for knowledge about Man and his behavior can be perverted to serve the cause of suppression. When Ivan Petrovich Pavlov, a Russian veterinarian, demonstrated that he could train dogs to slaver on command, the dictator Stalin saw in this a possible way to control the thoughts and actions of men. Thus Russian psychology was born and subsidized.

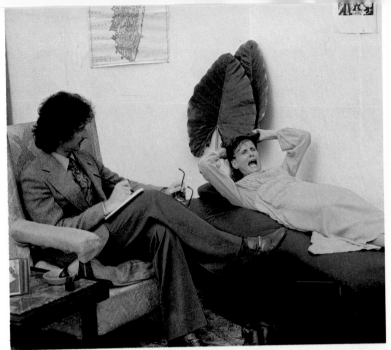

Sigmund Freud felt that all of Man's troubles came about because he was sexually inhibited. While this may have seemed true in the straight-laced Victorian era, we know now that Freud failed to provide a workable way for Man to better his condition.

Psychology and psychiatry have not provided an answer to the problems which Man has. Today, despite the efforts of these subjects, we have increasing violence and crime in the world.

The physical sciences, meanwhile, have left the humanities far behind. Einstein's theories of matter and energy resulted in the development of weapons which can destroy everyone on earth.

Yet Man has not had workable knowledge about *himself* and his fellows that he could *use* to live better, to be happier, to be more tolerant of his fellows, to really understand himself and the world around him.

Now, such a technology does exist. Man's hope for a better life, and his long search for knowledge, has finally culminated in a workable technology: SCIENTOLOGY.

Before Ron was 10 years old, he had become thoroughly educated both in schools as well as by his mother.

So it was that by the time he was 12 years old, L. Ron Hubbard had already read a large number of the world's greatest classics. He had a great interest in history and mankind's delvings into causes and laws underlying the nature of things.

In the 1920s Ron studied the work of Sigmund Freud. His teacher was Commander Thompson of the United States Navy Medical Corps who had studied under Freud in Vienna.

But Freud's theories to release people from human problems did not answer for Ron the questions he had.

Ron sought to find knowledge and understanding that people themselves could use to handle their own problems.

In 1925 Ron went to the Far East to find out if there was wisdom there. He journeyed throughout Asia exploring its cities and remote villages, getting to know the peoples' customs and beliefs.

He travelled up and down the China coast several times in his teens. He ventured from Ching Wong Tow to Hong Kong and inland to Peking and Manchuria. In Peking Ron met old Mayo, last of the line of magicians of Kublai Khan.

Deep in the hills of western China, Ron visited the lamaseries. There he conversed with monks and made friends with them and the people.

In the isolation of the high hills of Tibet, even native bandits responded to Ron's honest interest in them and were willing to share with him what understanding of life they had.

On the other side of the world in the South Pacific Islands, Ron continued his search into the beliefs of various cultures and the nature of things in general. He came to respect a wide number of peoples and their ways of living.

At one point Ron explored a "haunted" cave and revealed that the source of some ghostly rumblings was actually an underground river. This discovery relieved the natives who for some time had been frightened by the unknown river's sounds.

Ron's quest took him deep into jungles where he located an ancient burial ground in Polynesia, a place steeped in the tradition of heroic warriors and kings. Though his native friends were fearful for him, Ron explored the sacred area — his initiative based on doing all he could to know more.

With the death of his grandfather, the Hubbard family returned to the United States and, after intense study at Swavely Preparatory School in Manassas, Virginia and at Woodward Preparatory School in Washington, D.C., Ron enrolled at the George Washington Engineering School in the fall of 1930.

At George Washington University, Ron took one of the first nuclear physics courses ever taught in the United States.

With the knowledge of many peoples acquired by his world travels and explorations, Ron realized that if Man were to handle the atom sanely for optimum survival, he would first have to learn to handle himself.

While still at the University, Ron became aware there was more to life than science had dreamed of. He knew that neither the spiritualistic East nor the materialistic West had full understanding of the nature of life and the condition of Man. Ron made it a part of his life's work to synthesize and test extant knowledge from the ancients onward for what was observable, workable and rewarding to Man when applied to his life and problems.

As a student, barely 20 years old, Ron supported himself by writing. Within a few more years, he had established himself as an essayist, technical article writer in sports and aviation magazines, as well as becoming a professional photographer.

Over fifteen million words written by Ron have been published and are in print.

Beliefs as foreign to most as voodoo, practiced with fetishes and communication by trance with ancestors and deities, were examined by Ron in the West Indies.

This was yet another field where Ron established communication firsthand with hitherto unfamiliar cultures and surroundings.

Another location covered by Ron's researches was the pioneer territory of Alaska. He studied and understood the ways of the Tlingit Indians who talked to him of the thunderbird. According to their mythology this huge bird produced thunder by flapping its wings and lightning by opening and closing its eyes.

Out of the tremendous body of data he had acquired, he organized and honed many facts. Ron wrote later: "Workability rather than idealism was consulted."

The breakthrough came when he found that the basic single thrust of life throughout history was that Man, in common with all species, was striving to *survive* and that "survival might be defined as an impulse to persist through time, in space, as matter and energy" and that "by survival is meant everything necessary to survival including honor and morals and other things which make life bearable."

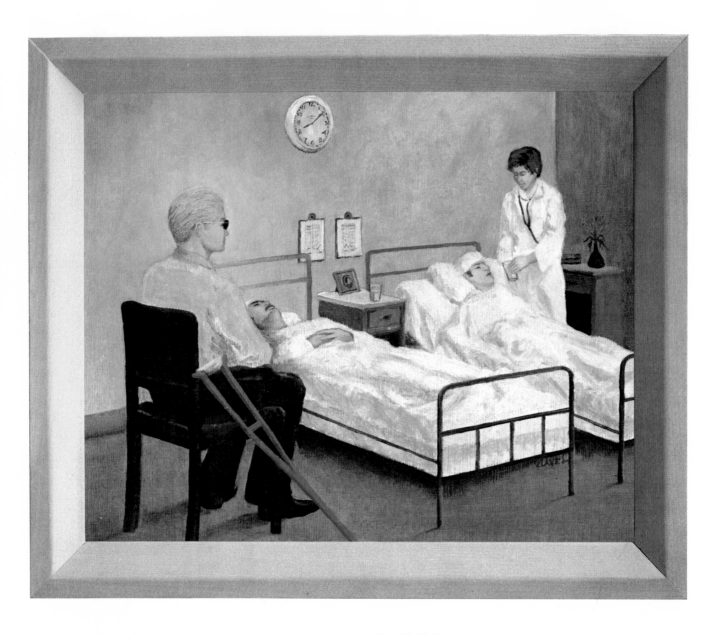

In 1941 Ron was ordered to the Philippines (which he had known as a youngster) at the outbreak of World War II.

He survived the early war in the South Pacific. He saw enough of war at first hand to be sickened by it. In 1944, crippled and blinded he found himself in Oak Knoll Naval Hospital. Using the extensive education in the field of the human mind that he had received earlier from Commander Thompson, Ron developed techniques that would help him overcome his injuries and regain his abilities.

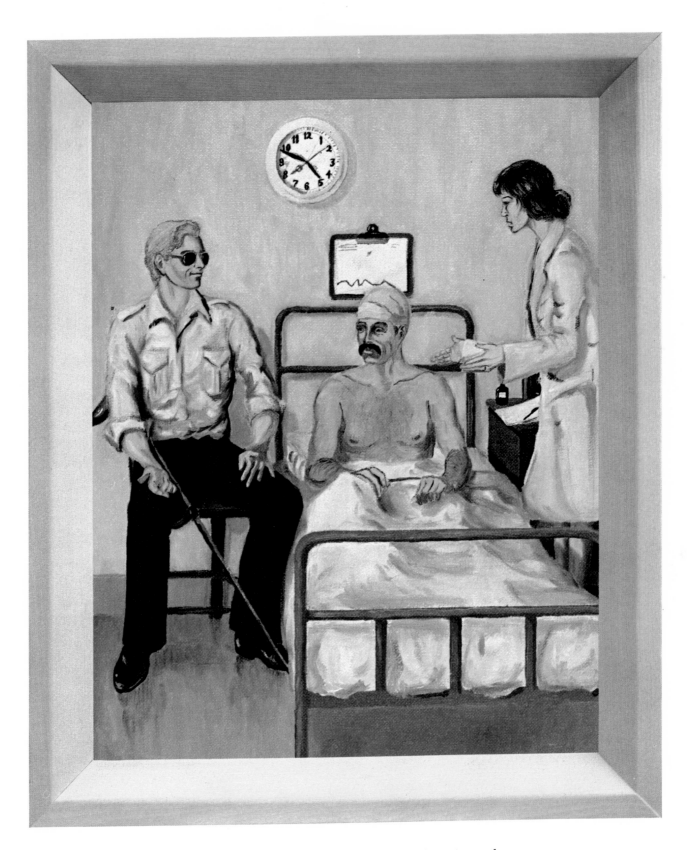

Ron concluded that the results he was obtaining could help others toward greater ability and happiness. During this period some of the basic tenets of Dianetics and Scientology were first formulated.

He made the vital discovery that you can always get function or thought to monitor structure; in other words, the mind can change the body but the body only slightly alters the mind.

Ron now knew that if Man were to handle his physical and emotional problems, the mind was the area to address.

By 1947 he recovered fully, a fact that shook the medical and psychiatric officers of the United States Navy's Retiring Board. Their fixed ideas and practices had received a hard blow.

In 1948 Ron wrote *Dianetics: The Original Thesis,* his first formal report of his discoveries about the mind and life.

This book presented data and case histories of successes achieved through addressing the mind to improve the livingness of a person. Such psychosomatic ills as hypertension, combat fatigue, apathy, rage, myopic astigmatism and chronic skin rash had already been handled in these cases.

A grass roots interest in Dianetics spread. Letters began to pour in from many countries asking for clarifications and advice. Answering them was becoming a full-time occupation.

What was needed was a complete popular text on the subject which would answer all questions.

In 1950 Ron wrote *Dianetics: The Modern Science of Mental Health* which defined the anatomy of the mind and a technology called auditing that was making people feel healthier and happier.

Providing a truly workable school of the mind which would predictably improve the human condition, *Dianetics: The Modern Science of Mental Health* leapt to the top of the New York Times best-seller list and just stayed there.

Almost immediately thousands of readers began to apply the data from the book and Dianetic groups sprang up across the country.

With *Dianetics: The Modern Science of Mental Health* translated into many foreign languages and an international best seller, the route was mapped for others to travel and find for themselves happiness and regained abilities.

Few books in modern times have had the outstanding success that *Dianetics: The Modern Science of Mental Health* enjoys. After becoming a best seller in 1950 and continuing to sell widely through the years, today — 28 years later — it is again a Number One best seller!

But Ron's work did not end in 1950. He found additionally that there was something that "animated" the mind which he described as "the personality and beingness which actually *is* the individual." Thus was Scientology born.

The word Scientology (the science of knowing how to know to the fullest extent) is derived from the Latin *scio*, know, and the Greek *logos*, the word, or outward form by which the inward thought is expressed and made known.

The library of Dianetics and Scientology data has grown by many volumes over the past quarter of a century until today it constitutes towers of knowledge.

Ron has explained Scientology as "an organization of the pertinencies (the quality of being to the point) which are mutually held true by all men in all times, and the development of technologies which demonstrate the existence of new phenomena not hitherto known, which are useful in creating states of beingness considered more desirable by Man."

Working from the basic dynamic, Survive, Ron established the eight prime motivations called the dynamics, which are held in common by all men. From the first dynamic, urge toward existence as one's self, they go onward to procreation, the family, the rearing of children; groups, including nations and races; Mankind; all life forms whether animal or vegetable; the physical universe; the thought dynamic; and lastly the eighth, infinity or God dynamic.

Addressing each of these areas of life broadly and successfully, Ron's worthwhile accomplishments have brought him many honors and awards from high officials of governments and groups around the world.

With the help of a staff of secretaries to handle his mail, Ron finds time to maintain a correspondence with thousands, to answer questions, to help people everywhere accomplish their goals.

Ron's Standing Order No. 1 is: "All mail addressed to me shall be received by me. I am always willing to help. By my own creed, a being is only as valuable as he can serve others."

You can always write to Ron.

Scientologists are known for their goodwill. They have the ability to help themselves and others handle life and gain a positive outlook toward the future.

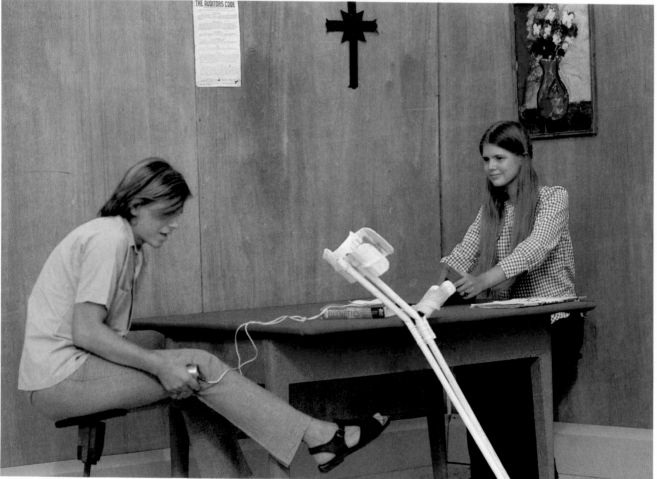

Dianetics and Scientology are not used to set a bone or shut off a pumping artery or stitch a gash. However, a professional auditor, working calmly with an injured or ill person, can assist him to recover faster and to regain good morale.

Neither the auditor nor the E-Meter can cure or heal anything — but with their assistance, an individual learns how to help himself get back his personal strength.

There are thousands of case histories of people who have remarkably gained better physical condition and energetic livingness through Dianetics and Scientology. With these proven technologies the individual learns how to reduce his difficulties.

The stress of today's world can take away one's enjoyment of life and peace of mind.

With Dianetics and Scientology auditing you'll become more able through understanding yourself and your environment.

The E-Meter is simply an extremely sensitive instrument that registers areas of difficulty and areas of enjoyment when your attention scans across these thoughts. The auditor uses the E-Meter as a guide in applying the technology to another.

The preclear soon realizes that life can be better and happier.

If one is to succeed in business and accomplish one's personal goals, calmness and efficiency are vital. These are qualities people actually attain through Dianetics and Scientology.

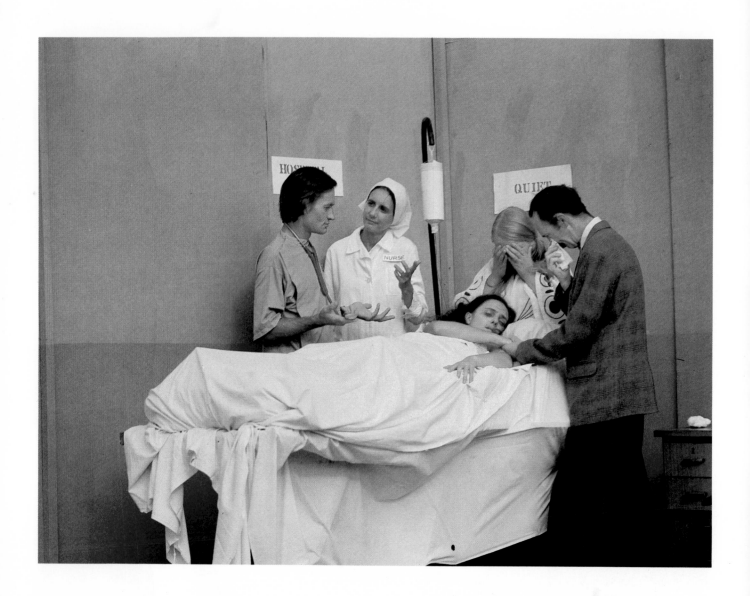

At times people become ill and medical therapy is unable to better their physical condition. The medical profession has known of the existence of psychosomatic illnesses for years but has no workable technology to handle them.

"Psycho" refers to mind and "somatic" comes from the word *soma* which means body. Thus psychosomatic illnesses are those caused by the effect of the mind on the body. They manifest themselves on the body as sporadic or chronic discomfort and pain.

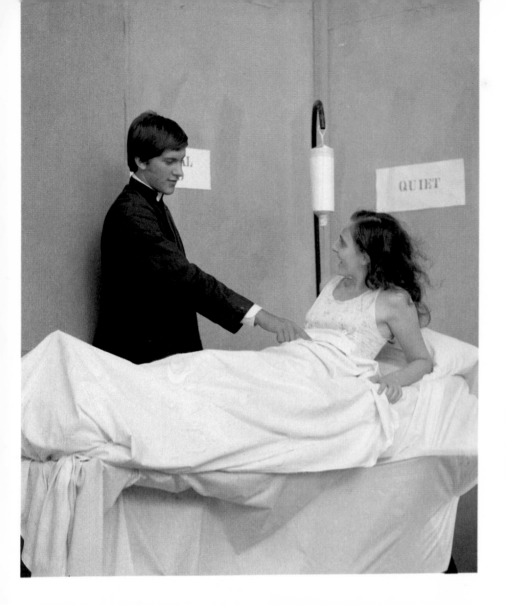

A skilled Scientologist can help a person achieve release from pain. Even a person's will to live can be recovered by a simple action called a Touch Assist — which assists the person to get into better communication with his body.

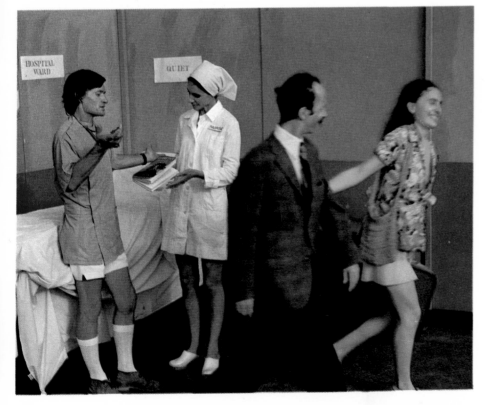

Thorough and complete assists improve the *rate of healing* so that the person returns to normal faster.

An assist is not engaging in healing. What it is doing is assisting the individual to heal himself or be healed by another agency by removing his reasons for precipitating, and prolonging his condition and lessening his predisposition to further injure himself or remain in an intolerable condition. This is entirely outside the field of 'healing' as envisioned by the medical doctor.

Ron describes a suppressive person as one with certain behavior characteristics who suppresses other people in his vicinity. When such a person exists in an area, a trained Scientologist applies special technology used in detecting and handling him so as to protect himself and others from harm.

Being informed on the subject of suppressive persons (the antisocial personality), the Scientologist is able to share his data with the uninformed. *Introduction to Scientology Ethics* gives readers a rundown on the attributes of both social and antisocial personalities.

Once they are detected suppressive personalities can be handled, thereby creating a safer atmosphere in which to live and work. Ron notes: "As there are 80 per cent of us trying to get along and only 20 per cent trying to prevent us, our lives would be much easier to live were we well informed as to the exact manifestations of such a personality."

Those who can't handle life self-confidently with communication will resort to handling it with force or violence. Communication is the interchange of ideas between people and is the basis of harmonious relations with others.

Of communication, Ron says: "Communication is not only the modus operandi, it is the heart of life."

Under the guidance of a trained Scientologist, it is possible to attain comfortable communication. In doing simple but very precise communication drills or Training Routines (TRs), the person gains better trust of himself and others.

Often the ability to communicate better motivates a person to expand his activities. He finds he makes new friends easily and has a more relaxed response to life.

Drugs essentially are poisons. The degree they are taken determines the effect.
A certain amount acts as a sedative and control factor. A larger amount acts
as a poison and can kill one dead.

With good confront and tolerance of people, skilled Scientologists have a successful record of helping drug users. Using Dianetics' and Scientology's abundance of resources such as Touch Assists, drills and auditing, people can be freed from the harmful effects of drugs, thus becoming more themselves and interested in optimum survival.

It is possible to come off drugs without the dreaded "withdrawal symptoms" — the prospect of which often makes an addict remain on drugs. Auditing in fact is the only successful means ever developed for handling drug damage.

This is one of the major breakthroughs made by Dianetics and Scientology. Putting sanity into handling the drug problem is of prime importance to this, and future generations.

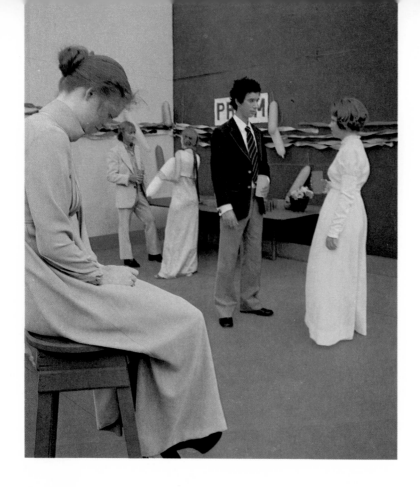

Social activities make some persons nervous, shy and insecure.

Participation in groups or harmonious relations with others may appear difficult.

With auditing a person experiences pleasure as he gets to know himself better and finds an increased understanding of life. Self-confidence and greater happiness are restored to him.

Scientology helps you to be more *yourself* in social situations, calm and self-confident.

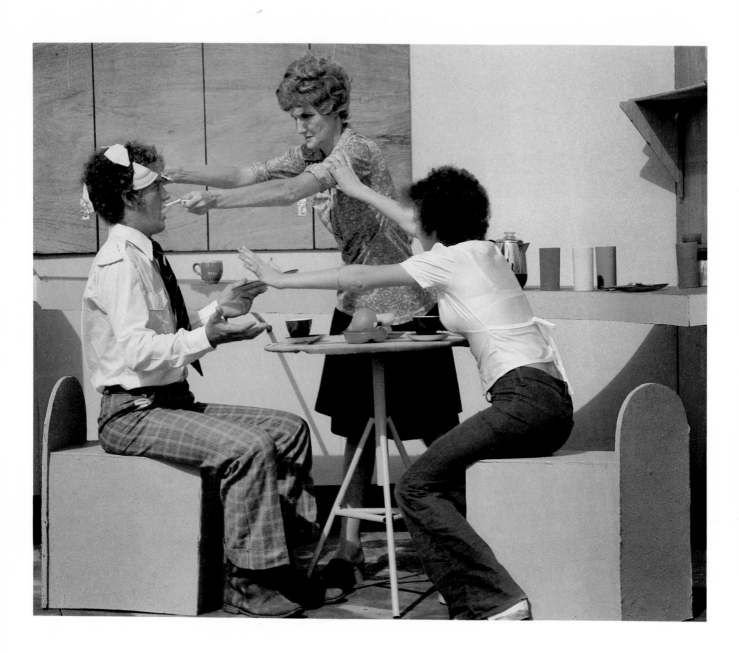

Have you ever experienced or known of insane situations in life similar to this one?

Auditing — the technical side of Scientology and Dianetics — is easy to learn. Gradiently, one becomes skilled in using many processes which, when applied directly to another person, produce changes whereby a new way of life can be created, or an old way of life can be understood and better endured or altered.

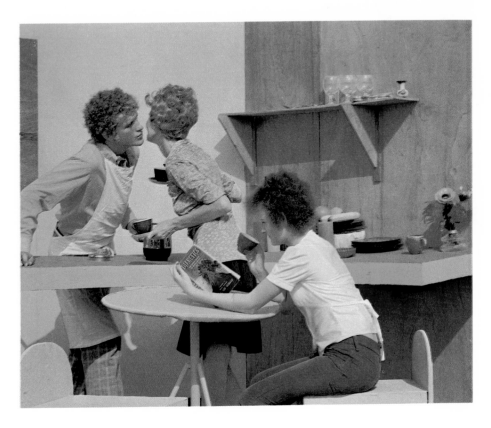

A renewed sense of individual worth restores sanity, tolerance of each other and love to the family.

Another area where a person's sense of personal worth can diminish is as he or she grows older. There can be a loss of self-confidence — perhaps even a lack of purposefulness in an older person's life.

Knowledge at whatever age brightens up the individual as he goes about enjoying the fruits of his discoveries and sharing them with others.

If one really wants to know more about himself, he should study *Dianetics: The Modern Science of Mental Health* written by Ron in 1950 and still today, 28 years later, a Number One best seller!

Nothing validates the success of Dianetics more than the continuing and increasing sales of this book which *Publisher's Weekly* recently called "perhaps the best-selling non-Christian book of all time in the West."

By applying Dianetics' and Scientology's proven technologies, the person becomes more versatile and creative. Knowledge of himself is available to the beginner through the reading of such a widely acclaimed and lasting book as *Dianetics: The Modern Science of Mental Health.*

Groups exist which seek to grab absolute socio-economic power and control of our society through war. The engineering of such disasters is destructive to Man's strong desire for peace and to his very life.

Dianetics and Scientology open new possibilities for people to learn to resolve problems other than by killing each other.

In our society we seek knowledge of what would bring peace, first among which is knowing ourselves and others and a study of Man's basic intentions which are good. In an early essay, Ron wrote: "Scientology and Scientologists are not revolutionaries. They are evolutionaries. They do not stand for overthrow. They stand for the improvement of what we have."

Dianetics and Scientology offer ways for self-improvement for individuals from all walks of life. Broad application of these technologies, extended throughout society, would lead from individuals to groups and ultimately would influence and increase mankind's potential.

Dianetics and Scientology believe that all men of whatever race, color or creed were created with equal rights. For all there can be a happier future of which Ron writes: "The better side of life or persons or dreams or hopes *is* attainable." Through training and auditing, the individual can measure his own progress by increased ability to handle himself and his environment."

It happens that people find they don't trust those they work with.

These feelings of mistrust can be carried over to other areas of life and cause interpersonal upsets.

A way to re-establish harmonious relations with others is available through knowing Scientology principles and technology. The course rooms as well as the auditing rooms of Scientology organizations across the planet are filled with many people seeking and achieving self-improvement.

Having successfully completed some Scientology basic training, the individual applies what he has learned about harmonious relationships with others and salvages his marriage. "A marriage," Ron reminds us, "is something you have to postulate into existence and keep created, and when you stop working at it it will cease."

Knowing *how* to bring harmony to personal relationships influences all areas of life for the better. One of the rewards can be a greater enjoyment of your work and your fellow workers.

Comfortable communication is one of the gains made with Scientology training. It is an attribute that establishes good working morale in the group.

NO. BUILDINGS BUILT

PETER H. MORLEY
ARCHITECT

Scientology offers ways to handle problems in all aspects of life — business as well as personal ones. Initiative and alertness are increased with training, enabling the individual to steadily increase his production and thus realize greater rewards.

Upsets can ruin one's own happiness and make harmonious relations with other people impossible.

From Dianetics and Scientology training you acquire auditing skills. With the help of the E-Meter, you address the troubled person with specific procedures that are designed to relieve stress in the areas of upset and difficulty.

People recognize quickly that self-improvement has taken place in a person who has had Dianetics and Scientology auditing. The person who has been helped by auditing will, in turn, try to help others. He *knows* the technology works.

One of the basic Scientology courses is the Communication Course in which students practice TRs (Training Routines). An objective of TRs is the person increasing his ability to confront which Ron explains as "an action of being able to face. If one cannot, if he avoids, then he is not aware. And aware means 'marked by realization, perception and knowledge'."

When family problems are present due to the behavior of an alcoholic member, they can be handled using Scientology knowledge of human affairs. It is needless and harmful to *not* have the know-how to resolve familial upsets with sanity and goodwill.

A trained Scientologist has raised his ability to confront and handle problems, inside or outside the family, with self-confidence. Under his guidance, love and understanding can replace confusion and conflict.

The distressed person can be audited with the proven technology of Scientology and Dianetics, reducing the area of confusion which has been driving him into undesireable, often insane actions.

Thousands of alcoholics have thrown away the bottles upon completion of their auditing programs. Gradiently they have attained freedom from mental torment or periods of irrational or insane conduct that have plagued them in the past.

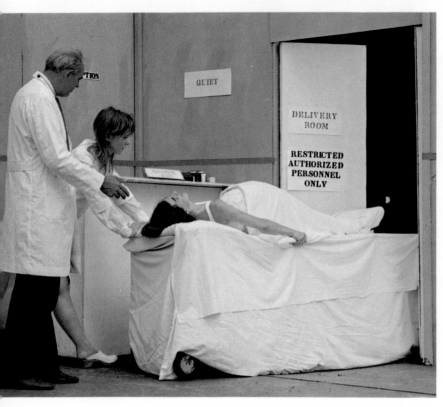

To most people, having a child brings joy . . .

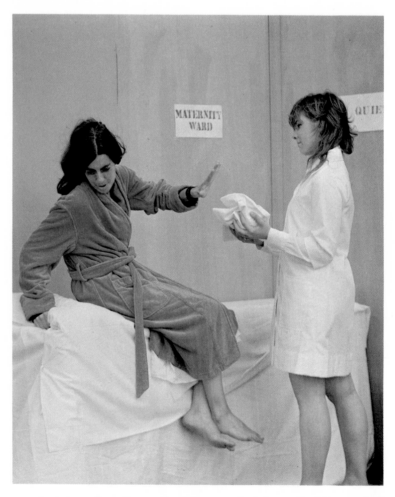

. . . but to a few the postpartum period (meaning the period following childbirth) is unhappy.

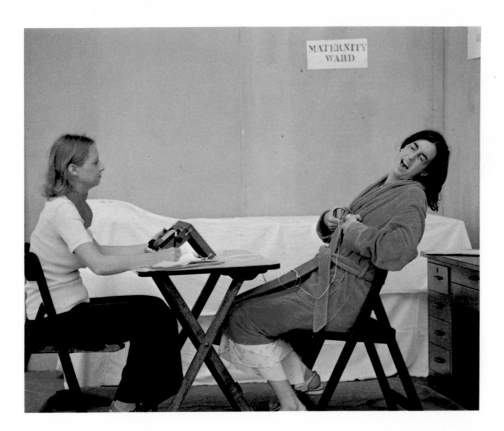

To handle postpartum cases of this nature, the auditor has the mother go over the circumstances of the birth. This frees her from confusions and hostilities by locating the source of these feelings. Disagreements or unhappiness connected to the event vanish and the mother experiences relief.

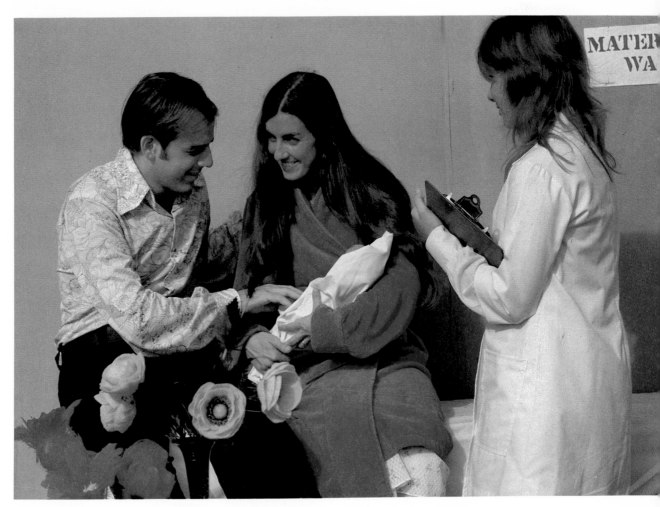

Besides increased love in the family, there is an additional gain made from postpartum auditing which is a positive outlook toward the future.

Concerning the family, Ron writes: "An adult has certain rights around children which the children and modern adults rather tend to ignore. The main consideration in raising children is the problem of training them without breaking them. It is possible to reform a child's attitude toward existence. Scientology increases the beingness and potentialities of beingness of the child in present time in order to secure the capabilities of the child in the future."

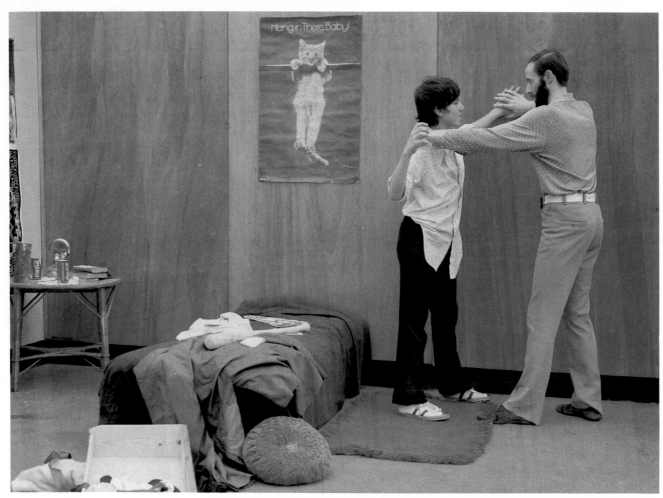

A parent who has basic Scientology training can do simple Objective Processes (dealing with body motions, observing and touching objects) with his son or daughter. These bring the person more into present time, put him into better communication with people and the environment and increase his ability to *have* things for himself.

Ron has said: "The *scarce* commodity in the world today is tolerance." It is one of a trained Scientologist's greatest assets. With tolerance and a knowledge of fundamental truths of life, he can assist many people.

The use of Dianetics and Scientology data in the home creates a safe environment for children to grow and can be part of a good education that they will apply throughout life.

It is easy to put these processes to work in groups, small and large. The amount of help an individual can deliver with these processes is priceless. As Ron has said of the trained person: "He is giving men back to themselves, and there is no greater gift."

When personal problems are handled, an individual of any age experiences a renewed sense of personal worth. He feels more self-confident and enjoys participating in group and social activities.

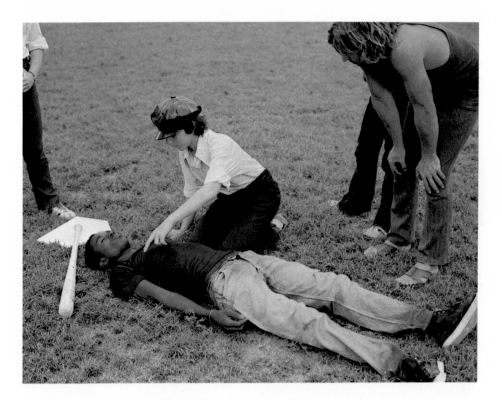

How to give a Touch Assist to an injured person is easily acquired in studying Scientology basics. Touch Assists result in faster recoveries from injuries, operations and emotional shocks.

Both parties win with Scientology. The person who received help achieves better physical condition rapidly. The one who delivered the service experiences a feeling of pride — from a simple Touch Assist that can be given on the spot anywhere.

Today we have more police administration and more sophisticated law enforcement weapons than ever before, yet the world's crime rates continue to rise.

In the interest of protection and security, easily learned Scientology basics (such as the ability to confront and handle situations quickly) can make a difference in the safety of lives. In many cases a Scientologist can prevent criminal actions from taking place.

"If one can confront," Ron says, "he can be aware. If he is aware he can perceive and act."

From his research work on the nature of Man, Ron found: "Man is basically good but can act badly."

That there is a minority percentage in society known to have antisocial tendencies is recognized and dealt with in Scientology. Training enables one to handle problems caused by such personalities. Willingness and skill in communicating with anyone, even those hostile to you can prove beneficial indeed.

A person's reaction to life and the environment are represented in Scientology by the Tone Scale: a scale of the various emotional tones, common to us all, from the highest to the lowest. These are, in part, serenity (the highest level), enthusiasm (as we proceed downward), conservatism, boredom, antagonism, anger, covert hostility, fear, grief, apathy. It is these emotions put into play which give us behavior at its various levels.

While it's true that TRs (Training Routines) are among the first skills a beginning Scientologist learns, they are of such importance that they continue to be practiced daily by the highest skilled auditors in the world. This is the ability to *be* there with another person and to communicate comfortably with him in any circumstance.

With successful training, the individual begins to come up the tone scale. He commences to have characteristics and potentialities found near the top of the scale such as outflow, reaching, certainty, creativeness and greater ARC (affinity, reality, communication) with others.

The extensive work that Scientologists perform in communities includes programs for reducing crime, protecting the mentally ill, establishing and ensuring patient's rights in hospitals, helping the aged and working in the field of education. These programs have won wide recognition for the administrative and processing technologies of Dianetics and Scientology.

Ron points out: "Scientology is a *workable system*." The successes of Scientology technologies applied to people of widely varied backgrounds have been attested to by individuals who have had auditing and training. A selection of these Success Stories is contained in the volume *Success with Scientology*.

If a world without insanity, without war and without crime seems a bit unbelievable to you, Scientology recognizes that it is only by improving conditions, a step at a time, that these goals will be accomplished. One person in a family improves himself and love is increased in that family; one bettered organization in a community leads the way for others; one improved city offers a safer environment, and so on. Thus improvements toward sanity, peace and honest citizenry become real and believable.

In locating and identifying the causes of criminality and war, Ron has noted they "are only a composite of individual aberrations. People who believe otherwise are just being irresponsible for their share. Further, one man or one woman failing to take his or her share in the general responsibility which makes society sane works as a further subtractive from group or world effectiveness. On the day when we can fully trust each other, there will be peace on earth. Don't stand in the road of that freedom."

A skilled Scientologist has ample self-confidence to assume leadership roles in career and group activities.

He has Ron's words to guide him in his work: "The highest quality leader who would bring the most to the group would work toward open and clean communication lines. He would attempt to effect the greatest affinity amongst the group and with the group. He would act only with the highest level of agreement with the group. And he would pay the strictest attention to the ethics of the group."

The common denominator, Ron found, of all psychosis is that the person "does not know what is going on in his environment and does not know what is going on inside himself. It is all unknown and therefore unobservational — unobserved." Another characteristic is the person's avoidance of both present time and a future, and a shifting into the past.

Rehabilitative work with individuals in institutions has proven that Ron's technologies are so broad and workable that they can raise the sanity level of anyone.

In 1969 The Citizens Commission on Human Rights was formed by the Association of Scientologists for Reform, a non-profit corporation. C.C.H.R. primarily concerns itself with issues involving the rights of mental patients, involuntary commitment and treatment, and reform within the field of mental health.

Scientology auditing can rehabilitate a person's power of choice as well as his ability to determine his own actions. As the degree of rationality of an individual increases, he is more able to have a positive outlook to the future and act accordingly.

Writing on criminality, Ron says: "Man is basically good. When going upon some evil course he caves himself in. Whether theft or threat or fraud is used, the criminal think is to get something without putting out anything; it permits him to receive without his contributing. Honesty is the road to sanity. You can prove that and do prove it every time you make somebody well by auditing him."

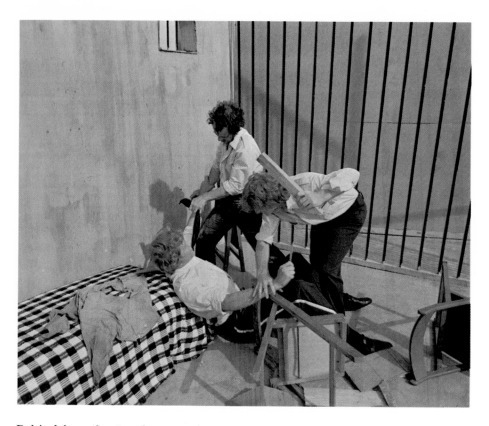

Behind bars the tough guys often get tougher but they don't get better. To improve, these people must be reached with Scientology technology which will enable them to handle their problems in a sane and just manner, and become productive members of society.

A Scientologist is one who understands. His technical skill is devoted to the resolution of the problems of life. He believes, with Ron, "that man is basically good, that he is seeking to survive, that his survival depends upon himself and upon his fellows."

When somebody finds out a few more things about life, about himself, and about others and gets a grip on the situation, he has less trouble in his environment. He thinks he can do more about life. This sort of change in him is brought about with Scientology auditing.

Scientology is a workable technology based upon much heretofore undiscovered knowledge about Man and life. Its organizations cover the earth; its staff members are friendly, productive people. Meet them, talk with them.

The Dianetics and Scientology library is extensive. Begin by reading some books by L. Ron Hubbard, Founder.

Professional films can be seen and enjoyed. Ask to see them.

Free Personality Tests are available. They are fun to do. A trained Scientologist will evaluate it and go over the results with you.

Scientology is open to all people everywhere.

Find out for *yourself* as much as you can about Scientology.

Have you ever thought you would like to explore more in order to *know* more about yourself and life?

Here is what Ron has to say to you: "Scientology is the track of knowing how to know for yourself. I have seen life from the top down and the bottom up. I know how it looks both ways. And I know there *is* wisdom and that there is hope."

What is Scientology?

A Description of Scientology

When one has made a truly basic and fundamental discovery in any field, many lesser discoveries proceed thereafter and many "firsts" occur.

This has been the case with Dianetics and Scientology. Scientology was founded some thirty years ago in the early 1950s by L. Ron Hubbard after many years of research and study into philosophy, science, religions and the living of life in many parts of the globe.

From earliest times, L. Ron Hubbard had been intrigued by the mysteries of life and by the apparent dominion over life exercised by death and its many minions. His interest was (and always is) the increase of living by the living and the freeing from deathlike circumstances of those entrapped in them by their own errors and by authoritarians of all kinds: criminals, the (uninstitutionalized) insane, self-seekers in power, the ignorant—all those that desire and work to bring about *less* living for Man. He desires that people who limit themselves by their own fixed ideas and unawareness be given a chance to free themselves in order to expand their own livingness and to help others do the same.

The word "Scientology" is taken from Greek and Latin roots and it signifies "the study of knowing, in the fullest sense of the word." One who studies Scientology learns to know how to know. Knowledge is defined in Scientology as certainty.

In its practice, Scientology is an applied religious philosophy. "Applied" is defined in the *Oxford English Dictionary* as "Put to practical use; practical as distinguished from *abstract* or *theoretical*." Everything in Scientology is directed towards workability and effectiveness—that which when applied correctly and exactly works to bring about the desired results for individuals and their environ-ments so as to improve conditions of existence for all. Anything which is not workable (doesn't bring about desired results which better conditions) is not Scientology.

"Religion" is defined as "Any specific system of belief, (worship), conduct, etc., often involving a code of ethics and a philosophy" (*Webster's New World Dictionary*). The word religion itself can embrace sacred lore, wisdom, knowingness of gods and souls and spirits. Scientology deals with the human spirit; the spirit is *you* existing with but actually independent of your mind and your body, and it is addressed because it has been found through research conducted on the most rigorous scientific basis that the soul or spirit does exist and has the capacity or potential capacity to resolve all problems which affect it, whether physical, mental or spiritual.

Scientology is a philosophy. It is the study of and contains knowledge of "the principles of human action or conduct; ethics" and is part of "that department of knowledge or study which deals with ultimate reality, or with the general causes and principles of things" (quotes from the *Oxford English Dictionary*) and is in fact *the* philosophy which most exactly and fully answers to such a description.

" 'Religious Philosophy' implies study of spiritual manifestations; research in the nature of the spirit and study on the relationship of the spirit to the body; exercises devoted to the rehabilitation of abilities in a spirit." (from the *Dianetics and Scientology Technical Dictionary*) The technology of Scientology is the means by which the philosophy of Scientology is put to practical use by an individual.

There have been, through the ages, reflecting Man's endless search for the truth about himself in order to make a better future for his fellows and descendants, many attempted systems for the handling of life's problems. There are and have been many religions. And as many philosophers and philosophies. These are men and movements which searched for ways to improve livingness and to overcome the barriers which limit it or reduce it to impotence. The Founder of Scientology acknowledges many of them in his books as having contributed to the opening of the door to what he has developed into the applied religious philosophy of Scientology.

Earlier systems, religions and philosophies, and some still existing, originated in many cases in good faith and with the best intentions. But when examined objectively in the light of conditions obtaining today on this planet, they must be seen to be far from uniformly successful. Civilizations have come and gone; problems plague every individual, family, group, nation, and the whole planet. Crime, insanity (institutionalized or not), ignorance and unhappiness persist in the wake of failures to handle many situations that make life more difficult than any reasonable person would think is necessary. Up to now, Man has not succeeded in bringing about for everyone unvarying help in handling these problems of existence, to increase individuals' abilities uniformly, to make stable and extensive self-improvement possible for everyone. Broadly and generally, Man has lacked understanding of life and the peace of mind of such understanding. He has been unable, up to now, to provide any individual regardless of race, color, creed, capacity or character with an exact scientific workable technology by which he can assess, evaluate and work out the problems not only of daily life but of life as a whole. Life as a whole is made not by gods or by fate; it is the summation of what every individual makes it or agrees that it is.

Some make of life the opportunity to improve conditions; some put up with it as it is, hoping it will pass them by; and some work on making life worse for others in any way they can.

Many religions, philosophies and systems, in the hands of lesser men than their originators, have been used to make life *more* difficult for Man. Some of them have been downright destructive of Man's understanding and ability, happiness and dignity. They have given the whole field of spiritual knowledge and endeavor a bad name by their example. Amongst the worst of these is modern psychology (which teaches that the soul does not exist) and its offshoots psychoanalysis and barbarous psychiatry. The totality of the beingness of Man does *not* consist of a meat body with a brain. He is an immortal being and his immortality can be restored to him.

The door to which L. Ron Hubbard came many years ago, that when opened by him led to the development of the applied religious philosophy of Scientology capable of fully restoring Man's immortality to him, was his basic discovery of the dynamic principle of existence. The dynamic principle of existence is SURVIVE. All life has the urge to survive. If life is not activated by the urge to survive, it is instead making the attempt to SUCCUMB, but the amazing thing is that someone bent on succumbing is doing just that because in his aberrated condition he conceives his succumbing as his way of surviving. There is a gradient of succumbing, from just a little bit to the final succumb which is death—the finite limit of succumb for a body. The gradient of survival ranges from the tiniest effort to survive to the realization of one's fullest survival potential,

including immortality. There is no finite limit to survival potential for an immortal being.

Applying this discovery to further research, and using his training as an engineer and as a philosopher, L. Ron Hubbard developed first a science of the anatomy and operation of the mind called DIANETICS. This word is taken from the Greek and means "through soul." It is the study of the working of the survive-succumb impulses working through the mind. As he developed means to help an individual remove from his mental processes those hidden parts in it which tend to make him succumb—parts of the mind based on pain and unconsciousness—and achieved great success with those means (read about them in *Dianetics: The Modern Science of Mental Health*, still a best seller nearly thirty years after its publication as a best seller in 1950, and in other books) he came across incontrovertible scientifically-validated evidence of the existence of the human soul. Further research into this phenomenon —*you*, in fact—developed into Scientology in which L. Ron Hubbard discovered not only the characteristics of the human soul or spirit (called in Scientology the thetan), but laws of life itself, laws which underpin the actions and activities of beings and all life forms in this universe, the knowledge and application of which increase the survival of individuals, families, groups, Man as a whole, the animal and vegetable kingdoms, the physical universe itself, the spirit, and makes possible a resolution for each individual of his relationship with the Supreme Being. From these discoveries were developed technologies that bring about increase of ability to perceive and make use of these laws in order to improve conditions and bring about more survival—more life.

Since every man, woman and child *is* a thetan, Scientology applies to all and can be applied by all.

It is observed, and experienced by many, that some men object to others surviving at all, being so fixated themselves on succumbing. They are merely afraid that their own dark deeds and evil intentions (the manifestations of their convictions that all others must succumb with them) will be made evident to those they seek to control unless these are prevented from becoming more able and perceptive and knowing. Their message is "You must die because I am dying. But you must die before I do." Scientology can help such men but prefers at this point to address itself to those decent beings who, despite what their past errors may be, desire honestly to find both hope and help for themselves and their fellows. Naturally Scientology becomes a target for those who do not wish hope or help for anyone, and has learned to safeguard its integrity by means of training its practitioners so thoroughly that they do not depart from its disciplines and by administrative activities that ensure the codes of Scientology are applied. Elsewhere in this volume you will read of the Church's handlings of those who have sought to deter her from her mission.

Scientology embraces all humanitarian and religious and scientific efforts to better Man's lot, and is the direct descendant of all such efforts through history that were genuinely intended to bring about increased survival, and did bring some hope to Man even though those hopes were not uniformly realized. While Scientology has made such tremendous breakthroughs in the study and knowledge and handling of life, it does not forget those who helped pave the way to understanding in days gone by. You will find them sincerely acknowledged by L. Ron Hubbard in his works. Elsewhere in this volume you will find information on how Scientology churches throughout the world are not only active in their own right in the field of the betterment of various conditions in society at large but are cooperating as well with many other organizations also active in social and religious programs.

The Accomplishments of Scientology

At no time has L. Ron Hubbard promised people anything, or claimed anything for Dianetics and Scientology. His writings are a record of observations and research and are offered by him as such.

What he has researched and developed, he has reported and others have used it.

One of his most common sayings is "what is true for you is what is real to you."

Others, a vast multitude of them, thousands of fully qualified observers, have found that what was true for them was very real in Dianetics and Scientology. It is they, not Ron, who make the claims for the subjects and who have heralded its breakthroughs.

What are these breakthroughs for which so much has been claimed, besides those mentioned already? Below are given some of the more major ones. All are thoroughly documented.

Scientology is not only the first body of knowledge in which the precision of science is applied to the humanities, but in which it is applied to the nature and behavior of the human spirit and its potential. Yet it is sufficiently simple that where it takes twelve years to train a psychiatrist to believe that there is no such thing as a spirit, several weeks of intensive Scientology training can permit a person to achieve results which he never dreamed of before, with a certainty he never knew he could experience. However, for a truly skilled Scientologist, the training period for the highest qualifications spans several years.

The first axiomatic construction of the basic laws of thought and behavior in Man was achieved by L. Ron Hubbard in the axioms of Dianetics and Scientology.

Scientology is the first to isolate the life unit that perceives and generates energy, a discovery comparable to the isolation of the nucleus in atomic physics.

Scientology was the first to prove that I.Q. and intelligence can be improved and are not inherent in a person.

The reactive or subconscious mind was first workably discovered and isolated in Dianetics and Scientology.

Moreover it was the first to isolate and classify accurately the twenty-four parts of the human mind. Prior to Scientology only the brain, the body, Freud's subconscious and Pavlov's stimulus-response law were known. Scientology has clarified these four and has discovered an additional twenty parts, any of them more important to Man in his efforts to bring peace and order to his environment and Earth.

Scientology was the first to determine accurately the honesty and potential character of people by invariable instrumental means.

And it is the first technology of the mind and spirit to subject itself to the most severe validation tests.

In Scientology, a new state or condition for Man which exceeds earlier concepts of Man's potential was first established. This alone in Scientology remains expensive due to the skilled attention it requires.

Scientology was the first applied system of bettering individuals to give the highest importance to increasing the individual's ability to communicate, and to develop techniques which deliver that result. The ability of an individual depends on his ability to communicate. This interpretation of ability as communication is entirely new.

It is the first to make whole classes of backward children averagely bright using only drills the teacher can do for a few minutes each day.

It proved conclusively for the first time that physical illness can stem from mental or spiritual disturbances, a fact hitherto only held as a theory and very seldom demonstrated.

Dianetics is the first development that removes traumatic barriers from the path of healing. It changes and improves the rate of healing, in fact. Few betterment activities have been so widely successful and so uniformly helpful as Dianetics.

It was first established in Dianetics that function monitors structure, despite widespread medical belief to the contrary. The mind can change the body. "Mental blocks" are capable of obstructing medical treatment of a really physical nature. The proof is that when one even reduces the mental block slightly, medicines such as antibiotics or hormones will now be effective when they were previously ineffective on some patients. Scientology was the first to define the mechanistic limits of medicine and give the medical doctor a tool.

Scientology is the first to make a technical breakthrough in the subject of psychosis (meaning a definite obsessive desire to destroy). In 1970 the actual cause of psychosis was isolated, and in ensuing years this has proven beyond doubt to be totally correct. Man has never been able to solve the psychotic break. In fact, human beings are actually afraid of a person in a psychotic break and in desperation turn to psychiatry to handle. Psychiatry, desperate in its turn, without effective technology, resorts to barbarities such as heavy drugs, ice picks, electric shock and insulin shock which half kill the person and only suppress him. The fact remains that there has never been a cure for the psychotic break *until now*.

Scientology is the first to isolate the precise barriers to study and the means to detect and remove them, including the basic cause of ineptitude or lack of ability to apply knowledge. Within the body of data on study are found the basic reasons why a person gives up a study, becomes confused and unable to learn, why knowledge gets lost, and why a person has trouble with his personal relationships— and his own mind as well as other subjects.

It is the first also to develop an orderly, gradient approach to study that can be applied at all ages and grades, to all subjects, permitting the child or student to advance at his own pace while giving him the means to increase his pace without sacrificing any certainty in the knowledge he gains. With this came also the solutions to the mutinous and rebellious conduct which had become the order of the day in modern schools.

In Scientology is found the first and only completely workable means of handling drug addiction, of fully eradicating the harmful effects of drug-taking on the body and mind, and of getting addicts off drugs without convulsions.

Scientology was the first to define by acknowledged clinical test, the importance of the effects of aspirin and other pain depressants and soporifics on the mind and on the nervous system, and to be able to erase them.

The basic nature of Man is discovered for the first time, in Dianetics, rather than postulated or hazarded since that basic nature can be brought into action in any individual completely. And that basic nature is found to be uniformly GOOD.

It was, moreover, first found in Scientology that the spirit is the source of all creation. And for the first time it becomes possible for the spirit, normally attached with little awareness to the mind and body, to be detached therefrom with great ease and absence of discomfort.

In so doing, it becomes fully apparent for the first time in Man's experience that the spirit (or thetan) is proved to be immortal and possessed of capabilities well in excess of those hitherto predicted for Man. The detachment accomplishes in the sober practice of science the realization of goals envisioned — but questionably, if ever, obtained — in spiritualism, mysticism and such fields.

Scientology is the first to enable an individual to be released from the very narrow limitation of having just one lifetime. This is a tremendous release for the individual because the significance and terrible consequences of death fall away. Death has lost its sting.

The first insights into the *basic* laws of organization and their codification into useable form has been accomplished by Scientology. By their use and application any group may be successfully de-aberrated and its expansion ensured. They apply equally valuably to the organization of a person's own life and his family. Man did not really know the principles of organization any more than he knew what made his mind work before Dianetics was published. Scientology has the first and only really workable means of measuring the survival potential of any human being in his existing state and of predicting his behavior accordingly in terms of characteristic actions towards survival or succumbing. And of course, the means of increasing his survival potential results in predicted and exhibited betterment of his actions towards the survival of himself, his dependents, his associates, his groups.

The first breakthrough in centuries of work by thinking men has been achieved by Scientology in the field of logic. Hitherto, logic has only existed as itself, lacking a useable definition of *il*logic with which logic should be compared for full understanding of what it, logic, really is. Illogic has now been broken down into its basic component parts, greatly facilitating the proper perception and discovery of data relevant to a problem and its resolution, be it a problem in personal life or in organization, or any administration.

Scientology is the first to discover the means of measuring accurately and objectively the real value of a group

member's contribution to the viability of the group. No longer need the unproductive or lazy worker or executive be rewarded for a contribution he never makes, or the stellar producer be ignored because he treads on precious toes or wears the wrong tie. When the latter person is neglected or punished, the viability of the group suffers irredeemably, just as it is when the unproductive is rewarded with increased status and responsibility that he did not earn and uses only to undermine the organization that trusts him to assist it.

The specific States of Conditions in which one operates his own personal life and manages the operation of a job, or gauges the state of an organization, the state of a family, the state of a government, or of a planet, were first discovered and described in Scientology, along with the sequences of steps used in each State of Condition which, when followed, carry one to the next higher State of Condition. The several states themselves form a sequence. When the steps of any one condition are followed one can then go on to the steps of the next higher condition. Doing so permits one to exercise power in his areas of responsibility. If one is in one State of Condition but does not follow the steps for that state, he will surely fail. Individuals, firms, governments and nations fail for this reason. These States of Condition and the steps for each exist as part of the woof and warp of the universe we live in.

Scientology has developed the first uniformly workable technology of ethics which can be applied by any individual for himself or for his group, and by the group, with an ease modified only by the degree to which ethics has been lacking in the area.

Scientology is the first to discover the cause of war, and the cause of conflict between any individuals. It is commonly thought that "it takes two to make a fight." This is found to be incorrect. The principle behind this is at the root of the decline of any civilization now dead and gone. The application of the technology which handles the causes of war and personal conflict is learned by the Scientologist.

Scientology has given the first workable definition of art, answering the questions What is art? How good does a work of art have to be? Why do some works of art elicit a poor or no response? The answers to these questions clarify what is probably the most uncodified and least organized of all fields. Scientology's approach results in improved art and improved appreciation.

It is very evident that each of the above "firsts" is something that leads to increased life and livingness for anyone, and that most of them actively diminish the influence of death or deathlike factors in life which act as stops and distractions to life.

Scientology helps one handle persons, environments and situations.

Scientology is used on life and its forms and products.

A Scientologist operates within the codes of Scientology.

Scientology is in two parts. The philosophy — the books, the lectures, bulletins, policies, anything found in L. Ron Hubbard's many years of published research; and the technology, whereby the philosophy can be put to practical use by any individual who studies the materials.

As such, its use can be applied to the field of education, to one's own life, to the family unit, to social reform in many fields, to handling communication problems, past upsets, problems and much, much more. "Religion is a part of living" has always been Scientology's watchword, and this is proven by the application of the technology in many different fields of life.

Secular use of the technology in new and diversified fields has grown considerably over the years—particularly in programs concerning education and drug rehabilitation.

A Scientologist is a first cousin to the Buddhist, a distant relative of the Taoist, a feudal enemy of the enslaver, and a bitter foe of the German, Viennese and Russian defamers of Man, otherwise known as psychiatrists and psychologists.

The religion of the Scientologist is freedom for all things spiritual in all fields of life. There must be adequate discipline and knowledge to keep that freedom guaranteed.

Our ability belongs to all worlds everywhere.

This book, *What Is Scientology?*, becomes increasingly important when one considers the vastness of its potential application to a troubled world.

Scientology's Position in a Troubled World

To the sane and analytical man, it often seems as though the madness surrounding our lives is all encompassing and relentless. The senselessness of today's society's compulsive attempts at self-destruction make it appear as though the reenactment of the Fall of the Roman Empire is only hours away. All of the reoccurring symptoms of ancient Rome are here: a reactive suppression of religion and of those religious figures that offer hope; fields of mental and physical health dominated by destructive madmen; education of the young fundamentally nonexistent; usage of drugs and alcohol enforced by the governing administration and idealized by the entertainment media; desperate experimenting with wierd mental practices—mysticism, hypnotism, the esoteric, the occult —trying to get out and away from consciousness.

The present direction of our sensibilities became thunderingly illuminated when, in January 1978, a young American attempted to promote an event: he offered to take on a wild Bengal tiger, armed only with a knife, and with him in the nude, in an arena that was "ideally suited for television." Apparently the only reason that the event was cancelled was because the Society for the Prevention of Cruelty to Animals and some naturalist groups felt that it would be cruel and unfair to the tiger.

We are lacking only a modern Nero to fiddle as the flames consume the cities.

The enormous failures of those that have been granted the authority to serve as examples to us all, and thence to correct the glaring problems that abound, are without end. Today the betrayal of our "leaders in the fields" of education, psychology and psychiatry, government and law enforcement, has seemingly left us with no stable guideposts. The apparency is that we are without visionaries and leaders in the midst of the greatest battle for survival we have known. The generals in this battle have been exposed as perverse, incompetent and suppressive. The field soldier appears in today's scenario as being forlorn and abandoned, standing on a lonely distant hill, observing the setting sun with his fist shaking in the air. He is screaming at the audacity of the sun going down for another day when once again he had nothing to say about it. Totally the effect of forces only dimly viewed, the screaming soldier retreats to darkness and the solace of a quart of brew.

Do these statements seem a bit extreme, perhaps theatrical, stressing only the negative? Well, consider these statistics:†

The crime rate has risen over 786% since 1957, yet in 1979 the U.S. government will spend 4 billion, 211 million dollars on the administration of justice in the U.S. for that year, and the crime rate will only continue to soar.

$70 billion dollars annually is poured into America's public schools yet they are an abysmal failure. Some studies show that one out of every five adults does not possess the minimal reading, writing and calculating skills necessary to function in society. Some 23 million American people are classified as functionally illiterate.

100,000 people are given shock treatment every year, though no one knows how these treatments work. Studies have been made which reveal brain damage after ECT, but it is considered irrelevant.

A study of psychiatric diagnosis and the patient's future behavior showed that for every case with a correct evaluation by a psychiatrist, there were 326 incorrect evaluations done.

Of 400 cases of violent crime recently reported in the press, it was found that the instigators of the crimes had recently been under psychiatric care.

A study of patients committed to New York's Bellevue Psychiatric Hospital for crimes of bodily harm showed that these patients increased their commission of such crimes by 200% following psychiatric treatment and subsequent release.

Of 114,552 first admissions, 14,168 people died in United Kingdom psychiatric institutions. This is a 12% average death rate.

In New South Wales, Australia, government statistics revealed that 4,000 people were unnecessarily admitted to mental institutions in one year (1974).

One out of every 10 American children are being drugged almost daily with federal and state aid and approval because they are active and not docile. Termed "hyperactive" (a term recently created by psychologists), these children are being given Ritalin, Stelazine and Thorazine. These drugs have known dangerous side effects. They are also addictive.

In England, between 75,000 and 125,000 people are dependent on barbiturates. In 1971, of the 78% of suicides

†Reference sources for the statistics that follow are: FBI Uniform Crime Reports; Los Angeles Herald Examiner, April 4, 1978; ABC TV show, "Medicine and Madness," May 26, 1977; Los Angeles Free Press, June 1977; Freedom, the independent journal published by the Church of Scientology; The Sun, New South Wales; 1973 Committee on Public Health and Safety Report; "Drugs and Drug Rehabilitation" by K. J. Pitt.

resulting from medically prescribed drugs, all but one occurred within a month of the last visit to the doctor.

In Sweden, a nation with a soaring suicide rate, 83% of those persons committing suicide have received psychiatric "care."

A Harvard Medical School professor states on record that 1,200 patients died under shock treatment in one year. Another doctor estimates 5,000 have died under ECT in a year.

Yet regardless of these condemnatory statistics, the psychiatric industry and its proponents continue to demand and receive an ever increasing federal and private income revenue.

Is it any wonder that our proverbial sane and analytical man, in the face of this ever expanding nightmare, appears ready to succumb? The psychiatrist, the educator, the politician arrogantly proclaim that "ultimately we animals are all doomed." At first, the sane man resists and fights this pronouncement. He attempts education and improvement for his family and self, but finds that the schools know of no way to teach him how to study and learn. They offer drugs for his children so that it will be "easier to handle them."

He flees the schools and struggles to get to his home, fearing that at any moment he may be robbed or even killed, as the police are helpless in protecting him from the violence in the streets. He pays enormous taxes to support the FBI, the CIA and his local police, but somehow feels that they are useless, yet knows not what else to do.

He feels despondent as his problems in life increase and the value of his earned income radically decreases. In desperation he seeks help from a psychiatrist. After taking most of his remaining money, the psychiatrist suggests drugs, electric shock and, if that should fail, offers experimental psychosurgery. Fleeing from the psychiatrist he again attempts to return home, this time to get beaten and robbed by young hoods barely in their teens. He crawls home only to find that the government has taken his sons to fight some new war that no one understands nor can explain to him.

Betrayed, battered, bruised, broken in body and spirit, our once sane and analytical man hears a knock on the door which breaks the silence of his quiet overwhelming despair. It is the social welfare worker, who offers him money if he will just stay home and not move nor work anymore. He turns on the television set and slowly sinks, with profound apathy, into the chair. The house lights grow dim and there are only the sounds of ambulances and sirens carting off the broken and damaged from the nearby streets.

Psychoanalysts attempt to explain it away by implying that it is all only a recent phenomenon, due to a present "psycho-social revolution." Somehow it will soon all pass, they say. But we know that it will not just pass, as some simple phasic behavior. It will not just magically get better, no matter how often we are assured of this by those in power.

Scientology and Scientologists know and understand both the nature of the society's malady and the way in which an individual can rise above it all, and yet simultaneously be responsible for the dis-ease and the handling of the suppressive factors which cause it.

In the works of L. Ron Hubbard, in his extensive published books, tapes and literature, there occurs the resolution of these seemingly overwhelming problems faced by today's society.

It is there to be learned, understood and used, exactly as written and spoken.

The study and application of Scientology is the way out.

There is an alternative to the madness which surrounds us.

2

The Actual Services of Scientology

The various organizations of Scientology offer a great many services to their members. This section attempts to give a comprehensive cross section of the services which are offered and the relative availability of each service. There may be some differences in organizations in various parts of the world from what is described here but this should serve to show what can typically be expected.

The services described here are laid out in a gradient of "beginner" who just wants to know what Scientology is about on up to the most advanced levels for dedicated Scientologists of long standing. One will find that these services cover a very broad range of subjects especially in the area of life and living, relationships with other people, work, success, finance and money. In general any service offered in Scientology is geared to enable one to be able to change unwanted conditions in life and increase one's inherent abilities towards making a better life.

As Scientology continues to expand this list of services can be expected to expand.

Beginning Services

The following services can reasonably be expected to be offered by any Scientology Church, Mission, Counseling Group and field practitioner. Exact contents may vary with locale.

Introductory Lecture: A brief description of Scientology and what it is with some basic principles of Scientology and how they can be applied to life.

Scientology Books: Books by L. Ron Hubbard which lay out the fundamental principles of Scientology and Dianetics and their applicability to life.

Tape/Film Lecture Courses: Taped or filmed lectures by L. Ron Hubbard in which he discusses the principles of Scientology and Dianetics.

Personal Efficiency Course: This course varies in content but is usually a series of lectures and demonstrations of key Scientology principles and how they can be applied to one's own life. One is invited to test out these principles outside of class time in a personal situation of his own to prove the workability of the principle just

learned. The entire course stresses *using* in life what one has studied and personally verifying the effectiveness of Scientology.

Group Processing: The application of Scientology auditing techniques to groups of people. The processes used can increase awareness and make one feel brighter, more alert and more cheerful. A supervisor directs the processing.

Co-Auditing: Students are taught some of the most fundamental processes of Scientology and how to apply them to others. They are then paired up to give and receive the processes, which gives them the reality of auditing another as well as the benefits of the processing.

HAS (Hubbard Apprentice Scientologist) Course: A course on communication and what it is with drills on how to communicate better in life.

HQS (Hubbard Qualified Scientologist) Course: Trains a student on data on how to assist another person who is ill or injured or in some distress to bring them some relief. Also covers some Scientology processes which are co-audited before the end of the course.

Mini Courses: These are many and varied but cover such subjects as money, marriage, jobs and work, music and the arts. Each takes various Scientology principles and applies them to bring about improvement and success in each of the areas.

Livingness Repair Rundown: This is a brand new Rundown to be used by Missions of the Church of Scientology in the handling of new public. This Rundown isolates and addresses the major area the individual has run up against in life that is causing him difficulty, and handles it through a specially formulated program exactly tailored to the individual's need, enabling him to better handle his life.

New Era Dianetics Auditing: Dianetics is the forerunner of Scientology. It is used to deal with the effects of "psychosomatic" ills and to aid in the recovery from illness or injury by alleviating emotional distress and upset. In July 1978 L. Ron Hubbard released his phenomenal New Era Dianetics technology to Scientology organizations all over the world. He has overhauled older Dianetics extensively so that there is up to 80% more gain to be had, and thus created a better Dianetics section of the Bridge.

Intermediate Services

One can expect to find the following auditing services at any Scientology Church, Mission, Counseling Group and field practitioner.

Word Clearing: L. Ron Hubbard found that the basis of any inability to study or apply what one has learned can be traced to one or more words not understood in one's studies. By locating and getting defined those words that weren't understood one can experience a remarkable resurgence in one's ability to study a subject and in actually using what one has learned. There are many forms of word clearing but they are all geared to finding the words misunderstood and clearing up the dull, sleepy, "don't want to" feelings that people get when reading or listening to something.

New Era Dianetics Drug Rundown: A major breakthrough in 1978, New Era Dianetics Drug Rundown is tailored to each individual pc, directed to freeing him from the compulsion or need to have drugs. It takes up and handles the harmful effects of drugs, alcohol and medicine, and it is very smooth auditing.

New Era Dianetics Case Completion: A pc who has completed the New Era Dianetics auditing program has had such amazingly beneficial actions as four new rundowns plus a number of other actions directed toward eradicating undesirable conditions. The end phenomena of New Era Dianetics auditing is a truly well and happy human being.

Straightwire Auditing: The processes on this level when applied result in a better recall of the past and a realization that one won't get any worse.

Communications Release: Also called Grade 0, this level of auditing when applied by an auditor results in the ability to communicate freely with anyone on any subject.

Problems Release: Also called Grade I, this level gives one the ability to recognize the source of problems and make them vanish. One is released from problems.

Relief Release: Also called Grade II, this level gives one relief from the hostilities and sufferings of life by enabling one to get rid of past feelings of guilt for actions one has done that one wishes one hadn't done or ac-

tions that one should have done but didn't. This would also include all the efforts to "cover up" what had occurred.

Freedom Release: This is also called Grade III, and it extensively handles past upsets which may still be affecting one's behavior today. The result is freedom from the upsets of the past and ability to face the future.

Ability Release: This level, also called Grade IV, handles one's fixed ideas and opinions which block success in areas of life. The result is moving out of fixed conditions and gaining abilities to do new things.

Expanded Dianetics: This level usually comes after Grade IV but can go wherever it will be most beneficial to the individual and his progress. Developed in recent years by L. Ron Hubbard, its results are freedom from cruel impulses and chronic unwanted conditions and ability to act in an optimum manner without restraint. This level is available in most organizations but not all, as it requires specially trained staff.

Other Auditing Actions: There are many other types of auditing which are geared to handle individual problems that a person might have. These do not replace the need for the standard Grade 0–IV auditing.

    Student Rehabilitation Auditing: Recovers one's ability to study and learn any subject. Removes the difficulties that prevent study.

    Marriage Co-audit: Enables a husband and wife to get back into communication and through communication resolve the marriage problems they are having.

    Method One Word Clearing: A form of word clearing that clears up problems one had in studying subjects in the past by finding the misunderstood words in the subject and can actually recover the knowledge one once had about the subject.

    The "Bright Think" Rundown is a powerfully simple process that handles any inability to think and talk brightly, and brings the person effortlessly into present time.

    PTS Auditing: In Scientology PTS means Potential

Trouble Source and refers to the type of person who has frequent "ups and downs," i.e. someone who feels great one day and badly the next, or who gets ill often for no apparent reason. This auditing helps to locate the source of this "roller coaster" and get it handled. Makes one more stable.

Confessional Auditing: Often difficulties in areas such as marriage, work, money, music and the arts can be handled by locating things one has done in the area for which one feels guilt causing a withdrawal from the area. This type of auditing handles those feelings and restores the desire to participate again. It can be specially adapted to any area of life.

Introspection Auditing: Handles the tendency of a person when faced with a particularly overwhelming and emotionally distressing event or series of events to withdraw or introvert into oneself. The end phenomena of this rundown is the person extroverted, no longer looking inward worriedly.

Assist Auditing: Can be done at any time and is used to assist a person to recover rapidly from an injury or illness or an emotional occurrence such as the death of a loved one or loss of something of great personal value.

Intermediate Training Services

The following courses can usually be found available in any Scientology Church or Mission. A Dianetic Counseling Group would have the Dianetics courses listed below.

Student Hat: Trains one on how to study successfully and how to resolve study difficulties before they defeat one's willingness to study. This course is vital for the study of Scientology courses and would be of great benefit to any student.

Primary Rundown: This course consists of thoroughly clearing the definitions of many basic words especially the small words such as "of," "at," "so," etc. and results in a person who can get the exact concept of what he reads and can literally visualize the materials he studies and becomes what is called in Scientology a "Super-Literate."

Grammar Course: Some people have trouble defining and clearing words because they don't know the basics of grammar and thus can't tell what nouns and verbs and adjectives are. This is a short course to handle any trouble with grammar.

Extension Courses: These are courses that can be done at home and are based on the various books by L. Ron Hubbard. Questions and exercises accompany each chapter of the book being studied and are sent in to the nearest organization for grading.

Basic Dianetics Books Course: Enables a person to get a firm grasp of Dianetic fundamentals by training him thoroughly in the basic books on the subject of Dianetics. A good deal of this material also forms many of the basics of Scientology.

Hubbard New Era Dianetics Course: New Era Dianetics (N.E.D.) is a summary and refinement of Dianetics based upon 30 years of experience in the application of the subject, and additional research and breakthroughs made by L. Ron Hubbard. The student studying it and the auditor practicing it will find that if he follows its precision drills with precision he will be able to handle life and the spirit as never before. As this course contains many new skills to be learned, auditors who have been trained in Dianetics before need additional training to deliver New Era Dianetics.

TRs Course: TR stands for Training Regimen or Routine and the full set of TRs comprise the fundamental drills on how one audits another person and gets the results

desired. These drills are the basis of auditing. Scientology Missions would also have this course.

The following services are available only at Churches of Scientology.

Hubbard New Era Dianetics Course Supervisor's Course: Trains the student in how to supervise the New Era Dianetics Course so that one can run the course in a Dianetic Counseling Group for others to study.

Word Clearing Co-Audit Course: Trains a student in the technology of word clearing which is a sweepingly fantastic discovery in the field of education. It removes study barriers and leads to a restoration of doingness which depends upon the restoration of understanding on the misunderstood word.

Class 0 (Hubbard Recognized Scientologist): This training level thoroughly covers communication, what it is and how to handle it, and trains a student how to audit a person to Grade 0, Communications Release. There is also a section on word clearing for those who have not yet been trained on how to word clear.

Class I (Hubbard Trained Scientologist): Trains a student on the data of understanding and handling problems. A graduate of this course is able to audit another person to Grade I, Problems Release.

Class II (Hubbard Certified Auditor): This level deals with understanding and handling feelings of guilt people might have because of things they have done. A graduate of this level can audit another person to a Grade II, Relief Release.

Class III (Hubbard Professional Auditor): Trains a student in recognizing and handling the upsets of others. The student when complete is able to audit another person to Grade III, Freedom Release.

Class IV (Hubbard Advanced Auditor): On this level a student is trained to handle fixed ideas and opinions in others that sometimes make them irrationally set in their ways. The student when complete can audit another person to Grade IV, Abilities Release. There is also a section on handling a person who has frequent ups and downs and lacks stability.

The training levels above from Class 0 to IV are often called the Academy Levels and are most often studied consecutively as a group.

Class IV Graduate (Auditor and C/S) Course teaches not only advanced auditing skills and data, it trains one to case supervise for any and all actions through grade IV. In addition the auditor is trained to deliver and C/S two new rundowns: The New Int Rundown and The "Bright Think" Rundown.

Expanded Dianetics Course: Offered to public only in certain Scientology Churches that have a Hubbard Graduate Dianetic Specialist on staff to supervise or oversee the course, as only persons specifically trained in Expanded Dianetics may run it or use it. Trains a person to understand and handle irrational behavior in others and chronic unwanted conditions. A graduate of this course can audit a person to produce the results just described.

Hubbard New Era Dianetics Graduate (Case Supervisor) Course: This course trains the student in the use of vital data necessary for the complete handling and case supervision of Dianetic sessions.

Class IV Graduate (Auditor and C/S) Internship is geared to pure doingness. It requires the person to audit and C/S and polish his skills on all of the O-IV actions and two new rundowns, as taught him on the Class IV Graduate Course.

Expanded Dianetics Case Supervisor Course: Trains the person in the supervision and correction of Expanded Dianetics auditing.

HMCSC (Hubbard Mini Course Supervisor Course): A short course on the fundamentals of supervising a classroom and running a course for students.

HPCSC (Hubbard Professional Course Supervisor Course): An expanded course on the techniques of course supervision covering in particular the supervision of practical application.

Co-Audit Supervisor Course: Trains the student in how to run a co-audit for any number of people. Includes all the techniques of handling students who are co-auditing.

Internships: A fundamental of Scientology training is that a graduate must be able to successfully apply what he has learned. The way this is done is to have the course graduate interne for some time until his work matches that of a veteran. An internship is required to make a course graduate's certificate a permanent one. Internships are offered for all the following training levels:
New Era Dianetic Auditors
New Era Dianetic Case Supervisors
Class IV Auditors
Class IV Graduates (Auditor and Case Supervisor)
Expanded Dianetic Auditors
Expanded Dianetic Case Supervisors
Mini Course Supervisors
Professional Course Supervisors.

Organization Executive Course (Org Exec Course): Trains one in how to run an organization covering all aspects of finance, production, personnel, promotion, sales, quality control, distribution and management. The material is based on Scientology principles and is applicable to any type of organization or business.

Org Exec Course Internship: As covered above the trainee gets practical experience applying what he has learned under the watchful eye of experienced executives.

Other Business Courses: There are a number of courses generally available covering finance, leadership, how to do investigations, targeting out programs for expansion, salesmanship and statistical management. These courses are added to from time to time and are generally available.

Advanced Auditing Services

The following services are to be found only in certain Scientology Churches due to the nature of the services. The types of organizations which offer these services are called either Advanced Organizations or Saint Hills (named after the original organization in England called Saint Hill which first offered these services). Organizations of this type can be found currently in Los Angeles, California, U.S. and Copenhagen, Denmark and East Grinstead, England.

Grade V Release: Also called the Power Processes, requires an auditor of considerable skill and is a prerequisite to higher level services.

Grade VA Release: Also called Power Plus, this level is the final Grade before the preclear commences solo auditing.

Solo Setups: These setups are varied and are simply those auditing actions that a person needs to prepare him for the upper auditing levels.

Solo Course: While this is a *course*, it is a prerequisite

to the auditing levels to follow, as they are all "solo" auditing levels, in that the person does the auditing himself. This course trains one in how to solo audit.

Grade VI Release: This is the first of the solo levels and on this level a person audits himself to achieve a return of powers to act on one's own self-determinism and a freedom from dramatization.

Clearing Course: The state of Clear is attained by completion of the Clearing Course at an Advanced Organization. A Clear has no vicious reactive mind and can be at cause knowingly on the first dynamic (optimum survival for self).

OT Levels: "OT" means Operating Thetan; the levels are the solo auditing levels OT I through OT VIII. When a being once more has recovered his full abilities and freedom, a state much higher than Man ever before envisioned is attained. This state is called Operating Thetan. An OT is knowing and willing cause over all eight dynamics of life. There are perhaps 15 levels above VIII fully developed but existing only in unissued note form, pending more people's full attainment of OT VI, OT VII, and OT VIII.

The following services are currently only available at the most senior Church of Scientology in Clearwater, Florida. They do not necessarily require all the above levels first but are done as most benefits the individual.

Case Completion Auditing: Fills in anything that may have been missed at any lower level and stabilizes results previously achieved. This level varies from individual to individual as to what is required and how long it takes. This level and the following levels are delivered by very highly trained auditors.

New Vitality Auditing: Handles those elements of personal instability which cause a person to be less himself. A highly trained auditor locates the major points of stress and when complete results in a great resurgence for the individual.

New Era Dianetics For OTs Rundown was developed especially for Dianetic and Scientology Clears who have completed the Grade of OT III. L. Ron Hubbard's most major breakthrough since 1968 when he released OT III, it can only be delivered at Advanced Organizations and at Flag Land Base by Class IV, OT III Advance Course Specialists. The end phenomena of "NED for OTs" Rundown is: Cause over Life.

L-10 Auditing: The "L" stands for list and L-10 is the designation given to this service. A precision technology that is delivered by a specially trained class of auditor—Class Xs. It handles doingness and causativeness with 23 separate, powerful actions, resulting in the increase of an individual's general ability, perception and memory.

L-11 Auditing: A level consisting of 6 powerful actions to locate and handle the major personal difficulty on a person's case. Delivered by a highly skilled auditor, it is also called the New Life Rundown as it gives to an individual a new life in truth.

L-12 Auditing: A new and vital rundown which L. Ron Hubbard has acknowledged as the most startling breakthrough in Scientology auditing since 1967. Again it is delivered by the most highly trained Class X-XII auditors. In handling very fundamental aspects of a person's beingness, L-12 was developed to make a fully extroverted and stable thetan.

As Scientology continues to expand more services may be developed and would then be added to this list.

Advanced Training Levels

The following services are available from the same organizations which offer the advanced auditing services.

Hubbard Class IV Advanced Courses Specialist is a Class IV, OT III auditor who has had specialized training to be able to administer to OT IIIs and above the "New Era Dianetics for OTs" Rundown, a major breakthrough based on research discoveries made by L. Ron Hubbard in 1978.

Saint Hill Special Briefing Course (SHSBC): First offered at the original Saint Hill in England, this course is an advanced auditor level and gives the student the chronological development of the materials of Dianetics and Scientology since the first books went into print in 1948. A graduate of this course is a Class V Hubbard Validated Auditor.

Senior Saint Hill Special Briefing Course: This course gives the studnt the materials of a number of the more modern techniques to complement his thorough study of the basics on Class V. A graduate of this course is a Class VI, Hubbard Senior Scientologist.

Class VII (Hubbard Graduate Auditor): A very highly skilled level, this course deals with the delivery of the Power Processes, Grades V and VA. The course is only available to staff members and is not a prerequisite for other training levels which the public may take.

Class VIII Course (Hubbard Standard Technical Specialist): The Class VIII Course trains a student on the exactness and precision of Dianetics and Scientology technology and how the exact application of the technology will always get the result.

Class IX Course (Hubbard Advanced Technical Specialist): This level provides an update of the technology developed and released since the Class VIII Course. It brings one fully up-to-date on auditing.

Class VI Case Supervisor Course: Trains the student in the supervision and correction of auditing at the level of Class VI, thereby ensuring the proper application of the materials.

Class VII Case Supervisor Course: Available only to contracted staff, this level trains a student in the supervision and correction of the auditing of Grade V and VA, the Power Processes. It is not a prerequisite to further case supervisor courses.

Class VIII Case Supervisor Course: Trains the student in the application of 100% standard technology to all cases.

Class IX Case Supervisor Course: This course covers all forms of case supervision up to Class IX auditing skills.

HSCSC (Hubbard Senior Course Supervisor Course): The comprehensive supervisor course which covers all the materials developed by L. Ron Hubbard on the supervision of students and courses.

Internships: Again the granting of a permanent certificate as a graduate of any of the courses requires an internship under a skilled veteran to ensure that one can actually apply what one has learned and with success. Internships are offered for all the following courses:
Class VI Auditor
Class VI Case Supervisor
Class VII Auditor
Class VII Case Supervisor
Class VIII Auditor
Class VIII Case Supervisor
Class IX Auditor

Class IX Case Supervisor
Senior Course Supervisor.

Flag Executive Briefing Course: This is a comprehensive course given on the skills of managing an organization and being an executive. Covers in detail the application of Scientology principles to the field of operating an organization.

Flag Executive Briefing Course Internship: The student gets practical experience as an executive to ensure that he can apply what he has learned.

Data Series Evaluators Course: Based on major breakthroughs in the field of logic, this course covers how one can locate and handle the exact cause of difficulty an organization is having.

Data Series Evaluators Course Internship: The practical experience of applying the data of the course to produce successful results.

Establishment Officer Course: Trains one in how to establish an organization and build it up with personnel and materials and how to get people to do their jobs successfully whether they are experts or novices.

The courses following are available only at the most senior Scientology organization in Clearwater, Florida. Where noted the course is only available for staff.

Class X Course: Trains a student in how to deliver the auditing level of L-10. Currently this course is available to staff only.

Class XI Course: Trains the student in the techniques of

delivering the auditing of L-11. Currently available to staff only.

Class XII Course: On this level the student learns the theory and auditing skills necessary to deliver L-12. Currently available only to staff.

Class X — XII Case Supervisor Course: Trains the Class XII auditor how to supervise and correct the application of these highly skilled levels.

Internships: There are internships to perfect the student's ability to apply the materials studied as on all lower level training. Again a highly skilled Class XII verifies each of the following:
Class X Auditor
Class XI Auditor
Class XII Auditor
Class X-XII Case Supervisor.

Public Relations Course: A course that applies the principles of Scientology to the field of public relations and which consists of what PR procedures are, their correct application, and their assistance to an organization so that it can expand, prosper and be viable.

Senior Executive Briefing Course: This course is the most comprehensive course offered on the application of Scientology techniques to management and being an executive. The management courses mentioned earlier are prerequisites for this course.

This list covers all the major courses and auditing services. This list will expand as more services are developed and released.

Other Services

While all the above cover the general scope and availability of auditing and training services, there are other services which Scientology organizations make available which do not fit exactly into these categories. The following list covers these other services one can expect to find in any Counseling Group, Mission or Church.

Church Services: Scientology churches do provide weekly services for the public and staff.

Chaplain's Help: There is a public chaplain who is available to aid those who are having difficulty. The chaplain also offers his services as a mediator in disputes. He is first and foremost the friend of all public, for any upset they might want to resolve.

Qual Consultation: The Qualifications Division of the organization has a consultant who is technically trained and serves to assist people who are having trouble with their training or auditing.

Review Auditing: Available to handle any difficulties

one is having that can be resolved through some short auditing action. This is particularly used to assist solo auditors who have run into something that needs help to resolve.

Cramming: This action comes from the word "cram" which to a student means to study something intensively. In this action a trained person isolates any trouble a person might have in applying what he has learned by finding exactly what was not understood and then correcting that exact thing. The result is one can then successfully apply the entirety of the materials.

Ethics: Ethical conduct and high ethical standards are maintained by providing this service to the public. It assists them in acting in an optimum manner that ensures them maximum benefit from their services.

Staff Training: All Scientology staff are trained on the materials necessary to do their job. There are many such courses available to staff on how to do the various jobs in an organization.

Summary

The above gives a general outline of the myriad services that are available to the public and the areas they cover. The general availability is as described with the addition that any of the lower level services can usually also be

found in the higher organizations. Again this list is complete up to this time but can be expected to expand as new services that the public want are developed and released.

3

The Effectiveness of Scientology

The following pages contain successes that people over the world have experienced through the application of Scientology technology.

When a person completes a Scientology service, they are asked to write a success story telling what gains or knowledge they have acquired from the service they've completed. This also serves as an indicator of the quality of service delivered, and shows where correction is needed if a person is dissatisfied with the service. The intention is, of course, to always see that a person is satisfied upon completing a service.

In some instances, months after a person has completed a Scientology service, they are written to and asked if they might write a success story about any gains or wins they've had since completing their service, through applying the data or gains they've acquired. This is also very important because a person should continue to have success in applying the Scientology data he learns long after completing the service. Again, the idea is to see that a person achieves everything he wanted and more from each Scientology service completed.

Of the more than a quarter of a million Scientology success stories written each year, a typical few have been chosen here from the various levels of training and processing.

Training

Communication (Comm) Course

I can hardly express in words and deeds the tremendous benefits that I gained in the attainment of my present goals as a businessman from just completing this initial course. I am fortunate to have found Scientology, an event that will definitely mark my rebirth and literally start me off on a new adventure of my life. My companions and I, although few at present, are aware of the tremendous potentialities of Dianetics and Scientology in being able to provide the magic touch of enlightenment to our people and pave the way to wisdom, advancement, peace and well-being.

Brig. General (Ret.) ATF

The Brigadier General (Ret.) is one of the top businessmen in Pasay City in the Philippines.

_____

The main thing I gained from the Communication Course is the ability to communicate. In that the purpose of the course was to do this I am completely satisfied with the results. Coming from an Ivy League educated background, I had assumed that a $16,000 investment meant that I already knew how to communicate. However, I was wrong to a great extent. Major educational systems do not teach "being there" as the basis for good communication. A parrot is not necessarily in good communication. Using misunderstood words in communication creates confusion and loss of interest.

One other major insight I gained from the Communication Course is that communication is not limited to words, speech, books or TV. Communication is going on constantly and to be able to communicate well gives a being more control over his life, and a greater awareness in general of life's possibilities.

W R

_____

Since I have started on the Communication Course life appears very much alive! My enthusiasm to go out and accomplish more goals increases more each day. I have had several wins in my personal life simply due to my own added ability and desire to confront *all* experiences in my life.

J G — Los Angeles

Before I became interested in Scientology I was heavily involved in an introverted, drug-oriented world. I had trouble even talking to my best friends. I didn't understand what they said and never tried to. I became tongue-tied and could never express myself or my ideas. I was an angry person inside.

After the first night I was on the Communication Course my life made a drastic change. It was fantastic. I talked to people I've never talked to before. I was able to be in a real world even with people that I wished not to be with. What I mean is that before the course I would withdraw and go into my own little world.

Now that I've finished the course I feel I can use the drills. I've learned to communicate to anyone who can hold onto reality and not become irrational. I feel great!

R G

From the time that I first started the Communication Course up until the time I finished, I knew that it had something to offer me. What I didn't expect was to experience such amazing wins from the course in so short of a time. I started the course so that I could be able to handle all the hang-ups in life much better than I had been. One thing that has improved a great deal is my shyness. Before I started course I was a much shyer person than I am now, especially when it comes to confronting and communicating with new people. However now I can confront anyone and I can communicate with them easily and feel a lot more comfortable. I have been able to apply the drills I've done on this course to life and they have worked.

Scientology has changed my life to the point where I want to continue on. At first I wasn't sure but after I've seen what this one course has done for me, and how happy it has made me, I can imagine what the other courses can do. Scientology is the only thing that can provide people with the technology and give them the tools to survive and get the most out of life.

A C

HQS (Hubbard Qualified Scientologist) Course

The HQS Course has been for me more practical and applicable than four years of college. It is a contentment to know you are affiliated with a group of good and dedicated people who work with a technology that can only bring tremendous success to anyone who cares to use it. Thank you.

P L

Prior to being introduced to Scientology, P L was just growing tired of the "drug scene." Currently, he runs four successful businesses, including a restaurant.

Having taken the HQS Course I have gained increasing awareness and understanding of myself and others, and of the (our) universe and environment. I am very aware that Scientology can and will change and better conditions on

this planet. Since being in Scientology I have been becoming increasingly happier and more able to pursue the things I want in life. And I know this is only a taste of what's to come. My hope has been restored. I encourage others to take this course, it works!

L R — New York

Student Hat

I used to think I could study just about any subject and *pass* the exam. Now I know that I can study any subject and *apply* the data. My glibness has really shattered on this course. Now I have started liking my job again; a lot of things have cleared up on the way. This course is worth a fortune.

G M — Montreal

I just finished one fantastic course and I feel great about it. My trouble in school was that I never knew how to study. I was always the kid with cheat sheets in the desk. And instead of writing a report by myself I'd copy the data verbatim from the source.

I now know HOW TO STUDY and if someone can learn to study then they can learn about anything they want to and do it. I never knew before how important proper study technology is, but now I love it. I'd never be without it.

E B M

Primary Rundown

Believe it or not, I didn't really know any of the words when I did the Student Hat. I had had courses at the graduate level in linguistics and I couldn't really define 'a' 'the' ... I've rediscovered my love for reading and writing. I study about twice as fast now.

It may take you a while to finish the Primary Rundown, but you save so much time for the rest of your life in handling paperwork and writing reports that it will buy thousands of hours later in which you can relax and enjoy yourself. A lot of teachers and business people are harried by their paperwork. As a Super-Literate, you can have time left to do what you are supposed to be doing and what you enjoy doing on your job. I can go through fifty student weekly reports in a few minutes and see what's there. I handle my administrative duties as a teacher much faster.

I think everyone should try it.

S C — Los Angeles

New Era Dianetics Course

This course was great! The data was so easy to learn. I am very excited about this technology and can hardly wait to put it to use. Thank you, Ron, you did it again.

S D — New Mexico

Well this course certainly will make a lot of difference in handling cases. It's fantastic to apply all those new actions. I even am very eager as a pc to go back in session and do the whole Bridge from the bottom again. I'm sure I can get 100% more gains out of it.

G A—Florida

This was a great course and I had many wins on the auditing part and receiving it as a pc. What a powerful set of processes! I'm looking forward to auditing it every day.

I V—Europe

Auditing the New Era Dianetics is really great! The exactness is so much more than it ever has been, that the wins and gains are so much more too. Thank you L. Ron Hubbard for the technology to really handle thoroughly a person on Dianetics. It is really a privilege to be one of the first to complete this course!

S W—Florida

I really saw my pc change before my eyes and observed a remarkable physical change from running one engram chain with New Era Dianetics tech. I am really seeing the true results of Dianetics.

J M—California

Well, a really fabulous course. I had a couple of *very* big wins on this, and assorted wins generally, both as an auditor and a pc. My biggest one is the fact that I really feel like an auditor, I feel very confident in my knowledge of the tech and its workability and that feels real good!

I was also able to help another person, who was previously a stranger to Dianetics and Scientology, to get enough subjective reality that he has started the Communications Course and has become a Scientologist himself.

C C—Florida

New Era Dianetics Case Supervisor Course

What a great course. L. Ron Hubbard has done it again! The technology will definitely ensure *everyone* gets the gains and miracles available. Thank you, Ron.

R M T—Florida

Fabulous course! The New Era Dianetics technology is completely thorough and handles pcs. It is a joy to supervise the auditing of pcs on New Era Dianetics.

M W—California

Expanding from Dianetic auditor to Dianetic Case Supervisor is a very rewarding gain. It's great to have certainty that you can handle one preclear and his reactive mind, but much more powerful to have certainty on handling many preclears and their reactive minds via the auditor. Having this skill, I really gained certainty in myself,

my knowledge of the technology and my ability to use the technology to help others. And helping others is what I've always most wanted to do.

J P

Co-Auditing

Co-auditing on the Dianetics Course was one of the most rewarding experiences of my life.

As a new Scientologist I found the data on the reactive mind and how it can prevent happiness and cause unwanted pains, sensations, emotions and attitudes to be fascinating and horrible. I wanted to do something to help myself and my friends to get rid of our reactive minds.

On the Dianetics Course, I learned how to audit others to be well and happy, but that idea was not totally real to me until I started co-auditing.

It was amazing to listen to my preclear tell me incident after incident from her past and see the relief she experienced when she found the source of the difficulty we were working on. One spectacular win was when she got rid of a stomach pain she'd had for years—and it didn't come back.

We'd take turns, I'd audit her in the morning and she'd audit me in the afternoon. Each session was such a win for us both that it was difficult to tell who was getting audited. We both felt great conquering our own and each other's reactive mind.

I also co-audited with several other students and it went the same way—big wins for both preclear and auditor.

I thoroughly recommend co-auditing as the way to advance oneself. There are so many advantages in learning to be effective in handling another's reactive mind as well as your own. And the friendships made while co-auditing are something very, very precious.

S M—Pennsylvania

Word Clearer Course

I really enjoyed getting this course under my belt. I'd never before really appreciated what a fantastic body of technology word clearing constitutes, nor had I appreciated the very important role that word clearing plays in all aspects of Scientology practice and life.

I've already had great success word clearing people, and I'm looking forward to just doing a whole lot more.

R S—England

Level 0

This was a fantastic course. If everybody did it, there would not be problems with communication on this planet. My profit from this course has been enormous. A fog is gone.

J M—Denmark

Just finished Level 0. It was great! I've been a professional singer for twenty-five years and have never communicated. I realized that I have never inflowed communication.

But have only attempted to outflow with little success. I know I can now duplicate and receive communication from others and not be on such an incessant outflow.

D H

_____

Wow! This is the best course I've taken. By the time you have finished this course you *know* communication.

I had a lot of fun doing this level and it was well worth waiting for. This course is vital to understanding life. Since I've done this course I have become much more aware of my own and others' communication and I know when something is wrong and how to repair it and get into better communication with others. This course is a real gas.

R L — England

Level I

What a level; how to get rid of problems. I always wondered why I had so much trouble solving them. Now I know where to look.

I have also discovered why I didn't want to get involved in helping people. "Failed help," i.e. failing to help them, really made me feel bad. It's very important data and increased my certainty as an auditor.

J N H — England

_____

After Level I, I found I had a much greater understanding of why people had problems and a new avenue of help was open for me. I could now help others solve their problems by directing their attention to the source of those problems. The data I got on Level I has been invaluable to me.

K K — New York

Level II

I have just completed Level II. The data is phenomenal! This level really has started making changes in the way I handle my family, my friends and of course my preclears.

There were a lot of unanswered questions that had popped up which finally got answered here!

J M

Level III

I've gotten a lot from my previous Scientology courses, but Level III gave me a very important key to understanding life. It's very simple data and very effective. My understanding is increasing daily and I am heartily thankful for the technology.

M G — Denmark

Level IV

I first came into Scientology when I was living in Paris. Life hadn't been very stable for me until then. I used to get

pretty ill. I'd had rheumatic fever; I suffered from sinusitis. I lacked purpose. Although I had many possessions I wasn't happy, got upset easily and was hung up with my losses.

Since coming into Scientology I've become happy and healthy; I have no problems or major upsets, feel I can handle a lot and have a purpose in life. When you're changing mental and physical conditions for the better, the sky's the limit! My rheumatic fever and sinusitis have gone for good.

But my biggest wins have been as an auditor — seeing people change in front of my very eyes. Their complexion becoming healthy, their cheeks rosy, their expression happier and their lives more ethical as their auditing brought them the insight to handle unethical situations in their lives. I recommend Scientology training for the simple reason that to have abilities is not enough if you don't have any data about life to align those abilities with.

M S — Tel Aviv

_____

I now have so much technology under my belt. It's great. Being a medical doctor, in the past I have had considerations about making myself known as a Scientologist. The major win that I have had in doing these training levels is that I now have the undeniable certainty of the validity and an awareness of the importance of Scientology technology. This means that I am letting it be known far and wide that I am a Scientologist. Any problems with critics are minimal compared with the value of letting it be known that I am a trained member of the only really, really, really worthwhile group on the planet.

S D, M.D. — England

Level IV Interneship

I have completed the Level IV Interneship and I feel it is a real achievement. My knowledge of the basics is such that I don't think of them while auditing. I have a certainty of application and a presence that have enabled my preclears to achieve signal results.

N F — Auckland

_____

This internship was excellent. I gained total certainty on the technology and that feels great. This has been an experience I will never forget. My responsibility level has come up even higher. There are many people who helped tremendously. Thanks.

P J — Portland

Expanded Dianetics Course

I have always been certain that Scientology works, but prior to completing the Expanded Dianetics Course I was acutely aware of the fact that there were some people that I was not really capable of helping very much. What made this awareness even more acute was the fact that the very people that I was unable to help were the people who were most urgently in need of help.

The Expanded Dianetics Course gave me all the data I needed to be able to help anyone handle his most severe aberrations, especially chronic unwanted conditions. On a more personal level, those portions of my own behavior which I consider to be aberrated and my own chronic unwanted conditions are no longer unconfrontable to me. I am very certain that the technology will handle them. So I have much more free attention which used to be tied up in worrying about my own aberrations. They are no longer a mystery to me. And understanding the source of my aberrations I am a much freer and more able being.

J P

Expanded Dianetics Case Supervisor Course

This was a terrific course. It's a great feeling to know that you can guide a fellow being out of the worst dilemma into the clear where he/she belongs with simple logical technology.

R A — Germany

Saint Hill Special Briefing Course

I have heard over 350 tapes by L. Ron Hubbard. I have read all of the books of Dianetics and Scientology in chronological order and now feel very calm and confident about the knowledge I have.

All the loose ends I was hardly even aware of have been tied up. Questions I had not phrased yet were answered. Fixed opinions by the ton took a nose dive. And I can evaluate situations better — no more "leap before you look!"

I do recommend this course for anyone who calls himself "Scientologist." You will achieve a stability and certainty well worth having. What a base for further auditing, training and handling of the universe!

A C — England

Being on the Briefing Course is most satisfying because I know I can now deliver the phenomenal results of Scientology to others. I really love auditing — there's nothing like it.

I taught school for fifteen years in an attempt to get others to communicate better by teaching them another language, French. Scientology is of such a vastly greater magnitude! When I found there was real help I was eager to have it for myself and to give it to others.

Another thing I have gained is being able to handle my children better. In general, the children are more self-reliant now. Each has become more aware of his share of responsibility to the family. Having the data of Scientology to align their experiences, they are all increasingly happy with life.

A S — Los Angeles

When we look at the data on the Saint Hill Special Briefing Course and when we look at the world, with all its violence and war, we can see clearly that people don't understand each other. They don't communicate between themselves, they are entrapped. People will fight for an idea or a symbol and the only thing they achieve is destruction of others, then of themselves, and eventually of their own goal.

So here in Scientology we learn the fundamentals of understanding, of communication, of judging situations and so with this knowledge we feel we can bring some peace and some understanding amongst people.

C D T — Paris

Senior Saint Hill Special Briefing Course

The Senior SHSBC filled in all the missing pieces for me. I went from feeling life is really a mystery to knowing what it's all about. Since doing the Briefing Course I haven't actually come into a situation that I haven't been able to handle. I've gone from knowing things are not going to go right, to knowing things of course *are* going to go right!

G Z — Philadelphia

Class VI Internship

It's hard to know where to begin! This was a super action indeed. I couldn't begin to describe all the gains I personally had from this internship. But to name a few: I have experienced enormous improvement in my ability to confront and handle and help people, and have also attained a great level of stability. But the most important thing to me personally is the self-confidence and personal integrity that I now feel. I feel strong and capable in life as well as when auditing. Truly priceless wins.

P A — Oregon

Solo Auditor Course

The adventure of Scientology — it's like a treasure hunt — except that you don't have to wait until you come to the end before finding the treasure. It's strewn all along the way. The gains in awareness and perception I have had on the Solo Auditor's Course have improved my auditing ability tremendously.

I have every confidence in myself and the technology to get me Clear now. What an exciting adventure — it gets better as you go.

M W — Perth

Class VII Course

I have just studied the Class VII Course most thoroughly and I had the most incredible realizations while doing it. Power Processing is so simple and precise and that makes it truly powerful for the preclear and the auditor!

Well, here I am ready to give Power to my preclears who will simply love it. Every preclear truly achieves power — it's a beautiful sight.

T V H — Germany

Class VIII Course

This is a beautiful course. All the basics and simplicities of the technology are contained in it. Auditing becomes very simple. To the extent that it becomes simple it becomes effective. It is the added complications that make it look difficult and ineffective, and I lost some of those, for sure.

A G — Copenhagen

One night I saw the Class VIII Course students filing out of their special classroom. Some were old friends. All were bright and serene and had a look as if they'd just experienced something wondrous. I stopped an old friend and asked, "What's it like on the Class VIII Course?" He laughed freely and said, "Incredible" and walked on. It wasn't what he said, but how he looked—exhilarated and serenely powerful, that made me decide right there "I want on that Class VIII Course!"

The course is incredible!

The special tapes are amazing.

I left that course with power, awareness and understanding to spare!

With certainty from the course, I applied my newfound powers and abilities and things flowed and glowed right for me, my friends and those around us. Relationships rekindled and blossomed; hopes thought lost were realized.

This all happened a few years ago and has continued. Today, I am happier and healthier than ever and the future looks bright and exciting.

C B — Los Angeles

HSST (Hubbard Specialist of Standard Tech)

I feel every Class VIII should do the HSST. The step between Class VIII and HSST is the difference between knowing how to audit well and knowing for certain that what processes you are auditing on a preclear will produce maximum gain. A Class VIII who wants to be a professional auditor is really depriving himself of an entirely different viewpoint if he doesn't do the HSST.

T E

Class IX Course

Scientology has been my favorite subject ever since I first started learning about it. On the Class IX Course I arrived at a point of knowing that I am an expert on this subject. I can use the full scope of Scientology effortlessly, not only in helping people with auditing but in life as well. The philosophy and its application belong to me personally. That is how I feel and it makes me feel both proud and happy, as well as very capable and sure of myself.

Soon after I finished the Class IX Course, my best friends found that their marriage was breaking up and they came to me for help. A year ago, I would have sent them to someone "who would know what to do." Now *I* knew what to do. I was able to trace the mass of confusion they were in down to the original point where it began and at that point the whole problem evaporated. We unlocked eight years of unhappiness in one hour. I was conscious of what I was doing at each step we took.

Having the power to help my friends like this when help is *really* needed is what I wanted when I came into Scientology. And the trip up the line has been as wonderful as the prize at this end.

D D — Minnesota

Class X Course

The Class X Course is an education into an extraordinary piece of technology. It is brilliantly put together by L. Ron Hubbard, in his usual genius and he has pushed this technology to such a high degree of expertise that no other technology, past or present, can approach it. I feel it's an honor to be able to have this opportunity to use and apply this data.

M C — Perth

Class XI Course

This was a great level—very simple, very dynamic, very precise. I learned a tremendous amount from this action. And it was a fun course. My deepest thanks to all who helped.

K C — England

Class XII Course

Doing the Class XII Course was the crowning point of my studies. I can understand people. I can communicate to them. I like them. After I did this course, I was promoted to an executive position. The data I have acquired has made me a far more effective executive than I ever thought possible. Those people who work for me can tell the difference. L. Ron Hubbard has done a brilliant job and once again I have personally verified the effectiveness of his data.

J E — New York

Cramming

During the last few years I have studied a vast amount of the technology of auditing. Some students, of a lower level of training, consider me an expert. I have had people come to me with, "What would you do if . . . ?" Many times I knew what to do. A few times the suggested situation was something I had not thought of before and could not immediately figure out. For a while I carried these uncertainties around unable to find any reference which answered the particular question. In one visit to Cramming with these questions I was referred to the exact references which answered those questions. I restudied those references.

As a result I've noticed that my attention is a lot more free, unencumbered by these little questions in the corners of my mind that were keeping me from having full attention on the work I was doing. This action also had the side effect of raising the respect I had for myself as an auditor. (It had diminished with each new uncertainty.) And also it has renewed my security in the completeness of this technology.

S B — Berkeley

Organization Executive Course

Many chamber of commerce staff members feel it's very much like trying to do a delicate operation with thick gloves on. The Organization Executive Course takes the gloves off. The data gives you the ability to handle other people with precision. The data is vital when one's only method of handling community situations is through the revitalization of the purposes of others.

At the time I entered Scientology, I was climbing the corporate ladder without regard for how many "dead bodies" resulted along the way. My view of ethics was, "He who had the power to make it happen is right."

The night I went for my Introductory Lecture was the night following my divorce, another fatality to this corporate climb. I didn't really believe that it was either possible or important to be happy. Just strong, and therefore safe.

After some auditing, I quit that game. Since that time I have been very happy and now remarried.

I have played the game in business, in government and in community organizations, and I know that I can get to the top in any of them.

J W – St. Louis

J W from St. Louis is the manager for World Trade and Agri (agri is short for agricultural) Business for the St. Louis Chamber of Commerce.

The libraries are full of thousands of books on organization management. But L. Ron Hubbard in just a few volumes called the Organization Executive Course has distilled the basics—the laws that are the foundation for all these other works—and made them immediately accessible, without having to wade through all the irrelevant material. They contain all the data necessary to make any business expand as far as you want to go.

H W – Kansas

H W is a member of the Kansas Economic Commission.

Flag Executive Briefing Course (FEBC)

After I'd done the OEC (Organization Executive Course) I had a very clear idea of how to set up and operate and expand towards its ideal scene, a Scientology organization or any ethical organization. Actually I didn't think there was much more to know about running a business or organization, but doing the FEBC soon disabused me of that attitude. It taught me that an organization is an alive and flexible thing and that it is necessary to change and adapt it to varying circumstances and customer demands. I realized that with my basics on organizations really understood from my OEC studies I could now "play the tune" by being flexible and creative without violating the basic concept of the organization.

So for anyone who wishes to better organize his business or group I can thoroughly recommend the FEBC. You'll find it to be a dynamic and stimulating experience and you'll wonder what became of all those business and organizational problems that used to plague you!

B W – London

Data Series Evaluators Course (DSEC)

I have been working with the Data Series and the technology of the Data Series Evaluators Course for over five years now. This is the greatest group technology I have ever learned to use as a being *ever* in my entire past. Though I have held many different posts in Scientology

organizations and before that, in the business world, there is no other post that has given me so many wins as that of an evaluator, not only regarding my job, but across all areas of my life.

When you can do a standard evaluation using the technology of the DSEC you can handle any situation whether it be on your job or in your everyday life.

This course is a must for every being regardless of what you do or your occupation. L. Ron Hubbard says that the moment you apply "humanoid thinking" to the subject of evaluation, you lose. Well what does that mean? It means that you, as a being, learn to think and act logically—*way* above the humanoid norm.

It is incredible to think there is a course that can train you to think logically and act logically based on logical conclusions in all areas of life. But it is true because it works every time when applied standardly.

H F

Mini Course Supervisor Course

Just before I got into Scientology, I had been working as a teacher. I had earned a Master's degree in Education and had confidently gone into the classroom to teach the children. I immediately found out that what I had been taught in the university had very little to do with the realities of managing a large class of unruly children. My beautiful lesson plans fell to pieces as I tried to cope with the ones who couldn't learn and with the ones who wouldn't learn.

I left teaching after one year feeling that it was an area of failure in my life.

Then a few years later I took the Mini Course Supervisor Course in order to learn my new job as a supervisor of a Scientology course in Los Angeles. On the course I practiced the skills of communicating and confronting. For the first time, I was able to FACE the students themselves, not some idea I might have had of them. I also learned the exact reasons for the "inability to learn" and the "unwillingness to learn." I learned to handle those conditions very simply. As soon as I finished the course, I began my year running the class. All my previous troubles with teaching had clearly evaporated. Far from being a failure, running that class was the happiest experience in my entire job history.

I know now that I could teach anybody anything. What I had been missing as a teacher was actually very little, but without it I failed. The Mini Course Supervisor Course taught me exactly what I needed to know to succeed at teaching and I am grateful for the data.

D D – Berkeley

Prior to taking the Basic Study Manual and the Mini Course Supervisor Course I was satisfied with my teaching abilities. Now I am extremely proud of them.

Using L. Ron Hubbard's study and supervising technology in my classroom produces amazing results. My students learn more quickly and retain instead of memorize. The level of interest on the students' part has risen to enthusiasm; and that in itself is quite remarkable considering I teach accounting, the school's most dreaded subject!

The students of the College of Business recently selected me as the *Outstanding Faculty Member 1976-77*. In addition, students fight to get into my classes and my classes are always overflowing while other classes remain half empty. My dropout rate is negligible while other teachers average 30 to 40 per cent.

I find teaching so much more challenging and keep amazing myself by figuring out new ways of applying the materials on these courses.

What a brilliant, eager-to-learn society we would have if everyone knew and used L. Ron Hubbard's study technology.

J A
Instructor of Accounting
University of South Florida

Hubbard Professional Course Supervisor Course

This was tough, but I wouldn't have missed doing it for the world. My confront on people and groups has come way

way up. I feel really thrilled to bits about the whole course. I can really supervise and do it well. I know exactly how a course should run. Many many thanks to all who helped.

K B — England

Hubbard Senior Course Supervisor Course

I have never had such certainty and ability on any one area as I now have on course supervision. I have done a lot of things but never with the certainty and professional capacity I now have. Thank you.

M R — Los Angeles

———————

Processing

Livingness Repair Rundown

When I first heard of this Rundown I wondered how one could get his Livingness repaired. I felt the things that had happened to me were in the past and better left forgotten. I thought time had healed what was in my past enough for me to carry on. Well, I was surprised to find time stood still in many places with all the emotion and pain just as powerful as the day it happened. Just to rid myself of that was enough, but what was fantastic was finding the real reasons why things happened and why I felt uncertain towards many things. With the ability of my auditors my attention was guided to many areas where I had made irrational decisions and unevaluated conclusions.

It's great to repair the past using the intelligence I have today and to get rid of fears and other upsets that affected me which I thought had long since been forgotten. The greatest wins I had were the cognitions I am still having using my past as a personal text. I have a new viewpoint of my life and the lives of others. I'd like to thank my auditors for their intelligence, ability, understanding and guidance which made my successes possible. I know now which direction I'm headed in and the certainty makes me feel good inside. I couldn't say enough about this technology which has repaired my past.

B B

———————

I did this so quickly I'm in awe! My abilities increased daily. Many unwanted feelings are gone so they aren't there to hold me back. I'm so much more extroverted and my confidence is returning. I don't dwell so much on what I don't have or can't do. My confront on these things is coming up. And what I can do and have is getting better. I feel more enthusiastic about everything and I feel good about communicating with others. I like to! My admiration and affection for others is so much greater now. I feel great. I feel good about *allowing* myself to be enthusiastic and extroverted and excited 'cause that is me!

I want other people to have this feeling and discover

Scientology. Those reservations I had are gone. A thousand thank you's!

L R — New York

New Era Dianetics Auditing

Well I just had my first session of New Era Dianetics auditing. The exactness of this new technology is fantastic. I felt that the auditor could and did zoom in on those unwanted areas in my case and handled them once and for all. There was no doubt that the things I wanted handled were truly handled for me without worrying about them ever again. I would like to thank L. Ron Hubbard for this marvelous technology and the wins are just what he says they are.

T C — Florida

———————

I am *really* happy and winning. These recent Objectives have enabled me to be more in communication with my environment and more in present time. Many thanks to my auditor for her standard application of L. Ron Hubbard's miraculous technology.

C G — New York

———————

New Era Dianetics is GREAT! I am able to find many drug items that were untouched before and this is very rewarding.

M R — Florida

———————

New Era Dianetics is GREAT! I really enjoyed it. It was good to handle all the things connected with my rash. I have always wanted to do this and New Era Dianetics has made it possible.

P E — California

———————

On New Era Dianetics auditing I had a cognition on how the reactive mind works and I could really see what's happening with a pc. I had many good wins in my auditing and I feel lighter and happier. New Era Dianetics is great.

M V — Canada

This New Era Dianetics session was fantastic. A "cold" that had hung on for two weeks just totally blew. L. Ron Hubbard's New Era Dianetics tech is truly miraculous.

M C — California

New Era Dianetics auditing has meant a complete turnaround for me. Where I ran regular Dianetics slowly before, I now run New Era Dianetics fast and smoothly. My self-doubts about being able to run well as a pc have totally vanished. In particular I've had a lot of gain running the New Era Dianetics Drug Rundown, handling a whole group of items that acted like drugs, and which I never touched upon before.

Thanks, Ron, for such incredible technology — it's given me some great wins and cognitions.

B D — Arizona

ARC Straightwire

I can testify with all the confidence at my command that I have completed ARC Straightwire, which was both exhilarating and most satisfying. My wins have been tremendous on reality, perception and understanding. Life for me now will be so much more interesting and productive. And furthermore, much of the memory I had lost has now returned but on a high level of reality and understanding in comparison to yesteryear. Thank you.

A B — Canada

Communications Release

I work for Continental Airlines and after my Communications Release I received an outstanding written appraisal from my supervisor, which had never been given to any woman in my office before; a complimentary letter from a customer; and a raise in pay some months before it was due by seniority. It was also an amount much greater than is usually given. In addition to this, I got a promotion to a job that is usually given to people with more experience than I have! My co-workers now seem to place a greater value on my opinions and often ask for my assistance. I shall always be grateful to Scientology for making these things possible.

E K — Los Angeles

After fifteen years of an *absolute inability* to communicate on any level, this past Tuesday I was able to take my sister in my arms and know she and I were able to communicate. I wasn't looking for or planning it, it was (and is) just there. It was one of the most beautiful things I have ever experienced.

G Z — Philadelphia

Problems Release

I've had a major change in my life during this action. I have always had trouble recognizing the source of a problem. I knew where there was one but without the source I couldn't handle it. Now I can and my speed in handling things has tripled because of it. I'm feeling 100% better and because of the above realization my viewpoint on life itself has changed for the better.

D P — Florida

Relief Release

I have never seen anything like this! This level of auditing release is called Relief, and a more accurate name was never given. I have had, on this level, more change and expansion than I ever dared believe. I am free of the hostilities and sufferings of life and all I can say is, it's impossible to realize how vast a change that is until you do it yourself.

H R — New York

Freedom Release

It's very nice to be able to look at the future in a *bright* way, especially when you haven't done so for a very, very, long, long time. It's like having a new future or something to put into it.

J P V — Paris

On this processing I experienced great feelings of freedom as I know what causes of upsets are, know how to handle them and am thus no longer hindered from looking and handling the future. Thanks to this marvelous technology. I just loved the processes of this level.

I L — Munich

Ability Release

I have just completed Scientology Grade IV, Ability Release.

How wonderful, I feel that every step taken on the Scientology ladder continues to unfold the wonders of this great technology, and one realizes its importance to mankind.

My thanks to the auditor who was really "GREAT," her patience and knowledge left one in no doubts. Also, my greatest thanks to the Founder, L. Ron Hubbard.

May Scientology go from strength to strength.

Rev. A T C — England

Rev. A T C is a Minister of the Established Church of England.

WOW!
This grade is really a "powerhouse" grade! The gains I

now have were before "beyond my wildest dreams." Thank you.

                                        S C — New York

S C is an internationally known bass guitarist. In recent years, since becoming a Scientologist, he has won many awards as a musician and is recognized by many as the top bass guitarist in the world. He is an active Scientologist.

PTS Rundown

I am very stable. I have stably expanded upward since my rundown — in auditing *and* out. My attention is again mine to play with. Thank you for helping me. I've gotten off the roller coaster. Merci!

                                        T D — Virginia

Confessional Processing

What a fantastic feeling to be free of harmful acts I've done, which I did such a good job of justifying in the past. I gained such a beautiful win regarding my relationship with my family. I realized without a doubt that I have two wonderful parents who care and love me deeply. I came to grips with what I did to hinder the relationship and since my big cognitions, the space at home is clean and loving. I feel so much more able in creating a safe and honest space with people, it feels tremendous!

                                        C M — New York

Word Clearing

Incredible — this action gives me a feeling that I can *have* knowledge in a lot of fields. I feel really great. Thanks so very much to my auditor.

                                        S M — Los Angeles

It's absolutely essential in studying anything to know the correct meanings of words.

A big win for me as I never believed any one definition was that important. It is! Thanks.

                                        K R — Montana

Expanded Dianetics

I've just finished Expanded Dianetics. The gains I've had have been phenomenal. I've lost the need to keep a constant watch on myself. The need to be "careful."

I can *trust* me. And you!

It feels good.

                                        P D

I'm delighted with the smooth handling and validation

I've received. I am certain that I can now operate without withholding myself as I know that I am "good"!

I feel I will be a much greater asset to those around me because of completing Expanded Dianetics.

                                        L A — New York

Power Processing

I can look at things that I couldn't look at before and look at them very realistically. It's amazing to me — things I used to not be able to confront, I can now look at very easily! I need about two hours less sleep at night now. I feel great and wake up bright and shiny.

                                        L S — Berkeley

Power Plus Processing

On completion of Power Plus Processing I feel very calm and stable and sure of my own abilities.

                                        J C — Vancouver

The world after Power Plus Processing is bright and shiny, the people, the sun, the places — life.

I gained familiarity with everything, with everyone.

                                        D Z — Mexico

Grade VI Release

Before I heard of Scientology I had spent several years reading and studying other philosophies: Adler, Steiner, Annie Besant, astrology, nature cure, etc. Each has their merit, and are all based on credible observation. But, I and fellow students accepted they were, at best, approximations of the truth.

On Grade VI, I discovered for myself as anyone else will, if they follow the instructions, that what L. Ron Hubbard says is true, is true. Also, that Scientology is a technology as logical as mathematics and factual as chemistry.

For myself I now know why my own and other people's behavior follows (or followed) the pattern it does (or did) and am happy that I have broken free of the trap at last.

                                        N M — London

Clear

I'm Clear — through and through. It's a state I've dreamed of and planned for now for two years. It is better than I hoped for. "Inside" I'm calm, peaceful and very happy. I can so easily be around others and myself with no inner voice telling me what to do, how to act and what to say. Truly a state of great freedom.

                                        C S

OT I

I have just completed OT I. What a great level this is. It's a beautiful state. The world looks new and fresh and so pleasant. My relationship with people is better. And I feel so very good.

M G—Melbourne

OT II

This is an increasing ability to confront—knowingly. I feel very much myself.

S P—Mexico

OT III

I have gained tremendous ability, perception and stability from this level. More than any other I have done.

D E—Florida

OT III Expanded

I am very happy having finished the level of OT III Expanded. It has been the most important step for me until now. I have really had great gains on this level. My awareness has increased immensely and my responsibility has grown. I now know who I am. It has been quite a bit of work but I've also had very much fun on this level. I am very thankful to all who have helped me to attain this goal.

K K—Denmark

OT IV

This level was simply fascinating and very refreshing. I feel very clean and have a tremendously increased love for my fellow man. It is a personal goal I've wanted for a long time. The gains are completely stable.

L T

OT V

I recall a time when I was about five years old. It was spring, the snow had melted and I was playing in a meadow. The ground was damp and spongy beneath my feet, the smell of plants growing was thick in the air. For an hour I watched a grasshopper going about his business. I recall the fascination I felt for the world around me.

With the completion of OT V, I again have that fascination. It's beautiful.

L M

OT VI

This level gently grooves you in to being able to use, self-determinedly the abilities attained from doing the previous levels. And it takes a bit of getting used to the speed at which a person can operate—not being governed by the laws of the physical universe. I find I can move freely. Matter, energy, space and time are no longer barriers to my freedom.

The steps from the bottom levels of Scientology to the top are really the greatest adventure anyone could wish for. My sincere thanks to all who help make it so.

M W—England

OT VII

When I was a child and when I was growing up I often pondered on the miseries of life as well as the absurdities. I frequently wished that my life would hurry up and get over because it wasn't really what I wanted. Unfortunately there was no complaint department to which I could turn in my life for a better or more satisfying model.

Five years ago I picked up a book (*Dianetics: The Modern Science of Mental Health*) which offered a new model, even if one already had a used one.

Today I completed OT VII. I could never have imagined one could ever achieve such a state. I'm powerful and ready to pursue life as I have never been able to do before. What thanks can you give a man who has made this all possible?

J S—Los Angeles

Student Booster Rundown

This auditing is really what it says it is. My study ability has almost doubled, and I feel as if I have no stops on studying. I also cleared up a lot of other things about life in general that have been barriers in the past. I feel all set up for future study and auditing.

J B—Philadelphia

_____

I don't know where to begin—I had so many wins. This processing took me from a true wreck back to true me and *happy to be me*. I feel very much more confident and aware and I'm eager to study everything now—even calculus and Greek!

A R

New Vitality Rundown

The new experience of life since doing the New Vitality Rundown is beyond words. I feel like I'm living—for me—for the very first time. It's a *new vitality* that I feel. My capacity to live and to grow is there like never before. It's like a new energy that I create. I can't believe it. A new awareness of granting life to things around me, and to people, and to allow others to grant life as well.

This is all *new* to me. It's like living all over again, with a responsibility and peace.

M C — California

L-10 Auditing

If I remember correctly, I started into L-10 with a question, "Who am I?" Well, I got my question answered. I emerged from the other side of L-10 with certainty of myself. I've had a tremendous lot of wins on this L-10, it's packed full of goodies. I can move full steam ahead and not be afraid or feel I have to hold back. I am ethical and whole, no longer have missing pieces.

B A — Denver

L-11 Auditing

Completing this rundown has given me a whole new viewpoint of life. I feel like a brand new baby with a whole fresh life before me — only more so, as most new babies don't start out this clean and fresh, much less have the benefit of their past experience, as I do. Life truly has begun at forty for me — thanks to the New Life Rundown.

F M — St. Louis

L-12 Auditing

This was the most wonderful auditing I ever had. My awareness and perceptions have risen to levels I didn't know existed. I am totally cleaned from past influences. I can hold my position in space whatever happens. I am clean, powerful and raring to go and get things done.

A R — Sweden

———————————

Ethics

In 1973 I was working part-time making minimum wages, barely enough money for myself and my child to keep a roof over our heads and food in the house. There seemed to be no possibility of a better job or even raising my status in the present one. Caring for a child was rather limiting in the jobs I could accept. I didn't feel I would ever be able to make enough money to do the courses I wanted to do.

I had been sick for a week with every symptom of a cold turned up to full volume. My supervisor against my protest insisted it was an ethics matter and sent me to see the Ethics Officer. The Ethics Officer gave me some information to read about difficulties and their causes. Then, between my coughs and sneezes he asked me some questions about my illness, the people I was associated with and earlier times I had had such a cold.

Two things happened during the course of this discussion with the Ethics Officer. First, during that twenty minutes or so, my cold almost entirely disappeared. The sneezing stopped, the earache and head pressure went away, my body cooled off, my running nose became possible to breathe through, my eyes ceased tearing and were no longer sore, the pain in my chest disappeared, the sore throat diminished and the coughing trickled away to almost nothing.

Second, during the next two months I was able to cause some changes at work which resulted in my quadrupling my salary while working at the same job! And to this day (some four years later) I have had no slightest thought of not being able to make all the money I'd ever need to do whatever I wanted to do.

As a side effect, a long time fear I'd had (no matter where I worked — a fear of losing my job) entirely vanished. In fact, all employers I've had since then have rather begged me to stay!

S B — New York

———————————

4

An Advised Course of Action for Training

The Classification Gradation and Awareness Chart shows the courses to be done to get up the "Bridge" (a term originating in early Dianetics and Scientology days to symbolize travel from unknowingness to revelation) to a high level of skilled application of Scientology technology.

Movement across the Bridge is done gradiently, a step at a time. One then can progress at a rate of speed that is appropriate to his ability and always be assured of arriving at the far end of the Bridge.

Over the years, a great deal of experience has been ac-cumulated in training individuals on the courses available and this chapter seeks to give an advised course of action for training based on the successes of the more experienced supervisors in Scientology.

Following is the portion of the Classification Gradation and Awareness Chart which lists the various courses to be taken and the results which can be obtained from the training levels. This parallels the processing side of the Classification Gradation and Awareness Chart which gives the route to Clear and OT and which is covered in the next chapter.

CLASSIFICATION GRADATION AND AWARENESS CHART OF LEVELS AND CERTIFICATES

FOR DIANETICS AND SCIENTOLOGY TRAINING

This chart describes the route to human recovery and expansion of one's ability and power as a spiritual being. The field of human recovery belongs to Dianetics. Above this is Scientology, which brings an individual to higher states of being and ability.

Now, starting with the first introductory level (bottom line at left) read across the columns and find out what is accomplished, where it can be obtained and why it is important. Note that the introductory levels are not prerequisites, but are there to help one begin and become familiar with fundamentals. Continue reading the chart by moving up one level, and reading across the columns, and moving up to the next and across the column.

-4 NEED OF CHANGE

AWARENESS CHARACTERISTICS	AUDITOR AND CASE SUPERVISOR CLASSES	CERTIFICATE	COURSE	PREREQUISITES
	BOOK AUDITOR	HBA HUBBARD BOOK AUDITOR	NONE	NO PREREQUISITE
	NOT CLASSED	ANATOMY OF THE HUMAN MIND COURSE CERTIFICATE	ANATOMY OF THE HUMAN MIND COURSE	NO PREREQUISITE
	NOT CLASSED	HAS CO-AUDIT CERTIFICATE	HAS CO-AUDIT	NO PREREQUISITE
	NOT CLASSED	INTRODUCTORY COURSE CERTIFICATE	INTRODUCTORY COURSE	NO PREREQUISITE
	NOT CLASSED	RECOGNITION CERTIFICATE	FREE INTRODUCTORY LECTURE	NO PREREQUISITE

LEVELS BELOW NEED OF CHANGE — FROM HUMAN TO MATERIALITY

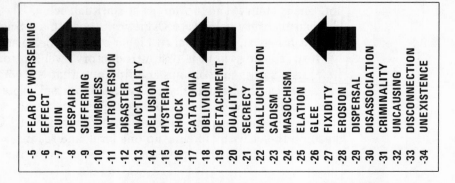

-5 FEAR OF WORSENING
-6 EFFECT
-7 RUIN
-8 DESPAIR
-9 SUFFERING
-10 NUMBNESS
-11 INTROVERSION
-12 DISASTER
-13 INACTUALITY
-14 DELUSION
-15 HYSTERIA
-16 SHOCK
-17 CATATONIA
-18 OBLIVION
-19 DETACHMENT
-20 DUALITY
-21 SECRECY
-22 HALLUCINATION
-23 SADISM
-24 MASOCHISM
-25 ELATION
-26 GLEE
-27 FIXIDITY
-28 EROSION
-29 DISPERSAL
-30 DISASSOCIATION
-31 CRIMINALITY
-32 UNCAUSING
-33 DISCONNECTION
-34 UNEXISTENCE

31

TEACHES ABOUT	SKILLS TAUGHT	WHERE OBTAINED	END RESULT
APPLICATION OF DIANETIC AND/OR SCIENTOLOGY DATA IN LIFE	APPLICATION OF DATA IN DIANETICS AND SCIENTOLOGY BOOKS	CHURCHES AND MISSIONS OF SCIENTOLOGY DIANETIC COUNSELING GROUPS	ABILITY TO HELP SELF AND OTHERS THROUGH THE APPLICATION OF DATA CONTAINED IN BOOKS OF DIANETICS AND SCIENTOLOGY
OBSERVATION AND UNDERSTANDING OF THE FUNDAMENTALS OF THE HUMAN MIND	NONE DEMONSTRATIONS OF THE PARTS OF THE HUMAN MIND	CHURCHES AND MISSIONS OF SCIENTOLOGY DIANETIC COUNSELING GROUPS	ABILITY TO OBSERVE AND UNDERSTAND THE BASIC MECHANISMS AND ABERRATIONS OF THE HUMAN MIND
HAS CO-AUDIT PROCESSES	ABILITY TO CO-AUDIT	CHURCHES AND MISSIONS OF SCIENTOLOGY DIANETIC COUNSELING GROUPS	REALITY ON GAINS ACHIEVABLE THROUGH CO-AUDITING
BASIC SCIENTOLOGY PRINCIPLES AND THEIR APPLICATION TO LIFE	NONE	CHURCHES AND MISSIONS OF SCIENTOLOGY DIANETIC COUNSELING GROUPS	INVOLVED AND INTERESTED IN SCIENTOLOGY
ELEMENTARY POINTS FROM DIANETIC OR SCIENTOLOGY DATA	NONE	CHURCHES AND MISSIONS OF SCIENTOLOGY DIANETIC COUNSELING GROUPS	RECOGNITION OF DIANETICS AND SCIENTOLOGY AS WORKABLE WAYS TO BRING ABOUT CHANGE AND IMPROVEMENT

32

-1 HELP

-2 HOPE

-3 DEMAND FOR
IMPROVEMENT

CLASSES	CERTIFICATE	COURSE	PREREQUISITES
NEW ERA DIANETICS AUDITOR	HUBBARD NEW ERA DIANETICS AUDITOR HNEDA (PROVISIONAL)	NEW ERA DIANETICS COURSE	STUDENT HAT
NOT CLASSED	HUBBARD GRADUATE OF STUDY TECHNOLOGY	THE STUDENT HAT	NO PREREQUISITE
NOT CLASSED	HUBBARD QUALIFIED SCIENTOLOGIST HQS	HQS COURSE	NO PREREQUISITE
NOT CLASSED	VOLUNTEER MINISTER	THE VOLUNTEER MINISTER'S HANDBOOK	NO PREREQUISITE
NOT CLASSED	HUBBARD EXTENSION COURSE GRADUATE	HUBBARD EXTENSION COURSE	NO PREREQUISITE

TEACHES ABOUT	SKILLS TAUGHT	WHERE OBTAINED	END RESULT
DIANETICS: ITS DEVELOPMENT AND REFINEMENTS, NEW ERA DIANETICS PRECISION TECHNOLOGY	NEW ERA DIANETICS AUDITING PROCEDURES AND RUNDOWNS	CHURCHES AND MISSIONS OF SCIENTOLOGY DIANETIC COUNSELING GROUPS	THE SKILL AND KNOWLEDGE TO MAKE A TRULY WELL AND HAPPY HUMAN BEING
THE FUNDAMENTAL PRINCIPLES OF LEARNING AND EDUCATION	HOW TO STUDY EFFECTIVELY	CHURCHES AND MISSIONS OF SCIENTOLOGY DIANETIC COUNSELING GROUPS	HOW TO STUDY EFFECTIVELY
CO-AUDITING AND HOW TO HELP OTHERS WITH AUDITING	TRS 0 TO 4, TRS 6 TO 9 CO-AUDITING ON OBJECTIVE PROCESSES	CHURCHES AND MISSIONS OF SCIENTOLOGY	PERSONAL CASE IMPROVEMENT AND ABILITY TO HELP OTHERS WITH AUDITING
HELPING YOUR FELLOW MAN	ASSISTS, HANDLING ETHICS AND PEOPLE ON DRUGS, MARRIAGE COUNSELING AND MANY OTHER SUBJECTS	HOME STUDY COURSE OR CHURCHES OF SCIENTOLOGY	ABILITY TO HELP ONE'S FELLOW MAN ON A VOLUNTEER BASIS
BASICS OF DIANETICS AND SCIENTOLOGY	NONE	GIVEN BY MAIL ALL CHURCHES OF SCIENTOLOGY	ABILITY TO UNDERSTAND THE FUNDAMENTALS OF LIFE AND EXISTENCE AND IMPROVE YOUR OWN LIFE

CLASSES		CERTIFICATE	COURSE	PREREQUISITES
9 BODY 8 ADJUSTMENT 7 ENERGY	**CLASS III AUDITOR**	HUBBARD PROFESSIONAL AUDITOR HPA (PROVISIONAL)	ACADEMY LEVEL III COURSE	HCA CLASS II (PROVISIONAL)
6 ENLIGHTENMENT 5 UNDERSTANDING 4 ORIENTATION	**CLASS II AUDITOR**	HUBBARD CERTIFIED AUDITOR HCA (PROVISIONAL)	ACADEMY LEVEL II COURSE	HTS CLASS I (PROVISIONAL)
3 PERCEPTION 2 COMMUNICATION	**CLASS I AUDITOR**	HUBBARD TRAINED SCIENTOLOGIST HTS (PROVISIONAL)	ACADEMY LEVEL I COURSE	HRS CLASS 0 (PROVISIONAL)
1 RECOGNITION	**CLASS 0 AUDITOR**	HUBBARD RECOGNIZED SCIENTOLOGIST HRS (PROVISIONAL)	ACADEMY LEVEL 0 COURSE	STUDENT HAT
	VALIDATED NEW ERA DIANETICS CASE SUPERVISOR	HUBBARD NEW ERA DIANETICS GRADUATE (VALIDATED)	NEW ERA DIANETICS GRADUATE (C/S) INTERNESHIP	HNEDA (VALIDATED) HNEDG (C/S) (PROVISIONAL)
	NEW ERA DIANETICS CASE SUPERVISOR	HUBBARD NEW ERA DIANETICS GRADUATE HNEDG (PROVISIONAL)	NEW ERA DIANETICS GRADUATE (C/S) COURSE	HNEDA (PROVISIONAL)
	VALIDATED NEW ERA DIANETICS AUDITOR	HUBBARD NEW ERA DIANETICS AUDITOR HNEDA (VALIDATED)	NEW ERA DIANETICS INTERNESHIP	HNEDA (PROVISIONAL)

35

TEACHES ABOUT	SKILLS TAUGHT	WHERE OBTAINED	END RESULT
INCREASING FREEDOM THROUGH HANDLING UPSETS IN LIFE	ABRIDGED STYLE AUDITING, HANDLING RUDIMENTS, TWO-WAY COMM, REHABS, AUDITING BY LISTS, LISTING AND NULLING	ACADEMIES OF SCIENTOLOGY	ABILITY TO AUDIT OTHERS TO GRADE III FREEDOM RELEASE
PRODUCING RELIEF THROUGH HANDLING OVERTS AND WITHHOLDS	GUIDING STYLE AUDITING, O/W PROCESSES, PREPCHECKING	ACADEMIES OF SCIENTOLOGY	ABILITY TO AUDIT OTHERS TO GRADE II RELIEF RELEASE
PROBLEMS AND THE HANDLING OF THEM	MUZZLED STYLE AUDITING, OBJECTIVE PROCESSES AND PROBLEMS INTENSIVES	ACADEMIES OF SCIENTOLOGY	ABILITY TO AUDIT OTHERS TO GRADE I PROBLEMS RELEASE
WHAT COMMUNICATION IS AND HOW TO IMPROVE COMMUNICATION	LISTEN STYLE AUDITING COMMUNICATION PROCESSES	ACADEMIES OF SCIENTOLOGY	ABILITY TO AUDIT OTHERS TO GRADE 0 COMMUNICATIONS RELEASE
CASE SUPERVISION AND PROGRAMMING OF NEW ERA DIANETICS	FLUBLESS CASE SUPERVISING OF NEW ERA DIANETICS	CHURCHES OF SCIENTOLOGY	A FLUBLESS NEW ERA DIANETICS CASE SUPERVISOR
CASE SUPERVISION AND PROGRAMMING OF NEW ERA DIANETICS	CASE SUPERVISING (C/SING) OF NEW ERA DIANETICS	CHURCHES OF SCIENTOLOGY	ABILITY TO CASE SUPERVISE NEW ERA DIANETICS
NEW ERA DIANETICS AUDITING	FLUBLESS NEW ERA DIANETICS AUDITING	CHURCHES OF SCIENTOLOGY	FLUBLESS NEW ERA DIANETICS AUDITOR
TEACHES ABOUT	SKILLS TAUGHT	WHERE OBTAINED	END RESULT

CLASSES	CERTIFICATE	COURSE	PREREQUISITES
NEW ERA DIANETICS AUDITOR FOR OTs	HUBBARD ADVANCED COURSES SPECIALIST HACS	ADVANCED COURSES SPECIALIST COURSE	HAA CLASS IV O.T. III
PERMANENT CLASS IV GRADUATE (AUDITOR AND CASE SUPERVISOR)	HUBBARD CLASS IV GRADUATE (AUDITOR AND CASE SUPERVISOR)	CLASS IV GRADUATE (AUDITOR AND CASE SUPERVISOR) INTERNESHIP	CLASS IV GRADUATE (AUDITOR AND CASE SUPERVISOR) COURSE
CLASS IV GRADUATE (AUDITOR AND CASE SUPERVISOR)	HUBBARD CLASS IV GRADUATE (AUDITOR AND CASE SUPERVISOR) (PROVISIONAL)	CLASS IV GRADUATE (AUDITOR AND CASE SUPERVISOR) COURSE	HNEDA PROV. HNEDG PROV. HAA CLASS IV
PERMANENT CLASS IV AUDITOR	HUBBARD ADVANCED AUDITOR HAA	CLASS IV INTERNESHIP	HAA CLASS IV PROV.
CLASS IV AUDITOR	HUBBARD ADVANCED AUDITOR HAA (PROVISIONAL)	ACADEMY LEVEL IV COURSE	HNEDA PROV. HPA CLASS III PROV.

11 ACTIVITY
10 PREDICTION

TEACHES ABOUT	SKILLS TAUGHT	WHERE OBTAINED	END RESULT
NEW ERA DIANETICS FOR O.T.s	AUDITING OF NEW ERA DIANETICS FOR O.T.s RUNDOWN	FLAG	ABILITY TO AUDIT NEW ERA DIANETICS FOR OTS RUNDOWN
THE NEW INTERIORIZATION HCOB SERIES, THE NEW 1978 CLASS IV RUNDOWNS, THE TECHNOLOGIES OF WORD CLEARING, CONFESSIONALS, PTS HANDLING, PREPARED LISTS AND ALL THE REMAINING MATERIALS OF CLASS 0 TO IV	FLUBLESS C/SING AND AUDITING OF ADVANCED CLASS IV PROCESSES, PROCEDURES AND RUNDOWNS	ACADEMIES OF SCIENTOLOGY	AN EXPERT AND FLUBLESS AUDITOR/CASE SUPERVISOR OF ALL CLASS IV AND ADVANCED CLASS IV PROCESSES, RUNDOWNS AND ACTIONS
	C/SING AND AUDITING ADVANCED CLASS IV PROCESSES, PROCEDURES AND RUNDOWNS		A CASE SUPERVISOR TRAINED TO C/S EXPERTLY FOR ALL THE RUNDOWNS AND ACTIONS UP THROUGH GRADE IV / A SENIOR AUDITOR SKILLED IN THE EXPERTISE OF DELIVERING THE NEW RUNDOWNS AS WELL AS THE MANY OTHER RUNDOWNS AND ACTIONS UP THROUGH GRADE IV
LEVEL 0 TO IV PROCEDURES AND EXPANDED GRADES	FLUBLESS AUDITING OF LEVEL 0 TO IV PROCEDURES AND EXPANDED GRADES	ACADEMIES OF SCIENTOLOGY	A FLUBLESS CLASS IV AUDITOR
INCREASING ABILITIES THROUGH HANDLING SERVICE FACSIMILES	DIRECT STYLE AUDITING, SERVICE FACSIMILE PROCESSING	ACADEMIES OF SCIENTOLOGY	ABILITY TO AUDIT OTHERS TO GRADE IV ABILITY RELEASE

38

| | 14 CORRECTION |
| 13 RESULT |

CLASSES	CERTIFICATE	COURSE	PREREQUISITES
CLASS V AUDITOR	HUBBARD VALIDATED AUDITOR HVA (PROVISIONAL)	SAINT HILL SPECIAL BRIEFING COURSE	CLEAR, HNEDA OR CLASS IV, HNEDA
PERMANENT EXPANDED DIANETICS CASE SUPERVISOR	HUBBARD GRADUATE DIANETIC SPECIALIST CASE SUPERVISOR HGDS CS	EXPANDED DIANETICS C/S INTERNESHIP	EXPANDED DIANETICS C/S COURSE
EXPANDED DIANETICS CASE SUPERVISOR	HUBBARD GRADUATE DIANETIC SPECIALIST CASE SUPERVISOR HGDS CS (PROVISIONAL)	EXPANDED DIANETICS C/S COURSE	HNEDG PROV. EXPANDED DIANETICS COURSE
PERMANENT EXPANDED DIANETICS AUDITOR	HUBBARD GRADUATE DIANETIC SPECIALIST HGDS	EXPANDED DIANETICS INTERNESHIP	EXPANDED DIANETICS COURSE
EXPANDED DIANETICS AUDITOR	HUBBARD GRADUATE DIANETIC SPECIALIST HGDS (PROVISIONAL)	EXPANDED DIANETICS COURSE	HNEDA (VALIDATED) CLASS IV GRADUATE COURSE AND INTERNESHIP

12 PRODUCTION

39

TEACHES ABOUT	SKILLS TAUGHT	WHERE OBTAINED	END RESULT
CHRONOLOGICAL DEVELOPMENT OF SCIENTOLOGY FROM 1950 TO 1967 WITH FULL THEORY AND APPLICATION	GRADE 0 TO IV AUDITING AT SAINT HILL STANDARDS	SAINT HILL HUBBARD COLLEGES OF SCIENTOLOGY	AN EXPANDED LOWER GRADES AUDITOR WHO HAS FULL KNOWLEDGE OF, AND ABILITY TO APPLY THE TECHNOLOGY
THE UNIQUE TECHNOLOGY OF EXPANDED DIANETICS ITS USE OF DIANETICS IN SPECIAL WAYS FOR SPECIAL PURPOSES ITS APPLICATION IN HANDLING SPECIAL CASES AND PEOPLE WHO GIVE THEMSELVES TROUBLE OR HAVE TROUBLE	FLUBLESS C/SING OF EXPANDED DIANETICS	SAINT HILL HUBBARD COLLEGES OF SCIENTOLOGY CONTINENTAL ACADEMIES OF SCIENTOLOGY AND AUTHORIZED ACADEMIES OF SCIENTOLOGY	A FLUBLESS EXPANDED DIANETICS CASE SUPERVISOR
	C/SING OF EXPANDED DIANETICS		ABILITY TO CASE SUPERVISE EXPANDED DIANETICS
	FLUBLESS AUDITING OF EXPANDED DIANETICS		A FLUBLESS EXPANDED DIANETICS AUDITOR
	AUDITING OF EXPANDED DIANETICS		ABILITY TO AUDIT OTHERS TO EXPANDED DIANETICS CASE COMPLETION

40

CLASSES	CERTIFICATE	COURSE	PREREQUISITES
PERMANENT CLASS VII CASE SUPERVISOR	HUBBARD GRADUATE AUDITOR CASE SUPERVISOR HGA CS	CLASS VII C/S INTERNESHIP	CLASS VII COURSE AND INTERNESHIP
PERMANENT CLASS VII AUDITOR	HUBBARD GRADUATE AUDITOR HGA	CLASS VII COURSE AND INTERNESHIP	CLASS VI INTERNESHIP CLEAR ONLY AVAILABLE TO SEA ORG OR 5-YEAR CONTRACTED ORG STAFF
PERMANENT CLASS VI CASE SUPERVISOR	HUBBARD SENIOR SCIENTOLOGIST CASE SUPERVISOR HSS CS	CLASS VI C/S INTERNESHIP	HNEDG (VALIDATED) CLASS VI C/S COURSE
CLASS VI CASE SUPERVISOR	HUBBARD SENIOR SCIENTOLOGIST CASE SUPERVISOR (PROVISIONAL) HSS CS	CLASS VI C/S COURSE	HNEDG PROV. CLASS VI COURSE
PERMANENT CLASS VI AUDITOR	HUBBARD SENIOR SCIENTOLOGIST HSS	CLASS VI INTERNESHIP	CLASS VI COURSE
CLASS VI AUDITOR	HUBBARD SENIOR SCIENTOLOGIST HSS (PROVISIONAL)	SAINT HILL SPECIAL BRIEFING COURSE	CLASS V COURSE

20 EXISTENCE
19 CONDITIONS
18 REALIZATION
17 CLEARING
16 PURPOSES
15 ABILITY

TEACHES ABOUT	SKILLS TAUGHT	WHERE OBTAINED	END RESULT
THE POWER AND POWER PLUS PROCESSES	FLUBLESS POWER PROCESSES C/SING	SAINT HILL HUBBARD COLLEGES OF SCIENTOLOGY	A FLUBLESS POWER CASE SUPERVISOR
	FLUBLESS POWER PROCESSES AUDITING		A FLUBLESS POWER AUDITOR
SCIENTOLOGY SETUP AND REPAIR PROCESSES AND RUNDOWNS UP TO CLASS VI	FLUBLESS C/SING OF CLASS 0 TO VI ACTIONS	SAINT HILL HUBBARD COLLEGES OF SCIENTOLOGY	A FLUBLESS CLASS VI CASE SUPERVISOR
	C/SING OF CLASS 0 TO VI ACTIONS		ABILITY TO CASE SUPERVISE CLASS 0 TO VI ACTIONS
	FLUBLESS CLASS VI AUDITING		A FLUBLESS CLASS VI AUDITOR
	THE FULL APPLICATION OF SCIENTOLOGY GRADES, REPAIR, SETUPS, ASSISTS AND RUNDOWNS UP TO CLASS VI		A SUPERB AUDITOR WITH FULL PHILOSOPHIC AND TECHNICAL COMMAND OF MATERIALS TO CLASS VI

CLASSES	CERTIFICATE	COURSE	PREREQUISITES
PERMANENT CLASS IX CASE SUPERVISOR	HUBBARD ADVANCED TECHNICAL SPECIALIST CASE SUPERVISOR HATS CS	CLASS IX C/S INTERNESHIP	CLASS IX C/S COURSE
CLASS IX CASE SUPERVISOR	HUBBARD ADVANCED TECHNICAL SPECIALIST CASE SUPERVISOR HATS CS (PROVISIONAL)	CLASS IX C/S COURSE	CLASS IX COURSE
PERMANENT CLASS IX AUDITOR	HUBBARD ADVANCED TECHNICAL SPECIALIST HATS	CLASS IX INTERNESHIP	CLASS IX COURSE
CLASS IX AUDITOR	HUBBARD ADVANCED TECHNICAL SPECIALIST HATS (PROVISIONAL)	CLASS IX AUDITOR COURSE	CLASS VIII COURSE
PERMANENT CLASS VIII CASE SUPERVISOR	HUBBARD SPECIALIST OF STANDARD TECH HSST	CLASS VIII C/S INTERNESHIP	HNEDG (VALIDATED) CLASS VIII C/S COURSE
CLASS VIII CASE SUPERVISOR	HUBBARD SPECIALIST OF STANDARD TECH HSST (PROVISIONAL)	CLASS VIII C/S COURSE	HNEDG PROV. CLASS VIII COURSE
PERMANENT CLASS VIII AUDITOR	HUBBARD STANDARD TECHNICAL SPECIALIST HSTS	CLASS VIII INTERNESHIP	HNEDA (VALIDATED) CLASS VI INTERNESHIP CLASS VIII COURSE
CLASS VIII AUDITOR	HUBBARD STANDARD TECHNICAL SPECIALIST HSTS (PROVISIONAL)	CLASS VIII COURSE	HNEDA PROV. CLASS VI

21 SOURCE

TEACHES ABOUT	SKILLS TAUGHT	WHERE OBTAINED	END RESULT
ADVANCED PROCEDURES AND DEVELOPMENTS SINCE CLASS VIII	FLUBLESS C/SING OF CLASS IX	SAINT HILL HUBBARD COLLEGES OF SCIENTOLOGY	FLAWLESS STANDARD CASE SUPERVISION OF CLASS IX PROCEDURES AND RUNDOWNS
	CASE SUPERVISION OF CLASS IX		ABILITY TO CASE SUPERVISE CLASS IX PROCEDURES AND RUNDOWNS
	FLUBLESS CLASS IX AUDITING		A FLUBLESS CLASS IX AUDITOR
	CLASS IX AUDITING		ABILITY TO AUDIT ADVANCED PROCEDURES AND SPECIAL RUNDOWNS
CLASS VIII PROCEDURES APPLICATION OF 100% STANDARD TECH TO ALL CASES	FLUBLESS C/SING OF 100% STANDARD TECH	ADVANCED ORGANIZATIONS AND SAINT HILL HUBBARD COLLEGES OF SCIENTOLOGY	FLAWLESS CASE SUPERVISION OF ALL CASES
	C/SING OF 100% STANDARD TECH		A FLUBLESS CLASS VIII CASE SUPERVISOR
	FLUBLESS CLASS VIII AUDITING		A FLUBLESS CLASS VIII AUDITOR
	CLASS VIII AUDITING		ABILITY TO HANDLE ALL CASES TO 100% RESULTS

POWER ON ALL 8 DYNAMICS

CLASSES	CERTIFICATE	COURSE	PREREQUISITES
PERMANENT CLASS XI CASE SUPERVISOR	CLASS XI CASE SUPERVISOR	CLASS XI C/S INTERNESHIP	CLASS XI C/S COURSE
CLASS XI CASE SUPERVISOR	CLASS XI CASE SUPERVISOR (PROVISIONAL)	CLASS XI C/S COURSE	CLASS XI COURSE
PERMANENT CLASS XI AUDITOR	CLASS XI AUDITOR	CLASS XI INTERNESHIP	CLASS XI COURSE
CLASS XI AUDITOR	CLASS XI AUDITOR (PROVISIONAL)	CLASS XI COURSE	CLASS X COURSE
PERMANENT CLASS X CASE SUPERVISOR	CLASS X CASE SUPERVISOR	CLASS X C/S INTERNESHIP	CLASS X C/S COURSE
CLASS X CASE SUPERVISOR	CLASS X CASE SUPERVISOR (PROVISIONAL)	CLASS X C/S COURSE	CLASS X COURSE
PERMANENT CLASS X AUDITOR	CLASS X AUDITOR	CLASS X INTERNESHIP	CLASS X COURSE
CLASS X AUDITOR	CLASS X AUDITOR (PROVISIONAL)	CLASS X COURSE	CLASS IX COURSE ONLY AVAILABLE TO SEA ORG STAFF

TEACHES ABOUT	SKILLS TAUGHT	WHERE OBTAINED	END RESULT
L-11 NEW LIFE RUNDOWN	FLUBLESS C/SING OF L-11	FLAG	A FLUBLESS CLASS XI CASE SUPERVISOR
L-11 EXPANDED	C/SING L-11	FLAG	ABILITY TO CASE SUPERVISE L-11
NEW LIFE EXPANSION RUNDOWN	FLUBLESS AUDITING OF L-11	FLAG	A FLUBLESS CLASS XI AUDITOR
	AUDITING L-11	FLAG	ABILITY TO AUDIT L-11
L-10 OT	FLUBLESS C/SING OF L-10	FLAG	A FLUBLESS CLASS X CASE SUPERVISOR
AN UPPER LEVEL RUNDOWN, THE BASIC TECH OF WHICH COMES FROM RESEARCH INTO INCREASING OT POWERS	C/SING L-10	FLAG	ABILITY TO CASE SUPERVISE L-10
	FLUBLESS AUDITING OF L-10	FLAG	A FLUBLESS CLASS X AUDITOR
	AUDITING L-10	FLAG	ABILITY TO AUDIT L-10 OT

AWARENESS CHARACTERISTICS	AUDITOR AND CASE SUPERVISOR CLASSES	CERTIFICATE	COURSE	PREREQUISITES
↑	PERMANENT CLASS XII CASE SUPERVISOR ↑	CLASS XII CASE SUPERVISOR	CLASS XII C/S INTERNESHIP	CLASS XII C/S COURSE
	CLASS XII CASE SUPERVISOR ↑	CLASS XII CASE SUPERVISOR (PROVISIONAL)	CLASS XII C/S COURSE	CLASS XII COURSE
	PERMANENT CLASS XII AUDITOR ↑	CLASS XII AUDITOR	CLASS XII INTERNESHIP	CLASS XII COURSE
	CLASS XII AUDITOR ↑	CLASS XII AUDITOR (PROVISIONAL)	CLASS XII COURSE	CLASS XI COURSE

TEACHES ABOUT	SKILLS TAUGHT	WHERE OBTAINED	END RESULT
L-12 THE FLAG OT EXECUTIVE RUNDOWN	FLUBLESS C/SING OF L-12	FLAG	A FLUBLESS CLASS XII CASE SUPERVISOR
	C/SING L-12	FLAG	ABILITY TO CASE SUPERVISE L-12
	FLUBLESS AUDITING OF L-12	FLAG	A FLUBLESS CLASS XII AUDITOR
	AUDITING L-12	FLAG	ABILITY TO AUDIT L-12

Auditor Training

A student who is training with the intent of becoming an auditor is advised to do a basic course first, then do the Student Hat Course. It is extremely important that the Student Hat Course be done as that is where the student really learns the technology of how to study and what the barriers are that can impede study.

It is vital that the Student Hat Course is done prior to beginning on major auditor training courses as time after time, study difficulties have been traced to students not fully understanding the materials on this course.

After a student has completed the Student Hat Course, he or she is recommended to receive Method One Word Clearing at the next opportunity. Method One Word Clearing is the action to clean up all misunderstood words in previous subjects one has studied. Students who have had this auditing early on in their training have had the least amount of difficulties in grasping the materials on their courses. This auditing can be done in the Hubbard Guidance Center (HGC) or on a co-audit basis, as part of Level 0. (Level 0 includes the materials on word clearing and communication.)

The first major course which is a mandatory step in auditor training is the New Era Dianetics Course.

Many students however have taken the Hubbard Qualified Scientologist Course before commencing this level. The HQS Course is a fairly short course and gives a student a chance to both give and receive Scientology processing.

The New Era Dianetics Course offers for the first time the New Era Dianetics data. It trains the student in the skills and knowledge he needs in order to make a truly well and happy human being. For best results, the student must not skimp on practical application and on the various training drills on this course, in particular the training drills called TRs. TRs are a precise training action putting a student through laid out practical steps, gradient by gradient, to teach a student to apply with certainty what he has learned.

TRs are very basic to auditing and must be learned well. A very high percentage of any difficulties auditors have had in auditing stems from not doing these drills to complete certainty on their application.

After the student has completed the Hubbard New Era Dianetics Course, it is advised that the student then does the New Era Dianetics Internship. On the internship, the interne perfects his skill as an auditor and gets the opportunity to see the complete workability of the technology through his pc's gains.

Experience has shown that auditors who have done a thorough New Era Dianetics Internship have little difficulty in later training and internships as they have a firm foundation.

After completion of the New Era Dianetics Internship, the student then goes into Academy Levels 0-IV. Again, the student will have no problem if he studies per Scientology study techniques learned on the Student Hat — making sure that he does not pass words he does not

understand, and does not skimp on his TRs, E-Meter handling drills and practical application including co-auditing.

After the student has finished his Academy Levels he should then go onto the internship.

After finishing the Class IV Internship, the Class IV Graduate (Auditor and Case Supervisor) Course and Internship are done.

The student then can either go onto the Expanded Dianetics Course or go to a Saint Hill Organization and do the Saint Hill Special Briefing Course. The Expanded Dianetics Course includes valuable technology that every auditor should know in order to be able to fully handle preclear cases. It is a must in the training of every auditor who is intent on becoming a professional auditor.

After the student has completed the Expanded Dianetics Course, an internship should be done. It has been found that interning after each level of training gives the best results and is the smoothest route up the Bridge.

The Saint Hill Special Briefing Course gives students a full understanding of the theory and developments of Scientology technology. As there is a great deal of tapes to be listened to and written materials on the course, the study technology as learned on the Student Hat must be adhered to in order to ensure maximum speed through the course.

After the Saint Hill Special Briefing Course, the student goes onto the Senior Saint Hill Special Briefing Course and Class VI Internship.

The next training course which should be done after this is the Class VIII Course, unless the auditor is a five-year contracted staff member in which case the Class VII Course and Internship can be done first.

The Class VIII Course is the course where an auditor learns the exact handling of all cases to 100% result and is a sharp, rapid standardization of auditing. The course lasts only a few weeks and is a period of intensive study. The Class VIII Internship should follow and then the Class IX Course and Internship. Auditors in the Sea Organization (Sea Org) at the Flag Land Base then continue onto Class X, XI and XII courses and their internships.

The above lays out what has been the most commonly successful training program done by those that are now highly skilled and successful auditors. The sequence is as follows:

HAS Course or Basic Scientology Course
HQS Course
Student Hat Course
Method One Word Clearing
Basic Dianetics Books Course
Hubbard New Era Dianetics Course
New Era Dianetics Internship
Academy Levels 0-IV
Academy Levels Internships
Class IV Graduate (Auditor and Case Supervisor) Course
Class IV Graduate (Auditor and Case Supervisor) Interneship

Expanded Dianetics Course
Expanded Dianetics Internship
Saint Hill Special Briefing Course
Senior Saint Hill Special Briefing Course
Class VI Internship
Class VII Course and Interneship (five-year contracted
   staff only)
Class VIII Course
Class VIII Internship
Class IX Course
Class IX Internship
Class X-XII Course and Interneships (for Sea Org
   auditors).

Any difficulties students may encounter in their training and progress up the training bridge have been traced back to a few major areas of weakness in the students' training—all of which can be easily handled by application of Scientology technology.

The most frequent area of trouble is in the application of study technology itself. The Student Hat Course teaches a student how to study, and how to handle any barriers to study encountered, so that all the material is easily comprehended and can be applied by the student.

Method One Word Clearing handles study difficulties due to earlier misunderstood words in subjects studied previously.

To fully handle study difficulties, the Primary Rundown should be done. A person who has done this course can read comfortably and instantly translate word data into concepts and so can study accurately and swiftly and can then do the actions. It is advised that this course be done at the student's earliest opportunity and prior to commencing on auditor training courses where possible, especially if the student has any amount of difficulty with study. Method One Word Clearing is a prerequisite to the Primary Rundown.

Students who have taken drugs prior to Scientology sometimes run into difficulties in their studies and in receiving Method One Word Clearing and are advised to get their Drug Rundown completed early on in their training. This auditing action can easily be co-audited while the student is receiving Dianetic training.

The next area of difficulty that some students have fallen into is not studying with the purpose of their studies in sight and then skimping on practical application. Not fully doing the practical drills and student auditing is a pitfall that students run into. Students who have "quickied" their studies in this manner oftentimes have losses in their ability to apply the materials of their courses, and do not continue with their training.

Students have fallen into this pitfall by various pressures to get through their training quickly and have then lost from view the purpose of their training.

Experience has shown that the best way to continue up the training Bridge quickly is by application of Scientology study technology and thoroughly doing the practical and auditing requirements on the course checksheets.

When doing practical requirements on the courses, students "twin" up and drill each other in the various processes. If this is done properly and per course material in-

structions, the student invariably has great wins when auditing pcs.

Some students have had trouble in evaluating relative importances on course materials and spend long periods of time trying to learn everything there is to know about the subject even at the most basic levels. This has made courses drag on endlessly in some instances. The technology to handle this phenomenon is covered in the Student Hat. There is a drill on the subject of evaluation of relative importances which can be done to handle this.

Another pitfall that some students have fallen into is that of not keeping in their own ethics on courses. Ethics is defined as: the study of the general nature of morals and the specific moral choices to be made by the individual in his relationship with others. There are certain rules and regulations which must be adhered to in order for results and gains to be gotten from training, e.g. not partaking in alcoholic beverages when one is a student, sufficient rest, adherence to course schedules, and of course the policy on not passing misunderstood words. When the student does not adhere to these rules and regulations, he will have trouble in study and grasping the materials. This then becomes an ethics matter, as the whole concern of ethics is to make it possible for technology to go in. (When this has been accomplished, that's as far as an ethics action is taken.) When a student's ethics are in regarding his studies, it has been found that he does not easily get off his purpose of getting trained and he makes it up the Bridge.

Money and time considerations have been problems students have run into. Some students have allowed difficulties in these areas to slow them down from getting up the Bridge or have dropped their studies indefinitely to handle these areas.

Experienced supervisors have found that money and time considerations almost invariably enter into the picture as stops in training when students have gone past misunderstood words and have not applied study technology. When a student does not fully grasp the subject he is studying, he easily becomes estranged from it and it becomes increasingly more difficult for the student to make time and money for his training. Experienced supervisors have found that time and money problems usually easily resolve when the student is cleared up on words that he has passed that he did not fully understand.

Students who use basic Scientology technology in their lives and work generally find these problems easily handled. The communication cycle, completion of cycles of action, ARC triangle (which are all basic Scientology data learned as early on as the HQS Course) have proven beneficial to students in improving their ability to handle work. The application of this technology in fact buys time for students to continue with their training.

There are many examples of students going even further into this and applying Scientology administrative technology to their jobs as found in the Org Exec Course Volumes.

The successful application of this technology has given many the opportunity to continue with their training without money or time problems.

Supervisor Training

The duty of a supervisor is the communication of the data of Scientology to the student so as to achieve acceptance, duplication and application of the technology in a standard and effective manner. The supervisor may or may not be a graduate and experienced practitioner of the course he is supervising but he must be a trained course supervisor. He is not expected to teach. He is expected to get the students there, rolls called, checkouts properly done, misunderstoods handled by finding what the student doesn't understand and getting the student to understand it.

As in auditor training, there is a gradient scale of courses and internships to train a supervisor. But in training a supervisor, the subject matter of the training is to get the supervisor-in-training to really grasp study technology and to be able to get it applied standardly in a course room.

As in auditor training, there has been much experience accumulated on the best route to train a top-notch supervisor.

Following has been one of the most successful training routes:

Basic courses leading to an understanding of the basic
    elements of Scientology (such as HQS Course)
TRs Course
Student Hat Course
Word Clearing Course
Method One Word Clearing
Mini Course Supervisor Course
Supervisor Internship
Hubbard Professional Course Supervisor Course
Supervisor Internship
Primary Rundown
Hubbard Senior Course Supervisor Course
Supervisor Internship.

Then on to auditor training and internships.

The areas which experienced supervisors have found to be the common areas in any supervisor troubles are as follows:

TRs and presence as a supervisor not sufficiently drilled, supervisor internships and practical not done adequately with enough obnosis drilling and practical experience supervising in the course room, supervisor trainees not fully grasping the subjects of study technology and word clearing technology.

In order to avoid these pitfalls, experienced supervisors have recommended that supervisor trainees do a good thorough TRs Course including TRs 0-IV, Upper Indoc (Indoctrination) TRs and Administrative (Admin) TRs. These drills and supervisor drills included on the Supervisor Course checksheets should be drilled thoroughly without "quickying" them so that the student is able to confront and handle real situations when they come up in course rooms. Insufficient attention to these drills by students is a major source of any difficulties that supervisors have had in their internships and in actually supervising when they have graduated from their training.

The most efficient method of training has been found to be doing internships after each level of training. This very much is the case in supervisor training and thorough internships should be done until the supervisor trainee can handle course rooms with ease. The student should do plenty of Supervisor Drills so that he can spot and handle any manifestations of out study technology or bypassed misunderstood word phenomena and keep the students winning on their courses and studies.

The supervisor trainee should drill hard on spotting and handling the three barriers to study (misunderstood words passed, skipped gradient, improper balance of mass and significance). According to experienced supervisors, students who have drilled heavily on these things have done extremely well as supervisors. The drilling is all covered in the supervisor courses and it is important that students thoroughly do all the actions called for on the checksheets.

Not fully grasping the subject of study technology itself and gaining a subjective and objective reality on the workability of word clearing technology is a trap that students can run into. This situation is easily bypassed if the student does the Student Hat Course and makes very sure that he does not pass any word that he does not understand and he uses the study technology fully as covered in the lectures by the Founder included in the course. The student should also get his own Method One Word Clearing at the first opportunity. The Primary Rundown is a necessary step in training a supervisor as well, as this is the course where the supervisor fully gets all the study technology with real certainty in its application.

To handle any weakness in the application of word clearing technology, a supervisor should include in his training a Word Clearers Course and actually do the various methods of word clearing until he can do this action with certainty and results.

By following the advised course of training of Student Hat, TRs, Method One Word Clearing and Word Clearers Course, supervisor courses and internships with the full application of study technology, the route to a fully trained supervisor is an easy route.

Case Supervisor Training

A Case Supervisor is that person in a Scientology church who gives instructions regarding, and *supervises* the auditing of preclears. The Case Supervisor (C/S) has to be an accomplished and properly certified auditor and a person trained additionally to supervise cases. The C/S is the auditor's "handler." He directs the auditor on what to do, corrects his application of the technology when necessary, and keeps the auditor calm and willing and winning. The C/S is the preclear's case director. His actions are done for the preclear.

The C/S training route is likewise laid out in a pattern of course and internships for each level.

Following is the best sequence of training levels to train a C/S:

Auditor training up through New Era Dianetics
  Internship completion
New Era Dianetics Graduate (Case Supervisor) Course
New Era Dianetics Graduate Case Supervisor
  Internship
Academy Levels 0-IV
Levels 0-IV Internships
Class IV Graduate (Auditor and Case Supervisor)
  Course
Class IV Graduate (Auditor and Case Supervisor) Internship
Expanded Dianetics Course
Expanded Dianetics Internship
Expanded Dianetics Case Supervisor Course
Expanded Dianetics Case Supervisor Internship
Saint Hill Special Briefing Course
Senior Saint Hill Special Briefing Course
Class VI Internship
Class VI Case Supervisor Course
Class VI Case Supervisor Internship
Class VII Case Supervisor training included in the Class
  VII training for those who have done previous Case
  Supervisor training (five-year contracted staff only.)
Class VIII Course
Class VIII Internship
Class VIII Case Supervisor Course
Class VIII Case Supervisor Internship
Class IX-XII auditor training, Internships, Case
  Supervisor Courses and Internships.

Experience has shown that internes and experienced auditors make the best C/Ses with the least amount of difficulty in getting through their training.

Also, experience has shown that the best method of C/S training is to do the various levels of C/S training in sequence and not to skip the lower levels of training.

Case Supervisor internships are important to be done thoroughly as are the other types of internships already mentioned. A wise Case Supervisor interne has his work checked by an experienced C/S so that he can undergo any needed correction on the internship itself. Then when he graduates he has real certainty on his application of the technology.

Executive Training

An executive is one who obtains *execution* of duties, programs and actions in an organization to further the aims and purposes of that organization.

Executive ability is similar to administrative ability in that it requires an ability to formulate and apply policy which will result in the safe, efficient and profitable running of an organization. However, executive ability also implies being able to get others to get the work done and being able to get policy known and used.

The Org Exec Course includes the policy formulated in Scientology that has been proven successful over the years in the expansion of the church.

The Org Exec Course including OEC Volumes 0-7 and Management Series Volume is available for any individual to study. The best sequence for study on this course has been found to be to do the Volume 0 OEC Checksheet, the Volume 0 Internship, Volume 1 OEC Checksheet, then Internship, etc. This ensures a proper balance of mass and significance and gives the student practical experience in getting policy into application in an organization.

As in auditor, case supervisor and course supervisor training, a student learning to be an executive must first do the Student Hat Course so that the technology of study is known and can be followed in the student's executive training. Method One Word Clearing should also be received prior to commencing on executive training, so that previous areas of study difficulty are cleared up.

A TRs course, including Administrative TRs, is also important in the training of any executive early on in his training. An administrator in the Church of Scientology is actually an "auditor" on the Third Dynamic, only he "audits" lots of people. Experience has shown that ex-
ecutive trainees can fail if they have not been thorough in their drilling of TRs. Admin TRs were specifically designed to train administrators and should not be skimped. The purpose of these TRs is to train the student to get compliance with and complete a cycle of action on administrative actions and orders, in spite of the randomities, confusions, justifications, excuses, traps and insanities of the Third and Sixth Dynamics, and to confront such comfortably while doing so.

A serious error that an executive trainee can make is not getting trained on the basic technology of Scientology such as how to handle work, ARC triangle, communications, etc. Without these basics and a general knowledge of the workability of Scientology technology, an executive trainee will find it difficult in the practical application of getting policy in. So basic courses leading to an understanding of Scientology technology and the applications of it, is a must in the training of any executive.

A recommended sequence of executive training is as follows:

Student Hat Course
Basic course leading to an understanding of basics of
  Scientology
TRs Course
OEC Volumes 0-7, Management Series and Internships
  after each volume
Data Series Evaluators Course
Data Series Evaluators Course Internship
Primary Rundown
Flag Executive Briefing Course
Flag Executive Briefing Course Internship.

Some executives have chosen to do the Management

Series Volume of the OEC as a first step after doing their Student Hat Course and receiving Method One Word Clearing. They had found that this was the most successful training route for them as the various series included in the volume, e.g. Establishment Officer Series, Organizing Series, Personnel Series could be put to immediate use and actually covered how to handle the problems they were running into daily in their own businesses.

Summary

Training to be a top-notch auditor, C/S, supervisor or executive is an easy task with the gradient levels of training available.

As can be seen from the preceding chapter, many people have had great success on the foregoing training routes. Students have no problem in progressing up the training Bridge when they apply Scientology study technology fully and study with the purpose of *application* of the materials.

5

An Advised Course of Action for Processing

Auditing as well as training is done on gradients. A gradient is defined as a gradual approach to something taken step by step, level by level, each step or level being of itself easily surmountable so that finally, states of being which are seemingly "too high above one" can be achieved with relative ease.

Auditing gets rid of unwanted barriers that inhibit, stop or blunt a person's natural abilities as well as gradiently increasing the abilities a person has so that he be-

comes more able, and survival, happiness and intelligence increase enormously.

The route to Clear and OT is clearly defined on the Gradation Chart. The chart maps out the various auditing levels, gives the awareness characteristics of each level, and covers the inabilities lost and abilities gained at each level.

Following is the portion of the Classification Gradation and Awareness Chart showing the processing levels to Clear and OT.

CLASSIFICATION GRADATION AND AWARENESS CHART OF LEVELS AND CERTIFICATES

FOR
DIANETICS AND SCIENTOLOGY PROCESSING

This chart describes the route to human recovery and expansion of one's ability and power as a spiritual being. The field of human recovery belongs to Dianetics. Above this is Scientology, which brings an individual to higher states of being and ability.

Now, starting with the first introductory level (bottom line at left) read across the columns and find out what is accomplished, where it can be obtained and why it is important. Note that the introductory levels are not prerequisites, but are there to help one begin and become familiar with fundamentals. Continue reading the chart by moving up one level, and reading across the columns, and moving up to the next and across the column.

AWARENESS CHARACTERISTICS	PRECLEAR GRADES OR STATE OF BEING	NAME OF STATE	PROCESSES AUDITED	SUBJECT AUDITED
-1 HELP	NEW ERA DIANETICS CASE COMPLETION	NEW ERA DIANETICS CASE COMPLETION	NEW ERA DIANETICS RUNDOWNS ON LOCKS, SECONDARIES AND ENGRAMS	LOSSES BY DEATHS OR SEVERE CHANGES IN PC'S LIFE. ANY UNWANTED SENSATIONS, MISEMOTIONS, SOMATICS OR PAINS. DISABILITIES, VALENCES
	NEW ERA DIANETICS DRUG RUNDOWN COMPLETION	NEW ERA DIANETICS DRUG RUNDOWN COMPLETION	NEW ERA DIANETICS DRUG RUNDOWN. FULL AND COMPLETE AUDITING OF HARMFUL EFFECTS FROM DRUGS, MEDICINE & ALCOHOL	ATTITUDES, EMOTIONS, SENSATIONS AND PAINS (AESPs) CONNECTED WITH TAKING AND PRIOR TO TAKING DRUGS, MEDICINE AND ALCOHOL
	NEW ERA DIANETICS OBJECTIVES	NEW ERA DIANETICS OBJECTIVES COMPLETION	NEW ERA DIANETICS OBJECTIVE PROCESSES	TO ORIENT PC IN PRESENT TIME, DROP OUT PAST AND IMPROVE HAVINGNESS
-2 HOPE	LIVINGNESS REPAIR COMPLETION	LIVINGNESS REPAIR COMPLETION	TWO-WAY COMM AND PROGRAMMED HANDLING	ADDRESSES THE INDIVIDUAL'S HANDLING OF LIVINGNESS
-3 DEMAND FOR IMPROVEMENT	HAS CO-AUDIT	HAS CO-AUDIT COMPLETION	HAS CO-AUDIT PROCESSES 1 AND 2	TONE RAISING, CONFRONT, HAVINGNESS
-4 NEED OF CHANGE	GROUP PROCESSING COMPLETION	GROUP PROCESSING COMPLETION	GROUP PROCESSES	ANY GROUP PROCESSES

LEVELS BELOW NEED OF CHANGE — FROM HUMAN TO MATERIALITY

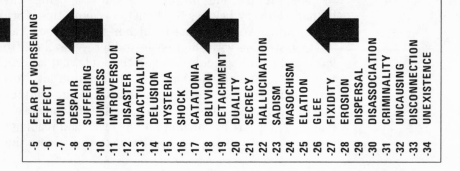

-5 FEAR OF WORSENING
-6 EFFECT
-7 RUIN
-8 DESPAIR
-9 SUFFERING
-10 NUMBNESS
-11 INTROVERSION
-12 DISASTER
-13 INACTUALITY
-14 DELUSION
-15 HYSTERIA
-16 SHOCK
-17 CATATONIA
-18 OBLIVION
-19 DETACHMENT
-20 DUALITY
-21 SECRECY
-22 HALLUCINATION
-23 SADISM
-24 MASOCHISM
-25 ELATION
-26 GLEE
-27 FIXIDITY
-28 EROSION
-29 DISPERSAL
-30 DISASSOCIATION
-31 CRIMINALITY
-32 UNCAUSING
-33 DISCONNECTION
-34 UNEXISTENCE

ABILITY GAINED	CLASS OF AUDITOR REQUIRED	WHERE OBTAINED	TRAINING REQUIRED	PREREQUISITES
A TRULY WELL AND HAPPY HUMAN BEING	HNEDA (PROVISIONAL)	CHURCHES AND MISSIONS OF SCIENTOLOGY DIANETIC COUNSELING GROUPS	NO TRAINING REQUIRED BUT NEW ERA DIANETICS COURSE RECOMMENDED	NEW ERA DIANETICS DRUG RUNDOWN COMPLETION
FREEDOM FROM HARMFUL EFFECTS OF DRUGS, MEDICINE AND ALCOHOL AND FREE FROM NEED TO TAKE THEM	HNEDA (PROVISIONAL)	CHURCHES AND MISSIONS OF SCIENTOLOGY DIANETIC COUNSELING GROUPS	NO TRAINING REQUIRED BUT NEW ERA DIANETICS COURSE RECOMMENDED	TRs COURSE NEW ERA DIANETICS OBJECTIVES COMPLETION
IN PRESENT TIME AND HAVINGNESS OF PRESENT TIME ENVIRONMENT	HNEDA (PROVISIONAL)	CHURCHES AND MISSIONS OF SCIENTOLOGY DIANETIC COUNSELING GROUPS	NO TRAINING REQUIRED	NO PREREQUISITE
AWARENESS OF ABILITY TO CHANGE CONDITIONS	CLASS III OR ABOVE	CHURCHES AND MISSIONS OF SCIENTOLOGY	NO TRAINING REQUIRED	NO PREREQUISITE
DEMAND FOR IMPROVEMENT	HAS CO-AUDIT SUPERVISOR COURSE GRADUATE	CHURCHES AND MISSIONS OF SCIENTOLOGY	NO TRAINING REQUIRED	NO PREREQUISITE
AWARENESS THAT CHANGE IS AVAILABLE	GROUP AUDITOR	CHURCHES AND MISSIONS OF SCIENTOLOGY	NO TRAINING REQUIRED	NO PREREQUISITE NOT A MANDATORY GRADE

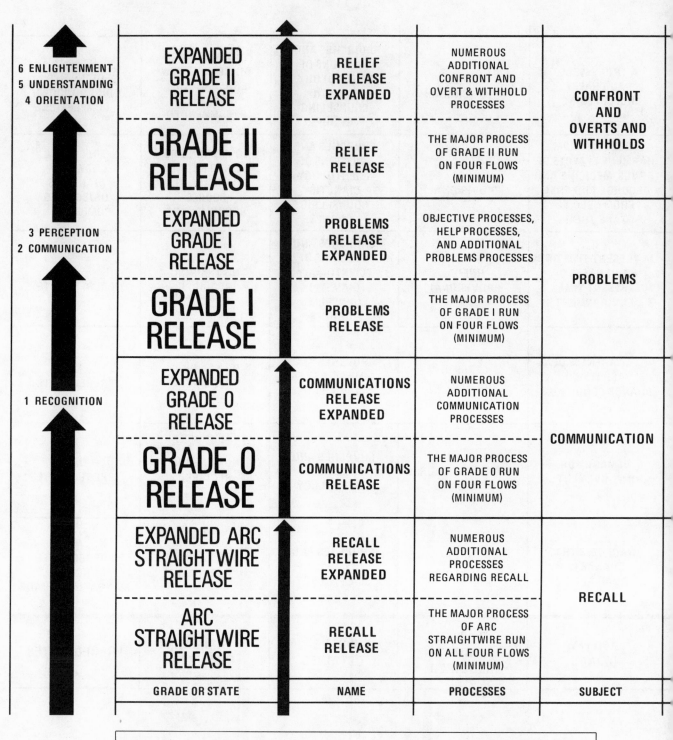

GRADE OR STATE	NAME	PROCESSES	SUBJECT
EXPANDED GRADE II RELEASE	RELIEF RELEASE EXPANDED	NUMEROUS ADDITIONAL CONFRONT AND OVERT & WITHHOLD PROCESSES	CONFRONT AND OVERTS AND WITHHOLDS
GRADE II RELEASE	RELIEF RELEASE	THE MAJOR PROCESS OF GRADE II RUN ON FOUR FLOWS (MINIMUM)	
EXPANDED GRADE I RELEASE	PROBLEMS RELEASE EXPANDED	OBJECTIVE PROCESSES, HELP PROCESSES, AND ADDITIONAL PROBLEMS PROCESSES	PROBLEMS
GRADE I RELEASE	PROBLEMS RELEASE	THE MAJOR PROCESS OF GRADE I RUN ON FOUR FLOWS (MINIMUM)	
EXPANDED GRADE 0 RELEASE	COMMUNICATIONS RELEASE EXPANDED	NUMEROUS ADDITIONAL COMMUNICATION PROCESSES	COMMUNICATION
GRADE 0 RELEASE	COMMUNICATIONS RELEASE	THE MAJOR PROCESS OF GRADE 0 RUN ON FOUR FLOWS (MINIMUM)	
EXPANDED ARC STRAIGHTWIRE RELEASE	RECALL RELEASE EXPANDED	NUMEROUS ADDITIONAL PROCESSES REGARDING RECALL	RECALL
ARC STRAIGHTWIRE RELEASE	RECALL RELEASE	THE MAJOR PROCESS OF ARC STRAIGHTWIRE RUN ON ALL FOUR FLOWS (MINIMUM)	

6 ENLIGHTENMENT
5 UNDERSTANDING
4 ORIENTATION

3 PERCEPTION
2 COMMUNICATION

1 RECOGNITION

Many many processes exist on the Grades 0 to IV on which a preclear may need to be audited to achieve the full ability gained for a Grade. However, a typical and ideal program is as above — receiving Quadruple Grades (major process of each Grade) and receiving Expanded Grades after Expanded Dianetics, then moving on up through the rest of the Grades to Clear and OT. But Expanded Grades may be done after New Era Dianetics Drug Rundown or New Era Dianetics Case Completion. If they are not done after Quadruple Grades per the ideal program they can be done after Power Processes but before Solo, and after OT III, IV, V, VI or VII.

Expanded Dianetics can also be received before the Scientology Grades after New Era Dianetics Case Completion.

ABILITY GAINED	AUDITOR CLASS	WHERE OBTAINED	TRAINING REQUIRED	PREREQUISITES
RELIEF FROM HOSTILITIES AND SUFFERINGS OF LIFE	CLASS II OR ABOVE	HUBBARD GUIDANCE CENTERS, OR AS A STUDENT ON AN ACADEMY OR SAINT HILL COURSE OR AS AUTHORIZED	NO TRAINING REQUIRED BUT CLASS II AND ABOVE RECOMMENDED	EXPANDED GRADE I RELEASE -------- GRADE I RELEASE
ABILITY TO RECOGNIZE THE SOURCE OF PROBLEMS AND MAKE THEM VANISH	CLASS I OR ABOVE	HUBBARD GUIDANCE CENTERS, OR AS A STUDENT ON AN ACADEMY OR SAINT HILL COURSE OR AS AUTHORIZED	NO TRAINING REQUIRED BUT CLASS I AND ABOVE RECOMMENDED	EXPANDED GRADE 0 RELEASE -------- GRADE 0 RELEASE
ABILITY TO COMMUNICATE FREELY WITH ANYONE ON ANY SUBJECT	CLASS 0 OR ABOVE	HUBBARD GUIDANCE CENTERS, OR AS A STUDENT ON AN ACADEMY OR SAINT HILL COURSE OR AS AUTHORIZED	NO TRAINING REQUIRED BUT CLASS 0 AND ABOVE RECOMMENDED	EXPANDED ARC STRAIGHTWIRE RELEASE -------- ARC STRAIGHTWIRE RELEASE
KNOWS HE/SHE WON'T GET ANY WORSE	CLASS 0 OR ABOVE	HUBBARD GUIDANCE CENTERS, OR AS A STUDENT ON AN ACADEMY OR SAINT HILL COURSE OR AS AUTHORIZED	NO TRAINING REQUIRED BUT CLASS 0 RECOMMENDED	NEW ERA DIANETICS DRUG RUNDOWN – AND ANY OTHER NEEDED NED ACTION AT CS DISCRETION
ABILITY GAINED	AUDITOR CLASS	WHERE OBTAINED	TRAINING REQUIRED	PREREQUISITES

Left margin scale (bottom to top):

7 ENERGY
8 ADJUSTMENT
9 BODY
10 PREDICTION
11 ACTIVITY
12 PRODUCTION
13 RESULT
14 CORRECTION
15 ABILITY
16 PURPOSES
17 CLEARING

GRADE OR STATE	NAME	PROCESSES	SUBJECT
SOLO AUDITOR	SOLO AUDITOR	SOLO DRILLS AND ASSISTS	SOLO DRILLS AND ASSISTS
SOLO SETUPS	SOLO SETUP COMPLETION	AS DESIGNATED BY THE CS	AS ORDERED BY THE C/S
GRADE VA RELEASE	POWER PLUS RELEASE	THE POWER PLUS PROCESSES	POWER PLUS
GRADE V RELEASE	POWER RELEASE	THE POWER PROCESSES	POWER
EXPANDED DIANETICS COMPLETION	EXPANDED DIANETICS CASE COMPLETION	EXPANDED DIANETICS PROCESSES AS DIRECTED BY CASE SUPERVISOR	PROCESSES OF THE LEVEL AS ORDERED BY CS
EXPANDED GRADE IV RELEASE	ABILITY RELEASE EXPANDED	ADDITIONAL ABILITY PROCESSES	SERVICE FACSIMILES AND FIXED CONDITIONS
GRADE IV RELEASE	ABILITY RELEASE	THE MAJOR PROCESS OF GRADE IV RUN ON FOUR FLOWS (MINIMUM)	SERVICE FACSIMILES AND FIXED CONDITIONS
EXPANDED GRADE III RELEASE	FREEDOM RELEASE EXPANDED	NUMEROUS ADDITIONAL PROCESSES ON CHANGE AND ARC BREAKS	CHANGES IN LIFE AND ARC BREAKS
GRADE III RELEASE	FREEDOM RELEASE	THE MAJOR PROCESS OF GRADE III RUN ON FOUR FLOWS (MINIMUM)	CHANGES IN LIFE AND ARC BREAKS

ABILITY GAINED	AUDITOR CLASS	WHERE OBTAINED	TRAINING REQUIRED	PREREQUISITES
ABILITY TO SOLO AUDIT	SOLO AUDITOR	ADVANCED ORGANIZATIONS	NO TRAINING REQUIRED BUT HNEDA RECOMMENDED	GRADE VA RELEASE
FULLY PREPARED FOR SOLO AUDITING	CLASS IV OR ABOVE	ADVANCED OR SAINT HILL ORGANIZATIONS	NO TRAINING REQUIRED	GRADE VA RELEASE
RECOVERY OF KNOWLEDGE	CLASS VII	SAINT HILL ORGANIZATIONS	NO TRAINING REQUIRED	GRADE V RELEASE ATTESTED BEFORE VA IS AUDITED
ABILITY TO HANDLE POWER	CLASS VII	SAINT HILL ORGANIZATIONS	NO TRAINING REQUIRED	NEW ERA DIANETICS DRUG RUNDOWN AND OTHER NEEDED NEW ERA DIANETICS ACTIONS AS DIRECTED BY THE CS GRADE IV RELEASE
FREEDOM FROM CRUEL IMPULSES AND CHRONIC UNWANTED CONDITIONS. ABLE TO ACT WITHOUT RESTRAINT	EXPANDED DIANETICS SPECIALIST	HUBBARD GUIDANCE CENTERS AS AUTHORIZED	NO TRAINING REQUIRED	NEW ERA DIANETICS FULL PC PROGRAM
MOVING OUT OF FIXED CONDITIONS AND GAINING ABILITIES TO DO NEW THINGS	CLASS IV OR ABOVE	HUBBARD GUIDANCE CENTERS OR AS A STUDENT ON AN ACADEMY OR SAINT HILL COURSE OR AS AUTHORIZED	NO TRAINING REQUIRED BUT CLASS IV AND ABOVE RECOMMENDED	EXPANDED GRADE III RELEASE - - - - - - - GRADE III RELEASE
FREEDOM FROM THE UPSETS OF THE PAST AND ABILITY TO FACE THE FUTURE	CLASS III OR ABOVE	HUBBARD GUIDANCE CENTERS OR AS A STUDENT ON AN ACADEMY OR SAINT HILL COURSE OR AS AUTHORIZED	NO TRAINING REQUIRED BUT CLASS III AND ABOVE RECOMMENDED	EXPANDED GRADE II RELEASE - - - - - - - GRADE II RELEASE

GRADE OR STATE		NAME	PROCESSES	SUBJECT
21 SOURCE	OT VII PROCESSES	SECTION VII O.T.	O.T. VII PROCESSES	SECTION VII O.T.
	NEW ERA DIANETICS FOR OTS	CAUSE OVER LIFE	NEW ERA DIANETICS FOR O.T.s RUNDOWN	AS SPECIFIED IN THE MATERIALS OF THE RUNDOWN
	OT III	SECTION III O.T.	O.T. III	SECTION III O.T.
20 EXISTENCE	OT II	SECTION II O.T.	O.T. II	SECTION II O.T.
	OT I	SECTION I O.T.	O.T. I	SECTION I O.T.
19 CONDITIONS	CLEAR	CLEAR	CLEARING MATERIALS	THE REACTIVE MIND
18 REALIZATION	GRADE VI RELEASE	WHOLE TRACK RELEASE	R6 EW	THE WHOLE TRACK

63

ABILITY GAINED	AUDITOR CLASS	WHERE OBTAINED	TRAINING REQUIRED	PREREQUISITES
SECTION VII OT PROCESSES EP	CLASS IV, O.T. III ——— SOLO AUDITOR FOR SOLO SECTION	ADVANCED ORGANIZATIONS	O.T. VII COURSE	O.T. III
CAUSE OVER LIFE	CLASS IV, O.T. III ADVANCED COURSES SPECIALIST (ACS)	FLAG AND ADVANCED ORGANIZATIONS	NO TRAINING REQUIRED	O.T. III OR ABOVE
SECTION III O.T.	SOLO AUDITOR PREFERABLY HNEDA AND CLASSED	ADVANCED ORGANIZATIONS	O.T. III COURSE	O.T. II
SECTION II O.T.	SOLO AUDITOR PREFERABLY HNEDA AND CLASSED	ADVANCED ORGANIZATIONS	O.T. II COURSE	O.T. I
SECTION I O.T.	SOLO AUDITOR PREFERABLY HNEDA AND CLASSED	ADVANCED ORGANIZATIONS	O.T. I COURSE	CLEAR GOOD RECORD AS A SCIENTOLOGIST
ABILITY TO BE AT CAUSE OVER MENTAL MATTER, ENERGY, SPACE AND TIME ON THE 1ST DYNAMIC (SURVIVAL FOR SELF)	SOLO AUDITOR PREFERABLY HNEDA AND CLASSED	ADVANCED ORGANIZATIONS	CLEARING COURSE	GRADE VI RELEASE
RETURN OF POWERS TO ACT ON OWN DETERMINISM — FREEDOM FROM DRAMATIZATION	SOLO AUDITOR PREFERABLY HNEDA AND CLASSED	ADVANCED ORGANIZATIONS	SOLO AUDIT COURSE	GRADE VA RELEASE SOLO SETUPS

64

AWARENESS CHARACTERISTICS	PRECLEAR GRADES OR STATE OF BEING	NAME OF STATE	PROCESSES AUDITED	SUBJECT AUDITED
	OT IX AND ABOVE	AS ISSUED	TO BE RELEASED	UPPER LEVEL O.T. SECTIONS
	OT VIII	SECTION VIII O.T.	O.T. VIII	SECTION VIII O.T.
	OT VII	SECTION VII O.T.	O.T. VII	SECTION VII O.T.
POWER ON ALL 8 DYNAMICS	OT VI	SECTION VI O.T.	O.T. VI	SECTION VI O.T.
	OT V	SECTION V O.T.	O.T. V	SECTION V O.T.
	OT IV	SECTION IV O.T.	O.T. IV	SECTION IV O.T.
	OT III EXPANDED	SECTION III O.T. EXPANDED	O.T. III EXPANDED	SECTION III O.T. EXPANDED

ABILITY GAINED	CLASS OF AUDITOR REQUIRED	WHERE OBTAINED	TRAINING REQUIRED	PREREQUISITES
SECTION IX O.T. AND ABOVE	AS ISSUED	FLAG AND ADVANCED ORGANIZATIONS	O.T. COURSES AS ISSUED	FULL O.T. VIII AND ABOVE
SECTION VIII O.T.	SOLO AUDITOR PREFERABLY HNEDA AND CLASSED	FLAG AND ADVANCED ORGANIZATIONS	O.T. VIII COURSE	NEW ERA DIANETICS FOR O.T.s AND FULL O.T. VII
SECTION VII O.T.	O.T. VII, CLASS IV OR ABOVE	ADVANCED ORGANIZATIONS	O.T. VII COURSE	O.T. VI
SECTION VI O.T.	SOLO AUDITOR PREFERABLY HNEDA AND CLASSED	ADVANCED ORGANIZATIONS	O.T. VI COURSE	O.T. V
SECTION V O.T.	SOLO AUDITOR PREFERABLY HNEDA AND CLASSED	ADVANCED ORGANIZATIONS	O.T. V COURSE	O.T. IV
SECTION IV O.T.	O.T. III, CLASS VIII ——— SOLO AUDITOR FOR SOLO SECTION	ADVANCED ORGANIZATIONS	O.T. IV COURSE	O.T. III EXPANDED
SECTION III O.T. EXPANDED	SOLO AUDITOR PREFERABLY HNEDA AND CLASSED	ADVANCED ORGANIZATIONS	O.T. III COURSE	O.T. III AND O.T. VII PROCESSES

What Can Realistically Be Expected to Be Met with in Processing

Many thousands of Scientologists have attained the states of being and the grades as defined in the Gradation Chart.

The abilities gained can be expected to be achieved after one has received the auditing of each level. This has consistently proven to be so in thousands of cases.

The Bridge is actually very easy to travel if one simply does the levels step by step with the intention of making it up the Bridge.

As Scientologists have routinely been receiving auditing and achieving the abilities stated on the Gradation Chart, a great deal of experience has been accumulated on exactly what preclears might anticipate upon receiving auditing. Based on this data, this chapter is written with the intention of giving helpful advice on how to proceed to receive processing. It includes recommendations as to how a preclear can progress with his processing, in terms of the Gradation Chart and avoid needless problems while enroute.

First Action

The very first thing a preclear should do when beginning auditing is to acquire a basic understanding of Scientology and the mechanics of the mind.

There are various ways this can be done as covered in the bottom section of the training side of the Classification Gradation and Awareness Chart. They include such things as attending an Introductory Lecture, reading a basic book such as *Dianetics: The Modern Science of Mental Health* and/or doing a basic or Introductory Course on Scientology.

A HAS Co-Audit can be done as a first action in Scientology, wherein the individual acquires both an objective and a subjective reality on the workability of the subject.

There are various basic courses which can be done. The Communications Course is recommended. Many have found that by doing TRs 0-4 they have been able to handle their own environment better and have thus been able to move faster in their auditing. TRs 0-4 is part of the Special Drug Rundown which handles the ill effects of having taken drugs. A course which includes TRs 0-4 is advised for anyone who has taken drugs in the past.

The HQS Course includes both TRs and co-auditing on Objective Processes (processing which extroverts a person) and Recall Processes (processing which improves one's memory). This course can be taken by someone who is currently on drugs and is trying to come off of drugs. When done in conjunction with the use of large doses of vitamins, it has been demonstrated as successful in thousands of cases.

It is important to note though, that whereas Scientology and Dianetic auditing have handled many physical disabilities in the process of increasing a person's natural abilities, this is not the purpose of Scientology and Dianetic auditing. Anyone with physical and medical problems should consult with a medical doctor trained in the handling of medical problems. Anyone having physical difficulties should have a medical checkup before commencing his auditing. Scientology does not specialize in the healing of sick people. Its major interest is the improvement of innate abilities and the enhancement of the spiritual being.

Training

Processing proceeds more rapidly when a preclear has read *Dianetics: The Modern Science of Mental Health*, and has done the Basic Dianetics Books Course or has had auditor training in New Era Dianetics.

New Era Dianetics auditing is a new and much more precise version of Dianetics, based upon recent research and breakthroughs made by L. Ron Hubbard. New Era Dianetics will allow cases to progress faster. It produces better and more lasting results from the beginning right on up the Bridge. It makes all gains attained in Dianetics and Scientology even more *pronounced*.

Preclears who have been trained as auditors themselves have the least amount of problems in their own auditing. There are many instances of an individual taking a Dianetics course and after auditing others has then had his own auditing go smoother and faster.

It is recommended therefore, that you receive training as an auditor, though it is not a requirement.

Half of the gains available in Scientology can be obtained from training and people who have done the training route to Clear have found their gains very stable. They have acquired the technology on the handling of their own lives and environments as well as having achieved the end results of each auditing level.

An individual who trains as an auditor can co-audit up the Grade Chart. An individual who co-audits up the Bridge may occasionally need a review in the HGC by an experienced and professional auditor. This may happen in that students, in the process of learning the techniques are not fully experienced auditors.

Once in a while, pcs who have signed up for auditing in an HGC have had to wait for their auditing as the auditors have been booked up. This has been occasionally true of a few organizations, not all, and these organizations are working hard to train up more auditors to handle the demand. This could possibly be encountered as one progresses up the Bridge to Clear.

For the most part, Scientology organizations give very good service and one can achieve one's processing goals easily by obtaining professional auditing in an HGC.

Preclear Hat

There are simple rules that a pc must abide by in getting auditing so as to achieve the most gains.

These rules are covered in a policy letter entitled "Pc

Hat" which is easily obtained from Directors of Processing in Scientology Churches and Missions. Often a preclear's difficulties in progressing smoothly have been traced simply to the lack of abiding by these rules. These rules are very simple such as getting sufficient rest, not engaging in an irregular Second Dynamic (the dynamic which includes families, children and sexual activities) while receiving auditing, not taking drugs or alcohol when receiving auditing, not doing dishonest things when receiving auditing, not engaging in other practices such as hypnotism, etc. These rules are laid down so that the pc is alert as possible and can make the most gains in his auditing.

Also, a preclear upset with individuals, or connected to anyone invalidating his gains, should stay away from these people when receiving auditing. If this is the case, the preclear should report this to the Director of Processing for relay to the Case Supervisor. Persons who are connected to antagonistic people in their environment do not make good gain. There are many ways to handle this, though. There is a new cassette tape lecture called "Can We Ever Be Friends?" given by a minister of the Church which should be sent to antagonists in a person's environment to handle any antagonism to his/her gains and activities in Scientology. (It should be noted this is not the only public for this particular tape lecture.) A person who is not retaining his gains is PTS. A PTS person is a person or preclear who "roller-coasters," i.e., gets better, then worse. This occurs only when his connection to a suppressive person — SP (a person who is opposed to Scientology and any betterment activities) or group is unhandled and in order to make his gains from Scientology processing permanent, appropriate handling must be done. This can be handled by an auditing action called the PTS Rundown, education on PTS/SP Detection, Routing and Handling Course as directed by the Case Supervisor and Ethics Officer of the Church.

For the best gains, an individual should receive auditing intensively, at least 12½ hours per week. The maximum results can be achieved in this manner as otherwise if a pc only has a couple of hours of auditing a week, time will be spent each session on handling problems and upsets which can occur in everyday life and less time will be available in addressing the actual processes of the levels which a pc must obtain on his route to Clear.

By getting auditing intensively, experience has shown that pcs go up the Bridge more quickly with less amount of auditing.

Application of Scientology to One's Environment and Life

One of the major causes of difficulty individuals have found in moving up the Bridge is not applying Scientology to their own lives and environments. For example, experience has shown that failure to apply Scientology ethics technology to one's environment will cause an individual to become too enturbulated to make rapid advance up the Gradation Chart.

Simple things like using the ARC triangle, completing cycles of action, using the communication cycle and staying away from people who invalidate one's gains have been basic to making rapid headway up the Bridge. Surveys have shown that individuals who have used Scientology and its administration technology in their lives have improved the success of their businesses and family life.

Money and time problems that pcs have can be handled, and have been in a great many instances, by the application of Scientology basics and administration know-how as found in the Org Exec Course Volumes.

Keeping "one's ethics in" or keeping discipline in on himself so that pro-survival actions are done along the dynamics is a very basic key to your progress in auditing. The Second Dynamic in particular has been found to be upsetting if one is not ethical in that area. It is advised that you apply Scientology basics to troubled areas and discipline where necessary so that you do not engage in irregular Second Dynamic activities while receiving auditing.

Auditing handles difficulties individuals have on the various dynamics and increases an individual's own self-determinism in handling one's life, but in the meantime, while a person is undergoing auditing it is best for the person to exercise some discipline in his own environment.

As an individual travels up the Bridge, he will find it increasingly easy to handle his environment and his own life and he can realistically expect to achieve the gains as stated on the Gradation Chart for each level.

Exchange

Preclears don't generally make as good progress as they could when their exchange is out on one or more dynamics. A person who doesn't produce can get mentally or physically ill. The best exchange in many cases has been found to be exchange by giving another auditing. There have been cases of individuals not progressing as well as they wished, until they started auditing and helping other persons, at which time their own gains increased substantially.

If an individual is having trouble in the area of exchange, there is a simple remedy for this called Exchange by Dynamics. This is a service which is offered by the Church of Scientology and is a very simple action. Whole lives have been changed for the better as a result of it.

Honesty Counts

Sometimes, preclears have withholds which get in the way of rapid progress up the Grade Chart.

A withhold is an unspoken, unannounced transgression against a moral code by which the person was bound, and it is restraining self from communicating.

Withholds knowingly kept from auditors can slow down case gain. It is not the intent and purpose of auditing to find a pc's secrets but rather to get a pc to confront his own case and troubles. If a person is withholding something, he is not looking at it and therefore, there is something which he is not confronting. Communication failures in these areas will cause processing to go slower, and the pc will not achieve the gains possible.

So it is advised that an individual be honest and straight with his auditor. It is in the best interest of the pc and the auditor treats all session reports as confidential.

Summary

The route up the Bridge to Clear and OT is achieved by going up the levels, step by step, as laid out in the Classification Gradation and Awareness Chart.

If individuals follow this route exactly as mapped out and are honest in their auditing and lives, going up the Bridge is easy and the gains immense.

6

Any Reasons for Failures and their Correction

Society has had enough of false solutions.

The general culture has been muddied up by psychological and psychiatric propaganda and actions since the last century.

Commitment, incarceration and control are key words in the handling of the world's mentally ill. Additionally, every effort to have psychiatric and psychological propaganda included in areas of living has been made.

While the rest of us have tried to get on with life, the psychiatrist and psychologist have infiltrated the fields of law, education, religion, politics, family and personal relations dictating what is "good for us."

Mental health jargon has found its way into the language. "Bizarre," "paranoid," "schizophrenic," "sick," "psychologically maladjusted" and many more have become part of nearly everyone's vocabulary.

Psychiatrists and psychologists diagnose both the living and the dead. Personal consultation is not required. Among those on whom judgement has been passed are: Mary Baker Eddy, Winston Churchill—no friend of psychiatry, William Shakespeare, Isaac Newton, Beethoven, Ezra Pound, Senator Barry Goldwater, and Jesus Christ.

Headline-hitting diagnosis for personalities pushes the terminology into everyday language. All oddities of human behavior receive comment on innumerable talk shows and in magazines.

An idea in circulation begins to shape itself and be refined by those who so desire it, in reality. Thus eccentricity or being just plain different can be classed as mental illness and treated as such.

Problems in living then become problems in nonconformity. Some unfortunate members of society easily acquire the label of "mentally ill"—the alcoholic, criminal,

aged, or drug addict. Being classified as sick provides a convenient way to suspend them from society pending treatment.

Of late, this practice has gotten even bolder. We now have community mental health centers for more "convenience."

The idea that the whole world could be used as an experimental proving ground for enforced psychological treatment has been confirmed by senior psychiatric consultants.

Dr. Howard P. Rome of the Mayo Clinic, United States, and a former president of the American Psychiatric Association is on record as follows: "Actually, no less than the entire world is a proper catchment area for the present day psychiatrist, and psychiatry need not be appalled by the magnitude of the task."

Canadian psychiatrist Dr. Brock Chisholm, architect of the World Federation for Mental Health has stated: "Psychiatry must now decide what is to be the immediate future of the human race; no one else can. And this is the prime responsibility of psychiatry."

Some would say this is playing God; others, playing both judge and jury. Either way actions support the words.

Under Hitler, the German psychiatric profession turned from experimentation to murder. It was a warning to the world of what could happen if rigid controls were not enforced. Under the Nazis some 300,000 German mental patients were put to death as having lives devoid of value.

The story is well known and documented.

Furthermore, German psychiatrists helped in the Final Solution program. Supporting the killings they ably assisted in the deaths of millions more.

But before damning the Nazis, it should be remembered

that representatives of the world's mental health movements watched with great interest the steps being taken by fellow professionals in Germany.

In England, the magazine *Lancet* ran articles in 1933-34 on Nazi Germany's eugenics, castration and sterilization programs.

But psychiatric propaganda was not solely confined to eugenics. Other areas of society were being undermined also. Dr. John Rawlings Rees, consulting psychiatrist to the British Army at Home, stated at an annual meeting of the National Association of Mental Health—then called the National Association of Mental Hygiene: "We have made a useful attack upon a number of professions. The two easiest of them naturally are the teaching profession and the Church; the two most difficult are law and medicine."

In Germany at this time, they drank beer to celebrate the death of the 10,000th mental patient at Hadamar Institution.

When the war was over, psychiatrists were busier than ever. The World Federation for Mental Health was formed, every group quickly switched from 'mental hygiene' to 'mental health' and the Nazi days were smoothed over.

The World Federation set out to examine "how many people were made mentally ill by the wrong kind of religion?" In England, Lord Adrian of the Eugenics Society stated, "Preventative health services are bound to interfere with individual liberty ... and ... must ... to supervise the lives of people who would like to be let alone."

Across the world, the mental health propagandists put their act together. Dr. Francis Cloutier of France, when asked if psychiatry had anything to offer and whether it was possible to raise the level of mental health, replied that answers to such questions were outside the field of traditional psychiatry.

Propaganda for shock treatment and lobotomy increased. A trail of mutilated people were left across the world. A Harvard Medical professor said that 1,200 patients died under shock treatment in 1969. Others put it higher; 5,000 is estimated by one doctor.

Or as Dr. Russell Barton of the United Kingdom Mental Health Association put it publicly on television, "I have no wish to impose any unpleasant treatment on anybody, but sometimes the treatments we have aren't pleasant."

Dr. Anthony M. Graziano summed up: "In the mental health industry, illness is our greatest product."

The problems of life manifest themselves in many ways, but for each one of these manifestations psychology and psychiatry attempts to cut out something, take away something or suppress something. No thought is paid to giving an individual something in place of what was taken. The end result is always less individual.

The theory that psychology in schools will help educate children, the theory that psychiatric evidence in courts is better than criminal codes, in the office and factory— scrutinizing personnel, and infiltration into the home and family are all hollow statements.

The results: high crime rate, high divorce rates, condemned industrial management, increased terrorism, murderers released from institutions who then commit further murders, operations on the brain leaving the patient worse, and a whole plethora more.

Each time a crime against humanity is committed, we all die a little.

Scientology is faced with picking up the pieces of a broken society. It is not easy to stand up against such overwhelming odds. It has taken a brave look at the world. What makes it possible to do so is that Scientology has a workable technology.

Scientology gives something back.

The technology we have WORKS to definite positive predictable results. Results are obtained if one has honestly studied, understood and applied the technology.

There are various types of errors that can be made by the individual in both TRAINING and PROCESSING. The following is a description of these, and how they are easily corrected.

Failures in Scientology Training

Failure To Get Any Scientology Training: There is tremendous gain available from the study of Scientology, both case gain, and increased ability to handle life and others. There has never previously been a concise and accurate technology of life and betterment, and so most people don't know how much benefit there is to be had from the study of Scientology.

At least reading all the basic books of Dianetics and Scientology is a must. Some persons entering Scientology would prefer to have processing only and do not intend to become professional auditors or professional Scientologists. But even for a preclear a basic understanding of life is essential. This is available in the basic books and basic courses of Scientology.

To many the words "study" or "training" remind them of past failures and losses. Many "know" that they can't study or learn. Past schooling and education have become so bad that today students can "graduate" from high school unable to read! Not until Scientology has there been a precise technology of how to study. Do not assume that because one was unsuccessful in study in the past, that one can't learn or is not a good student. With Scientology study technology anyone can learn. With processing anyone can increase their intelligence and memory. With Scientology it is now possible for anyone to study and learn successfully.

Past Study Failures: Having had failures as a student prior to Scientology a person can become so convinced that he cannot study that he/she won't try to study again, or when attempting to study runs into past failures and doesn't progress. There are various student remedies and processing available which free the person from study failures of the past, and allow him to start studying anew.

Having Studied Subjects "Similar" to Scientology: Persons who have studied the mind, the spirit or Man, prior to Scientology, are likely to enter Scientology with fixed ideas and misconceptions—often with so many confusions and disagreements from these earlier subjects that it is impossible for them to learn. Formidable and undefined words and terms in earlier subjects, false data in earlier subjects, mysteries and questions left unanswered in earlier subjects, all prevent the student from learning that subject, or from learning any similar subject in the future.

But with Scientology word clearing and Scientology processing this can be handled and the student can then go on to study successfully in the future.

Punishment in Education: Because no study technology existed before Scientology, other means such as force, duress, punishment and humiliation were resorted to by some. These actions reduce self-determinism and intelligence. Through Scientology processing such bad experiences are easily erased.

No Purpose for Studying: A person will not study or learn if he is studying without a purpose. No purpose for studying usually stems from having been made to study against one's determinism in the past, having been taught useless data or subjects in the past, having been made to attend school for a time period or until a certain age. Past failures to study before Scientology can make it seem so hopeless that one loses one's purpose. Former miseducation resulting in loss of purpose can be rapidly erased through processing resulting in a rehabilitation of one's purpose and desire to study and learn. Scientology data and courses are for use and are found immediately useful by Scientology students in their everyday lives. This too gives one a purpose for studying.

Dishonesty or Out-Ethics in Study: Many have been taught to crib or cheat in school. Often as there was no way to successfully learn, or because the materials being taught were useless there may have seemed to be no reason not to be dishonest in study. Persons with a dishonest study history will tend to bring their bad habits into their Scientology studies and may try to cheat on exams, falsify their progress in study, check off items on courses or checksheets as done when they aren't, or as passed when they are not. Such bad habits are quickly handled with a student confessional and with regained integrity, the Scientology student is able to study honestly and succeed.

Studying for the Wrong Reason: Rarely, a person with bad motives will seek to study for some harmful purpose or ulterior motive. In this frame of mind the person is actually unable to learn or duplicate well and is in very poor case shape himself. This is easily detected and can be remedied with Scientology processing directed toward the handling of bad motives and the rehabilitation of the person's basic goodness.

Studying for Status: In society diplomas and certificates are sometimes only used for reasons of status or authority, and often don't mean that the person is competent in the subject. Approaching a Scientology course only to get a certificate to impress others with is a mistake. Scientology courses are totally oriented toward the understanding and ability to use the materials. Certificates are awarded and validated on evidence of competence.

Incomplete Courses: A person starting and failing to complete course after course in school and in life will arrive at a point where he is so hung up in earlier incomplete cycles and failed studies that he can no longer approach or study

a new subject. Scientology study technology and processing rapidly resolve this.

A Scientologist having carried this habit over into Scientology will get a resurgence on taking up the first incomplete course and completing it or resolving the reason for not completing it.

Trick Methods of Studying and Memory Systems: As there has not been any way to resolve study difficulties before Scientology, many trick methods and memory systems have been developed in an effort to get around the inability to understand or retain data. A lot of students develop their own methods or systems. These are no substitute for understanding and being able to use the data and are of no assistance. With Scientology study technology any difficulties in study or with understanding the data are readily resolved and there is no need for such systems.

Mixing the Study of Scientology with Study of Other Practices: This can be very confusing to the student who attempts it as other practices do not define the words and terms they use, often contain erroneous or false data, often omit important data. Confusions from other practices are easily cleaned up in Scientology but there's no point in accumulating more. If these practices were workable, Man would not be in the condition he was in before Scientology.

Disagreements and Confusions about Materials being Studied: These invariably stem from either a failure to apply Scientology study technology to what one is studying or from tremendous confusions and disagreements in faulty subjects one has studied in the past. If any current study difficulty does not easily resolve by using Scientology study tech, then it is a matter of earlier confused studies. These are rapidly handled with processing.

Students' Guide to Acceptable Behavior: This is a list of rules that Scientology students abide by for their own and other students' benefit. Its use prevents such things as classroom distractions which would prevent one's own or another student's progress.

Studying While Being PTS: This is an error as the study of Scientology improves one's abilities. Being connected to someone antagonistic to oneself or betterment of any kind will result in a conflict. Therefore, persons who are in this situation are not trained on Scientology courses without first handling and resolving the PTS situation. The Ethics Officer will enable anyone to do this and a course on the subject exists which gives all the data necessary to handle.

A variation of this is a person who has been taught so badly that his education actually suppressed him. Teachers dedicated to invalidating their pupils, subjects so confusing or useless that studying them made one feel stupid are examples of this. Such experiences are easily erased with processing.

Sometimes there are persons who hang around the fringes of Scientology who like to impress others with their pretended knowledge or wisdom. These do not use what they hear or read to help others with but only for poor motives such as impressing others, making others seem ignorant, etc. Persons like this usually know very little actual Scientology data and what they have picked up is always misduplicated. A favorite trick of such is to tell others things which are strange, bizarre or mysterious. It may sound impressive, but usually results in upsetting people or at least violating their reality. Do not be overwhelmed or impressed by them. Report them to the Ethics Officer and get your data from Scientology.

Verbal Data: Pre-Scientology subjects and studies are full of what is called "verbal data"—some subjects deal exclusively in verbal data. By "verbal data" is meant data passed on by word of mouth rather than from the original books or materials. It is always altered in the passing on, sometimes so severely that the original meaning or data is completely lost. The only way to get the original data in unaltered form is from the person who developed or researched the subject. In order to ensure that Scientologists only get pure Scientology, only books, tapes, bulletins and other written materials by L. Ron Hubbard are used for study. Explaining, interpreting, altering or passing on Scientology data verbally is completely forbidden. Instead only the written and taped materials by the Founder are used so that Scientologists get the Source data.

Studying While in Poor Physical Condition: Students in Scientology do not study while sick, ill, too tired or hungry as these would prevent one from studying well and are easily handled or prevented.

Studying While in Poor Emotional or Case Condition: A person emotionally upset or distraught cannot put his attention on study and so does not do well in study. Scientology processing quickly resolves these conditions, increases intelligence and memory enabling one to study well.

Drugs and Study: Drugs prevent successful study. Students in schools, colleges and universities are frequently seriously impaired mentally by drugs. Stimulants used to keep one awake do not aid but impair the mind and prevent successful study. Persons who have taken hallucinogenic drugs are usually so adversely affected that they cannot study or learn at all. The taking of drugs while on a Scientology course is therefore forbidden.

Persons who have taken drugs are given processing on the Drug Rundown to erase the damage done by drugs and to rehabilitate the person mentally and emotionally.

Eyesight or Eyestrain: If the effort to read causes strain the student cannot study well. This difficulty is resolved by special Scientology processes.

Thinking One Knows it all Already: A preconceived idea that one already knows it all and therefore has nothing to learn is a barrier. It usually stems from having been disillusioned too often with former subjects. Processing remedies this.

Pretending or Falsifying Prerequisites: Scientology courses state what prerequisites are needed to successfully study that course. Attempting to falsify or pretend that one has studied and can apply materials covered in earlier courses would result in failure. Processing raises integrity and the recognition that there is so much valuable

data in Scientology soon brings about honesty in the student.

The prerequisites of courses and the arrangement of Scientology courses in an orderly sequence prevents failures that could occur from trying to study material out of sequence or trying to study advanced materials before more basic materials have been grasped.

Trying to Study without Studying Scientology Study Technology: This is the most common cause of any student failure there is. The brilliant research done by L. Ron Hubbard into the field of study itself, making it possible for study and learning to be 100% successful is all contained in Scientology courses on study. There is the Basic Study Manual, the Student Hat Course and the Primary Rundown. These materials are vital for any student and are therefore studied early in one's Scientology studies. Any student seen to be having difficulty with study should be immediately checked for not having studied the technology of study.

Misunderstood Words: So vital is it that students do not go past misunderstood words, that Scientology classrooms contain dictionaries, reference books, the supervisors are trained to help students find and clear misunderstoods and trained word clearers are available who can assist further with word clearing using an E-Meter as an aid. Students are required to own their own dictionaries and reference books and materials. Any errors that could be made by students in clearing words can be quickly handled with processing.

Students blowing from, giving up on or failing on courses are all directly traceable to errors or failures to use study tech and can be quickly located and handled by a supervisor or auditor using an E-Meter.

Misunderstood Words in Earlier Studies: As the discovery of the importance of the misunderstood word and the importance of fully clearing meanings and definitions was discovered by L. Ron Hubbard, earlier pre-Scientology subjects and schooling are full of misunderstood words and confusions. These in most people are so great as to make study very difficult if not impossible. A process called Method One Word Clearing fully handles this, making it possible for Scientology students to approach and study any subject regardless of past poor education or study.

Wrong Reasons or Explanations or "Whys": Giving a person a wrong reason or wrong explanation for something can be very upsetting. These are commonly called "Wrong Whys" in Scientology. As an example a teacher may have told a pupil that the reason he was having difficulty in study is because he was "lazy" or "stupid" or "came from a bad background" or any other wrong reason. These are called "Wrong Whys" and can cause a person to hang up and even get quite misemotional. A correct "Why" on the other hand results in immediate improvement for the student. Techniques known as "Correcting Wrong Whys" and "Why Finding" are available to Scientologists and result in magical improvement.

Not Owning Own Materials: Not having the textbooks and materials prevents the student from reference to the materials. Therefore on Scientology courses the student is required to purchase or own the necessary texts.

Not Getting Confusions or Questions Clarified: A student who goes on trying to study over unanswered questions or confusions won't get far. Scientology supervisors are trained to handle these by locating the cause of the confusion and helping the student to understand and grasp the materials being studied.

Studying out of Sequence: Scientology courses are arranged in the best sequence for optimum study. Checksheets are used for this purpose. Not using a checksheet or trying to do a course in different order than arranged on the checksheet can prevent success. It is simply handled by doing the course in the sequence given on the checksheet.

Not Interning: As most study or education prior to Scientology consisted of theory only and no chance to apply or use the materials under supervision, many failures resulted. Scientology is for use and is very practical. Therefore internships are made available where the student can practice the materials of the course to full proficiency, under supervision.

Not Communicating to the Supervisor: Scientology supervisors are very approachable and willing to help their students. Just because some teachers discouraged their pupils from communicating is no reason not to approach a Scientology supervisor. Whenever a student experiences any difficulty on a Scientology course the supervisor is there to help.

Short Cuts: Short cuts to learning such as trying to speed up recorded lectures, trying to read fast, not taking the time to fully grasp one piece of data before going on to the next, skipping parts of a course, etc., are not short cuts at all. These only bring failure, and are handled by going back and fully redoing the materials skipped or skimped.

Too Simple or Too Complex Dictionaries or Reference Books: A dictionary that is too small to give the full meaning of a word, and a dictionary that is so complex as to be confusing are alike going to give a student trouble. Scientology course rooms contain a range of dictionaries and reference works to overcome this, and materials exist in the study tech which teach a student how to correctly use dictionaries and reference works.

Not Continuing on to Next Course: This is listed here as an error as so often Scientologists who have put off further training or study until later, remark that when they did do the next course they wished they had done it sooner. And as Scientology gives the knowledge of life itself the sooner one gets this understanding the better off he is.

Failures in Processing

Not Getting Processing: The biggest error a person could make would be not getting any processing at all; and thereby missing out on the vast increases in ability, happiness, intelligence, improvements in personality, relationships with others, and capacity to live and enjoy life, that result from processing.

There are various misconceptions which could prevent a person unfamiliar with Scientology from enjoying its benefits. There have been various therapies, treatments, beliefs that Man has tried in the past. Sometimes with poor or no results, or even ending up worse off than before. As a result one could easily give up hope that any betterment is possible, or expect another failure, perhaps even become so disillusioned as to believe that anyone or anything that offers help is going to be another betrayal. Persons who have tried and failed to better themselves or others in the past are likely to shun or attack anything that offers help or freedom. They may confuse Scientology with other practices or treatments that have failed. Should you encounter such a person, ask whether he or she has encountered anything previously that seems similar to Scientology or to processing. Discuss with the person previous attempts to help or better himself, herself or others. This will bring about a recognition that such failures belong to other practices, not to Scientology and that no matter how similar these may have seemed to the person that Scientology is new, unique and different.

Another possible cause for not getting processing is making the error of believing false rumors put out by vested interests, or persons with something to hide. The true disposition and characteristics of this type of person are outlined fully in *The Volunteer Minister's Handbook* by L. Ron Hubbard.

Persons with low havingness, low acceptance level, may think that they could not afford processing, or put off processing until they "can afford it" and thus go without its benefits. Processing raises acceptance level and the ability to earn and have money. Such persons can be processed directly on their ability to have money. There is co-auditing available, where the person takes a course in auditor training and teams up with another co-auditor, and the two process each other under the supervision of an experienced Scientologist. Co-audits are available at Churches and Missions.

Not wanting processing is invariably caused by a different reason than the reason being given, especially if the person is misemotional. This is easily handled by discussing with the person why he/she doesn't want auditing. Few or many reasons may be given, but the right reason will show up accompanied by a dissipation of misemotion and good indicators will appear, with the person now wanting processing.

Not Getting Enough Processing: Sufficient processing will handle any unwanted condition, or recover any lost ability. Other considerations such as having to be completed by a certain time or date, considerations of how long it should take, other commitments, etc., can be a limiting factor in how much processing the person gets. Even a small amount of processing will result in improvement, but may not be sufficient to accomplish what the person wanted to achieve.

There are many many cases where it has been proven that continuing on further with the same process or type of process always gets the result in the end. As one gets processed wins and gains occur. With further processing more wins and gains add up to bigger ones. And continuing processing results in the biggest wins and gains of all. Don't discontinue processing because the full result one is looking for has not been immediately achieved. Continue on and the full result and much more will be yours. When one hears that a process or block of processing did not accomplish all that was asked for, always check into whether the process was continued long enough to its full result, how much processing was done, whether all the processes of that particular type or subject were run. Very often you will find it was a matter of lack of persistence, or ending off too soon, and that continuing the process or processes will give all that was expected and more.

Not Getting Intensive Processing: The best results are obtained from processing done intensively. A session once a week or days between sessions is not as effective as intensive processing done on consecutive days. Various restimulations and the usual knocks and setbacks of life occur between sessions spread far apart. These often need handling at the beginning of the session and thus valuable processing time is spent. The best way to handle this is with intensive processing. Of course getting any processing, even sessions days apart is better than none, but intensive processing gives the best results.

Some people have put off getting processing until something goes wrong and then getting short assist-type processing to handle. While assists are very effective in a time of need, these do not result in rapid progress up the Grade Chart. And as Scientologists move up the Grade Chart they invariably find that less and less "goes wrong" anyway. So one should not put off processing until "something goes wrong," but should concentrate on case advance up the Grade Chart.

Knowing that one has a case condition that needs to be handled and putting it off until later can be an error. The sooner conditions are addressed with processing the sooner they are resolved.

Not Understanding Processing: It is an error to be processed while not knowing or understanding some aspect of what is being done, or what one is asked to do. For example one should look up the definition of the word "processing," and other words and terms immediately connected with processing such as "auditor," "preclear," "session," etc. in the *Dianetics and Scientology Technical Dictionary.* A preclear who is being audited while not understanding what is going on can become mystified, puzzled, can even become critical of the auditor or auditing and blow from being audited. This is handled by clearing the definitions of misunderstood words the preclear was audited over, and clearing to full understanding the most common words and terms used in auditing. A person new to Dianetics and Scientology is well advised to read the basic books on the subject as this will help his progress in processing. Getting trained on Dianetics and Scientology courses is an excellent adjunct to processing; much case gain is obtained from study of Dianetics and Scientology alone.

It is an error to be processed on a process or command that one does not understand. One cannot answer the question if he doesn't understand it. If the auditor uses a word or term you don't know the meaning of, speak up so it can be cleared up.

Persons who have been involved in earlier mental or spiritual practices or studies of the mind usually enter Scientology with great confusions and misconceptions. A person who has studied psychology may think the mind is the brain, or that he is his body and not a spiritual being. Such a person being very confused with false ideas would have great difficulty in processing (as well as in his everyday life) until these misconceptions and confusions are cleared. He would not only be confused but would also have lots of disagreements. Fortunately this is easily handled by clearing up the words and terms in the subject or subjects he studied prior to Scientology, followed by a basic education in Dianetics and Scientology.

Education and schooling have deteriorated so much in recent times that many people do not even understand very common words in their own language, let alone the words in the subjects they have studied. Method One Word Clearing fully resolves this and gives a huge increase in the ability to grasp what one hears and reads as well as considerable return of memory and even skills one may have had and lost.

A person who hasn't read the Classification Gradation and Awareness Chart may not understand the direction and purpose of his processing, or understand which aspects of his case are handled at various grades and levels.

While one does not have to be a trained auditor to be processed, study and training in Dianetics and Scientology enhance processing results. It is a big error to be processed over a mystery, confusion or misunderstood word, and it is a mistake for a preclear not to get training in at least the basics of Scientology.

A "foreign language pc" by which is meant someone being processed in a different language than their own, can encounter words they do not understand, and should get these clarified. If possible they should get audited in their native language, but provided care is taken to clear the meanings of words, they can successfully be audited in a language learned later in life.

Errors About the E-Meter: Misunderstandings about, lack of knowledge of or even confusing this confessional aid with other instruments or machines can get in the way of processing.

Some preclears have not known not to wear rings — these can cause false needle reactions. Washing hands with a strong detergent before a session can change the tone arm reading. Relaxing or letting go of the cans during a session, tightening one's grip or waving one's hands around, will give false readings or reactions. Some preclears have even tried to influence the meter for various reasons. If the cans are too large or too small to be held comfortably, one's hands can get tired and this acts as a distraction from processing. Wearing unduly tight clothing or shoes can give a false reading. So can being tired or hungry.

These errors can result in puzzlement for both auditor and preclear alike and reduce the effectiveness of processing temporarily. One can get a basic understanding by reading *The Book Introducing the E-Meter* and if any of these errors have occurred in one's processing, technical procedures exist which will rapidly handle any upset or discomfort, and restore the latent gain of processing in which such errors were made. It is far easier for a preclear to tell the auditor that his hands are getting tired, or that the cans are too large to be held comfortably, than to spend time finding this out and perhaps suffer needless discomfort. However, auditors are trained to detect and quickly handle these.

Not Communicating to the Auditor: It is a serious error for a preclear to withhold from an auditor. It prevents case gain, results in a critical attitude and can cause a blow or departure from processing. It is easily remedied in processing by getting these withholds off.

Some preclears have felt that they would look bad or that the auditor would think less of them, if they were to tell the auditor certain things about themselves and so withhold these. And some have felt that no one would understand and so didn't tell. Auditors are very understanding, and have heard the same or similar things from many preclears and are not upset or influenced against the person by what he or she may say. Withholds invariably seem much worse to the preclear before he tells the auditor, often these are magnified out of all proportion, but when told, the withholds seem small and cease to make the preclear's life a misery.

Past experience has taught people that they will be punished if they reveal their sins, mistakes or errors. Auditors abide by the Auditor's Code and never do this.

The definition of "in session" is: *interested in own case and willing to talk to the auditor.* Therefore withholding from the auditor, or being unwilling to talk to the auditor, prevents a preclear from being "in session" and inhibits case gain. As past experience may have made one less willing to communicate, even though one wants to, there are processes which can be run which will enable one to overcome any reservations or shyness about communicating. So even if it seems impossible or difficult, tell your auditor and he can help you by making it easier.

Some preclears have not realized that it was important to tell the auditor their cognitions. This can result in the preclear being upset through lack of acknowledgment of his increased awareness. Even where this has occurred it is easily handled in processing resulting in rehabilitation of the cognitions and gains and tremendous relief.

It is a mistake not to communicate changes which occur on a process, such as changes of emotion, somatics, pictures or incidents that come up. Auditors are trained to handle these and it is vital for the auditor to know this data. It enables the auditor to do a better job of auditing the preclear and saves auditing time. This includes errors of: getting upset about something and not telling the auditor, trying to decide whether something was important enough to tell the auditor, not telling the auditor something for fear it might hurt the auditor's feelings, trying to puzzle something out instead of telling the auditor, feeling that something was wrong or incorrect and not telling the auditor, feeling bad and not telling the auditor, having a win or feeling very good and not telling the auditor, not telling the auditor how one really felt, having a sickness or illness or other undesirable or unwanted condition and not telling the auditor, not being fully honest or even lying to the auditor, suppressing something so it "won't come up in session," trying to cover up an upset,

problem, worry or withhold, pushing things aside to "save time" in auditing, not telling the auditor good or bad indicators, saying one is not tired or hungry before or during a session when one is, telling an auditor something else to cover up a withhold or overt, pretending something is better or worse than it is to the auditor, trying to be a "good pc" or "cooperative pc," being "obliging," not telling the auditor when one doesn't understand something in the session, and any other way of not being in free communication with the auditor. Preclears who have made these errors can simply make this known, and the Case Supervisor can get it handled in processing which will bring full relief and restore all the latent gain from earlier auditing.

Not Being Interested in One's Case or the Session: Being processed while one's attention and interest is on something else other than the process being run is self-defeating. If the preclear tells the auditor of this it can be easily handled. A lot of times this situation is due to an actual real present time problem such as: a preclear coming to session knowing that the parking meter will run out and worrying about it instead of putting another coin in the meter, or needing to go to the W.C. and trying to put it off until later, wondering or worrying about something when a phone call would handle, finding a chair uncomfortable to sit in yet trying to stick it out instead of changing the chair, wearing tight or uncomfortable clothing or shoes while being audited, being hungry yet trying to put off eating until after the session, during a session thinking of something one must do later and trying to remember it through the rest of the session instead of asking the auditor to make a note of it and to remind one after the session is over. These errors distract one's attention from his case and the process being run, and auditing time is too valuable to waste when a few minutes would handle the matter so one's attention is free to put on the session.

Another way that this can occur is where the preclear has something which is very important to him to get handled; sometimes so important that he judges his success in auditing by whether this changes. A somatic such as an ache in the knee which the pc wants to get rid of and after every session tests out his knee to see if it still aches. Very often such things are not communicated by the preclear for whatever reason and so are called "hidden standards." Because it is not communicated by the preclear to the auditor, it does not get taken up in auditing, and because it is of such importance to the preclear his attention can be so fixed on the hidden standard that he cannot easily take his attention off it and so has difficulty being audited on anything else. Any pc who has something that he wants auditing to handle, or has something he measures his case gain by, or if he has his attention fixed on some part of his case or life, should make this known so that it can be taken up in processing and handled.

There are many processes which address and handle such things. Some persons who had a hidden standard have concluded that auditing didn't work, or didn't work on them, when maybe the auditor was running processes to improve the preclear's ability to communicate and the preclear was "checking his stomach to see if it still hurt when he thought of Grandma." So anyone feeling that they are not making progress in processing can be asked how he or she measures case gain and you'll be surprised at some of the answers.

Another variation of this is the person getting processing for some other reason than has been stated. An extreme of this is the person who has given up in life and is waiting to succumb. As Scientology processes are directed toward survival, a pc headed toward succumb will be in conflict with the auditing itself. Recognize that persons in conflict with processing or in conflict with Scientology are only in this conflict because they have goals or purposes which are destructive or directed toward succumb. The same applies to persons critical of or antagonistic toward Scientology. But because Man is basically good, underneath these sub-optimum purposes are constructive purposes and so processing will salvage these, too.

Trying to Handle One's Own Case: Having acquired a little data on Scientology processing one could imagine that he knew enough to handle his own case. One could try to "self-audit" which has proven unsuccessful. Some try to tell the auditor what to do or what to run on them. Some figure about their case or processing trying to solve it all themselves. This approach does not work and people have been trying to figure out what was wrong with them most of their lives to no avail. Auditors and Case Supervisors are trained in the processes of Scientology and know how to do the best for the preclear. Misguided efforts to help by self-auditing or trying to run the session by the preclear only slow things down. Not answering the process question or not doing the auditing command but instead doing something else is a variation of this. If the auditor asks the preclear to recall a particular type of incident that is what the preclear should do, not try to find a different type of incident or do something else entirely, as doing so prevents the process from being run, and so reduces the results of the processing. Should a preclear find himself doing this he should inform the auditor. Or if he doesn't understand why the process is being done, or thinks a different process should be run, he should inform his auditor of this so that it can be handled, right away with no loss of auditing time.

Another variation of this is the preclear who feels critical or out of agreement with the auditor or what is being run. Don't waste time feeling critical or out of agreement and not saying so, or waste time criticizing and complaining. Say so when you notice anything like this so it can be handled then and there.

Auditing is a team activity and the preclear can help himself to make better and faster gains by keeping the auditor informed and working together with the auditor as a team. As the preclear becomes more familiar with auditing, these errors of trying to do it differently or thinking there's a better or faster way cease to occur as reality on the effectiveness and gains from processing occur.

Another form of this error would be for a preclear to doubt his own reality or memory and compare his own recall with other persons or try to find dates or content of incidents from relatives or other persons or books. Even if data from others conflicts with one's own reality it would be a mistake to assume one's own data is wrong. Most persons who have not had processing have poor memory and do not duplicate well. Even history books often conflict with each other and are often altered versions of what actually occurred.

Engaging in Other Practices: Scientology processing is a precision activity and therefore cannot be mixed with other practices without reducing its effectiveness. Scientology is at its best when purely and standardly applied. It is not enhanced by meditation, yoga, trying to analyze one's id, attempting self-hypnosis, or practicing or mixing any other practice, therapy or self-help method with Scientology. There have been many many different practices and therapies around for a long time, yet Man is today generally in poor plight, showing there has been a lack of success in improving his condition. Some past therapies and practices have been destructive. So don't mix Scientology with these or engage in them between sessions as only a reduction of the gains available from Scientology processing can result. Some pcs have tried getting audited by more than one auditor at once, some love to discuss or talk about their cases to someone else between sessions, some have tried to "audit" themselves between sessions. Some have tried experimenting with processes or pieces of Scientology data they have picked up. A skilled auditor can readily untangle this, but why spend valuable processing time this way when it could be spent on case advance? Persons who make this type of error can appear to be very mysterious cases. Any case that seems to be different or reacting in a mysterious way is suspected of and asked if the person does some practice or exercise between sessions or even if he or she is talking about case or "being audited" between sessions.

Among the long list of former therapies and earlier practices are those which being forceful, painful, or which sought to make the person less self-determined, were harmful or aberrative. A person who has indulged in or been treated in any of these will be resistive to processing, or any other effort to help, until the effects of these are run out. Scientology is not only a precision activity with invariable success when purely applied, but it also is a means of undoing and releasing one from any past experience with harmful "therapy."

Being Processed or Trained While PTS: Persons who are connected to someone antagonistic toward themselves or Scientology will not be able to hold onto their gains from processing and this is the only reason for any loss of gain. This mechanism is described in Scientology technical materials and the processing of persons who are PTS is forbidden by policy. The method of handling and resolving this condition of PTS is fully covered in the "PTS/SP Detection and Handling Course." Yet because a person who is PTS may not believe the situation can be handled or because they don't understand the subject of PTSness, or because they felt there was something shameful about being PTS, or for fear of consequences sometimes withheld it, many who are PTS have not revealed it and tried to be processed anyway. However, a trained Scientologist can quickly recognize the symptom of loss of gains or rollercoaster and direct the person to correct handling of the condition. Technology exists to enable a person, connected to someone hostile or antagonistic, to handle that person to a resolution of the conflict or antagonism. A course exists which educates and trains one on the subject to put him more at cause over it. And processing exists which runs out the experience of having been connected to suppressive persons or groups. All one has to do is to go to a

Scientology Church or Mission and avail oneself of the technology.

For example, a Scientologist's father was antagonistic to his son, and sought to control his son by offering to give him money, then withholding the money in an effort to force his son to take up the profession he himself had failed in. The father seeing Scientology as a threat to his plans (as it would enable the son to be self-determined and live his own life), told the son he could have the money when he gave up Scientology. The son mistakenly once again did what his father told him only to have the promise broken again. All the son would have to do is recognize that he was connected to someone ill-intentioned toward him, and who had no intention of helping him in any way and he could then begin to handle the situation to the benefit of both himself and his father. Sometimes as in this instance a person will keep himself connected to a suppressive person for fear of what it would cost to handle, or for an ulterior motive. Yet what a price to pay for loss of freedom, happiness and the ability to be oneself when all one needs to do is to ask for the technology on the subject of PTSness.

Being Antisocial, Out-Ethics: Persons who are chronically antisocial, or involved in a harmful or criminal activity will not permit themselves to be helped and work just as hard at damaging themselves as they do others. The description and explanation of such persons is contained in materials listed under subjects of "Suppressives," "Antisocial Personality" and all these materials are available in the "PTS/SP Detection and Handling Course." As such a person is motivated by destructive purposes he is against anything which tries to help or improve people and so will sometimes attack Scientology because it does help people. Scientology can help even suppressive persons by enabling them to get rid of destructive goals and purposes and restoring their own basic goodness. But by committing overts against their fellows and by trying to damage Scientology it becomes harder and harder for such persons to accept help, especially from those they have sought to harm. Therefore, it is a serious mistake to try to attack Scientology or to try to harm it or its members in any way. All such attacks have been futile but the persons behind them have made themselves that much harder to help.

It is similarly a mistake to be involved in any contra-survival or out-ethics activity. As Man is basically good, he won't permit himself to get more able if his intentions are bad, and this prevents case gain until the person reforms and ceases to commit continuous overts against his fellows. But through processing this person can find and handle the reasons why he "had to do such things" or "couldn't stop himself" from doing them. So powerful is this principle that it even inhibits the progress of Scientologists should they become involved in upsets or misunderstandings, quarrels or overts and withholds from each other. Using the technology of ethics, and cleaning up their overts and withholds from each other, their ARC and progress in Scientology are enhanced. But any overt against another Scientologist or against a Scientology organization, such as harsh words, stealing a book, not paying a donation for service received, will prevent case gain or progress until the matter is put right, and all one has to do is to see the local Ethics Officer about it.

An extreme of this is a person belonging to a group with harmful or suppressive aims. Such persons are required to disavow and handle their connections before participating in Scientology, as until they do so there is little hope for their betterment. Yet by taking this up with an Ethics Officer this, too, can be handled.

Similarly failing to adhere to basic rules of decency, failure to follow the laws of the land, not making restitution for wrongs, not doing all possible to put right a grievance are errors which would impede one in Scientology. Amongst Scientologists these are rare as the practice of Scientology results in a higher level of ethics and integrity. No matter how bad one may consider he or she has been, Scientologists are very ready to forgive and so one should not make the mistake of withholding his errors or failures.

Unauthorized Case Actions: Trying to audit oneself between sessions; being "audited" by another between sessions, "trying out" pieces of data or processes, obtaining or seeking confidential technical data above one's level are all restimulative and can cause a case to deteriorate, appear mysterious or hang fire, until these are located and corrected. One should not do these or permit them to be done to oneself or others. If such have occurred report it so the correct repair can be done.

Sometimes students new to the subject are keen to try processes or techniques on others. Scientology works to the degree it is exactly applied. The answer is to get trained to audit the processes correctly and don't experiment or fool around. The overt of impairing another's case progress would hang up one's own case progress.

Any instances which do occur should be reported to the Ethics Officer who would dissuade the offender, and reported for the person's case folder so any bypassed charge can be quickly repaired.

Getting Nonstandard Processing: Scientology maintains high standards of training and competence for its auditors, and awards certificates where these have been earned. Its organizations discourage untrained or unqualified persons from processing others. Scientology processes produce 100% gains when done standardly. To go to someone who has not been trained for processing is to court failure.

Persons who have not been trained in Scientology processing yet try to process others are unethical. Sometimes unethical persons have stolen Scientology processes or data and tried to use them, sometimes calling it Scientology, sometimes pretending they invented it. They are short-lived as they invariably alter the processes and data and so it no longer works. Such persons are recognized by:

(a) not having certificates issued by the Church of Scientology

(b) not calling what they are doing Scientology but something else

(c) having changed the processes or data from L. Ron Hubbard's books, tapes and bulletins.

You can always ask to see an auditor's certificates, and can always ask your nearest Scientology organization about the credentials of anyone offering or delivering processing.

If you have been unfortunate enough to have gone to an

unqualified person for processing, go to a Church of Scientology and make a full report on the matter and get some standard processing to repair errors made, so that you can enjoy the spectacular results of standard auditing.

Drugs and Drug Reversion: As drug abuse is widespread and due to the impairment of memory, intelligence and sanity caused by drugs, persons who have taken drugs do not respond well in life or in processing until the effects of drugs have been handled. Continuing to take drugs while trying to be processed would defeat the purpose of the processing, as drugs reduce awareness and self-determinism and often produce hallucinations.

Scientology has a drug program which is the only effective way known to enable drug takers and even addicts to come off drugs stably; and processing completely releases the person from the effects of drugs and rehabilitates him into a condition better than he had prior to taking drugs. Drugs do not aid processing results. Some medicines contain hallucinogenics or other drugs and therefore should not be taken during processing.

Disability Payments, etc.: A person taking a disability payment or compensation for an ailment or injury should make this known when starting out in Scientology. Scientology improves ability and gets rid of unwanted conditions. Persons entering Scientology who received a disability payment, and started processing have improved and then sagged until it was found and handled in their processing. It would be better to make anything like this known in the first place.

Undisclosed Illness or Condition: Very often persons new to Scientology consider that it is bad or shameful to admit to things they have wrong with them. This can cause frustration in processing as the person is not in full communication with the auditor and is actually trying to use the processing to handle something different (and unknown to the auditor), than what the processing is being addressed to. Any data relating to a person's case is kept confidential and the sooner the preclear tells the auditor of anything of this nature the faster and better his processing will be.

Falsifying or Pretending Attainments: Persons who have not yet experienced case gains from processing, and who are anxious to impress others have been known to try to pretend case gains or attainments not made. Trying to rush through processes or sessions; trying to skip basic lower level auditing actions in order to get onto higher levels, claiming to have already done actions that haven't been done, finding out what the end result of a process is and trying to fake it, even falsely declaring or attesting to things not actually done—these invariably show up and need to be corrected. Scientology processes and procedures are exact in application and result and are laid out in their proper sequence on the Grade Chart. There is no short cut to Clear or OT. Over the years many who were poorly informed in the subject have hopefully tried to "quickie" their way up, or to pretend lower grades and levels not actually attained. This makes higher levels appear not to work and of course they don't work without lower grades fully in. The answer is honesty and getting the lower levels and basics properly done.

Quitting Processing, Refusing Processing: Persons "processed" by an unqualified person, or who have made any of the errors described so far can make the conclusion that processing does not work, or does not work on them, that he or she is a "different" or "difficult" case, overlooking the fact that standard Scientology processing has not been done on them. This can be very upsetting and discourage the person into giving up or even refusing to have further processing. Persons in this frame of mind are often misemotional and do not readily find or state correct reasons or causes for things. In fact if the person is misemotional you can be sure that he is giving or has been given a wrong reason for the upset. The right reason for any upset or misemotion when found will bring in good indicators and enable the person to do something constructive to handle the situation. No matter how bad or how black things may seem it is always possible to locate and repair the departure from standard Scientology which caused the upset. Upsets always occur on a departure from standard Scientology processes or techniques. Often it only takes minutes by a professional auditor to change a severe upset into glowing smiles of relief. It is a grave mistake not to get this done, or to leave without getting such a simple action done. Even though the errors leading to upsets were caused by uninformed or nonstandard misuses of Scientology techniques or data, most organizations will repair these upsets free of charge. It is foolish to leave an upset unhandled when the means of resolving it is so easy and so available.

Not Recognizing Extent of Progress

Usually persons new to Scientology have so many things they want to get rid of, so many things they want to change, so much they want to improve that it would be hard to even communicate all of them. As fast as one unwanted condition disappears with processing, they are onto the next and getting it handled. Because the things that have been handled are no longer bothering the person, and because he is interested in handling the rest of the things wrong with him, it is easy to lose sight of just how much has been handled, how successful his processing has been so far. Yet an inquiry into the person's condition, outlook in life, complaints and difficulties that he had prior to Scientology, compared with how he is doing now will usually give a list of miracles enough to amaze even the most pessimistic.

Finally the most basic error one could make is not to get processing or not to get enough processing. There is no condition which will not resolve with processing. There are a vast number of different processes and techniques which cover every situation, difficulty, inability or trouble a person could encounter in life, and all of these can readily be handled with Scientology. A person relatively new to Scientology will be amazed at the vast number of ways that it can be applied with miraculous results. Don't fail to use it and deny yourself the benefits of it. No matter what the difficulty is, inquire of your nearest Church or Mission and you'll find there is a Scientology process or technique or method to handle it.

The greatest error of all is not using Scientology on every possible occasion.

Scientology Ethics

7

"**Ethics** is a code of agreement amongst people that they will conduct themselves in a fashion which will attain to the optimum solution of their problems."

— L. Ron Hubbard

The effectiveness of Scientology has been demonstrated for over twenty-eight years, at this writing. It has given Man the truth about himself, his spiritual nature, his vast potential abilities, and his reactive mind which has hitherto limited his native ability and held him back from full achievement of his goals.

Momentous as the above discoveries by L. Ron Hubbard have been, even they have been surpassed by his discovery of a technology, applicable to everyone, which enables Man for the first time to achieve his full abilities, rid himself of his reactive mind, and freely set and reach his long sought goals.

The various Churches and organizations of Scientology and Dianetics are the custodians of this technology which is daily being applied to the improvement of Man's spiritual abilities and thus the making of a better civilization of which we all can be proud.

This is a great responsibility, and coupled with it is the Church's responsibility to ensure honest application by all Scientologists of the technology solely for the benefit of mankind.

This responsibility is carried out through the use of Scientology ethics policies. Ethics policies are levelled primarily at making auditing and training honest and flawless.

Thus, persons who receive Scientology auditing and training at a Scientology Church or Mission can be confident that the services they receive will be standard and fully effective and that ethics will be applied to make it so if a departure occurs.

All executives and staff members of Scientology organizations are charged with the responsibility of keeping the technology firm and unalterable, both in study of it and application to another by pastoral counseling (auditing).

To do otherwise would be unethical, or out-ethics.

OUT-ETHICS is defined as: an action or situation in which an individual is involved contrary to the ideals and best interests of his group. An act or situation or relationship contrary to the ethics standards, codes, or ideals of the group or other members of the group. An act of omission or commission by an individual that could or has reduced the general effectiveness of a group or its other members. An individual act of omission or commission which impedes the general well-being of a group or impedes it in achieving its goals.

Thus there are ethics standards and codes of agreement in Scientology that prevent out-ethics individuals and groups from altering the truth or misusing the technology of Scientology and Dianetics.

These standards and agreements are found in the ethics policies of the Church which are available for all to read and understand in the Organization Executive Course

Volumes 0 and 1, on sale at any Church of Scientology bookstore or Publications Organization.

Scientology ethics policies also provide justice actions for Church members and organization staff:

JUSTICE is 1. Moral rightness; equity. 2. Honor; fairness. 3. Good reason. 4. Fair handling; due reward or treatment. 5. The administration and procedure of the law.

There are CHAPLAIN'S COURTS to resolve matters of dispute between individuals, which may be utilized by staff personnel, preclears, students, or any Scientologists.

BOARDS OF INVESTIGATION are called by certain executives in Scientology organizations to investigate and help discover the cause in any conflict, poor performance, or down statistic areas of production. Also they are convened to investigate unusual improvements in an organization or its production statistics to isolate the reasons or changes which brought about the improvement and recommend policy or directives and commendations on those responsible so that such improvements become a matter of record and are continued.

An ETHICS HEARING is used to obtain data for further action or inaction in the case where doubt exists as to whether an ethics-actionable offense has occurred by a staff member.

An EXECUTIVE ETHICS HEARING is used for the same purpose where the person in question is an executive of an organization.

A COURT OF ETHICS is convened where statistics and known evidence exist which show that an offense per the Church's ethics codes has been committed by a staff member.

An EXECUTIVE COURT OF ETHICS is convened for the same reasons as above where the offender is an executive.

A COMMITTEE OF EVIDENCE is convened in cases of more severe out-ethics and offenses per the Church's ethics codes and is the only one of the above justice bodies that can recommend cancellation of certificates and awards or expulsion from the Church.

A COMMITTEE OF EVIDENCE FOR REVIEW may be requested by any person who was an interested party in a Committee of Evidence and feels he was unjustly penalized. It is convened and held solely to go over the evidence found by the original committee and may only recommend that a new Committee of Evidence be convened or that the penalty be changed.

The various actions listed above consist of one or more impartial members strictly adhering to rules of evidence and Church policy in order to make recommendations which, when carried out, resolve the out-ethics situation, get ethics in, and Church policy followed.

As Scientology ethics developed over the years and was applied to the rehabilitation of out-ethics individuals, it was found to have a technology of its own. In 1968, an incredible breakthrough was made by L. Ron Hubbard in isolating the natural law which explains the cause of violence and conflict amongst individuals, groups and nations. Simple but powerful technology now exists to eradicate the harmful, even disastrous effects of the instigators behind the scene of conflict and chaos.

The application of this technology concerning what is known as the THIRD PARTY LAW,† has been stunningly effective in resolving attacks against the Church, as well as conflicts between individuals and other group activities.

But ethics technology goes even farther—into the realm of spiritual ethics. For instance, it is out-ethics for a person to interfere with or invalidate another's spiritual advancement or progress. The one interfered with or invalidated may lose his spiritual gains and feel depressed.

The person who does the interfering or invalidating to stop the other from getting better is in fact committing a suppressive act against the improvement of Man's spiritual ability and thus is going directly against the purpose of the Church.

A person who continually does the above is known as a SUPPRESSIVE PERSON and is recognized by the traits of his antisocial personality.

The other person, who had made spiritual gains and then had them invalidated or was interfered with in his spiritual progress by the suppressive person, would at first have been happy and winning in life and then felt depressed and that he had lost something of value. Not realizing what has happened or who suppressed him (as it can be done very covertly) will cause him to become misemotional over these losses and perhaps violent and troublesome to those around him. This manifestation describes the POTENTIAL TROUBLE SOURCE, which means that the person is connected to a suppressive person whom he has not as yet recognized or handled.

As Scientology is for *everyone*, its ethics technology also includes the handling of the PTS and even the suppressive person, to get them on the road of stable spiritual gain. The techniques developed by L. Ron Hubbard for this, correctly and exactly applied, produce startling changes for the better in these types of persons.

Ethics technology on a spiritual level is used also when a person lets his own ethics go "out" or fails to get it "in." This normally occurs when a person commits an overt act and then withholds it:

OVERT ACT: 1. An overt act is not just injuring someone or something; an overt act is an act of omission or commission which does the least good for the least number of dynamics or the most harm to the greatest number of dynamics. 2. An intentionally committed harmful act committed in an effort to resolve a problem. 3. That thing which you do which you aren't willing to have happen to you.

WITHHOLD: 1. A withhold is an unspoken, unannounced transgression against a moral code by which the person was bound. 2. The unwillingness of the preclear to talk to the auditor or tell him something. 3. A withhold is something that a person believes that if it is revealed it will endanger their self-preservation. 4. When the person should be reaching and is withdrawing that's a withhold. 5. A withhold is a withhold if it is a violation of the mores the preclear has subscribed to and knows about. 6. A withhold is something the preclear did that he isn't talking about. 7. A withhold is

†For a full rundown on the THIRD PARTY LAW, see *The Volunteer Minister's Handbook*.

what the preclear is withholding and it does not have to include what the preclear considers is a withhold. 8. It is restraining self from communicating. 9. Is always the manifestation which comes after an overt. Any withhold comes after an overt.

By doing this he goes out of communication with his fellows and becomes less effective at his job. It is then time for a spiritual counseling action known as a CONFESSIONAL, wherein a minister has the person tell what overt acts he has done. After applying standardly the technology of a confessional, the person will be back in communication and feel much more at cause in life, and as a result will do much better at his job.

So in the scope of Scientology ethics, there are not only codes and agreements, but a precise technology powerful enough to handle attacks upon the Church or its individual members, and also keep Scientologists themselves clean of overt acts and withholds.

One of the most important and far-reaching discoveries made by L. Ron Hubbard in the field of ethics technology has been that of the actual Conditions of Existence (or operating conditions) existing in the physical universe. Hitherto unsuspected, these conditions affect every person, family, group, business, company, society, country, race, species, spiritual being, and form the ethics basis of life itself.

As one moves up these conditions, he becomes less out-ethics and more ethical, his exchange with others becomes less of an overt and more valuable, and his productivity and morale come into existence and increase markedly.

The proven, effective way to gauge or determine what operating condition a person or activity is in is the method in use by policy in Scientology organizations, which is to operate entirely on valid STATISTICS of production for each person in the organization based on his post purpose and what he contributes in order for the organization to survive better. When a person's statistic is rising, he is helping the organization to survive and is thus *protected* by ethics.

On the other hand if the statistic is seen to be level or falling, or is found to be dishonest or false, or if nothing is produced, or the actions on the post are going against the organization's survival and expansion, then ethics must be applied either by the person or the organization to remedy the situation.

By basing a condition assignment solely on valid statistics, a person is encouraged to demonstrate his competence in contributing to the survival of the organization, and since "personality" or "opinion" play no part in the assignment, those who do not contribute to the survival and expansion of the organization are quickly located and their ethics gotten in.

Operating by statistics is not limited only to Scientology organizations. A statistic, by definition is a number or amount compared to an earlier number or amount of the same thing. Statistics refer to the quantity of the work done, or the value of it in money. Operating by statistics can, (and should) be done in any endeavor or walk of life to improve the quantity, quality and viability of the activity.

The full list of Conditions and the exact FORMULAS which must be applied to get out of a condition and up to the next higher one, and the laws governing what happens when formulas are misapplied or wrongly used exist in *The Volunteer Minister's Handbook*. If a person studies these and applies the correct formula for the condition he is in, and continues to do so as he rises up through the conditions he will eventually arrive in a true condition of Power.

At this operating state, he will be of greatest value to himself, his family, group, business, company, society, country, race, and species and as a spiritual being have his ethics fully in.

In summary, Scientology ethics has a truly remarkable technology of its own discovered, researched, and developed by the Founder of Scientology, L. Ron Hubbard, which does not have "punishment" or "incarceration" as an end result; but rather the *full* handling of the out-ethics situation, rehabilitation of those involved, and the carrying out of a precise series of technical steps which get in the person's ethics, increase his exchange, productivity and contribution, and lead to spiritual enhancement. A person whose ethics are *in* will be able to give and receive full benefit and maximum gain from the training and processing technology of Scientology and Dianetics and thus more readily achieve his goals.

The effectiveness of Scientology ethics technology and its success is demonstrated in the following excerpts of statements from those who have applied it. These are representative of the thousands of such statements that have been received by the Church from all over the world.

On the General Use of Scientology Ethics Technology

This has been one of the most successful actions I've done in Scientology. The purpose of ethics isn't to make you wrong—it's to make you ultimately right. There is no "punishment" and everything I did (amends work, application of the condition formulas, etc.) played its part in getting me to the state of beingness where my responsibility and awareness have soared.

W S — Canada

I feel I am quite a changed person after this ethics cycle. For the first time in my life, I feel completely stable and at cause over all parts of my life. I would like to validate L. Ron Hubbard for having understood, codified, and communicated the basic laws of life contained in the ethics policies and technology. Having this has enabled me to reach a whole new state of beingness.

M M — England

I just had a fabulous ethics handling. It totally exteriorized me as a being and I became certain of myself again. Thank you Ron for the data that makes understanding this universe possible.

J C — U.S.A.

On the Use of a Chaplain's Court

Two parishioners, R.M. and L.M., a husband and wife, were having trouble with their marriage, and actually were on the brink of divorce. As they had four children, this was a very serious affair. They agreed to a Chaplain's Court, and I, as chaplain, had them sit down and go over the marriage vows and the original purposes and agreements they had at the time of getting married. This got them in real communication with each other for the first time in quite a while. I then had them confront each other and alternately tell overt acts and withholds on the other. After thirty minutes they were laughing together at how silly they had been. I had them then spot the ethics condition their marriage was in and drew up a program with them to apply the correct formulas all the way to Power. They left the court thanking me for saving their marriage. It has now been three months since the court and they have brought me a full write-up of all their program steps complete. As they left my office today, each praised the ethics technology of L. Ron Hubbard and with arms around each other, said together "We're in Power," looked at each other, kissed, waved to me and walked out to where their smiling children were waiting, still arm in arm. What more can I say? This ethics technology is POWERFUL!

A R — U.S.A.

On the Use of Ethics Policies

Our organization was having difficulty with its financial planning and promotional activities. A Board of Investigation was called by an executive of the organization to fully investigate the matter and make recommendations as to what should be done to resolve the situation. The board was composed of three staff members who were familiar with policy but not directly on financial or promotion lines. The board discovered that cross-policy was being set on financial planning and promotion by persons in those areas who had not studied the full financial and promotion policies of the organization. A study program was recommended and carried out while financial and promotional planning was placed under an experienced executive until the persons concerned learned the correct policies and could take back their responsibility for it. The result has been greatly increased financial and promotional success and affluent expansion for the organization.

S F — U.S.A.

A Court of Ethics was called on R.N., a student, by the Church for commission of technical errors in his pastoral counseling of another student. He admitted to having violated standard technology, and was assigned a condition and a full retrain on the technology he had failed to apply. Since working through the conditions and retraining, his counseling has been excellent and the same student he had

erred with has now gotten the best spiritual gains of his life from R.N.'s counseling.

D M — New Zealand

On the Use of The Third Party Law

There was continual conflict between G.A. and P.H. They could not agree on anything and got into heated arguments in public. Several reports came to me as Ethics Officer of their conflicts upsetting and distracting other staff members. I called them in and had each read The Third Party Law material, then asked them the questions designed to locate the person who was promoting the conflict. It only took a few minutes and suddenly at almost the same instant, both realized *who* was promoting the conflict. I called in the person and when confronted with the evidence, she broke down and confessed to promoting and actually encouraging the conflict to both G.A. and P.H. separately as it gave her continual excuses and justification for not doing jobs assigned and getting off work because of "headaches" "caused" by the arguments. It was found she had also done this to her mother and father to cover up bad things she had done as a child. A Confessional was done to clean up all her overt acts and withholds and she now has no compulsion to be a third party and is productive on post. G.A. and P.H. are best of friends and work together in full agreement as a team. The Third Party Law is an amazing piece of technology!

R A — U.S.A.

On The Handling of Potential Trouble Sources

I can hardly believe how much better I feel after handling two situations in my life that were making me a potential trouble source. My life has changed and I feel much saner and happier. Thank you Ron, for the ethics technology and especially for being there and helping so many people including me.

J P — U.S.A.

My handling as a PTS was the most stupendous action I have ever had. It has handled one whole lifetime of continuous losses. Now I can *win* as I do not have to have the validation of another to be proud of myself or my accomplishments. With the suppressive person recognized and handled, I now can *be, do,* and *have* on my own self-determinism in the present, and not be drowned in the unwarranted invalidation of the past.

D R — U.S.A.

By studying the ethics policies concerning potential trouble sources and suppressive persons and doing the handling of my own PTS situation, I have gained the ability to not get involved or become effect of suppression and to understand completely the phenomena. I also feel that I have become happier, saner and more things are easier to confront. My integrity has been raised. My thanks go to L. Ron Hubbard for the technology.

M H — U.S.A.

For the first time in twenty-four years I am not a potential trouble source. I struggled with this for years and had given up on even trying anymore until the standard tech of Scientology ethics was used to handle it and guide me through the situation. Now I've had new realizations about my life and am totally at cause and can handle anything. I'm not stuck in the past anymore and my perceptions are improving to an incredible degree.

C C — U.S.A.

S.N. was a potential trouble source. He lost gains, felt depressed, and had chronic somatics in his leg (hip area) that kept him from walking and which had no discoverable physical or medical reason for being there. I was asked by a minister of the Church of Scientology to do a standard potential trouble source handling with him. During the handling he recognized a source of suppression in his life since childhood and is now doing the final technical handling steps to resolve it completely. The initial steps of the technology have been startlingly effective and have changed his life completely. He has been in Scientology only six weeks and now has a full reality on the power and workability of ethics technology. I enclose his written statement he gave at the conclusion of the initial handling steps of his PTS situation.

P S — U.S.A.

I must say I feel wonderful and super-fantastic now. There is a reason—ethics handling. It's just amazing. Now I no longer have that mysterious pain in my hip that wouldn't let me walk. It was connected to my being spiritually suppressed and when I recognized the source of suppression it vanished! The ethical way is the *only* way when it comes to *my* spiritual future.

S N — U.S.A.

On the Handling of Overt Acts and Withholds

Cleaning up my overts and withholds has been a fabulous action which has made me feel clean, calm, and relaxed. I know *I* can create and have a fresh start in *life*. My integrity has been restored. I can now look outward fully again, whereas before, I was interiorizing into the things I'd done which I later regretted. This is truly a fabulous feeling. My thanks to L. Ron Hubbard for this excellent technology.

H V — Germany

Getting off my overts is the most incredible and workable thing I've ever seen. Looking at my own overts,

confronting them, and communicating them is like initiating a new life, full of happiness and revitalized purposes. By committing overts and withholding them I also withheld my spiritual power but now it has returned, and I feel better than ever!

A C — U.S.A.

The hardest hardest thing to do was to confront what I had done in the past. I shunned taking responsibility for my actions. I couldn't even tell anybody about those few withholds that I had been carrying around with me since I was six years old. But now, I could tell anybody! How easy! But I never realized that until I understood the technology of overts and withholds and ethics. I feel like I've been given a second chance and am ready to start anew. Only *this* time I have L. Ron Hubbard's ethics technology to back me up!

M C — U.S.A.

I feel great! This was a very life-giving and revealing action for me. Getting off my overts and withholds has raised my confront and responsibility level tremendously. I am way up in spiritual tone and my eyesight has improved. I feel terrific!

L F — England

On the Receiving of Confessionals

I had so many wins and cognitions during the Confessional that I can't remember them all. But the biggest thing of all is that I am CLEAN, totally CLEAN. I have no withholds anymore. *Any*body could ask me *any*thing, and I wouldn't flinch, tell lies, change the subject, avoid answering, or back off from telling the truth. No more withholds! I've confronted and taken FULL responsibility for *every*thing. I got off *every*thing and in doing it I took complete responsibility for it all, which I learned is the only thing that really gets one spiritually clean. I didn't just come clean on the major things or on the little ones, I came clean on *every*thing. It's an utterly fantastic feeling! It was a bit hard at the start. I didn't want to confront it—but it quickly became not only easy but very very pleasurable. As the Confessional progressed I went exterior many times, my perceptions increased, and I ended up stably exterior with greatly increased perceptions. My deepest gratitude to my minister for his thoroughness and above all to L. Ron Hubbard for this fantastic technology.

K K — U.S.A.

I had a very excellent Confessional recently and from this was able to clean up seven years of overt acts which has been holding me back, and which I was totally unable to confront. This was a truly great action and very much needed and wanted.

A V — South Africa

It's amazing not to have any withholds. There are no bars imprisoning me. I used to wonder how it would feel to have another chance at life and a good clean start. Well, everyday now is like a *new* day and a *new* chance to make my life go right. Thanks, Ron.

R R — Australia

On the Application of Condition Formulas

I have had incredible spiritual gains as a result of doing ethics conditions formulas. My eyesight and spiritual perception have improved and I feel very *in*-ethics.

J M — Canada

This was the best thing I could ever have done. I have just applied the conditions formulas in relation to my family. The affinity I have now for my wife and child is really high and I feel totally clean and in-ethics towards them. I'm a new *me* off to a new start with *my* family. Ethics conditions really work!

C H — Australia

My wife and I applied the conditions formulas to our marriage (which was getting a bit rocky) at the Church of Scientology under a minister's guidance. Ever since then, my life has been *smooth*. I have never loved my wife more, nor have I ever loved life more. We don't criticize and nag at each other anymore, and I've never been more proud of her, or myself, for that matter. I see nothing ahead but smooth sailing in our marriage! Thank you Ron, for the fantastic technology.

D H — U.S.A.

Applying ethics technology and especially conditions formulas has saved my business. A year ago I was ready to quit and was confronted with situations at the office daily that I (at the time) thought only money in large quantities could handle, which I didn't have. Then I met a Scientologist who steered me to the Church bookstore where I bought the whole Organization Executive Course Volumes and Management Series. By the time I had read Volume 0, I had put in statistical management and ethics technology in my business. By proper application of conditions formulas I managed to bring the business out of the red and into the black. Now I've had to expand into larger premises and have three branch offices in other cities! Business is great! And I'm now taking night courses at the Church with my whole family. What a change in less than a year! I strongly urge anyone who hasn't read and applied ethics technology to get on the bandwagon. It works!

B R — U.S.A.

In conclusion, Scientology ethics is best described in the words of the Founder, L. Ron Hubbard, written in January 1951:

"Ethics are distinct from morals. Ethics are the factors of survival as they reasonably and currently apply to the problem. Honesty, derivably, is the highest level of survival."

8

The Social Services of Scientology

As the average citizen of a big city today gazes out of his high-rise apartment window, he will see drug addicts and pushers lining the street below and will hear police sirens screaming on their way to the scene of a mass murder. Tattered alcoholics will be sleeping on nearby park benches while others search through piles of garbage in search of their daily bread. The paper boy will scream "Read all about it" and the headlines will tell of overdosings and mysterious deaths in the local mental hospital. A young teenager will be stabbed in a back alley after a showdown of two local gangs.

Our average citizen will probably close his window, draw the curtains, and mix himself a stiff drink. When he was young he dreamed that Man could improve his plight, but now that he is older and wiser he knows the ways of the world and realizes that life must go on and there is nothing he can do.

And is this the case or has our average citizen grown disillusioned and cynical? What chance does mankind have to solve the serious problems that he is faced with today? Will Man better his condition or will he go up in an atomic mushroom?

Down through the ages Man has grappled with social ills and now and then a determined few have made progress. Traditionally, it has been the role of religion to provide Man with answers that he could not find elsewhere, and men of religion have often striven to improve social conditions and have met with success.

In the early 1900s Gandhi, affectionately called Mahatma meaning Great Soul, was honored by the people of India as the father of their nation.

He developed a method of social action, based on the principles of courage, nonviolence and truth which was followed to free India from British control.

Since 1950 the Church of Scientology has involved itself in social reform and is currently taking action to create a safer, saner society where all men are able to exercise their fundamental rights to live, with dignity and respect.

Drug and Alcohol Rehabilitation

The Narconon Program

As you read this book there will be someone taking heroin for the first time. Someone else will be committing a crime to get his daily fix or beginning his first prison sentence for selling drugs or dying from an overdose of barbiturates.

You may feel this has nothing to do with you, that no one in your family thinks of taking drugs. But the fact is that drug abuse is not restricted to a closed shop of "down and outs." It can hit anywhere.

Society now faces such a terrifying increase in drug abuse that the future of our entire social order is under threat. Drug abuse directly or indirectly affects us all.

The Cost of Drug Abuse

The cost of this malaise in the senseless loss of lives, property stolen or destroyed, is on a steep incline. The cost in terms of human misery is beyond calculation. It has bogged down judicial systems and tied up legislative bodies in endless debate over the nature of the problem and the possibility of a solution.

National economies have felt the ill effects of the problem, both in terms of the direct cost to society and in the wastage of manpower, time and money which must be spent by law enforcement and correctional agencies, judicial and legislative bodies, social services and welfare agencies, medical and hospital emergency facilities, and city and national governments, in their seemingly hopeless efforts at protecting us from the effects of drug abuse. All of these resources should be utilized for more productive activities.

For the addict himself drugs are a prison with no escape. He sees his day-to-day existence as a death watch, hardly caring that the next hit may be his source of extinction. One addicted person spoke of his life in this way:

"I have been addicted for 7 1/2 years and have been desperately looking for years for an appropriate possibility to become free of it. The drugs, heroin and morphine, made me physically and mentally so broken that I sometimes believed I would perish because of it. I have heard from acquaintances who also have been drug addicted how deeply they themselves sank."

Another addict states:

"I myself have been an addict of eleven years. Several of my friends during this time died of overdoses and I myself have twice just barely escaped death. For years I constantly suffered depression and didn't actually believe anymore that someday I could learn to live another kind of life again."

The heartbreak upon the family of an addicted person, forced to watch the disintegration of their loved one, is expressed by one mother who says:

"My family was absolutely desperate and overcome with illness by our daughter's nervous stress. Here in Berlin I tried all possible things to get my daughter free from drugs: among other things a treatment for drug addicts in a hospital, six weeks therapeutical conversation, both without success. I was only one person in sixty thousand parents . . . ."

The Drug Problem

Drug abuse was once considered a symptom of Western society. Now it has become epidemic across the planet.

In September, 1976, the "National League of Cities" conference of mayors in the United States found that a total of 48 per cent of the 328 mayors in the United States rank drug abuse as one of their cities' most crucial problems.

The authorities are baffled. Most have come to see drug abuse as a problem without a solution. The *Los Angeles Times* April 11, 1976 states:

"Most experts in the drug field recognize that the public would like an easy solution to the complex problem of addiction, but they say there are not any easy solutions.

They have tried just about everything over the years but it has been one failure after another."

The failure of the existing system in solving the problem of drug related crime is shown by an FBI report "Crime In The United States 1975." Total recidivism among prisoners released in 1972 after serving sentences for narcotics crimes was as high as 65 per cent. The same report reveals that one out of every 500 persons arrested in the United States in 1975 was charged with crime related to narcotics.

The statistical relationship between criminality and drug addiction shows that as the addiction rate increases there is a drastic growth in crime. In the United States:

"Police estimate that addicts are responsible for 50 per cent of all serious crimes. Total property loss from addict theft has been estimated conservatively at more than 15 billion dollars a year nationally."

The Attorney General for California, Evelle J. Younger, is convinced that California is "losing the war against drug abuse." He further states:

"California has approximately one million drug abusers. 110,000 to 120,000 of these are addicted to heroin (require tons of heroin a year to support their habit). 525,000 offenses were committed in California in 1975 to support drug abuse. Forty per cent of the income producing crimes in Los Angeles are drug related. One California resident out of forty is a victim of drug-related crime each year."

Alex Macdonald, British Columbia's Attorney General has estimated that 65 per cent of all crimes in the province are narcotic-related and addicts are stealing $18 million a month to pay for their habit.

The appalling loss of lives from drug addiction is also a rising statistic. "In 1975, 98 persons died of drug abuse in Toronto, Canada." "In 1976, 325 West Germans, 59 Frenchmen, 50 Italians and 18 Swedes died from heroin overdoses. And this year, country after country, the body count is running well ahead of last year's pace." According to Richard Shaw, chief toxicologist of San Diego, California County Coroner's Office there was a 300 per cent increase in drug deaths in San Diego between 1974 and 1976.

The drug abuse problem unresolved for more than a decade, continues to intensify daily. There are those who approach the escalative statistics with an air of being prepared to be bored again. It is difficult to countenance the large scale misery they signify. Unfortunately an attitude of mind guarantees no immunity from the ramifications of the problem. One can only speculate on the effects it will have for the society of our future.

Scientologists Take Action

Scientologists are no longer willing to stand by and watch drug abuse consume our society. They are contributing their time, money and services to actually do something about abuse. They are working directly with the addicted person twenty-four hours a day until he gets through withdrawal. They are going into prisons to work directly with the inmates. They are working personally with correctional agencies, parole officers, prison officials and concerned citizens to effectively achieve something in the field of drug abuse and drug related crime.

They have been liaising closely with Narconon in their goal to eradicate drug abuse. The time for debate on the subject is past. It is now time for positive action. Narconon is the vehicle for getting through the problem to a society free of drug abuse.

Narconon

What It Is and How It Started

Narconon (non-narcosis) is a nonprofit organization using the drug rehabilitation technology of L. Ron Hubbard. Narconon is dedicated to the prevention and reduction of drug abuse and drug related crime. The specific purpose of the program is the rehabilitation of former addicts, narcotics users, criminals and ex-convicts who have been involved in drug abuse. It has as its goal the alleviation of the drug abuse problem in society by

(a) establishing residential programs in the community for withdrawal and drug rehabilitation;
(b) establishing youth institutional programs for rehabilitating those involved in drug abuse;
(c) establishing prison rehabilitation of inmates involved in drug abuse, and
(d) establishing any other rehabilitation modalities in the future which will further Narconon's overall purposes.

Narconon was founded in 1966 by Mr. William Benitez, then an inmate of the Arizona State Penitentiary, whose addiction history had spanned nineteen years.

Narconon Founder Speaks

Benitez explains:

"My failure to come off drugs wasn't due to not wanting to, believe me I really tried. I read and read ... Freud, Jung, Menninger—and studied one philosophy after another, everything I could get my hands on to find out about myself. I underwent psychiatric aid and participated in all sorts of programs and as time went on, I knew less about myself instead of more. The only thing that kept me from putting a gun to my head was that I knew someday I would make it. I felt so sorry for my friends who were constantly trying to get off drugs. I wanted to help them and yet I couldn't even help myself ... I was so tired of the life of addiction, thieving, prostitution and all (the turmoil) that goes with it. On my fourth and last trip to Arizona State Penitentiary, I was tried as a habitual criminal which sentence carried a mandatory fifteen years to life, of which I received fifteen to sixteen years. It was at this point that I began to go into agreement with the idea that once you were an addict, you remained an addict."

A prisoner gave Benitez a copy of *Fundamentals of Thought* by L. Ron Hubbard, which explained mechanisms of thought and the components and functions of communication. Immediately, he recognized the workability of this technology and studied intensively for fifteen months, before initiating a course.

Benitez founded the Narconon Program on the basic applied principles set out in L. Ron Hubbard's book. "When first applied to a pilot group at Arizona State Penitentiary in 1966, it consisted only of the basic communication exercises. Yet, seven out of ten of the first group in their own words, "made it." Their success spread at grass roots level to other prisons, and drawing on further research by L. Ron Hubbard, the program was expanded."

In 1967, prison officials granted permission for any inmate to join the group, and thereafter Narconon was opened to anyone who had the desire to change his life for the better.

Benitez wrote to L. Ron Hubbard who gave his encouragement in expanding the program. The Church of Scientology in Phoenix assisted by donating materials so that inmates could continue their work and help others in the penitentiary.

The Expansion of Narconon

The program continued to expand. By 1970, William Benitez had been released from prison and came to Los Angeles to assist in opening the National Office of Narconon. This bureau became known as Narconon U.S., and commenced a program of expansion throughout the United States. This growth was aided by the leadership of Lieutenant Colonel Mark Jones (U.S. Marine Corps Retired) who undertook the preparation of standardized course texts and directives utilizing the works of L. Ron Hubbard as applicable to the field of drug rehabilitation. These materials helped make it possible for interested and qualified individuals to implement further Narconon programs with the same good success.

Initial programs in California institutions, such as California's Rehabilitation Centre in Norco, California; California Men's Colony in San Luis Obispo, and Youth Training School proved very successful.

The ten-month program at the Youth Training School was evaluated by its officials. The evaluation showed that disciplinary offenses of the control group increased 10 per cent during the second five month period, while those of the Narconon group decreased by 81 per cent. The grade average of the control group increased from C to C plus, while that of the Narconon group increased from C- to B-.

Ron Randall, parole agent from California Department of Youth Authority has said:

"I am very impressed by some of the gains I have seen in wards placed in Narconon. One of the most dramatic changes I ever noted was produced in a ward who had failed to show improvement in other local drug treatment programs. At Narconon he made rapid and outstanding improvement. The improvement was due to the Narconon Program alone since all other factors remained constant."

In May, 1972, a Narconon Program was started at the Ventura School for Boys and Girls in Ventura, California. This program continued to grow and later received funding from the California Youth Authority.

A representative from the California Youth Authority, Robert J. Farrell, parole agent, says:

"As one of our more congenial community resources, Narconon has produced results with some of our wards, where other programs have failed. It is reassuring to have an organization such as Narconon that meets the needs of our parolees and goes a little beyond — they care."

A pilot program, with governmental support, was started in May 1972, at the Delaware Correctional Centre. This program expanded and for the next three years received State and Federal funding support, for its two programs at Delaware Correctional Centre and Sussex Correctional Institute in Sussex, Delaware.

A recent evaluation of the Delaware Correctional Centre showed a recidivism rate of 64 per cent for those not on the Narconon program, while only 16 per cent of those that completed at least two courses of the Narconon program returned to prison.

The National Office continued to promote Narconon broadly, and more programs were started. At this point, Narconon was receiving assistance from the Church of Scientology. Parishioners of the Church donated books and other needed materials to various prisons beginning Narconon programs. Supervisors from Scientology organizations were utilized, as they had an understanding of how the communication drills which are the basis of Narconon's program should be run.

In 1972 also Narconon opened its first residential programs. It then became possible to take the person still on drugs through the withdrawal program, and other Narconon courses. This expansion was an important step for Narconon as it brought all stages of rehabilitation into the safety of a residential environment.

Albert W. Hilburger, attorney from New London, Connecticut has said:

"Without equivocation, of all the social agencies with which I have had contact over the past two years, Narconon is the one to which I turn when all other possibilities have vanished. It is staffed with youthful, outgoing, knowledgeable and dedicated men and women who can communicate properly with their "clients." Let me offer my highest possible commendation: that this is the number one social agency serving the community in the reduction of crime and drug abuse."

Narconon Today

At the time of writing there are thirty-one Narconon programs thoughout the world. By the time you read this book there may well be more, for the demand increases daily. A full directory listing is in Chapter 17.

Narconon Services

Narconon provides services to those who are addicted to drugs of any kind.

The definition of drug is: a substance other than food which when taken into the body, produces a change in it. If the change assists the body, the drug is a medicine. If the change produces harm, the drug is a poison.

Addiction means: slavishly following or unable to give up a habit, strongly inclined. Thus the type of drug is not relevant. It may be alcohol, narcotics, tranquilizers or any other forms.

Narconon is for anyone who is honestly looking for a better way of life. It is for those who seriously want to stop taking drugs or alcohol and in some cases to stop breaking the law because of drugs. It is for those who are genuinely looking for a way out of the trap.

Narconon is well aware that many individuals may have previously attempted to end their drug addiction through other programs, many of which employ psychiatric methods. For this reason, any person who genuinely wants to come off drugs may not be prevented from joining a Narconon program for reasons of past psychiatric treatment.

Rehabilitation in Narconon is *not* only aimed at getting the addicted person off drugs, but also at giving him sufficient awareness and certainty of himself to remain off them.

Narconon provides real help to the addicted person or inmate by getting him functioning again and back into the mainstream of life as a responsible and contributing member of society.

The aim of Narconon is an addict in better condition than before he commenced taking drugs, knowing he will not deteriorate.

There are several graduated steps of the Narconon program which help the individual to achieve these aims.

(1) WITHDRAWAL PROGRAM

The first step in the rehabilitation of an addict is withdrawal from drugs. Narconon provides drug-free withdrawal with twenty-four hours per day supervision, supplemented by a balanced diet, vitamins and liaison with the medical profession as needed.

Withdrawal usually takes three days to a week. During this period, the addict is given personal counseling and exercises called "objectives." These simple mental and physical exercises assist him in directing his attention onto the external world and simultaneously reduce his personal pain and discomfort immensely. The addict is given close support and has completely open communication with Narconon staff. With the Narconon method, withdrawal is confrontable.

(2) NARCONON BASIC COURSE

Narconon has found that most drug users have difficulty in controlling their attention and are unable to confront other individuals or their environment.

The Narconon Basic Course involves "communication and confront" exercises which focus his attention on the present time environment and increase his ability to communicate and relate with other people. These include practical exercises in which Narconon students work in pairs to assist each other successfully through each drill or exercise.

(3) NARCONON STUDY COURSE

This course evolved because a large number of Narconon students discovered their drug-taking was linked with frustrations in the area of education. A majority of drug users either cannot study successfully, or are capable of reading and studying but unable to relate what they have studied to life, and therefore feel a sense of purposelessness in learning.

Through Narconon's study techniques the student learns about the barriers or problems one may encounter while studying and how to overcome them. By the end of the course he knows how to learn, and he can apply what he has learned to any area of life. These skills of literacy and an ability to study also enhance his employment prospects.

(4) NARCONON OBJECTIVES COURSE

In the Narconon Objectives Course the student learns to apply the communication materials in greater depth. He learns the basic skills necessary to evaluate his relationships and activities, deciding whether they are constructive or detrimental to his character and purposes.

The course also helps the student to observe the effect of his actions on himself and others, and to recognize that often the real satisfactions in life come about through his own work and creativity rather than what is done for him or to him. In this way, his willingness to take on responsibility increases.

(5) COUNSELING

The final step of the program is one-to-one counseling. During this part of the program, the ex-addict works with a trained Narconon counselor to find and resolve specific problems relating to his drug taking. It is evident that the drug user is trying to solve some problem in life through the use of drugs. These problems can be broadly classified as things the individual wants to achieve and is not achieving, or things he wants to avoid and cannot. Through counseling, the person finds and fully resolves problems he had before and during his drug history. The end result of counseling is a person who has no inclination to use drugs to achieve what he wants. He is now free to return to the mainstream of society as a responsible citizen, with no further involvement in the criminal justice system or drug abuse. The person is now in better condition than before he commenced taking drugs and knows he will not deteriorate.

(6) ONGOING MEDICAL CARE

The long-term use of drugs creates extremely destructive effects on the addict's body. Unfortunately, he is often unaware of this physical damage since the drugs themselves cause suppression of pain. It is therefore possible for major diseases and illnesses to go undetected. Severe malnutrition is also common. Close liaison with medical doctors ensures that medical conditions are detected and handled with speed. Competent medical care, a balanced diet with nutritional supplements, physical exercises, and sufficient rest are a vital part of the Narconon program.

Because Narconon delivers its services within prisons and in residential facilities, there are some obvious structural differences in running these programs. For this reason, the Narconon prison program and the Narconon residential program have been placed in separate categories.

The Narconon Prison Program

The Narconon prison program is run within the prison or correctional facility. From statistical studies and personal experience in dealing with inmates, experience has shown that the key to rehabilitative success is voluntary participation. The program is intended for inmates with drug problems who request to be on the program and are accepted.

The hours of the Narconon program in prisons vary depending upon the regulations for each facility. Space for the program is set aside by the prison controllers and trained Narconon supervisors and staff are brought in to run the classes. Not infrequently, individual Scientologists or Scientology ministers volunteer their time to supervise the courses run in prisons.

The courses offered within the Narconon prison program are the Narconon Basic Course, the Narconon Study Course, and the Objectives Course. Upon completion of the Narconon courses, inmates often wish to become trainee supervisors and assist in running the programs themselves. For this reason the Narconon Supervisor Course is available on request. The procedures are relatively easy to supervise. The supervisor must maintain good control and discipline in the class, ensuring through observation that the people are really participating, and examining each one to ensure he has achieved the skill he should attain.

The entire Narconon prison program is designed to prepare the inmate for his transition into society. Narconon graduates are also assisted with finding meaningful vocations and pursuing successful careers once released.

Narconon's prison programs have been highly recommended by officials in the field of corrections. Joan W. Simmons, Classification Officer of the Canadian Penitentiary Service has written:

"The Narconon programme is the only programme I have observed to produce quick and stable results in assisting addicts to give up their dependency on drugs. I have been employed in Corrections since 1964 and have had the opportunity to participate in and observe varied treatment programmes for addicts, but this is the first programme that I have observed to achieve what it claims to achieve."

In Sweden Narconon also works closely with community agencies. A good example is the service offered to prison officials whereby ex-inmate drug addicts are permitted to count their time on the Narconon program as time served on their sentences.

Narconon Community Programs

Narconon offers its services in the community in the form of street or residential programs. Both programs offer the same services except that in the residential program, addicts live in the Narconon facility. As suitable premises are located all programs become residential. Staff are rostered so that appropriate services are available day and night.

All Narconon courses provided in street and residential programs are drug-free withdrawal; the Narconon Basic Course, the Study Course, the Objectives Course and one-to-one counseling. Courses are run daily and it is optimum for the student to reside with the Narconon community throughout the program. As he goes through the program he gradually becomes more a part of the group, and contributes to the house, his fellow students and to Narconon. As each student progresses, his responsibility level rises.

Frequently upon completing the program the student will elect to stay with Narconon and become a staff member.

Dave Cunningham, a councilman for Los Angeles has said of the program:

"It is one of the few programs which has enabled drug/alcohol abusers to evolve a rational, humanistic approach to social and personal tensions. Narconon has proven its success inside institutions and on the streets. It is well staffed and well organized; people associated with its programs are dedicated and cooperative. I therefore highly recommend Narconon."

An English doctor feels that the Narconon program in Bracknell, England, is an asset to his community; he says:

"In several cases the mental and physical states after just a few weeks here, have been quite strikingly better, and the prospects of a genuine, ultimate cure, are to me, far better than I would have expected.

"It is my definite opinion that a permanent Narconon Centre at 'The Close,' Bracknell, would provide a very important and useful service to the community, and would be a credit not only to the organizers and 'managers,' but also to those granting the requested planning permission."

Stanley F. Hazleton, MB., BS., MRCS., LRCP.

And in Sweden Dr. Frede Petersen of Nykopings Hospital found that young drug addicts on the Narconon program made definite improvements:

"We are able to state that Narconon through their work have been able to achieve a substantial change in the behavior of these young people and their personality development even though it has not resulted in freedom from drugs in all cases yet. I believe though that a continued stay at Narconon gives good hope of a future free from drugs and at the same time a stable foundation for a positive personality development in these people."

Narconon Personnel

Narconon personnel have the common denominator of wanting to help individuals get off drugs so they can lead purposeful lives. They are willing to actually do something about drug abuse. They are dedicated individuals who chose to work with Narconon because it has proven itself in the rehabilitation field.

It is for these reasons that people join the staff of Narconon. In some cases they are Scientologists. In many other cases, the personnel are individuals who have progressed from addict to ex-addict and from there to become a contributing staff member. The following statement given by an ex-addict who now works with Narconon is typical of countless others:

"Before I came to Narconon I was a heavy criminal and a drug addict. I had done a lot of time in and out of jails and drug programs. None of these helped me stop using drugs or committing crimes. I had always pictured myself as a 'hope to die, dope fiend.' I couldn't foresee myself going a day without drugs. Now that I have been through the Narconon program, I have stopped using drugs and committing crimes. Above that I have no desire to start them again. Before I could never be trusted with money. Now I work in Treasury as a Narconon staff member. I have more confidence in myself now, than I ever had before. I would really like to thank Narconon and its staff for giving me back myself."

Each Narconon staff member receives basic Narconon training as well as specific training for the position he will hold. The need for more personnel increases as more Narconon programs are established. There are many staff positions available and anyone desiring to help, a few hours a week or full-time, will be warmly welcomed.

Narconon Funding

Narconons have received financial assistance from city, state and national governments. Funding has been given by correctional agencies, Probation Department offices of Youth Services and Departments of Health as well as City Council.

Donations have been given to Narconon by private foundations, civic groups, businesses, concerned individuals and Scientologists.

In Sweden and Germany individual addicts are funded to go through the Narconon program by the Social Boards. The amount of funding varies from travel expenses to a daily allowance for each participant on the program.

How to Start a Narconon Program

Anyone interested in pioneering a Narconon program should contact the nearest Narconon program or the Continental Office.

The Narconon office will give assistance to anyone wishing to start a Narconon. Their Narconon consultants are ready to give guidance at any time.

The first thing you will need to do is recruit individuals interested in working in the field of drug rehabilitation. These individuals, your future staff, will be trained by Narconon.

Once one has the support of a willing and able staff, one has the basics of a Narconon group. It's these individuals who will be working directly with the addicts using their knowledge of the Narconon methods, to assist the addict in becoming a contributing member of society.

Assistance is given in obtaining suitable premises and ensuring that all local regulations and requirements are met.

You will need course materials in order to run your course, and you will need to contact the people who wish to be rehabilitated. Available from the Narconon office are the Narconon Student Manual, Narconon Basic Picture Book, Narconon Study Manual, Narconon Technical Manual, Basic Manual for Narconon Supervisors, Withdrawal Specialist Manual, Objective Exercises Manual and Handling Problem Students Manual.

Donations may be needed for beginning expenses and course materials. The Narconon consultant will give you help on how to go about obtaining donations as needed.

In many cases the local community has assisted in donating furnishings, bedding, food and sometimes money to new Narconon programs.

The Narconon consultant will help you in finding referral agencies in your area and will give you other information on how to go about finding addicts desiring your help.

Narconon consultants give their full support to new as well as existing programs at all times.

What Does Scientology Do to Help Narconon

Many Scientologists are personally working in Narconon to help participants through the rehabilitation process. Some are full-time staff and others work as part-time volunteers in community programs and prisons.

Scientology Churches and Missions are always willing to help Narconon and its staff by helping out with supervisors to Narconon courses, when needed.

Narconon is acquiring donations for premises or materials and helping in the recruitment of staff for the programs. Scientology Churches have donated materials, furniture and supplies to Narconon programs, and also can give administrative advice.

The Church of Scientology fully endorses the Narconon program which has a purpose in common with the overall aim of Scientologists:

"A civilization without insanity, without criminals and without war, where the able can prosper and honest beings can have rights, and where Man is free to rise to greater heights."

Congressman Ronald V. Dellums of the California House of Representatives states:

"I would like to offer in this letter, my enthusiastic endorsement of the narcotics rehabilitation program operated by Narconon . . . .

"I sincerely believe that it has developed a comprehensive approach to the problem of addiction, which if widely accepted, would represent the first substantial attack on this problem to be mounted in this country.

"I am particularly impressed with the manner in which the Narconon concept extends itself to those areas of institutional life that are most often neglected in the development of social programs.

"The fact that many outstanding citizens have volunteered to serve with your organization, as members of your Board of Directors and as volunteers in the program is further evidence that you are working effectively and imaginatively to deal with the serious problems of narcotics addiction in this society. I commend you for your efforts."

Narconon is successfully rehabilitating addicts and prison inmates and is being recognized as the group that is handling the problem of drug abuse.

The Road Out

"There are two ways to escape the raw deal that this universe sometimes hands out. One is to go to sleep or become wholly unreal and forget it.

"The other is to attain a calm serene beingness that is proof against the knocks and arrows of misfortune.

"The first method has distinct liabilities. However, it is the most usual route taken by human beings who find the going too rough.

"Alcohol, drugs, self-hypnotism, are all men have been proven to use. The only real trouble with them is that one wakes up into the same world but a bit weaker, a bit redder of eye, feeling a bit worse.

"The drug or other knocks on the head didn't change the universe any and one is still in it, still catching it, probably with an even lower resistance to it. So the first method is not a very good one.

"The second method, the ability to rise above it all has long been preached.

"But unfortunately there wasn't any readily available technology to accomplish it.

"It's one thing to hear that we should rise above it all and quite another to do it.

"The road out is the road of increased awareness. It is not a wholly painless road.

"Those who had already taken the road down had a rough time going up again. If they increased their awareness enough they would arrive at a high level where they were at cause and in which they could not only cope with their environment but could prosper in it, well above the reach of suffering.

"But how to get them up from the point to which they had already gone down? I was finally able to map an easy road which could be travelled despite drugs, despite the starting point, and of course that made it easier for everybody. That road begins with the Narconon Course.

"I would feel pretty bad if a lot of good guys had to live with the road blocked.

"Like anybody else I have had my own share of slings and arrows over the years and I know what it is like.

"It isn't all that easy to help one's fellows and to be helped in return. But the end product is itself worth a lot of slings and arrows.

"The road out is the way up.

"I hope you make it.

"Best of luck
L. Ron Hubbard"

Article written on 22nd September 1969 by L. Ron Hubbard for Narconon, Arizona State Prison and published in their *Narconon Newsletter Issue VI.*

The Educational Programs

Can you remember when you were a child and you stewed apathetically in a hot classroom watching the minute hand dawdle around the clock?

And can you recall the joy of approaching summer when you knew you would be free at last from the prison of school, free to do what you wished rather than listen to your teacher droning on about the crops grown in China?

And then there was the feeling of impending doom as summer drew to an end, as the days of exploration and adventure ran out, and you once again were faced with the thought of endless monotonous lectures with only a twig on a nearby girl's pony tail to liven things up.

And now if you are an adult and have your own children, how are they faring in the educational machine? Do you have to threaten them in order to get them to do their homework, which you can't understand anyway because it's New Math? Does it require blood, sweat and tears to force your kids to go to school?

And what about the rest of the world? The headlines read "Plummeting I.Q.s . . . National Average Drops Significantly," "Scholastic Test Scores Drop For Second Straight Year." Once we had ideals of high standard education for all, yet each year student test scores drop, there are more school dropouts, less people achieve their goals and careers in life, and crime and illiteracy rates zoom up. Man travels to the moon and he masters the atom but he has not conquered the classroom.

Teachers have been blamed, parents have been blamed, and so now the curriculum, the examination system, the size of schools, television. There have been a host of reasons for the failure and a multitude of solutions. Yet the student continues to score lower and lower.

In the United States there are twenty million adults and seven million teenagers who cannot read. This means they cannot understand enough written English to pass a driver's test or fill out a job application—let alone read a chapter in a book.

For adults the inability to read means job failure and broken homes, for juveniles it means increasing delinquency or involvement in crime.

In the United Kingdom, which has likewise a problem of a known three million illiterates, Mr. Jack Ashley, M.P. for Stoke on Trent, put a plan to the Home Secretary to beat the terrible problem of vandalism which is defacing Britain. The annual cost of vandalism in Britain is a staggering £100 million. Broken windows, smashed desks and chairs and extensive damage to toilet fittings are regularly reported in many schools. In a study carried out by psychologist Ludwig Lowenstein in cooperation with the National Association of School Masters in Britain on 1,844 schools, it was found that there were 6,349 acts of pupil violence and a total of 37,470 disruptive incidents recorded during the two months recorded by the survey. Remember that it takes only one pupil bent on creating problems to bring an entire class to the point of disruption, with the probable result a drop in the educational standards. Somewhere along the line standards have slipped. No longer do children look up to their teachers, nor, in too many cases do they respect any form of authority. Headmasters dismiss instances of students attacking teachers as "nothing unusual."

In South Africa the struggles between black students and the authorities in 1976 erupted into bloody slaughter with thousands of black children boycotting schools, police and antiriot squads encamping in black townships and student leaders and school children being arrested.

In the United States, 1976, the *Los Angeles Times* ran (one of three) articles headed "School Standards Decline. Fewer Basics, More Electives lead to Drop in Student Scores."

"Declining student achievement and rampant inflation in the nation's schools and colleges are largely the result of widespread and pervasive erosion of academic standards within the American educational system. The drop in standards was the result of a shift in social and educational values during the 1960s—a shift to which schools and colleges both succumbed and contributed by reducing the number of basic academic classes, weakening graduation requirements and emphasizing electives that are academically less demanding. All of these things—curriculum shifts, drops in requirements, grade inflation, rising absenteeism—began in the mid-1960s and then swept through the educational system at an unprecedented rate. It was not until the 1970s, however, that they had their sharpest impact in the nation's schools and colleges."

Dr. William A. Marra, a Professor of Philosophy at New York's Fordham University, told some 200 symposium attendees, December 1975, of the problems that confront poorly educated freshmen. He called for a return to basic skills and legitimate subject matter in public schools. When students are unable to cope with college studies, Professor Marra reviews the subjects they should have mastered in high school instead of pondering over the impact of social adjustment, peer group acceptance, rap sessions, group thinking, the cold war, raunchy literature and sex instruction. He tells his students "Your teachers deceived you and betrayed you; they deceived and betrayed you and your parents whose taxes dearly paid for your education." Dr. Marra told his audience "They solemnly nod their heads and agree with me."

A further indication of increasing educational decline is the number of colleges which are forced to rewrite their textbooks on a lower reading gradient to accommodate poorly educated students.

Tom Williamson, editor-in-chief of the college department of a publishing house in New York, said last year,

"It's generally understood that most college freshmen now come in with a ninth grade reading level. Obviously, you want books they can understand, so you make adjustments. We're downgrading our language."

Therefore in education the field is very messed up, in spite of 120 billion dollars alone in the United States being spent on it, despite a myriad of solutions from well-intentioned educationists, psychologists and teachers and despite frantic actions from anxious parents demanding better education methods for their young.

The Answer

So what is there that is effective, what could improve this bleak picture and lead to a reversal of these worldwide trends?

In the early 1960s L. Ron Hubbard thoroughly researched the barriers to study, learning and reading. In 1964 the now internationally used technology of study and learning was released. This is known as the STUDY TECHNOLOGY.

The definition of study is: the absorption of knowledge for the purpose of application.

The definition of technology is: the method of application of an art or science as opposed to mere knowledge of the science or art itself.

The study technology is the *how* to study and learn—and the how to study is senior and superior to what is studied.

The study technology is even more basic than study itself and is currently a missing educational link.

In researching this method of study, L. Ron Hubbard also located the sequence of actions which occur when the basics of the study technique are violated. This sequence is germane to the situations rampant today across our planet.

The sequence is that when a student fails to understand some part of a subject, be it a word, or a symbol, then that subject ceases to make proper sense to him. He starts to withdraw from it and becomes inattentive and rebels against it. He then resorts to disruptive acts which become more and more violent as he is forced to continue to study the subject. The final act will be to leave.

A teacher trained in this educational technology presents his materials in such a way that this sequence does not occur. If there is a point of misunderstanding, he is able to handle it and so avoid the phenomena which would follow.

In the 1960s various individuals who contacted the Scientology study technology used it in the field of education and reported great success and improvement in learning amongst their students.

In 1971 the first educational organization began in California when a student of Scientology who had been using the study technology of L. Ron Hubbard realized that this technology was indispensable. Students of Scientology were having continuous successes with their studies—none of the problems that are taken for granted in the educational field existed in Scientology colleges and classrooms. These students were learning, winning, quickly completing their courses and satisfied with their production and accomplishments. So started the organiza-

tion called Applied Scholastics to get the study technology of Mr. Hubbard applied outside the Churches of Scientology to remedy people's failures in study.

Training courses were offered to teachers and professors in the basics of study technology and how to apply it. Today there are now seven similar Applied Scholastics organizations in the United States alone which offer services to public schools, universities, private schools, to industrial teachers, college students and children. The United States headquarters of Applied Scholastics is in Los Angeles. A list of the organizations can be found in Chapter 17.

1975 and 1976 saw great expansion as new groups took up these methods. Related organizations were established in the United Kingdom, Canada, Africa, Denmark, Switzerland, France, Mexico and South America.

Any person who wishes to create such a group need only contact his nearest Education Center in the "List of Organizations" chapter. He will then be given course materials and assistance in setting up his group.

Help is given in the form of passing on successful methods of getting people on course, running a course and ensuring that students are winning on their course. Training services are offered by Education Centers to those wishing to set up a group so that they can learn to apply the study technology.

The beginning activities of the groups are often held in living rooms of private homes, play centers or school rooms. Elaborate facilities and large financial reserves are not needed to start an education group.

Assistance will be readily given by established education groups at any time it is requested by the new group or its staff.

Services Offered by Education Organizations which use L. Ron Hubbard's Study Technology

Various services are offered by the organizations which use the study technology depending on the need of the client: Teacher's Course, Reading Course, Dictionary Course, Children's Study Course, Basic Study Course and Subject Rehabilitation.

Each course is based on the researches into education and study by L. Ron Hubbard.

Teacher's Course

This is a service for teachers who may wish to improve their teaching standards. The course is divided into theory and practical sections.

The theory section provides the teacher with the basic theory of study and its phenomena, and also answers and provides remedies to such questions as: Why are some students such slow learners and others not; why do students become disruptive, disinterested, play truant; why does a class go wild; why can't this student read; how does one give that individual attention students need in a classroom of thirty and control the whole class, so learning can occur?

The practical sections of the course contain exercises and drills which enable the teacher to apply the theoretical data comfortably with ease, so that by its standard application the teacher can control the classroom and have receptive students who are eager to apply the data they study.

Student Courses

A student enrolling in a study technology organization is first interviewed in order to isolate his areas of difficulty. Depending on what is found in the interview the student is then enrolled on one of the following courses:

(A) *Reading Course*

This service is designed for those students who either wish to improve their reading ability or for those who fall short on their reading ages. Students who wish to do other services but whose reading ability is insufficient are also placed on the Reading Course.

The supervisor first works on an individual basis with the student so that the exact first point of difficulty is located. Then the student proceeds forward from that point on a gradient level per the study technology Reading Course. The course breaks down the subject of reading, starting from the basics and becoming gradiently more complex in stages which can be easily assimilated by the student.

(B) *Children's Study Course*

The child learns the basics of study, the "how" of study, so that he can learn any subject and be able to apply what he has learned. The child learns to recognize the barriers to study and their manifestations so that he will himself know when he encounters a study difficulty, and he will know what to do to overcome it.

The course consists of thirteen books, a glossary of terms and is accompanied by a teacher's manual of instructions on how to run the course together with a set of tests to be given the children. Every child takes this service as it is the study technology which enables him to study and apply the data of any further subject he takes on.

(C) *Basic Study Course*

This service is a higher gradient of the Children's Study Course done in more depth. It is designed for older students so they learn how to apply the study technology to their high school or university courses.

(D) *Subject Rehabilitation*

Once a student has learned how to study he is then capable of remedying and improving his study of any subject. On an individual basis the supervisor first locates the point in the subject where the student first encountered difficulty. The student proceeds from that point onwards using the study technology under the guidance and supervision of the supervisor to fully rehabilitate his grasp on the subject until he comprehends it and can apply it.

Counseling

A consultancy service is offered to teachers who have trained in the technology and are now applying it in their schools and colleges. This service assists with the standard application of the technology. It ensures the expected results are achieved. Applied Scholastics counselors do not advise on the school curriculum but only on the methods of teaching. This is a recent service.

Publics Serviced by the Groups

There is a variety of publics who have been serviced over the years by the education groups. These range from individual teachers and children, parents who wish to learn the technology to assist with their children's study and individual college and university students.

Administrators and community personnel both at county and state levels have been serviced. State and private schools, universities, colleges, education centers and school districts have received programs delivered in their own premises.

There are many organizations and individuals working to improve the field of education. Applied Scholastics and related organizations are willing to work alongside them, giving them their full support as their goals and purposes are the same.

Educational Funding

Various sources of funding exist in different countries for educational programs.

Requirements for funding proposals differ according to the country, state, province or local community where the education group operates.

To find out if there are funding opportunities for your program, contact your nearest educational center (see "List of Organizations" chapter). If there is no center nearby, write to your Continental Education Center. They will gladly furnish you with the information and assist you in applying for funding.

Expansion

The news of the phenomenal success of this technology has reached far and wide. Correspondence is continuously coming in from individuals wanting to know how they can be trained in L. Ron Hubbard's study technology and how they can initiate education groups.

Recent enquiries have come from Nigeria, Kenya, Israel, South America and Iceland. Enquiries from Europe are increasing rapidly resulting in new centers being established.

Schools

The principles used by Applied Scholastics in the United States met with such phenomenal success in the early 1970s that many individuals dreamed of setting up alternatives to the public schools system.

One such visionary, Mrs. Bonnie Bishop, realized her dream by forming the Apple Schools network in 1974. Her first "Apple" in Los Angeles, California started with fifteen students in two rented rooms in a local Methodist church. By the end of the following academic year, school enrollment had increased by 800 percent.

Today Apple has expanded onto a forty-two acre campus in the Los Feliz residential area of Hollywood. Its curriculum covers grades from kindergarten through to high school.

The Apple Schools offer a unique educational opportunity. Besides teaching the basic three "R's," too often neglected in today's schools, the study technology is applied throughout the child's school career with the stress on the individual student's progress.

Checksheets

Specific use of the study principles is made with "checksheets" for every grade and subject. This ensures that neither the fast nor the slow student is penalized. Instead each is encouraged to better his own production and knowledge. The stress is on the application of what is learned so that the child is acquiring skills he can use in life.

He finds that by applying L. Ron Hubbard's study technology he can learn any subject he wishes, be it a sport, mastering a musical instrument or any other subject.

The checksheet system is a specific tool of this technology. Its use ensures that a proper sequence of learning occurs. Emphasis is on the student's genuine understanding and ability to apply what has been learned.

Today the Apple network has expanded to eight schools in the U.S.

Apple's Contribution to World Peace in the United States

Apple has a school record noticeable for its lack of upset, vandalism and dropouts. Drugs, violence and crime, which have become grave and heartbreaking problems in so many schools, are not a part of Apple. They get almost 100 percent attendance in one year. There was only one dropout in one year. Those who teach with the network and the parents who send their children to Apple Schools know that these schools create a safe environment for the children and give them the opportunity to prepare for a purposeful and rewarding career. This is indeed a ray of hope for the future, not only for Apple graduates but for America and the world.

Other Schools

Other schools have also started and are applying the same principles. They are:

The Ranch School, Oregon, The Delphian Foundation, Oregon, The Pumpkin School, U.S., Freinet Institute, Mexico, and also the Innovative Program School, Los Angeles.

Africa

One of the most rewarding and satisfying expansions in the use of L. Ron Hubbard's study technology has occurred in Africa. Despite the strife and unrest within the continent, tremendous demands have been made for courses for black, colored and Indian children and adults. Black, colored and Indian teachers, students, teachers' associations, school boards and governments have also asked for courses.

Large numbers of teachers have eagerly attended training classes under sometimes primitive conditions. The appreciation and increased hope and human dignity resulting from these programs is touching. Here are some of these teachers' remarks:

"I stand like a warrior to conquer all difficulties I have come across with much ease. The entire world has become a phenomenon that needs restudy and to be observed with a different perspective. . . ."

The light of understanding is shining in parts of that dark continent and will soon shine even more brightly as more and more of her people learn and apply the study technology of L. Ron Hubbard to their lives and education systems. This way can the hope and promise of more peaceful times be spread across Africa.

In one of his lectures on study L. Ron Hubbard stated: "The situation with regard to success in life depends upon a subject called study. If you can't learn anything, you can't find out how to do anything. Study operates as the door, open or closed, to learning how to handle life. If a student can't learn anything, then, of course, he won't be able to do anything, regardless of the attitude he has toward the human race, or his wish to do something for people or his desires in any way, shape or form. These would all be buried by the fact that he couldn't learn anything."

L. Ron Hubbard opened his lecture on the problem in education given in 1964 with these words:

"A culture is held together solely and only by education whether that education is achieved by experience or teaching.
"The amount of money invested by governments in education is enormous and is in fact usually the largest budget next to armaments. With a considerable sum being spent on the education of an individual, the burning question is: Has he become educated?"

Many hundreds of people in countries around the world are working to give an affirmative answer to that question, by learning and applying L. Ron Hubbard's study technology in their communities and schools. With education comes understanding and with understanding many wonderful things can be accomplished. Together the peoples of all races, colors and creeds can bring the dream of world peace into being.

The Church of Scientology and the Education Centers using this fantastically effective and workable technology are working hard to increase the contribution to world peace. Your help and contribution will be warmly welcomed and valued.

The Human Rights Program

Psychosurgery

"Well over 100,000 persons have already been subjected to psychosurgery around the world, including 20,000 in England, perhaps 50,000 in America, many many thousands in Canada. We are now in the midst of a resurgence, including multiple forms of psychosurgery upon hyperactive children. It is time to take action before this revival takes on the proportions of the first wave that peaked in the 1950s." (U.S. Congressional Record February 24, 1972, Vol 118 quotes from Dr. Peter R. Breggin, Washington School of Psychiatry.)

Psychosurgery is but one of many brutal and barbaric psychiatric treatments. Psychosurgery, such as lobotomy and leucotomy, is the intentional destruction of healthy brain tissue for the purposes of altering behavior. Its effects are permanent and irreversible.

Different sects of psychosurgeons attack different areas of the brain for different reasons. Psychosurgery operations are performed for symptoms ranging from drug addiction, homosexuality, frigidity, intolerable pain, fear, schizophrenia, hyperactivity in children, depression, obsessive gambling, to even political radicalism.

After forty years psychosurgeons are still not in agreement as to technique or amount of destruction and psychosurgery remains experimental by definition.

Several psychiatrists speak out against psychosurgery saying:

"The more I study the functions of the brain, the more I am left in no doubt that I have no knowledge whatsoever about what the brain is or what it does. To do a destructive operation on an organ of such infinite complexity and delicacy in our present state of ignorance is like kicking a piece of machinery in an attempt to make it work." (Dr. Henry Rollin, M.D., D.P.M., Consulting Psychiatrist, Horton Hospital, Epsom.)

Dr. Harry Sullivan, a medical doctor, stated in 1940: "These sundry procedures, (the Freeman lobotomy, the Metrazol and camphor convulsive treatments, the electroshock, the block method and so forth), produce 'beneficial' results by reducing the patient's capacity for being human. The philosophy is something to the effect it is better to be a contented imbecile than a schizophrenic."

Dr. Patrick McGrath, a Broadmoor Physician Superintendent says: "I now have grave ethical doubts about the use of irreversible procedures when reversible ones are in our hands, and I also have grave ethical doubts about the validity of consent to such methods by forcibly detained patients."

Psychosurgery Case History

The effects of psychosurgery are devastating not only for the patient but also to the families of patients who must care for them. Countless lives have been ruined by these barbaric operations, psychiatry's offering to humanity.

A husband tells the pitiful story of the physical and mental destruction suffered by his wife and of the painful existence they have led since her operation:

"My wife had the operation (prefrontal leucotomy) in 1957. Thereafter she became a completely different person. I noticed definite personality changes and severe mental disturbances. She began drinking heavily and proceeded to neglect the home. I was unable to trust her with money and she would pick up with anybody who was prepared to buy her drinks. This was totally out of character, as she had been a very good wife prior to this.

"From this time forth she was in and out of hospitals many times. Another operation was suggested whereby a deeper cut in the frontal lobes should be made, which was said would cure the trouble. I resisted this suggestion until 1964. . . .

"After this operation my wife became very seriously mentally affected. She suffered epileptic fits, became doubly incontinent and apathetic. The anxiety neurosis was still present. She would accuse people who came to the house of assaulting her. She became incapable of keeping the house clean and even eventually began to lose her balance and use of her left hip and leg. In 1967 she was confined to a wheelchair. In 1967 I was compelled to give up my job in order to constantly attend her. I was training to be a trade union official at this time and had I been able to proceed with this career I would no doubt have been in a well-established position by now.

"When she has been in mental hospitals the irrational fears and apathy have greatly increased. I feel however that she is slowly deteriorating all the time.

"In 1964 as a result of the second operation, an infection developed in the skull. My wife was treated by a doctor two years for this complaint and eventually had to have another operation to remove a portion of infected bone at Atkinson Morley Hospital.

"Since 1957 I feel that my wife has not been capable of managing her own affairs. She has twice been admitted to hospital for emergency treatment after suicide attempts, and although lucid for periods, her condition is not sufficiently stable for it to be said that she is capable of managing her own affairs.

"In 1950 my wife was suffering from anxiety neurosis. Twenty-three years later, after three operations and electric shocks etc. and being continuously in and out of mental hospitals, she is far worse than before this treatment began. Her weight during this period has gone down from 8 stone to 6 stone 7 lbs. Her condition now points to the opinion that she has suffered irreversible brain damage due to two leucotomies and infection requiring operations, and electric shocks, deep coma insulin treatment; she is now a wreck."

Sidney Edward Davey
Saltfleet by Louth Lincs

Mrs. Davey's case unfortunately is not unique in the files of the Citizens Commission on Human Rights. Psychiatry has produced many "cures" such as hers.

Shock Treatment

Another psychiatric cure-all is the electric shock treatment. Shock treatment, or electro-convulsive therapy (ECT) was "discovered" by Ugo Cerletti, a professor of psychiatry at the University of Rome. He seized on the idea when observing electrically induced convulsions in hogs being prepared for slaughter at the slaughterhouse and then calculated how much current would be needed to send a human being into convulsions without killing him.

His first patient was a man arrested for loitering. The following are Cerletti's own words of his first human experiment with electric shock treatments.

"This subject was chosen for the first experiment on induced electric convulsions in Man. Two large electrodes were applied to the frontoparietal regions, and I decided to start cautiously with a low intensity current of 80 volts for 0.2 seconds.

"As soon as the current was introduced, the patient reacted with a jolt and his body muscles stiffened; then he fell back on the bed without loss of consciousness; he started to sing abruptly at the top of his voice, then he quieted down.

"Naturally, we who were conducting the experiment, were under great emotional strain and felt that we had already taken quite a risk. Nevertheless, it was quite evident to all of us that we had been using too low voltage. It was proposed that we should allow the patient to have some rest and repeat the experiment the next day. All at once the patient, who evidently had been following our conversation, said clearly and solemnly, without his usual gibberish: 'Not another one. It's deadly!'

"I confess that such explicit admonitions under such circumstances, and so emphatic and commanding, coming from a person whose enigmatic jargon had until then been very difficult to understand, shook my determination to carry on with the experiment. The electrodes were applied again, and a 110 volt discharge was applied for 0.2 seconds."

ECT, Its Procedure

Today it is estimated that 50,000 people a year are subjected to ECT in the United States alone.

Techniques of administration vary, but the general procedure is as follows:

Medication is applied in the mouth to reduce the risk of suffocation and other complications. Dentures, hairpins and jewelry are removed to avoid injury during the convulsions. Graphite jelly is applied to the head where the electrodes will be placed, to increase conductivity and prevent burning of the flesh. A muscle relaxant drug is given to reduce the risk of bone dislocation and fractures. This causes almost complete paralysis, including respiratory paralysis, so that the subject's breathing must be assisted artificially. The electrodes are put in position and the psychiatrist releases 70 to 175 volts of electricity for one tenth to one and a half seconds. The electricity penetrates the skull into the brain. The subject's mouth opens and a rubber gag is inserted to protect his teeth and prevent him from biting or swallowing his tongue.

As can be seen from the procedures for reducing injury, the process of electro-convulsive treatment is violent. This torture invented and used by psychiatrists is given in the name of help to patients suffering from depression. In most states and countries, ECT can be given without the patient's consent. This is an obvious violation of human rights.

Electric shock treatments are effective in one respect, they very successfully produce loss of memory. Frequently, memories of several years prior to the treatment are totally erased. Often patients no longer remember their homes, families, names, or the skills learned in the period obliterated through shock treatment. A person's past, his knowledge and his experiences are taken from him—information vital to his personality and his future. This alone can kill a person.

Psychiatry is responsible for these deaths.

Ernest Hemingway, one of the literary minds of our century, bitterly complained that his mind and life were being destroyed by ECT. After his second set of ECT treatment, Hemingway told A. E. Hotchner, author of *Papa Hemingway:* "They are taking away my memory. They are destroying my livelihood. I have nothing to live for if I cannot write. It was a brilliant cure but they lost the patient. It's a bum turn, Hotch, terrible."

Thirty days after the "treatment" Hemingway took his own life.

What killed Hemingway? Psychiatry.

Psychiatry

Psychiatry, the word, comes from the Greek "psyche" which means spirit or soul, and "iatry" which means healing. Yet the goal of psychiatrists today cannot by any stretch of the imagination be considered the healing of the soul when they employ such torturous treatments as psychosurgery, electric shock treatments and psychotropic drugs. The underlying principle behind such treatments is that Man is an animal rather than a spiritual being, for you clearly don't tie a spirit down and hack it with a knife.

The history of modern psychiatry began with research at Leipzig University in the late nineteenth century. In 1879 Professor Wundt, working under Bismarck, forwarded the idea that Man did not have a soul, that Man is a stimulus-response mechanism. From this came Pavlov's techniques of behavior modification and conditioning, based on the principle that Man can be trained like an animal and must be controlled. This is the philosophy which paved the treacherous way for Nazi Germany and Communist Russia.

Today a person can be picked off the street or taken from his own home, labelled "mentally ill and dangerous," and incarcerated in a mental institution. It is ridiculously easy to be committed to an institution, and thoroughly difficult to get out. Once in the institution, a patient, sane or insane, voluntary or involuntary, is generally stripped of his rights. He is at the mercy of the psychiatrists, and psychiatrists are not renowned for mercy.

A large percentage of mental patients are hospitalized without need. The Australian Health Commission published a report stating that Australian hospitals hold 22,000 patients a year, 10,000 of which could have been kept out of hospitals.

However, once in an institution, the difficulty is in getting out. In Austria 60 per cent of the 11,184 patients have been institutionalized for two years, and 50 per cent for more than ten years. Only 6 per cent are voluntary patients.

Psychiatry has been trying to control our society by elevating itself as the priesthood in mental healing. It has spread itself into all areas of society, leaving its path littered with casualties. Those who oppose its methods are attacked as "insane," those who refuse to cooperate are given its treatments. Its deaths are carefully masked and its abuses well justified by "expert opinion." Those unaware of its true nature put faith in its false promises, those who know only some of its masked evil find it terrifying; those who are willing to confront it for what it is recognize an obstacle in Man's forward progress to a saner society, and they then arrange to overcome it.

Scientologists Take Action

Psychiatrists until 1950 had virtually carte blanche to tinker with peoples' heads in the name of mental healing. In that year L. Ron Hubbard's *Dianetics: The Modern Science of Mental Health* was released, the cornerstone of a twenty-eight year campaign by Scientologists to expose the bankrupt technology of modern psychiatry.

Scientology organizations and individual Scientologists take a strong stand against psychiatric abuse, as evidenced by the Code of a Scientologist.†

Scientologists have formed a group specifically to handle psychiatric abuse. The group is the Citizens Commission on Human Rights.

The Formation of the Citizens Commission on Human Rights

The Citizens Commission on Human Rights (CCHR) is an international organization dedicated to the elimination of psychiatric abuse and the restoration of human rights for all individuals.

The Citizens Commission on Human Rights believes that mental patients constitute the most oppressed and least represented minority group across the world. In recognition of this, and the practical considerations of choosing an area of operation which is not too broad to enable the actual achievement of proposed goals, CCHR primarily concerns itself with issues involving the rights of

†The full Code of a Scientologist is contained in Chapter 14.

mental patients, human experimentation, involuntary commitment and treatment, and reform within the field of mental health.

CCHR has an international membership of laymen and professionals of various faiths and political convictions joined together by the common respect for the rights and dignity of the individual. The Commission has many attorneys, medical doctors, psychiatrists, and civil rights workers who maintain memberships or advisory positions with CCHR.

The Citizens Commission on Human Rights was formed in mid-1969 by the Reverend Kenneth J. Whitman of the Church of Scientology and Washington, D.C. attorney John Joseph Matonis. Dr. Thomas S. Szasz, a professor of psychiatry at the Upstate Medical Centre, New York University, and the author of *Manufacture of Madness, The Myth of Mental Illness, Law, Liberty and Psychiatry*, was the first consulting psychiatrist for the Commission.

In the United States, the Citizens Commission on Human Rights is a member group of the Association of Scientologists for Reform (ASR), a nonprofit organization. In all other countries across the world, CCHR is sponsored by the Church of Scientology.

Since 1969 when the first chapter began, CCHR has expanded to major cities in the United States with chapters in many other countries.

The Victor Gyory Story

One of the very first actions which the Citizens Commission on Human Rights undertook was the successful release of Victor Gyory from Haverford State Hospital in Philadelphia in 1969.

Gyory was a Hungarian refugee who immigrated to the United States. He was taken from his quarters to Bryn Mawr Hospital with superficial wounds to his wrists. From Bryn Mawr he was sent to Haverford State Hospital, a mental institution.

Since Gyory spoke very little English and no one at the institution spoke Hungarian, psychotherapy had little effect. The staff then tried drugs, and he continued to speak "incoherently." The only thing left was electro-convulsive shock treatment. He was stripped naked, placed in an isolation cell without food, and in the morning he was brought to a room, strapped to a table and given electric shock. He was given shock treatment every other day for quite some time. He was never allowed a court hearing although he requested one.

The Citizens Commission on Human Rights stepped in, John Joseph Matonis (chief counsel for CCHR) took his case to court and revealed that one of the treating psychiatrists was not certified to practice psychiatry, being only a general practitioner. A continuance was granted for the court proceedings so that Dr. Thomas Szasz could undertake a psychiatric examination of Gyory. Victor Gyory had been diagnosed by the hospital psychiatrists as being schizophrenic with paranoid tendencies and had been ordered to receive three shock treatments a week for depression. Upon examination of Victor Gyory, Dr. Szasz found him sane and was willing to testify to his sanity.

When the court recommenced, he was quickly granted a writ of *habeas corpus* (free the body) by the hospital before

Dr. Szasz could testify. This case was a significant test case into the constitutionality of electro-convulsive therapy which the patient was being given against his will.

And also as the hospital released him upon service of the writ, the case in fact challenged the constitutionality of his commitment to the institution.

Victory Gyory was held against his will, drugged and forceably given shock treatments because he didn't speak English. His story is not unique. It is one of thousands of cases of injustice, torture and suffering resulting from psychiatric methods. By putting itself above the law, this experimental branch of the medical profession has become a nightmare for thousands of human beings. Some have contacted the Citizens Commission on Human Rights for assistance and assistance has been given them.

Psychiatric Conditions Across the World

CCHR has found that conditions in psychiatric institutions around the world are commonly appalling. In a majority of institutions patients are subjected to brutal treatments such as ECT and psychosurgery. Experimentation on patients is not uncommon while dangerous and often deadly psychotropic drugs are increasingly used as chemical straitjackets. CCHR has many cases of patients appealing for help after having been beaten or forceably electric shocked as punishment for refusing to take such drugs. Pleas for release from patients and their families are taken up by Commissions around the world.

British Member of Parliament Christopher Price has spoken out against these drugs: "I think that what is broadly happening is that the psychotropic drug has replaced the padded cell in our mental hospitals. Now they have drugs to damp people down and turn them into zombies."

The number of ex-patients coming forward with their stories of psychiatric abuse in each country where CCHR operates cannot be ignored, and the causes of these atrocities are not "side effects" and accidents, but psychiatric treatment and the subject itself.

CCHR Public Services

CCHR has successfully secured the release of mental patients from mental institutions where they have been imprisoned. When a patient or a relative asks CCHR for help in releasing an individual from a mental hospital CCHR goes into action, often utilizing its legal and medical advisors.

CCHR has also assisted in bringing their abusers to court. This not only acts as a deterrent to others commiting the same act but gives some compensation for the suffering inflicted on the patient. Each lawsuit is a further step towards bringing justice and hope to the victims of maltreatment and to the future of thousands more.

CCHR is always willing to give assistance to any individual. However to handle individual cases could limit CCHR's effectiveness in the achievement of real reform. CCHR thus finds it necessary to also engage in reform activities with the purpose of restoring human rights to many hundreds of people in an area.

INFORMING THE PUBLIC

Only by widely informing the public, legislators and public officials of instances of abuses and the brutality and ineffectiveness of many psychiatric treatments and practices, can the urgent need for legislation be exposed. Only by legislating to bestow and protect basic rights of patients, can we achieve these reforms.

CCHR therefore provides the service of informing the public of the need for changes in the field of mental health through lectures, newsletters, reports, public hearings of the Commission, symposiums, open meetings and public demonstrations.

HOSPITAL INVESTIGATIONS

Another activity frequently undertaken by CCHR chapters is the touring and investigation of mental hospitals. These activities have produced restored human rights in many countries.

By touring hospitals, noting abuses, unsanitary conditions and violations of regulations, comprehensive reports can be made to the proper authorities. As a result corrective actions have been taken, and facilities and patient care improved.

OFFICIAL ACTION

Many public and government officials are giving their support to CCHR chapters when factual information is brought to their attention. For example, in 1971 a St. Louis, Missouri chapter exposed illegal drug experimentation on patients, which was being done without the patients' consent at the Missouri Institute of Psychiatry.

CCHR submitted the facts to the Department of Health, the Governor of Missouri, State legislators and Congress, and national media reported the information. As a result the Director of Mental Health enforced regulations on human experimentation. The Department was fully supported by the Governor. A further result was the loss of the majority of State and Federal funding of the Missouri Institute of Psychiatry, for allowing these illegal experiments.

The reform did not stop there. The Governor followed up by endorsing an investigation into all the psychiatric hospitals in the area; the Mental Health Commission was reorganized to include medical doctors and laymen and excluding many of its psychiatrists. Human experimentation ceased at the Missouri Institute of Psychiatry thanks to increased public and legislative awareness of the importance of human rights and the need to guard them.

CCHR is proud to have contributed to the protection of countless mental patients from the fate of dangerous involuntary drug experimentation.

MULTI-STATE INFORMATION SERVICE EXPOSED

A large psychiatric computer program called the Multi-State Information Service, which contained detailed records of the history, diagnosis and treatment of voluntary and involuntary patients was brought to public awareness by the Citizens Commission on Human Rights. The

Commission made a full submission on this matter to government agencies and it was utilized by Senator Sam Ervin's Committee on Constitutional Rights. This information was then brought to full public view in the media.

MENTAL PATIENTS PHYSICALLY ILL

From documenting many cases of abuse, CCHR has found over and over the staggering accuracy of L. Ron Hubbard's discovery "that many of those suffering from 'mental illness' have long-standing, undetected physical illnesses or injuries." Upon treatment of these physical afflictions, the person would become saner. With proper medical examinations and treatments in institutions, patients can be treated physically and avoid unnecessary physically damaging psychiatric treatment. The effects of lobotomy, ECT and psychotropic drugs are not so easily cured.

DECLARATION OF HUMAN RIGHTS
FOR MENTAL PATIENTS

The Citizens Commission on Human Rights has written and distributed a Declaration of Human Rights for Mental Patients. This is used to inform legislators and the public of the rights a mental patient deserves. It can and has been used to form laws granting those rights to patients and should be posted in hospitals so patients can see and be informed of the rights to which they should be entitled.

These rights may in no way be violated by anyone for whatever reasons and in particular these rights cannot be subjected to modification by reason of professional or political opinion. If the state has determined through a fair jury trial that it has the right to detain anyone for so-called mental illness or deficiency, then it must provide the services, facilities and staff to properly care for those whom it has detained. If the state cannot properly provide such, then it has no right to so detain anyone on the basis that it is for the individual's welfare that he is detained. These rights are deemed absolutely essential for human conditions. Any other conditions are inhuman and should not be tolerated, condoned or supported.

REFORMS THROUGH LEGISLATION

CCHR has found that a majority of the current mental health laws have few if any provisions to protect the rights of the mental patient. One of the rights to which all patients are entitled is that of refusing treatment.

In August of 1976, California passed an act limiting the use of ECT and psychosurgery. Under this law a patient must be given full information on electric shock therapy and psychosurgery and must give his consent before it can be administered. He has the right to refuse treatment and cannot be put under duress or loss of privilege for refusing. At any time before the treatment (should he still desire it after having full data on side effects) the patient may withdraw his consent for the treatment either verbal-

ly or in writing. Psychosurgery is forbidden in any circumstances on minors as is electric convulsive therapy banned for children under twelve years of age.

The Citizens Commission on Human Rights played a vital part in getting this law passed; CCHR presented submissions, furnished legislators with information on the effects of ECT and psychosurgery and documented cases of abuse, as well as testifying at legislative hearings, working in cooperation with other groups and meeting personally with many legislators. The passage of this law was a significant achievement in human rights and for the mental patients of California. Using this success as a precedent, many other CCHRs have proposed similar legislation in the United States and countries around the world.

Legislative reform, through the passage of such laws gives the patient the right to refuse treatment and in this way to control his own future, and makes it increasingly difficult for forced psychiatric treatment to occur.

The Commissions have hundreds of cases of abuses similar to those mentioned in this book. Many other major accomplishments have been made by eradicating psychiatric abuse and restoring human rights. The accomplishments given in this chapter give an overall view of the activities with which CCHR is involved and the services they offer. A full catalogue of the Commission's cases and accomplishments would fill many volumes.

CCHR Funding

CCHR in the United States is a nonprofit corporation funded entirely by donations and memberships. In other countries, CCHR receives financial assistance from the Church of Scientology in addition to donations. The Commission incurs expenses from printing and distributing reports and submissions, holding symposiums, producing newsletters and brochures apart from miscellaneous expenses. Donations are always welcome and memberships can be purchased from any CCHR chapter.

How to Start a CCHR

Anyone wishing to start a CCHR should contact their nearest CCHR chapter. Forming a CCHR does not take a lot of expertise nor does it require extensive researches. All that is needed is willingness and desire to do something to eliminate psychiatric abuse and restore human rights. CCHR members have written up successful actions on setting up a Commission, documenting abuses, what to look for in touring hospitals, and various other pointers you may need.

Information packets based on previous CCHR activities will be given to you in order to study how to document abuses, tour hospitals and ways to enlist support and assistance from your local community.

Enlisting the aid of other individuals, medical doctors, and attorneys to help you with CCHR will be the first step in establishing a group.

One person alone cannot change the mental health system, yet a group of dedicated individuals working towards a common goal can accomplish miracles. CCHR is such a group.

Committee on Public Health and Safety

The Problem

"The total medical care expenditure in the United States in 1972 was $83.4 billion, of which $77.3 billion was spent for personal health services, and the rest for construction of facilities and research. The total compares to only $12 billion in 1950."

(From a slide show *Behind the Crisis of Health Care*, by the American Friends Service Committee.)

The cost of health care is skyrocketing. The cost of getting sick is a matter of growing concern.

The Committee for National Health Insurance has published the amazing fact that the average American family works one month out of the year to cover the costs of medical bills for his or her family.

Yet the consumer is not getting his dollar's worth. Substantial evidence points to a decline in health care.

This is a very serious situation.

Scientologists are applying themselves to this problem by working with The Committee on Public Health and Safety (COPHS). A society cannot function well, when many of its members are physically ill. The chronic problem of "how do I possibly pay my medical bills" takes a person's attention away from worthwhile activities he could otherwise pursue. These are active concerns of the Committee.

Another important matter is examining why ineffective medical care continues to be offered to people who pay their bills and don't improve. Is a workable alternative being withheld for reasons of vested interest in perpetuating a failed order?

The Committee on Public Health and Safety was formed in 1972 in response to mounting requests for health and safety information which was not being provided by governments, and private agencies.

Regional Committees have compiled and disseminated existing data which was specifically requested by the public. They have also researched and published data which was concealed or played down by food, drug and medical organizations. The Commitee investigates and issues reports on public complaints received by the Public Health area, and assists in obtaining and accomplishing required reforms.

The Committee on Public Health and Safety, based in the United States, is a member group of the Assocation of Scientologists for Reform, a nonprofit corporation.

It is composed of doctors, chiropractors, attorneys, concerned citizens and Scientologists.

The Services to the Public

COPHS publishes a newsletter providing information on health care, including developments in health legislation, brief summaries of reports on health issues and listings of forthcoming conventions, meetings, lectures and symposiums and their content. The newsletter also publishes the results of research that COPHS has recently undertaken and contains a brief statement of recent COPHS activities. Thus it provides comprehensive information and contact on all aspects of health care.

COPHS Investigations

Because of rising health care costs and frequent lack of results, COPHS has done an extensive study in the area of health care. Members interviewed doctors, medical society members, legislators, lawyers, insurance professionals, government officials, nutritionists, chiropractors, journalists, acupuncturists, medical administrators, psychiatrists, religious leaders and the public. All agreed that getting sick is very costly. Further investigation revealed the reason. The American Medical Association, who took charge of the medical profession over a hundred years ago in an alleged attempt to improve the quality of care, has instead created a dog-in-the-manger monopoly which has jeopardized the lives of millions of Americans.

Investigation by COPHS revealed that the American Medical Association and its close connections in the pharmaceutical industry have created a powerful political lobby which operates as a dominating force in limiting the kind of health care available to the public.

Essentially it is this health care monopoly which militates against alternative forms, such as chiropractic, nutrition and vitamin therapy, osteopathy, and others, which de-emphasize medication and are therefore a threat to drug companies and the AMA, who retaliate by trying to suppress competition. By doing so they deny freedom of choice to individuals.

The Federal Trade Commission has asked the Committee on Public Health and Safety to submit a report on the AMA and its involvement in the health care issue, in conjunction with a proposed report on antitrust law violations by the AMA.

COPHS Funding

The Committee on Public Health and Safety is funded entirely by donations and memberships. Anyone who desires to contribute can mail a check to the COPHS of their choice (see the listing in Chapter 17).

How to Start a Committee on Public Health and Safety

If you are interested in working with COPHS or in starting a Committee on Public Health and Safety, contact any COPHS. It is not necessary to have training in the medical profession; to work with COPHS, you need only to be interested in increasing the quality of health care for our society.

The Aged, Mentally Retarded, Alcoholics and Prison Reform Programs

In the course of a day serious crimes are committed all over the world. People are killed in the streets in alcohol-related traffic accidents, elderly people die forgotten in nursing homes, and mentally retarded children reach out for some human understanding and are given mind-altering drugs.

These seemingly unrelated areas have a common denominator. These four major problems faced by mankind today, crime, alcoholism, care of the aged and the mentally retarded may seem unrelated but the Church of Scientology has found that one insidious force has become involved in dealing with these difficulties and in fact perpetuating them. This is psychiatry, which has cultivated the image of an authority on social ills.

A brief look at the inception of psychiatry will throw light upon this situation. In the 1800s, a man named Pavlov did some experiments on dogs and developed the theory of stimulus-response. He found that if he rang a bell and then showed a dog food, the dog would salivate. After repeating this a number of times, he found that the dog would salivate upon hearing the bell even without any food being present. Thus the dog was programmed to respond to the stimulus of a ringing bell. And this taken one step further was the beginning of the theory that Man is a stimulus-response mechanism that will respond to being savagely jolted with electric current or having sections of his brain excised.

Such psychiatric practices as electric shock treatment, psychosurgery and the use of mind-altering drugs, have been found by members of the Church of Scientology to be in frequent use in the treatment of the aged, alcoholics, criminals and the mentally retarded. As an answer to these abuses, the Church has been active in forming and giving aid to social reform groups which (1) seek to expose and stop psychiatric (and other) abuses which are a violation of Man's basic rights, (2) strive for the passage of legislation that will prevent these abuses and (3) work in the community to establish proper facilities for the treatment and rehabilitation of the aged, alcoholics, criminals and the mentally retarded.

The membership of these groups consists largely of non-Scientologists who have the above goals, and who are working with Scientologists to achieve them.

In the United States, a group of Scientologists formed the Association of Scientologists for Reform (ASR) which is a separately incorporated group from the Church of Scientology. This Association sponsors the various social reform groups throughout the U.S. which are seeking proper treatment for the aged, alcoholics, criminals and the mentally retarded.

Care for the Aged

For instance, in the field of treatment for the aged, a group called the Gerus Society was begun in 1968 by Scien-tologists in Los Angeles who saw the need for improved care for elderly persons in the U.S. Since that time similar groups have started in other major U.S. cities and the various chapters have been active in exposing poor treatment conditions for the aged, and demanding change.

Spread unevenly across the United States there are over 21 million elderly people — those people over sixty-five years. The number of these senior citizens increases by 2.1 per cent a year and forms a growing proportion of the total U.S. population.

California Defense Attorney for the Elderly, Paul Morentz, wrote the foreword for a recent Gerus publication *Rewards of Old Age:*

"For some time now, there has been legislation regarding the care and treatment of the elderly. Recently, it has come to light however, that not only are these laws not enforced, but that severe abuses are being committed against the elderly. The resulting scene is one of tragedy as the human rights of our elderly are sacrificed so others can fill their pocketbook. Abuses must be exposed, and as they are, these abuses must be corrected. We who care must align our goals and work as a solid unit for even better legislation and for strict, competent enforcement of that legislation."

Over sixty per cent of nursing homes across America do not meet Federal standards according to the Department of Health, Education and Welfare. Dr. J. Raymond Gladue, of the American Association of Nursing Homes Physicians, testified to Congress that the care in nursing homes is "either very poor or scandalous."

These are standards that have been on the books and unenforced by the Department of Health, Education and Welfare since 1967.

Perhaps the most prevalent abuse of the aged found by Scientologists is the excessive use of psychiatric mind-altering drugs in their "treatment." In one case a patient sent from a state mental institution to a nursing home as part of the de-institutionalization program, had been given fifteen types of medication for some years. Some of these drugs obviously duplicated each other, yet the physician and the nursing homes could not decrease them. Not surprisingly, the man was addicted.

The Scientologist Social Reform Groups for the Aged hold the opinion that the elderly deserve better care than that which they frequently receive in nursing homes. Socrates held that society may well be judged by the manner in which it cares for its elderly. These people have worked hard and painfully throughout their lives to help create a better society for the following generations. They deserve special care. If we won't do it now for them, who will do it for us?

Alcoholism

The second area of concern of Scientologists' social reforms is that of treatment for alcoholics. A group called the National Alliance on Alcoholism Prevention and Treatment (NAAPT) was formed in Los Angeles, California, by Scientologists who found that alcoholics were being subjected to cruel and inhuman treatment.

In an initial report published by the Alliance, the group described an imaginary city that contains all the alcoholics in America in order to adequately portray the magnitude of the problem today. Within the structure of "Alcoholic City U.S.A." we can see the degree to which all areas of society are affected, and the desperate need for effective rehabilitation of alcoholics.

"Alcoholic City" is large, with a population of ten million people people, ranking the largest city in the world after Shanghai and Tokyo. Five per cent of the inhabitants of "Alcoholic City" are "skid row," the remaining ninety-five per cent are employable. Seventy per cent of the city area would be classed as "respectable neighborhoods."

The inhabitants of this city have a high crime rate, amounting to almost 3 million arrests yearly, which means one-third of the city is in legal trouble. If we have only one policeman for every 250 people (roughly the average of New York City) we would need 40,000 policemen for "Alcoholic City," and they would be required to handle over 9,000 homicides and over 6,000 suicides each year. The residents, most of whom drive, injure over a million people yearly in auto accidents and one and a half-million are disabled. Twenty-eight thousand lose their lives through the problem drinker.

Now where are monies allocated in this city? The cost to the taxpayer in the arrest, trial and maintenance of jails for problem drinkers is enormous—one billion dollars or more yearly. There would be over three billion dollars in property damage and medical expenses per year. Two billion dollars goes towards health and welfare services and over ten billion dollars would be lost in man hours to industry, government and the military due to the alcoholic's inability to hold down a job.

Of the finance allocated to treatment for the citizens of "Alcoholic City," much will be wasted. The individual may go to a mental hospital and be treated for a "mental illness." The cost would be $7,500 per patient per year or, if all the city dwellers were patients, $75,000,000,000 a year. All of this would be wasted since alcoholism is not a "mental illness."

So here we have "Alcoholic City U.S.A.," which gives a graphic picture of the seriousness of the problem of alcoholism. And yet, when Scientologists have examined what is being done to reduce the problem they have found that all too often alcoholics are treated in a similar vein as the aged, with mind-altering drugs, shock treatment, and other psychiatric brutalities.

The problem is summed up by Anna Twomey, who is a counselor at Boston City Hospital in the U.S.

"I've been working in the field of alcoholism for twenty-seven years, seventeen of them as a counselor in the Boston City Hospital. The heavy use of drugs for the rehabilitation of alcoholics and the millions of dollars wasted each year in Massachusetts on ineffective methods of treatment and types of research that benefit only the researcher, and not the alcoholic, must be stopped.

"It is high time we stop playing games with the lives of the thousands of sick and suffering alcoholics in Massachusetts and start putting all our efforts into programs that are proven effective. I thoroughly believe NAAPT is one group that is doing just that."

Another individual who has worked with the NAAPT is Rev. William A. Kaufman, Executive Director of the Christian Rehabilitation Center in North Carolina, U.S. According to Rev. Kaufman:

"Alcoholism is not a 'psychiatric sickness' and should not be treated as such. Good medical, nutritional and socializing influences are much needed in solving the problem of alcoholism and drug addiction. I have found through my work as a professional in the alcohol rehabilitation field, that establishing a new desire and determinism to 'be somebody' and setting a goal to be achieved in life are the first steps toward recovery."

As Rev. Kaufman points out the essential thing in helping an alcoholic is to treat him as a human being, and work to increase his self-respect and trust in himself and others. Members of the NAAPT have found that counseling by recovered alcoholics is very successful in helping the alcoholic to stop drinking. By relating to a fellow human being he ceases to see his own problem in isolation. By talking to another who has had the same problem, the alcoholic realizes that there is a road out.

On the other hand, the common psychiatric "solution" to the alcoholic's problem is to prescribe tranquilizing drugs. Dr. I. A. Pursch, Captain, Medical Corps, and Chief of the Alcohol Rehabilitation Service of the Naval Regional Medical Center in Long Beach, California, has supported the NAAPT in its stand against the use of mind-altering drugs. According to Dr. Pursch, "One of the primary manifestations of the well trained, conscientious physician's ignorance about alcoholism is the frequency and the extent to which alcoholic patients are being treated by tranquilizer medications, both before and after they have been clearly diagnosed as having alcoholism."

As with the treatment of the aged, another psychiatric control mechanism used on alcoholics is shock treatment. A registered nurse and recovering alcoholic who had received shock treatments told the NAAPT in New England her story:

"Prior to leaving home my daughter and I agreed the one thing I would not receive was shock treatment. She was young and maintained her stand but my written permission negated her refusals.

"I had an adverse reaction to the shock treatments. After five treatments I very vaguely recall Dr. Stebbins telling me that the next alternative must be lithium therapy, then in an experimental stage. I was discharged feeling ghastly, worse than upon admission. I was on lithium, Librium, Elavil, and Valium. I experienced a complete loss of memory in areas such as financial obligations, names of people, complete years of events, and professional ability. I was always frightened that I might never recover.

"Two days after my discharge I was readmitted to intensive care in a comatose state. Three months later I returned home and stayed more or less out of work for two years."

Many such stories have been gathered by the NAAPT in its drive to expose psychiatric abuse in the treatment of alcoholics.

Prison Reform

The third area of concern for the Scientologist in social reform is the rehabilitation of criminals. Out of growing awareness and concern about rising crime, the Committee to Re-Involve Ex-Offenders (CREO) was formed in the United States with similar groups in other parts of the world. The groups have found that current prison systems do not rehabilitate or correct criminals and thus do nothing to emend criminality.

The purpose of the Scientologist prison reform groups are similar to those of the other social reform groups:

(1) To safeguard against, expose, and seek the correction of abuses to the fundamental rights of men as granted by Almighty God and as guaranteed by the Constitution of the United States of America and the Universal Declaration of Human Rights of the United Nations in regard to the custody and treatment of prisoners.

(2) To establish and promote the acceptance of ethical codes in the area of criminal rehabilitation where any man has used his power or authority to enslave, harm or lessen the freedom of others.

(3) To conduct educational programs, organize study groups and/or committees to give lectures, to publish and circulate magazines, books and pamphlets and employ other media dealing with such activities.

(4) To establish educational and vocational training centers in the community for the rehabilitation of offenders and ex-offenders.

(5) To work with other individuals and organizations of similar objectives.

The abuses uncovered by Scientologist reformers include overmedication, use of shock treatment and beatings. One group in the United Kingdom is currently mounting a campaign against brutalities in prisons controlled by the Home Office, a department of the government. Criminon documented the case of an old woman who was beaten before being put in prison, imprisoned for thirty days in excess of her term and on her release was offered £125 if she would take no action against the Home Office for the injustice. She has refused the money and is bringing a legal suit.

Another case documented by Criminon is that of an ex-prisoner, David Thomas, who told about psychiatric treatment he had received in British prisons:

"I was transferred to Wormwood Scrubs in May 1967

and was put into the psychiatric wing. After a short while I was again given drug treatment. During my time at Wormwood Scrubs I was continually on drugs. I felt just like a vegetable. I felt extremely degraded whilst in prison and the drugs seemed to make me feel worse. I was transferred to Grendon Underwood Prison psychiatric wing in April 1968. I was eventually released in July 1968. After my release I would regularly go out and buy drugs. I felt I could not manage without them. I was in great fear of prison and felt the need for drugs, whenever I thought of prison.

"The situation I am now in is that when reminded of my experience in prison I then need the drugs to calm me down. However when I am on the drugs I then become self-destructive and injure myself.

"On one occasion four years ago I attempted suicide by drugs as I had become so depressed over my experience. Prior to being in prison I was a normal family man who got on extremely well with my wife and children. I am now aggressive and wound up and cannot control my self-destructive impulses. I never experienced these impulses prior to my imprisonment.

"Prior to my imprisonment I had not taken drugs. I had never had psychiatric treatment and never attempted suicide."

Criminon interviewed Thomas' wife who corroborated her husband's statement and said "he had become like a zombie since he had been on drugs and was drinking far more heavily than he used to."

A friend of David Thomas' who had known him for fourteen years told Criminon:

"Prior to his imprisonment in 1965, I found him to be a normal, active and healthy man. He was always able to find himself work. I do not recall him ever being depressed and he would have no more than a couple of pints of beer whilst out with friends.

"Since his release from prison in 1968, David Thomas has seemed to me to be a totally changed person. He is now unable to cope without excessive drink."

Thus we see the product of psychiatry in prisons.

Care of the Mentally Retarded

The final area with which Scientologists' social reforms are dealing is treatment for the mentally retarded. A group called the Task Force on Mental Retardation came into being with the realization that difficulties reported by parents of retarded children in obtaining care for their children were not isolated.

The complaint of one parent led to an investigation of facts which caused further investigation and began a trail leading into a morass of budget changes, personnel changes, antiquated laws, frustrated public servants, and apathetic parents tired of "fighting the system."

The Task Force was formed on December 10, 1971 by Rev. G. Bruce Ford of the Church of Scientology of California. He was joined by a special education teacher, an engineer and father of a retarded boy, a teacher and mother of six, and an educational executive.

This initial group and similar chapters in other parts of the world have found that the public considers a mentally retarded person has no value and must be a burden on the rest of the population. This idea is formulated without reference to the facts. The mentally retarded person when he is trained, *can* work and make his contribution to society.

Before proceeding further, mental retardation should be defined, as its definition, causes, and cures have continued to be highly disputed within the field. This has added to the confusion and diversity in diagnosis, treatment and care of the mentally retarded.

Even the label "mental retardation" has been disputed along with its connotation of mental illness. Dr. George Lee, British authority on retardation says:

"The word adds to the confusion that exists all over the world. It brings fear and dismay into peoples' minds because they don't differentiate between the retarded and the mentally ill. The retarded are among the most innocuous of all God's creatures, they can't be numbered among the violent."

A simple definition of mental retardation as written by the American Association of Mental Deficiency is: "subaverage functioning which originates in the development period and is associated with impairment in adaptive behavior."

The National Association for Retarded Citizens in the United States says the mentally retarded are those who develop at a below average rate and experience unusual difficulty in learning, social adjustment, and economic productivity.

Over 200 causes for the "affliction" known as mental retardation have been recognized. Physical factors (brain damage, tumors, genetic impairment, neurological poisoning etc.) mental, spiritual and social factors are seen to play a part.

As with the aged, alcoholics and criminals, the psychiatrists have involved themselves in the treatment of the mentally retarded. The Task Force on Mental Retardation has found that the psychiatric battery of "therapies" including heavy drugging, shock therapy, and bizarre behavior modification techniques have virtually no favorable effect on the retarded person. On the other hand, the love, understanding and effective practical training which he desperately needs are not provided by the psychiatrist.

Scientologist reformers have uncovered abuses of the mentally retarded. In Nevada, a woman related to the Task Force the case of her retarded son who was institutionalized at a Nevada mental hospital, and his subsequent death there in 1967. The eleven year old boy was housed with older patients some of whom were known to be violent. On one occasion the boy was thrown against a wall by a particularly violent inmate and suffered a broken jaw and eye damage. According to the child's mother, hospital personnel attempted to "cover up" the case. She also reported her child received excessive dosages of the dangerous drug Thorazine (up to 550 mgs).

During the night the child was confined to his bed with the use of "restraining devices." One night he became tangled in the apparatus and subsequently died of asphyxia "due to a faulty restraining device" according to the local coroner.

Another case which the Task Force investigated at this same Nevada mental hospital concerned the use of "punishment therapy" on a mentally retarded girl.

Dr. Robert Quilitch who administered the treatment admitted that it was a "last ditch attempt" to handle the girl, Carol Sue Loeser, and that even psychosurgery had been contemplated. In Carol Sue's case a "shock stick" was utilized in punishing unwanted and disruptive behavior provoked by the doctor involved. (A "shock stick" is an identical device to cattle prods used to control and train animals.) Dr. Quilitch asserted that the treatment was safe and effective and justified, by the failure of earlier modes of therapy applied to Carol Sue. He admitted to the Task Force that one of the girl's major temper tantrums centered on her inability to make herself understood, due in part to a cleft palate.

Upon visiting Carol Sue, the Task Force observed her terrified response upon being addressed by the ward doctor—she immediately jumped up as if she had been stung—or perhaps shocked. The similarity between this result and the conditioning of Pavlov's dogs is painfully obvious.

The mentally retarded have a longer history of maltreatment than any other human minority. In ancient Greece infanticide was practiced on mentally retarded children. During the Middle Ages the mentally retarded were usually locked up in filthy asylums, or executed as witches, and subjected to every form of torture; Martin Luther and John Calvin decided that the retarded were the children of Satan and had no right to survive. More recently, in Nazi Germany, the retarded were classified as "life devoid of value," and systematically gassed, starved to death, and cremated in special ovens at the state's mental hygiene facilities.

While such treatment is condemned today, in many areas of the world conditions for the retarded can still only be described as deplorable.

How to Start a Social Reform Group

If you are interested in joining a social reform group like the ones described here simply contact the director of the group nearest you (see Chapter 17). He or she will tell you what you can do to contribute and can give you reports compiled by the various groups and other introductory data which will help you get started.

You may be interested in starting your own group in the area where you live, in which case you can also contact the nearest group director for guidance on how to proceed. He or she will provide you with information on the social problem you will be working with, effectiveness of existing programs and reforms possible. The director will also put you in touch with any Scientologists in the area. They will be very willing to work with you to get something done about abuses in the community.

The existing reform groups have been effective in achieving social reforms and will give assistance in determining what actions you will need to take in your local area and will relate to you what they have found most effective in similar situations.

You can then find out what is happening in your community regarding treatment or care for the type of people you want to help. You can determine what treatment programs exist which are effective and which programs are abusive and should be exposed.

Eventually you will be helping to pass legislation that will put an end to abusive treatment and ensure that the aged, alcoholics, criminals and the mentally retarded are given the care and rehabilitation they deserve.

This may seem like a great deal to take on, but the question is "If I don't do something about this, who will?"

Man keeps hoping that someone else will solve the problems that confront him and so these problems daily grow worse.

It is the philosophy of L. Ron Hubbard, the Founder of the Church of Scientology, that if one is to lead a truly full life, he must take responsibility for those less fortunate than him, rather than forsaking them and leaving them in the hands of cruel men who seek only to control and subdue. And it is this philosophy that the Scientologist social reformers practice in their daily lives by exposing abuses and setting them right. You are welcome to contribute to this cause.

L. Ron Hubbard has said:

"Your potentialities are a great deal better than anyone ever permitted you to believe and with this attitude, despite the immensity of the task, one can make changes for the better in society.

"My purpose is to bring a barbarism out of the mud it thinks conceived it and to form, here on earth, a civilization based on human understanding, not violence. This is a big purpose. A broad field. A star high goal. But I think it's your purpose too."

According to a 1970 report issued by the President of the United States Committee on Mental Retardation, one of every thirty retarded persons, some 250,000 people, are cared for in institutions in the kind of "environments experienced by prisoners of war." The Committee report cites physical maltreatment, abusive use of drugs, prolonged periods of isolation and restraint, overcrowded and deteriorating living areas, and a generally low esteem for the dignity of those being served. The Committee recommended that the "model residential environment should provide a warm, stimulating social setting devoid of any form of dehumanizing conditions" and noted that such a model did not exist in any one of the fifty American states. Scientologist reformers make similar recommendations:

(1) That ALL the retarded receive an education.
(2) That the education and training given to a retardate be of value to the child coping with the world around him.
(3) That the hospitals for the retarded work to remove the institutional image and adopt a more pleasant, cheerful, and humane image.
(4) That institutionalized children and adults who can

benefit from a community life be placed in the community — as soon as possible.
(5) That the shortage of "trained professionals" be alleviated by employment, full or part-time, of parents, students and others who care. A study should be made to see if better utilization of professionals could be made. The Task Force believes that love is the major factor in obtaining a response from any child.
(6) That long-range planning be begun to establish socio-economic residential communities within the overall community, for the retarded to live as normal a productive life as the bulk of society.

Description of Services

The four types of Scientology reform groups described above offer a variety of services to the community. They release publications which describe existing local treatment conditions, and make recommendations for their improvement. Members of the group are available to the media.

The groups have researchers who provide data on existing laws and regulations governing treatment for the various groups. The researchers can also provide data on adverse effects of treatments and on some effective alternatives.

Another function of the different groups is to provide help in documenting specific abuses which may involve securing medical records and having testimony notarized.

Relatives or friends of an alcoholic, criminal, etc., who is institutionalized will often desire to have the person removed and can contact a Scientology reform group for assistance. The group assists with the legal arrangements necessary to remove the person and will help in relocating him in a secure environment.

The groups will also help in researching, writing, proposing legislation and getting it passed to ensure that the aged, alcoholics, criminals and the mentally retarded do receive the help they need.

In addition, members of these groups work within communities to set up proper treatment facilities. They can help with arranging funding for programs, working out a regimen of treatment which will be effective and in many other ways.

All miscellaneous services available are:

(1) Advice on which local facilities provide the best care.
(2) Providing speakers for school classes or events, civil group seminars, etc., who will discuss treatment, conditions and the need for reform.
(3) Aid in investigating, exposing, and stopping abuses of people's rights in institutions, via newsletters, public hearings, symposiums, demonstrations, etc.

A complete list of all Social Reform Groups, giving their addresses and telephone numbers (where available), is contained in Chapter 17 of this book.

Bibliography

Alcoholism Report, The. (JSL Reports, Vol. II, No. 19). United States, July 26, 1974.

Breggin, Dr. Peter R., Washington School of Psychiatry. *U.S. Congressional Record, Volume 118, February 24, 1972.*

Chavetz, Morris E. and Demone, Harold W. Jr. *American Handbook of Psychiatry Problems to Control Alcoholism.* Caplan G., Ed.

Church of Scientology. *Freedom, The Independent Journal of the Church of Scientology*, United Kingdom Issue Number 54. Church of Scientology, June 1976.

Coroner's Office, Toronto, Canada. *Coroner's Office Annual Report for 1975.* Toronto.

Cunningham, Dave—(Letter to Claude Martinez). Councilman 10th District, City of Los Angeles, California, October 22, 1975.

Dan Golenpaul Associates, New York, New York. *Information Please Almanac.* Atlas and Yearbook, 28th Edition 1974. New York: Dan Golenpaul Associates, 1975.

Dellums, Ronald V. (Letter to Greg Zerovnich). Member of Congress, House of Representatives, California 7th District, April 24, 1973.

Department of Health, Education and Welfare. *First Special Report to the U.S. Congress on Alcoholism and Health* from the Secretary of Health, Education and Welfare. (DHEW Publication No. HSM, 73-9031.) U.S. Federal Government, December 1971.

Elkins, Henry. *Testimony given to the Citizen's Commission on Human Rights Los Angeles.*

Farrell, Robert J.—Letter from. Parole Agent, California Youth Authority, April 19, 1977.

Federal Bureau of Investigation. *Crime in the United States.* Published by the Federal Bureau of Investigation, 1975.

Freeman, Walter, M.D. and Watts, James W., M.D. *Psychosurgery in the Treatment of Mental Disorders and Intractable Pain.* Springfield, Illinois: Thomas, 1950.

Gerus Society, U.S. *Quality of Care.* Prepared by the Gerus Society, 1975.

Globe and Mail, Toronto, Canada. *A Cautious Heroin Test.* Toronto.

Hilburger, Letter from Albert W. Attorney, New London, Connecticut. April 16, 1975.

Hotchner, A. E. *Papa Hemingway.*

Hubbard, L. Ron. *Dianetic Registration.* Hubbard Communications Office Policy Letter 12 June 1969.

Los Angeles Times, Addiction—Will There Ever Be a Solution. Los Angeles: Los Angeles Times, April 11, 1976.

Los Angeles Times, California Losing War Against Drug Abuse. Los Angeles: Los Angeles Times, January 13, 1977.

McGrath, Dr. Patrick, Broadmoor Physician Superintendent. *Wokingham Times*, England: February 5, 1976.

New England Elderly Demands Society, sponsored by the Church of Scientology. *The Institutionalized Elderly: Human or Animal?* New England Elderly Demands Society.

Newspaper Enterprise Association. *World Almanac and Book of Facts.* New York, New York: Newspaper Enterprise Association, 1974.

Oberosterreichische Nachrichten, September 24, 1976.

Prevention Resource Bulletin, Vol. 1, No. 5, Winter 1.

Randall, Rod—Letter from. Parole Agent, Department of Youth Authority, April 19, 1977.

Rollin, Dr. Henry, M.D., DPM—Eng. Consultant Psychiatrist, Horton Hospital, Epsom. *British Clinic Journal.* February 1974.

Simmons, Jean W.—Letter from. Classifications Officer, Canadian Penitentiary Service, June 24, 1974.

Sullivan, Harry Stack. *Concepts of Modern Psychiatry.* 3:73, February 1940.

Sun, The (Australian Newspaper), December 11, 1975.

Szasz, Thomas. *From the Slaughterhouse to the Madhouse.*

Task Force on Mental Retardation. *Mental Retardation in Nevada.* Las Vegas, Nevada: Task Force on Mental Retardation, August 1974.

Upton, Jonika (Nazareth Hospital, New Mexico, 1958, age 16) Shock quotes. *Madness Network News.* Statement on the use of shock treatment made before the San Francisco Mental Health Advisory Board hearing, January 20, 1975. April 1975.

U.S. Department of Transportation. *The National Counter Measures Program.*

U.S. Federal Government. *Alcohol and Alcoholism: Problems, Programs and Progress.* (NIAAA, U.S. Department Health, Education and Welfare—DHEW—Publication No. HGM 72-9127.) U.S. Federal Government: Revised 1972.

U.S. Senate. *Developments in Aging: 1973—January through March 1974.* A report of the Special Committee on Aging.

Van Nuys News, Van Nuys, California, U.S. *Kickbacks to Nursing Homes Told.* Van Nuys: Van Nuys News, January 30, 1975.

9

The Effectiveness
of Scientology's
Social Services

Citizens' Commission on Human Rights

Editorial

Kudos to the Scientologists!

Had it not been for unswerving devotion to a cause, and dogged persistence, the ugly details of mistreatment of mental patients in at least some of California's mental hospitals never would have seen the light of day.

The catalyst in the seven-year effort to expose the shameful — yes criminal treatment of patients by some staff, including highly-paid psychiatrists and administrators — is the Citizens' Commission on Human Rights, 1600 North La Brea Avenue, Suite 107, Hollywood. Supported by the Association of Scientologists for Reform, much of the day-to-day investigative work which led finally to the state probe was conducted by Rev. Heber C. Jentzsch and Staffer Mike Quinn.

Matters came to a head last September when the Commission's Mental Health Task Force blew the whistle on the unconscionable acts of indifference, brutality, and perhaps sadism rampant in some of the institutions, including Metropolitan Hospital, Norwalk, where in June a 19-year-old patient, Mark Holcomb died of injuries found by a coroner's jury to have been caused "at the hands of another person other than by accident."

Hospital records reported the young man died of "aspiration in his own vomit while restrained and drugged . . ." The hospital director, Dr. Carl Ellis — removed three months later after the case was publicized — denied responsibility for the death, merely repeated that the hospital needed "more personnel," despite the fact mental health funding in Los Angeles County zoomed from $16 million in 1968, to $84 million in 1976, while patient "delivery days" declined 75%. Of those monies, psychiatrists and professional services "eat up 92% of the budget" with patients getting 4.6% for their care.

The Commission believes, rightly, that no amount of money will correct staff brutality — behavior so utterly without feeling that this incident could take place, as recorded in a statement by Cara Brandt:

"My grandmother, Lucy Brancato, went to Metro on June 8, 1965, because of depression. She was put in a locked ward. On Oct. 1, 1967, she received shock treatments. On Oct. 9 she left the hospital by climbing a fence and went to the home of my grandfather. She pleaded with him not to take her back. She had bruises all over her body. She said they had hurt her bad. He took her back because he couldn't believe they would do something like that. The hospital said they didn't know how she was bruised. Two weeks later she disappeared. My grandfather was notified by telegram. The hospital said they searched for her everywhere. On Nov. 7, two weeks later, she was found dead in a clothing closet 7 feet off the ground, where she could not have climbed with linen stacked neatly in front of her. Within 15 minutes she had been sent to the Chapel of Memories in Norwalk . . . My grandmother died in degrading conditions—my grandfather died of a broken heart two months later."

Joining the Citizens' Commission in a demand for state intervention are three groups representing some 12,000 California attorneys. Their position was stated by Attorney Mary Ann Bannan of Public Council, a public-interest law firm, who criticized the "isolation from the outside world" which had marked the confinement of Mark Holcomb before his death.

"We think the difficulty in obtaining access to persons in mental hospitals is critical," she said. "Until the doors of these institutions are opened to public scrutiny, there is no realistic expectation that they can be held accountable for treatment of patients. Patients are not allowed to have visitors, to make phone calls, to receive or send mail. They are denied access in many instances to the most basic means of communication. This situation cannot be therapeutic . . . We fear that too often hospitals use the pretext of confidentiality to conceal mistreatment of patients. Confidentiality should not mean coverup . . ."

The Commission on Human Rights has called upon the California Legislature to examine these issues: (1) Treat or release laws; (2) forced drugging laws; (3) involuntary commitment law; (4) the need for competent medical facilities and medically-trained personnel "instead of a warehouse of drugging and brutality unseen by the public, and quashed by the administration of mental health hospitals.

"When a patient can die in his own vomit, when deaths can occur unattended without inquest because it happened in a mental hospital, when three women patients at Metropolitan can have their hips broken in a space of four days, and when a woman can die in a closet and be there two weeks and nothing done about it — there is a grave need for action," said the Scientologists' task force.

We couldn't agree more! And to the everlasting credit of these stalwart citizens, the light has been focused on the evil doings inside these institutions. It is devoutly hoped that citizen pressure will not relent until the whole disgraceful mess is cleaned up.

— D.C.M.

Support Offered

Columbia Missourian
4 November 1973

Psychiatry Institute Shaken by Controversy

By Kathy Cunningham
Missourian Staff Writer

ST. LOUIS — An issue that may be the biggest controversy in the stormy history of the Missouri Institute of Psychiatry is now in the public arena.

The 11-year institute background has been sparked with debate and speculation, usually concerning funding priorities and facilities. Now the issue is research, and in particular drug research using patients as subjects.

Although few persons were

About 3,000 pages of documents relating to research at the institute were found in a trash can.

aware of the situation, Dr. George A. Ulett, former director, established extensive drug research programs at the institute. Most of the projects were funded by pharmaceutical companies and used state patients as experimental subjects.

For all practical purposes, clinical research involving drug experimentation has stopped at the institute. It was halted in August after Dr. Harold Robb, director of the Missouri Division of Mental Health, sent out a new set of guidelines regarding patient consent for clinical experimentation at state facilities.

DR. ROBB DENIED that the regulation was directed at the institute. He said the rules apply to all state hospitals. He did admit, however, that the release of the guidelines, which had been in the drawing stage for about six months, was speeded up a bit after a former institute patient released about 3,000 pages of research documents found in a trash can at the facility.

The former patient and his son gave the documents to Dr. Fred Rock of the Church of Scientology in St. Louis. Dr. Rock took the documents to Dr. Robb before approaching the news media last summer.

Dr. Rock's church group stresses the right to personal freedoms, and he saw the release of information about institute activities as a step in obtaining more rights for mental patients.

What was really going on at the institute and the research conducted by Dr. Ulett, institute director from December 1972 until his hasty resignation in September, was relatively unknown. The papers, from Dr. Ulett's personal files over a 15-year period, revealed a close relationship between him and pharmaceutical manufacturers.

When Dr. Ulett was a member of the medical school faculty at Washington University in St. Louis and director at Malcolm Bliss Hospital, a mental facility in the St. Louis City Hospital system, he received research money from drug companies.

DRUG COMPANY CHECKS from this period were made out to the "Neuromedical Foundation: Ulett Epilepsy Research Project."

When the institute was created in late 1962, about the time Dr. Ulett became director of the Missouri Division of Mental Health, research funding from pharmaceutical manufacturers was directed through the Psychiatric Research Foundation of Missouri.

Dr. Warren Thompson, institute administrator and executive director of the Psychiatric Research Foundation until June 1973, said all funds were transferred to University channels in 1965.

One of the documents in Mr. Rock's possession refutes the assumption that all research funding was administered through the University. A Jan. 2 letter, written on Psychiatric Research Foundation stationery, from Thompson to Dr. Ali Keskiner of the institute staff states:

"All donations to the Psychiatric Research Foundation must be unrestricted and no promises, expressed or implied, must be made to a drug house that an investigation of a particular drug will be made and reported to that drug house in consideration of their making such contribution."

THIS LETTER IMPLIES funds for institute research projects, often grants in excess of $1,000, were coming through the foundation. Thompson concluded the letter by saying:

"The foundation deducts a 10 per cent overhead cost on all donations and establishes an account with an appropriate designation for your endeavors with 90 per cent allocation of the donation."

Dr. Ivan Sletten, acting director of the institute since Dr. Ulett's resignation, attempts to downplay the emphasis on drug research and Dr. Ulett's involvement with it.

Dr. Sletten defended the institute and said, "We have a sound humanitarian program. Our teaching and clinical activities are important to both the Division of Mental Health and the Food and Drug Administration."

MR. ROCK SENT copies of Dr. Ulett's papers to Congressman James Symington, D-2nd Dist., a member of the House Subcommittee on Public Health and Environment. As a result, the FDA is conducting an investigation of the institute and its practices.

It was shortly after the investigation was begun and Dr. Robb established the new guidelines for obtaining patient consent that Dr. Ulett and Dr. Turan M. Itil, institute director of research, resigned.

113

JOHN A. SHARP
REPRESENTATIVE, DISTRICT 38
11320 BLUE RIDGE EXTENSION
KANSAS CITY, MISSOURI 64134

COMMITTEES:
EDUCATION
CONSTITUTIONAL AMENDMENTS

MISSOURI
HOUSE OF REPRESENTATIVES
JEFFERSON CITY 65101

February 14, 1974

Rev. Frederick M. Rock
Missouri Church
of Scientology
4225 Lindell Blvd.
St. Louis, Missouri 63108

Dear Rev. Rock:

I just wanted to drop you a brief note to thank you
for the numerous materials your church has sent me
regarding the abuses in human experimentation of
Missouri's institutions for the mentally ill and
mentally retarded. Your church has performed a
great public service in this regard.

I certainly support efforts to assure that the
individual rights of those treated for mental illness or retardation are not violated in the name of
medical progress.

Sincerely,

John A. Sharp

JAS:mr

From MICHAEL O'HALLORAN M.P.

HOUSE OF COMMONS
LONDON SW1A OAA

25 March 1977

Mr. Michael Stern,
Secretary, Citizens Commission on Human Rights,
68 Tottenham Court Road, W.1

Dear Mr. Stern,

Thank you for your letter of 22 March and the
attached copy of the petition which is to be
presented in Parliament by Mr. David Price.

I do share your concern at psychosurgery and will
speak to Mr. Price about what support I can give.

With best wishes,

Yours sincerely

MICHAEL O'HALLORAN

PETITION

To the Honourable the Commons of the United Kingdom of Great Britain and
Northern Ireland in Parliament assembled. The Humble Petition of we the
undersigned.

SHEWETH

1. That experimental brain operations (psychosurgery) are being
    performed on mental patients in National Health Service
    hospitals.

2. That the World Health Organization (May 1976) has condemned
    psychosurgery as ethically doubtful due to the uncertainty of
    its results and its lack of a firm theoretical basis.

3. That a U.S. court in 1973 labelled psychosurgery as "clearly
    experimental, poses substantial dangers to research subjects
    and carries substantial unknown risks".

4. That the back wards of our large mental institutions are
    "littered with the wrecks of humanity who, in the heyday of this
    operation 20 years ago, were given little or no option but to
    undergo prefrontal leucotomies for a variety of psychiatric
    conditions". These patients must be maintained with National
    Health Service monies for the rest of their lives.

5. That psychosurgical operations have been performed on mental
    patients for a wide variety of psychiatric conditions from
    homosexuality and gambling to aggression and hyper-activity
    in children.

6. That psychosurgeons disagree on what areas of the brain to
    destroy to bring about the personality changes they are seeking.

7. That there is informed psychiatric opinion in this country that
    there is insufficient knowledge about the brain to justify
    destructive operations upon it.

8. That the use of irreversible procedures on mental patients
    when reversible psychiatric procedures are available is
    unethical.

9. That information on the use of psychosurgery in the U.K. is
    being withheld from the public.

10. That the request by the Royal College of Psychiatrists for
    £50,000 to conduct an experiment involving psychosurgery
    on 100 patients was turned down earlier this year by the
    Medical Research Council as scientifically inadequate.

11. That the Government is to consider changes in the 1959
    Mental Health Act in the next session of Parliament and that
    among the changes to be considered is the ethics of the
    use of irreversible procedures on mental patients.

Wherefore your Petitioners humbly pray that this Honourable House will
bring about an immediate moratorium on the use of psychosurgery in
National Health Service hospitals pending the results of a public inquiry
into its use and results in the U.K.

And your Petitioners, as in duty bound, will ever pray, Etc.

Name   Address

Legislation Passed

REPLY TO:

☐   DISTRICT OFFICE
    2435 FOREST AVENUE
    SAN JOSE, CALIFORNIA 95128
    (408) 241-6900

☐   CAPITOL OFFICE
    ROOM 4144
    STATE CAPITOL
    SACRAMENTO 96814
    TEL: AREA CODE 916
    445-4253

COMMITTEES
    EDUCATION
    CHAIRMAN,
        PERMANENT SUBCOMMITTEE
        ON HIGHER EDUCATION
    HUMAN RESOURCES
    URBAN DEVELOPMENT AND
        HOUSING

Assembly
California Legislature

JOHN VASCONCELLOS
ASSEMBLYMAN, TWENTY-THIRD DISTRICT

◆ 13

Attachment #2 — Components of AB 1032

The major components of AB 1032 are:

1.   Informed Consent — Defines informed consent; prescribes the kinds of information that must be directly communicated to the patient by the doctor regarding the proposed treatment; requires the Department of Health to develop a standard consent form.

2.   Psychosurgery — Defines psychosurgery (those operations, including lobotomy, which are performed for the purposes of modification of behavior, personality, etc., rather than for a physical disease of the brain); requires a three physician review board to review the case and patient and agree unanimously with the treating physician's choice of treatment and that the patient has the ability to give informed consent and has in fact given it according to the bill's requirements; prohibits psychosurgery from being administered to anyone under 18 years of age.

3.   Electro Convulsive Treatment — Defines ECT as any electroconvulsive treatment which depends on the induction of a convulsion by any means.

   a) Involuntary patients — Requires informed consent of patient, plus a review of the patient's treatment record by two physicians (one must have personally examined the patient) who must agree with the treating physician's determination; requires in addition that the patient's attorney or an appointed public defender agrees as to the patient's capacity to give informed consent; if the patient is incapable of giving consent, a court must substantiate that determination and if so, authorize a responsible relative or guardian to give informed consent according to law's requirements.

Attachment # 2 — Components of AB 1032

—2—

b) <u>Voluntary patients</u> — Requires informed consent of patient plus review by one other physician of the patient's <u>ability</u> to give informed consent. If the reviewing physician agrees the patient is capable, no further review may take place and the treatments proceed. If the reviewing physician disagrees, then the patient reverts to the procedures required for an involuntary patient.

c) <u>Minors</u> — ECT is forbidden for minors under 12 years of age. Persons between 12 and 16 may receive ECT only if emergency, lifesaving treatment and a review board of three child psychiatrists agrees with that diagnosis. At that time all other provisions of the bill must also be met.

ECT shall never be performed if the patient is deemed capable of giving informed consent and refuses to to do so.

4.   <u>Postaudit review</u> — There shall be postaudit review of all facilities in which ECT is performed.

5.   <u>Penalties</u> — Physicians who intentionally violate this law are subject to a penalty of not more than $5,000, and such violation shall be grounds for investigation and revocation of license by the Board of Medical Examiners.

6.   <u>Monitoring</u> — Regular reporting (with full protection for confidentiality) of use of such treatments, through director of health.

#   #   #

Drug Rehabilitation Needed

Congress of the United States

House of Representatives

RONALD V. DELLUMS, 7TH DISTRICT, CALIFORNIA

DISTRICT OF COLUMBIA COMMITTEE
CHAIRMAN, SUBCOMMITTEE ON EDUCATION
ARMED SERVICES COMMITTEE

WASHINGTON OFFICE:
1417 LONGWORTH BUILDING
WASHINGTON, D.C. 20515
(202) 225-2661

BARBARA J. WILLIAMS
ADMINISTRATIVE ASSISTANT

DISTRICT OFFICE:
201 13TH STREET, ROOM 105
OAKLAND, CALIFORNIA 94604
(415) 763-0370

DONALD R. HOPKINS
DISTRICT ADMINISTRATOR

24 April 1973

Mr. Greg Zernowich
4955 Desmond Street
Oakland, CA 94608

Dear Mr. Zenowich:

I would like to offer this letter to express my enthusiastic endorsement of the narcotics rehabilitation program operated by Narconon. Having had the opportunity to discuss and study the very unique aspects of this program, I sincerely believe that it has developed a comprehensive approach to the problem of addiction, which, if widely accepted, would represent the first substantial attack on this problem to be mounted in this country. I am particularly impressed with the manner in which the Narconon concept extends itself to those areas of institutional life that are most frequently neglected in the development of social programs, namely the Armed Services and the prison. As supplements to the residential programs, it is my opinion that these additional thrusts carry the rehabilitation programs to an area of human activity that desperately needs to be reached if problems are to be met before they contribute to the burdens already borne by existing programs in urban areas.

There are other aspects of Narconon which I regard as equally remarkable, but which I will not elaborate on here, such as the emphasis upon helping the individual cope with his environment by focusing upon the building of adequate self images, and developing a realistic evaluation of his role as an individual and his responsibilities as a component of the social structure. The fact that many outstanding citizens have volunteered to serve with your organization as members of your Board of Directors and as volunteers in the program is further evidence that you are working effectively and imaginatively to deal with the serious problems of narcotics addiction in this society. I commend you for your efforts, and pledge my good offices to do whatever is within our ability to assist you in any way possible.

Sincerely,

Ronald V. Dellums
Member of Congress

RVD/jyh

EXCERPTS FROM N. HOOD AFFIDAVIT 29 JANUARY 1974

COUNTY OF LOS ANGELES)
) ss
STATE OF CALIFORNIA)

I, Nathan Hood, hereby swear that the following statements are true
to the best of my knowledge.

That I began to use cocaine, methadrine, and heroin in 1961 and
that I became a heroin addict in 1966.

That in the years between 1966 and 1975 I spent a total of 8 years
in and out of various California prisons from Folsom to Tehachapi.

That I learned of the Narconon Drug Rehabilitation Program while an
inmate at California Correctional Institution at Tehachapi.

That since completing and graduating from the Narconon Program, I
have certainty that I will never again use drugs or other narcotic
substances and that I now have more self respect, self confidence,
and the ability to take responsibility for once again becoming a
useful and productive member of society.

BY MY HAND AND SEAL this 31st day of May, 1976.

SUBSCRIBED AND SWORN TO BEFORE ME this _31_ day of May, 1976.

notary public

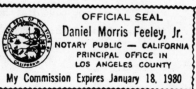

OFFICIAL SEAL
Daniel Morris Feeley, Jr.
NOTARY PUBLIC — CALIFORNIA
PRINCIPAL OFFICE IN
LOS ANGELES COUNTY
My Commission Expires January 18, 1980

Prison Reform Needed

STATUTORY DECLARATION

I, Anthony Blyth of 105 Aberfeldy House, John Ruskin Street,
Camberwell Gate, London do solemnly and sincerely declare as
follows.

1. I was imprisoned in Wormwood Scrubs in December 1966. I was
    released on the 17th of September 1974. During my imprisonment
    I was transferred around 24 times and was detained in several
    prisons including Parkhurst, Wandsworth, Albany, Gartree,
    Hull, Leeds and Maidstone.

2. After I had been in prison only a few weeks, I was given drugs
    named valium, tuinal and chloral after shouting at a prison
    officer. The doctor, whose name I do not remember, said it
    was to calm me down.

3. The number of drugs I was given was gradually increased and
    within one year I was on the following drugs:-

    > Mandrax
    > Librium
    > valium
    > largactil
    > pheno-barbitone
    > tuinal
    > artane
    > chloral

4. Whilst I was on these drugs my body went totally numb and I felt
    like I was floating. I felt really agitated and touchy and would
    blow up over stupid little things. I felt very emotional and out
    of control. The drugs made me shake and I had no grip at all.

5. In Parkhurst in February 1968, several prison officers came into
    my cell. The officers were, Hudson, Watson, Arnell "Punchy" Smith
    and Leurd. They put me naked into a straight jacket and injected
    me in the neck with a long needle. I do not know the name of the
    drug but it made my whole body shake.

6. On the same day, these prison officers, whilst I was in the
    straight jacket, put a long scaffold plank down my back under
    the jacket. The plank with me attached to it, was then propped up
    against the wall at 45 degrees, so that I was facing the floor and
    with my feet not touching the ground. If I moved or coughed the
    plank would fall and I would end up on my face.

7. On one occasion in 1968 whilst I was in Parkhurst, I refused to take the drugs and was put in isolation for refusing. The Medical Officer in Parkhurst was a Dr. Cooper.

8. In October 1969, after the Parkhurst riot, I was so badly beaten that I had to have 47 stitches in my head and on my face.

9. On a few occasions in Parkhurst in 1969 and 1970, Hudson Watson, Arnell, Leurd and "Punchy" Smith urinated in my food and then told me after I had eaten it.

10. When I was in Maidstone Prison in 1973, I had a heart attack whilst on drugs. Previously I had been extremely healthy and an avid sportsman. I had never before had heart trouble.

11. I was given drugs from a few weeks after the beginning of my sentence until the day of my release in September 1974. I am still on the Mogodon and take 7 or 8 a night. I cannot sleep at all without them.

AND I make this solemn declaration conscientiously believing the same to be true and by virtue of the provisions of the Statutory Declarations Act 1835.

Declared at *26/8 Walworth Road*)   *T Blythe*
SE17 ith London Borough of)
Southwark)
This *19ᵗ* day of *April* 1977.)

Before me,

A Commissioner for Oaths.

J. H. Sampson
A Commissioner For Oaths.

Reforms Needed in Treatments of Alcoholics

TRANSLATED EXCERPTS FROM LETTER OF ALCOHOLIC CASE DENMARK.

Name: Rita Moller (case)
Address: Ruten 21, Tingbjerg Bronshoj 2700

1. Has been institutionalized about 30 times through the years.
9. Concerning medicine I have been experimented with - I have had so much
    medicine, that I cannot remember them all. 50 ml truxal times 5 a day
    plus 25 ml Stemetil in 1½ year, where I became so ill of this medicine
    that they thought I was schizophrenic, which I knew I wasn't - it was
    the medicine.

    At last I got 40 different pills a day with 10 different mixtures, and
    all that medicine made me very ill, I was controlled in a way - if I
    was too happy, I had to take pills to get me calmed down, if I was down,
    I got pills to get me up - in an unnatural way.

10. I have received ECT - 12 times. It was a doctor Degn, who gave it
    to me in 1950.

17. The best help one can get as an alcoholic is a place where alcoholics
    can come and be together with other alcoholics who are rehabilitated
    and through communication and group therapy, learn really to understand
    the problem.

    There ought to be real treatment homes, where you of course have to have
    some activities, so that the people have something to do, and these
    committed alcoholics should have a lot of help, as many conversations and
    group therapies by very understanding people, who really want to help
    them, so they get their self confidence back - after the stay there,
    there must be some places where they can go, so they are not tempted
    to start all over again.

    If this help should be available, there must be money available, and they
    can be hard to get and get state support, and help from the commune -
    may be by selling notes, you can win with, or apply for support.

                              Kind regards

                              Rita Moller

                              Rita Moller

Reforms Needed for the Retarded

EXCERPTS FROM H. R. DAVIS
AFFIDAVIT 10 FEBRUARY 1977.

1   Henry R. Davis of San Francisco, California being duly
2   sworn this 10th Day of February, 1977 hereby deposes and says:
3   The following is a statement of the conditions existing at
4   Central State Hospital while I worked there. With this statement
5   I hope to show the general neglect, the low level care and
6   treatment, and some of the abuse of patients that I became aware
7   of.
8   My ward was ward 5 in the Boland Building. This ward was
9   for mentally retarded boys from ages 14 to 18. I worked the night
10 shift from 11 PM until 7 AM. I have also worked with the
11 mentally ill in other wards and buildings of the hospital.
12 Some of the patients were in wretched condition. I have
13 seen patients, one in particular, deteriorate down to nothing.
14 One patient in particular was a 17 year old boy who weighed 69
15 pounds when he died. Nothing was done for these patients except
16 to house them, feed them, drug them and let them outside to
17 play. There was nothing therapeutic being done for them. There
18 was nothing done to raise their ability to care for themselves.
19 Central State Hospital represented a very sad state of
20 affairs. It is a prison for some people. It is a home for others
21 who can not make it anywhere else. The medical care was slip-shod.
22 The patients in the Boland building and in other areas of the
23 hospital were kept tranquilized all the time. Thorazine,
24 Phenobarbital, Mellaril, Ritalin were some of the drugs given.
25 The patients either got stimulants to get them going or tran-
26 quilizers to calm them down.
27 I declare under penalty of perjury that the above
28 statements are true and correct.
29
30
31   Henry R Davis
32   _____
33
34 Subscribed and sworn to before me
35 this 10ᵀᴴ Day of February 1977
36
37   Hilda Lockridge
38 _____
39 Notary Public
40
41
42
43   OFFICIAL SEAL
        HILDA LOCKRIDGE
        NOTARY PUBLIC-CALIFORNIA
44   CITY AND COUNTY
        OF SAN FRANCISCO
45   My Commission Expires Dec. 11, 1979

Reforms Needed for the Aged

<u>AFFIDAVIT</u>

I, Clyde Roach of 1481 Harvard St. N.W., being duly sworn, do hereby affirm that the following statements are true to the best of my knowledge.

My elderly mother, Mrs. Florence A. Roach was forcibly taken to her bank by 3 strangers approximately 6 years ago and forced to withdraw $1500.00 from her savings account for them. She had a nervous breakdown as a result and entered D.C. General Hospital.

Persons at D.C. General Hospital suggested that I place her in St. Elizabeth's Hospital as she was, at times, rather confused. I felt that she might receive good care at St. Elizabeth's so I committed her on the grounds that she was mentally incompetent.

Prior to her admittance to St. Elizabeth's, my mother never needed drugs or medication; however since her admittance to St. Elizabeth's, she has been given constant sedatives by the physicians there. Her bodily needs have also been neglected. Her fingernails were like claws until I recently cut them. Her hair is never oiled now (she is a black woman) and was dry and brittle and breaking off until I visited her and greased it myself. The skin on her shoulders, neck and arms were also very dry until I oiled them. One nurse there acted indignant when I began to groom her. I replied that what I was doing was necessary as no one else was taking care of her properly.

My mother used to have two gold plates in her mouth, one for her upper teeth and one for her lower teeth. These were removed and never returned to her. She was told they would be replaced but never were. This was 3 or 4 years ago. She now has no teeth, as a result.

Her feet are full of corns and callouses but nothing is being done about them by the nurses at the hospital.

My mother broke her hip at the hospital last summer and was placed out of the geriatric building and into another building at St. Elizabeth's to have surgery and have it set. I had to sign the papers for her surgery. She is still sore from this. I believe that a nurse on her geriatric ward broke her hip. It is apparent to me that there could have been no other way that this could have happened. There was a nurse on her ward who was rather mean to her who is no longer there.

My mother continues to live at St. Elizabeth's Hospital. She is not mentally ill and, despite the sedation, quite coherent. She needs to enter a proper home in the community.

I authorize the use of this affidavit by the Gerus Society or any of its assigns for the purpose of protecting other elderly persons from the violation of their personal rights.

Clyde Boaen

Subscribed and
Sworn before me this
_27th_ day of

April , 197_7_

Scarlette P. Gaines
Notary Public

Scarlette P. Gaines
Notary Public of D. C.
My Commission Expires February 14, 1981

Working Towards Legislation

WESTERN SUN

EDITION OF THE EVERETT HERALD

EVERETT, WASHINGTON, WEDNESDAY, MARCH 30, 1977

85th Year No. 76

60 Pages

They didn't like a bill, so they helped to change it

Two young men determined to help prisoners have at least made a dent in the political system of Olympia.

Chris Finn of the Committee to Reinvolve Ex-Offenders and Steve Kozachik, director of the Citizens Commission on Human Rights, have been fighting the original version of HB 13 since it was introduced in mid-January.

The bill pertains to getting treatment — mental and physical — from outside the walls of prison. The "treatment release" program, as outlined in the first bill, put the program in the hands of the superintendent of a correctional institution.

Finn said that merely amounts "to a system whereby the warden could order treatment as a condition of parole," violating the freedom of choice guaranteed even to felons.

The young men got the ear of Rep. Ron Hanna D-Tacoma, who helped them rewrite the bill.

politics

Jack Morgan
political writer

Now there's substitute HB 13, which lists a whole host of protections for prisoners who participate in treatment release.

Two key parts say the prisoner must meet "minimum security requirements" and the treatment program "shall

Wednesday, March 30, 1977, Everett Herald

have previously been demonstrated to be effective, safe and beneficial to persons."

Both Finn and Kozachik have concerns about current psychiatric treatment programs and Finn is preparing a study on the effectiveness of mental programs prisoners participate in.

He says a study by Dr. Arthur Zitrin of New York University School of Medicine shows that people committed to New York's Bellevue Psychiatric Hospital for committed bodily harm increased their commission of such crimes by 200 per cent following treatment and release.

Finn doesn't know about this state's programs, but he's determined to find out and said he expects to complete a report in about a month.

In addition, the young man has been asked by the House Institutions Committee to help write new legislation that will establish genuine rehabilitation centers.

PROPOSED SUBSTITUTE HOUSE BILL NO. 13
2/25/77

1 AN ACT Relating to treatment release; and adding new sections to
2 Chapter 72 RCW.
3 BE IT ENACTED BY THE LEGISLATURE OF THE STATE OF WASHINGTON:
4   NEW SECTION. Section 1. The Secretary of the Department of
5 Social and Health Services is authorized to place on treatment
6 release prisoners convicted of a felony, and committed to the
7 Department of Social and Health Services by the Superior Court.
8 Treatment release shall be permitted under the following conditions.
9   (1) That the prisoner meets minimum security status
10 standards, as prescribed by the Department of Social and Health
11 Services;
12   (2) That application for treatment release is made by the
13 prisoner;
14   (3) That the prisoner gives informed consent to the
15 treatment in writing and prior to such consent;
16   (a) the prisoner be given access to legal counsel upon
17 request; and
18   (b) that he be fully advised of the benefits, possible
19 negative side effects of treatment and consequences of not
20 receiving the treatment.
21   (4) That the prisoner be able to refuse treatment at any
22 time.
23   NEW SECTION. Sec. 2 (1) Treatment employed pursuant to
24 this Act shall have previously demonstrated to be effective,
25 safe and of benefit to persons.
26   (2) Treatment response, and follow-up data shall be
27 collected to facilitate the evaluation of treatment
28 effectiveness.
29   (3) Treatment employed shall be constantly reviewed by a
30 responsible person who shall terminate such treatment when it is
31 deemed no longer of benefit to the prisoner.
32   NEW SECTION. Sec. 3. Records shall be maintained on all
33 treatment administered pursuant to this Act, including informed
34 consent documents. The department of Social and Health Services
35 shall regularly inspect such records to ensure accuracy and
36 completeness. Prisoners shall have reasonable access to
37 treatment records maintained pursuant to this Act.
38   NEW SECTION. Sec. 4. Notwithstanding other provisions of
39 law, participation in treatment release alone shall not effect
40 reduction in the minimum term of sentence as established by the
41 Board of Prison Terms and Paroles.

Responses to Social Reform Reports

STATE OF CALIFORNIA—HEALTH AND WELFARE AGENCY RONALD REAGAN, *Governor*

DEPARTMENT OF HEALTH
CAMARILLO STATE HOSPITAL
BOX "A"
CAMARILLO, CA

March 8, 1974

Reverend G. Bruce Ford
National Chairman
Task Force on Mental Retardation
Church of Scientology
2723 West Temple Street
Los Angeles, California   90026

Dear Bruce:

Thank you for the opportunity to review your report to Governor
Reagan on Mental Retardation in California Part II "Community Ware-
housing on Mental Retardation in California". You have made the
problems of a complex area of the delivery of services to the
mentally retarded very clear. The recommendations on page iii of the
summary and page 30 of the body of the report must certainly be
supported by everyone concerned with the mentally retarded. Your report cannot help but have profound impact on the public and the
legislators. It is a notable contribution to human welfare by the
Task Force on Mental Retardation sponsored by the Church of Scientology
of California.

Some unhappiness might be expressed at the sentence on page ii of the
summary, "There is no doubt that most of these former patients and
retardates are better off in the community under local care than they
were stagnating at the State hospitals...." because we did have individual treatment programs and special training for the mentally retarded even prior to the Regional Center concept and the reorganization
of State hospitals on a program basis. This could be documented by the
Camarillo State Hospital plan for its Mental Retardation Program entitled "Blueprints for Life: Education for Living," which our then
Medical Director, Dr. Louis Nash, circulated in Sacramento prior to

- 2 -

the selection of Camarillo as the location for a new Mental Retardation
Program. This program was actually implemented when we received our
first mentally retarded residents in August of 1967. We have 16 mm
sound and color films of our training programs to document that they
were in no way "stagnating." The body of the report contains much
recognition of the current hospital programs which is appreciated. You
might wish to make it more au courant by reporting the Director of the
Department of Health as Dr. William Mayer replacing Dr. Stubblebine
and some references to current legislation such as AB 2262.

We all support your efforts publicizing the need for workshops for the
mentally retarded and for the establishment of "programs" in community
residential facilities. We will be happy to assist in the establishment
of such programs in any way that we can. Actually at Camarillo we are
already doing this in various ways in association with local board and
care facilities as well as on the larger scale of work with the Area
Boards. One of the most important and satisfying aspects is the joint
effort of both hospital and community. We have long been working to be
considered a part of the community and a phase in the continuum of treatment and training for the developmentally disabled as well as a long-term
resource for the multiply handicapped. It seems as though the hospitals
are finally being regarded in this way and as community resources for
training and assistance in the establishment of programs.

Congratulations on your major production. It reflects the vast amount
of time and effort you have put into its composition. It is very
impressive.

Sincerely,

Jacqueline Montgomery, Ph.D.

Jacqueline Montgomery, Ph.D.
Community Liaison Representative

JM:lf

REPLY TO:

☐   SACRAMENTO OFFICE
STATE CAPITOL
SACRAMENTO, CALIFORNIA 95814
(916) 445-8077

☐   DISTRICT OFFICE
515 VAN NESS AVENUE
SAN FRANCISCO, CALIFORNIA 94102
(415) 557-0784

COMMITTEES
Housing and Community
Development
Human Resources
Transportation

Assembly
California Legislature

WILLIE L. BROWN, JR.
MEMBER OF THE ASSEMBLY, 17TH DISTRICT
SAN FRANCISCO

January 23, 1976

Reverend Dorothy Broaded
Director
The Gerus Society
840 South Carondelet, No. 2
Los Angeles, CA   90057

Dear Reverend Broaded,

I have received your recent letter regarding the
services you provide to aged people of California.
I am familiar with your operation and have nothing
but praise for your efforts in this field.

It goes without saying that you have captured the
essence of effective public advocacy. Your approach
recognizes that a group of individuals united and
dedicated to a cause they really believe in are the
most effective instruments in changing public policy
in California.

I share your concern about the plight of the aged
and stand ready to assist you in any way possible.

Thank you for taking the time to write and I look
forward to hearing from you in the near future. Best
wishes to all of you for the coming year.

Sincerely,

WILLIE L. BROWN, JR.

WLB:agy

131

United States Senate
WASHINGTON, D.C. 20510

October 6, 1975

COMMITTEES:

APPROPRIATIONS
BANKING, HOUSING AND
URBAN AFFAIRS
SPECIAL COMMITTEE ON AGING
SELECT COMMITTEE ON
STANDARDS AND CONDUCT

OFFICES:
2003 F. KENNEDY FEDERAL BLDG.
BOSTON, 02203
617-223-7240

421 OLD SENATE OFFICE BLDG.
WASHINGTON, D.C. 20510
202-224-2742

Mr. Ron Savelo
New England Director
The National Alliance on Alcoholism Prevention
    and Treatment
448 Beacon Street
Boston, Massachusetts   02115

Dear Mr. Savelo:

Thank you for your letter and for sending me a copy of
Alcoholism: Treatment Without Degradation published by NAAPT.

The recommendations for treatment of the alcoholic proposed
by NAAPT are provocative. I share your concern for restoring to
health the many alcoholics who are not able to lead normal lives
because of their drinking problems. I commend you for your work
in this field and I hope you will continue to share your good ideas
with me.

Again, thank you for writing.

Sincerely,

Edward W. Brooke

EWB:md

Effectiveness Revealed

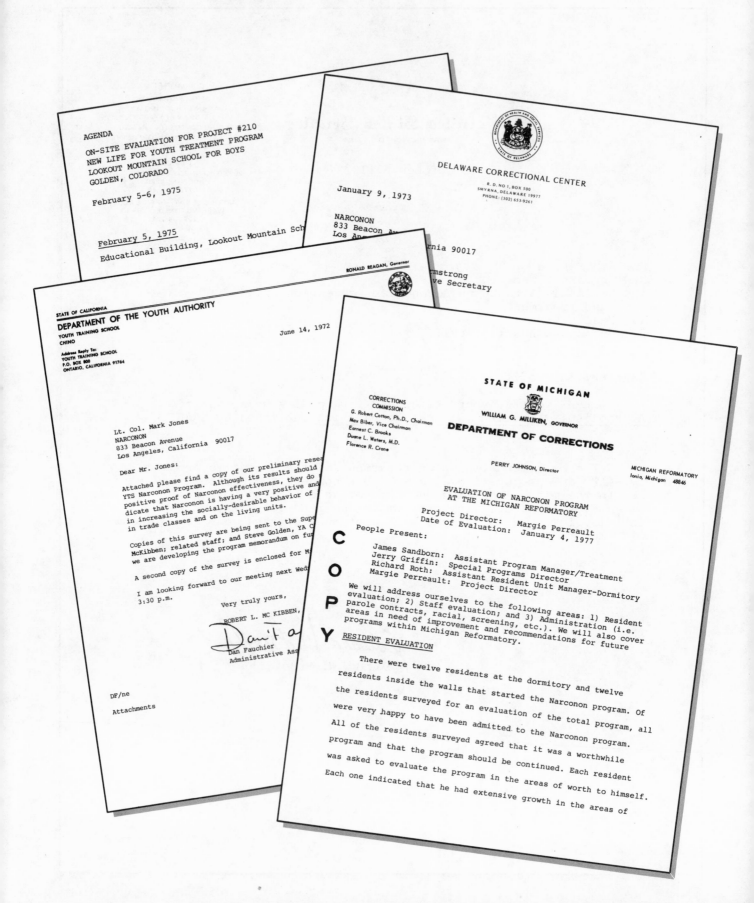

AGENDA
ON-SITE EVALUATION FOR PROJECT #210
NEW LIFE FOR YOUTH TREATMENT PROGRAM
LOOKOUT MOUNTAIN SCHOOL FOR BOYS
GOLDEN, COLORADO

February 5-6, 1975

February 5, 1975

Educational Building, Lookout Mountain Sch

DELAWARE CORRECTIONAL CENTER
R. D. NO 1, BOX 500
SMYRNA, DELAWARE 19977
PHONE: (302) 653-9261

January 9, 1973

NARCONON
833 Beacon A
Los An
ornia 90017

rmstrong
ve Secretary

RONALD REAGAN, Governor

STATE OF CALIFORNIA
DEPARTMENT OF THE YOUTH AUTHORITY
YOUTH TRAINING SCHOOL
CHINO

Address Reply To:
YOUTH TRAINING SCHOOL
P.O. BOX 800
ONTARIO, CALIFORNIA 91764

June 14, 1972

Lt. Col. Mark Jones
NARCONON
833 Beacon Avenue
Los Angeles, California 90017

Dear Mr. Jones:

Attached please find a copy of our preliminary rese
YTS Narconon Program. Although its results should
positive proof of Narconon effectiveness, they do
dicate that Narconon is having a very positive and
in increasing the socially-desirable behavior of
in trade classes and on the living units.

Copies of this survey are being sent to the Supe
McKibben; related staff; and Steve Golden, YA C
we are developing the program memorandum on fu

A second copy of the survey is enclosed for M

I am looking forward to our meeting next Wed
3:30 p.m.

Very truly yours,

ROBERT L. MC KIBBEN,

Dan'ta

Dan Fauchier
Administrative Ass

DF/ne

Attachments

STATE OF MICHIGAN
WILLIAM G. MILLIKEN, GOVERNOR
DEPARTMENT OF CORRECTIONS

CORRECTIONS
COMMISSION
G. Robert Cotton, Ph.D., Chairman
Max Biber, Vice Chairman
Earnest C. Brooks
Duane L. Waters, M.D.
Florence R. Crane

PERRY JOHNSON, Director

MICHIGAN REFORMATORY
Ionia, Michigan 48846

EVALUATION OF NARCONON PROGRAM
AT THE MICHIGAN REFORMATORY

Project Director: Margie Perreault
Date of Evaluation: January 4, 1977

People Present:

James Sandborn: Assistant Program Manager/Treatment
Jerry Griffin: Special Programs Director
Richard Roth: Assistant Resident Unit Manager-Dormitory
Margie Perreault: Project Director

C O P Y

We will address ourselves to the following areas: 1) Resident
evaluation; 2) Staff evaluation; and 3) Administration (i.e.
parole contracts, racial, screening, etc.). We will also cover
areas in need of improvement and recommendations for future
programs within Michigan Reformatory.

RESIDENT EVALUATION

There were twelve residents at the dormitory and twelve
residents inside the walls that started the Narconon program. Of
the residents surveyed for an evaluation of the total program, all
were very happy to have been admitted to the Narconon program.
All of the residents surveyed agreed that it was a worthwhile
program and that the program should be continued. Each resident
was asked to evaluate the program in the areas of worth to himself.
Each one indicated that he had extensive growth in the areas of

EXCERPTS FROM OFFICIAL EVALUATIONS OF NARCONON.

This program has been very beneficial to the residents and staff of the Michigan Reformatory. We have proven that this program can have a definite effect on behavior modes, learning skills, and interpersonal relationships of residents that are in the program. It is hoped that Central Office can add the full expense of this program into the new budget year.

STATE OF MICHIGAN
Evaluation of Narconon Program
January 4, 1977
Page Nine

CONCLUSION

1. Of the Experimental Group all were doing well in terms of the criteria of rehabilitation.

2. The Control Group was not doing well in terms of the four criteria of rehabilitation.

3. The Narconon rehabilitation programme does substantiate its claims and as other lay groups appeals to its clientele on the factors of workability towards the varied personality differences it must treat.

NARCONON DRUG REHABILITATION
PROGRAM EVALUATION
A follow up Study
SARAH M.E. HEWITT B.A. PSYCHOLOGY
CUM LAUDE

The experimental group of Narconon participants showed an observable, measurable
... decrease in incidents of misbehavior, and
... increase in positive school behavior

to a greater degree than did the control group

DEPARTMENT OF THE YOUTH AUTHORITY
State of California
Youth Training School Chino

Education, the Solution to a Country's Problems

EXCERPTS FROM EDUCATION ALIVE SUCCESS STORIES.

With dignity and pride, I express my sincere gratitude to Ron Hubbard for his wonderful methods in his study technology.

Difficulties are not encountered by teachers alone but by children as well. For the children the technology is a real master, for they actually realise that the classroom actually belongs to them.

Once more I say "Bravo" to Education Alive for gone are the days when children were deprived of their privilege to prove their worth.

> M.K. Mampuru
> Vice-Principal
> Maetjiebulo Higher Primary School

Follow up action on fifteen of the students shows most pleasing results already. It is clear to me that Education Alive technique is bound to produce a most pleasing revolution in Education. Children are able to work with profit for long, long hours. During a one-week long teach-in, up to five weeks work has been done by the children.

> Mr. A.M. Murashiki
> National Secretary
> Rhodesian African Teachers Association

As a teacher the EDUCATION ALIVE children's course has done wonders to me. I now feel that I am a bold, confident and eager teacher.

I believe I will never have any difficulty in helping out children in their study. The technology of this course will also be used in the family.

Long live the Education Alive Children's course. The course deserves its name - EDUCATION ALIVE.

> Mabataung Makhalemele
> from the first Teachers
> Course held in Lesotho.

Already I notice a decrease in absenteeism from my maths classes. Children who used to arrive reluctantly and who were too bored to attend at all now come willingly and on time. I have in my class children who failed last year and are now repeating the subject, as well as those who are in my class for the first time; already I notice that those repeating are working better and grasping faster than those who are considered to be brighter.

> Mr. R.A. Feldman
> Eersterust High School
> Eersterust
> March 23, 1977

Expansion of Education Alive

In March 1976 Education Alive stepped into South
Africa to bring education to a troubled country.
Since then it has expanded to 44 schools and 223
teachers finished the "Teacher's Course".

SUCCESS STORY

Three cheers to the originator and the person who was responsible
for the title of this field of study. For there is none other
more fitting. The result of this study is what the name implies.
It turns the ignition on, as it were, the inanimate becomes
alive, real and full of meaning.

Personally I have had innumerable gains, of which I would like
to make mention of only three, that to me are of prime importance. Firstly, it has boosted my morale to such an extent that
I feel quite confident to confront and successfully handle any
problem that might come my way, be what it may. Secondly, it
has brought me to the realisation that the human mind has full
control over the physical body. Thus, one is able to determine
one's fate. Thirdly, as a teacher, it has become very real to
me that whatever I try to impart to the students, for whose
progress I am responsible, can only become real to them if every
single word has been understood and mastered. Only then can the
information become useful and be applied in everyday life.

Once again, may the saints responsible for the spread of
Education Alive have great success in getting these facts
known to every living human being on Earth. It would, like a
magic wand, turn Hades into a living Paradise.

                              Ruth E. Williams
                              from the first course
                              run in Cape Town for
                              Coloured Teachers.

What the Children Think

SUCCESS STORY

EFFECTIVE EDUCATION ASSOCIATION

NAME: Murray Ewing

ACTION COMPLETED: Study course

I liked the course. I like studying. I know about misunderstoods and not understoods and if I get mixed up I'll look the word up in the dictionary and make sentences. It will help me at want to do will know h studying.

I hereby give my permiss
in whole or in part, or
of the publications of t

SIGNATURE: Murray

ADDRESS: 'Daledene'
East

FORENINGEN FOR
FFEKTIV GRUNDUDDANNELSE

SUCCES   Dato: 13/10

Marianne Nielsen 12 år

ordbogskursus

det er gået så godt jeg er så glad for at jeg blev
fordi jeg har tænkt mig at bruge det alle
steder jeg er, og jeg kommer snart igen,
komme her igen og jeg
af det jeg har
ordbog og have
min mor
af de svære ord.

ianne

APPLIED SCHOLASTICS
SUCCESS

name Cynthia Temple
action Dictionary Course   date 6-23-77

I really liked taking the
Dictionary Course. It helped
me to spell better and understand
better. I'm happy!

YOU HAVE MY PERMISSION TO PUBLISH THIS SUCCESS STORY
IN FULL OR IN PART.

I feel that I am now a better, clever student, and will face schooling with a smile. This term my friends will see a new Clement and be surprised with what I am going to do, because I am going to try not to fail one class test in future, and I am going to please my teachers with my work, and do my homework regular, and study more often so that I may become a clever student and a smart one.

Clement Stander
Eersterust High School

I am very grateful for taking up this course, because I have learned a lot especially the art of how to study. I always had the problem of how to study, now I am glad I took up the course for I have learned very much and which I will not easily forget.

I have now learned how to study by using a study kit and that also helps me not forget the things which I have studied.

Glenrose Watsmann
Eersterust High School

I have not only been educated, but been kept out of the street and mischief. The only thing I disliked was to stop working.

Johnny Haes
Eersterust High School

In the future I will use all the things that I learned in this course, and I will see to it that my friends will follow my footsteps and we will improve in the subjects we wrote before this course.

I think if it was not for the friendly and helpful supervisors I would not have learnt as much as I have learnt now.

Nadine Roberts
Eersterust High School

After ten years of not knowing anything, I'm finally learning how to spell and read. Thanks to everyone.

Dana Steely

The Learn How to Learn Course has showed me how to learn by myself and I really enjoyed the course.

L. Ron Hubbard must be a real smart man.

David Cantrell

What the Parents Think

EXCERPTS FROM PARENTS' SUCCESS STORIES

I'm delighted to have this opportunity to relay to anyone who will give me an hour or two, the fantastic results and wonderful changes that have occurred in my son Fred Arcoraci since his attendance to Applied Scholastics Inc.

Now the results are just incredible, not only is he happy about going but he smiles. He is looking forward to *returning* to school. Isn't that *great!!*
— Connie Boyle

In June of this year Matthew completed the study course at EEA [Effective Education Association] where he learnt to understand and apply the study technology of L. Ron Hubbard.

I noticed a considerable improvement in his ability to understand the meanings of words and to study.

His school work improved greatly following this and he became more confident in his ability to do it.

In September he was readily accepted for his new school and has shown himself to be one of the more able pupils in his class.
— Mark D. Roberts

Alexander has just completed ten hours of reading coaching at EEA. His main problem before he began was that he had been away from school for about three weeks at the beginning of last term, and had fallen behind the rest of the class in his reading, which upset him a great deal.

After the first four hours of coaching, he had caught up with the rest of the class, but more importantly, his own confidence had returned, and he was really enjoying reading again. Over the past two weeks, I have observed that most days when he gets home from school, he will pick up a book and start reading to me, without any suggestion from me. This he would never have done before.

I am delighted with the progress he has made, not only with the actual reading itself, but with his enjoyment of going to EEA, and his enthusiasm about learning generally.   — R.M. Allen

Thank you so much for helping Stephen to really enjoy reading. Previously he had shown no interest in wanting to read, but after just one hour of coaching he was enthusiastic, happy and very eager to communicate thoughts and ideas. It is indeed a miracle to realize that learning can be fun and to see how study technology can produce enthusiasm for wanting to continue with a subject that previously had created difficulties.
— Christine Yardley (Mrs.)

EXCERPTS FROM TEACHERS' SUCCESS STORIES

The things I have gained from this course are innumerable. It has revolution-ized my entire being and I have emerged from it as if mentally re-born. I shall always consider my mental life as consisting of a period before the course and one after it. The world outside looks different from what it was before; it is brighter, clearer and more enjoyable to live in.

Now I know how much talent is locked up in every head — and I intend to reveal the talents of every pupil in my hands and tap it out for use in the entire world.

> — P.E.O. Rikhotse
> Principal, Alexandra High School
> Johannesburg, 7th April, 1977

This has been a great course for me. Apart from the considerable personal win of seeing I can make this work, I am fired with enthusiasm for the whole scheme and can see it will have revolutionary effects on our educational sys-tem and whole social structure as a result.

> — Dianne Kirby
> The Old Rectory
> Shelfanger, Diss. Norfolk

A subject I hated as a student I had to teach to pupils. It was awful. I was al-ways trying to avoid having to do it. Finally I used the idea of applying mass. It clicked. And now I can proudly state that both class and myself enjoy that particular subject tremendously.

My only dissatisfaction is that it should have been here sooner for I have wasted so many years. Thank you.

> — Ameen Lagardien
> Capetown Teacher
> 1976

10

Date Chronology of Scientology

Dates of Pioneer Movements in Expansion

The first Church of Scientology was registered in 1954. Even prior to this date and subsequently, pioneer movements in many countries have resulted in Scientology becoming known and established in the following countries:

Date	Country	Date	Country	Date	Country	Date	Country
1950	United States	1968	Sweden	1973	El Salvador	1976	Ghana
1950	Canada	1969	Germany	1973	Greenland	1976	Guam
1950	Scotland	1969	Greece	1973	Puerto Rico	1976	Hungary
1951	Australia	1969	Mexico	1974	Finland	1976	Italy
1952	Israel	1970	Brazil	1974	Nigeria	1976	Peru
1952	New Zealand	1970	Guatemala	1974	Switzerland	1976	Portugal
1953	England	1971	Austria	1974	West Indies	1976	Spain
1954	France	1971	Colombia	1975	Botswana	1976	Uruguay
1955	South Africa	1971	Wales	1975	Chile	1978	Costa Rica
1956	India	1972	Belgium	1975	Kenya	1978	Pakistan
1958	Norway	1972	Holland	1975	Philippines	1978	Saudi Arabia
1965	Japan	1973	Argentina	1975	Turkey	1978	Tahiti
1965	Rhodesia	1973	Bolivia	1975	Venezuela	1978	Zambia
1967	Denmark	1973	Czechoslovakia	1975	Yugoslavia		

Significant Dates in Scientology
Organization Development

1950 HUBBARD DIANETIC RESEARCH FOUNDATION, the first organization of Dianetics in the United States, located until 1951 in Elizabeth, New Jersey. This organization name was shortened by a successor corporation, the Hubbard Dianetic Foundation of Wichita, Kansas. Later it was reincorporated in Arizona and the original name, Hubbard Dianetic Research Foundation, was restored.

1951 FIRST TRAINING CENTER. L. Ron Hubbard trained Hubbard Dianetic Auditors in Wichita, Kansas.

FIRST OFFICE. Later, the above center of training was moved to Phoenix, Arizona which was the first office of Scientology that L. Ron Hubbard established. In 1954 it became the Hubbard Association of Scientologists International (HASI).

18 Feb. 1954 Church of Scientology of Los Angeles was founded.

28 Feb. 1954 Church of Scientology of Auckland was founded.

1954 ACADEMY TRAINING was fully established in Washington, D. C.

21 Jul. 1955 Founding Church of Scientology of Washington, D. C. was founded.

15 Nov. 1955 Church of Scientology of New York was founded.

11 Mar. 1957 Church of Scientology of Miami was founded.

11 Nov. 1957 Church of Scientology of Johannesburg was founded.

1 Dec. 1958 Church of Scientology of Durban was founded.

Spring 1959 SAINT HILL MANOR was purchased by L. Ron Hubbard. Located in East Grinstead, Sussex, England, it was to be used as a residence for him while in England and by HCO Worldwide as the communication center of Scientology.

1959 SCIENTOLOGY WORLDWIDE MANAGEMENT CONTROL CENTER was established at Saint Hill Manor.

1959 Church of Scientology Worldwide was founded.

26 Oct. 1959 Church of Scientology of Paris was founded.

19 Nov. 1959 INTERNATIONAL COUNCIL for Dianetics and Scientology was appointed to ensure the smooth running of Dianetics and Scientology throughout the world.

20 Jun. 1960 HUBBARD ASSOCIATION OF SCIENTOLOGISTS INTERNATIONAL UNITED KINGDOM was incorporated.

20 Jun. 1960 Hubbard Scientology Organization of London was founded.

20 Jun. 1960 HASI was established in Cape Town, South Africa.

30 Dec. 1960 HCO LTD was incorporated in the United States.

28 Jan. 1961 Church of Scientology of Cape Town was founded.

Apr. 1962 Church of Scientology of Port Elizabeth was founded.

26 Sep. 1962 HUBBARD SCIENTOLOGY RESEARCH FOUNDATION was established to further Scientology research.

4 Nov. 1963 Church of Scientology of Detroit was founded.

23 Nov. 1963 HASI LONDON was incorporated.

24 Jan. 1964 SCIENTOLOGY LIBRARY AND RESEARCH LTD. was established to safeguard and preserve all Scientology materials.

8 Dec. 1964 Church of Scientology of Hawaii was founded.

11 Jun. 1965 Hubbard College of Scientology Saint Hill Foundation was founded. Subsequently Foundations were established in all Scientology Organizations.

14 Oct. 1965 COLLEGE OF SCIENTOLOGY was formed with headquarters at Saint Hill in Sussex, England.

1 Jan. 1966 Church of Scientology of Seattle was founded.

1 Mar. 1966 THE GUARDIAN post was established. The purpose of the Guardian is: To help L. Ron Hubbard enforce and issue policy, and to safeguard Scientology orgs, Scientologists and Scientology.
ASSISTANT GUARDIAN post was created and to be appointed only by the Guardian.

1 Mar. 1966 Church of Scientology of California Worldwide Guardian's Office was established.

1966 Church of Scientology of California United States Guardian's Office was established.

1 Sep. 1966 FOUNDER L. Ron Hubbard resigned from the Board of Directors and post of Executive Director and was given the title Founder, to continue his writing and research.

11 Nov. 1966 Church of Scientology of Twin Cities was founded.

27 Jun. 1967 Church of Scientology of Austin, Texas was founded.

12 Aug. 1967 THE SEA ORGANIZATION was officially established. The Sea Organization is a fraternal organization existing within the formalized structure of the Churches of Scientology.

8 Sep. 1967 Church of Scientology of Toronto was founded.

18 Sep. 1967   Church of Scientology of Bulawayo was founded.

16 Nov. 1967   SAINT HILL MANOR was purchased by the Church of Scientology from L. Ron Hubbard.

27 Nov. 1967   The first Scientology Publications Organization was established in Saint Hill Manor, England.

27 Dec. 1967   ADVANCED ORGANIZATION was begun aboard the *Royal Scotman*. (This ship was later renamed the *Apollo*.)

23 May 1968   ADVANCED ORGANIZATION, EDINBURGH, Scotland was established to deliver Clear, OT I, II, III, IV, V and VI.

17 Jun. 1968   Church of Scientology of San Francisco was founded.

17 Jun. 1968   Hubbard Academy of Personal Independence of Edinburgh was founded.

Jun. 1968   Scientology Publications Organization moved from Saint Hill Manor to Edinburgh, Scotland.

5 Aug. 1968   ADVANCED ORGANIZATION expanded to Los Angeles, California.

13 Aug. 1968   AMERICAN SAINT HILL ORGANIZATION opened in Los Angeles, California.

31 Oct. 1968   Church of Scientology of Las Vegas was founded.

5 Nov. 1968   Church of Scientology of Denmark was founded.

12 Dec. 1968   Church of Scientology of Pretoria was founded.

1969   Church of Scientology of Denver was founded.

31 Jan. 1969   Church of Scientology of Adelaide was founded.

14 Feb. 1969   Publications Organization moved from Edinburgh to Copenhagen, Denmark.

16 Apr. 1969   Church of Scientology of Goteborg was founded.

7 Jul. 1969   ADVANCED ORGANIZATION DENMARK was founded to service the European and African areas.

7 Jul. 1969   Church of Scientology of Saint Hill Europe was founded.

17 Jul. 1969   Church of Scientology Celebrity Centre of Los Angeles was founded, to service celebrities.

22 Jul. 1969   Church of Scientology of Copenhagen was founded.

17 Aug. 1970   ADVANCED ORGANIZATION UNITED KINGDOM moved from Edinburgh, Scotland to Saint Hill, Sussex, England.

15 Oct. 1970   Church of Scientology of Munich was founded.

13 Nov. 1970   FLAG MANAGEMENT BUREAU was established as the key management body of the Sea Organization to oversee the completion of approved plans, programs and targets.

19 Nov. 1970   CONTINENTAL LIAISON OFFICES (CLOs) were established as the central authority for their areas through which all orders to an organization were channeled.

20 Jan. 1971   Hubbard Scientology Organization of Plymouth was founded.

11 Feb. 1971   Church of Scientology Publications Organization U.S. (formerly a liaison office) became fully established as an organization.

22 Feb. 1971   Hubbard College of Scientology Advanced Organization Saint Hill United Kingdom was established.

9 Mar. 1971   Church of Scientology of Buffalo was founded.

13 Mar. 1971   Church of Scientology of Boston was founded.

31 Mar. 1971   Church of Scientology of Vienna was founded.

31 Mar. 1971   Church of Scientology of Stockholm was founded.

13 Apr. 1971   Church of Scientology of San Diego was founded.

19 Aug. 1971   FLAG REPRESENTATIVE NETWORK was established, the purpose of which is: To safeguard that those actions necessary to the prosperity of an area or org are implemented and continued.

14 Sep. 1971   Church of Scientology of Portland, Oregon was founded.

27 Jan. 1972   Church of Scientology of St. Louis was founded.

21 Mar. 1972   Church of Scientology of Sydney was founded.

6 Jun. 1972   Church of Scientology of Vancouver was founded.

18 Aug. 1972   Church of Scientology of Malmo was founded.

17 Oct. 1972   Church of Scientology of Perth was founded.

8 Nov. 1972   Flag Operations Liaison Office West U.S. was established.

8 Nov. 1972   Flag Operations Liaison Office East U.S. was established.

12 Dec. 1972   Church of Scientology of Melbourne was founded.

1972-1973   FLAG OPERATIONS LIAISON OFFICES (FOLOs) were established in the place of Continental Liaison Offices (CLOs). FOLOs were established for Eastern United States, Western United States, United Kingdom, Europe, ANZO (Australia, New Zealand, Oceania) and Africa.

6 Sep. 1973   Church of Scientology of Amsterdam was founded.

Nov. 1973   Pacific Area Estates Hotel Organization for Scientologists was established.

144

WHAT IS SCIENTOLOGY?

12 Mar. 1974	Hubbard Scientology Organization of Manchester was founded.
13 Mar. 1974	Church of Scientology of Montreal was founded.
13 Mar. 1974	Church of Scientology of Ottawa was founded.
22 Mar. 1974	Church of Scientology of Sacramento was founded.
13 Mar. 1975	Church of Scientology of Chicago was founded.
16 Mar. 1975	Church of Scientology of Philadelphia was founded.
15 Apr. 1975	Church of Scientology Universal Media Productions was established.
6 Dec. 1975	FLAG LAND BASE. Flag moved from the Flagship *Apollo* to the Fort Harrison Hotel in Clearwater, Florida. Here, the Flag Service Organization is known as the "Mecca of Technical Perfection" and is available to Scientologists all over the world.
6 Dec. 1975	Flag Land Base Estates Organization was established to cater to the needs of public and staff of the Flag Land Base.
5 Feb. 1977	LRH COMMUNICATOR NETWORK INTERNATIONAL was established in Los Angeles, California, ensuring that the technology and policies of the Founder are applied, and applied correctly.
Feb. 1977	Cedars Complex was purchased by the Church of Scientology as a major centre for Scientology in the Los Angeles area.
27 Sep. 1977	The first of the Los Angeles Service Organizations, Church of Scientology of Los Angeles, moved into Cedars Complex.
8 Dec. 1977	Cedars Complex Estates Service Organization was established.
12 Feb. 1978	The pattern and duties of the LRH COMMUNICATOR NETWORK INTERNATIONAL were streamlined. Powers and command channels of the network were finalized and laid down in policy.

Founding Dates of Missions of the Church

WESTERN UNITED STATES

Date Founded

25 Feb. 1971	Mission of Los Gatos, Los Gatos, California
25 Jun. 1971	Mission of Riverside, Riverside, California
15 Sep. 1971	Mission of Berkeley, Berkeley, California
15 Sep. 1971	Mission of Davis, Davis, California
15 Sep. 1971	Mission of Phoenix, Phoenix, Arizona
15 Sep. 1971	Mission of the Meadows, Las Vegas, Nevada
27 Oct. 1971	Mission of Albuquerque, Albuquerque, New Mexico
27 Oct. 1971	Mission of Tucson, Tucson, Arizona
1 Dec. 1971	Mission of Orange County, Tustin, California
20 Jan. 1972	Mission of Richardson, Richardson, Texas
20 Jan. 1972	Mission of Salt Lake City, Salt Lake City, Utah
8 Feb. 1972	Mission of Westwood-Wilshire, Los Angeles, California
25 Feb. 1972	Mission of Honolulu, Honolulu, Hawaii
23 Mar. 1972	Adams Avenue Mission, San Diego, California
19 Apr. 1972	Mission of South Bay, Redondo Beach, California
24 Apr. 1972	Mission of El Paso, El Paso, Texas
9 Nov. 1972	Mission of the Valley, Sherman Oaks, California
2 Jan. 1973	Mission of Palo Alto, Palo Alto, California
2 Jan. 1973	Mission of Sacramento, Carmichael, California
2 Feb. 1973	Mission of Castro Valley, Castro Valley, California
2 Feb. 1973	Mission of Chula Vista, Chula Vista, California
2 Apr. 1973	Mission of Davis-Sacramento, Sacramento, California
1 Jun. 1973	Mission of East Bay, Oakland, California
29 Nov. 1973	Mission of Amarillo, Amarillo, Texas
29 Nov. 1973	Mission of Walnut Creek, Walnut Creek, California
7 Dec. 1973	Mission of Houston, Houston, Texas
7 Dec. 1973	Mission of Pasadena, Pasadena, California
10 Jan. 1974	Mission of Boulder, Boulder, Colorado
10 Jan. 1974	Mission of Lake Tahoe, South Lake Tahoe, California
10 Jan. 1974	Mission of the Southwest, Dallas, Texas
15 Feb. 1974	Mission of Long Beach, Long Beach, California
21 Mar. 1974	Mission of Davis-Portland, Portland, Oregon
21 Mar. 1974	Mission of Davis-Sheridan, Sheridan, Oregon
21 Mar. 1974	Mission of Santa Clara, San Jose, California
5 Apr. 1974	Mission of Fresno, Fresno, California
24 Jul. 1974	Mission of Washoe Valley, Reno, Nevada
10 Sep. 1974	Mission of Colorado Springs, Colorado Springs, Colorado

10 Sep. 1974	Mission of Golden Gate, San Francisco, California
12 Sep. 1974	Mission of Las Vegas, Las Vegas, Nevada
10 Jan. 1975	Mission of Santa Rosa, Santa Rosa, California
10 Apr. 1975	Mission of Anchorage, Anchorage, Alaska
11 Apr. 1975	Mission of San Antonio, San Antonio, Texas
16 Sep. 1975	Mission of Burbank, Burbank, California
16 Sep. 1975	Mission of Santa Barbara, Santa Barbara, California
30 Oct. 1975	Mission of Santa Fe, Santa Fe, New Mexico
15 Jan. 1976	Mission of Mountain View, Mountain View, California
4 Mar. 1976	Mission of Steamboat Springs, Steamboat Springs, Colorado
11 Mar. 1976	Mission of Vista, Vista, California
24 Jun. 1976	Mission of Edmond, Edmond, Oklahoma
24 Jun. 1976	Mission of San Francisco, San Francisco, California
1 Jul. 1976	Mission of Chico, Chico, California
12 Aug. 1976	Mission of Monterey-Carmel, Monterey, California
16 Sep. 1976	Mission of Reseda, Canoga Park, California
24 Feb. 1977	Mission of Los Feliz, Los Angeles, California
13 Mar. 1977	Mission of Stockton, Stockton, California
17 Mar. 1977	Mission of Manhattan Beach, Manhattan Beach, California
24 Mar. 1977	Mission of Wilshire, Los Angeles, California
21 Apr. 1977	Mission of Phoenix, Phoenix, Arizona
2 Jun. 1977	Mission of Greeley, Greeley, Colorado
9 Jun. 1977	Mission of Beverly Hills, Los Angeles, California
6 Oct. 1977	Mission of San Mateo, San Mateo, California
10 Nov. 1977	Mission of San Luis Obispo, San Luis Obispo, California
5 Jan. 1978	Mission of Bellevue, Bellevue, Washington
5 Jan. 1978	Mission of Kentfield, Kentfield, California

EASTERN UNITED STATES

29 Jun. 1971	Mission of Cambridge, Cambridge, Massachusetts
3 Jan. 1972	Mission of Delaware Valley, Marlton, New Jersey
20 Jan. 1972	Mission of New York, New York, New York
20 Jan. 1972	Mission of Orlando, Orlando, Florida
23 Mar. 1972	Mission of Flemington, Flemington, New Jersey
22 Jun. 1972	Mission of Cleveland, Cleveland Heights, Ohio
2 Jan. 1973	Mission of Westchester, Putnam Valley, New York

1 May 1973	Mission of Fort Lauderdale, Fort Lauderdale, Florida
1 Jun. 1973	Mission of Charlotte, Charlotte, North Carolina
1 Jun. 1973	Mission of Waterbury, Waterbury, Connecticut
7 Dec. 1973	Mission of Fifth Avenue, New York, New York
21 Mar. 1974	Mission of Erie, Erie, Pennsylvania
19 Aug. 1974	Mission of Albany, Albany, New York
10 Sep. 1974	Mission of Putney, Putney, Vermont
10 Sep. 1974	Mission of New Britain, Berlin, Connecticut
10 Oct. 1974	Mission of Elmira, Elmira, New York
17 Oct. 1974	Mission of East Manhattan, New York, New York
10 Dec. 1974	Mission of Arlington, Arlington, Virginia
1 Jan. 1975	Mission of Cincinnati, Cincinnati, Ohio
8 May 1975	Mission of Columbus, Columbus, Ohio
15 May 1975	Mission of New London, Groton, Connecticut
27 Aug. 1975	Mission of New Haven, Woodbridge, Connecticut
16 Oct. 1975	Mission of Van Hornesville, Van Hornesville, New York
8 Dec. 1975	Mission of Bayshore, Bayshore, New York
4 Mar. 1976	Mission of Atlanta, Atlanta, Georgia
25 Mar. 1976	Mission of Tampa, Tampa, Florida
2 Apr. 1976	Mission of Marshfield, Marshfield, Massachusetts
4 Jun. 1976	Mission of Washington, Washington, D.C.
10 Jun. 1976	Mission of Coral Gables, Coral Gables, Florida
9 Sep. 1976	Mission of Baton Rouge, Baton Rouge, Louisiana
6 Nov. 1976	Mission of Bethesda, Bethesda, Maryland
16 Dec. 1976	Mission of Toledo, Toledo, Ohio
30 Dec. 1976	Mission of Virginia Beach, Virginia Beach, Virginia
9 Jun. 1977	Mission of Palm Beach, West Palm Beach, Florida
14 Jun. 1977	Mission of Worcester, Worcester, Massachusetts
29 Sep. 1977	Mission of Rochester, Rochester, New York
22 Dec. 1977	Mission of Dayton, Dayton, Ohio
22 Dec. 1977	Mission of North Manhattan, New York, New York

CENTRAL UNITED STATES

15 Sep. 1971	Mission of Chicago, Villa Park, Illinois
15 Sep. 1971	Mission of Peoria, Peoria, Illinois

27 Oct. 1971	Mission of Lakeview, Chicago, Illinois
27 Oct. 1971	Mission of Omaha, Omaha, Nebraska
26 Oct. 1972	Mission of Anderson, Anderson, Indiana
2 Feb. 1973	Mission of Kansas City, Kansas City, Missouri
14 Dec. 1973	Mission of New Hope, Minneapolis, Minnesota
15 Feb. 1974	Mission of Huron Valley, Ann Arbor, Michigan
13 Jun. 1974	Mission of Carbondale, Carbondale, Illinois
27 Mar. 1975	Mission of St. Charles, St. Charles, Missouri
13 May 1976	Mission of Champaign-Urbana, Champaign, Illinois
20 Jan. 1977	Mission of Birmingham, Birmingham, Michigan
24 Mar. 1977	Mission of Racine, Racine, Wisconsin
7 Apr. 1977	Mission of Milwaukee, Milwaukee, Wisconsin
2 Jun. 1977	Mission of Highland Park, Highland Park, Illinois
8 Sep. 1977	Mission of Indianapolis, Indianapolis, Indiana
12 Jan. 1978	Mission of Flint, Flint, Michigan

CANADA

23 Mar. 1972	Mission of Vancouver, Vancouver, British Columbia
28 Aug. 1974	Mission of Windsor, Windsor, Ontario
22 May 1975	Mission of Edmonton, Edmonton, Alberta
22 Apr. 1976	Mission of York, Toronto, Ontario
28 Jul. 1976	Mission of London, London, Ontario
27 Oct. 1977	Mission of Ontario, Kitchener, Ontario
12 Jan. 1978	Mission of Quebec, Quebec
3 May 1978	Mission of Calgary, Calgary, Alberta

UNITED KINGDOM

29 Jan. 1970	Mission of Birmingham, Moseley, Birmingham, England
1 Aug. 1970	Mission of Helensburgh, Helensburgh, Dunbartonshire, Scotland
15 Sep. 1971	Mission of Swansea, Glamorgan, Wales
20 Jan. 1972	Mission of Southampton, Botley, Hants, England
18 Sep. 1975	Mission of Leeds, Leeds, Yorkshire, England
6 Nov. 1975	Mission of Hove, Hove, Sussex, England
9 Sep. 1976	Mission of Bristol, Bristol, Avon, England
15 Sep. 1976	Mission of York, York, England

EUROPE

9 Nov. 1971	Mission of Le Bois D'Oingt, Le Bois D'Oingt, France

13 May 1972	Mission of Munich, Munich, West Germany
30 Oct. 1972	Mission of Brabant, Brussels, Belgium
5 Jun. 1973	Mission of Franken, Heilbronn, West Germany
29 Nov. 1973	Mission of Hamburg, Hamburg, West Germany
21 Mar. 1974	Mission of Frankfurt, Frankfurt, West Germany
21 Mar. 1974	Mission of Versailles, Versailles, France
10 Sep. 1974	Mission of Angers, Angers, France
10 Oct. 1974	Mission of Frankfurt am Main, Frankfurt am Main, West Germany
21 Nov. 1974	Mission of Bern, Bern, Switzerland
10 Dec. 1974	Mission of Helsingborg, Helsingborg, Sweden
28 Aug. 1975	Mission of Basel, Basel, Switzerland
28 Aug. 1975	Mission of Zurich, Wirkel, Switzerland
19 Sep. 1975	Mission of Haldenstrasse, Luzern, Switzerland
25 Sep. 1975	Mission of Geneva, Geneva, Switzerland
25 Sep. 1975	Mission of Lucerne, Lucerne, Switzerland
25 Sep. 1975	Mission of Vienna, Wien, Austria
2 Mar. 1976	Mission of Lowenstrasse, Zurich, Switzerland
2 Mar. 1976	Mission of Neue Bruecke, Stuttgart, West Germany
4 Mar. 1976	Mission of Stuttgart, Stuttgart, West Germany
3 Jun. 1976	Mission of Nymphenburg, Munich, West Germany
29 Jul. 1976	Mission of Lyngby, Lyngby, Denmark
16 Sep. 1976	Mission of Fribourg, Fribourg, Switzerland
2 Dec. 1976	Mission of Arhus, Arhus, Denmark
24 Mar. 1977	Mission of Horgen, Horgen, Switzerland
26 May 1977	Mission of Lyon-Sarcey, Le Chana-Sarcey, France
23 Jun. 1977	Mission of Köln, Hansaring, West Germany
14 Jul. 1977	Mission of Brussels, Brussels, Belgium
13 Oct. 1977	Mission of Hässleholm, Hässleholm, Sweden
10 Nov. 1977	Mission of Klosterstrasse, Klosterstrasse, West Germany

AUSTRALIA AND NEW ZEALAND

20 Feb. 1972	Mission of Melville, Melville, West Australia
21 Feb. 1972	Mission of Christchurch, Christchurch, New Zealand
10 Dec. 1974	Mission of Ellerslie, Auckland, New Zealand

PUERTO RICO

26 May 1977	Mission of Puerto Rico, San Turce, Puerto Rico

AFRICA

12 Jul.	1977	Scientology and Dianetics Center, Johannesburg, South Africa
14 Jul.	1977	Mission of Johannesburg, Sydenham, Johannesburg, South Africa

SOUTH PACIFIC

7 Apr.	1977	Mission of Guam, Agana, Guam

Dates of Church Contributions to Social Reform

The following includes contributions by individuals and organizations outside the Church, who use the technology of Scientology.

19 Feb. 1966   Narconon founded for the reduction of crime and drug abuse in the United States.

Aug. 1968   *Freedom*, Scientology's independent newspaper founded.

Dec. 1968   Citizens Commission on Human Rights, United Kingdom, founded.

1969   Citizens Commission on Human Rights, Canada, founded.

16 Mar. 1969   Citizens Commission on Human Rights, United States, founded.

May 1969   First ever Human Rights Prayer Day held, London, England.

2 Dec. 1969   Victor Gyory released—first mental patient released by the Citizens Commission on Human Rights.

15 Mar. 1970   Criminon founded in New Zealand.

7 Apr. 1970   Aged Reform Group founded in New Zealand.

17 May 1970   Mentally Retarded Reform Group founded in New Zealand.

20 May 1970   Narconon, the nonprofit organization dedicated to handling drug abuse, is incorporated in the United States.

12 Nov. 1970   Narconon London begun.

22 Mar. 1971   Narconon Canada founded.

26 Aug. 1971   Psychiatric Practices Bill returned by Legal Commission as unconstitutional for the first time in history of Rhodesia.

6 Dec. 1971   Task Force on Mental Retardation (TFMR) founded in the United States.

1972   Citizens Commission on Human Rights founded in Europe.

1972   Aged Alcoholics Group founded in Europe.

25 Jan. 1972   Criminal Reform Group founded in the United States.

23 Mar. 1972   Narconon founded in Sweden.

18 May 1972   Citizens Commission on Human Rights founded in Australia.

28 Jul. 1972   Applied Scholastics Institute founded in the United States.

14 Jan. 1973   Narconon founded in the United Kingdom.

4 Mar. 1973   Thanksgiving Service at Saint Hill Chapel in Sussex, England, to commemorate the federal recognition of the Church in Australia.

8 Apr. 1973   Denmark Human Rights Prayer Day held.

17 Jun. 1973   Sweden Human Rights Prayer Day held.

7 Aug. 1973   Citizens Commission on Human Rights founded in Germany.

25 Oct. 1973   Narconon was registered in Berlin.

10 Nov. 1973   Narconon started in Berlin.

3 Dec. 1973   The National Commission on Law Enforcement and Social Justice, founded in Canada.

14 Feb. 1974   Citizens Commission on Human Rights founded in Denmark.

1 Mar. 1974   Gerus Society (Reform for the Aged) started in the United States.

1 Mar. 1974   City of Los Angeles highly commended Narconon.

May 1974   Munich Human Rights Prayer Day was held.

16 May 1974   United Kingdom Police Reform Group, National Society for Crime Reduction and Social Justice, founded.

18 May 1974   Germany Commission for Police Reform founded.

29 Jun. 1974   Canada National Conference on Human Rights and Social Reform.

30 Jun. 1974   Human Rights Prayer Day held in Canada.

5 Jul. 1974   Committee to Re-Involve Ex-Offenders (CREO) founded in Germany.

16 Jul. 1974   Social Reform Groups for Aged, Alcoholics, Criminals, Mentally Retarded, founded in Canada.

19 Jul. 1974   United States Police Reform Group, National Commission on Law Enforcement and Social Reform (NCLE) founded.

25 Aug. 1974   Human Rights Prayer Day held in the United States.

29 Nov. 1974   Citizens Commission on Human Rights founded in Paris.

14-20 Dec. 1974   Narconon Week in Harahan, Louisiana.

10 Feb. 1975   Criminal Reform Group founded in Australia.

29 May 1975   The West German Government Advisor commended Narconon.

30 May 1975   Association for Scientologists for Reform (ASR) incorporated.

17 Jun. 1975   Commission for Citizen Protection against data misuse founded in Germany.

5 Jul. 1975   United Kingdom National Conference of Social Betterment and Reform.

6 Jul. 1975   Human Rights Prayer Day in the United Kingdom.

23 Sep. 1975   Massachusetts Department of Correction thanked the Committee to Re-Involve Ex-Offenders for their help.

4 Oct. 1975   Human Rights Prayer Day held in Africa.

22 Nov. 1975   European Conference on Social Cooperation and Peace held in Denmark.

23 Nov. 1975   Human Rights Prayer Day in Denmark.

8 Jan. 1976   Criminal Rehabilitation Group (RURI) founded in Denmark.

8 Jan. 1976   A Bill was passed in New York limiting psychiatric funding.

28 Feb. 1976   Narconon Day in New London, Connecticut.

26 Apr. 1976   The Publications Board in South Africa ruled that *Peace and Freedom*, the Scientology publication which released articles on psychiatry in South Africa, was not an undesirable publication. This was a major step in the direction of freedom of speech in South Africa.

4 May 1976   Commission for Police Reform founded in Germany.

25 May 1976   FEGU (Education Centre) started in Denmark.

8 Jul. 1976   Aged Reform Group founded in Australia.

11 Aug. 1976   Select Committee on Correction, California Legislative Assembly supported CREO (Committee to Re-Involve Ex-Offenders).

24 Aug. 1976   International Conference and Prayer Day in Anaheim, California, United States.

27 Aug. 1976   Church of Scientology spiritual counseling was recognized as acceptable training for a child by the Federal Minister for Youth, Family and Health in Germany.

29 Aug. 1976   First International Human Rights Prayer Day was held in the United States.

2 Sep. 1976   Major exposé of murders of mental patients at Los Angeles Metropolitan Hospital.

21 Sep. 1976   California Law AB 1032 was passed limiting the use of electro-convulsive treatment (ECT) and psychosurgery.

9 Nov. 1976   Citizens Commission on Human Rights incorporated in New Zealand.

2 Feb. 1977   Mentally Retarded Reform Group founded in Australia.

15 Feb. 1977   Citizens Commission on Human Rights founded in Amsterdam.

16 Feb. 1977   Criminon founded in Denmark.

28 Feb. to 2 Mar. 1977   Citizens Commission on Human Rights reported on State Committee probing into the deaths at Creedmore Hospital in New York.

26 Apr. 1977   District of Columbia Nursing Home regulations were amended by the Committee on Human Resources after representations by Gerus (Reform for the Aged).

21 May 1977   A moratorium on psychosurgery was held in New South Wales, Australia.

24 May 1977   The electro-convulsive treatment (ECT) machine was removed from Lake Alice Hospital in New Zealand.

24 May 1977   Narconon was founded in France.

13 Jul. 1977   Police Reform Group was founded in France.

Dates of Biographical Listings on
L. Ron Hubbard

1972	*Community Leaders of America*
1972	*International Authors and Writers Who's Who*
1972-1977	*Sussex and Kent Authors Today*
1973-1977	*Dictionary of International Biography*
1973-1979	*Marquis Who's Who in the South and Southwest*
1975-1978	*International Who's Who in Community Service*
1975-1978	*National Social Directory*
1976-1977	*CBS News Almanac 1977*
1976-1977	*Marquis Who's Who in the World*
1976-1978	*The Writers' Directory*
1976-1978	*Marquis Who's Who in America*
1977	*Men of Achievement*
1977-1978	*Marquis Who's Who in Religion*
1978	*Marquis Who's Who in the East*

Dates of
Important Awards and Recognitions of the Founder,
the Church of Scientology
&
Secular Groups Using the Technology
Developed by the Founder

FOUNDER AWARDS

	TITLE	PRESENTED BY
1915	Blood Brother of the Blackfoot (Pikuni) Indians	Blackfoot (Pikuni) Indians
1923	Eagle Scout Badge (12 years old)	Boy Scouts of America
1940	Explorer's Club Flag for geological expeditions	Explorer's Club New York
1971	International Who's Who in Community Service Award	Board of Directors of International Who's Who
1972	Community Leader of America	Editorial Board of American Biographical Institute
1973	Men of Achievement Diploma for Distinguished Service	Chairman of the Board
2 Sep. 1973	International Who's Who in Community Service Diploma of Honour	Committee of Awards and Editor
25 Apr. 1974	Plaque from Acapulco	Mayor of Acapulco, Mexico
28 Oct. 1974	Highest Certificate of Merit	Governor of Louisiana
1975	Community Leaders and Noteworthy Americans Award; Bicentennial Edition 1975-1976	Editorial Board of American Biographical Institute
11 Apr. 1975	Certificate of Merit (one must demonstrate he has saved a life to receive it)	Mayor of New Orleans, Louisiana
1976	Certificate of Inclusion in Who's Who in America	Marquis Who's Who
Jun. 1976	Certificate of Recognition and Gratitude	Governor of Puerto Rico
28 Aug. 1976	International Social Reform Award	Applied Scholastics Apple School Education Alive Gerus Society Dignity for the Aged Truth Campaign Expansion Consultants Narconon The Church of Scientology Dianetic Information Group Better Education Supplementary Teaching Association Citizens Commission on Human Rights Society for Safety in Mental Healing Alcoholism Rehabilitation Committee Humanization of Treatment of Alcoholics National Alliance for Alcoholism Prevention and Treatment Association for Rehabilitation of Alcoholics Committee for Reform of Conditions for the Aged Task Force on Mental Retardation Purpose-Committee for the Mentally Handicapped Self Development Communities for the Retarded National Commission on Law Enforcement and Social Justice Committee to Re-Involve Ex-Offenders Committee on Public Health and Safety
9 May 1977	Ingrams West Award for *Dianetics: The Modern Science of Mental Health*, the 27 year No. 1 Best Seller	Ingrams West Trade Publishers

Jun. 1977	1977 Community Leaders and Noteworthy Americans Award	Community Leaders of America
17 Jun. 1977	Tully Marketing Business Administration Award	Tully Marketing

PROCLAMATIONS

21 Nov. 1974	Narconon Awareness Month	Mayor of Gretna, Louisiana
27 Nov. 1974	Narconon Week	Mayor of New Orleans, Louisiana
24 Feb. 1975	Scientology Day	Mayor of Tustin, California
8 Jul. 1975	L. Ron Hubbard Day	Mayor of Gretna, Louisiana
7-14 Sep. 1975	Scientology Education Week	Mayor of Houston, Texas
28 Feb. 1976	Narconon Day	Mayor of New London, Connecticut
10 May 1976	Scientology Education Week	Mayor of El Paso, Texas
15 Jul. 1976	Dianetics and Scientology Day	Mayor of Westwego, Louisiana

KEYS TO CITIES

1970	Key to the City of Long Beach	Mayor of Long Beach, California
Apr. 1974	Key to the City of Austin	Mayor of Austin, Texas
Sep. 1974	Key to the City of New Orleans	Mayor of New Orleans, Louisiana
Oct. 1974	Key to the City of Westwego	Mayor of Westwego, Louisiana
Nov. 1974	Key to the City of Baton Rouge	Mayor of Baton Rouge, Louisiana
Nov. 1974	Key to the City of Kenner	Mayor of Kenner, Louisiana
Nov. 1974	Key to the City of Harahan	Mayor of Harahan, Louisiana
Dec. 1974	Key to the City of Donaldsonville	Mayor of Donaldsonville, Louisiana
Jan. 1975	Key to the City of Jefferson Parish	President of Jefferson Parish, Louisiana
Jan. 1975	Key to the City of Crowley	Mayor of Crowley, Louisiana
Mar. 1975	Key to the City of Dallas	Mayor of Dallas, Texas
May 1975	Key to the City of Arlington	Mayor of Arlington, Texas
May 1975	Key to the City of Carrollton	Mayor of Carrollton, Texas
Jul. 1975	Key to the City of Gretna	Mayor of Gretna, Louisiana
Jul. 1975	Key to the City of Groves	Mayor of Groves, Texas
Jul. 1975	Key to the City of Port Arthur	Mayor of Port Arthur, Texas
Aug. 1975	Key to the City of Houston	Mayor of Houston, Texas
Aug. 1975	Key to the City of Albuquerque	Mayor of Albuquerque, New Mexico
Aug. 1975	Key to the City of Fort Worth	Mayor of Fort Worth, Texas
Sep. 1975	Key to the City of Santa Ana	Mayor of Santa Ana, California
1975	Key to the City of Beaumont	Mayor of Beaumont, Texas
1975	Key to the City of Galveston	Mayor of Galveston, Texas
1975	Key to the City of Port Neches	Mayor of Port Neches, Texas
1975	Key to the City of Waco	Mayor of Waco, Texas
May 1976	Key to the City of El Paso	Mayor of El Paso, Texas

HONORARY CITIZENSHIPS

20 Sep. 1974	Honorary Citizenship of Kenner	Mayor of Kenner, Louisiana
24 Sep. 1974	Honorary Citizenship of New Orleans	Mayor of New Orleans, Louisiana
15 Oct. 1974	Honorary Citizenship of Baton Rouge	Mayor of Baton Rouge, Louisiana
29 Oct. 1974	Honorary Citizenship of Westwego	Mayor of Westwego, Louisiana

27 Nov. 1974	Honorary Citizenship of Harahan	Mayor of Harahan, Louisiana
23 Dec. 1974	Honorary Citizenship of Donaldsonville	Mayor of Donaldsonville, Louisiana
1975	Honorary Citizenship of Beaumont	Mayor of Beaumont, Texas
1975	Honorary Citizenship of Galveston	Mayor of Galveston, Texas
1975	Honorary Citizenship of Santa Fe	Mayor of Santa Fe, New Mexico
7 Jan. 1975	Honorary Citizenship of Crowley	Mayor of Crowley, Louisiana
16 Jan. 1975	Honorary Citizenship of Jefferson Parish	President of Jefferson Parish, Louisiana
21 Mar. 1975	Honorary Citizenship of Dallas	Mayor of Dallas, Texas
28 Apr. 1975	Honorary Citizenship of Duncanville	Mayor of Duncanville, Texas
2 May 1975	Honorary Citizenship of Richardson	Mayor of Richardson, Texas
2 May 1975	Honorary Citizenship of Arlington	Mayor of Arlington, Texas
2 May 1975	Honorary Citizenship of Carrollton	Mayor of Carrollton, Texas
28 Jul. 1975	Honorary Citizenship of Port Arthur	Mayor of Port Arthur, Texas
Jul. 1975	Honorary Citizenship of Gretna	Mayor of Gretna, Louisiana
29 Jul. 1975	Honorary Citizenship of Groves	Mayor of Groves, Texas
6 Aug. 1975	Honorary Citizenship of Houston	Mayor of Houston, Texas
15 Aug. 1975	Honorary Citizenship of Fort Worth	Mayor of Fort Worth, Texas
26 Aug. 1975	Honorary Citizenship of Lubbock	Mayor of Lubbock, Texas
26 Aug. 1975	Honorary Citizenship of Amarillo	Mayor of Amarillo, Texas
27 Aug. 1975	Honorary Citizenship of Albuquerque	Mayor of Albuquerque, New Mexico
15 Sep. 1975	Honorary Citizenship of Riverside	Mayor of Riverside, California
15 May 1976	Honorary Citizenship of El Paso	Mayor of El Paso, Texas

ADDITIONAL AWARDS

14 Jan. 1975	Honorary State Representative State of Louisiana	Speaker of the House, House of Representatives, Baton Rouge, Louisiana
15 Jan. 1975	Honorary State Senator State of Louisiana	Lt. Governor and President of Senate, Louisiana
3 Jul. 1975	Ambassador of Goodwill	Chief of the Cherokee Nation
6 Aug. 1975	Certificate of Appreciation from the City of Houston	Mayor of Houston, Texas
9 Aug. 1975	San Antonio Alcalde Award	Mayor of San Antonio, Texas
26 Aug. 1975	Colonel Aide de Camp	Governor of New Mexico
Sep. 1975	Ambassador of Goodwill, San Bernardino	Mayor of San Bernardino, California
Nov. 1975	California Assembly Award	California State Assembly
Jan. 1976	Plaque of Recognition	Mayor of Tustin, California
28 Jan. 1976	Award for Distinguished Services to the People of California	California State Assembly
Jun. 1977	Mexico Achievements Award	Institute of Applied Philosophy Institute of Dianetics Technology Organization of Dianetics Cultural Association of Dianetics Technological Institute for Education Freinet Institute Publications Organization of Applied Philosophy Publications of Dianetics Centre of Dianetics Dianetics Institute of Guadalajara University of the Arts

27 Jun. 1978   National Life Achievement Award for excellence   Illinois Society for Psychic Research
               in enhancing the study, public knowledge, and
               growth of psychic and spiritual awareness data

Aug. 1978   Award for outstanding example of duty,   International Professional Association
               responsibility, dedication to truth and a true
               professional approach toward all endeavors

CHURCH OF SCIENTOLOGY & SECULAR GROUPS AWARDS

Date	Presented to	Title	Presented by
23 Nov. 1968	Church of Scientology	Citation for Patriotic Policies in Support of Our Nation	Department Commander of Veterans of Foreign Wars of the United States
20 Jan. 1970	Narconon	Commendation	Division of Correction, Honolulu, Hawaii
11 Oct. 1973	Rev. Duke Snider & members of the Founding Church	Commendation	Office of the U.S. Attorney, Dept. of Justice
14 Oct. 1973	Church of Scientology	Commendation	Mayor of Los Angeles, California
1 Feb. 1974	Founding Church of Scientology	Commendation	District of Columbia, City Council
1 Mar. 1974	Narconon	Commendation	City of Los Angeles, California
14 Apr. 1974	Rev. Arthur Maren & Freedom Newspaper	Commendation	Senator Edward Kennedy
11 Oct. 1974	Ben Gibson, Executive Director, Narconon New Life	Commendation	California State Assemblyman, Frank Holoman
17 Oct. 1974	Church of Scientology, Mission of Ardmore, Pennsylvania	Commendation	Elwyn Institute (for Disabled Children)
4 Dec. 1974	Narconon	Athletes for Narconon Week	Mayor of Palo Alto, California
14-20 Dec. 1974	Narconon	Narconon Week	City of Harahan, Louisiana
3 Aug. 1975	Church of Scientology, Los Angeles	Commendation	KNBC Radio
29 May 1975	Narconon	Commendation	West German Government Advisor
1975-1976	Rev. Kenneth Whitman, National Editor of Freedom	Entry in *Who's Who In Religion*	Marquis Who's Who
15 Jan. 1976	Church of Scientology, San Francisco	Commendation	Protestant Chaplain California Medical Facility
2 Feb. 1976	Church of Scientology Mission of Zurich	Commendation	Swiss Association for Cerebrally Paralyzed Children
19 Feb. 1976	Church of Scientology, San Francisco	Commendation	Alameda Welfare Department
10 Jun. 1976	Church of Scientology	Commendation	Berkeley Area Interfaith Council
8 Jul. 1976	Sylvia Cain of the Founding Church of Scientology	Commendation	Rep. Walter Fauntroy
1976	Church of Scientology	Certificate of Award	Florida Alliance Against Repression
27 Oct. 1976	Des Popham, Church of Scientology	Commendation for charity concert	Veteran's Administration, Bay Pines, Florida
8 Dec. 1976	Eric Barnes & members of the Church of Scientology Mission of San Francisco	Commendation for fund raising	St. Jude's Children's Research Hospital
22 Dec. 1976	Nicole Payette & members of the Toronto Church	Commendation	Harold Lawson Residence Toronto Association for Mentally Retarded
2 Dec. 1977	Church of Scientology of Riverside	Commendation	Clean Community Systems Committee, Riverside Chamber of Commerce

Dates of Government Actions
Concerning Scientology

THE INTERNAL REVENUE SERVICE

1956 The Founding Church of Scientology in Washington, D.C. applied to the Internal Revenue Service (IRS) for tax exemption from Federal income taxes. The IRS granted this application due to the fact that the Church was incorporated as a religious and educational organization.

2 Jan. 1957 The Church of Scientology of California was granted tax exemption by the IRS.

26 Jul. 1957 The Church of Scientology in New York became tax exempt.

1958 The Federal tax agency sent the Founding Church a letter withdrawing their tax exempt status.

1958 Scientology attorneys duly filed a protest against the IRS ruling and asked for reinstatement of tax exemption. The IRS refused.

The Founding Church filed suit in the U.S. Court of Claims.

7 Jun. 1967 The IRS revoked the tax exemption of the Church of Scientology in New York.

5 Jul. 1967 Nine years after the suit of 1958 had been filed by the Founding Church, the trial began. After six days of testimony, the court ruled that the Church was not entitled to tax exemption.

The Founding Church immediately filed a petition for amendment of judgment or a rehearing.

1968 A year later the case was heard. The court concluded that the Founding Church was not entitled to tax exemption and dismissed the petition.

18 Jul. 1967 The IRS revoked the tax exempt status of the Church of Scientology of California.

7 Nov. 1969 The IRS revoked the tax exempt status of the Church of Scientology of Florida.

26 Mar. 1970 The IRS revoked the tax exemption of the Church of Scientology of Hawaii and the Hawaiian Church sued the IRS to regain its exemption.

2 Sep. 1970 S. B. Wolfe, Director of the Audit Division of the IRS, issued a confidential supplement to their manual, instructing district offices to be alert to identify any Scientology-type organizations filing returns.

27 Jan. 1971 The Church of Scientology of Michigan had its tax exemption revoked by the IRS.

27 Feb. 1971 The Founding Church in Washington, D.C. petitioned the U.S. Government in the Court of Claims and once again did not receive exemption.

20 Oct. 1971 The IRS determined that the Church of Scientology in Washington state was not tax exempt.

5 Sep. 1973 The IRS petitioned the court to enable them to check the financial records of the Church of Scientology of California for the years 1968-1969, and to depose the President of the Church. At this time, negotiations were in progress for tax exempt status for the years 1964-1967.

12 Jan. 1975 The Church of Scientology of Washington state regained tax exempt status.

4 Jun. 1975 The Court ruled that the Church of Scientology of Hawaii is classed as a tax exempt organization.

After the favorable court decision on the Hawaiian Church's tax case, a precedent was set and the following Churches were declared tax exempt:

17 Jun. 1975 Church of Scientology of Portland

1 Jul. 1975 Church of Scientology of Miami

18 Jul. 1975 Church of Scientology of Buffalo

18 Jul. 1975 Church of Scientology of Detroit

18 Jul. 1975 Church of Scientology of New York

22 Jul. 1975 Church of Scientology of Boston

30 Jul. 1975 Church of Scientology of Las Vegas

4 Aug. 1975 Church of Scientology of St. Louis

1 Sep. 1975 Church of Scientology of Sacramento

5 Sep. 1975 Church of Scientology of Texas

29 Apr. 1976 On December 30, 1971, the IRS had assessed the Church of Scientology of Texas for income tax for the years 1964-1967. The Church filed a complaint against the assessment and the court ruled that no additional taxes were due.

WASHINGTON, D.C.

20 Mar. 1959 The Food and Drug Administration (FDA) enrolled a secret agent, Taylor Quinn, on the Academy of the Founding Church of Scientology in Washington, D.C. His assignment was to gather material which would be used to show that the E-Meter was used to diagnose and treat disease.

1963 The FDA filed in the United States District Court, asking for the seizure and condemnation of the E-Meter.

Judge William B. Jones ordered a warrant to be issued, authorizing the seizure of the E-Meters.

4 Jan. 1963 The Founding Church of Scientology, a religious center at 19th and R Streets, was

desecrated, looted and terrorized by a group of United States Marshals and deputized longshoremen acting for an agency of the Federal Government (FDA).

The agents removed thousands of copies of Church books, texts, recorded sermons and even ransacked the Church's archives.

3 Apr. 1967   Four years later, the FDA charges were tried. The first trial resulted in a general jury verdict for the government, and District Judge John Sirica ordered destruction of the seized E-Meters together with the printed material.

5 Feb. 1969   Attorneys for the Church immediately appealed the case. The U.S. Court of Appeals reversed the lower court's verdict, ruling that the Founding Church of Scientology was indeed a bona fide religious organization.

1971   The FDA filed a petition for rehearing and this was granted. No new evidence was presented at the second trial; however, the District Court found in favor of the government once again.

24 Nov. 1971   Attorneys for the Church filed notice of appeal.

1 Mar. 1973   U. S. vs. Hubbard E-Meter case was heard again. Judge Gesell presided and the Court of Appeals recognized the validity of the Church's First Amendment Rights as a religion. The court ordered that all seized materials were to be returned to the Church. The E-Meter became a bona fide religious artifact.

23 Oct. 1973   The literature and E-Meters were returned to the Church. A ceremony was held by the Church representing the denouement of the longest case ever fought by the FDA, in which the Church won successfully, having proved to the Court of Appeals that the materials which had been seized were indeed religious paraphernalia.

8 Jul. 1977   The Churches of Scientology in Washington and Los Angeles were raided by the Federal Bureau of Investigation (FBI). The FBI seized thousands of documents, which the Church had obtained under the Freedom of Information Act.

30 Jul. 1977   The Church filed complaints and the government was forced to return all documents. The raid was declared illegal and in violation of the First Amendment of the Constitution of the United States.

AUSTRALIA (STATE OF VICTORIA)

1962   Dr. E. Cunningham Dax, Chairman of the Victoria Mental Health Authority, wrote to every Minister of Health in Australia, citing what he considered to be the dangers of Scientology.

Aug. 1963   Victorian Health Minister R. W. Mack issued a statement asking people who thought

they had proof of illegal practices by Scientologists to contact the Crown Law Department.

Not a single person came forward with a complaint against Scientology.

17 Oct. 1963   Hon. J. Walton, M.L.C., delivered an anti-Scientology speech to the Victorian Legislative Council, calling for a full governmental inquiry into the practices of Scientology.

27 Nov. 1963   The Victorian Governor in Council appointed a Board of Inquiry to "inquire into, report upon and make recommendations concerning Scientology as known, carried on, practiced and applied in Victoria."

The Board consisted of one man, Kevin Victor Anderson, Q.C., a senior member of the Victorian Bar. Appointed Counsel to assist the Board in conducting the inquiry was Gordon Just.

21 Apr. 1965   The Board of Inquiry concluded its hearing.

5 Oct. 1965   Anderson tabled his report in Parliament. It denounced Scientology in toto.

7 Dec. 1965   The Victorian Legislature passed what was called the Psychological Practices Act, 1965. The principal aim of the Act was the banning of Scientology. It was at first informally known as the Scientology Prohibition Bill.

7 Dec. 1965   Within one half-hour of the passage of the bill, police raided the Scientology headquarters in Melbourne, confiscating some 4,000 documents, personal files and books.

28 Apr. 1970   The Hubbard Association of Scientologists International issued a writ in the Supreme Court in the State of Victoria against Anderson and Just, charging them with misfeasance, breach of duty and recklessness in the conduct of the inquiry into Scientology.

The Victorian legislature passed a retroactive law which conferred absolute immunity upon Anderson and Just. It was entitled Evidence (Boards and Commissions) Bill and amended the Evidence Act, 1958.

12 Jan. 1971   A Scientologist was exempted from military service due to being a member of a religious organization.

12 Feb. 1973   The Government of Australia proclaimed the Church of Scientology to be a religious body that can perform marriages.

14 Apr. 1973   Tribunal in Victoria granted the Church of the New Faith (Church of Scientology) the use of premises in the City of Caulfield to carry out religious and social activities and declared it a "place of worship."

12 Dec. 1973   The Church of Scientology in Melbourne became incorporated as a Church.

12 Dec. 1973   Tax exemption was granted to the Church of Scientology because it is a religion.

23 Apr. 1974   All restrictions on Scientologists becoming immigrants in Australia were lifted.

12 Jun. 1975   The Attorney General of Australia lifted the ban on the word "Scientology."

13 May 1977   The first Minister of the Church of Scientology became registered as an authorized celebrant in Victoria.

WESTERN AUSTRALIA

Jan. 1967   Health Minister G.C. MacKinnon of Western Australia told newsmen that he would call for a nationwide ban of Scientology at the Health Ministers Conference to be held in April at Perth.

Apr. 1967   MacKinnon had the subject of Scientology put on the agenda for the Conference of Health Ministers but was unable to get agreement from all Ministers for joint Commonwealth-State legislation against Scientology.

1968   A Bill, similar to the one passed earlier in the State of Victoria, was introduced in the Parliament of Western Australia. It prohibited the practice and teaching of Scientology.

                 During a lengthy debate of the Bill, H. Graham, deputy leader of the Opposition, stated "When a Labour Government is elected — whenever that might be — high on the list of priorities will be the repeal of this rotten piece of legislation."

1969   Police raided the Church of Scientology in Perth and confiscated materials. Fourteen Scientologists and the Hubbard Association of Scientologists International were prosecuted for "practicing Scientology."

18 Nov. 1969   At the trial, the Association presented no evidence, stating that it had no case to answer. The court upheld this contention and dismissed the case, showing the Scientology Prohibition Act to be unenforceable.

2 Dec. 1970   The Court of Western Australia declared a Scientology minister exempt from military duty because he was a minister of a religious body.

17 Oct. 1971   The Church of Scientology in Western Australia was incorporated as a Church.

18 Jan. 1973   With the first Federal Labor Government elected in Australia in twenty-three years, the new Attorney General in Canberra, Senator Lionel Murphy, recognized the Church under the Australia Commonwealth Marriages Act.

25 May 1973   The Scientology Prohibition Act of Western Australia was repealed, nulling past measures against the Church and making it within the law to practice and teach Scientology.

6 Sep. 1973   Restrictions on the word "Scientology" were lifted.

12 Dec. 1973   Tax exemption was granted to the Church of Scientology because it is a religion.

Aug. 1976   Mr. Herbert Graham, a former Deputy Premier of Western Australia, publicly apologized for the conduct of Western Australia in passing the prior legislation against Scientology.

SOUTHERN AUSTRALIA

1968   The Scientology Prohibition Act was passed, making it illegal to practice Scientology.

31 Jan. 1969   The Church of the New Faith (Church of Scientology) became incorporated as a Church in Adelaide.

12 Feb. 1973   The Government in Australia proclaimed the Church of Scientology to be a religious body that may perform marriages.

12 Dec. 1973   Tax exemption was granted to the Church because it is a religion.

11 Mar. 1974   The Scientology Prohibition Act was repealed.

14 May 1975   Due to the Prohibition Act of 1968, the name "Scientology" could not be used by the Church, and it was instead called the Church of the New Faith. Finally, this name was replaced by the proper name of the Church — the Church of Scientology of Southern Australia.

NEW ZEALAND

28 Jun. 1968   A petition was presented to Parliament, requesting that a Board of Inquiry be set up to investigate Scientology and requesting legislative action. The petition was referred to the Select Committee on Social Services, who recommended that the inquiry be held.

3 Feb. 1969   By Order in Council, the Commission was set up. Sir Guy Richardson Powles and E.V. Dumbleton were appointed members of the Commission with G.S. Orr as Assisting Council.

                 The Commission sat for eight days, during which they heard twenty-seven witnesses.

30 Jun. 1969   The Report of the Commission was submitted to the Governor-General of New Zealand. It recommended that no legislative action be taken against Scientology.

BRITAIN

25 Jul. 1968   The Minister of Health, Kenneth Robinson, stated: "The Government is satisfied, having received all available evidence, that Scientology is socially harmful."

                 The following administrative action was taken against Scientology:

                 "a) The Hubbard College of Scientology and all other Scientology establishments, will no longer be accepted as educational establishments for the purpose of Home

Office policy on the admission and subsequent control of foreign nationals;

b) Foreign nationals arriving at United Kingdom ports who intend to proceed to Scientology establishments will no longer be eligible for admission as students;

c) Foreign nationals who are already in the United Kingdom, for example, as visitors, will not be granted student status for the purpose of attending a Scientology establishment;

d) Foreign nationals already in the United Kingdom for study at a Scientology establishment will not be granted extensions of stay to continue those studies;

e) Work permits and employment vouchers will not be issued to foreign nationals (or Commonwealth citizens) for work at a Scientology establishment;

f) Work permits already issued to foreign nationals for work at a Scientology establishment will not be extended."

27 Jan. 1969   An inquiry into Scientology was set up by Richard Crossman, Secretary of State. The inquiry was to be conducted by Sir John Foster KBE, QC, MP Conservative Member for Northwich. It was to be conducted by Sir John alone and not under statutory powers, therefore no one would be required to give evidence.

7 Dec. 1970   The ex-Minister of Health, Kenneth Robinson, admitted under cross-examination in court that he had never verified any bad reports on Scientologists, but had used his "sixth sense" to adjudicate whether a report was true or not.

31 Dec. 1970   The inquiry was concluded by Sir John Foster and he submitted his Report a few months later. The principal recommendations of this Report are:

a) That psychotherapy (in the general sense of the treatment, for fee or reward, of illnesses, complaints, or problems by psychological means) should be organized as a restricted profession open only to those who undergo an appropriate training and are willing to adhere to a proper code of ethics, and that the necessary legislation should be drafted and presented to Parliament as soon as possible;

b) That the fiscal privileges enjoyed by religious bodies should be reviewed which not only satisfy the present criteria but also have a substantial following in the United Kingdom and engage in genuine and overt acts of worship.

Sir John Foster went on to say in his findings that Scientologists who are entitled to enter the United Kingdom under the Aliens Order should be allowed to study Scientology in the United Kingdom so long as no laws are being infringed.

22 Dec. 1971   The Foster Report was published.

9 May 1973   Yvonne Van Duyn, a Dutch Scientologist, was stopped from entering the United Kingdom by immigration officials. She was declared an "undesirable" as she was coming to work for the Church of Scientology.

Per Article 48 of the Treaty of Rome, an EEC National (EEC – European Economic Community) should be allowed to work where they so wish within the Common Market. An application for a declaration by way of summons in the Chancery Division was applied for in order to get a decision on Article 48 of the Treaty of Rome. The Vice Chancellor referred the case to the European Court of Justice for the decision on the points in question. The European Court of Justice decided that Van Duyn could enforce Article 48 of the Treaty of Rome, that in not granting Van Duyn leave to enter, the Home Office must take into account her personal conduct and that the Home Office could take into consideration her involvement with an organization when considering her personal conduct.

1977   A Notice of Motion has now been filed to have the case re-referred to the European Court of Justice to get a proper decision on the government meaning of "public policy" upon which they rely their case per Article 3 of Directive 64/221.

The case is also being readied for a preliminary trial on the Administrative law issues before the United Kingdom court.

25 Jan. 1977   One of the recommendations of the Foster Report was to enact legislation to regulate the ethical conduct of psychotherapy.

The Church of Scientology submitted a submission on the ethical conduct of professional psychotherapists to the Minister of State for Health, Mr. Roland Moyle, under the view that until legislation was passed concerning psychotherapists nothing would be done by the British Government to lift the restrictions enforced by the Home Office.

Nov. 1977   *The Diaries of a Cabinet Minister* by Richard Crossman was published. In it, Mr. Crossman stated that he had met with Kenneth Robinson in 1968 – and there was no evidence against the Church.

Nov. 1977   Former Home Office Minister, Mr. Alex Lyon, stated he had tried to get the ban lifted, but it was being kept in place by the Department of Health, although they could give no good reason for it.

RHODESIA

1968   The Control of Goods Act prohibited any importation of material which "promotes or relates to the practice of Scientology." No E-Meters could be imported without written permission of the Minister of Law and Order.

24 Jul. 1975   The above act was taken to the Court of Appeals who ruled that the Control of Goods

Act was invalid. This decision recognized the religious bona fides of Scientology in Rhodesia.

SOUTH AFRICA

28 Mar. 1969   Dr. De Wet, the then Minister of Health of South Africa, established a nine member Commission of Inquiry into Scientology.

28 Apr. 1969
to
2 Dec. 1970   The inquiry was held. The Church of Scientology's official case to the Commission was based on the following issues:

a) The nature of the attack on the Church which has had similar pattern throughout the world.

b) The financial, ethical, organizational and advertising aspects of the Church.

c) The Church's role in the field of community relations and social work.

d) The religious nature of Scientology.

3 Feb. 1972   Jan Hendrik du Plessis, who had testified heavily against the Church at the inquiry, admitted to perjury and corrected all of the false statements which he had relayed to the Commission.

The Report of the Commission was tabled. The findings and recommendations of the Commission omitted the official case of the Church.

1973   Dr. S. van der Merwe, Minister of Health, stated that the Government does not accept or reject the Commission's report, and that it was up to the members of the public to decide for themselves on Scientology. He published the report "for the information of members of the public."

1974   The Republic of South Africa passed the "Medical Dental and Supplementary Health Service Professions Bill." This bill has a section on the registration of psychologists or any practice that would aid the mental state of individuals as well as the use of devices for the purpose of aiding others. This act was an affront to the Church of Scientology in South Africa.

9 Oct. 1974   The Publications Control Act was passed by Parliament. This act states that any production, importation, distribution or possession of certain undesirable publications or objects is prohibited unless cleared through a committee.

7 May 1975   On orders from the Minister of the Interior of South Africa, the Johannesburg Church of Scientology was raided by two police officers. The Church's newspaper *Peace and Freedom* was confiscated and the Church was charged with an offense contrary to the Publications Act. The newspaper contained articles attacking psychiatry in South Africa.

1 Aug. 1975   The newspaper *Peace and Freedom* was found to be an "undesirable publication" by the Publications Committee.

26 Apr. 1976   The Church took the matter to the Publications Appeal Board, who came to the conclusion that although psychiatrists had been criticized in the publication, they did not constitute "a section of the inhabitants of the republic" capable of being damaged as a group. The Board ruled that *Peace and Freedom* newspaper was not an undesirable publication.

1976   A Mental Health Act (passed in April 1973) enabled individuals to become detained in mental institutions against their will and by authority other than their own. This act was amended in 1976 to include a section which prohibited the publishing of sketches and photos of any mental institution or patients, or to publish false statements concerning mental institutions, patients detained, or the administration of the institution. This was a direct attack on the Church of Scientology's newspaper *Peace and Freedom*. *Peace and Freedom* printed and exposed atrocities and unbearable conditions in the South African mental institutions.

6 Jun. 1977   Nigel Tasker, a Scientology social worker was arrested and charged with dealing in dagga, inciting a person to commit an offense, trespassing on a mental institution, and publishing photos of patients. Mr. Tasker had been in the process of investigating ways and means of bettering conditions in institutions and in amending the health laws, when he discovered the patients were using dagga. He had notified the proper authorities but was charged nonetheless.

15 Aug. 1977   The Nigel Tasker case was dismissed and he was found not guilty.

1977   The Attorney General tried to prosecute the directors of the company publishing *Peace and Freedom*, despite the Publications Board decision in April 1976.

Sep. 1977   All charges were dropped against the directors of the company publishing *Peace and Freedom*.

GERMANY

Oct. 1973   The Bavarian Ministry of Education and Culture recognized Scientology as a bona fide religion.

4 Apr. 1974   The Church of Scientology in Germany won a libel case in which the judge recognized the Church as a religious community.

27 Aug. 1976   The German Federal Ministry of Youth Health and Family recognized the Church of Scientology ministerial training as qualifying for certain exemptions and grants.

11

The Victories of Scientology

"O ye that love mankind; ye that dare oppose not only the tyranny stand forth: every spot of the old world is overrun with oppression. Freedom hath been hunted round the globe. Asia and Africa have long expelled her—Europe regards her like a stranger, and England hath given her warning to depart. O! receive the fugitive, and prepare in time an asylum for mankind."

Tom Paine (1736-1809)

Tom Paine was a man who believed in liberty and civil rights. He had apparently a deal of influence upon the writers of the Declaration of the Rights of Man and of Citizens made by the National Assembly in France in 1789 and still, in theory, the cornerstone of the French Constitution. Paine also had an influence on those who drafted the earlier Declaration of Independence of the fledgling United States of America in 1776. The ideas enshrined in those documents shine no less brightly with the passage of time despite the many abuses we have seen, whilst lip service is paid to them. Although the political ideals are commonplace and respectable in the Western world of today—they form to a large extent the basis of the declarations and conventions promulgated by the United Nations—at the time they were considered radical, disreputable and abominable in the "proper" quarters.

A tremendous goal, freedom within just laws, it was naturally not acceptable to those persons who preferred and indeed could probably only conceive of a society ruled through force and suppression.

In Europe this goal was swiftly swallowed and lost in interminable wars and the glorification of them through the political philosophy of Hegel and his followers. Napoleon, Bismarck, Hitler and Stalin amongst others sought and obtained an undesirable goal—death—for vast numbers of men, women and children.

In America, the torch of liberty still burns, although it has shocked the touching faith of many to find recently that it did not necessarily burn in the Capitol nor within the ranks of government agencies. Not all Americans were surprised, however. That this should be the case is no real surprise to a trained Scientologist.

In *Dianetics: The Modern Science of Mental Health*, a section on Judiciary Dianetics pointed out that "jurisprudence and its adjudications are constructed on the cornerstones of right and wrong, good and evil." Definitions of these are inherent in Dianetics: by these definitions a correct solution can be reached with regard to any action or actions of Man.

This section continued:

"The fundamental test of rationality is the ability to differentiate right from wrong. The fundamental factors in establishing censure are good and evil. Without precision definition of these four factors any structure of law or judgment is rendered forceless and becomes involved through its introduction of arbitrary factors which seek to adjudicate by introducing errors to nullify errors. Penal codes which will answer all needs can only be written where precision, scientific definitions exist for the four factors, and civil equity which will not lead to injustice can only then be established and formulated."

The same chapter pointed out that:

"We are here at a bridge between one state of Man and a next. We are above the chasm which divides a lower from a higher plateau and this chasm marks an artificial evolutionary step in the progress of Man.

"The auditor is at that bridge; when cleared he will be at its higher end. He will watch much traffic cross. He may see customs, laws, organizations and societies attempt to avoid the bridge but, being swept along, tumble into a nothingness below.

"In his attitude towards his preclears or toward society at large, he can gain nothing by reprimanding and judging past error in the light of current sentience. Not only can he gain nothing, but he can inhibit progress. It is a remorseless fact that the attack upon unreason has begun. Attack unreason, not the society or the man."

A Scientologist does not act for himself alone. Seeking optimum survival across the dynamics the Scientologist when confronted with a problem of livingness seeks to achieve the optimum solution. This is "the solution which brings the greatest benefit to the greatest number of dynamics." The dynamics being eight in number, a Scientologist seeks to act ethically, rationally seeking the optimum survival not just for himself or his family, but also for the group, the nation, mankind and the other dynamics.

This means that Scientologists tend to be socially conscious persons keen to promote social reforms, be it in their own neighborhood, on the wider scale of a national reform, or on the still wider international scale. What happens to mankind as a whole (the Fourth Dynamic) is of vital importance to Scientologists. Scientologists know of the vital necessity of communication, affinity and reality in understanding problems across the dynamics, and they also know of the "top triangle" (Knowledge, Responsibility, Control) and its value.

Scientologists also are well aware of the fact that "Man's primary fight is with those elements which oppress him as a species and bar his thrust toward high goals. Man's fight is with the elements, with space and time, and with species which are destructive to him. He has hardly begun his conquest. He is just now armed with tools enough and science enough to make good his conquest of the universe. He has not time to bicker and indulge in tantrums and yah yah across back fences about atom bombs."

Why is it then that Churches of Scientology have acquired the reputation of being more ready to bring disputes before courts than any other ecclesiastical body and, it is sometimes alleged, more than any other organized body of any kind? Why are Scientology's lawsuits almost a regular feature of the international press? Why did a Scientology Church file a conspiracy suit against the United States Government claiming $750 million damages in early 1977? Why do American Churches of Scientology figure amongst the most regular and tenacious users of the provisions of the American Freedom of Information Act? Why was a British Member of Parliament sued for defamation? Why was the British Government hauled before the European Court by a Dutch Scientologist?

Why did the Government of Victoria (a small state in Australia) pass a retroactive law specifically intended to prevent a suit brought by a Scientologist from coming to trial?

Why are certain individuals in Sweden facing suits for agitation against religious minorities?

Why should a church sue in court at all? Is this not in fact counterproductive? Does this not lose friends for Scientology?

To put it bluntly it has been said that it is bad public relations for Scientology to go to law. One has often heard this said. It is one point that is almost certain to be raised by the average newspaper reporter, when, in encountering Scientology for the first time, he hears from his (no more knowledgeable) colleagues dark rumors that he will be sued and harassed in court for years, or that the newspaper's libel insurance premium should be considered when he comes to write his feature.

An amusing anecdote exists where it is reported that a State Tax Office in the United States was asked why it had not chosen to "investigate" the local Scientology Church. A harassed department head is supposed to have said "The Australian Government tried to wipe them out. They beat the Australian Government. The British Government tried to wipe them out. They beat the British Government. The IRS (United States Internal Revenue Service, the national tax agency) tried to wipe them out. They beat the IRS. Now tell me why this office should get into an unnecessary fight with them?"

When this question is asked, it can only be asked in the absence of knowledge of the real history of Scientology and in a mistaken understanding of the purpose of law.

It is hoped that some of the former history will be clarified by the remainder of this chapter and elsewhere in this book. The latter point should be clarified at this time.

In a truly democratic society the law does not exist solely for the benefit of the ruling class or group as is the case to the degree that they fall away from the ideals of Paine and Jefferson. It exists for the benefit of the people, to ensure that their rights and obligations are fulfilled. To the extent that a legal system fails to do this, then to that extent the society moves away from freedom towards eventual totalitarianism.

United States of America

The Church of Scientology's often controversial relationship with certain agencies of the United States Government has been a matter of public record for some considerable time.

The Church's first major encounter with the U.S. Goliath began early in 1963 when the Food and Drug Administration (FDA) under its chief council, Goodrich, organized a raid in force, with drawn guns, upon the unsuspecting premises and staff of the Founding Church of Scientology in Washington, D.C.

The purpose of the raid was to seize a quantity of the Church's pastoral counseling aids (E-Meters) and several tons of Church literature, including the basic books of Scientology.

The apparent grounds for the raid were that the vast quantities of Church literature seized by the FDA constituted "labeling" of the E-Meters, was "misleading," and thus the E-Meter was "misbranded." For those readers who are not familiar with the ostensible functions of the FDA, it is necessary to explain that one of the FDA's responsibilities is to ensure that all foods and medicines etc. are properly labeled, describing their contents accurately for the guidance of the ultimate consumers of these foods and drugs. As a matter of practice over the years the FDA managed to extend the concept of labeling beyond mere "labels" on; for example a jar of honey sold in a health food store, to include literature which, sold in the same shop, extols the virtues of honey as a folk medicine for various minor ailments, or as something which is generally beneficial to eat. Any such claim in the literature which might conflict with the orthodox allopathic medical opinion of the day, as personified by the American Medical Association and its various interests, thereby might become "misbranding" of the hapless honeypots. The fact that the honey contains the same materials that bees have put into it for thousands of years is, of course, not the point.

It is thus, perhaps, not altogether remarkable that the FDA should seek eventually to extend its jurisdiction into the area of religious and philosophical literature which might be claimed (and indeed was claimed) to amount to mere labeling for a confessional aid used by a church in its ministry. It is only remarkable if one is unable to make the necessary logical and semantic disjunction with a clear conscience; food and drugs—church and pastoral counseling, the two categories of thing are not compatible.

The Founding Church was unable to make this leap of credulity, and in the end, so was the U.S. Court of Appeals.

But the law is not swift in its operation. To achieve the final victory over the FDA, the Church had been forced to involve itself in ten years' worth of costly litigation before the Court of Appeals found for the Church in a decision handed down on March 1st 1973. (And this again was quite some time after Goodrich had been caused to resign from the FDA.) In this sparsely worded judgment the Court of Appeals recognized the validity of the Church's First Amendment Rights as a religion to protection from the government's "excessive entanglement with religion" and ordered all E-Meters and seized literature to be returned to the Church.

It was a curious document. The earlier decision of the District Court was a carefully worded one. The Appeal Court found itself empowered to amend only the essential provisions of this decision. The case had been heard at first instance before Judge Gerhardt Gesell, whose father and grandfather were both prominent psychologists at the famous Gesell Institute, and for whom the very subject of Dianetics and Scientology obviously ran counter to all ingrained notions of the workings of Man's mind.

Many years later, in 1976 Judge Gesell was to admit his personal prejudice against Scientology at a hearing in a Freedom of Information action brought by the Church.

All in all, the FDA's action against the Founding Church's E-Meters and the Church's subsequent victory was a milestone in Scientology's legal history in the United States. It was not a straightforward case. From the time of the raid in 1963 the case had been tried and lost at first instance in 1967; successfully appealed in 1969 and remanded for retrial; retried and lost in 1971; and then appealed and finally won by 1973, bringing with it a full recognition of Scientology's rights as a religion in the United States and another victory for the First Amendment of the Constitution.

The Churches of Scientology have also maintained a running battle with the IRS since that organization took it upon itself to join the battle and revoke the nonprofit status of all Churches of Scientology in July 1967.

An arbitrary decision, this second major attempt to hinder Scientology's development in the United States by the United States Government resulted in a great deal of hard fought litigation across the length and breadth of America from that day on. An intolerable burden on any organization, it was nevertheless shouldered and carried by the U.S. Churches of Scientology with success.

Added to the routine coercive measures sought to be invoked against the Church—high assessments annually, threats of jeopardy seizures etc., were the attentions of the Special Services Staff (SSS) of the IRS, a "dirty tricks" intelligence unit designed to put stumbling blocks in the way of progress of certain litigants or those on the notorious White House "Enemies Lists." (Not surprisingly, Scientology was on ex-President Nixon's "Enemies List".)

A pattern of harassment of the Scientology Churches by the IRS was detected and documented. Consistently and relentlessly legal measures were taken to demonstrate clearly this conduct before the courts. The courts, disbelieving at first, began to get the message.

Finally at the deposition of an IRS agent in the Hawaii Church's tax case, in mid-1974, it was proved that the IRS' revocation of that Church's tax exempt status was not based on any factual or evidenciary basis whatsoever. Indeed, it was shown that at the time of the revocation an intensive IRS inspection had shown that all financial matters were in apple pie order, but the tax exempt status was denied nonetheless.

This marked the turning point in the Church's relationship with the IRS. Faced with the certainty of a court loss at appellate level in this case the IRS finally consented to communicate and negotiate with the Church. As a result, at the beginning of June 1975, the Hawaii Church achieved its full nonprofit status (June 4th 1975).

This was a spectacular conclusion to several years of court work in Hawaii, and it was followed in rapid succession by the resolution of tax exempt status for other "similarly situated" American Churches of Scientology. At the time of writing twelve other U.S. Scientology Churches have received back their due nonprofit status from the IRS, and there are more on the way through the official machinery.

June 16, 1975—Portland Church receives its exemption; June 19, 1975—Seattle Church receives its exemption; July 14, 1975—Florida Church; July 18, 1975—Michigan Church, Buffalo Church; July 22, 1975—Boston Church; July 30, 1975—Nevada Church; August 4, 1975—Missouri Church; September 1, 1975—Sacramento Church; September 5, 1975—Texas Church; Church of Scientology Washington State January 12, 1976; New York Church March 28, 1977.

In addition to these federal exemptions, Churches and Missions in the United States have obtained literally hundreds of local and state tax exemptions as a result of the full recognition of Scientology's religious nature and its benefit to the public of its community. These would include corporation taxes, property taxes, income taxes, sales taxes, etc., each one obtained representing in its way a victory for Scientology. For in each case, an official body has been brought to an understanding of Scientology's nature and goals, often over the top of entheta and confusions previously existing. Each one represents a further acceptance of Scientology as an indispensable part of the community.

A similar acceptance of Scientology's indispensability came from the courts when in 1971 the U.S. Post Office revoked bulk mail permits for Scientology and attempted to deny Scientology's religious status to achieve this. Finally after a hearing the court ruled in favor of the Church and directed the Post Office to behave.

In 1973 the Churches of Scientology in the United States, as well as around the world, became aware of the devastating effect of false reports about Scientology collected, maintained, and used in secret files by government agencies. As any Scientologist would quickly realize, false data, when collected on a subject by a government agency, would act destructively. The validity of the data being uninspected, each time the subject is raised the falsity is consulted and a necessarily irrational response results. The secretness of the file prevents inspection or correction of the data.

This accounted for a great deal of the irrational behavior of government agencies not just as regards Scientology, but also in many other matters. The files, having been well and deliberately poisoned by interested sources, acted as self-perpetuating sore spots, seeding and refueling themselves with their own feedback as time went on.

Just as with any lie, the only handling is for each point to be carefully examined and the truth established, at which time any upsets or difficulties should rapidly resolve.

An extensive and systematic use of the Freedom of Information Act (and similar state provisions where existing) was put into effect by the Churches of Scientology in America, to gain access to these official data banks, with the aim of correcting all false data, thus enabling governmental agencies to become sane on the subject of Scientology, and capable of communicating accurately.

This has resulted in very many courtroom engagements over data that government agencies wish to withhold from the public and Scientology, for of course it is not necessarily easier for a government agency to confess its errors and omissions than it is for an individual. Indeed, it may be a good deal more difficult. Pitched battles have raged in full-scale trials over the production of a half-dozen documents. Such a case took place with the Drug Enforcement Administration, which in its time has disseminated some remarkable false information about Scientology.

With this agency, at first "few documents were releasable," then some, then many. Finally at trial, all but four or five were released, giving rise to an opportunity for correction to be done. As for the remaining four or five documents, the Judge held that he was not entitled by law to disclose these, but if he were, he would have disclosed them as they contained "silly and innocuous information." This case is, at the time of writing, under appeal concerning the last few withheld items, so the battle is not yet over.

Despite agency reluctance, hundreds of thousands of documents have been released as a result of Freedom of Information Act suits being filed and fought. Many corrections have been obtained, amongst which the U.S. Labor Department's correction is perhaps the most spectacular at present. Scurrilous allegations from an unreliable source of drug usage and gunrunning were authoritatively corrected by this department, after these false "facts" had emerged from a Freedom of Information suit. Yet for years, personnel at the department read and doubtless believed this false data each time they wanted to handle a Scientology matter in the course of their business. It can be imagined what effect data of that nature had on their treatment of Scientology matters.

Actions like this, of which there are many, can be seen in a wider context than just another victory for Scientology. The biggest victory is the growing consciousness of the need for ethical data usage such that government departments may be more careful to get correct data correctly used in the future, not only in relation to Scientology but to the whole community. Each step of this nature is a step further towards sane and rational government, a boon to all men, not just Scientologists.

U.S. Government agencies currently being handled in this way include the FBI, the CIA, the IRS, the Defense Communications Agency, the Justice Department, the Department of Defense, Interpol and of course, the FDA.

This list is not exhaustive. The same is being done with numerous state agencies up and down the land, and other federal agencies, to attain the end result of more rational government.

Of course, in the process of locating these false and secret data, which may reflect adversely on the agency, a reaction can be expected. Thus it was on the 8th July 1977 the FBI, following in the footsteps of the FDA some fourteen years earlier, raided simultaneously the Churches of

Scientology in Los Angeles and Washington, D.C. at 6:00 a.m. and 9:00 a.m. respectively, breaking down Church doors and creating a frightful mess. They seized over 100,000 confidential Church documents and made off with them. But only three weeks later, on the 30th July, the District Court in Washington, D.C. ruled decisively that the raid was illegal and unconstitutional—all documents stolen from the Church in D.C. were ordered to be returned. Some two weeks later the District Court in Los Angeles followed suit and ruled that the raid in Los Angeles was also illegal and unconstitutional, and that all stolen documents were to be returned to the Church in Los Angeles.

These were very substantial victories both for Scientology and the Constitution of the United States. They also show that the law, well used, is the last recourse of all. And to keep it that way, it must be constantly created and used by the public.

Ministerial Recognitions

It is also helpful to realize that a very important aspect for the recognition of Scientology and its indispensable role in the community is reflected in the official attitude to those who are chosen to serve as ministers of the Church. This is important because in any civilized community certain relationships have been found to have been of long-term survival value to the community in helping to establish the stability of the society. Such relationships as husband and wife, doctor and patient, attorney and client, minister and penitent have long carried considerable privileges at law, as these relationships are considered worthy of greater protection and encouragement than others, for example, vendor and purchaser, policeman and public. Such privileges have been hard won over the centuries and are not to be considered lightly.

The recognition of Scientology ministers by the government or the courts is therefore a very important and very fundamental recognition for Scientology in society. It was thus particularly significant for Scientology in the United States that recognition of its ministers was tested and approved in the field of exemption from military service, at a time when the war in Vietnam was at its height.

In Barr v. Weiss 293 F. Sup 7 (1968) a decision of the United States District Court for the Southern District of New York, decided on 26th August 1968 by Tenney, District Judge, the Petitioner Aaron Barr sought a writ of *habeas corpus* to restrain his alleged unlawful detention by the United States Army and to obtain judicial review of the denial by the Army of his application for discharge based on his status as a full-time student of the ministry in the Church of Scientology. In granting the application for a writ of *habeas corpus* and ordering the discharge of the petitioner from the United States Army Reserve forthwith, the court said, *inter alia*:

"By denying petitioner's application solely on the basis of the exclusion of the Academy of Scientology from the 'approved list' an exclusion that may have resulted from the school's failure to submit the required information rather than from academic deficiency, the Army capriciously neglected to consider either the standards set by the Academy of Scientology or the established character of the Church of Scientology of New York.

"As noted herein, the Church of Scientology of New York is a duly recognized religious corporation under the laws of the State of New York. It has been in existence since November 15th, 1955 .... The duties and functions of its ministers are similar to those of the clergy of other religious denominations. Their ministers hold services every Sunday, officiate at funerals, christenings and weddings, counsel their parishioners, and conduct confessionals. The Church has three ministers duly licensed by the State of New York as well as other ministers licensed by other states. There are some fifty full-time students in the Academy of Scientology who devote approximately thirty-five to forty hours per week to their training. Their course of study includes instruction in the basic tenets of their Church and its system of ethics, and on the methods of counseling parishioners as to their personal, spiritual and ethical affairs. In order to qualify as a minister, students must pass oral and written examinations.

"Inasmuch as petitioner complied in all respects with the applicable Army regulations, and since the Army's determination was arbitrarily reached, this Court directs that petitioner's application for a writ of *habeas corpus* be granted and petitioner be discharged, from the United States Army Reserve forthwith."

This decision was upheld on appeal by the U.S. Court of Appeals for the Second Circuit (412 F.2d. 338 [1969]).

In United States v. Richard Joseph Engle, an action in the United States District Court, Southern District of Indiana, Indianapolis Division, the Defendant Engle was indicted for failing to report for military service; he defended the indictment on the grounds that he was a duly ordained minister in the Church of Scientology. By a motion to dismiss dated 21st September 1972, the United States Attorney, the prosecuting authority, moved to dismiss the indictment in the following terms:

"Motion to Dismiss.
Comes now the United States of America, by Counsel, and moves the Court to dismiss the indictment in the above captioned cause.

"In support of this motion, the United States of America, by Counsel, shows the Court that:

"1. The Defendant, Richard Joseph Engle, alleges that he is a duly ordained Minister in the Church of Scientology.

"2. The Defendant, Richard Joseph Engle, alleges that he executes his ministerial duties from seventy to eighty hours per week.

"3. Some of the Circuits† which have had occasion to examine the religious status of the Church of Scientology have determined that the organization should be recognized as a religious organization, and

"4. It appears that the Selective Service System should recognize the Church of Scientology as a religious organization, even though the Selective Service System does not now do so.

"Wherefore the United States of America, by Counsel, moves the Court to dismiss the indictment filed in the above captioned cause."

The Court duly granted the motion and dismissed the indictment.

Since that time, the United States Army by its Chaplain School situated at Fort Hamilton, New York, has accepted the religious status of the Church of Scientology. The policy of the U.S. Army is that "Commanders at all levels have a responsibility to provide religious activities which serve the needs of persons of all faiths within their commands."† In accordance with this policy the Army Chaplain School publication *The Newer Religions* contains information concerning Scientology for the use of Army Chaplains.

In the United States, the Military Selective Service Act of 1967 permits persons, who conscientiously object to military service to be assigned by the Selective Service System to "civilian work contributing to the maintenance of the national health, safety or interest" for a period of two years.

The Selective Service System now recognizes employment with the Church of Scientology as work "contributing to the maintenance of the national health, safety or interest."

There have been many other major victories for Scientology in the United States. And of course there have been many smaller ones too. But a milestone in the development of Scientology in the United States came in the case of Lake v. U.S.

In June Margaret Lake v. United States of America, in Rescission Proceedings under Section 246 of the Immigration and Nationality Act, a decision of the Nationality Service, decided on 19 October 1972, by oral decision of the Special Inquiry Officer, (File A 18-232-265; Kansas City) Lake, an Australian citizen, applied for permanent residence status in the United States on the grounds that she was a minister in the Church of Scientology of Missouri. Her application was at first granted, but subsequently revoked on the grounds that the Church of Scientology was not a bona fide religious organization in the United States. Lake appealed, the sole issue being whether the

Church of Scientology is a bona fide religious organization. Allowing the appeal, the Special Inquiry Officer of the Immigration and Nationality Service gave judgment in the following terms:

"These proceedings were brought about by a Notice of Intention to Rescind† dated December 15th, 1970. On January 4th, 1971, Mrs. Lake requested the present hearing. The Notice of Intention contains thirteen numbered factual allegations in support of the conclusion that Mrs. Lake was not in fact a minister of religion of a bona fide religious organization. There is no question raised in the enumerated paragraphs as to Mrs. Lake's qualifications as a minister. The only question is whether the Church of Scientology is a bona fide religious organization in the United States. I will limit my decision to that issue.

"I am at a loss to understand on the basis of thirteen numbered factual allegations how one could draw the conclusion that the Church of Scientology is not a bona fide religious organization.

"The burden of proof upon the Service in a rescission proceeding is a heavy one (Waziri v. U.S. INS 392 F. 2d 55 [9 Cir 1968]).

"In Matter of M. 5 I & N Dec 172, the Salvation Army was held to be a bona fide religious organization in the United States within the meaning of the predecessor statute to 101(a) (27) (D) (1). The criteria in making that determination was set out as follows:

"... has been incorporated under the laws of many of the states in this country; is a worldwide religious organization having a distinct legal existence; a recognized creed and form of worship; a definite and distinct ecclesiastical government; a formal code of doctrine and and discipline; a distinct religious history; a membership, not associated with any other church or denomination; officers ministering to their congregation, ordained by a system of selection after completing prescribed courses of training; a literature of its own; established places of religious worship; religious congregations and religious services; a Sunday school for the religious instruction of the young; schools for the preparation of its ministers, who in addition to conducting religious services, perform marriage ceremonies, bury the dead, christen children, and advise and instruct the members of their congregation.

"I believe that this criteria has been substantially met by the respondent's (Mrs. Lake's) presentation. The Service failed to establish by clear, convincing and unequivocal evidence that the Church of Scientology is not a bona fide religious organization in the United States. I am satisfied therefore that the respondent was lawfully accorded permanent residence status."

This case, in much the same way as the draft cases, illustrates the general recognition of Scientology's indispensability in the community, through the recognition of its ministers for immigration purposes. The granting of special status for ministers who wish to enter and work in the United States is a reflection of society's knowledge that a minister is of benefit to the wider community.

---

†See glossary.

†Student Handout H 22026/12-1 U.S. Army Chaplain School: *The Newer Religions*, July 1972.

†i.e. the Notice of Intention to Rescind Mrs. Lake's previously granted immigrant status, on a number of stated grounds.

Keeping Scientology Available

One of the most important victories that Scientology has achieved is that of perpetuating itself indefinitely without altering or losing the truths upon which it is based.

There are those antisocial individuals who would seek to pervert or prevent communication from Scientology reaching into the public who have not yet heard of Scientology. One of the usual ways of carrying out this purpose is by means of widely published entheta, of defamation, from what the ordinary public may frequently choose to consider "reliable sources." Thus it is, in order to maintain communication with the public, Churches of Scientology are alert to sue whenever defamatory materials are published broadly.

An example of this is a libel suit brought against *Confidential Magazine* for the publication of falsehoods in 1970. However, in July 1971, the suit was interrupted when the magazine became insolvent. It was then bought by the publisher of the paperback version of *Dianetics: The Modern Science of Mental Health* who agreed to print accurate articles concerning Dianetics in the magazine's last edition.

Likewise the magazine *Swank* had chosen at about the same time to publish false data about Scientology but by July 1971, contemporaneously with *Confidential Magazine*, the suit was interrupted by the dismissal of the editor. The new editor then agreed to settle the case, and published a factual article on Scientology as part of the settlement.

Whereas libels published in a magazine are often relatively transient in nature, those published in a book are "more permanent in nature," and often regarded as more authoritative because of its format by the unthinking reader. As a matter of practice, as more time is invested by an author and by publishers in the production of a book than in the production of a magazine article, it is also recognized by the courts that it is somewhat more difficult to ask that a book be not distributed on the grounds of defamation. Nonetheless, the Churches of Scientology in the United States have succeeded in limiting and finally preventing publication of four such works. The first of these was a book by George Malko. The suit resulted in the publishers settling out of court for a substantial sum by way of damages, and a letter of apology from the publishers containing an undertaking that the book should not be distributed further (settlement date: October 11th, 1976).

A second such book, which proved a much easier court proposition, was that published in 1971 by one Paulette Cooper. This book was somewhat simpler to handle than the previous one because the allegations made in it were far more outrageous and susceptible to exposure as falsehood. The exact text of the settlement of the cases which arose from the publication of this book included a full, signed retraction of a very large number of false statements made by the author, as well as an undertaking not to write about Scientology again in the future. The final settlement of these cases occurred just before trial was due to commence on December 5th, 1976. Some seven cases were involved in this matter altogether, including actions brought in other countries where the defamatory work had been published.

The third book was published by a then internationally known pornographer, in 1972, one Maurice Girodias. He evidently needed and sought a fast buck at that time from the instant controversy which he felt might here be created were a book of this nature to be published about Scientology. The book contained major falsehoods, and was highly defamatory.

A number of legal cases began in the United States and the United Kingdom. The legal fighting was fierce and during it, before any final resolution could be made, Girodias' publishing house, Olympia Press, went bankrupt. Copies of the books distributed were few in number, and the remainder were held by the foreign printers against the debt owed them by Olympia Press. By mid-1973 the matter was won.

Similarly, a suit against Holloway House publishing company in August 1971 was brought concerning a book, covering various subjects but containing defamatory statements in one chapter about Scientology. Finally, the publishers settled on the 28th July 1975, paying a substantial sum in damages, and undertaking to destroy all books in their possession containing the chapter on Scientology. The publishers undertook not to reissue the book with that chapter in it, and the case was dismissed with prejudice.

In acting against defamatory books it is important to remember that the very word "defamatory" means "apt to bring one into public hatred, ridicule, odium or contempt" and that for a suit to be successful in this field, statements complained about must be both defamatory and false. There is actually no justification for putting false data into the public arena, especially when concerning something as important and beneficial as Scientology. There is already sufficient false data in our society today without more such being allowed to roam unchecked. Although it may be considered selfish by some that the Churches of Scientology should sue for defamation to protect their own good name, it should be realized that the wider ramifications of defamatory data mean that drug addicts who could have been saved through one of the drug rehabilitation techniques offered by a Church-sponsored group, may not now approach the Church and may die as a result; a marriage that could have been saved by the application of Scientology may fall apart because the defamatory data prevents those in difficulty from coming to a Scientology Church; families may split up because the false data has been believed by one or other member of the family, etc.

Even in this regard then, the Church of Scientology acts from a wider viewpoint than perhaps do most plaintiffs in the field of defamation.

An example of this is perhaps best shown by the incidents following the Church of Scientology of California's purchase of large properties in Clearwater, Florida, in order to set up an Advanced Training Seminary there, at the end of 1975. The Mayor of the local town, who was running for higher political offices, took great pains to cause a stir in the locality, presumably to make himself better known and to gain votes. His gripes were taken up by two local newspapers, and a great deal of commotion was caused in a very short time. The prompt action of filing suits against the Mayor and against the two local newspapers involved, calmed the scene down relatively quickly. The matters raised were canvassed calmly through the means of written pleadings and briefs in the cases. Gradually the enturbulence died away in the City of Clearwater; and finally after a year or so, in the first few months of 1977, all the actions were finally settled advantageously one after the other. Peace reigned again in the small community of Clearwater.

Australia

Dianetics and Scientology have existed in Australia since the early 1950s. They did not become news in Australia until the early 1960s when various interested parties sought to make them newsworthy in an undesirable way by means of a carefully orchestrated black propaganda campaign. This resulted eventually in a degree of social enturbulation in Victoria (a small state in Australia) such that "an inquiry" appeared necessary to "investigate" Scientology. This inquiry was something of a group trauma, particularly as it was conducted in the most injudicious fashion by Kevin Anderson Q.C. The net result was that Scientology was ostracized from society in Victoria by 1965 and the practice of Scientology for fee or reward was forbidden by law for a period. Two other Australian states, Western Australia and South Australia became involved in the upset. In the latter two states Scientology was actually prohibited per se by law in 1969.

The situation then at the end of the 1960s looked grim. But auditing and training never ceased. And Church activities carried on as normal, in defiance of the unconstitutional laws.

Legal actions were then brought by the Church and others against Anderson for defamation. The impact of these suits was so great in the State of Victoria that that State's legislature found itself obliged to pass a retroactive law granting the Tribunal of Inquiry (i.e. Anderson) immunity from suit. This Act, it was admitted during the Parliamentary debates, was solely for the purpose of preventing the Scientology Church from likely success in its suit against Anderson.

Following the enactment of the legislation in Western Australia, the police in Perth raided the Church of Scientology there twice at the beginning of 1969. After the second raid in which they seized all available records, including an unidentifiable shopping list, fourteen Scientologists and the Hubbard Association of Scientologists International were prosecuted for "practicing Scientology." The prosecution sought to get all cases handled at the same time but the court in Perth ruled that each should be heard separately.

The first case to be brought was that against the Hubbard Association of Scientologists International (HASI). At the trial the Perth police submitted all the evidence they had seized, to support their contention that the Association was guilty of practicing Scientology. The Association presented no evidence, stating that it had no case to answer. It lost at first instance, but immediately appealed, steadfastly alleging that it had no case to answer. It was a tremendous moment when the full court of Western Australia agreed with the Association's contention.

The court said, "It is not enough to put in a whole mass of material, merely upon the basis that it was seized upon the premises—said to be or to have been occupied by the Defendant...it was not a legitimate or fair way of proceeding...." The case against the Association was dismissed and after a period of waiting, the cases against the fourteen individuals were also dropped, as the prosecuting authorities thought better of their conduct.

This decision on November 18, 1969 was a milestone for Scientology in Western Australia, as it clearly demonstrated that the law passed, seeking to suppress Scientology, was unenforceable. And quite properly so. That a modern state can conceive the idea of legislating a religion out of existence whilst claiming to guarantee freedom of religion under its Constitution, and then follow this up with police raids and large seizures, is a very sad reflection on the ethical condition of any state. The Scientologists involved took a firm line in defending themselves successfully. This has probably made a greater contribution to the welfare of Western Australia than might commonly be expected. For had they given in, a precedent would have been set for a course of events which would not have ended with Scientology. It also demonstrates how strongminded citizens and a firm judiciary can counter effectively any destructive hysteria from a confused executive or legislature, stampeded into action unwisely by the activities of one or two antisocial personnel in their midst.

Sir John Foster, K.B.E., Q.C., MP said of this Australian legislation some years later in 1971: "(this) appears to me to be discriminatory and contrary to all the best traditions of the Anglo-Saxon legal system."

In August 1976, Mr. Herbert Graham, Deputy Premier of Western Australia, apologized publicly for Western Australia's conduct towards Scientology in passing the legislation. Having vigorously opposed it at the time he described the day of its passage as "the blackest day in the political history of Western Australia." When his party was returned to power, the law was immediately repealed.

But before the final recognition of Scientology in Australia, there was still a long hard road to walk.

The next major victory of Scientology in Australia came in the end of 1970 when one of the Church's Assistant Guardians, who had applied for exemption from military service as a minister of the Church, was granted exemption by the Court of Petty Sessions held at Perth, Western Australia on the 2nd December 1970.

The applicant, Jonathan Gellie, claimed that he was entitled to exemption from military service on the grounds that he was a minister of the Church of the New Faith (which was the name of the Church of Scientology in Australia). In allowing his claim for exemption, the court said, *inter alia:*

"Section 29 of the National Service Act of 1951 to 1968 provides that certain persons are exempt from liability to render service under the Act so long as the condition or status on which the exemption is made continues. One class of persons so exempt is 'Minister of Religion.'

"The applicant in this matter, Jonathan Gellie, a person registered under the Act, applied to the Department of Labor and National Service for exemption from liability to render service on the ground that he was a Minister of Religion.

"In support of his application the applicant gave evidence and stated that he had completed a course of training with the Hubbard Association of Scientology in Perth and obtained a certificate dated the 30th May 1970 from an organization called 'The Church of Scientology of California' indicating that he had been ordained as a Minister of the Church.

"He later received a certificate from the Church of the New Faith Incorporated, Adelaide, South Australia, dated the 18th August 1969, which indicated that Jonathan Gellie had been selected and ordained as a Minister of the Church with power to practice Divine Counseling, to give Spiritual Advice, to hear confessions and to officiate at Marriages, Funerals, Baptisms and other sacraments and to perform all other duties that may devolve thereon as Minister of the Church.

"*The applicant said that there was no significant difference between the Church of the New Faith and the Church of Scientology.* Evidence to this effect was also given by a Mr. Marc Harrison a barrister and solicitor of South Australia.

"The applicant stated that since March 1970 he had been employed on a full-time basis as a Minister of the Church of the New Faith and apart from casual laboring work once a month his sole source of income was from the Church. Most of his time was spent in counseling the members and also visiting those who were sick. He and their other Ministers conduct services once a week on a Sunday in premises in Hay Street for a group of people of an average number of sixty. Since March 1970 he has conducted about one service in four. These services are commenced by a chaplain who preaches to the congregation and reads the creed of the Church of Scientology. There is reference in this creed to God and the Soul of Man. After this a minister reads text from the writings of L. Ron Hubbard, the Founder of Scientology and explains to the group. A prayer for 'Total Freedom' is then read. This prayer says:

"'May the author of the universe enable all men to reach an understanding of their spiritual nature. May awareness and understanding of life expand, so that all may come to know the author of the universe. And may others also reach this understanding which brings Total Freedom.' Notices are then read and the minister moves

among the group discussing various matters and the formal part of the service is then concluded.

"Having carefully considered the evidence, called on behalf of the applicant which evidence was not contradicted and which I accept, the submissions made by counsel and the various authorities quoted, *I came to the conclusion that in the context of the National Service Act the Church of the New Faith is a religion. It has a creed which makes reference to God, its objects speak of a God and a human spirit and it believes in the immortality of the spirit. Its creed and objectives indicate a belief and a reverence for a divine power.*

"Marriage, christening and burial services are conducted by its ministers who dress in a similar fashion to the ministers of other religions and when the adherents meet, their services are conducted in an orderly and dignified manner.

"*From the evidence that has been produced I consider that, on balance of probabilities the Church of the New Faith is a religion . . . .*"

This decision signaled another huge step forward for the Australian Church. As has been mentioned earlier concerning American victories of Scientology, the recognition of a minister as exempt from military service by virtue of his profession, is one of the most fundamental and most important recognitions of Scientology's indispensability within a community.

These two substantial recognitions from the judiciary for Scientology in Australia, paved the way for Scientology's full political and legal recognition in the Commonwealth of Australia. This came after much campaigning. On the 7th February 1973, a letter from the Attorney General of Australia, Mr. Lionel Murphy, announced that the Church would henceforth be a recognized denomination for the purposes of the Marriage Act 1961-1966, which enabled the Church to nominate persons for registrations as authorized marriage celebrants.

This wise move came from the Federal Government of Australia, and heralded the end of the ill-advised repressive legislation in Western Australia and Southern Australia. It also heralded the coming of a new era for Scientology in Australia, and a complete reversal of the state of affairs from some nine years earlier.

The effect of formal governmental recognition is widespread. The Scientology Act of 1968 in Western Australia had been repealed by the 25th May 1973. It was followed a year later on the 11th April 1974 by the South Australian Parliament, who passed an Act to repeal the Scientology (Prohibition) Act 1968. This left only the Psychological Practices Act in Victoria which purported to prevent the practice of Scientology for fee or reward in that state. However, the Act also ruled that none of its provisions would apply to recognized ministers of religion, and thereby with the federal recognition, became at once invalid insofar as its purpose was to prevent or hinder the expansion of Scientology. Scientology's relation with the Federal Government of Australia thus was finally normalized.

Scientology's dealings with the media followed much the same pattern at much the same time. Initially subjecting Scientology to heavy libels, resulting from the lies and commotion of a few individuals, the press eventually needed to be sued or presented with threat of suit. Finally the picture changed and Scientology's relations with the media improved greatly.

Numerous correction articles have been obtained through the use of legal actions: for example, the *Sunday Times*, Perth, correction article of 26 December 1971 which corrected a false rumor that Scientology had been banned in the United Kingdom; the *West Australian*, Perth, correction article of 29 February 1972 correcting a false report that the Scientologists in Perth charged with practicing Scientology had been found guilty, when in fact the verdict had been reversed; the *Dandenong Journal*, Melbourne, printed an apology in the 20th June edition and paid a substantial sum by way of damages for their error in criticising the President of the Church of Scientology in a manner which exceeded the bounds of propriety; the *Daily News*, Perth, published a correction article on the 6th September 1975 concerning a false report on an English legal action; the *Sun-Herald* of Sydney published a correction article on 14 December 1975 correcting false allegations concerning Scientology; the *Daily Mirror*, Sydney, did the same on the 17th October 1975; the television corporation, ABC, broadcast an apology on the 13th December 1976 in which they expressed their regret for having defamed Scientology in a news program.

The list is not exhaustive. Each of these corrections may be a small matter in itself, but taken one after the other, and caused by the use of legal action etc., they provide a calming influence in an enturbulated area, and permit a media relationship to be normalized. It is in fact the application of real justice in the public arena.

With the basic picture of Scientology secured in Australia, perhaps the best moment came in May of 1977 when the first minister of the Church of Scientology was registered in the State of Victoria, by the Government of Victoria. Victoria was the state where the trouble originated. Victoria was the place that took the most active part in maintaining the controversy about Scientology in Australia and it was thus unsurprising that the State of Victoria would try to hold out against the Church longer than anyone else. Although recognized federally, as mentioned above, in 1973, the Church was unable to get a minister registered in Victoria. No real explanation was ever given of the delay despite frequent and repeated correspondence, and finally the Church decided to seek recourse before the newly formed Administrative Appeals Tribunal. The Tri-

bunal were seized of the problem of the nonrecognition of Scientology ministers in Victoria, and the lack of legal grounds for this. The Tribunal asked Victoria for an explanation. Almost immediately the government of Victoria gave in and registered the first minister, recognizing both the Church and its own folly in persisting with untenable religious harassment.

References were made earlier to the Church of the New Faith being Scientology's official corporate name in Australia. The circumstances of the selection of this name are unusual. It is a story in itself. Concomitantly with the endeavors to suppress the practice of the religion of Scientology in Australia childish steps were also taken to suppress the very word "Scientology." Administrative orders were issued in the various states which prohibited the use of the word "Scientology" in the names of any corporations existing in those states. Accordingly, the Church of Scientology was obliged to change its name in order to comply with the requirements of these ill-considered regulations.

Following its recognition in 1973 by the federal government and persistent legal work, these foolish prohibitions were lifted, and the Church of Scientology has now proudly reverted to its real name.

In fact, the atmosphere changed throughout Australia for Scientology. Federal tax exemption was granted in December 1973, all previous restrictions on Scientologists becoming immigrants in Australia were lifted on the 23rd April 1974 by the Minister for Immigration, and by January 1975 the Australian Tourist Commission was writing to the Church of Scientology strongly recommending Australia as a suitable location for the Church's International Prayer Days and Social Reform Conferences. Difficulties with planning permissions which had previously existed, miraculously disappeared (Caulfield, Melbourne, Planning Decision of 14 April 1973, which permitted the use of premises in Melbourne as places approved for religious activity). And so it went. One by one the various difficulties were handled, following from the federal recognition and the tacit rejection by all the Australian State Governments and the Federal Government, of the notorious "Anderson Report."

Now Scientology and Scientologists are free to uphold and practice their beliefs, even in the State of Victoria, Australia.

The United Kingdom

The history of Scientology in the United Kingdom follows a pattern of development similar to that in other countries but with distinctively British touches.

The first Scientology Church appeared in the United Kingdom in the early 1950s and the first Scientology chapel to be registered as a place of religious worship was in London in 1957. Those who are not familiar with British practice in the matter of Marriage Registrations etc., should realize that in the United Kingdom the place where

a marriage ceremony is to take place is registered, rather than the minister, which is the case in most other Commonwealth countries.

Scientology's progress was orderly and steady in the United Kingdom until the mid-1960s when the overspill from the FDA action in the United States, and more particularly the Victorian Inquiry in Australia, began to reach England.

At this time the British press became active, stimulated by various stories that were being circulated. The main center of agitation against Scientology in the United Kingdom was a private association, the National Association for Mental Health, who had good contacts within the British Health Ministry. With skillful manipulation a hullaballoo was caused in the United Kingdom about Scientology, based on alleged "evidence" which was of such a "sensitive nature" that it could never be released, nor challenged.

This hypothetical evidence became the center of an enormous controversy concerning Scientology in the United Kingdom in 1967 and 1968. The Minister of Health, Kenneth Robinson, publicly requested that Scientology be subjected to "the harsh glare of publicity."

What happened is now ancient history. As a result of political pressure, the British Government announced a ban on foreign Scientologists entering the United Kingdom. No trial had been held, no prosecution had been started, no inquiry had been undertaken, no chance had been given for Scientology to present the true facts. Somewhat like *Alice in Wonderland,* the sentence came first and then came the trial.

This seemed a somewhat uncharacteristic move for the British Government, which was commonly regarded as being very liberal in most respects. However, most informed opinion strongly criticized the government's action at this time as being "contrary to the best Anglo-Saxon legal traditions," and to the moral traditions of "fair play."

Nevertheless some of the more sensational sections of the press followed the finger pointed by Kenneth Robinson. And at this point the Church of Scientology in the United Kingdom, through force majeure, started on its formidable role as a litigator in the courts.

Within a couple of years, the Church of Scientology's willingness to fight legal actions in order to clear its name in public, was renowned throughout the United Kingdom. The Church took a very serious view of any defamatory statements made about it.

Why so "sensitive"? Shakespeare understood this phenomenon, and put it lucidly into words in "Othello," Act III, scene 3:

"Who steals my purse steals trash;
'Tis something, nothing;
'Twas mine, 'tis his, and has been
Slave to thousands;
But he that filches from me my good name
Robs me of that which not enriches him
And makes me poor indeed."

Perhaps the most remarkable Scientology case in the United Kingdom, was the libel action brought against the British Member of Parliament, Geoffrey Johnson-Smith. Johnson-Smith had, on television, publicly repeated statements made by the Minister of Health concerning Scientology in Parliament on the 25th July 1968. The statements were prima facie defamatory, but the key issue in bringing the suit against Johnson-Smith was whether or not he was protected by the same Parliamentary privilege from suit for defamation as that attached to the Minister when he made the statements originally. The action came to trial towards the end of 1970 and lasted for thirty court days.

In the end, the court found that the privilege accorded to the Minister did extend to Johnson-Smith to the extent he could be said to be commenting on the Minister's statements.

During the course of the case the former Health Minister, Kenneth Robinson, who had instituted the ban on Scientology, admitted under cross-examination that he acted from his "sixth sense," rather than from any verified data, in coming to his decision about matters pertaining to Scientology. This was quite a remarkable admission for a Minister of Her Majesty's Government, and a revealing insight into the modus operandi of the British Government. This may help to explain some of the economic difficulties that the British Government are having in managing the country in the 1960s and 1970s. It certainly explains the difficulties Scientology has had in treating with this government.

The Church of Scientology in the United Kingdom was well-satisfied with the results of this case and considered it worth going through the whole trial in order to establish that one piece of evidence. For it must be realized that the United Kingdom knows no Freedom of Information Act and governmental information is covered by the "Official Secrets Act" and so there is no way to get information out of the government except by costly law suits as in this case. Thus the Geoffrey Johnson-Smith case in actual fact created a tremendous impact on the United Kingdom picture, to Scientology's benefit.

The Church of Scientology became recognized in the public eye as a strong defender of its own right to survive in a country which preaches freedom of religion, thereby helping to see to it that the same treatment is not meted out to others. It is in fact not unlikely that when, in the late 1970s, there were attempts to have the government take some action against followers of another minority religion, the government was very reluctant to do so because of its experience in dealing with the strongly motivated Church of Scientology.

Scientology's dealings with the government in the United Kingdom present an interesting aspect of the development of Scientology in that country. Following the imposition by "decree" of the ban on alien Scientologists entering the country, various legal actions were taken to confirm the rights of various foreign Scientologists who were at that time already in the country.

An action was brought on behalf of some fifty staff and students at the Hubbard College of Scientology at Saint Hill, East Grinstead, Sussex, and as a result of this action, the Home Office, apparently feeling persecuted, consented to allow those already present in the United Kingdom to remain to complete their studies.

This was followed in short order by the case of Schmidt and Another v. the Secretary of State for Home Affairs, where Schmidt sought to challenge the legal validity of the ban. Having done nothing illegal or damaging to the United Kingdom's interests himself, the action could well be said to have put English law on trial. It may be said that the law failed the test. For when the matter came before the Appeal Court, it was held that the Secretary of State for Home Affairs had the power to exclude any person "for good reason, for bad reason, or for no reason at all." Thus English law's much vaunted "fair play" proved to be a hollow sham in the area of immigration, where government by decree is the only standard. It has been suggested that this conduct may be contrary to international conventions concerning human rights and free communication internationally. However, the British Government's actions have not yet been challenged on this ground in court.

Following the Schmidt v. Home Secretary case, it became apparent that because of this decision there was no legal remedy immediately available to Scientology against the ban. However, there is more than one way to skin a rabbit. As mentioned earlier, when the ban was introduced with no trial, no inquiry, and no evidence produced against Scientology, there was something of an outcry amongst informed public opinion about the arbitrariness and capriciousness of this action. Tremendous pressure of public opinion built up against the ban.

Scientologists and their supporters demanded a hearing. For at no time had Scientology been given the right to answer its accusers, or present its own view of the matter. Finally, after the Minister of Health, Robinson, had been removed from his Cabinet post, the new Home Secretary, Richard Crossman, decided that an inquiry would be called even though it was after the event. As he said some years later, he set up the inquiry because he "felt the Scientologists had a legitimate grievance" and had been "singled out."

The announcement of the inquiry came on the 27th January 1969. Sir John Foster Q.C., M.P., was appointed as a one-man Commission of Inquiry, and chose nonjuridical means for conducting the inquiry. He heard no witnesses, although he did examine documentary evidence. The Foster Report was finally published on the 21st November 1971. His conclusions were unequivocal. Sir John found that the actions taken by the British Government in 1968 "were not justified." He recommended that the ban be lifted and that the various other restrictive measures taken which were also not justified, should be reviewed.

This was hailed by the media and public opinion as a major victory for Scientology in the United Kingdom. It was certainly a vindication of Scientology's consistent view that the ban was, in Sir John Foster's words, "wrong in principle." From that time, the British Government went into a paralysis and was unable to take any action. For six years the British Government allegedly "considered the matter" but was apparently unable to face up to what it had done to Scientology.

This became so obvious that it actually assisted Scientology to get a wider acceptance from the public in the United Kingdom. Knowing that no evidence has been published against Scientology, knowing that Scientology was exonerated by Sir John Foster's inquiry, and knowing the general state of the United Kingdom administration, it was apparent that an injustice of some magnitude was committed. The government's actions then, contrary to their intentions, contributed to the expansion of Scientology in the United Kingdom, by giving it in fact far greater publicity than it had had before.

At the time of writing, the Church of Scientology is engaging in further litigation in endeavors to locate the basic false reports that caused the upset in the late '60s to occur. To this end, actions have been brought against the Metropolitan Police, Interpol, and the Department of Health and Social Security, and others.

However, no commentary on Scientology's victories in the United Kingdom would be complete without mentioning what happened to the National Association for Mental Health (NAMH). This association, it will be recalled, was apparently the source of most of the difficulties in the late 1960s and the association's purposes were to further interests of psychiatry in the United Kingdom. For about a year prior to November 1969, there had been a high rate of new membership in the National Association for Mental Health. In about September 1969 two members submitted motions which were highly critical of the association, for discussion at the Annual General Meeting. Suddenly many new applications for membership were made, and then the association froze membership. Finally on the Friday before the Annual General Meeting on the 12th November 1969, nine last-minute nominations were received at the Association's headquarters for persons who wished to stand for office in the governing body of the NAMH. All these persons were Scientologists. Instantly the Association Council of Management "expelled" every member who had joined the association in the previous year, just two days before the Annual General Meeting.

An hour before this meeting, in a dramatic appeal to the High Court some of the expelled members obtained an injunction to prevent the Annual General Meeting being held, on the grounds that the Council of Management of the Association had dismissed them in violation of the rules of natural justice.

This whole situation caused a tremendous amount of media and public interest, and the issues of psychiatric abuses suddenly became the subject of national debate. In the end, this had the effect of causing the association to reform itself to some extent and currently, ironically, it is found to be urging many of the same reforms of psychiatric treatment that Scientology has always sought. This turnaround in attitudes, which is actually a substantial step towards social reform in this area, is perhaps one of Scientology's most interesting victories in the United Kingdom. Certainly Scientology's persistent efforts to expose abuses in the psychiatric field in the United Kingdom, and to bring about reforms, had its effect.

Since the time of the Johnson-Smith case, the Church of Scientology in England became known as having some expertise in the field of the law of defamation, and prepared to bring a suit for any published defamatory falsehood.

One of the most significant of these was the action brought against the *Sunday Times* for a dreadful libel published on the 6th October 1969. This article was written by a reporter named Alexander Mitchell and was based on false information apparently deliberately planted.

Failing an instantaneous correction, a writ was issued on 22nd October, and finally a correction was printed on the 28th December in the *Sunday Times*, the Church of Scientology having obtained its retraction, its costs, an undertaking not to publish the same or similar libels again, and having obtained an inspection of the *Sunday Times* source documents, to assist in correcting the false data. This article had been widely distributed around the world. The retraction and undertaking, particularly as they were obtained in such short order, were thus a very important victory for Scientology in the United Kingdom.

There are many other examples of this type of action. For example, at Christmas 1969, *Queen Magazine* published a defamatory article, written by an American author, Paulette Cooper. This article became the subject of a suit and the net result was a statement of apology in open court from the *Queen Magazine*, with costs and damages paid to the Church on 12th March 1971.

A similar defamatory publication concerning the American author Paulette Cooper was the book called *The Scandal of Scientology* which comprised a collection of various scattered bits of newspaper entheta, none of which in fact were true. This book was unwittingly published in the United Kingdom by F. W. Woolworth & Co. Ltd. and a suit was brought for this publication. It rapidly settled and Woolworths apologized, as did the American publishers of the book, Tower Publications Inc. This apology and retraction is a matter of public record, and the statement in open court was made on the 9th June 1976.

Yet another example occurred when the *Observer* published a libel on the 7th December 1969 concerning some tragic events in the United States, to which it was alleged Scientology had a connection. Although a writ was never issued, under threat of action a rebuttal of the original article was rapidly published in the *Observer*, and the Church's legal costs were paid by the newspaper. Should more examples be needed, the *Economist* published in an article of the 1st February 1969 passages which suggested, inter alia, that Scientology had "lost" defamation proceedings which it had brought. In fact this was not the case, and after a short action, the *Economist* admitted that they were in error on this point, and apologized for it. This was not a major action by any means, but of course it shows that the Church of Scientology is prepared to take action whenever a statement which is false and defamatory goes beyond the bounds of fair comment.

It is not only the ordinary commercial press that makes errors when reporting on Scientology. The magazine *Month* published a libel concerning the Church of Scientology in its January 1970 edition. The defamatory material in this publication was actually based on the statements published by the *Sunday Times* earlier, but the retraction had not been made prior to the printing of this edition of *Month.* In a way it was a classic demonstration of how a false report in the media is picked up by other media and passed on. The editor of *Month* was concerned to realize that he had published false and defamatory materials, through relying on what he considered to be a "reliable source." Accordingly a suitable retraction was published in the May 1970 edition of *Month.* There are numerous other such examples, which it would perhaps be unnecessary to recount in detail at this point.

The examples given above clearly show how defamatory material can be spread from media to media and how many lay persons can pass on false and defamatory data quite unwittingly, as did F. W. Woolworth & Co. It can be seen that false information can thus be transmitted rapidly throughout the society, particularly where the publication is in a permanent form such as in a book, or in a wide-ranging form such as on the electronic media. It is perhaps not always realized how quickly and easily false information can be disseminated on a wide scale in society. This information may be taken as a stable datum by the society, wrongs and injustices may result, and the society become a bit more turbulent and confused.

Considering the message of hope and help that Scientology brings to society, and all individuals in it, it can be seen that it is important that false data about Scientology should be corrected with truth as quickly as possible. Again, as in the constitutional issues encountered in the United States, the law is the last recourse of the individual.

Let us look at the unhappy example of the *Shropshire Star.* On the 20th November 1971 this newspaper wrote an article attributing libelous remarks to Lord Denning, the Master of the Rolls.† These remarks were in fact made by the opposition counsel during the heat of a case, and were merely referred to by Lord Denning. As a result of legal measures a retraction was printed in the newspaper and a sum was paid to cover the Church's costs, on the 20th March 1972.

Showing that not only the small newspapers can make errors of fact easily, it should be noted that the *Daily Telegraph* itself misattributed these remarks to Lord Denning and was also obliged to publish a retraction. The date of the retraction is 8 March 1972. In this case, fortunately, it was unnecessary to institute legal action.

There are many other such examples: the *Manchester Evening News,* paid a substantial sum in settlement of a defamation action brought in respect of a libel published in their newspaper article of the 22nd December 1971. The *Morning Telegraph* as a result of defamatory misreporting in December 1971, made the same error as the *Shropshire Star,* and settled with a retraction published and all legal costs paid. The Holmesdale Press Limited, publishers of the *Crawley Advertiser,* settled in June 1970 with the publication of a statement in the newspaper, an undertaking to the Church not to republish the said or similar libels and having paid the Church's costs in respect of a libel published in that newspaper in 1967.

The New English Library published a book early in 1970 on several pages of which were mentions of Scientology, falsely connecting it up with various "hippie" cults in California. The publishers at first denied that any of the passages in the book were defamatory, but nevertheless, eventually settled for an admission in open court that the facts were in error, and tendered their apologies to the Church. A sum by way of damages was paid, and the Church obtained its costs.

So too when the authors and publishers of a book published in the early 1970s in the United Kingdom called *The Great Beast,* a biography of Aleister Crowley. The author of this book endeavored falsely to demonstrate how some principles of Scientology were "connected with" the tenets of black magic. It came as no surprise to find that the author of this book was connected with the false data which led to the publication of the *Sunday Times* article mentioned earlier. Finally the defendants made a statement in open court admitting that their allegations were baseless, agreed to correct the words complained of, and undertook not to publish them in the future. A sum was paid by way of damages and the Church received costs.

†The senior Judge of the English Court of Appeal.

Perhaps one of the more remarkable victories of Scientology in the United Kingdom does not arise from a defamation action brought in the courts to clear Scientology's name. Instead it was an action brought against the Church by the World Federation for Mental Health (WFMH), a private organization, which had been characterized by the *Freedom* newssheets as a vast psychiatric conspiracy aiming to dominate and control governments by the use of degrading psychiatric treatment and misleading advice.

The WFMH sued twice in order to get Scientology to withdraw its allegations, but the Church succeeded in striking both actions out, on the grounds that the WFMH had no reputation to be injured. Very substantial costs were later awarded to the Church by the court, and the WFMH then moved to Canada, where execution of these costs owed to the Church would be that much more difficult. As it was apparent that the WFMH was directly connected to most of the attacks on Scientology for many years (the ban was put on while the WFMH had a congress in London) this was considered to be a most decisive victory — the biter bit.

If there have been more defamation actions brought by Scientologists in England than in any other country, it is perhaps a result of two factors in particular. The first would be the encouragement given to the media by the former Minister of Health, who exhorted them to "expose" Scientology to the "harsh glare" of publicity; and the second is perhaps the fact that the rule of official secrecy in England has made the media become somewhat apathetic on the subject of factual and accurate reporting, and more often than not, they have had to make do with speculative data in the absence of factual information. Taken together, these factors virtually guarantee upsets and trouble in society.

Apart from the media who may be lacking concrete data, there are others who seek to profit from "bad news."

One of these was Maurice Burrell, who sought to publish a book concerning Scientology, purporting to explain what it is and what it does. The book had a cover which made it resemble a Scientology publication, but inside were a number of adverse commentaries and erroneous statements concerning a number of the Church's legal actions pending at that time in the United Kingdom. This latter in fact amounted to contempt of court, as it was capable of adversely influencing potential jurors in these cases. Accordingly, a motion was brought before the court taking Burrell and his publishers to task for their contempt. The motion was granted. In this way the interests of both Scientology and the justice system in the United Kingdom were forwarded by the Church's prompt action in preventing a contempt of court from being perpetuated, causing possibly irreparable damage to all concerned. It also served as a caution to those who might otherwise be careless of such matters.

The pornographer Girodias has been mentioned earlier in this chapter. Suffice it to say that he sought to publish his book, not only in America, but also in the United Kingdom. Actions were immediately brought both in England, where the publishers resided, and in Scotland where the printers actually had the books, and a complicated and hard-fought legal battle resulted. Although the results in England were ambivalent, in Scotland the court was disposed to grant an injunction against the printers preventing them from distributing the books, which injunction remained in place. In England, due to Olympia's (publishing house) activities in the course of the litigation, the Church brought a motion for contempt of court, which was successful. The court then ordered Olympia to pay the Church £1500 costs. The firm had some difficulty in obtaining this, but finally did so. However their publications finally proved too much even for the liberal British authorities, and some 90 per cent of their stock of pornographic works was seized by the police, and after a court hearing, was ordered to be burnt.

This was the last straw and the firm went bankrupt; the printers in Scotland pulped all copies of the book available in order to recoup as much of their costs as possible; and by the end of 1973 the matter was essentially over.

Africa

The Church of Scientology in Rhodesia has faced peculiar problems, owing to the political situation and the modus operandi of the Rhodesian Government.

No effort was made towards pretense or reasonableness by the government, and regulations were passed in 1968 under the Control of Goods Act 1954, which provided that no one should import into Rhodesia any document or register or gramophone record or tape recording etc. which "promotes or relates to the practice of Scientology." The same section also ruled that no E-Meters may be imported without the written permission of the Minister of Law and Order. Although the regulations were passed in 1968, by Ministerial delegated legislation, rather than by Acts of Parliament, the matter was not finally settled in a Court of Law until it came before the High Court of Rhodesia in July 1975.

In a remarkable trial, William Looij appealed against a prosecution brought against him by the state on ten counts, one of which was the alleged breach of the import of Scientological materials regulations, and the remaining were various alleged breaches of the Law and Order (Maintenance) Act, as a result of small peaceful demonstrations, and the publication of broadsheets criticizing the Rhodesian Government.

The literature complained of was alleged to be "subversive" in that it sought to criticize the seizure and burning of Scientology books by the Rhodesian police, and the seizure of a Holy Bible, which was part of the Ministerial training course.

In a most memorable judgment, the Appeal Court ruled that the Control of Goods Act was not an Act intended or designed to confer the power to prohibit wholly or partially the dissemination of religious, philosophical, political or other ideas. The court pointed out that "the right of people to have access to ideas is jealously guarded in all democratic societies." Indeed, it pointed out, "This is an aspect which sharply distinguishes a democracy from an autocracy and it is inconceivable that the legislature responsible for this Act could have intended it to be so used as the power to control the dissemination of ideas . . . ." The court then proceeded to hold the regulations of 1968 to be ultra vires (beyond the powers allowed) and therefore invalid.

The court then ruled that the statements alleged to be "subversive" were no such thing. The court upheld the right of members of the public to criticize, even in scathing terms, the actions of the government elected for the time being under its democratic constitution. The court pointed out that subversion is an extremely serious offense, and it is so serious that it can only be committed when the statements alleged to be subversive are established beyond reasonable doubt to be made with the intention of undermining, not only the government for the time being, but the system or constitution under which that government was elected and operated.

This decision recognized the religious bona fides of Scientology in Rhodesia, and removed the main suppression on Scientology in that country i.e. the prohibition of importing Scientology materials to Rhodesia and the seizure of them once they were there.

It represents the most major victory for Scientology in Rhodesia, and guarantees that Scientology will be available in that country for those who wish to take advantage of it. It has also shown that the courts are prepared to stand up against the executives' over-zealousness where fundamental rights to freedom of religion and religious practice are at stake.

South Africa

Scientology's development in South Africa has followed a similar but somewhat different path from that in Rhodesia. In South Africa there are a number of distinctly different racial and ethnic groups which are separate and distinct from each other. Scientology expanded well in South Africa until the late 1960s, at which time the local South African chapter of the mental health front groups, the South African National Council for Mental Health, began to create discord in the area. Following the example of the Australians, and later the British, the South Africans held their own inquiry into Scientology. Although the inquiry lasted for several months at the beginning of the decade, it is perhaps chiefly noted in South Africa for the fact that psychologists and psychiatrists sat on the Commission, and that the chief witness, a former policeman called J. H. Du Plessis, gave startling and dramatic evidence against Scientology, all of which was blatantly false. Following the inquiry, but prior to publication of its results, Du Plessis, arrested in London for a minor fraud offense, confessed that he had lied and perjured himself throughout the inquiry. Two other hostile witnesses did the same thing, though less dramatically. This robbed the inquiry of many of the effects it had hoped to create. As far as Scientology was concerned, it continued on in South Africa delivering training and pastoral counseling for its parishioners throughout the inquiry, and expanding and growing all the while.

But although the inquiry was complete, Scientology still had suppression to confront and overcome. The Scientology publication Peace and Freedom ran into difficulties. Having published articles critical of psychiatry in South Africa, it became labeled an "undesirable publication" and was so declared by a government notice published on the 1st August 1975, under the auspices of Section 13 of the Publications Act of 1974. This endeavor to censor Peace and Freedom's exposures of psychiatry failed when the matter was taken to the Publications Appeal Board on the 26th April 1976. After a spirited hearing, the Publications Board came to the conclusion that although psychiatrists had been criticized, they were not a group such as to constitute a "section of the inhabitants of the republic" capable of being damaged as a group. Accordingly the Appeal Board ruled that the newspaper was not an undesirable publication. This was a major blow in the direction of freedom of speech in South Africa, in an area, psychiatry, where the domination over government is quite strong and there are constant attempts to censor the press on this subject.

In early 1976, the South African Freedom exposed the abuses of South African mental institutions, which were run by a private firm and used as free black labor in order to do light industrial work for a profit. The scandal of these South African labor camps was the subject of press investigation, from Sweden to the United States and beyond. Although the story was angrily denied by the South African health authorities, and the private firm which ran these camps, the evidence published by such bodies as the United Nations has not been refuted. Accordingly, a law was quickly passed to prevent photographs being taken of mental institutions or mental patients by those who were not members of the major South African press unions. This, as debated in the South African Parliament, was entirely intended to prevent Scientology from speaking up and exposing the indescribable conditions of alleged mental patients within the Republic of South Africa.

But it did not silence Scientology's campaign against

psychiatry. In late 1976 a Scientology social worker discovered a mental hospital in which drug smuggling to the patients was being undertaken by the staff. Marijuana was being couriered freely into the hospital. The reporter complained to a Member of Parliament who raised questions which were ignored. The social worker then took it to a national newspaper who investigated the matter further themselves and published it (with photographs) to the chagrin of the psychiatric profession and the Ministry of Health. A shocked South African population watched in fascination as in retaliation, the social worker was prosecuted for (a) drug running and (b) having pictures taken of mental patients and mental institutions. As of course he had done neither, the case was dismissed on August 15th, 1977.

Scientology's endeavors to expose the abuse of psychiatry in South Africa continues unabated. Assistance is given where needed to persons wrongly incarcerated in mental hospitals. Several have been released after legal advice has been obtained for them by the Church.

Despite the fact that the Publications Appeal Board had ruled that the *Peace and Freedom*s were not undesirable publications, the Attorney General early in 1977 decided that nonetheless he would prosecute the directors of the company publishing *Peace and Freedom*, for publishing "undesirable materials." In view of the Publications Appeal Board's decision, this prosecution seemed doomed to complete failure and to expose the prosecution as essentially an harassment action. Such was indeed the case, and in September 1977 all charges were finally dropped.

New Zealand

Scientology in New Zealand has had several victories, the most major of which was the fully successful handling of a government inquiry into Scientology, which arose, stimulated by the Australian example, in 1969. This inquiry is distinctive amongst all others in that it was fairly and judicially conducted throughout, and came to conclusions which were eminently satisfactory for all parties concerned, including Scientology in New Zealand. The net result of this inquiry was that government relations in New Zealand were better than ever before. Currently Scientology is recognized as a religion there, and its ministers are also recognized by the State. Scientolgy's progress there is now steady and uninterrupted.

Canada

One of the most notable Canadian victories was brought about on March 21st 1974. On that date the Court of Appeals in British Columbia granted an interim injunction restraining a Vancouver broadcasting corporation (Radio NW Limited) and others from continuing or repeating on radio broadcasts the libelous remarks concerning the plaintiff which they had earlier published, and wished to repeat in subsequent programs. This was a substantial victory and it had the distinction of being a major, clear-cut, court recognition of the religious bona fides of the Church of Scientology in Canada.

The action of limiting the activities of sources of defamation, as has been seen earlier in this chapter, is one of importance. One major Canadian source was a woman by the name of Nancy McLean. Nancy McLean had signed a contract with the Church of Scientology of Toronto undertaking not to utter entheta statements about the Church or any member of the Church.

Nevertheless, she did publish further defamatory statements and an injunction was sought by the Toronto Church and obtained on the 29th April 1974 in the Supreme Court of Ontario. As a result, this individual was ordered to refrain from making public statements on television or radio which might attack or defame or impugn the Church.

Two other such sources sought to create discord in the Canadian area but failed when the law was asked to determine the propriety of the matter. On the 17th February 1975, Sheldon Booksales Ltd., was found liable for substantial damages to be paid to the Church of Scientology of Toronto, for publication and circulation of a defamatory book, originating from England. The court further ordered that this firm should be perpetually restrained from publishing or distributing this entheta book any further. Costs were awarded to the Church.

A more significant victory still was achieved the same day, when a judgment was awarded to the Church of Scientology against Tower Publications Incorporated and Paulette Cooper, for the same book mentioned earlier in this chapter. On this occasion the court awarded substantial damages to the Church, with costs, having found that Cooper's book was defamatory and had injured the plaintiffs. This was the second judgment obtained by the Church of Scientology in an action brought against this book by Ms. Cooper.

Another victory obtained over an entheta book *Inside Scientology* is recorded in the judgment of the Supreme Court of Ontario dated 24th November 1975 where the Church of Scientology succeeded in obtaining judgment against the printers and distributors of the book, Oxley Central Services Ltd. Substantial damages were awarded for the defamatory content, and costs were awarded to the Church.

Two other books became the subject of legal action in Canada. The first was withdrawn in early 1974 (18th April).

A contemporaneous action against the second resulted in an offer of a public apology and withdrawal of the book.

Europe

Scientology's development in Europe has been somewhat slower than its development in the English speaking countries, simply because of the language barrier. Looking Scientologically, the continent of Europe presents a picture of a very large number of relatively small Third Dynamic national groups living in very close proximity to each other, but with completely different cultural and linguistic background and tradition. This area contains a large number of group engrams resulting from the many wars that have plagued Europe during the centuries. But once Scientology arrived in Europe in the early 1970s, it began to expand rapidly. This of course led to the inevitable conflicts with the more antisocial personalities in these countries, which seems to be part of the process of settling in in a new area.

Although these upsets are becoming "old hat" to Scientologists, they still do need handling in order that more commotion in an already turbulent society shall not occur. European courts, although operated on different principles from those experienced in the Anglo-Saxon jurisdictions, are, on the whole not much faster nor slower than other courts. Consequently as Scientology is fairly new in this area, many of its court battles on key issues are yet to come.

Nevertheless although immense victories lie ahead of Scientology in Europe, there are several that have already set the trend, and those of most interest have been set out below.

Sweden

Sweden in some ways differs from many of the other countries in the world in which a Scientology church is active. The Swedes are particularly proud of their Constitution, their constitutional guarantees for Freedom of Expression, Freedom of Religion and other such freedoms. In Sweden there have been, for hundreds of years, freedom of information principles in respect of official information, such as are only now beginning to become current in other countries. The tradition of liberalism is also inherent in Swedish society, although the society is socialistically oriented.

This liberalism is particularly noticeable in the area of freedom of speech and freedom of the press, and when statements are felt to go beyond the limits of decency, it is frequently very tricky to adjudicate where the line should be drawn between the interests of freedom of speech and freedom of religion.

Anomalously, Swedish law makes it very hard for "Idealistic Associations" to sue on the grounds of defamation. Nevertheless Scientology in Sweden did succeed in a libel action, when the newspaper *Expressen* printed highly defamatory articles in February of 1973. These articles attacked the teachings and beliefs of Scientology, and went beyond the bounds of reasonable criticism. Action was initiated and finally a relatively amicable settlement took place on the 10th of December 1973 and relationships were normalized.

One of the other highly developed awarenesses in Swedish society is that of international law. Sweden is often one of the first countries to ratify a Human Rights Convention as promulgated by the United Nations. Sweden is also one of the fastest countries to absorb the principles of an international convention into its own law. This is no mean feat, as it often takes other countries many years to implement such innovative provisions. In this respect, Sweden, in following the principles of international law, achieves a greater legal awareness than many other countries.

Thus, in Sweden, it has been possible to bring a type of legal action which more closely describes the activities of those who seek to create difficulties for Scientology, than may be found in other countries. It is possible in Sweden to bring a suit as a result of "agitation against a religious minority." The very word "agitation" describes almost exactly the activity of an antisocial personality in seeking to cause discord in an area.

This was obviously well known to those who drafted the international conventions on human rights, who were all too aware of the disastrous results that can accrue from prolonged, unhindered agitation.

In a number of precedent-setting cases, the Church of Scientology in Sweden succeeded in establishing the right of a plaintiff to sue for agitation in the Swedish court, based on the principles of international law. The Swedish Appeal Court three times confirmed the right of the Church, as a minority religious group, to bring such an action. (Church of Scientology Sweden v. *Se Magazine* — decision of 23 June 1976; Church of Scientology Sweden v. Kempe — decision of the Appeal Court of 23 June 1976; Church of Scientology Sweden v. Kristianstadsbladet — Appeal Court decision of 11 January 1977.)

However, as in all things legal, and has been shown to be particularly with the FDA case in the United States, it is a long way from starting an action to achieving final victory. As of this writing, the Swedish Supreme Court has not yet finally ruled on this point.

But it has been officially recognized and stated by the Swedish Government that the drug rehabilitation technology of Scientology is indispensible.

This statement was made in June of this year by the Swedish State Prosecutor who said so publicly and it made headlines in Sweden.

Denmark

Denmark is distinguished from other countries in the world by having very liberal press laws and the world's worst and most salacious newspaper, *Ekstra Bladet*, resident there. Fortunately, due to the language barrier and a limited number of Danish speakers in the world, most of the defamation is contained within the borders of Denmark. Scientology's legal history in Denmark has thus been preoccupied in the tussle with this particularly vitriolic newspaper. These are hard fought battles, in a country where rules of evidence are unknown to the courts. In these proceedings almost anything goes, rumor, gossip, hearsay or falsity. Nevertheless, while the battle rages in court, the Church of Scientology in the first of these cases to come before the Danish Supreme Court, won hands down in an action where *Ekstra Bladet*, strangely enough, had sued the Church's paper, *Freedom*, for defamation. However *Ekstra Bladet*'s suit was thrown out of the Supreme Court and the Church was awarded its costs (5th April 1977). It is thought this judgment may prove a major landmark in Danish legal history.

A colleague of a noted writer for *Ekstra Bladet*, one Gerda Vinding, joined the fray and on the 10th April 1974 wrote an article on Scientology which was printed in a newspaper *Vestkysten*. As the statements were defama-tory a suit resulted. Finally on March 15th 1977 the court ruled that the statements made by Gerda Vinding about Scientology were "null and void."

Likewise statements made by an Italian, one Mario Linares, and published in an article in *Ekstra Bladet* on the 4th September 1974, resulted in a libel action. Finally a judgment was obtained for the Church of Scientology on the 15th September 1975, where the various statements were ruled "null and void" and the Scientology Church was awarded substantial damages and costs.

Whilst final victory over such sources in Denmark has not yet been achieved by Scientology, it is reassuring to realize that as a result of Scientology bringing these matters to public attention, a major reform of the press laws was made into a reality in Denmark, enabling faster more effective corrections to be made by persons who are the subjects of articles containing false data.

During the course of this battle, on one occasion in 1973, one of the editors of *Ekstra Bladet* was sentenced to two weeks in jail and a fine as a result of an offense committed against the press law. It was no surprise to find out that this was the editor most involved in creating hostile press for Scientology.

Germany

Each country in the world has its own Third Dynamic agreement and its own ethnic "feel." Germany is no exception and has some very distinctive ethnic traits. A heavily industrialized nation, Germany seems to have a feel for laws and regulations perhaps more so than other European countries. Redesigned after World War II to be more in harmony with the ideals of the United Nations, Germany's constitution and laws have been carefully worked out to further the democratic interest as much as possible.

One of the laws in Germany that is very much pro-survival, is the Press Law (actually there is a different Press Law for each German State) which allows correction articles to be submitted to newspapers, where false information has been published by them. These correction articles have been placed time and again by the Church of Scientology in various newspapers, sometimes only with the use of a legal action, where it has been conceded that false data has been published about the Church of Scientology. A few examples of these should suffice for the record here: *Der Spiegel*, 31 January 1977; *Abendzeitung*, 24 February 1976; *Augsburger Allgemeine*, 8 October 1975; *Deggendorfer Zeitung*, 7 September 1973.

One of the earlier victories in Germany was obtained early in 1973 after Scientology had been heavily libeled by the internationally distributed magazine *Der Spiegel.*

The magazine, once sued, rapidly checked its data, found it to be false, and then settled on advantageous terms with the Church of Scientology (8 October 1973). Relationships with *Der Spiegel* were thus normalized.

Where correction articles are refused it may be necessary to bring an action against a newspaper for defamation. Such an action was brought against *Abendzeitung* of Munich, which resulted in a Declaration of Injunction whereby the newspaper undertook not to repeat any of the assertions made. This injunction was given as part of a successful settlement with the Church on the 12th July 1973.

A good court recognition of Scientology's religious bona fides came out of the successful defamation action against a German journalist Constanze Elsner, who had spread wild allegations to frighten her listeners and readers. She was enjoined from repeating these statements in a judgment of the 4th April 1974, Munich Court.

Something of a "stand off" resulted when the Max Planck Institute for Psychiatry in Munich brought legal actions against the Church of Scientology in Munich as a result of an exposure in the Church's newspaper *Freedom* of dubious psychiatric practices during the period of World War II. During the course of this litigation, the Max Planck Institute utilized all available resources to overwhelm the Church of Scientology in Germany. This private psychiatric institute even went so far as to invoke the aid of politicians, government ministries and police forces in order to apply pressure to the Church. Although the Max Planck Society is a huge organization of which the Institute of Psychiatry is but a small part, and although at the time of the suit in the early 1970s, the German Church was fairly small, nevertheless the Church fought the Max Planck Institute to a standstill in court, and the matter was finally forcefully settled by the court itself, on terms which were highly satisfactory. The date of the settlement was 18 March 1974.

In the meantime, Germany has been one of the most stringent legal battlegrounds for Scientology. At the time of writing, many cases are in progress, which it is intended should lead to major and significant victories for the Church.

One should not however become fixated on the courtroom battles but should also bear in mind the fact that Scientology has been recognized by the German Federal Ministry of Youth, Health and Family, in that its ministerial training qualifies for certain exemptions and grants (27 August 1976). Additionally, Scientology has been recognized as a bona fide religion by the Bavarian Ministry of Education and Culture (October 1973).

One of the most significant victories in Germany was the discovery and exposure of the reality of the Interpol network, and the corrupt purposes for which it was being used, by deliberate leaks from its mechanisms in Germany. As a result of actions taken following the discovery of false information being pumped into government circles by Interpol, Interpol has now been located and identified as one of the major enturbulation sources for mankind.

The false data distributed by Interpol and published in Germany about Scientology came about as a result of the Max Planck Institute's call for help to official sources as mentioned above. It is often said in England "It is an ill wind that blows nobody any good." In this instance, although the publication of this false data from Interpol had some damaging effect on Scientology at first, in the long run it has proven that it is likely to be beneficial. The effect of a falsely reporting, corrupt private international police organization on a society has been recognized and steps are being taken to rectify the matter by many responsible citizens and officials around the world.

It is anticipated that when this handling is complete, society will be a lot better off for having this international police "kingdom," which is currently subject to no one's jurisdiction or control, take some social responsibility for its actions and their consequences.

International

So far we have considered Scientology's victories in relation to various countries. Scientology has become an ethical force in the world to be reckoned with.

Internationally, actions have been brought to handle Interpol's corruption and false reporting, which causes endless suffering to many hundreds of thousands of people around the planet.

Scientology is also bringing actions internationally against various states for abuses of human rights. In this respect Scientology is in the forefront of social reform movements seeking to improve the status of human beings on this planet, that is to say, improving the existing scene on the level of mankind.

Scientology is constantly urging reforms in various fields of international law, and is prepared to bring the legal actions necessary for reform. In this way, reform of the existing scene for large numbers of the planet's population is achieved by court precedent, and practical steps are taken to upgrade human and civil rights around the world.

Scientology's greatest victories are doubtless yet to come. And every victory is an advance for understanding in an enturbulated world. Where losses occur they are short-lived triumphs for power in the ebb and flow of litigation. But where Scientology wins and gains ground, each such step is a step forward for mankind too.

12

The Volunteer Minister Program

In December of 1976, events were held in Churches of Scientology around the world to celebrate the publication of *The Volunteer Minister's Handbook*. This handbook came about as a result of research undertaken by L. Ron Hubbard which culminated in 1972, into the causes, prevention and resolution of today's soaring crime rate.

One of the most important factors in a society is, and has always been, its religion. It is unfortunate that to some the word *religion* has negative connotations. Yet in its purest form, religion simply means: the expression of Man's belief in a power or force which is separate from and above the condition of *human being*. Religion is that which gives direction to Man's ethical behavior, gives him his sense of community, morals and ethics.

L. Ron Hubbard discovered that the occurrence of a rising crime rate was concurrent with a decline in church attendance.

He found that people were not attending their traditional churches. They no longer sought the minister, or priest, or rabbi to give solace and guidance and minister to the solutions of life's problems.

Man's need in this area was obvious enough. Alcoholism, suicide, drug abuse, divorce, crime, were all soaring. But he knew of no sanctuary from it all, nor did he know of a place to go for the answers. He didn't know of anyone with understanding and with a workable means with which to handle these problems.

Thus L. Ron Hubbard decided to release *The Volunteer Minister's Handbook* and to make the workable technology of Scientology immediately available to everyone, at a very basic and fundamental level.

By studying, fully knowing and applying the data contained in the handbook, anyone who so intends then becomes a Volunteer Minister. The Volunteer Minister simply goes forth, encounters and confronts the problems of Man and life and the processes of living, and functions as a modern day missionary. Using what he has learned in the handbook, he encourages sanity and the resolution of ills across a muddied and troubled land.

Indeed, this handbook contains the results of hundreds of thousands of hours of research and doingness and the resultant technology, if applied without alteration, handles the almost endless misfortunes of Man.

A "bad" marriage, a friend's drinking problem, the reconciliation of two people's differences, failures in school, weakening relationships—the Volunteer Minister, armed with this handbook, can correctly deal with these and a myriad of Man's other ills.

To a world whose peoples were more troubled than perhaps ever before and where a declining affinity for life and an overwhelming confusion was threatening all, *The Volunteer Minister's Handbook* was published and released.

Within the first few weeks after release the sales of the handbook jumped to 10,000. It heralded the beginning of the Volunteer Minister.

Since then, the Volunteer Ministers have been rapidly expanding in number and have been contributing their time and newly acquired knowledge to the restoration of purpose and spiritual values to the lives of others, and in so doing have aided them in the resolution of the real day-to-day problems of life.

The Volunteer Minister accomplishes the seemingly miraculous by using the technology of Scientology to change conditions for the better for himself, his family, the group to which he belongs, his friends, associates, and ultimately for all of mankind.

It has been said that a society would do well to have more Volunteer Ministers than policemen. By focusing our attention on the awakening of the true spirit of Man, and his liberative aspects instead of on the criminal factors, we may yet survive to see a day dawning to illuminate a sane and joyfully productive planet.

It is not really so difficult. One begins by obtaining a copy of *The Volunteer Minister's Handbook*. He studies it at his own rate of speed and develops knowledge, from the handbook, of how to assist himself and his fellow man.

The handbook is specifically arranged in such a way that each section is a small specialized course, each with a checksheet of its own. One does these checksheets in order, as they are designed and arranged to bring about a continuously expanding understanding of the materials. There are twenty-one checksheets and sections of materials, covering such things as the Basics of Study Technology, Marriage and Children, Communication, and Public Relations.

Although the handbook is intended for home study, one is always welcome at a church of Scientology for assistance with any difficulties, whether in the study of the materials or in the actual application of the principles contained in the book.

In most churches of Scientology, there is a Volunteer Minister In-Charge, who will provide further assistance to the Volunteer Minister, should it be needed and requested.

What does the student minister do, once he has finished his home study?

Once the minister has completed his course of study within the handbook, and has completed the checksheets, he goes to his nearest Church of Scientology for examination and certification as a Volunteer Minister. At the church the newly certified Volunteer Minister is put in contact with other Volunteer Ministers, should he so desire, and is given any additional help that might be needed to facilitate his getting started in a practice.

How should the Volunteer Minister set up his practice?

In setting up practice as a Volunteer Minister, it must be remembered that central to the entire concept is that you can do something for your fellow man on a *voluntary* basis. It is assumed that you will need to continue working on your regular job. But realize that you will be there on that job with the knowledge contained within *The Volunteer Minister's Handbook*. You will find, amazingly, that there are many roads open and available to you as a Volunteer Minister, wherein you can practice the invaluable technology which you now have.

You may, for example, choose to set up a practice specializing in marriage counseling, and offer your services in your own home, in your own spare time. Or you may wish to specialize in the handling of drug abuse, which is so prevalent in society today. You would be contributing to aiding the millions of people who have "insurmountable" problems with drugs or alcohol.

The Volunteer Minister may decide to work with an already existing group of people who are working on a specific problem of today's society.

For example, a Volunteer Minister will find that most hospitals will welcome the assistance of a minister to help

with their patients, and that the patients most certainly welcome the visits of the Volunteer Minister. Here he will find that the section in the handbook called the Assists Pack offers a practical means with which to ease the pain and speed the recovery of those in physical distress.

A Volunteer Minister might offer his services at a drug rehabilitation center assisting people in coming off of drug usage and in helping them recover from the drug's harmful effects.

The technology studied in the Drug Rehabilitation Pack provides all that one needs to effectively assist in this. As there are some "rehabilitation centers" that are not truly interested in the recovery of the people entrusted to them, the Volunteer Minister should check with the Church of Scientology for the name and address of a center that truly wants to achieve the result of cured drug addicts and alcoholics.

Should one specialize in handling problems of a specialized nature?

This is really up to the individual minister. The most optimum manner in which to begin practice is by using the applicable data you have learned in the handbook, as you encounter difficult situations and problems in life.

Later you may find that you have had the most personal satisfaction in working to reconcile partners in a failing marriage, and that this is the area and the type of problem you feel is most vitally needful of your newly acquired skills. You might, then, decide to specialize in the handling of this and would get enrolled on more specialized courses available at the local Church of Scientology. You would learn how to become even more expert and professional in your handling of marriages. There are, of course, numerous courses available at any Church of Scientology in which to increase knowledge and enhance your ability in whatever field of endeavor you might choose.

How does one build up his practice?

A very successful Volunteer Minister started out by counseling one close friend. Later, when this person was well on the way to successfully handling his own life, the minister asked him to refer five friends that had similar problems to his. Within a few weeks, this Volunteer Minister could no longer readily handle the number of people contacting him with requests for assistance. He had to hire others to deal with the expansion.

What, if anything, should I charge?

This is entirely up to you. As a Volunteer Minister, you may choose to give your services for no charge, or you may request a donation for your time and service.

You would always, of course, remember to leave your card, so that the individual you have helped knows where to contact you for future assistance, or information.

What about groups?

As you progress in your practice as a Volunteer Minister, you will find that the people you have helped are now much more able and would themselves like to help others.

You simply get them to obtain their own copy of *The Volunteer Minister's Handbook* and get them started studying it. You can ensure that they get experience in applying what they learn by letting them aid you in the handling of some difficult situation.

This should be done gradually, giving the student minister relatively simple cases to start with. Then give him progressively more difficult cases as he advances in his studies.

As the number of Volunteer Ministers, student ministers and individuals requesting assistance begins to grow, you may find that you have developed a need for a more organized group in your area. You could establish a parish. You would begin by holding Sunday services in your home or other suitable location. The themes of the services would be relevant to your unique parish and their individual interests.

What is the relation of the Volunteer Minister to other churches?

As a Volunteer Minister you have an ecumenical duty to all the churches in your area. You should stay in good communication with ministers of other religions. You may even give sermons at other churches. The sermons must give *hope* and carry the message that *something can be done about the problems and difficult situations encountered in life.* The book, *A New Slant on Life*, by L. Ron Hubbard contains several essays which align to this.

What other things could a Volunteer Minister do in relation to other religions?

The Volunteer Minister could work with and assist the other ministers in his area. He may find that ministers without the technology contained in *The Volunteer Minister's Handbook* quite regularly come across situations that they don't know how to handle. As a Volunteer Minister you can help other ministers so that they can better help others.

What about individual counseling?

You will find that as a Volunteer Minister you can assist anyone with almost any problem or difficulty. Individual counseling is most effective when the person receiving counsel also studies the applicable portion of the handbook. In this way the person being helped not only will handle his present difficulty, but also will obtain the subjective technology with which to prevent a future recurrence of that difficulty.

Are there any restrictions as to what a Volunteer Minister can or cannot do in his ministerial functions?

No, there are not. Anything that a minister would do, a Volunteer Minister may do. Any area of life is a potential area for the Volunteer Minister's help.

Do I have to clear my actions with someone at the Church of Scientology?

A Volunteer Minister is not required to answer to any-one concerning his actions as a Volunteer Minister. However, you will find that there are people in the nearest Church of Scientology who are well trained in being able to assist you in anything that you might need, and also to offer you guidance in the course of action you choose.

What if there is no Church of Scientology near, or if I have a problem with which the local Church cannot help?

You can write to the *Volunteer Minister In-Charge, P.O. Box 23751, Tampa, Florida 33623 U.S.A.* He will be happy to be of assistance.

The Volunteer Minister's Program is comprehensive. Anyone can become a Volunteer Minister, if he so wishes. Anyone with a desire to help others can aid in bringing about sanity to this planet, through this program.

The Volunteer Minister can perform his ministerial functions whenever he wishes. He can do as much as he feels capable of. Regardless of the quantity of his products, he is one who is actively doing something to help improve conditions in the world. The Volunteer Ministers are a growing corps of persons from all stratas of all societies who know that this contributive work is pro-survival and is for the greatest good for the greatest number. The good works of the Volunteer Minister elevate us all.

Following are a few success stories from Volunteer Ministers around the world:

I have found the use of the data in *The Volunteer Minister's Handbook* workable enough to literally save a life. A few months ago at 2 a.m. in the morning, two neighbors rang my bell and told me that there was a young man out on the street unconscious. He had overdosed on drugs. I gave him a Scientology Locational Assist I had learned in *The Volunteer Minister's Handbook*, then walked him around as he became more conscious. He made it through and extolled the help I had given him to his family and the community. It was an incredible experience for me to know I had learned a way to actually help another through an exact technology. Now I feel able to be of service to many others.

L T

I am a physician and routinely I have used *The Volunteer Minister's Handbook*'s data to handle patients who are on drugs and medications, and who would like to resolve their drug dependency. I have used the Drug Bomb and CalMag formula constantly in my clinical work. I always use the data in the Training Routines section in confronting and handling people and situations, and I very often use Touch Assists in my practice, with great success.

D K

I have a strong intention to upgrade education in my community, and *The Volunteer Minister's Handbook* helps me to realize this goal. Recently I made a presentation, based on material in *The Volunteer Minister's Handbook*, to a prominent educational and religious leader who also handles children with learning problems and personal problems. He was fascinated with the data on the basic concepts about the mind, and PTSness, as well as the barriers to study. As a result he is going to utilize me to upgrade his current education rehabilitation project. (Also, he was extremely pleased that the material is *not* related to psychology or psychiatry which he despises.) As a Volunteer Minister I am having unusual acceptance in the field of education and community affairs.

M B

After learning some data from *The Volunteer Minister's Handbook* a friend of mine had some good wins with his mother, an 80 year old who had had severe arthritis for years. By using some simple Scientology techniques, she can now use her fingers for the first time in sixteen years. She can also now walk around without a walking frame, and is a much more cheerful and extroverted person.

J E

I read my *Volunteer Minister's Handbook* on how to give Touch Assists. I had read this before but wanted to brush up on it. Later I had to walk to the store. On the way back I heard a loud crash and turned to see a four-car collision. A Volkswagen bus had been involved in the accident and I noticed the driver was just sitting in the bus not moving and holding his head. I walked over to him and asked him how he was doing. He said he didn't know and seemed to be in shock. I told him I was going to give him a Touch Assist and gave him a brief idea of what it was before starting. By the time the ambulance arrived he appeared to be much better and was no longer in a state of heavy shock. It really felt good to have the knowledge to help an individual in a situation like this.

J C

On a consultancy basis I was called in by the chief administrator of a hospital in New York. He was desperate about his hospital's statistics and conditions. Using data learned from *The Volunteer Minister's Handbook*, I was able to help him spot and analyze the trouble sources. This made it possible for an efficient admin scale to be worked out whereby he will realize rapid improvement in his operation and steady progress toward realizing his administrative goals.

H A

Last night I had what was probably my biggest win as a Scientologist in the field. I was at work and I noticed that there was an extremely large group gathering across the street. I then saw a policeman pulling a girl aside. She was screaming at the police and writhing. They were helpless as far as calming her down. I assumed she was on drugs, so I walked over and immediately took control and applied some basic Scientology technology. She shortly calmed down to a point where the police were able to handle her. It is definitely powerful tech and I'm glad to know I have it. Thanks Ron for *The Volunteer Minister's Handbook*.

J F

As Chaplain, I employ *The Volunteer Minister's Handbook* on virtually every chaplain matter. I know that when policy and purpose are established, enturbulence will subside proportionately. So, I discover the situation, determine which Scientology stable datum hasn't been applied, find it in *The Volunteer Minister's Handbook* and have the parties concerned apply it. It works every time!

C B

I began using *The Volunteer Minister's Handbook* about three months ago. I was having a great deal of trouble making my marriage work and had requested a Chaplain's Court. The chaplain gave me a good study program to do, most of it in *The Volunteer Minister's Handbook*. It was wonderful. The data on marriage and children really enlightened me and I took a look at things about my Second Dynamic I'd not been willing to look at before. My husband and I are very happily reunited now and the whole family is doing fine. Then I was asked to be a volunteer chaplain. I've done many handlings now and have had no failures. I use *The Volunteer Minister's Handbook* as my bible. I've salvaged many marriages. It's a marvelous book. It really lays out that the tech is for use. *Use it* and *win*. I do. Thank you, L. Ron Hubbard.

J D

You can have similar successes.

Just start with the intention to help another. Find out more about The Volunteer Minister Program from a Church of Scientology, and then tell others.

It is important.

13

Holidays of Scientology

In common with many organizations, the Church of Scientology observes holidays in all areas of the world.

As the various Churches are located in many different countries, holidays fall on different days in varying areas.

From time to time, each national area additionally holds a conference on social reform—combined with a human rights service.

Internationally, the two major events are the birthday of L. Ron Hubbard, Founder of the Church, and the date of publication of Mr. Hubbard's major book—*Dianetics: The Modern Science of Mental Health.*

First published May 9th 1950, *Dianetics* has long been regarded as a key anniversary in the history of the Church.

Other landmarks and holidays follow in order by month. The year of founding of the various Churches is also given so that holidays appear in historical perspective.

JANUARY

1   New Year's Day.

4   Iceland Day, to celebrate the Church of Scientology incorporation there in 1975.

12   Vocation Day, Perth, in celebration of a 1971 Court of Justice decision that a vocation as a minister in the Church of Scientology is one legally recognized by the Courts of West Australia.

15   Efficiency Day, to celebrate the 1957 publishing of *Problems of Work* by L. Ron Hubbard.

16   Africa Day, to celebrate the recognition in 1975 of the Church of Scientology in South Africa.

20   Italy Day, to celebrate the incorporation in 1977 of the Hubbard Dianetics Institute, Milan.

25   Criminon Day, to celebrate the 1972 founding of Criminon, the prison rehabilitation program.

27   Founding Day, to celebrate the inception in 1961 of the Church of Scientology, Cape Town.

31   Founding Day, to celebrate the inception in 1969 of the Church of Scientology, Adelaide, South Australia.

FEBRUARY

5   Founding Church Day, Washington, D.C. On this day in 1969, the Founding Church of Scientology was recognized as a bona fide religion in the D.C. District Court.

7   Australia Day, to celebrate the recognition in 1973 of the Church of Scientology across Australia, by the then Federal Attorney-General, Senator Lionel Murphy. Scientology was recognized under Section 26 of the Commonwealth Marriage Act, 1961-1966.

18   California Day, to celebrate the inception in 1954 of the Church of Scientology in Los Angeles.

19   Narconon Day, initiated 1966. On this day William Benitez started a drug rehabilitation program in Arizona State Prison. Called

Narconon, the program was based on secular use of L. Ron Hubbard's communication technology. The program is now in use in some thirty separate locations across the world.

26   Saint Hill Day, to celebrate the 1966 opening of the Hubbard College of Scientology at Saint Hill Manor, East Grinstead, Sussex, England. The College can hold several hundred students and is currently being extended.

28   Founding Day, New Zealand, to celebrate the inception of the Church of Scientology in Auckland.

MARCH

1   G.O. Day, to celebrate the inauguration of the Guardian Office in 1966. The position of The Guardian was first established at Saint Hill Manor, East Grinstead, Sussex, England and was followed by the appointment of Assistant Guardians in all continents. The post is a lifetime appointment, and is the senior executive position in the world-wide Churches of Scientology.

5   CCHR Day, to mark the formation in 1969 of the Citizens Commission on Human Rights. Started in England, the Commission is now world-wide, and has achieved reforms in many countries to better the lot of the mental patient.

13   FOUNDER'S BIRTHDAY, to celebrate the birthday of L. Ron Hubbard, Founder of Dianetics and Scientology. Mr. Hubbard was born on this date in 1911, at Tilden, Nebraska. The day is internationally celebrated, and the Founder responds with a personal message to all Churches across the world.

24   Student Day, to celebrate the commencement of the Saint Hill Special Briefing Course in 1961. The course was begun at Saint Hill Manor, East Grinstead, Sussex, and in 1968 was expanded to the American Saint Hill Organization in Los Angeles, and then a year later to Copenhagen, Denmark.

30   Founding Day, to celebrate the inception of the Church of Scientology in 1972 in Amsterdam, Holland.

APRIL

1   Liberty of Conscience Day, Washington, D.C., to celebrate a 1965 ruling by a D.C.

District Judge that Scientology ministers may refuse to divulge confidences given them by parishioners.

4   Germany Day, to celebrate the recognition in 1974 of the Church of Scientology in Munich.

11   Repeal Day, South Australia. On this day in 1974, the Parliament of South Australia repealed the Scientology Prohibition Act.

25   New Zealand Day, to celebrate recognition of the Church in 1974 with Scientology ministers licensed to celebrate marriages.

MAY

1   Communication Day, to celebrate the publication of the first issue of The Auditor magazine at Saint Hill Manor, East Grinstead, in 1964.

9   MAY 9 DAY. On this day in 1950, the Founder of Dianetics and Scientology, L. Ron Hubbard published Dianetics: The Modern Science of Mental Health.
     This date is celebrated by all Churches and Missions internationally, as it is accepted as THE founding date of Dianetics and Scientology, and tributes to the Founder are paid in all Scientology organizations.

12   Founding Day Germany, to celebrate the inception in 1967 of the Church of Scientology in Munich.

13   Freedom of Worship Day, Victoria, Australia. In 1977, the first minister of the Church of Scientology in Victoria was licensed to celebrate marriages in Melbourne.

25   Repeal Day, West Australia. On this day in 1973, the Parliament of West Australia repealed the Scientology Prohibition Act.

26   Integrity Day, to mark the 1965 release by the Founder of his studies on ethics—the reason and contemplation of optimum survival.

JUNE

1   Parents' Day, to celebrate family unity obtained by many families as a result of Scientology. It is usually observed over the first weekend in June, and provides an opportunity for families to get together.

3   Teachers' Day, to celebrate the 1974 utilization of L. Ron Hubbard's study technology in Brixton, London, England, to help immi-

grant children. Courses and classes using this technology are now offered by several secular bodies. Also the establishment of Applied Scholastics in the U.S. and Canada, and Education Alive in Africa, are celebrated on this day.

4   Founding Day, Switzerland, to celebrate the inception in 1974 of the Church of Scientology in Basel.

6   Holland Day, to celebrate recognition in 1977 of the Church of Scientology in Amsterdam.

13   Founding Day, to celebrate the inception in 1965 of the Church of Scientology in Copenhagen, Denmark.

17   Japan Day, to celebrate the inception in 1965 of the Church of Scientology in Tokyo.

18   Academy Day, in celebration of the 1964 release of L. Ron Hubbard's study technology.

19   Incorporation Day, California, to celebrate the 1956 change of name from Church of Scientology to Church of Scientology of California.

JULY

5   Incorporation Day, BC, to celebrate the 1971 registration of the Church of Scientology in British Columbia, Canada.

7   Advanced Org Founding Day, to celebrate the opening of the Advanced Organization, Denmark.

15   Siberia Day, to celebrate the Church's first major stand against easy seizure and involuntary commitment in the United States. The Alaska Mental Health Act of 1955 was known as the "Siberian Bill."

17   Celebrity Day, to celebrate the 1968 opening of the International Celebrity Centre in Los Angeles.

AUGUST

5   Founding Day, to celebrate the 1968 opening of the Advanced Organization, Los Angeles.

12   Sea Org Day, to celebrate the establishment of the Sea Organization in 1967.

13   Founding Day, to celebrate the inception in 1968 of the American Saint Hill Organization in Los Angeles. The U.S. organization delivers the same services as the other two Saint Hills in England and Denmark.

18   Founding Day, to celebrate the inception in 1975 of the Church of Scientology in Greenland.

20   *Freedom* Day, to celebrate the publication in 1968 of the first issue of *Freedom* newspaper. Now published in many countries, *Freedom* has a two million plus distribution.

24   World Peace Day, to celebrate the 1976 anniversary of the Church's first International Conference for World Peace and Social Reform, held at Anaheim, California, and attended by 10,000 church members from all over the world.

30   ACC Day, to celebrate the anniversary in 1960 of the first Advanced Clinical Course held at Saint Hill Manor, England.

SEPTEMBER

1   Founder's Day, to honor L. Ron Hubbard, founder, Church of Scientology, and to recognize his resignation from the Church Directorship and official assumption of the title of Founder.

4   Clear Day, to mark the inauguration of the Clearing Course in 1965. Run initially at Saint Hill Manor, the course can now be taken at Advanced Organizations in the United Kingdom, the United States, and Denmark.

8   Canada Day, to celebrate the Toronto incorporation in 1967 of the national Church of Scientology in Canada.

11   Auditors' Day, to celebrate the counseling achievements of each year, hear new developments and provide an opportunity for auditors to get together. The event is usually held on the second Sunday in September.

15   Norway Day, to celebrate the incorporation in 1975 of the Church of Scientology in Oslo.

30   Incorporation Day, Washington, D.C., to celebrate the incorporation in 1955 of the Founding Church of Scientology.

OCTOBER

3   Celebration Day in Nova Scotia to celebrate the official recognition of the Church of Scientology in 1973.

9   Founding Day, to celebrate the inception in 1969 of the Church of Scientology, Stockholm, Sweden.

NOVEMBER

15   Saint Hill Day, to celebrate in 1967, the purchase of Saint Hill Manor, East Grinstead, from the Founder, to serve as the Church's international central office.

19   Celebration Day, to mark recognition in 1973 for the Church in the North West Territories, Canada.

20   Yukon Day, to celebrate recognition in 1973 of the Church of Scientology in the Yukon Territories.

25   Founding Day, to celebrate the opening in 1975 of the Clearwater complex in Florida.

DECEMBER

1   Founding Day, to celebrate the inception in 1963 of the Church of Scientology in Durban, South Africa.

9   Founding Day, to celebrate the inception in 1972 of the Church of Scientology in Manchester, England.

12   Founding Day, to celebrate the inception in 1972 of the Church of Scientology in Melbourne, Australia. Prior to this date, the Church was known as the Hubbard Association of Scientologists International — the HASI.

23   Children's Day, to mark the 1950 publication of *Child Dianetics* by L. Ron Hubbard.

24   Christmas Eve.

25   Christmas Day.

27   Founding Day, to celebrate the inception in 1968 of the Church of Scientology in France.

30   Freedom Day U.S., to celebrate the official recognition in 1974 of the Church of Scientology in the United States.

31   New Year's Eve.

14

The Creeds and Codes of Dianetics and Scientology

The creeds and codes of Scientology have provided the guidance of discipline necessary to withstand the temptations and distractions experienced in the cut and thrust of our battle for spiritual decency.

Man has for too long suffered under a school of thought —"Miceology"—which teaches one to conform to the environment. The Scientologist however knows that the real victory can only be achieved by *commanding* the environment and this is the task we have on our hands.

Many a religious body and professional activity has failed desperately for lack of correctly estimating the worth of its creeds or codes. Such provide the sturdy brace and mainstay, the intention to stay on course forwarding a purpose. Many groups, of course, don't have any codes at all but should; for example, while psychiatry might have a modus operandi, none of those conversant with this handling of the insane—the function of psychiatry—would call it a code intended to induce a better state of beingness in a patient.

In education too we discover an almost total absence of codified conduct beyond that laid down by school boards to regulate the social attitude of, and restrain possible cruelty in educators. Although education is very widespread, and indeed is the practice best accepted by this society for the betterment of individuals, it yet lacks any tightly agreed upon method or conduct codification for the relaying of data to the student. Custom has dictated a certain politeness on the part of the professor, or teacher. It is generally believed to be necessary to examine with rigor and thoroughness. Students are not supposed to whisper or chew gum, but education in general has no code designed to oil the flow of data from the rostrum to the student bench. On the contrary, a great many students would declare that any existing code was designed to stop any flow whatever.

If you were to make the best progress along any highway you would do well to follow the signs. In our creeds and codes we have a number of signposts, and if their directions are pursued a maximum of result will result. If they are not pursued, one is liable to find oneself over in the ditch, in need of a towtruck.

Here then are the creeds and codes of Dianetics and Scientology. Firstly the Creed of the Church of Scientology as laid down when the Church was formed on 18th February 1954. It remains ever popular and is the most in use in our Church services throughout the world.

THE CREED OF THE CHURCH OF SCIENTOLOGY

We of the Church believe:

That all men of whatever race, color or creed were created with equal rights.

That all men have inalienable rights to their own religious practices and
   their performance.

That all men have inalienable rights to their own lives.

That all men have inalienable rights to their sanity.

That all men have inalienable rights to their own defense.

That all men have inalienable rights to conceive, choose, assist and support
   their own organizations, churches and governments.

That all men have inalienable rights to think freely, to talk freely, to write freely
   their own opinions and to counter or utter or write upon the opinions of others.

That all men have inalienable rights to the creation of their own kind.

That the souls of men have the rights of men.

That the study of the mind and the healing of mentally caused ills should not
   be alienated from religion or condoned in nonreligious fields.

And that no agency less than God has the power to suspend or set aside these
   rights, overtly or covertly.

And we of the Church believe:

That man is basically good.

That he is seeking to survive.

That his survival depends upon himself and upon his fellows, and his attainment
   of brotherhood with the Universe.

And we of the Church believe that the laws of God forbid Man:

To destroy his own kind

To destroy the sanity of another

To destroy or enslave another's soul

To destroy or reduce the survival of one's companions or one's group.

And we of the Church believe:

That the spirit can be saved and

That the spirit alone may save or heal the body.

L. Ron Hubbard
Founder

Another valid though lesser known creed is that of the Founding Church of
Scientology of Washington, D.C. formed as a religious society on 21 July 1955.

CREED:

That God works within Man, his wonders to perform;

That Man is his own soul, basically free and immortal, but deluded by the flesh;

That Man has a God-given right to his own life;

That Man has a God-given right to his own reason;

That Man has a God-given right to free and open communication;

That the human spirit is the only truly effective therapeutic agent
   available to Man;

That a civilization can endure only so long as both spiritual and material needs
   find place within its structure.

Actually the first two creeds of all were written in January 1951 following a paper *Diagnosis and Repair of Groups* which was a study of the Tone Scale and mental equipment of the leader of a group.

The Credo of a Good and Skilled Manager is the most well known of the two. It appears in the book *How to Live Though an Executive*.

THE CREDO OF A GOOD AND SKILLED MANAGER

To be effective and successful a manager must:

1. Understand as fully as possible the goals and aims of the group he manages. He must be able to see and embrace the ideal attainment of the goal as envisioned by a goal maker. He must be able to tolerate and better the practical attainments and advances of which his group and its members may be capable. He must strive to narrow, always, the ever existing gulf between the ideal and the practical.

2. He must realize that a primary mission is the full and honest interpretation by himself of the ideal and ethic and their goals and aims to his subordinates and the group itself. He must lead creatively and persuasively toward these goals his subordinates, the group itself and the individuals of the group.

3. He must embrace the organization and act solely for the entire organization and never form or favor cliques. His judgment of individuals of the group should be solely in the light of their worth to the entire group.

4. He must never falter in sacrificing individuals to the good of the group both in planning and execution and in his justice.

5. He must protect all established communication lines and complement them where necessary.

6. He must protect all affinity in his charge and have himself an affinity for the group itself.

7. He must attain always to the highest creative reality.

8. His planning must accomplish, in the light of goals and aims, the activity of the entire group. He must never let organizations grow and sprawl but, learning by pilots, must keep organizational planning fresh and flexible.

9. He must recognize in himself the rationale of the group and receive and evaluate the data out of which he makes his solutions with the highest attention to the truth of that data.

10. He must constitute himself on the orders of service to the group.

11. He must permit himself to be served well as to his individual requirements, practicing an economy of his own efforts and enjoying certain comforts to the wealth of keeping high his rationale.

12. He should require of his subordinates that they relay into their own spheres of management the whole and entire of his true feelings and the reasons for his decisions as clearly as they can be relayed and expanded and interpreted only for the greater understanding of the individuals governed by those subordinates.

13. He must never permit himself to pervert or mask any portion of the ideal and ethic on which the group operates nor must he permit the ideal and ethic to grow old and outmoded and unworkable. He must never permit his planning to be perverted or censored by subordinates. He must never permit the ideal and ethic of the group's individual members to deteriorate, using always reason to interrupt such a deterioration.

14. He must have faith in the goals, faith in himself and faith in the group.

15. He must lead by demonstrating always creative and constructive sub-goals. He must not drive by threat or fear.

16. He must realize that every individual in the group is engaged in some degree in the managing of other men, life and MEST and that a liberty of management within this code should be allowed to every such sub-manager.

Thus conducting himself a manager can win empire for his group, whatever that empire may be.

L. Ron Hubbard
Founder

Published at the same time was The Credo of a True Group Member.

CREDO OF A TRUE GROUP MEMBER

1. The successful participant of a group is that participant who closely approximates in his own activities the ideal, ethic and rationale of the overall group.

2. The responsibility of the individual for the group as a whole should not be less than the responsibility of the group for the individual.

3. The group member has, as part of his responsibility, the smooth operation of the entire group.

4. A group member must exert and insist upon his rights and prerogatives as a group member and insist upon the rights and prerogatives of the group as a group and let not these rights be diminished in any way or degree for any excuse or claimed expeditiousness.

5. The member of a true group must exert and practice his right to contribute to the group. And he must insist upon the right of the group to contribute to him. He should recognize that a myriad of group failures will result when either of these contributions is denied as a right. (A welfare state being that state in which the member is not permitted to contribute to the state but must take contribution from the state.)

6. Enturbulence of the affairs of the group by sudden shifts of plans unjustified by circumstances, breakdown of recognized channels or cessation of useful operations in a group must be refused and blocked by the member of a group. He should take care not to enturbulate a manager and thus lower ARC.

7. Failure in planning or failure to recognize goals must be corrected by the group member for the group by calling the matter to conference or acting upon his own initiative.

8. A group member must coordinate his initiative with the goals and rationale of the entire group and with other individual members, well publishing his activities and intentions so that all conflicts may be brought forth in advance.

9. A group member must insist upon his right to have initiative.

10. A group member must study and understand and work with the goals, rationale and executions of the group.

11. A group member must work toward becoming as expert as possible in his specialized technology and skill in the group and must assist other individuals of the group to an understanding of that technology and skill and its place in the organizational necessities of the group.

12. A group member should have a working knowledge of all technologies and skills in the group in order to understand them and their place in the organizational necessities of the group.

13. On the group member depends the height of the ARC of the group. He must insist upon high level communication lines and clarity in affinity and reality and know the consequence of not having such conditions. AND HE MUST WORK CONTINUALLY AND ACTIVELY TO MAINTAIN HIGH ARC IN THE ORGANIZATION.

14. A group member has the right of pride in his tasks and a right of judgment and handling in those tasks.

15. A group member must recognize that he is himself a manager of some section of the group and/or its tasks and that he himself must have both the knowledge and right of management in that sphere for which he is responsible.

16. The group member should not permit laws to be passed which limit or proscribe the activities of all the members of the group because of the failure of some of the members of the group.

17. The group member should insist on flexible planning and unerring execution of plans.

18. The performance of duty at optimum by every member of the group should be understood by the group member to be the best safeguard of his own and the group survival. It is the pertinent business of any member of the group that optimum performance be achieved by any other member of the group whether chain of command or similarity of activity sphere warrants such supervision or not.

L. Ron Hubbard
Founder

There are three main codes very well-known to all Scientologists. Two of these are moral: one is the Auditor's Code which imposes definite regulations and ethical standards to be abided by in auditing at all times. The second is the Code of a Scientologist intended for adherence by all Scientologists. The third is the Code of Honor which is not moral but ethical and carries an entirely different emphasis as it is not enforced or enforceable. A higher and more visionary ethical code, as contrasted with an enforceable moral code, it must be practiced on an entirely self-motivated basis.

The code most subject to the evolutionary process has been the Auditor's Code. It is also the most publicized. Many changes and additions have occurred over the years and they are all included here.

As of this date the Auditor's Code is:

THE AUDITOR'S CODE

In celebration of the 100% gains attainable by Standard Tech, I hereby promise as an auditor to follow the Auditor's Code.

1. I promise not to evaluate for the preclear or tell him what he should think about his case in session.

2. I promise not to invalidate the preclear's case or gains in or out of session.

3. I promise to administer only Standard Tech to a preclear in the standard way.

4. I promise to keep all auditing appointments once made.

5. I promise not to process a preclear who has not had sufficient rest and who is physically tired.

6. I promise not to process a preclear who is improperly fed or hungry.

7. I promise not to permit a frequent change of auditors.

8. I promise not to sympathize with a preclear but to be effective.

9. I promise not to let the preclear end session on his own determinism but to finish off those cycles I have begun.

10. I promise never to walk off from a preclear in session.

11. I promise never to get angry with a preclear in session.

12. I promise to run every major case action to a floating needle.

13. I promise never to run any one action beyond its floating needle.

14. I promise to grant beingness to the preclear in session.

15. I promise not to mix the processes of Scientology with other practices except when the preclear is physically ill and only medical means will serve.

16. I promise to maintain communication with the preclear and not to cut his comm or permit him to overrun in session.

17. I promise not to enter comments, expressions or enturbulence into a session that distract a preclear from his case.

18. I promise to continue to give the preclear the process or auditing command when needed in the session.

19. I promise not to let a preclear run a wrongly understood command.

20. I promise not to explain, justify or make excuses in session for any auditor mistakes whether real or imagined.

21. I promise to estimate the current case state of a preclear only by standard Case Supervision data and not to diverge because of some imagined difference in the case.

22. I promise never to use the secrets of a preclear divulged in session for punishment or personal gain.

23. I promise to see that any fee received for processing is refunded if the preclear is dissatisfied and demands it within three months after the processing, the only condition being that he may not again be processed or trained.

24. I promise not to advocate Scientology only to cure illness or only to treat the insane, knowing well it was intended for spiritual gain.

25. I promise to cooperate fully with the legal organizations of Dianetics and Scientology as developed by L. Ron Hubbard in safeguarding the ethical use and practice of the subject according to the basics of Standard Tech.

26. I promise to refuse to permit any being to be physically injured, violently damaged, operated on or killed in the name of "mental treatment."

27. I promise not to permit sexual liberties or violation of the mentally unsound.

28. I promise to refuse to admit to the ranks of practitioners any being who is insane.

Auditor

Date

Witness

Place

L. Ron Hubbard
Founder

Historically the story of the Auditor's Code is fascinating. Initially the code comprised a chapter in the book *Dianetics: The Original Thesis*, written in 1948 and eventually published in 1951. It is of interest that there was no Church of Scientology at that time or for some years to come.

In those early times of *Dianetics: The Original Thesis*, *Dianetics: The Modern Science of Mental Health* and *Science of Survival*, the Auditor's Code was derived more or less from an ideal rather than from practical experience. In the ensuing years a great deal of auditing has been done which has contributed to the development of the Auditor's Code.

Following its earlier publication in the three aforementioned books, the Auditor's Code 1954 first appeared in Professional Auditor's Bulletins Number 38 and Number 39.

Over the next four years several additions were made to the Auditor's Code 1954, the first of which appeared in the book, *Dianetics 55!*

A further addition was released in Hubbard Communications Office Bulletin 1 July 1957 *Addition to the Auditor's Code*, and two more items were added when the Auditor's Code of 1958 was published.

On 14 October 1968 the Auditor's Code 1968 was issued as a Hubbard Communications Office Policy Letter. It was released in celebration of the 100% gains attainable by Standard Tech.

Hubbard Communications Office Policy Letter 2 November 1968 *Auditor's Code* added three more code items bringing the total number to 28, as shown earlier.

The Code of Honor first appeared in Professional Auditor's Bulletin 40 on 26 November 1954. It was not expected to be closely and tightly followed in that an ethical code cannot be enforced. Any effort to enforce the Code of Honor would bring it into the level of a moral code. It cannot be enforced simply because it is a way of life which can exist as a way of life only as long as it is not enforced. Any other use but self-determined use of the Code of Honor would, as any Scientologist could quickly see, produce a considerable deterioration in a person. Therefore its use is a luxury use, and which is done solely on self-determined action, providing one sees eye to eye with the Code of Honor.

The code clearly states conditions of acceptable comradeship amongst those fighting on one side against something which they conceive should be remedied. While anyone practicing "the only one" believes that it is possible to have a fight or contest only so long as one remains "the only one" and as that single identity confronts all of existence, it is not very workable to live without friends or comrades in arms. Amongst those friends and comrades in arms one's acceptability and measure is established fairly well by his adherence to such a thing as the Code of Honor. Anyone practicing the Code of Honor would maintain a good opinion of his fellows, a much more important thing than having one's fellows maintain a good opinion of one.

The only difference between paradise on Earth and hell on Earth is whether or not you believe your fellow man worthy of receiving from you the friendship and devotion called for in this Code of Honor.

THE CODE OF HONOR

1. Never desert a comrade in need, in danger or in trouble.

2. Never withdraw allegiance once granted.

3. Never desert a group to which you owe your support.

4. Never disparage yourself or minimize your strength or power.

5. Never need praise, approval or sympathy.

6. Never compromise with your own reality.

7. Never permit your affinity to be alloyed.

8. Do not give or receive communication unless you yourself desire it.

9. Your self-determinism and your honor are more important than your immediate life.

10. Your integrity to yourself is more important than your body.

11. Never regret yesterday. Life is in you today, and you make your tomorrow.

12. Never fear to hurt another in a just cause.

13. Don't desire to be liked or admired.

14. Be your own advisor, keep your own counsel and select your own decisions.

15. Be true to your own goals.

L. Ron Hubbard
Founder

The second of the two most important moral codes of the Church is the Code of a Scientologist. Evolved to safeguard Scientologists in general it is a stopgap to serve in the interim time when all Scientologists are not yet up to a level where they are content to receive for their opponents the logical targets of the subject itself, and for their randomity must pick out their companions in order to engage in a game.

With all Scientologists subscribing to this code Scientology will, itself, maintain its potent forward motion in our world and this universe.

The current Code of a Scientologist is that issued as Hubbard Communications Office Policy Letter 5 February 1969 *Press Policy, Code of a Scientologist*.

PRESS POLICY   CODE OF A SCIENTOLOGIST

1. To keep Scientologists, the public and the press accurately informed concerning Scientology, the world of mental health and society.

2. To use the best I know of Scientology to the best of my ability to help my family, friends, groups and the world.

3. To refuse to accept for processing and to refuse to accept money from any preclear or group I feel I cannot honestly help.

4. To decry and do all I can to abolish any and all abuses against life and mankind.

5. To expose and help abolish any and all physically damaging practices in the field of mental health.

6. To help clean up and keep clean the field of mental health.

7. To bring about an atmosphere of safety and security in the field of mental health by eradicating its abuses and brutality.

8. To support true humanitarian endeavors in the field of human rights.

9. To embrace the policy of equal justice for all.

10. To work for freedom of speech in the world.

11. To actively decry the suppression of knowledge, wisdom, philosophy or data which would help mankind.

12. To support the freedom of religion.

13. To help Scientology orgs and groups ally themselves with public groups.

14. To teach Scientology at a level it can be understood and used by the recipients.

15. To stress the freedom to use Scientology as a philosophy in all its applications and variations in the humanities.

16. To insist upon standard and unvaried Scientology as an applied activity in ethics, processing and administration in Scientology organizations.

17. To take my share of responsibility for the impact of Scientology upon the world.

18. To increase the numbers and strength of Scientology over the world.

19. To set an example of the effectiveness and wisdom of Scientology.

20. To make this world a saner, better place.

L. Ron Hubbard
Founder

During the early 1970s and up to present time a *Case Supervisor Series* of technical materials was produced. Included was the Code of a Case Supervisor.

THE CODE OF A CASE SUPERVISOR

This is the Code of a Case Supervisor as regards his auditors and their preclears for whom he is C/Sing.

1. I promise to know my Dianetics and Scientology totally cold up to the level at which I am C/Sing.

2. I promise never to look for some imagined error in tech data but always to look for and find the real error in the auditing, programming or C/Sing.

3. I promise never to treat a case as "different."

4. I promise that if I cannot find the reason why a session has failed from the folder that I will suspect a false auditing report and get the preclear asked about the session and get data as to why it failed.

5. I promise never to punish an auditor for querying a C/S.

6. I promise to refrain from discussing or mentioning data from preclear folders socially.

7. I promise to correct my auditors' application of tech positively without invalidation.

8. I promise that I will order the auditor to cramming or retraining for any flunked session.

9. I promise never to order an unnecessary repair.

10. I promise never to use repair processes to get case gain when the preclear needs the next grade.

11. I promise never to give verbal C/S instructions but always to write them down.

12. I promise never to talk to the auditor about the case.

13. I promise never to talk to a preclear about his case.

14. I promise to send the preclear to the Examiner or Director of Processing, to get data, if unsure why the folder has been sent up for C/S.

15. I promise never to be reasonable as a C/S.

16. I promise to maintain sufficient ethics presence to get my orders followed.

17. I promise never to issue involved repair orders.

18. I promise never to follow C/S advice from a preclear but I will accept the preclear's data.

19. I promise that I will ALWAYS read through the preclear folder before C/Sing a case.

20. I promise I will always have the folders of cases in trouble casewise, ethically or medically reviewed to find the out-tech.

21. I promise never to put a preclear on a grade to "solve his case."

22. I promise to always order a repair of a misaudited grade until the end phenomena has been achieved.

23. I promise to advance the preclear up the Grade Chart in the proper sequence.

24. I promise never to order a grade run that the preclear is not set up for.

25. I promise never to indulge in the practice of "hopeful C/Sing."

26. I promise never to C/S a session I cannot read but will instead return it to the auditor for clarification.

27. I promise to make every effort to find and point out an actual goof and send the auditor to cramming.

28. I promise never to invalidate or harass an auditor for a correct action or when no technical goof has occurred.

29. I promise to recognize and acknowledge a technically perfect session.

30. I promise to see that a preclear or Pre-OT who knows he has made an end phenomena is sent to Examinations and Certifications and Awards to attest.

31. I promise never to send a preclear or Pre-OT who hasn't made it to declare and attest.

32. I promise to see that preclears and Pre-OTs who haven't made it are handled until they have made that specific declare.

33. I promise to complete cycles of action on the preclear and never start a new one while an old one is still incomplete.

34. I promise to ensure that the auditors for whom I am C/Sing continue to improve in skill and training level.

35. I promise to maintain a standard of the highest professional conduct.

A Supervisor's Code was issued as Hubbard Communications Office Policy Letter 15 September 1967, *The Supervisor's Code*. It was extracted from the *ACC Manual* published in 1957 and revised by substituting the word 'Supervisor' for 'Instructor.'

THE SUPERVISOR'S CODE

The Supervisor's Code has been developed over many years' experience in training. It has been found that any time a supervisor broke one of the rules, to any degree, the course and training activities failed to function properly.

Teaching Scientology is a very precise job, and a supervisor must maintain the precision at all times to render the services he should to the students entrusted to his care.

A supervisor cannot hope to gain the respect or willingness of the student to be taught by him sitting there, spouting words and being an "authority" on the subject. He must know his subject and follow the Supervisor's Code to the letter. It isn't a hard code to follow, and it is a very practical one. If you feel you cannot honestly follow all of it, you should receive more training, and, maybe, more processing until you can make the code your own before attempting to train students in Scientology.

We have had the rules of the game of Scientology a long time, and now we have the rules of the game called training. Have fun!

1. The supervisor must never neglect an opportunity to direct a student to the actual source of Scientology data.

2. The supervisor should correct a student's mistake thoroughly and use good ARC while doing it.

3. The supervisor should remain in good ARC with his students at all times while they are performing training activities.

4. The supervisor at all times must have a high tolerance of stupidity in his students, and must be willing to repeat any datum not understood as many times as necessary for the student to understand and acquire reality on the datum.

5. The supervisor does not have a "case" in his relationship with his students, nor discuss or talk about his personal problems to the students.

6. The supervisor will, at all times, be a source point of good control and direction to his students.

7. The supervisor will be able to correlate any part of Scientology to any other part and to livingness over the Eight Dynamics.

8. The supervisor should be able to answer any questions concerning Scientology by directing the student to the actual source of the data. If a supervisor cannot answer a particular question, he should always say so, and the supervisor should always find the answer to the question from the source, and tell the student where the answer is to be found.

9. The supervisor should never lie to, deceive, or misdirect a student concerning Scientology. He shall be honest at all times about it with a student.

10. The supervisor must be an accomplished graduate of a Course Supervisor's Course.

11. The supervisor should always set a good example to his students, such as giving good demonstrations, being on time, and dressing neatly.

12. The supervisor should at all times be perfectly willing and able to do anything he tells his students to do.

13. The supervisor must not become emotionally involved with students of either sex while they are under his or her training.

14. When a supervisor makes any mistake, he is to inform the student that he has made one, and rectify it immediately. This datum embraces all phases in training demonstrations, lectures, and processing, etc. He is never to hide the fact that he made the mistake.

15. The supervisor should never neglect to give praise to his students when due.

16. The supervisor to some degree should be pan-determined about the supervisor-student relationship.

17. When a supervisor lets a student control, give orders to, or handle the supervisor in any way, for the purpose of demonstration or other training purposes, the supervisor should always put the student back under his control.

18. The supervisor will at all times observe the Auditor's Code during sessions, and the Code of a Scientologist at all times.

19. The supervisor will never give a student opinions about Scientology without labeling them thoroughly as such; otherwise, he is to direct only to tested and proven data concerning Scientology.

20. The supervisor shall never use a student for his own personal gain.

21. The supervisor will be a stable terminal, point the way to stable data, be certain, but not dogmatic or dictatorial, toward his students.

22. The supervisor will keep himself at all times informed of the most recent Scientology data and procedures, and communicate this information to his students.

I agree to follow and obey the foregoing code.

Signed: _____

L. Ron Hubbard
Founder

The following is the Code of a Sea Org Member. It has been distilled from the collected works of L. Ron Hubbard.

First released in tentative form on April 9th, 1971, it has been revised by surveys of Sea Org members and is herewith re-released in final form.

These rules are not new, on the contrary they are the traditional ones with which the Sea Org was built.

THE CODE OF A SEA ORG MEMBER

1. I promise to uphold, forward and carry out Command Intention.

2. I promise to use Dianetics and Scientology for the greatest good for the greatest number of dynamics.

3. I promise to help get ethics in on this planet and the universe.

4. I promise to do my part to achieve the Sea Org's humanitarian objective which is to make a safe environment where the Fourth Dynamic engram can be audited out.

5. I promise to uphold the fact that duty is the Sea Org member's true motivation, which is the highest motivation there is.

6. I promise to keep my own personal ethics in and uphold beyond all compromise the honor, integrity and true discipline that is the Sea Org's heritage and tradition.

7. I promise to effectively lead, care for and train those under my charge and to ensure they keep their own ethics in and if that fails to take action with fair and legal justice.

8. I promise to take responsibility for the preservation and the continued full and exact use of the technologies of Dianetics and Scientology.

9. I promise to exemplify in my conduct the belief that to command is to serve and that a being is only as valuable as he can serve others.

10. I promise to improve my worth to the Sea Org and mankind by regularly advancing my knowledge of and ability to apply the truths and technologies of Dianetics and Scientology.

11. I promise to accept and fulfill to the utmost of my ability the responsibilities entrusted to me whatever they may be and wherever they may carry me in the line of duty.

12. I promise to be competent and effective at all times and never try to explain away or justify ineffectiveness nor minimize the true power that I am.

13. I promise, at all times, to set a desirable example in appearance, conduct and production to fellow Sea Org members and the area in which I operate.

14. I promise to demand that my fellow Sea Org members not fall short of the ideals and spirit of the Sea Org.

15. I promise to do my part to protect and further the image of the Sea Org.

16. I promise to come to the defense of the Sea Org and fellow Sea Org members whenever needed.

17. I promise through my actions to increase the power of the Sea Org and decrease the power of any enemy.

18. I promise to make things go right and to persist until they do.

A lesser known code within the organizations of Scientology is the Letter Writer's Code published as Hubbard Communications Office Policy Letter 21 November 1961, *Letter Writer's Code*. This further enhanced the Church's communication lines.

THE LETTER WRITER'S CODE

1. Always answer a correspondent's exact questions.
2. Never get angry or misemotional with the correspondent.
3. Maintain two-way communication with the correspondent.
4. Be willing to grant beingness to the correspondent.
5. Do not justify organizational mistakes whether real or imagined.

6. Never fail to help at the correspondent's reality level.
7. Never imply or promise help where it is not real to you.
8. Never cut communication with a correspondent, once initiated.
9. Never Q and A with a correspondent: That is, never answer a bank communication with a bank communication.
10. Be willing to help the correspondent's life and livingness until he or she is Clear.
11. Never fail to answer a letter promptly: that is, within forty-eight hours.

L. Ron Hubbard
Founder

A Dianetic Family Code appeared in the book *Child Dianetics* in 1951. It listed some do's a family could observe to raise its tone.

THE DIANETIC FAMILY CODE

Check yourself and your family on these:

1. Do everything possible to maintain affinity, reality, and communication.
2. Use discipline based on understanding and computation rather than on compulsion.
3. Use the question, "Is it important?" before taking any precipitate action.
4. Realize that *any* invalidation of another's data adversely affects the ARC triangle.
5. Pass on information the other person should have instead of concealing the facts in the hope of saving the other some anguish, but do not burden the child with adult problems.
6. Remember, the family is a team and an ARC break with one member is a break with all.
7. Watch for possible key-in and restimulating phrases and actions, and avoid them until they can be erased.
8. Watch for control circuit phrases and avoid them.

L. Ron Hubbard
Founder

The Medical Liaison Officer's Code was published as Hubbard Communications Office Policy Letter 11 October 1970. This code was practiced on the ships of the Sea Organization where prescribed medical treatment had to be continued at sea. On the Flagship there was a fully operational clinic and a Medical Liaison Officer. The code is presented here to provide a basis of operation for Medical Liaison Officers and may be of interest to the Dianetically trained doctor.

MEDICAL LIAISON OFFICER'S CODE

1. I promise not to evaluate the physical symptoms of those on medical lines but instead to listen and then provide whatever information or direction is needed to result in a physical improvement.

2. I promise not to invalidate the reality of those on medical lines as to the state of their physical bodies but

to keep them producing and contributing to whatever extent they are realistically able.

3. I promise to administer only standard or proven medical treatment where indicated and not to deviate or experiment with unproven treatments or medications nor will I allow anyone else to do so.

4. I promise to keep all dental and medical appointments once made and to see that those who need to see a specialist or dentist see one.

5. I promise to see that those who are not getting proper food or rest do so, so that they become eligible for auditing.

6. I promise to see that the data needed to give proper care to those on medical lines is passed on or conveyed to whomever is giving it in my absence.

7. I promise never to sympathize with those on medical lines but to be effective.

8. I promise to complete all medical treatments started which are producing improvement in physical conditions and not to change the medication or treatment that is producing results for another.

9. I promise to refer anyone who by their actions are attempting to prevent a recovery to the Master at Arms (also known as an Ethics Officer) and to advise the Case Supervisor.

10. I promise never to abandon or neglect those under my care.

11. I reserve the right to refuse care to anyone who does not follow the directions given them to make them well or who repeatedly fails to keep appointments involving a medical series which must be given as scheduled to be effective.

12. I promise never to criticize or become angry with those on medical lines.

13. I promise never to provide a pain killer to anyone I feel would respond to an assist given by myself or another promptly.

14. I promise not to continue a treatment past the point it is no longer needed or no longer effective.

15. I promise to grant beingness to those on medical lines.

16. I promise to provide a safe, clean and comfortable environment for the unwell.

17. I promise to indicate to those on my lines which medications and treatments are curative ones and which are only intended to alleviate symptoms.

18. I promise not to enter comments, expressions or enturbulence into the environment of those on medical lines that would cause mystery, misunderstoods or fear of worsening.

19. I promise to encourage those on my lines who are responding well to be as causative and knowledgeable about their physical condition as is possible and never to present medicine as anything more than a technology that can be studied and learned by anyone of interest and ability.

20. I promise not to explain, justify or make excuses for any clinical mistake whether real or imagined but to correct it immediately.

21. I promise to estimate the current state of those on medical lines with reality and not to diverge due to other-determined influence or false or alarming reports.

22. I promise to follow all standard C/S instructions exactly and to obtain C/S permission before permitting the administration of any narcotic or drug rendering a preclear ineligible for auditing.

23. I promise to see that all dentists and medical specialists used to treat a preclear are competent in their skill and to base my decision on results only.

24. I promise to maintain high health standards in the environment and to see those I am responsible for are protected from the influence of poor health or safety standards.

25. I promise to use my knowledge of Dianetics and Scientology in all that I do.

26. I promise to keep excellent records and data on those on my lines and to keep the C/S advised.

27. I promise to prevent extreme health conditions from occurring by seeing that preventative or early care is given on time.

28. I promise to ensure anyone medically cured or under treatment receives processing as this alone ensures the cure remains a permanent one and shortens the time required for treatment.

Conclusion

As this volume demonstrates, the growth of Dianetics and Scientology has been truly phenomenal since *Dianetics: The Modern Science of Mental Health* was first published in 1950. Today the worldwide membership numbers in the millions and is accelerating more rapidly than ever. In a saddened world where ethics and discipline have been neglected, our codes have yet held us to our task.

Now we look to the future, to a snowballing expansion, far greater responsibility in social reform, technical advancements, administrative streamlining, greater coaction within Scientology itself and with other churches and groups. Codes, rights, duties, guides will all continue to evolve and play their part as vital aids to be used and not abused, to support each one of us in our endeavors to rehabilitate ourselves and our fellow man towards spiritual growth and freedom.

15

The Scientology Catechism

SCIENTOLOGY ORIGINS AND BACKGROUND

What does the word Scientology mean?

The word Scientology means "the study of knowledge" or the "science of knowledge" from the Latin *scio* which means know or distinguish, and from the Greek word *logos* which means reason itself or inward thought. So it means the study of wisdom or knowledge. It means "knowing how to know." The word was coined by L. Ron Hubbard.

Is Scientology in the dictionary?

Scientology is in many reference works. For example, the World Book Dictionary lists a definition of Scientology.

What is Scientology about?

Scientology is about people like you, and your family and your friends. It's about tolerance and love and being free enough to make things better. It is about certainty in life and living. It is about happiness.

The true story of Scientology is simple, concise and direct. It is quickly told:

1. A philosopher develops a philosophy about Man and life and death;
2. People find it interesting;
3. People find it works;
4. People pass it along to others;
5. It grows.

So the true story of Scientology is a simple story.

And too true to be turned aside.

How did Scientology start?

In 1950 L. Ron Hubbard published *Dianetics: The Modern Science of Mental Health.* This book covered the anatomy of the human mind, and a technology called auditing. It started a demand for Academies in which

people could study the discoveries outlined in that book. The book has remained a best seller ever since.

Realizing already at this stage that the mind in itself, no matter how liberated, was limiting and that there was something "animating" the mind, L. Ron Hubbard permitted the founding in 1950 of the Hubbard Dianetic Research Foundation to facilitate investigation into the realm of the spirit.

An astonishing number of characteristics and potential abilities of Man were unearthed in this course of study, and it was a difficult task which had to be painstakingly done to isolate the most important truths. By 1952 Hubbard found that he had isolated *élan vital*, the spirit, and thus was Scientology born.

Subjects which L. Ron Hubbard consulted in the organization and development of Scientology were a full knowledge of both Eastern and Western philosophical and religious thought; the physical sciences, including nuclear physics, and mathematics.

Scientology is a wisdom in the tradition of ten thousand years of search in Asia and Western civilization. It is an organization of the pertinencies which are mutually held true by all men in all times, and the development of technologies which demonstrate the existence of new phenomena not hitherto known.

This one-man effort is incredible in terms of study and research and is a record never approached in living memory.

How long has Scientology been in existence?

Scientology evolved from Dianetics which was launched in May 1950. The Church of Scientology was first registered in 1954 in California.

Why is Scientology called a religion?

Scientology is a religion by its basic tenets, practice, historical background and by the definition of the word "religion" itself. The following will help clarify the philosophical and practical aspects of religion.

Religious practice implies ritual, faith-in, doctrine based on a catechism and a creed.

Religious philosophy implies study of spiritual manifestations; research on the nature of the spirit and study on the relationship of the spirit to the body; exercises devoted to the rehabilitation of abilities in a spirit.

Scientology is a religious philosophy in its highest meaning as it concerns itself with Man and his relation to the Supreme Being and life, bringing Man to total freedom and truth.

Scientology is also a religious practice in that the Church of Scientology conducts basic services such as sermons at church meetings, christenings, weddings and funerals.

So Scientology is a religion in the most traditional sense. It deals with Man, the spirit, and is distinguished from material and nonreligious philosophies which believe Man is a product of material circumstances. Scientology does not demand blind faith but endeavors to help the individual discover past experiences and shed the trauma and guilt (sin) which encumbers him. He or she finds as they progress that they can confidently express the certainty they are a spiritual being.

Was Scientology called a religion to make it legal?

Dianetics, the substudy of Scientology, was operating quite legally before Scientology came into existence and became a religion. It is now some twenty-five years since the first Church of Scientology was registered. So, inasmuch as it was legal from the start, there was never any effort to "make it legal." Scientology is called a religion because that is what it is and the large membership of that day voted that it become a Church.

Why is Scientology a Church?

Both the modern day usage of the word "church" and the historical root justify the use of this word when referring to Scientology's organizations. It is not a word monopolized by Christian organizations. In modern day usage an extension has taken place whereby people speak of the Buddhist or Moslem Church, simply meaning the whole body of believers in a particular religious teaching.

There were churches ten thousand years before there were Christians, and Christianity itself was a revolt against the established church.

A church is simply a building that houses religious activities, a place of learning and attaining knowingness, and knowingness has always been considered sacred lore. As we are dealing with helping Man become more spiritually aware of himself and his family, as well as God, Scientology therefore is a church. In the most ancient tradition, it is symbolic of the thrust towards life of the dynamics or parts of life which total the number eight. We have a road that has been traveled by many. Traveling this road, they have found that they have, indeed, achieved greater success in life and greater happiness in the search for truth. Religion means basically the search for truth. Seeing that, Scientologists in the early '50s voted that a church be formed.

Scientology has been adjudicated a church by the various courts and government agencies of the United States, Australia, New Zealand, Sweden and many other countries as well as experts on religion.

What is the Mother Church?

The Mother Church is the Church of Scientology of California. It is the Scientology group where the highest levels of spiritual counseling may be attained and where research is conducted into as yet undeveloped areas of Scientology. Its headquarters are at St. Hill Manor, East Grinstead, Sussex, England.

Where are Scientology Churches and organizations located?

Scientology Churches and Missions exist all over the world. There are a great many Churches and far more Missions in various countries.

For a complete list, please consult the chapter on Scientology Churches and Organizations.

What does a Scientology Church or Mission actually do?

The Scientology Church's main activities consist of training in the Ministerial Academy and pastoral counseling or auditing on an individual basis. We also conduct Sunday services and chaplain's counseling. We help the individual become more able to help himself and to help others. This is done by training and counseling.

How active is Scientology in the Black communities and countries?

Increasingly more active. By the Creed of the Church, "all men of whatever race, color or creed were created with equal rights."

There are Scientologists of all races and religious backgrounds.

What is the Scientology Cross?

It is an eight-pointed cross representing the eight parts or dynamics of life through which each of us is striving to exist. These parts are: our urge to survive through ourselves; our families and procreation; through our groups; as mankind; through all living things; the physical universe; the spirit; and through realization and understanding of the Supreme Being. To be able to live happily and with respect in each of these spheres of existence is symbolized by the Scientology Cross.

The vertical plane of the cross depicts the path toward greater spiritual heights and the horizontal plane represents the need to help others in the world so we can reduce criminality, insanity and war and provide each of us a safer environment where there can be creation rather than destruction. As a matter of interest the cross as a symbol predates Christianity.

Does Scientology have prayers?

Prayers are read in all services. In addition, Churches in each country participate in an annual interdenominational Human Rights Prayer Meeting. The first international Human Rights Prayer Day was held in 1976. The first national one was held in 1969.

How does Scientology work?

Firstly, the philosophy of Scientology provides answers to many questions about life and death and gives people more wisdom and understanding. Secondly, it works by application of an exact technology on a precisely mapped path. By application of this technology in a counseling/auditing context, a person is able to remove barriers and unwanted conditions and so become more himself. As a person progresses his native abilities are successfully employed towards helping others.

That which is real to the person himself is all one is asked to accept of Scientology. No beliefs are forced upon him. By training and processing he finds out for himself.

What does Scientology accomplish?

Since Scientology is an applied religious philosophy, the stress is on application and workability. It addresses the individual and brings about self-improvement by increasing a person's awareness and ability to handle life. It differs from other religious philosophies in that it supplies the means through which a person can increase his ability to guide himself and cope with the problems and situations he and others face in life.

What claims do you make for Scientology?

Scientology helps Man become more able and brings about greater individual peace and happiness. It helps individuals do this through its unique counseling/auditing technology and its training in the philosophy of Scientology which is very much an *applied* religious philosophy.

Man has often been attracted to philosophies that sound very nice but even if an individual agrees with the idea that he should love his neighbor, he is not often able to do that. Scientology and Dianetics supply the tools with which he can, indeed, love his neighbor. Pastoral counseling is much more effective and much faster than any previous study.

We believe that each individual does have answers to various problems of living and simply needs the right questions to find the right answers for himself. Scientology supplies these questions.

How do people get into Scientology?

Usually by word of mouth, often by reading a book. Sometimes by meeting a Scientologist and seeing that they have "something"—an attitude to life, certainty, self-confidence and friendliness, which they would like to have. Fundamentally, because they would like to improve something in their lives or because they want to help others improve themselves and thus make a better civilization.

How does one become a Scientologist?

Usually by trying it firsthand. Often by reading a book and then studying a basic course or having some auditing. People find it works and their lives improve, and they continue on in their training and processing.

Is auditing like hypnotism and psychotherapy?

It was as a result of L. Ron Hubbard's investigation of hypnotism and all other mental practices that he saw the need for practical answers. In his first book, *Dianetics: The Modern Science of Mental Health*, he wrote he found hypnotism and psychotherapy dangerous and impractical.

Nearly all methods of alleged mental science are based on principles quite the opposite to Scientology. They treat Man as a "thing" to be conditioned, not as a thinking being who has answers and who can improve enormously.

Is Scientology a cult or a secret society?

Not at all. Scientology literature is freely available to anyone. There is no demand for the individual to withdraw from society; on the contrary, Scientologists become more involved.

We believe what is true for you is true for you, and one must seek answers for himself and observe for himself and then decide what is true for him. We promote the family unit and harmony. Further, individuals under eighteen years of age must have parental consent to be a member of the Church and in addition, even adults must be free of any encumbrances on membership, i.e. any close relative or family member who is antagonistic to their being a member. We hold no secret rituals nor have we altered the Bible in any way.

Even though there are confidential materials in the upper level courses, this only exists to ensure that a student does not impede his progress, or that of his friends, by studying the materials he is not yet qualified to handle.

By what means or method does Scientology differ from other religious philosophies?

Nearly all religious philosophies share a belief in Man's ability to live uprightly. In addition, one of the aims of Scientology is to achieve a world without insanity, war and crime.

In Scientology there is no attempt to change another's beliefs or to persuade the person away from his own religious practice. Scientology helps people to achieve their goals: (1) through reading the materials contained in the books and publications; (2) through the unique counseling technology called auditing (or pastoral counseling); (3) through training courses which utilize comparatively new discoveries in education. Scientology makes it possible for *any* religion to attain its goals and is therefore a religion of religions.

Does Scientology interfere with other religions?

Scientology is all-denominational in that it opens its membership to people of all faiths. Part of the Church's Creed states that "all men have inalienable rights to their own religious practices and their performance."

Many Scientologists attend services of the religion that they were born into and find that Scientology assists them to get more out of their religion. Many ministers, rabbis and priests have taken Scientology courses and have found Scientology principles entirely compatible with their religions.

Why do Scientologists want to help people?

Because every one of us working in Scientology has been helped enormously and we want others to share our wins and successes.

SCIENTOLOGY BELIEFS

Is Man a spirit?

Close your eyes.
Mock up (create) a picture of a cat.
Done?
That which is looking at the cat is you, a spirit.

How does one know Man is a spirit?

It is something for each individual to look at, observe, and come to a conclusion about by himself. We believe Man is more than a mind and a body and that it is he, himself, the spirit, who can control his mind and body.

Do you think your body would *do* anything by itself if it were not guided by you, the being?

What is the Scientology concept of God?

We have no dogma in Scientology and each person's concept is probably different. In helping a person to become more aware of himself, others, the environment and God, each person attains his own certainty as to who God is and exactly what God means to him. The author of the universe exists. How this is symbolized is dictated by your early training and conscience.

Why don't you teach about God?

We do—but not by dogma. In his book *Science of Survival*, L. Ron Hubbard writes: "No culture in the history of the world, save the thoroughly depraved and expiring ones, has failed to affirm the existence of a Supreme Being. It is an empirical observation that men without a strong and lasting faith in a Supreme Being are less capable, less ethical, and less valuable to themselves and society.

"A man without an abiding faith is, by observation alone, more of a thing than a man."

Can't God be the only one to help Man?

We take the maxim quite to heart that God helps those that help themselves. You have the answers to the mysteries of life; all you require is awareness and this Scientology can and routinely does teach you. Man asks for pat answers, he is used to doing this. Scientology requires that the person thinks for himself and thus learns wisdom.

Does Scientology believe in brotherly love?

Yes, and perhaps goes a step further. L. Ron Hubbard wrote that "to love is the road to strength and to love in spite of all is the secret of greatness, and may very well be the greatest secret in this universe."

Does Scientology recognize good and evil?

A very clear distinction is made between good and evil. Those actions which enhance survival of the eight aspects or dynamics of life; that is, survival for oneself, one's family and children, for one's group, for mankind, for all living things, for the physical universe itself, for the spiritual universe and for God, is good and that which destroys or denies any part of these aspects of life is evil. Decision making is then based on enhancing the majority of these dynamics of life.

Good may be defined as constructive. Evil may be defined as destructive.

Does Scientology believe Man is sinful?

Man is basically good but aberrated; he does harm or sins certainly—and reduces his awareness further by so doing.

Man often "solves" problems by harming himself and others.

Through Scientology he can confront his actions, erase the ignorance and aberration which surrounds them, and know and experience truth again.

All religions seek truth. Freedom of the spirit is only to be found on the road to truth.

Sin is composed, according to Scientology, of lies and hidden actions and is therefore untruth.

Will Scientology help one control his mind?

It will help—for you are not your mind or your body, and just as Scientology helps you to intelligently control all parts and conditions of existence, it helps put *you* at cause over your mind and life.

Is Scientology about the mind?

No. Scientology is about the individual himself as separate and distinct from the mind. Dianetics is about the mind, and is the most advanced mental science Man has.

Does Scientology believe in mind over matter?

Well, whose mind and what matter?
Scientology addresses you, not your mind, not your body, but you.
Some people do intriguing things with the mind. Some have it confused with the brain.
We do believe that *élan vital*, the spirit, is *potentially* superior to material things.

Does Scientology believe one can exist outside of the body?

Before entering Scientology many people experience the feeling of looking down on one's body, and by traveling the path in Scientology, this experience becomes nothing out of the ordinary. Believing that Man is a thetan (Greek for soul or spiritual being), it obviously follows that Man can exist outside of the body. Scientology believes that Man is not his body, his mind or his brain. He, a spiritual force, energizes the physical body and his life.

Scientology has proved, for the first time, that Man is a spiritual being, not an animal.

Does Scientology believe in reincarnation?

Reincarnation is a definite system and is not part of Scientology.

In the past the term reincarnation has mystified Man. The definition has been corrupted. The word has been taken to mean: to be born again in different life forms, whereas its actual definition is: to be born again into the flesh or into another body.

The existence of *past lives* is proven in Scientology.

Today in Scientology, many people have certainty in their past experiences, referred to as past lives, not as reincarnation. Individuals are free to believe or not. One can find out for himself. Self-discovery is part of Scientology.

What about past lives?

Past lives are not a dogma in Scientology.

Many Scientologists do believe in past lives as a result of their own past experiences recalled in counseling. With Scientology you are the judge of your own certainty in your past experiences, because you will know for yourself without reservation what they are. After all, you were there!

It is a fact that unless one begins to handle aberrations built up in past lives, he doesn't progress satisfactorily.

To believe one had a physical, or other, existence prior to the identity of the current body, replete with all of those philosophical manifestations, is hardly new—but it is exciting because, if true for you, one is responsible for the current state of affairs (he didn't simply inherit it from others before him) and will have to face the future he is creating.

What does Scientology think of other religions?

Scientology respects all religions. Each is a different road leading toward God and all faiths are good in that they encourage people to lead a religious life. Religion binds mankind in a common endeavor to reach wisdom.

Scientology does not conflict with other religions or other religious practices. Quite often Scientology Church members rekindle a greater interest than ever in the subject of religions—including the one of their baptism.

What does Scientology have to say about Christianity?

Christianity is one of the great religions of the world and Scientology supports its civilizing influence and respects the words of Jesus Christ.

Christianity is among the faiths studied in the Great Religions Course that is part of the Church of Scientology's ministerial qualifications.

Does Scientology believe in Jesus Christ and is there not redemption only through Christ?

There are probably many types of redemption. That of Christ was to heaven.

Jesus Christ was the Savior of Mankind, the Son of God and instructed his disciples to bring wisdom and good health to Man, and promised mankind immortality. In Scientology we believe in these three things Christ intended for Man. It is our mission as Scientologists, as it was Christ's disciples', to bring wisdom, good health and immortality to mankind.

There are many great religious prophets and leaders, each of whom has left a path toward God. Religious prophets are recognized in Scientology as the torchbearers of culture and civilization.

Does one have to give up one's religious practices and belief?

No, it has been said Scientology provides a practical means by which people can actually live up to the standards set by the prophets and religious founders who preceded us.

Membership in Scientology does not mean that there is any necessity to leave your church, synagogue, temple or mosque.

Does Scientology believe in charity and welfare?

It does. However, too much giving without there being any chance of returning that charity, in no matter how small a way, can degrade the dignity of people and cause harm. Scientology's welfare programs therefore encourage those receiving the charity to make some form of contribution by helping others so that self-respect can be maintained.

Does Scientology hold any political views?

Scientology is nonpolitical. By its Creed, "all men have inalienable rights to conceive, choose, assist and support their own organizations, churches and governments." The Church believes there should be separation of church and state but the two are mutually dependent upon one another. It is believed that there can be no great culture without affirmation of Man's spiritual nature.

Can children participate in Scientology?

Scientologists want their children to have Scientology available to them. There are often children's courses, children's choirs and study programs for young people. There are Scientology schools in several countries. Scientology Churches will only permit a minor to enroll for a course with written parental consent.

Do Scientologists have definite ideas about the raising of children?

There is a lot written about children in Scientology. Basically children are recognized as people and should be given all the respect and love granted adults. Dignity and purpose are native to the child.

It is already being observed that children raised in good Scientology homes are above average in ability and soon begin to understand how and why people act as they do, and so life becomes a lot safer and happier for them.

The concern of the Scientologist is purely with the beingness of the child, which is to say his spirit, his potentialities, and his happiness.

Why should one get better or change if the emotions and depressions are all part of life?

Mainly because depressions and such are not necessarily a part of life. One soon discovers in Scientology that these things considered as "part of life" in the past, can be handled. Happiness, you could say, is the overcoming of not unknowable obstacles toward a known goal. This feeling of happiness becomes a major part of a Scientology individual's life.

Why are people afraid to find out for themselves?

Scientologists are not afraid to find out for themselves, in fact, nothing in Scientology is taken on faith, but it is a matter of self-discovery for each individual. In the writings of L. Ron Hubbard, he has always encouraged a student of Scientology to approach with a skeptical attitude and not to believe something unless it is true for him in application.

Why can't one make up his own mind about it?

One can and indeed one should. There is no purpose served in studying Scientology because someone else wants you to. But having taken a good look at it and having thought you'd like to know more, the best thing is just to start.

What is real in Scientology for you is what you find in it that is real for you.

SCIENTOLOGY'S FOUNDER

Who is L. Ron Hubbard?

L. Ron Hubbard is an American educationist, philosopher, researcher, writer, explorer and Founder of Scientology and Dianetics.

See the photographic biography of L. Ron Hubbard in this book.

What sort of person is he?

He is an individual of great warmth and stature. He is full of adventure and his courage and concern for his fellow man has no bounds.

Is L. Ron Hubbard still alive?

Yes, very much so. His many published volumes, over eighteen million copies sold, are testimony to his presence and zest for life. Mr. Hubbard was born on March 13, 1911, so he is only in his sixties.

What is L. Ron Hubbard's role today?

L. Ron Hubbard is the Founder. This is obviously a lifetime appointment since he retired in 1966 from participating in the running of the Churches of Scientology on a day-to-day basis. He takes a very keen interest in our expansion and researches done by him are made available to the Church. L. Ron Hubbard is world renowned and respected as the Founder—a friend to all mankind.

Is it true that L. Ron Hubbard has withdrawn from Scientology?

No, he is still doing research and he is keenly interested in how Scientologists all over the world are progressing. He resigned as a director of the Church in 1966, and no longer actively runs each Church, but as the Founder he keeps in close touch with what Scientologists are doing.

What would happen if L. Ron Hubbard died?

All great religious leaders of the past have died. Their work flourished.

Men die, wisdom and ideas do not. As long as men and women communicate and read and use the knowledge L. Ron Hubbard has organized, Scientology will grow and serve mankind.

How did L. Ron Hubbard rise above the reactive mind when others didn't?

He applied to himself the principles he had found.

Where does L. Ron Hubbard live?

Since he was a little boy, he has roamed the world and has seen more of it than most other men. He still travels.

Does L. Ron Hubbard live on a ship?

He undertook an expedition to retrace ancient trade routes after he retired in 1966 and the work lasted several years. He has not lived on a ship for some time.

Is L. Ron Hubbard a millionaire?

L. Ron Hubbard is one of those fortunate people who never make problems over money. He inherited some wealth at an early age, but in the early 1930s became one of the highest paid writers in America, long before Dianetics.

He is probably a millionaire several times over from his book royalties. His public book sales are astronomical. Why would he need any other income?

He receives no royalties from the fees paid to organizations for training and processing. On the contrary, these organizations were forgiven any debt they ever owed him.

Does L. Ron Hubbard eat food, and sleep?

Oh yes—he has a body, and bodies need food and sleep to run well.

But at an age when most men have packed it up, Ron still outworks any of those around him. And sleeps less.

Is L. Ron Hubbard married?

Yes, he is happily married and for twenty-five years to Mary Sue Whipp Hubbard, and through this marriage they have three lovely children.

Why is only L. Ron Hubbard's name on the books?

Because he wrote them.

Why did he leave the United Kingdom?

L. Ron Hubbard left the United Kingdom in 1966, two years before the Scientology vs. institutional psychiatry controversy became a major political issue. He had already left on an expedition.

Two years after his departure he was informed that his visa would not be renewed. Since then there have been three changes of government in the United Kingdom and L. Ron Hubbard has had no reason to renew his visa.

How is it that one man discovered so much information?

He simply cared enough to want it and had the intelligence and persistence to find it.

Few men have been trained in all the Eastern philosophies and in the highest levels of Western science as well.

Was L. Ron Hubbard Jesus Christ?

L. Ron Hubbard personally states he is a man as others are men. He is a much loved friend and teacher.

Is Ron Clear?

Yes—in order to map the route for others he had to make it himself.

How is it that Dianetics and Scientology are based on one man's work?

L. Ron Hubbard, in the first pages of his second book, *Science of Survival*, states:

"Acknowledgment is made to fifty thousand years of thinking men without whose speculations and observations the creation and construction of Dianetics would not have been possible. Credit in particular is due to:

Anaxagoras	Thomas Paine
Aristotle	Thomas Jefferson
Socrates	Rene Descartes
Plato	James Clerk Maxwell
Euclid	Charcot
Lucretius	Herbert Spencer
Roger Bacon	William James
Francis Bacon	Sigmund Freud
Isaac Newton	Cmdr Thompson (MC) USN
van Leeuwenhoek	William A. White
Voltaire	Will Durant
Count Alfred Korzybski	

and my instructors in atomic and molecular phenomena, mathematics and the humanities at George Washington University and at Princeton."

Does L. Ron Hubbard make a lot of money out of Scientology?

No, not that Scientologists would begrudge him a fortune if he wanted one. Mr. Hubbard forgave Churches a thirteen million dollar debt in 1966 when he retired as Executive Director. He receives royalties on his books and considering just one book, *Dianetics: The Modern Science of Mental Health* has sold over 2.5 million copies, he has no need of money from the Church.

He has no need of money from Scientology and often protests efforts on their part to give him money. He even paid for all the research himself.

How much money does L. Ron Hubbard make from books?

His book royalties are very large indeed. His nonfiction and fiction is sold in bookstores the world over, in many languages. He has been published in over twenty pen names.

His publishers made $2,505,653 in the six months between October 1976 and March 1977 from sales of his materials.

Seventy-five per cent of his income comes from book royalties, the remaining twenty-five per cent from personal investments. He is possibly today's highest paid writer.

What does L. Ron Hubbard do these days?

He's writing scripts for lecture cassettes and instructional films.

You can buy the cassettes if you wish at Church of Scientology bookstores, and see the films as they are released, if you are a student in an Academy or a preclear receiving counseling.

SCIENTOLOGY ATTITUDES

How do Scientologists view life?

As a game. A game in which everyone can win and no one need lose. Scientologists are optimistic and believe there is hope for a safer world and a better civilization.

What moral codes do Scientologists abide by?

Scientologists have two moral codes: one is a code of practice called the Auditor's Code and the other is the Code of a Scientologist. The moral codes are enforced and degrees of discipline exist.

There is also an ethical code and that is the Code of Honor. The ethical code is not enforceable. Anyone practicing the Code of Honor would maintain a good opinion of his fellows, a much more important thing than having one's fellows maintain a good opinion of one.

Shouldn't people handle their problems themselves?

Yes, of course. This aspect is heavily stressed in Scientology. Scientology does not handle a person's problems for him, but helps *him* to handle the problems. Of course, you can go on from there to the point where people don't have the problems they had before. There are problems in life that one chooses, for example, deciding to learn a new skill. And there are problems thrust onto one by life. Ideally one handles problems causatively as the solver. Not as the effect or as part of the problem.

What is Scientology's view on drugs?

We don't moralize about drugs. Improperly used, at best they cause stupidity.

Medically prescribed drugs for physical illness are not frowned upon, but usually the medical treatment would be completed before you commence your training or auditing.

Drugs and alcohol are not permitted while on course or receiving counseling; they slow you up and make you less aware. Many Scientologists work in drug rehabilitation programs with great success.

Do you have any special dietary laws or have rules against smoking and drinking in Scientology?

No alcohol is allowed twenty-four hours prior to or during counseling sessions. Smoking is not permitted during sessions, or in class. Otherwise there are no stipulations regarding drinking or smoking.

Do Scientologists use medical doctors?

Scientology has long pursued the firm policy of sending the sick to the medical doctor. Any Scientologist sick with a physical condition is sent to his doctor for medical treatment, examination, etc. and has to show a letter from a doctor before resuming studies. Some of our larger Churches have a doctor or nurse on the staff, but it is more usual to visit the local doctor.

Does Scientology cure illness?

If you have a physical illness you should inform the Registrar. She will arrange for a competent medical examination and treatment under the care of a doctor. You may have Dianetic counseling while under the doctor's care.

When you are physically well you can begin your Scientology training and counseling.

If you refuse medical examination for physical illness, the Registrar will not permit you to enroll for training or counseling.

In Scientology does one have to sacrifice one's individuality?

No. Apparently, people, each one of them, are unique. They have in common problems and aberrations. As they become disentangled from the reactive mind they become more themselves, more unique, more individual. They are more tolerant and have a greater capacity to love their fellow man and incidentally to like themselves.

Psychology's greatest failure was the attempt by Pavlov, Skinner and others to mould Man in the role of a behavior-modified animal.

What can one benefit from Scientology?

Gains are innumerable. One of the first courses is a course in communication. We feel that the basic solvent for any situation lies in the ability of that person to communicate with his friends, his family, and his fellows and with himself. Benefits usually started by those who have taken the Communications Course include increased vitality in life, greater self-respect, personal happiness. The future is brighter than before.

What is Scientology's system of ethics?

L. Ron Hubbard has defined ethics as "reason and the contemplation of optimum survival."

The modern Westerner often has punishment as the force which provides ethical or moral conduct. In Scientology as in Buddhism the accent is on personal knowledge which gives strength to the principles of right conduct which in turn permit the growth of awareness and wisdom. Wisdom is aligned to what L. Ron Hubbard has termed the dynamic principle of existence, the common denominator of all life — Survival.

In Scientology, ethics is a rational system based on a number of codes of practice. There is the Auditor's Code which imposes definite regulations and ethical standards to be abided by in the counseling situation at all times.

There is also a Code for Supervisors in regard to training. There is the Code of a Scientologist. These codes and others are contained in Chapter 14 of this book.

L. Ron Hubbard points out: "Dishonest conduct is non-survival. Anything which is unreasonable in the conduct of interrelations among men could be considered unethical, since those things which are unreasonable bring about the destruction of individuals and groups and inhibit the future of the race."

Man has long postulated a means by which he could put himself on the right path without punishment for his weaknesses. As long ago as 500 B.C. religions recognized that confession frees a person spiritually from the burden of sin.

In Scientology we have found that a confessional (auditing) assists the person who has drawn away from his fellows and become divided amongst himself and society.

L. Ron Hubbard writes: "No man, who is not himself honest, can be free — he is in his own trap. When his own deeds cannot be disclosed, then he is a prisoner; he must withdraw himself from his fellows and is a slave to his own conscience."

Apart from the confessional there are the Conditions Formulas in Scientology's ethics system wherein a person determines his conditions in relation to parts of life and works out by self-discipline and help from others, his means to take responsibility for his transgressions and regain his integrity and composure.

What does "clear the planet" mean?

It means that Scientology's goal is a world without insanity, war and crime, in which Man regains awareness that he is himself, basically good, and regains his confidence. He seeks survival along all of the eight dynamics of life in accordance with his breadth of understanding.

What does suppressive person mean?

It means someone who has so little self-esteem and certainty that he protests and tries to prevent improvement in others. If others improve and become more able he feels threatened. A person like this can be upsetting to someone who is receiving spiritual counseling as he continuously undermines them and tells them that they have not changed, cannot change, will never change, except to become worse.

What is disconnection?

Disconnection was the action of helping persons to become exterior from circumstances or people that suppress them. At one time (between 1966-1968) this was done by formally writing a letter, which in some cases caused upsets.

It was not fully understood that disconnection was usually a temporary handling, to give the person a "breathing space" from a problem, while they found the true source of it.

It was also one of the penalties applied to Scientologists who behaved unethically.

Disconnection has been replaced since 1968 by ethics counselings, which are quick and effective and designed to assist a person to recover his ability to act both causatively and rightly.

Does Scientology actively promote for converts?

While Scientology is open to people of all religious denominations and beliefs, it does not attempt or wish to change any man's beliefs. It is freely available to everyone of whatever race, color or creed and is disseminated broadly in many different languages. One does not become a Scientology convert because one is not being asked to change beliefs. Persons who wish to leave Scientology may do so freely and may be returned all unused donations.

How does Scientology compare with other religions?

Scientology respects all religions and encourages all persons to understand their own religion more fully. In studying Scientology, many persons find their interest and understanding of religion to be helpful in rekindling interest in the one of their baptism. The approach in Scientology is a very practical, down-to-earth one and helps a person to answer for himself the age-old questions: "Who am I?" "What am I doing here?" "What is my goal in life?" etc. Some clergy of other denominations have — and do — study Scientology, and find no conflict with their beliefs.

Does one really need Scientology to do well in life?

That is a question that you will have to answer for yourself. However, a Scientologist's viewpoint is that while one might be able to do well in life, one can always do better and if you are interested in self-improvement, Scientology provides a tested route by which much can be attained.

Lots of people are doing quite nicely who have never heard of Scientology. The judicious question is: "Could they be doing better?"

Does one have to believe in Scientology?

No. To quote L. Ron Hubbard, "Anything that isn't true for you when you study it carefully isn't true."

SCIENTOLOGY ORGANIZATIONS

Scientology is a philosophy. Why does it need organizations?

Remember, Scientology is an *applied* philosophy.

In the early days organization was regarded as unnecessary. L. Ron Hubbard only became involved with the organizational aspect of Scientology reluctantly. He had hoped after the publication of *Dianetics: The Modern Science of Mental Health* to devote himself to his writing and research but the demand for his knowledge and services was too great. It was not until 1966 that he was able to resign his directorship and leave the management of Scientology Churches around the world to others.

Scientology organizations and Churches exist to apply the technology, and ensure that it remains a pure subject which delivers that which is promised in terms of spiritual awareness and result.

In an ideal world little or no organization would be needed but this world is not in an ideal condition. The adventure of self-discovery and learning available in Scientology can only be delivered if the teachings remain pure and free from interpretations and variation generated by vested interests. For example, psychology and psychiatry, both devoid of spirituality, and increasingly political in nature, sought to take over and utilize parts of Scientology technology for materialistic ends. They failed because they lacked the disciplines of Scientology.

Today, Scientology Churches around the world are organized into four activities: firstly, the administration of the organization; secondly, the delivery of courses and counseling; thirdly, the dissemination of Scientology and the beliefs of the Church and lastly, the worldwide social reform and rehabilitation programs of Scientology.

How many people work in a Scientology Church and is it a different type of organization?

The number of staff varies from church to church. There is at least one full-time minister in the small churches and as many as 200 staff in the larger churches.

Scientology organizations are basically service organizations. They operate according to Scientology organizational policies which are the principles by which the conduct of Scientology affairs are guided. Policy is derived from successful experience in forwarding the basic purposes, overcoming opposition, ending distractions and letting the basic purpose flow and expand.

What is the Guardian's Office?

The Guardian's Office is the administrative bureau for the Church. It handles public relations, finances, legal and social matters and is active in defending and seeing to the viability of the Church. Guardian's Office personnel are executives of Scientology.

What is Flag?

"Flag" in nautical terms means "the Flagship" or the vessel which gives orders to others. It is used by the Sea Organization to designate its headquarters.

What is the Sea Org?

It is quite similar to the religious orders of other churches. This missionary organization began in 1968. It once operated from a number of sea vessels. Its purpose was to assist L. Ron Hubbard with research of earlier civilizations and also to provide senior management courses. The quiet of a ship also enabled Ron to continue his research and writing of books in peace.

The Sea Organization is a fraternal organization existing within the formalized structure of the Churches of Scientology. It consists of highly dedicated members of the Church. These members take vows of service. The Sea Organization life-style of community living is traditional to religious orders.

The Sea Organization has no corporate structure or identity. The leadership of the Sea Org is found within the Church of Scientology of California (Flag Bureaux). Sea Org members work for the various independent Churches of Scientology. The individual Sea Org member would be an employee of whatever Church he worked for, and is subject as are all other employees of that Church to the Board of Directors.

The Sea Organization retains its name in celebration of the fact that the Founder's life was majorly connected with the sea. It exists to help L. Ron Hubbard and keep Scientology working.

Is it true that people in the Sea Org sign a billion year contract?

Yes, they do. It is a symbolic document which, similar to vows of dedication in other faiths and orders, serves to signify an individual's commitment to the goals, purposes and principles of the Scientology religion. The person has dedicated his life to working toward these ends and toward increased sanity and world peace.

How well paid are Scientology staff?

It varies from place to place. If you want to quickly make your fortune, you will feel a little out of place working in a Scientology organization. Scientology staff are motivated by a desire to help others and a vocation, a sense of duty. As long as they make enough to maintain themselves they don't worry about big personal earnings. The pay is adequate but not excessive. Recently, donations were increased so that staff member pay could better keep pace with inflation.

What is a minister of Scientology?

This is a person who has graduated from the Church's Great Religions Course and from other courses in Scientology covering subjects such as ethics, morals, communication, human understanding, the anatomy of problems, human upsets and traumas in life, and who has been awarded a validated Scientology certificate upon completion of these courses.

Having successfully passed examinations in these studies, the candidate must then gain considerable experience in counseling, taking an additional six months to two years. He must be able to conduct the usual functions — Sunday services, marriages, christenings, burials and chaplaincy duties. Finally, the candidate must pass the ethical and moral standards laid down by the Ministerial Board of Review whose purpose is to help safeguard Scientology, Scientology Churches and Scientologists by ensuring that ministers of the Church are and remain of good moral character, continue to uphold the codes of Scientology and apply standard technology in their counseling of parishioners.

Above all, the ethical tenets are adhered to by the minister of Scientology by his own determination, out of his belief in his own honor, and good reason, and optimum solution along the eight dynamics of life.

He is a minister devoted to and using Scientology, which is a practical religion that can be applied to all of life, and religion is the oldest heritage that Man has.

Are all Scientologists ministers?

No. Only those who decide to enroll in and study for the Scientology ministry for future ministerial work. Out of his own choosing, he has elected to help his fellow man by providing counseling (for he is someone with special knowledge in the handling of life), and by restoring spiritual values.

What are Field Staff Members?

They are missionaries who disseminate Scientology, sell books, courses and counseling services, and introduce people to the Church. They often support themselves in the field by receiving ten per cent payment from their local Scientology organization on the donations paid by those they select for Scientology services.

Why is everything copyrighted in Scientology often in L. Ron Hubbard's name?

For the reason that literally dozens of "new" discoveries presented in the last twenty years were originally plagiarized by "researchers" who did not acknowledge the true source of their materials. This puts a lie on the line.

It is a phenomenon of human behavior that if I steal something, an idea from you and present it as my own, I will then be very critical and destructive of you and very invalidative of your work.

The "new" theories of silence around an unconscious person, the measurement of *élan vital* in plant life, the communication formula, the concept of a variable I.Q., the

mental image picture are but a few of the discoveries made in Dianetics and Scientology which have been represented later by some "authorities" as their original work.

The work is open to all who reach for it but to ensure that the technology remains standard and workable it is necessary to ensure there are no lies or additives made.

So we copyright all Dianetics and Scientology materials.

Why is it people who work in Scientology don't seem to be interested in anything but Scientology?

Scientologists enjoy the work they do and this brings satisfaction and certainty. Many people go through life without a sense of purpose or a career but this is not true of Scientologists who are interested and participate in all manner of things — sailing, films, the arts, theatre, books, plays, sport, hobbies and many other leisure activities.

The fields of interest and talents you find in Scientology organizations would surprise you — Scientology is their major vocation, but not their only interest.

If you had a chance to change yourself and civilization so greatly, you would be interested as well.

Why are there so many young people in Scientology?

Many Scientologists are under thirty-five. We find that young Scientologists like the life-style working in the Church. It may be that due to the rapid expansion of Scientology they find that there are many opportunities to achieve responsible positions in the Church, quite rapidly.

However, there are many families that have three generations working in Scientology, so there are a great many older people in Scientology as well.

Did Scientology buy a large property in Clearwater, Florida for millions of dollars? What is it for?

It was purchased initially for United Churches, a church dialogue and unity program. The facilities are now shared with the Church of Scientology Flag Land Base which provides courses and counseling at a very high level of technical competence in ideal surroundings. Scientologists call it the mecca of standard technology. It is the friendliest place in the world.

It is the headquarters of the Sea Organization. It is not the headquarters of Scientology. These are in England.

Why does one have to fill out forms?

Forms such as surveys and routing forms help Scientology to understand what questions each individual has. A routing form is a system to simplify an individual's progress through the organization and to ensure that he does, indeed, get what he came in for. Basically it is a system of checks and balances to smooth your path.

What has to be done to get the organization to stop sending mail to one's old address?

All that is necessary is a note, postcard or phone call to the Director of Communications at the local Church and a correction will be made.

FINANCIAL STRUCTURE

Isn't it unusual, a church charging for service?

We never heard of a church that didn't!

There is no other form of tithing or financial contribution required of a Scientologist to the Church other than a donation based on the value of a course or counseling service. Scientology ministers do not get paid for officiating at weddings, funerals, naming ceremonies, etc. and derive their income solely from the course and counseling donations.

If Scientology is so good, why isn't it free?

Scientology is not owned by the government, and hopefully never will be. The Church earns its money for its expenses out of delivering courses and counseling. In this way, Scientology has expanded over the past quarter-century and can now make its benefits available to many, many more people.

Many Scientology services *are* free and the knowledge is free to all men.

Where does the money go?

If Scientology were owned by the government, only the taxpayer would pay. But thank heavens it isn't. It costs money to run organizations.

Ten per cent of all contributions received for training and counseling go to the Mother Church in England as a tithe to pay for the central administration and communications network. Also, money is used to open up new areas.

Scientology does more with its money than all other counseling services combined even when these are paid for by the government.

Why is auditing so expensive?

Auditing is only a small fraction of the cost of psychology, psychiatry and other social services. Go look at their price lists!

To someone who is becoming happier, more able, more aware and more successful, auditing seems to be worth far more than money. However, the auditing you receive is not just the hours in the chair with your auditor. The Case Supervisor spends many hours going over your folder before you even commence auditing and then throughout your auditing he studies your folder daily. Your auditor also spends a lot of time on your folder in addition to the time spent actually auditing you. There is a team of people engaged in providing the backup facilities to your auditor, some of whom you don't meet.

The difficulty is to find something in our technological society with which to compare a commodity which results in a completely revitalized life. Answers to the eternal questions of "What am I?", "Where am I going?" and "Where have I come from?" cannot be compared to products like washing machines, motor cars and television sets. Western man has perhaps not appreciated that the only security there is is that which lies within himself.

What about those who cannot afford to pay a donation?

There are many free counseling services and deserving charity cases are considered on their merits. But it's interesting that once a person begins to become more causative through Scientology he does not usually need or want charity, but prefers to exchange a valuable for something valuable. It is a matter of personal integrity. If you wish to be considered as a charity case please see the chaplain. Additionally, there are training scholarships available for bona fide ministers of other churches, certain medical practitioners and social workers in approved rehabilitation programs.

Details are available from the Social Coordination Bureau of the Church.

There are also books, books, books and free public lectures.

Is there a way of having Scientology services without making a financial donation?

Yes, but it is important to contribute in order to feel right and worthwhile. One can study in the Scientology Academy and receive counseling while studying to be a minister. This is a much more economical way than receiving private counseling on a one-to-one basis with a professional pastoral counselor/auditor.

How much does it cost to go Clear?

The usual donation for the Clearing Course at this writing is around $2300. Aside from the fact that the state is unattainable elsewhere, it would cost far more than that in any other practice.

There are also some preparatory auditing and training steps which must be done prior to enrolling on the Clearing Course. The Registrar at your local Church or mission can give you full details on these and answer any questions about donations.

Why does one have to pay in separate organizations for their services?

All Scientology Churches and Missions are autonomous and as such do not have interconnecting financial records or funds.

Is the organization profit making?

No. Scientology churches are not profit organizations.

SCIENTOLOGY BOOKS

What is the best book to read as a beginner?

Dianetics: The Modern Science of Mental Health, which is the best-selling Scientology and Dianetics book of all time and was on the *New York Times* Best Seller List for forty-two weeks when it was published in 1950. Today, twenty-eight years after original publication, it continues to be a best seller.

In 1977 *Publisher's Weekly* called *Dianetics: The Modern Science of Mental Health* "perhaps the best-selling non-Christian book of all time in the West."

This book gives the basics of Dianetics, the forerunner to Scientology, and provides a number of principles on which Scientology is based.

Are the books difficult to understand?

The books are quite easy to understand and have been written to truly communicate. L. Ron Hubbard's writing style seems to be very beautiful—it is friendly and it makes nothing out of pomposity.

Are the books expensive?

No, the books are offered at comparable cost to other texts in bookstores. Books by L. Ron Hubbard are in leading outside bookstores as well as within Scientology organizations.

What books should one read to get information about:

1. Past Lives: *Dianetics: The Evolution of a Science* and *Have You Lived Before This Life?*
2. How to bring up children: *Child Dianetics*
3. Human behavior: *Science of Survival*
4. Marriage: *Marriage Hats*
5. Anatomy of the Human Mind: *Dianetics: The Modern Science of Mental Health*
6. Understanding people: *Science of Survival*
7. Work: *Problems of Work*
8. Organization: *How to Live though an Executive*
9. Justice/Ethics: *Introduction to Scientology Ethics*
10. Study methods: *Basic Study Manual*
11. Scientology's general background: *The Phoenix Lectures*
12. Scientology for beginners: *The Fundamentals of Thought*
13. Dianetics' earliest fundamentals: *Dianetics: The Original Thesis*
14. The human mind: *Handbook for Preclears*
15. Scientology and the tradition of wisdom: *The Creation of Human Ability*
16. The Axioms and The Logics of Scientology: *Advanced Procedure and Axioms*
17. The Beingness of Man: *Scientology 8-8008*
18. The increase of Life Energy: *Scientology 8-80*
19. Scientology Scales (used in rating individual intelligence or achievement): *Scientology 0-8*
20. Man's Time Track: *A History of Man*
21. Dianetic research on the subject of the human mind: *Dianetics: The Evolution of a Science*
22. Communication: *Dianetics 55!*
23. The application of basic Scientology tech: *The Volunteer Minister's Handbook*
24. Scientology and Dianetics technical definitions: *Dianetics and Scientology Technical Dictionary*
25. Administration and management definitions: *Modern Management Technology Defined*
26. Dianetic technology through 1975: *Dianetics Today*
27. Self-help, with tests and processes based on the discoveries contained in Dianetics and Scientology: *Self Analysis*
28. The religious-historical roots of the Church of Scientology: *The Church of Scientology: Background and Ceremonies*

All of these books were written by L. Ron Hubbard. Over fifteen million words of his have been published and are in print.

How can one get happiness out of a book?

The key to happiness is knowledge and you will find quite a bit of knowledge is contained in Scientology and Dianetics books.

By knowledge we mean assured belief, that which is known, information, instruction, enlightenment, learning, practical skill. Knowledge is more than data; it is also the ability to draw conclusions.

DIANETICS

What is Dianetics?

Dianetics is the substudy of Scientology and deals with the reactive mind and an individual's unwanted sensations, psychosomatics, emotions, misemotions and considerations.

Dianetics is *not* psychiatry. It is *not* psychoanalysis. It is *not* psychology. It is *not* personal relations. It is *not* hypnotism. It is the route from aberrated human to capable human and in fact, both Dianetics and Scientology processes could be described as methods of "unhypnotizing" men to their own freer choice and better life.

What is the mind? Where is the mind?

The mind is basically a tool that an individual uses, something like a computer. One does not physically locate the mind but it is that portion of an individual's universe that contains pictures and memories of all moments of an individual's life. The human mind is a storage place of knowledge.

The book, *Dianetics: The Modern Science of Mental Health* deals with the anatomy of the mind, and the make-up of both the analytical mind and reactive mind.

A person has a reactive mind, so surely it serves a useful purpose?

It might have, eons ago, on a genetic line; however, it only serves to get a person in trouble at this time as it exerts force and the power of command over his awareness, purposes, thoughts, body and actions.

In Scientology it is a large forward step to find that the reactive mind vanishes before the strong spirit.

What is the difference between Scientology and Dianetics?

Dianetics means through the soul (from the Greek words *dia* and *nous*) and deals with the individual with relation to his mind. Scientology is the study of knowing how to know and deals with Man as a spirit as separate from his mind and body.

Dianetics and Scientology are *separate* subjects. They have in common certain tools like the E-Meter, TRs and auditor presence. But there it ends.

Dianetics addresses the *body*. Scientology addresses the thetan.

While a thetan can produce illness, it is the body that is ill.

Thus Dianetics is used to knock out and erase illnesses, unwanted sensations, misemotion, somatics, pain, etc. Scientology and its grades are *never* used for such things.

Scientology is used to increase spiritual freedom, intelligence, ability, to produce immortality. Considering Man as a spirit, we must enter the field of religion.

Why are the terms preclear, student and auditor used?

They are used to designate the function or purpose of each person's job.

A preclear is someone who is receiving spiritual counseling in order to find out more about himself and life and who has not yet attained the state of Clear.

A student is one who reads in detail in order to learn and then apply. His purpose is to understand the materials he is studying by reading, observing, and demonstrating so as to apply them to a specific result. He connects what he is studying to what he will be doing.

An auditor is one who has been trained in the technology of Scientology, who listens and computes and applies standard technology to preclears to help them achieve the ability gained as stated on the Gradation Chart. The word "auditor" is used, not "operator" or "therapist," because auditing is a cooperative effort between the auditor and the preclear, and the law of affinity is at work.

There are numerous words of its own in Scientology, and each one means a very definite and positive thing. Further, when you have a precision definition of these words, you get "a package of understanding." They are understandings which were never fully understood before, therefore they couldn't be otherwise than new words.

DIANETICS AND SCIENTOLOGY COURSES

What method of training does Scientology use on its introductory course?

The introductory course, known as the Personal Efficiency (PE) Course, consists of five evenings of live lectures that are informal and very easy to follow, explaining elementary Scientology to beginners.

From these lectures you make up your own mind as to whether Scientology makes sense to you, and is workable, and whether you wish to find out more about it.

What does the Communication Course consist of?

The Communication Course is a course in elementary communication and control. It consists of training drills on communication and to put the student at cause over the environment. Knowledge is of no real value unless it is applied; hence the emphasis on practical application of the data on courses. This is what gives a person certainty in any area. You work with other students on the drills and you have a trained course supervisor who will give you all the help you need.

What are the drills about?

The drills are based on the idea that if Man wished to get physically strong or stronger, no matter how strong he was, he would exercise. The same view is held as regards a person's ability to deal with life and to get even stronger, no matter how strong he is, in the game of life. The drills are simply exercises to bring about greater awareness and the ability to confront (the ability to be there comfortably and perceive) and to communicate freely with anyone.

How is the Communication Course run?

With a trained course supervisor in charge, you study materials on your own. You get checked to make sure you know them and you work with other students on practical drills, permitting you to associate and coordinate theory with actual doingness. The course is run on a checksheet which lists all the materials and drills of the course on an easy gradient. You work through your checksheet at your own pace so you are not held back by anyone slower than yourself.

Keep in mind that in Scientology courses, you have got nothing in your road to keep you from learning. So you learn rather fast.

How can one know the Communication Course will work, or be sure it will help one?

You can only know it will work and be sure it will help you by trying it out for yourself. Millions throughout the world have benefited by this course. If you follow instructions exactly and study the materials exactly as laid down, you too will benefit.

How old are the people on this course?

Scientology attracts people from all walks of life and all ages. Your fellow students will be from sixteen to eighty years old.

Can I sit in on a class first?

If it does not upset the schedule, the Registrar can often arrange for you to see a class at work. However, being a spectator is not what Scientology nor life is all about. And it is not the best criterion for whether something will work for you. The best way is to experience it yourself. For example, one could spectate at a roadside for years, but if one wants to know if cars are a viable form of transport, one takes a drive.

What other kind of courses are offered?

The courses follow a logical progression chart.

The Hubbard New Era Dianetics Course teaches Dianetic auditing and Dianetic assists. The course includes data on the human mind, mental image pictures, and as its basic principle, the exhaustion of all the painfully unconscious moments of a subject's life. By eradicating pain from the life of an individual, the auditor helps him become well and happy. In Dianetic assists, the auditor runs out the physically painful experience the parishioner has just undergone—an accident, illness, operation or emotional shock. This erases the "psychic trauma" and speeds recovery to a remarkable degree.

From courses to train one to become a Dianetic Counselor (auditor) one progresses from Level 0 to Level IV which are training levels in counseling technology. Level 0 trains one to counsel on the subject of communication, Level I on human problems, Level II covers the area of human transgressions and shortcomings which cause one to withdraw and to be afraid. On this level the counselor is taught to hear the equivalent of confessionals and to bring relief to people. On Level III one learns about resolving upsets in life and on Level IV the counselor is taught how people can regain the ability to better face the future and to allow others the right to choose their own paths and to make their own future. Once trained in both the theoretical and practical sections of Levels 0 to IV a counselor is able to audit people on each level or grade. (See the Gradation Chart in this book.)

The Saint Hill Special Briefing Course (SHSBC) has certain distinct purposes. The course was begun to do two things: (1) to study and resolve training and education; (2) to assist people who wanted to perfect their Scientology and be Scientology counselors applying standard auditing technology to help others. The latter has achieved worldwide recognition through people who have graduated from the SHSBC.

Internships are served in Scientology, an activity offered in which experience can be gained. As an example, the apprenticeship of an auditor is done as a Scientology Church intern; he is a course graduate who becomes an auditor by auditing extensively. This same application of experience is also true of Scientology's administrative courses.

The Primary Rundown consists of word clearing, a technique for locating and handling every misunderstood word the person has ever had, and study technology. It makes a student super-literate. Being a super-literate is like hearing and seeing and reading for the first time. Reading a text or instruction or book is comfortable. One has it in conceptual form. One can apply the material learned. It is a new state.

In addition, there is the comparative religions and practical theology course, the Minister's Course, where one studies the world's great religions as well as courses in marriage counseling, in leadership, organization, administration, data evaluating, international management, dissemination, public relations, ethics, morals and logic.

Upon completion of courses, certificates are awarded by the Hubbard Communications Office to designate study and practice performed and skill attained.

There are many courses to take on one's way to greater personal happiness, ability and freedom. You move at your own pace and each of your studies will change your life.

What specifically is the Minister's Course?

This course is studied by Scientologists who have already successfully completed at least one course in counseling. Texts for the Minister's Course include studies of the great religions of the world and selections from the great religious writings through the ages. A number of Scientology books and materials are studied including material to enable one to perform the Church's ceremonies.

Other sections of the course are devoted to the eight dynamics of life as applied to Man, the Creed of the Church and its ethical and moral codes which are the standards governing the conduct of the members of Scientology's ministerial profession.

How hard are these courses to do?

They are not hard at all. There is a proverb in Scientology that if it is not fun, then it is not Scientology.

Scientology courses are graded in easy stages and as you learn one skill you go on to learn a slightly more difficult skill. Uppermost in L. Ron Hubbard's study technology is the gradient: a gradual approach to something, taken step by step, level by level, each step or level being, of itself, easily surmountable—so that, finally, quite complicated and difficult activities or high states of being can be achieved with relative ease. This principle is applied to both Scientology processing and training and this is one of the reasons Scientology is so easy to learn.

How long do courses take?

It takes as long as it takes—meaning the person regulates his own progress—how long it takes him to apply his mind in order to acquire the knowledge or skill called for and obtain a stable result.

However, beginning courses take about one to two weeks, depending upon how much time an individual puts in, and his learning rate.

Where are the classes held?

Auditor training classes are held within the Academy of each Church of Scientology. Public introductory courses are held at the Church in the Public Division.

What is the schedule of a Scientology Academy?

Organization hours are seven days a week, from 9 in the morning to 10:30 at night. An individual can begin a course at any time and, as he is on a checksheet, he can move along that course as fast as he likes. The course hours are usually 9:00 a.m. to 6:00 p.m. and 7:30 p.m. to 10:30 p.m., and weekends.

Are Scientology staff properly qualified and university trained?

According to sociology studies there is a very high proportion of young university graduates and professional people in Scientology.

Auditors receive very intensive training to a far higher standard of competence than most university courses. Additionally, they perform their function under the Church's Auditor's Code, rules that ensure that preclears will get the greatest gains out of their processing.

To be trained as an auditor you will need a fairly high I.Q. and the equivalent education to U.S. high school graduation, or a European or British school matriculation.

Larger Scientology organizations are staffed by Scientologists qualified by their professional group or university in their job—whether it be teacher, lawyer, accountant, executive, writer, musician, actor or artist.

Scientology course supervisors are highly trained personnel whose responsibility is to eradicate any barriers or hindrances presented which distract the student from studying and then to get the course materials fully understood and applied by the student. Scientology supervisors operate under the Supervisor's Code, making it their duty to communicate the data of Scientology to the student so as to achieve acceptance, duplication and application of the technology in a standard and effective manner.

Trained management staff of Scientology have the skill with which goals, purposes, policy, plans, programs, projects, orders, ideal scenes, statistics and valuable final products in any activity are aligned and gotten into action. Scientology management consists of ethics, technology and administration as a balanced picture.

Yes, Scientology attracts and has in its ranks many ably qualified persons who have been trained to be true professionals—those who may do things pretty easily from all appearances, but who are actually taking care with each little bit that it is just right.

How can Scientology ministers be trained so quickly to be counselors of the Church of Scientology?

In the Church of Scientology students attend course from 9:00 a.m. to 6:00 p.m. with one hour for lunch. Therefore they are spending eight hours a day, five days per week on their studies. Many students also continue studying in the evenings and on weekends. A student on a Scientology course does not "flunk out" and he does not complete the course until he is absolutely capable of applying the data. Students are encouraged to move through their courses as rapidly as they can but with the assurance that they can apply the data fully.

For example, if a Scientology student is able to complete a course in four weeks at forty hours a week, he has put 160 hours into that particular course. This is far more than a college student in religious study or theology puts in on a course. In most universities a student has 60-75 credit hours in his major subject, with additional hours in varied other fields. As you can see, the student in Scientology gets twice that in one course. In short, we adopt a professional attitude towards our students, and keep them very busy. Education and training should be in the direction of accomplishing certain actions professionally. And professionals are distinguished by the fact that they work hard. So the state of mind with which a person approaches study will determine the results that person gets from the study.

What kind of training does an auditor have and how long does it take?

Thoroughness of auditor training is achieved on a gradient scale. It might alarm a student to look across the training chart and realize what he must be able to perform, but it should not, if he realizes that he is climbing a stairway of rather easy steps. The steps are each one of them easy and their gradient has been planned and experienced carefully. Therefore, no student is ever passed to the next step of these many steps before the supervisor is entirely certain that he has mastered the last step.

When a student is taught a datum, he is taught it with the understanding that it will clarify many other later and more complicated data. Thus, he is taught the simple datum thoroughly; he is taught fundamentals.

This is the power of Dianetics and Scientology: that of stressing single, simple truths. Thus in training we concentrate solidly and continually upon these fundamental truths.

There are both Dianetic and Scientology auditor courses available. In any auditor course, the student graduates by reason of excellent examination marks and well-done sessions on the interneship.

Auditor training usually begins with a course on how to study. The product of this course is a student who has a good working knowledge of study technology and thus can progress well in auditor training courses.

Auditor courses are divided into levels; each level consists of theory and practical sections, a combination of study and drills whereby the student applies and actually does what he has read about and learned.

There is an examination at the end of each level. If a 100% examination standard is met in each section, the student auditor/counselor undergoes an internship where he audits under the guidance of a senior supervisor.

Each level takes from one to three months to complete, depending whether one is studying full or part-time.

As a full-fledged graduate auditor using standard Dia-

netics or Scientology processes, you will have acquired confidence in yourself, in your tools, in your attitude toward preclears and in the results you mean and determine to achieve.

There is a mission for you as an auditor.

DIANETICS AND SCIENTOLOGY AUDITING

What is the difference between receiving auditing and training in Scientology?

The best reference to show you the difference between the two routes of auditing and training in Scientology is the Classification Gradation and Awareness Chart shown in Chapters 4 and 5 of this volume.

On the right side of the chart there are various steps called the states of release. Here in auditing you are working toward improving yourself and regaining recognition of your spiritual nature.

The left-hand side of the chart describes the very important steps of training on which one gains the knowledge and abilities necessary to deliver the grades of release to another. In training one is learning about various facets of life with a view to helping others.

These are two different paths that do parallel each other. Optimumly a person follows both paths.

The chart is a guide for the individual from the point where he first enters Scientology and shows him how and where he should move up in order to attain these releases and grades.

There is a bonus to training: when you are trained as an auditor you can use your knowledge to confront problems and resolve them for yourself *and* others. You have confidence and certainty, and others respect your judgment.

Scientology contains the entire map for getting the individual through all the various points on the chart and for getting him across the Bridge (a term originating in early Dianetics days to symbolize travel from unknowingness to revelation) to a higher state of existence.

Do all the people on staff in Scientology have auditing as well as training?

Yes, auditing of staff members is part of the exchange for their work in Scientology organizations.

Scientologists have a common reality that the realizations and gains obtainable from auditing and training are pearls without price. They encourage their children, their families and their friends to have the same.

Scientology is no ivory tower philosophy. It is an applied religious philosophy which has a proven workable technology, which is for *use*. It is meant for anyone who wishes to reach for it.

How is auditing best received?

Auditing is best received through a certified minister of the Church of Scientology in a Scientology Church or Mission, under supervision of a trained Case Supervisor.

Auditing is usually received in a 12½ hour intensive, defined as a single block of auditing sessions delivered within a short period of time on a set schedule.

There are common sense rules which are in your interests to keep, for example, you must see that you have sufficient rest, ensure that you are properly fed, etc. while on auditing lines.

Before being audited it helps for you to have done a basic course such as the Personal Efficiency Course or the Communication Course, both of which contain fundamental knowledge of Scientology.

How many hours of auditing a day will one receive?

This depends upon the Case Supervisor. A preclear is never audited once he is tired or has become hungry. Some people receive longer hours of auditing than others; between 2½ and 5 hours is average.

Has the technology of auditing changed since the early days of Scientology?

Yes, there have been considerable refinements made in the quality of training and auditing results. There is now an orderly gradient of case gain and abilities regained which permits anyone to predictably follow a well-mapped path to freely communicate with anyone on any subject as a well, happy person all the way to recovery of knowledge and the ability to be at cause over mental energy, space and time, and even more. Very early on the path you will find a new awareness of truth, and freedom from harmful effects or necessity to take drugs.

The amount of technical materials which exist in Dianetics and Scientology today on the subject of the spirit, mind and life, is extensive. For instance, there are about 25,000,000 words on tape in archives which provide the consecutive path of discovery. When placed chronologically with books, bulletins and policy letters and other issues, this gives a record of all discoveries and applications in these subjects.

The bulk of Scientology knowledge towers into mountains. It is accessible, in the main, to those who seek it.

In 1973 the Founder, L. Ron Hubbard, wrote: "The materials of Scientology are the result of forty-three years of search, coordination and application to millions. We are very rich in materials, in results and in the potential future. Into our brightest times we are expanding."

L. Ron Hubbard has never ceased to work untiringly on Scientology auditing technologies nor failed to carry forward a progress line which improved.

What is the E-Meter, how does it work and what does it measure?

The E-Meter is a shortened term for electropsychometer. It is a religious artifact used as a spiritual guide in the Church confessional or counseling session. It is an aid to the auditor or pastoral counselor in two-way communication with the preclear, locating areas of spiritual travail and indicating spiritual well-being in other areas.

In itself, this confessional aid does nothing. It is an electronic instrument that measures mental state and change of state in individuals, as an aid to precision and speed in auditing. The E-Meter is not intended or effective for the diagnosis, treatment or prevention of any disease.

The E-Meter is used to disclose truth to the individual who is being processed and thus free him spiritually.

What would one get out of auditing?

You would get out of auditing whatever you wanted to. In auditing you set your own goals of what you want to achieve and work toward those goals.

A person can achieve a reality on a change having taken place in himself for the better. He can recognize that he can now do things he could not do before. Auditing changes conditions for people.

A person can have measurable ability increases which can be tested. For example, Dianetics and Scientology (demonstrated by carefully controlled tests) greatly speed up reaction time. They also increase I.Q. rapidly and this can be verified by I.Q. test scores. As a person is audited he becomes quicker mentally.

Another test is the Oxford Capacity Analysis, a specially prepared graph which plots ten personality traits from a test taken by the preclear. Taken at intervals before and after auditing, the OCA graph shows the changes that have occurred.

Results like these are products gotten out of auditing. Such results bring *pride*.

How can one get auditing faster?

By just standardly having your sessions. Auditing takes as long as it takes but each and every session gets more charge handled for the person. By charge is meant anger, fear, grief or apathy contained as misemotion in the person's case. Auditing discharges this charge so that it is no longer there to affect the individual.

If your attention is on going faster you will actually impede your own progress because your attention will be on that rather than on what the auditor is asking you to look at. It is important for best results to stay "in session" —so that you are interested in your own case and willing to talk to the auditor.

Just ensure that you are properly nourished and rested and are abiding by the common sense rules in the booklet, *What Every Preclear Should Know*, so that you are always sessionable and ready to be audited.

Does auditing really work in all cases?

Scientology has some time since passed the point of achieving uniformly workable technology. The technology of Dianetics and Scientology is standard and does work in 100% of the cases in which it is applied standardly.

The only proviso is that the preclear must be there of his own determinism and that he abide by the rules for preclears during the period of his auditing to ensure optimum auditing results.

When do you audit somatics?

Dianetics and the Drug Rundown are used to audit somatics.

The word "somatic" is used in Dianetics to denote physi-cal pain or discomfort of any kind. Somatic means a non-survival physical state of being and is addressed with procedures to help the preclear become well and happy.

The Drug Rundown handles the use of drugs (including medical drugs, treatments and alcohol) to which pain and somatics are usually connected. By proven techniques it removes any previous harmful effects of drugs on an individual.

What can auditing cure?

Scientology is not in the business of curing things. Auditing is not done to cure the body or to cure anything physical and the E-Meter cures nothing. However, in the process of a person becoming happier, more able and more aware as a spiritual being through auditing, illnesses that are psychosomatic (meaning the mind making the body ill) in origin often disappear.

Scientology auditing is really not to be confused with various other therapies. It does not fit at all with psychiatry and it does not exist in the tradition of psychology.

The "psych-iatrist" and "psych-ologist" took their very names from religion since "psyche" means soul. But in this century, for example, psychology has been redefined as "the science of mind or mental phenomena or activities; the study of the biological organism as man and the physical and social environment" (Merriam Webster's Third International Dictionary, 1961). So in psychology there is no definition for "psyche." Somewhere along the way, in psychology, Man lost his soul!

Psychiatry and psychology modernly seek to relieve mental anguish by using drugs or hypnotism or physical means.

The Scientology minister has a responsibility to his people and those about him to relieve suffering. He has many ways to do this; auditing is one of these ways. He is quite successful in doing so and he does not need or use drugs or hypnotism or shock or surgery or violence.

In auditing, the person himself, is addressed—the psyche or soul, meaning the same as thetan—the being who is the individual and who handles and lives in the body. Auditing is done entirely to return to a thetan his causation, to restore his power of choice, and to free him. It is a process of self-discovery and new or regained abilities. You cannot have decent, honest or capable beings as long as they are in some way trapped and overwhelmed.

Can one go exterior?

Exteriorization is a subjective reality for each individual. Many Scientologists have been known to go exterior, some with scientific evidence as well, records of which exist in U.S. universities interested in this phenomenon.

At what level does one go exterior?

Exteriorization is the state of the thetan, the individual himself, being outside his body with or without full perception, but still able to control and handle the body.

This can happen at any time at all in auditing and is just one of the phenomena. When a person goes exterior, he achieves a certainty that he is himself and not his body.

How do you know when you reach a certain grade as a preclear?

Grade and level are the same thing but when one has a grade one is a preclear and when one has a level one is studying its data.

The Classification Gradation and Awareness Chart lists out the end attainments for each grade for a preclear. You will know when you have achieved each separate grade. In addition you will feel very, very good; you will have made many new realizations and will be invited to say whether you feel you have reached the particular grade or not.

Why does one have to wait six weeks for auditing if one took drugs?

Research has shown that it takes at least that long for the effect of drugs to wear off. It is not a moral decision, but a technical one. Quite simply, auditing is not as effective while drugs are in the system because the person on drugs is less alert, and may even be rendered stupid, blank, forgetful, delusive or irresponsible.

Do you take drugs when you are in Scientology?

Except for purely medical drugs, no. Drugs are usually taken by people to escape from unwanted emotions, pains or sensations. In Scientology these unwanted conditions get handled and people have no need to take drugs. Drugs dull a person and make them less aware. In Scientology our aim is to make people brighter and more aware.

Why should a person quit drugs?

This is best answered by giving some data on drugs.

Drugs essentially are poisons. The degree they are taken determines the effect. A small amount gives a stimulant. A greater amount acts as a sedative. A larger amount acts as a poison and can kill one.

All drugs dull one's senses and affect the reactive mind so that the person becomes less in control and more the effect of his reactive mind, a very undesirable state. This one sees quite readily after he's been in Scientology just a short time.

THE STATE OF CLEAR

What is Clear?

Clear is a state in which an individual is now in control over his own mental matter, energy, space and time. Or to put it in another way, he no longer reacts unknowingly, but acts knowingly.

Total absence of the reactive mind is the definition of Clear. The reactive mind is a portion of a person's mind which works on a totally stimulus-response basis, which is not under his volitional control, and which exerts force and the power of command over his awareness, purposes, thoughts, body and actions. This is what the procedures of Scientology are devoted to disposing of, for the reactive mind is only a burden to an individual.

Thus the stimulus-response type mechanisms no longer are part of his life. The completely cleared individual would have all his self-determinism in present time and would be completely self-determined.

One shouldn't under-valuate that the reactive mind is quite an adversary and therefore you can't over-value the state of Clear. It has never been achieved before.

What's it like to be Clear?

Like being brand-new, with tremendous increase in abilities. A Clear, in an absolute sense, would be someone who could confront anything and everything in the past, present and future.

How does one go Clear?

Simply by taking one's first step in Scientology or taking the next step up as shown on the Classification Gradation and Awareness Chart. The state of Clear is above the release grades (all of which are requisite to clearing) and is attained by completion of the Clearing Course at a Scientology Advanced Organization. The Church of Scientology Advanced Organizations are located at Los Angeles, California; St. Hill, East Grinstead, Sussex, England and Copenhagen, Denmark.

What is the quickest way to go Clear?

By simply following the Classification Gradation and Awareness Chart as laid out by the Founder, L. Ron Hubbard.

How long does it take to go Clear?

It takes anywhere from one year to two years to go from the bottom of the Grade Chart through the Clearing Course.

If one goes Clear, will one lose his emotions?

No, on the contrary, a Clear is able to use and experience any emotion. The painful emotions only have been released from his life. Clears are very responsive beings.

What can you do when you are Clear?

You can do far more than you envisage before Clear.

One is able to deal causatively with life rather than react to it. A Clear is rational in that he forms the best possible solutions he can on the data he has and from his viewpoint. A Clear can give you solutions that straighten out things that others are trying to and can only fight. He gets things done, accomplishes more.

Once you are Clear, do you stay Clear?

Yes. However, one can abuse any state of awareness and if abused, one could begin losing clarity. But this doesn't often happen.

Keep in mind that the state of Clear is not suddenly achieved but that you are very certain when the reactive mind has gone. Attained on a gradient, the person on the Clearing Course is getting rid of more and more of his reactive mind and going clearer and clearer until he becomes Clear—which is no reactive mind and no compulsion to make a reactive mind—and this state remains with a Clear.

A Clear is far more positive about things than he ever was before. This includes being positive that his state is stable.

Are Clears perfect?

No, they are not perfect.

A Clear has become the basic individual through auditing. The basic individual is not a buried unknown or a different person, but an intensity of all that is best and most able in the person.

Do Clears eat food and sleep?

Most definitely.

Do Clears get colds and get sick?

A Clear is very rarely ill. This doesn't say that a Clear in a body won't get sick, for the body is susceptible at times to various things.

However, to measure a Clear by his health is a big mistake because we're talking about the *individual*. Nevertheless, Clears are far more healthy.

If Clears have erased the reactive mind, why do they continue to get auditing?

There are impulses and considerations on other dynamics than the first for the Clear to handle. Going Clear handles the first dynamic which is the urge toward existence as one's self. Here we have individuality expressed fully. There are seven other dynamics which are addressed with auditing.

How does one know that he's not already Clear?

One simple way is to check and see if you still have thoughts that you don't wish to get.

Clear is not a status, it is a state of being.

THE STATE OF OPERATING THETAN

What is meant by OT?

This is an abbreviated term meaning "Operating Thetan." The word "thetan" in Scientology comes from the Greek word *theta* meaning soul or spirit. This, in essence, is you. OT is a state of being where one is able to operate causatively in the physical universe and is able to retain a position exterior from material factors, including one's physical body.

People on the OT courses are progressing to this state. When you are on your road to OT, it is a familiarity, it is a road of getting acquainted with yourself, the way you were once, and the way you are now, and fitting yourself into some sort of a framework with relationship to existence.

How would you describe the state of Operating Thetan?

OT (Operating Thetan) is a state of spiritual awareness in which an individual is more and more able to control himself and his environment. An OT is someone who is oriented to greater survival for himself, his family, groups, mankind, plants and animals, the physical universe, other spiritual beings and through God. An OT is at cause over time.

There are degrees of condition of a thetan. As the individual starts walking uphill gradiently from Clear to OT, he is integrating all of his experience, he is a being who is becoming more powerful, a proofed up being who is stable. And he being basically good responds to very decent impulses.

An OT does not go into a state of "total serenity" and withdraw from life to meditate. Rather, he knows the causes and effects of various things and how they're interwoven. So he experiences everything that he wants to experience and doesn't have to experience things that he doesn't want to ever experience. He's in actual fact a walking miracle who is himself comprehending all the miracles. It's quite a remarkable state.

Why are some parts of OT materials confidential?

Because an understanding of OT materials is dependent upon having fully done the earlier materials per the Classification Gradation and Awareness Chart. If one had not, some of the higher level material would not be understandable.

Releasing confidential data into unskilled or uneducated or unscrupulous hands would be dangerous. It belongs to those who have traveled the Scientology route exactly and must be available to them when they are ready.

Can OTs read minds?

You don't have to be an OT to "see" people's thoughts and intentions. You can probably recall a time you knew what someone was thinking or had done, but perhaps negated it, or felt it was not "good manners." But to answer the question bluntly—yes, with varying degrees of ability.

A SCIENTOLOGY CAREER

Can one audit as a career?

Yes. Dianetics and Scientology courses abound and there are Academy levels where individuals are trained to audit. As an auditor you can do something about life. There are millions of people on this planet who are in need of and desire Scientology counseling. It is a truly satisfying career. Auditors are very valuable and in great demand.

L. Ron Hubbard's opinion of auditors is well known: "I think of an auditor as a person with enough mettle to *do something about it.* This quality is rare and this quality is courageous in the extreme. It is my opinion that auditors are amongst the upper tenth of the upper twentieth of intelligent human beings. Their will to do, their motives, their ability to grasp and to use is superior to that of any other profession."

Of what value would it be to have my child trained as an auditor as a career?

It would firstly provide a young person with certainty and knowledge in dealing with every possible type of human problem, be it interpersonal, familial, organizational, ethical, moral or religious. Secondly, it would provide a career of fulfillment in aiding people from all walks of life to gain greater awareness and respect for themselves and others.

Auditors are in demand in every Church of Scientology and Mission of the Church, throughout the world.

Can one make Scientology a career?

Yes, there are thousands of professional Scientologists who work in Churches and Missions throughout the world. One can become a minister of the Church and perform counseling duties on a full-time basis. There is also employment in the Church's social reform organizations, in administrative work, in furthering dissemination and in publication of Church materials.

There are availabilities for making Scientology a career in nearly every single aspect of employment. Further, there is a developed Scientology technology in nearly every aspect of living—from the raising of children to resolving marriages, to publishing, accountancy work, executive work, and so on.

Not all Scientologists are professionals. Some very high executives and artists in the world have stated they would not know how to handle their jobs at all if they were not also trained Scientologists.

SCIENTOLOGY SOCIAL REFORM AND CONTROVERSIES, GOVERNMENT, WORLD

You say Scientologists are working doing good things for society in various countries. What are some specific examples?

If we gave you every documented example it would probably fill a room, so here are just a few activities in which Scientologists are working, in various countries. They work for the most part with non-Scientologists towards a common goal; many of the activities are sponsored by Scientologists, but not all.

AUSTRALIA

1. Citizens Commission on Human Rights (CCHR). Group collects data on psychiatric abuse, issues reports and handles cases.
2. Criminal Rehabilitation and Education Advancement Movement (CREAM). Fights for more humane methods to deal with criminals.
3. Society to Protect Privacy of Individuals: Working to reform the Australian Security Intelligence Organization (ASIO).
4. Action for Privacy Committee: Also to reform ASIO.
5. Committee for Freedom of Information: Working for an FOI Act, so people may have access to government files on them and the right to correct any false information contained therein.

NEW ZEALAND

1. Citizens Commission on Human Rights (CCHR). Group collects data on psychiatric abuse, issues reports and handles cases.
2. Criminon: Works for more humane treatment and rehabilitation of criminals.

UNITED KINGDOM

1. Citizens Commission on Human Rights (CCHR). Group collects data on psychiatric abuse, issues reports and handles cases.
2. Narconon: Community Drug Rehabilitation program with 80% success rate.
3. National Society for Crime Reduction and Social Justice: Works for police reform; especially of dossier system.
4. All Party Freedom of Information Committee: Working for an FOI Act in the United Kingdom so people may have access to government files on them and the right to correct any false information contained therein.
5. Effective Education: Educational program specializing in improving study abilities and handling problem students.
6. Alcoholics Rehabilitation: Working to improve conditions and rehabilitation facilities for alcoholics.
7. REHAB: Working to improve conditions for criminals.

8. Dignity for the Aged: Working to better conditions for the aged.

CANADA

1. Citizens Commission on Human Rights (CCHR). Group collects data on psychiatric abuse, issues reports and handles cases.
2. Committee on Institutional Psychiatry: Investigates and reports on psychiatric institutions.
3. Task Force on Alcoholism: Works to better conditions and rehabilitation facilities for alcoholics.
4. New Life for Senior Citizens: Works to improve conditions for the aged.
5. National Committee on Law Enforcement and Social Justice: Works for police reform. Especially interested in reform of the dossier system and Freedom of Information in Canada so people may have access to government files on them and the right to correct any false information contained therein.
6. Criminon: Works for more humane treatment and rehabilitation of criminals.
7. Task Force on Mentally Retarded: Works for better care and treatment of the mentally retarded.
8. Learning, Interest and Motivation: Education program specializing in the handling of study difficulties.

UNITED STATES

1. Citizens Commission on Human Rights (CCHR). Group collects data on psychiatric abuse, issues reports and handles cases.
2. National Society on Law Enforcement and Social Justice: Works for police reform. Especially interested in reform of the dossier system.
3. Committee on Public Health and Safety: Consumer protection group especially in area of medical malpractice.
4. Task Force on Mental Retardation: Works for better care and treatment of the mentally retarded.
5. Committee to Reinvolve Ex-Offenders: Helps in criminal rehabilitation, especially in their readjustment to the community once released from prison.
6. National Alliance on Alcoholism Prevention and Treatment.
7. Association of Scientologists for Reform: A legislative reform group to protect civil and human rights.
8. Gerus Society: Works for better care for the aged.
9. NEEDS (New England Elderly Demands Society): Works for better care for the aged.
10. Applied Scholastics: Education program specializing in handling children with study difficulties.
11. Narconon: Community and prison drug rehabilitation program with 80% success rate.

SOUTH AFRICA

1. Society for Safety in Mental Healing: Campaigns for rights of mental patients, and takes up cases of abuse in violation of UN Universal Declaration of Human Rights.
2. Self Development Committee for the Retarded: Works in getting mentally retarded Black and colored people out of health care into education.
3. Education Alive: Special program operating in Black, colored and Indian communities to help educate both children and adults.
4. Association for the Rehabilitation of Alcoholics (AFRA).

Helps to handle the rehabilitation of alcoholics and improve treatment facilities.

DENMARK

1. Medborgernes Menneskerettigheds Kommission (Danish equivalent of CCHR). Group collects data on psychiatric abuse, issues reports and handles cases.
2. Befolkningens Ret Til Uforfalsket Nyhedsformidling— BRUN (Peoples Right to Unfalsified News Distribution): Fights for press reform.
3. Landsbyskolen Pa Amager (City school on Amager): School specializing in new education and study methods.
4. Alkoholikernes Humanisering: To humanize treatment of alcoholics.

SWEDEN

1. Kommitten for Manskliga Rattigheter at Mentalt Sjoka (Swedish equivalent of CCHR). Group collects data on psychiatric abuse, issues reports and handles cases.
2. Narkonon: Community Drug Rehabilitation program with an 80% success rate.
3. Programmet for Mellankyrklig Dialogi i Sverige: A cooperative project between Swedish churches which works together in handling community and church problems.

GERMANY

1. Kommission fur Verstobeder Psychiatrie gegen Menscheniechte (Commission for Violation of Psychiatry against Human Rights — German equivalent of CCHR). Group collects data on psychiatric abuse and handles cases.
2. Narconon: Community Drug Rehabilitation program with 80% success rate.
3. Die Kommission fur Polizeireform (Commission on Police Reform). Research group especially interested in the circulation of false reports by police agencies and reform of this abuse.
4. Die Kommission zum Schutz des Burger gegen Datenmissbrauch E.V.: Group pushing Freedom of Information legislation, which will enable people to have access to and the right to correct government files on them.

AUSTRIA

1. Kommission fur Verstobeder Psychiatrie gegen Menscheniechte (Commission for Violations of Psychiatry against Human Rights — Austrian equivalent of CCHR).

FRANCE

1. Commission des Citoyens pour les Droits de l'Homme (French equivalent of CCHR). Group collects data on psychiatric abuse, issues reports and handles cases.

This list is by no means a complete one.

What is the Association of Scientologists for Reform? How does it fund itself?

The Association of Scientologists for Reform (ASR) is an incorporated group of Scientologists in America who are active in various areas of social reform. ASR sponsors groups. It is an outlet for Scientologists who have realized through Scientology that social responsibility is the key to helping others.

It is funded through donations by various agencies.

Do Doctors, Governments, Schools, Social Workers and other professional people use Scientology?

Yes, they do. There are members of all the above professions and institutions who are also Scientologists and apply their wisdom to improve their fields of endeavor.

A number of schools and universities in Europe, Africa, and in the United States apply L. Ron Hubbard's study methods.

Scientology is used on life and its forms and products. The chief uses of Scientology are in the fields of education, organization, mental health reform, social order and religion. Scientology is the first to give scientific meaning to these and thus professional people use it extensively.

Why has Scientology sometimes been so controversial with governments and the media?

No doubt the Egyptians considered the Jews controversial in Moses' time. The Christians were considered worse than controversial by the Romans.

We are a social reform movement as well as a religion. Scientologists live their beliefs as a matter of personal integrity. They expose rotten spots in society and use every legal means to oppose government agency intrusion into the lives of private citizens by mental health laws, secret dossiers, imprisonment without trial and other constitutional violations.

In the last decade the tide of public opinion has turned overwhelmingly in favor of Scientology. Eminent non-Scientologists such as Professor Thomas Szasz confirmed Scientologists' views on psychology and institutional psychiatry. Newspapers and TV publicized conditions inside mental institutions, considered unbelievable when Scientologists first documented them. And Watergate took the lid off the secret dossiers used by vested interests in government.

It is not a coincidence that in the last few years several national and international agencies have corrected their files and apologized for false reports they had spread about Scientologists.

Scientology has been attacked by specific governmental officials at times and in fact this was the subject of an entire book, *The Hidden Story of Scientology* written by distinguished American journalist, war correspondent and investigator-reporter, Omar Garrison. Garrison has documented the secret alliance between those governmental officials and organized mental health for the suppression of Scientology. The Church's mental health reform programs were regarded as a threat to the control of such organizations as the World Federation of Mental Health and its national branches.

While there have been a few individual members of government who have acted as spokesmen for mental health organizations, no government in the world is "against" Scientology.

Doesn't Scientology being a religion avoid taxes and intervention from governments?

From the time of Jesus Christ and before, being a religion has never saved a group from government intervention and our age is no exception.

For example, the Church of Scientology is liable for taxes in Britain but is no less a religion as thousands of Scientologists there can testify.

Surely a government wouldn't attack Scientology for no reason?

According to a recently published document from the American Senate Intelligence Committee many groups and individuals can fall afoul of government. "The unexpressed major premise of COINTELPRO (a project of the FBI) is that the Bureau has a role in maintaining social order. . . . combating those that threaten that order." Groups included in COINTELPRO's list of those that threaten social order are the National Association for the Advancement of Colored People and the local Boy Scout Movement.

No one was very surprised to find the Church of Scientology on former President Nixon's "enemy" list which as a matter of record listed twelve other social minded religious groups, including the National Council of Churches. (The "enemies list" was maintained by the IRS.)

We are not revolutionaries, we are humanitarians. We are not political. We ask, "Who objects to a group or company functioning better to produce a better civilization? Who objects to a race becoming sane and a stable asset to its communities? Who objects to a neighborhood smoothing out?"

Scientologists are in a position to help and do help bring about a betterment of the conditions of life. They have sufficient courage and integrity to work *within the law* to bring about ethical reforms in many areas.

Has Scientology been to court a lot of times?

Scientology and Dianetics have been to law around the world. It was often necessary in the early days to establish our rights under the law.

Scientology is no outlaw in a society, but is the catalyst of that society, and as such it may and should use every facility that society possesses to institute higher levels of beingness and activity. In other words, if a Scientologist finds somebody doing wrong in the field of healing, for instance, he has the full and complete right to use any and all police courts, legislation, to right that wrong.

Are there any laws against the practice of Scientology? Has it been banned?

There is no legislation against Scientology anywhere in the world. Organizations have had their troubles in the past, and Scientology has been considered very controversial since Scientologists were campaigning against the barbaric treatments meted out by institutional psychiatry and the violation of human rights by "authorities in the name of government" long before these issues were popular. In the middle 1960s the controversy reached a crescendo and in Australia three states passed legislation and Britain refused entry visas to alien Scientologists wishing to enter the country. If you are interested, the whole story has been written by Omar Garrison (who is not a Scientologist) in his book *The Hidden Story of Scientology.*

It's interesting to note that by the early 1970s Australia had granted federal recognition to the Church of Scientology and its religious bona fides. All bans have been lifted. This probably occurred as a result of the unpopularity of the law which permitted book burning and police entry without a warrant which made the legislation unacceptable to the great majority of Australians.

In England the outcry was such that the Minister responsible lost his post and a distinguished lawyer was appointed to inquire. He found the restrictions on entry of Scientologists into the United Kingdom were not justified:

"the mere fact that someone is a Scientologist is in my opinion no reason for excluding him from the United Kingdom, when there is nothing in our law to prevent those of his fellows who are citizens of this country from practicing Scientology here." This quote is from the official report laid before the British House of Commons.

Is Scientology like mental therapies such as group therapy, transcendental meditation, psychology, positive thinking and so on?

Scientology is different to these in a similar way that Judaism, Buddhism or Christianity is different. The religious philosophy of Scientology embraces all aspects of Man and his relationship with the physical and spiritual worlds.

Most mental therapies concentrate on some small aspect of life and livingness. When Scientology addresses life, it encompasses knowingness of life and broad understanding. To understand all would be to live at the highest level of potential action and ability.

In the case of psychology, it concentrates on behavior. Through Scientology's researches, we know that behavior in the individual is not of any great worry. It is what the person can be aware of, not his conduct, that is important. And one of Scientology's primary goals is increasing people's awareness of life itself.

Other mental therapies are normally concerned with the mind or the brain of Man; again, psychology is a good example. In Scientology the brain is viewed for what it is: another part of the nervous system which receives and sends impulses to body parts, and the mind is a communication and control system between the thetan (the person himself who is a spirit) and his environment. Therefore, Scientology is directed toward the *élan vital* or spirit of Man—the being who is the individual and who handles and lives in a body, and is separate from his brain and his mind.

Are there some people who say they don't like Scientology?

Millions of people do like Scientology. As a matter of fact the membership in Scientology is growing rapidly each year and is presently in the millions. The "don't likes" are the minority.

Do you know that there are certain characteristics and mental attitudes which cause about 20% of the population to oppose violently any betterment activity or group? This is factually true and since Scientology is engaged in and dedicated to improving conditions around the world, it is among those organizations which have been attacked.

Scientology is the fastest growing religion on the planet by actual surveys and statements by sociologists.

Why has the press now become far less critical of Scientology than previously?

A criticism is defined in Scientology as a hope that they can damage, with an inability to do so. Although Scientology's early years were accompanied by some measure of critical press, much has been done in recent years to correct erroneous impressions of the character of the religion. You will find that today there is a more informed press which generates a large number of accurate and favorable articles concerning Scientology and its many social reform efforts. Indeed, the early growing pains faced by Scientology were minimal in comparison to those faced by other young religions, notably Christianity, Mormonism and Christian Science.

Why has Scientology seemed to have had troubles over the years?

Any group that calls for reforms in the areas of vested interests like psychiatry and mental health is known to have controversy laid at its door and we, like the Quakers fighting for reforms in the slave trade, are no exception.

Today psychiatry is being inquired into in many countries. Citizens Commission on Human Rights, a member group of the Association of Scientologists for Reform, a nonprofit corporation, is very much the upcoming thing. It is dedicated to eliminating psychiatric abuse and to restoring human rights to all individuals.

Any controversy has been worth it to see the clean-up now beginning to take place.

How does Scientology view the deprogramming groups who "save" young people from religious groups?

Any parent who is concerned about the involvement of a person under eighteen years of age in Scientology has only to refuse to give parental consent for their studies. Even an adult with a family connection to someone antagonistic to their being in Scientology would not be permitted to work or study in the Church.

From what we have heard, deprogramming is a sordid business based on psychologists' techniques, developed for the military in brainwashing, and is probably actionable under civil or criminal law.

What about the alarming stories sometimes circulated of how Scientologists deal with their attackers?

Scientologists believe firmly in reasonable discourse and in the vast majority of circumstances, communication and good intention resolves almost any possible conflict.

To a Scientologist, communication is by thousands of per cent the senior in importance to affinity and reality. It is the more important in understanding the composition of human relations. Communication is the solvent of all things and Scientologists use it more than any other group to settle differences.

Scientologists stand up for freedom with responsibility; they are not owned or controlled by financial interests. L. Ron Hubbard kept the technology free from political, racial and commercial interests. The message of Scientology knows no national borders. Scientologists have used the democratic process, the court room and the public assembly to fight violations of human rights, unconstitutional government intrusion and exploitation of ignorance in a dozen countries. Add to this the fact that Scientology's growth and impact on society has been explosive in less than half a lifetime. Scientology has been opposed by the few who have a vested interest in ignorance, authoritarianism, and "readily controlled masses."

Psychology and psychiatry have become little more than political minions and control mechanisms in some countries.

Scientology was hit by a vicious media and political attack in the middle 1960s of international proportions. The Scientologists were put under a searchlight of public scrutiny and even the smallest action was magnified and distorted.

False reports abounded. Yet Scientologists stood firm and contested the battle by the two means open to them: through the courts and the public marketplace of ideas. The Scientologists won that battle, psychiatric horror stories were exposed, and some national and international "Mental Health" front groups disbanded or moved out.

Privacy against the computer and the "dirty dossier" became popular issues in a number of countries.

During that time provocateurs and "secret agents" tried to infiltrate Scientology organizations in a manner which would not have been credible to ordinary people prior to Watergate.

It may be true to say that some Scientology executives over-reacted at that time, but 99.9% of the gossip you may have heard was initiated at that time. Through lawyers and the confessions of instigators who developed a conscience, Scientology executives have gathered documentary evidence on all this. To quote Victor Marchetti who is not a Scientologist but a noted expert on the CIA and intelligence matters:

". . . most amazing to me were the documents that indicated that the CIA and its Deputy Director, Admiral Rufus Taylor, in 1968, were snooping on the Church of Scientology. At the time, I was the executive assistant to Admiral Taylor, and I cannot remember anything that would have caused the CIA to have any concern in the activities of your religious movement . . . other than idle, or perhaps mischievous, bureaucratic interest.

"In sum, I have the feeling, after reviewing all the material you provided to me and reflecting on past developments of this nation, that the Church of Scientology and its members were victims of government paranoia . . . not unlike that which was heaped upon other 'different' religious movements in times past. . . . the Mormons, the Amish, and similar independent groups. (And let us not forget that in another time and on another continent, another authoritarian regime . . . the Romans . . . once tried to squelch another new religious sect . . . the Christians.)

"Finally, I would like to commend the Church of Scientology for its faith in itself and its determination to work within the constitutional democratic system of our nation. It has fought the good fight against great odds openly and legally . . . and it has survived . . . which is more of a tribute to its membership than it is to our own government. By its tenacity and determination, the Church of Scientology has forced that government to adhere to the Constitution . . . something that will benefit all Americans in the long run."

Why is it that Scientology is against psychiatry?

Scientologists have disagreements with enforced psychiatric methods which include involuntary commitment, forced and heavy drugging, electroconvulsive shock treatment and lobotomy and other psychosurgical operations. Psychiatry is a profession which forces its "treatment" on others and Scientologists have seen too many of psychiatry's failures come to its Churches for help not to be concerned about the moral, physical and spiritual outrage being committed by this so-called profession.

A primary difference between Scientology and psychiatry is that psychiatry is authoritarian and tells the person what's wrong with him, often introducing a new lie. Scientology finds out what's wrong with the person from the person.

By the Creed of the Church of Scientology, the healing of mentally caused ills should not be condoned in nonreligious fields. The reason for this is that violent psychiatric therapies cause spiritual traumas and at best suppress problems in living. Scientology believes the entire asylum concept must be overhauled so there is rehabilitation rather than dehumanization. Psychiatry's unyielding role as savior of mental illness in the world is rejected by Scientology.

Scientology is not against all psychiatrists. Reform discussions on mental health take place regularly, and some psychiatrists are also members of the Church.

Why do some people say Scientology is harmful?

The common denominator of people with this belief is exposure to inaccurate reports, generated by some vested interest which feels threatened. Scientology stands for more knowledge, more understanding, more tolerance, more communication. Some vested interests consider this harmful.

Is Scientology trying to rule the world?

No. Scientology is encouraging people to attain their full individual potential and to assume greater responsibility for poor social conditions. Scientology does want to improve and reform the bad spots in society, and Scientologists believe there can be a better world. For example, the Citizens Commission on Human Rights has a national membership in laymen and professionals of various faiths and political convictions joined together by a common respect for the rights and dignity of the individual to which anyone can belong and work for the betterment of social conditions.

The Church of Scientology believes that religion can be a civilizing factor, as Buddhism civilized a barbaric Asia a long time ago.

Religion exists in no small part to handle the upsets and anguish of life. These include spiritual duress by reason of various conditions.

What is wrong with the world today?

Today this world suffers from an increasing incidence of neurosis brought about by a dependency upon mechanical things which do not think, which do not feel, but which can give pain to those that live.

The curse of this world is not actually its atom bomb, though that is bad enough. The curse of this world is the irresponsibility of those who try to depress all beings down to the low order of mechanically motivated, undreaming, unaesthetic things.

Scientology is a bitter foe of such defamers of Man.

How can Scientology do anything about the world situation?

By approaching and making the able individual in society more able and more certain of his abilities, and by continuing its successful expansion and social reform programs throughout the world.

Certainty is a wonderful thing. The road toward realizing what certainty is has led Scientology's investigations through many uncertainties. One had to find out what was, before one could find out what could be. That work is done. It is possible to bring people, each and every one, into higher levels of certainty. And bringing them into higher levels of certainty brings them into higher levels of communication, communication not only with themselves but with others and with the material universe. And as one raises that level of awareness, one raises also the ability to be, to do, to live, and in the process we can make a better world and a better civilization.

16

Statistics of Scientology

Introduction

This is a first attempt at a comprehensive survey of Scientologists. The aim is to establish an accurate statistical analysis on an international scale.

The results are being made available for broad, public distribution. They will also be used internally, as Scientologists tend towards an inquiring nature — be it for themselves, their families or the world around them.

Scientology is a bootstrap operation. One where each person goes at his own pace, finding out for himself, thus becoming more and more able to better his own conditions.

The tables in this first publicly released survey prove the point. The number of people giving up smoking, reducing their alcohol intake and ending off drug habits is quite remarkable.

To the well trained Scientologist, such miracles are standard. He has the technology at his fingertips to do all this — and more.

One can sit and wait for a solution to the problems of life. Some drop out entirely, others find remedies in drugs and alcohol. Others feel these are not answers, but do not know where to look.

The person who quietly confronts his problems is the person who will win.

In Scientology, as shown in the tables, there are many who have taken this broad, first step.

Society is geared towards being complex. People tend to flinch away from it. Then they experience a loss — becoming victims of their own flinch: next time things seem more impossible than ever.

But for those who are willing to front up to it, life can be more hopeful, can contain more meaning, and can become a pleasurable activity in all its many forms.

The tables released here contain data generally known to Scientologists. Never before has so much been put together for all to see.

Each statistic is backed by an individual story. For society is composed of individuals — and each statistic here represents one person, their win, their success.

The tables show individuals regaining self-respect, increasing peace and calm in their environment, and providing a safe home in which children can grow up.

Scientology presents an opportunity for each and every person to achieve more than he had ever dreamed.

For as the tables show already, many are having gains beyond their greatest expectations.

The data is here in Scientology for others to achieve the same.

Scientology & Dianetics Counseling Membership across the World

World Membership Figures	
Year	Number
1954	200,000
1959	1,800,000
1968	3,276,000
1977-78	5,437,000

Membership is defined as being persons with a current membership who usually, but not always, have enrolled upon a course of counseling or ministerial training. It does not for the purposes of this survey include buyers of Scientology books or postal correspondents.

Figures for 1954—1959 are estimated, based on data held in archives. They are as accurate as could be determined from data available — some of which was sparse. In 1968, a survey of all founding members was undertaken which provided accurate data on which an analysis could be based.

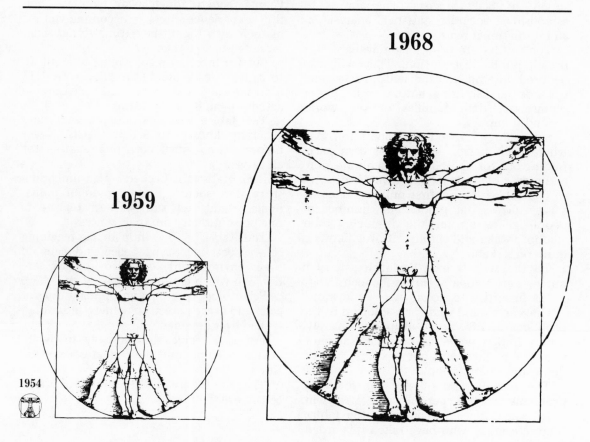

1968

1959

1954

1977 - 78

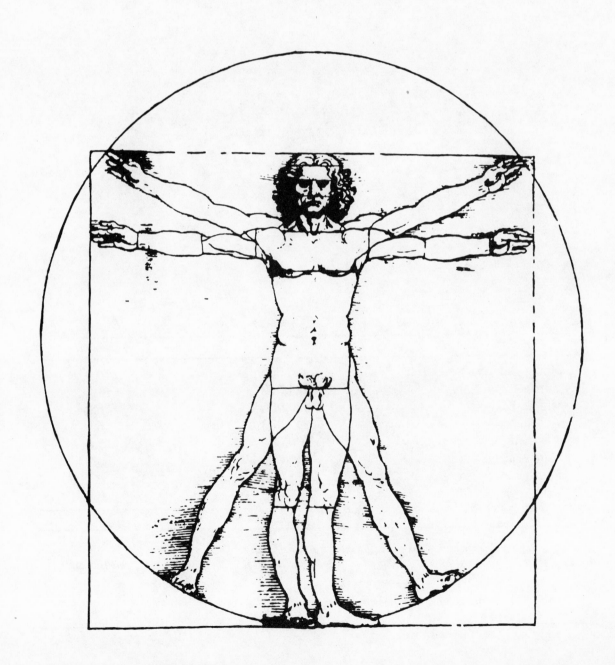

Church of Scientology World Membership Breakdown by Continent

June 1977

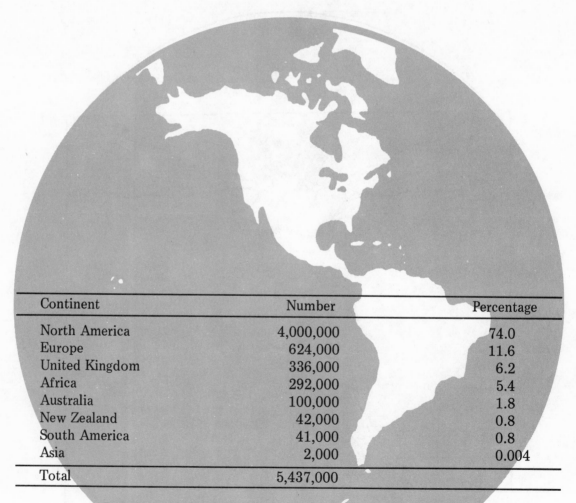

Continent	Number	Percentage
North America	4,000,000	74.0
Europe	624,000	11.6
United Kingdom	336,000	6.2
Africa	292,000	5.4
Australia	100,000	1.8
New Zealand	42,000	0.8
South America	41,000	0.8
Asia	2,000	0.004
Total	5,437,000	

Europe comprises the following countries: Norway, Sweden, Denmark, Holland, Belgium, France, Germany, Austria and Switzerland.

Africa comprises Africa continent.

Asia	0.004%
South America	0.8%
New Zealand	0.8%
Australia	1.8%
Africa	5.4%
United Kingdom	6.2%
Europe	11.6%
North America	74.0%

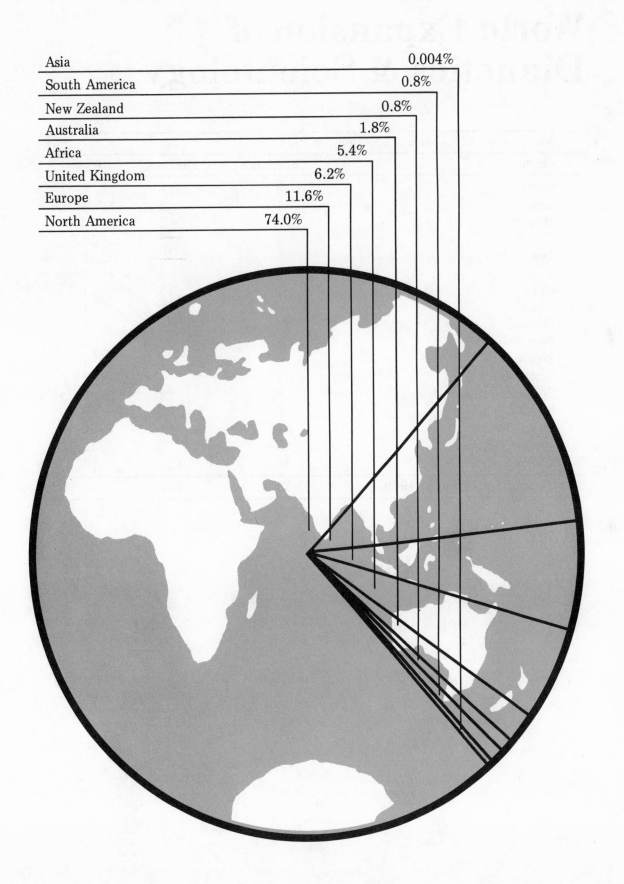

World Expansion of Dianetics & Scientology

Missions and Churches up to September 1978			
Country	Churches	Missions	Total
Australia	5	1	6
Austria	1	2	3
Belgium	--	2	2
Canada	5	8	13
Denmark	6	2	8
France	1	5	6
Germany	1	10	11
Guam	--	1	1
Holland	1	--	1
New Zealand	1	2	3
Puerto Rico	--	1	1
Rhodesia	1	--	1
South Africa	6	2	8
Sweden	3	2	5
Switzerland	1	8	9
United Kingdom	9	8	17
United States	38	118	156
Total up to September 1978	79	172	251

1954

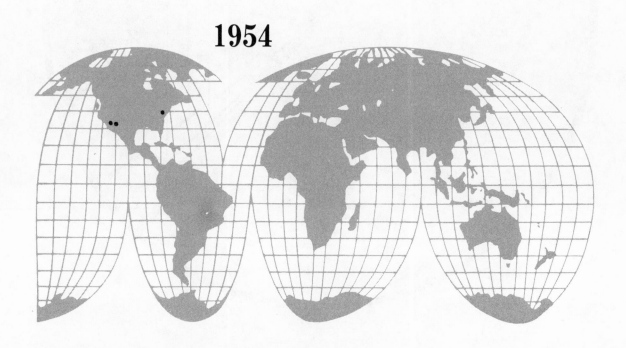

| Dianetic and Scientology philosophic study groups | | | |
Continent/Countries	Dianetic	Scientology	Total
North America	14	39	53
including Canada, United States, Mexico, Puerto Rico			
South America	5	5	10
including Argentina, Brazil, Colombia, Costa Rica, Guatemala, Venezuela			
Europe	6	43	49
including Austria, Belgium, Denmark, Finland, France, Germany, Greece, Greenland, Hungary, Italy, Netherlands, Norway, Portugal, Spain, United Kingdom			
Africa/Asia	--	18	18
including Ghana, India, Israel, Japan, Liberia, Nigeria, Pakistan, Saudi Arabia, Zambia			
Australia	1	3	4
Oceania	4	3	7
including Philippines, Tahiti, New Zealand			
Total	30	111	141

1977-78

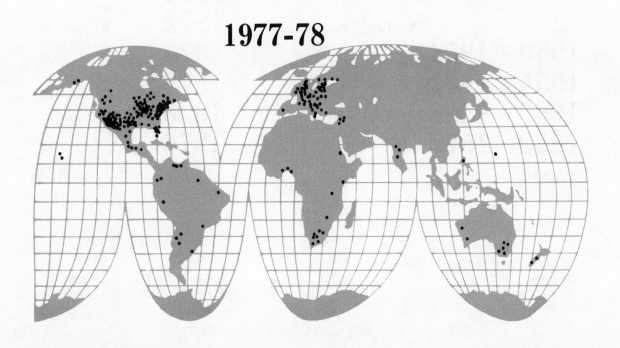

27 Years
of Scientology Growth

Church Establishment

1950-1977

Year	No. Established
1950 - 1954	3
1955 - 1959	7
1960 - 1968	14
1969 - 1977	52
Total	**76**

Establishment means legal incorporation under the laws of the country in which the Church or Mission is located.

Mission Establishment

1970-1976

Year	No. Established
1970	22
1971	20
1972	36
1973	25
1974	23
1975	30
1976	17
Total	**173**

1970, 1971 and 1972 include establishment of earlier missions.

1973 through 1976 are establishment of missions for those years only.

10 Years Cumulative Growth Churches & Missions

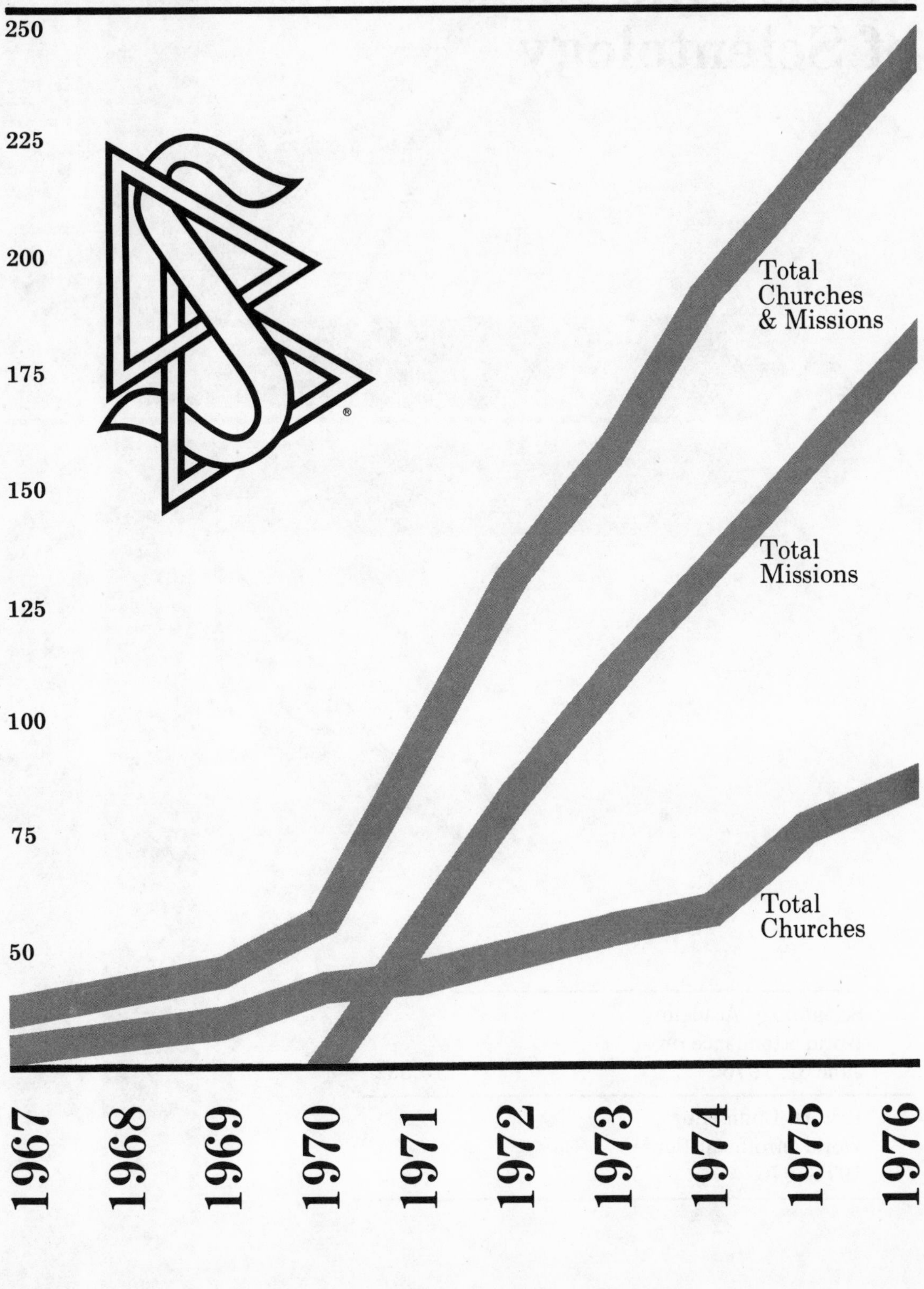

Total
Churches
& Missions

Total
Missions

Total
Churches

250

225

200

175

150

125

100

75

50

1967 1968 1969 1970 1971 1972 1973 1974 1975 1976

The Ministry of the Church of Scientology

Scientology Academy World attendance on June 31, 1976	10,532
Pastoral Counseling World enrolment figure 1975-1976	26,472

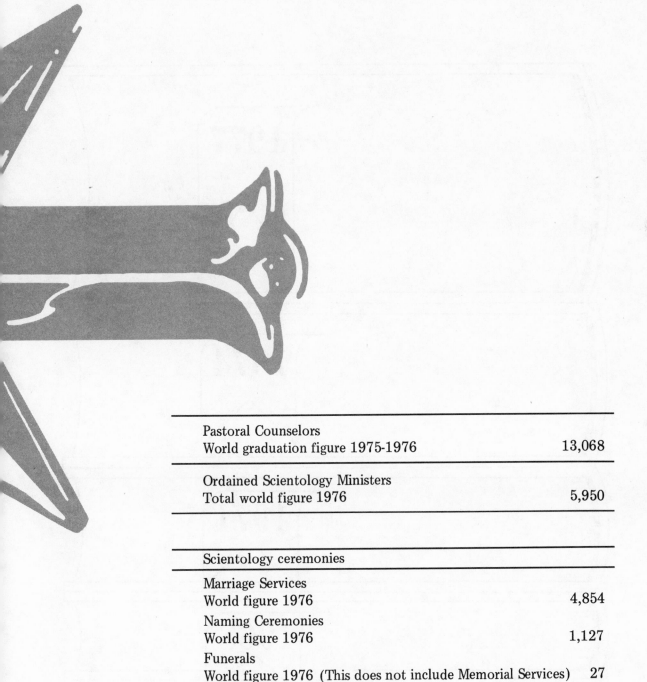

Pastoral Counselors World graduation figure 1975-1976	13,068
Ordained Scientology Ministers Total world figure 1976	5,950

Scientology ceremonies	
Marriage Services World figure 1976	4,854
Naming Ceremonies World figure 1976	1,127
Funerals World figure 1976 (This does not include Memorial Services)	27
Sunday Service Average number attending 1976	17,468

An average of one in 300 Scientologists attends Sunday service regularly.

Church of Scientology
Literature Distribution Figures

Since 1950, 171 different books on Dianetics and Scientology have been published and re-printed numerous times due to demand for them.

Since 1950, an additional 116 different books and booklets have been published. Most of these are based on the works of L. Ron Hubbard.

Since 1950, 18,795,680 Dianetics and Scientology books have been sold.

Magazine Distribution 1977	
Magazine	Distribution per issue
The Auditor	389,000
Advance!	95,000
Freedom	2,160,000
Source	56,000

The Auditor magazine is published monthly in 3 countries and circulated internationally.

Advance! magazine is published bi-monthly in 3 countries and circulated internationally.

Freedom is published 6 times a year in 14 countries in a variety of languages. Its readership is in excess of 6 million.

Source magazine is published bi-monthly and circulated internationally.

The Church of Scientology: Its Staff

Percentage Distribution of Church & Mission Staff

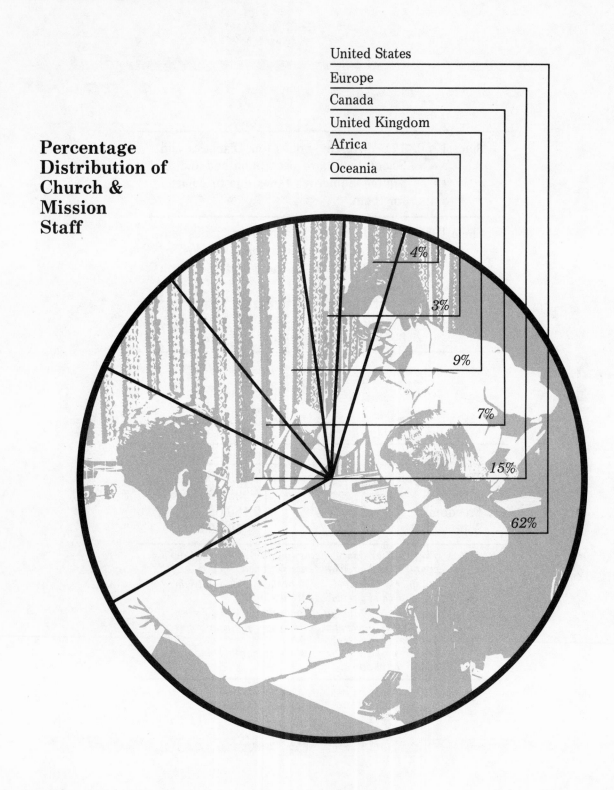

United States

Europe

Canada

United Kingdom

Africa

Oceania

4%

3%

9%

7%

15%

62%

Church and Mission Staff Total world figure June 31, 1977	**6,429**

Full-time Scientology Church and Mission staff
Country by country, 1977 figures

These figures do not include Volunteer Ministers or volunteer staff, nor do they include those aiding the Church's social reform activities.

Country	Church staff	Mission staff	Total staff
United States	2,795	1,246	4,041
Canada	319	116	435
United Kingdom	497	80	577
Germany	168	80	248
Denmark	235	20	255
Australia	193	10	203
Sweden	116	20	136
France	106	40	146
Africa	158	10	168
New Zealand	35	20	55
Switzerland	10	80	90
Austria	10	10	20
Holland	35	0	35
Belgium	0	20	20
Total	4,677	1,752	6,429

Full-time staff for Dianetics and Scientology philosophic educational groups
Country by country, 1977 figures

Country	Scientology	Dianetics	Total
Mexico	50	50	100
Israel	0	10	10
Brazil	0	10	10
Italy	5	5	10
Total	55	75	130

Church of Scientology Social Services

Non-Scientology groups utilizing the communication technology of L. Ron Hubbard	Geographical breakdown 1978	
Country	Rehabilitation groups Drugs	Rehabilitation groups Education
United States	22	25
Canada	4	1
United Kingdom	1	3
New Zealand	1	--
Germany	1	--
Sweden	1	--
Denmark	1	2
South Africa	--	4
Italy	--	3
Switzerland	--	1
Spain	--	1
Total	31	40

It should be noted that the use of this technology is purely in a secular capacity, and should not be confused with the theory and practices of the religious doctrines of the Church of Scientology.

Human Rights Groups Mental Health Reform	Geographical breakdown 1978
Country	CCHR*
United States	19
Australia	4
Canada	3
United Kingdom	5
Denmark	1
France	1
Sweden	1
New Zealand	1
Austria	1
Germany	1
Holland	1
Italy	1
Total	39

*CCHR: Citizens' Commission on Human Rights.

Freedom of Information Reform

Country	NCLESJ[1]	FOI[2]
United States	24	--
Australia	--	5
Canada	3	1
United Kingdom	3	1
Denmark	--	1
France	1	--
Sweden	1	--
Germany	1	3
Switzerland	1	1
Austria	1	--
Norway	1	1
Australia	--	1
New Zealand	--	2
Total	36	16

1. *NCLESJ: National Commission on Law Enforcement and Social Justice, seeks privacy and agency reform.*
2. *FOI: Freedom of Information, groups supported by individual Church members.*

Social Reform Groups
Geographical breakdown

Country	Criminon	TFA[1]	TFMR[2]	Aged[3]
United States	7	5	5	2
Australia	1	--	1	2
Canada	--	1	--	1
United Kingdom	1	--	--	--
Denmark	1	1	--	--
France	--	--	--	--
Sweden	--	--	--	--
New Zealand	1	--	--	--
Total	11	7	6	5

1. *TFA: Task Force on Alcoholism*
2. *TFMR: Task Force on Mental Retardation*
3. *New Life for Senior Citizens*

Vital Statistics of Scientologists Across the World

In June 1977, a survey of some 30,200+ Scientologists was taken in all geographical areas where the Church is located.

From the main survey, a random sampling of 3,028 surveys was undertaken, the results of which follow. The only arbitrary in the sampling was to ensure that all geographical locations were included from which responses had been received.

General Information

Breakdown of Scientology membership by age group June 1977		
Age group	Number	Percentage of respondents
Under 20 years	288	10.7
21-25 years	909	33.8
26-30 years	748	27.8
31-35 years	347	12.9
36-40 years	178	6.6
41-50 years	124	4.6
51-65 years	84	3.1
Over 65 years	10	.4
Total reporting	2,688†	

†340 of the respondents did not include their age.

Scientology members
Duration of membership

Duration	Number of people	Percentage
0-1 years	534	17.64
1-3 years	946	31.24
3-7 years	865	28.57
7-11 years	348	11.50
11-16 years	120	3.96
Over 16 years	138	4.56
No answer	77	2.44
Total reporting	3,028	

Method of introduction to the Church

First contact	Number reporting	Percentage
Friend/Relative	1,582	34.85
Word of mouth	1,048	23.08
Books	820	18.06
Personality test	458	10.09
Lecture	370	8.15
Advertisement	226	4.97
Sunday Service	35	.77
Total reporting	4,539†	

The Friend/Relative category divides into three approximately equal subcategories;
(a)   Introduction by accompanying a friend·or relative to a Scientology organization.
(b)   Book gift.
(c)   Respondent's personal curiosity after observing a "change" or "improvement" in a friend or family member.

†Several people gave more than one answer.

Training in Scientology & Dianetics

Scientology and Dianetics education
Level of certification

Type of certificate	Number	Percentage
Basic Scientology certificate	769	25.4
Scientology administration certificate	716	23.6
Dianetic counselor certificate	701	23.2
Scientology counselor certificate	775	25.6
No certificate	14	.5
No answer	53	1.7
Total reporting	3,028	

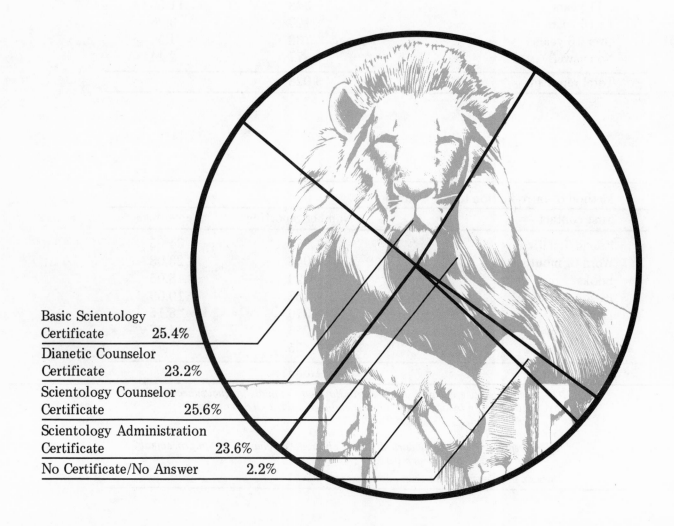

Basic Scientology
Certificate   25.4%

Dianetic Counselor
Certificate   23.2%

Scientology Counselor
Certificate   25.6%

Scientology Administration
Certificate   23.6%

No Certificate/No Answer   2.2%

Counseling in Scientology & Dianetics

Scientology and Dianetics counseling
Level of certification

Type of counseling	Number	Percentage
Basic Scientology counseling	1,009	33.3
Dianetic counseling	148	4.9
Lower level Scientology counseling	1,146	37.8
Advanced Scientology counseling	613	20.2
No answer	112	3.6
Total reporting	3,028	

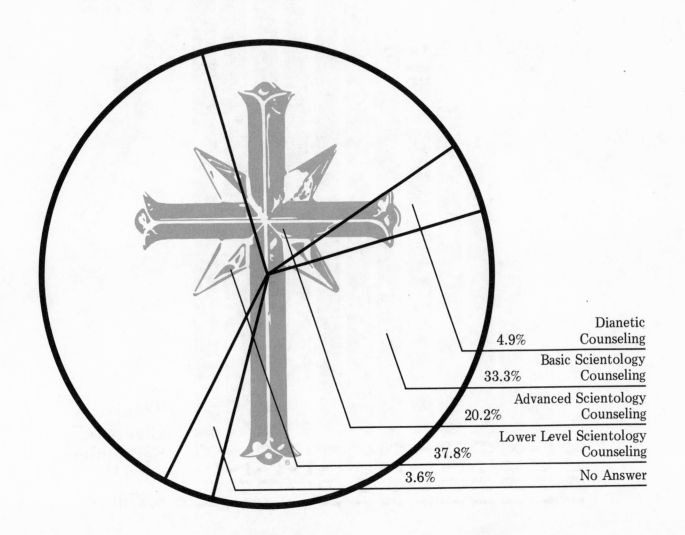

4.9% Dianetic Counseling

33.3% Basic Scientology Counseling

20.2% Advanced Scientology Counseling

37.8% Lower Level Scientology Counseling

3.6% No Answer

Number of Clears

cumulative   1966 to September 1978

The first graduation
from the Clearing
Course was
February
1966

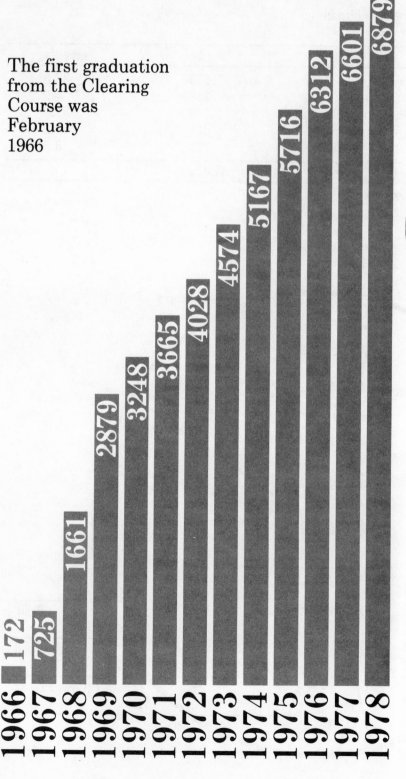

172
725
1661
2879
3248
3665
4028
4574
5167
5716
6312
6601
6879

1966
1967
1968
1969
1970
1971
1972
1973
1974
1975
1976
1977
1978

Total
Clears to
September
1978:
6,879

Educational Background

Scientology membership		
Educational background		
Type of education	Number reporting	Percentage
Secondary education	1,424	47.03
University education	1,133	37.42
Specialist education	421	13.94
No education reported	50	1.66
Total reporting	3,028	

Secondary education includes general basic schooling up to college or university entrance: covers high school, grammar, elementary, public, boarding and private schools.
Specialist education includes college, technical and art school.

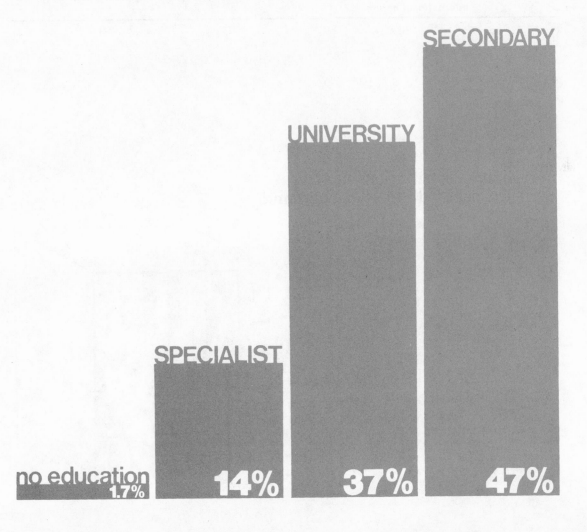

Social Background of Scientologists

Class — social status

Class	Number Reporting	Percentage
Middle	2,378	78.5
Upper	353	11.65
Working	251	8.29
No answer	46	1.55
Total reporting	3,028	

The social status breakdown here is assigned on responses to the survey. The criteria used is drawn from the Dictionary of Social Sciences (Tavistock, London, 1964). "Upper class" refers to the aristocrat and elite professional socio-economic class; "middle" denotes the intermediary between upper and lower; "working" covers unskilled manual labor. It should be noted that the figures given are of international nature.

Percentage Distribution
Skilled/Unskilled Labor Background

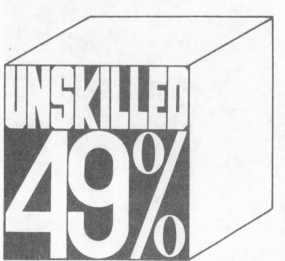

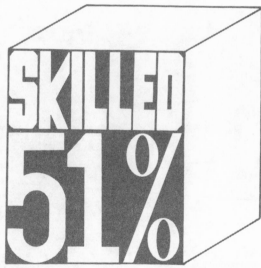

Occupational backgrounds

Type of occupation	Number reporting	Percentage
Arts	636	19.82
White collar	504	15.71
Blue collar	440	13.71
Student *(non-Scientology subjects)*	473	14.74
Technical *(includes all branches of engineering)*	297	9.25
Teaching	269	8.38
Armed Forces	183	5.70
No occupation	128	3.99
Medical *(includes nursing and dentistry)*	154	4.80
Sales and marketing	85	2.64
Professional sports	4	.13
Law	10	.31
Civil Service	7	.21
Other	18	.59
Total reporting	3,208	

Occupational gains as a result of Scientology
Nonspiritual benefits claimed by respondents

Type of benefit	Number reporting	Percentage
General improvement	705	23.28
More able/competent	568	18.75
More aware/understanding	194	6.41
Study ability improved	163	5.38
Communication ability improved	157	5.18
Higher tolerance toward life in general	79	2.61
No benefit reported	89	2.94
Nonapplicable, as no longer at that profession	1,073	35.43
Total reporting	3,028	

Religious Background

Scientology membership Religious background		
Belief	**Number reporting**	**Percentage**
Christian *(non-Roman Catholic; includes all other nonspecified Christian Churches)*	1,164	38.44
Roman Catholic	784	25.89
No religious affiliation	625	20.64
Jewish	199	6.57
Eastern *(includes Hinduism, Buddhism, Unification)*	53	1.75
Unspecified Christian faiths	25	.82
Others specified *(includes Greek Orthodox, Evangelical, Mennonite, Calvinist, Dukhobor, Mormon, Christian Science, Russian Orthodox)*	56	1.8
Methodist	11	.36
Scientologist	10	.33
Baptist	4	.13
No answer	97	3.2
Total reporting	**3,028**	

"Do you consider yourself still to be a practicing ——— ?" (from above list)

Yes _____   No _____   70% replied 'yes'.†

> †*Although the survey was not designed to elicit information as to whether a departure from an earlier religious practice preceded Scientology contact, the information has been included. A subsequent publication could fruitfully explore this area.*

Scientology membership Furtherance of religious belief		
Has Scientology helped further your religious beliefs	**Number reporting**	**Percentage**
Yes	2,297	75.85
No	402	13.27
No answer	313	10.33
Slightly	16	.53
Total reporting	**3,028**	

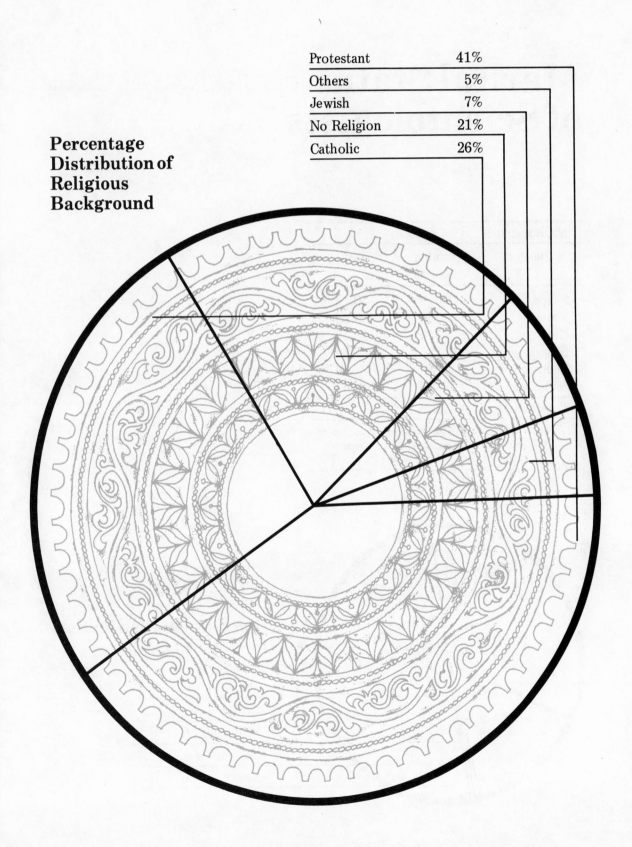

**Percentage
Distribution of
Religious
Background**

Protestant	41%
Others	5%
Jewish	7%
No Religion	21%
Catholic	26%

Marital Status of Scientologists

Marital status		
Status	Number reporting	Percentage
Single	1,519	50.16
Married	1,029	33.99
Divorced	320	10.57
Separated	125	4.12
Widowed	18	.59
No answer	17	.56
Total reporting	3,028	

Not all marriages, divorces, separations and widowhoods reported occurred after contact with Scientology.

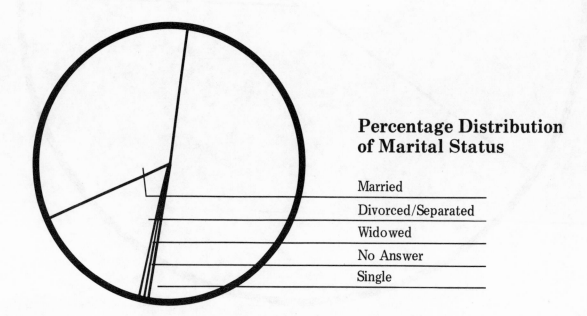

Percentage Distribution of Marital Status

Married

Divorced/Separated

Widowed

No Answer

Single

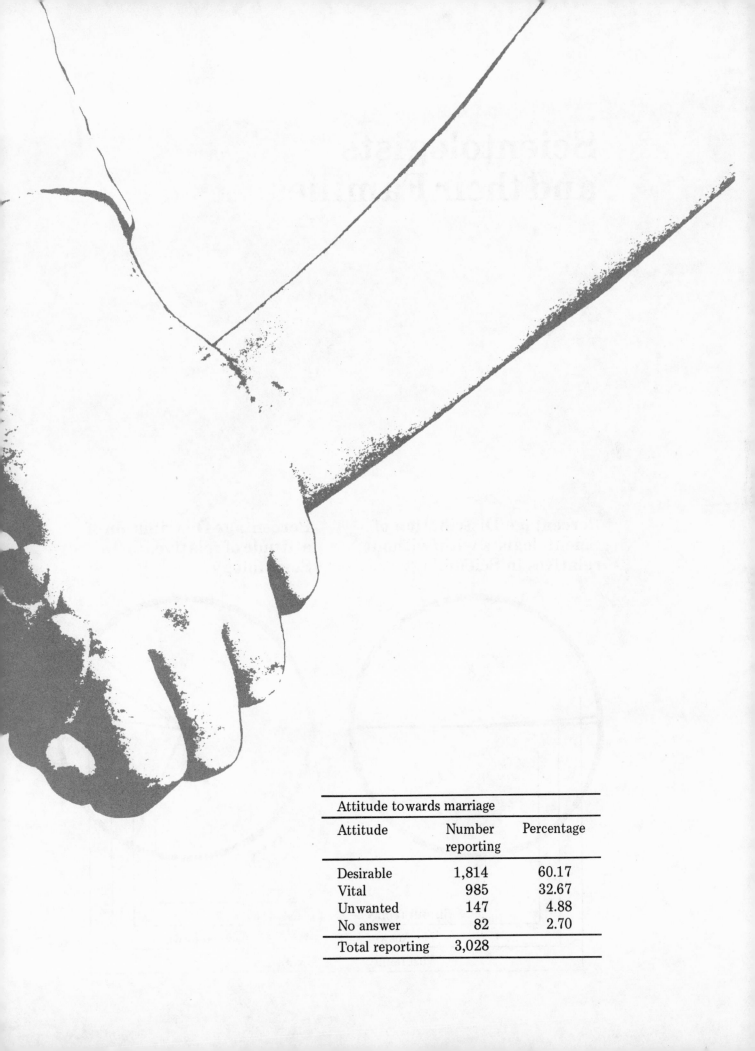

Attitude towards marriage		
Attitude	Number reporting	Percentage
Desirable	1,814	60.17
Vital	985	32.67
Unwanted	147	4.88
No answer	82	2.70
Total reporting	3,028	

Scientologists and their Families

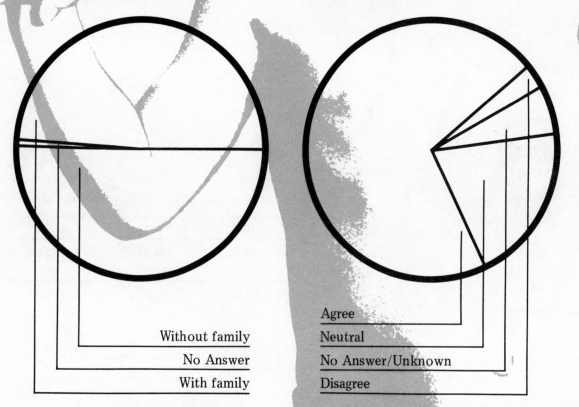

Percentage Distribution of Scientologists with/without relatives in Scientology

Percentage Distribution of attitude of relatives to Scientology

Without family

No Answer

With family

Agree

Neutral

No Answer/Unknown

Disagree

Scientologists with/without relatives in Scientology

Families in Scientology	Number reporting	Percentage
People with a family member in Scientology	1,477	48.8
People without a family member in Scientology	1,531	50.7
No answer	20	.7
Total reporting	3,028	

'Family' includes parents and/or other relatives of a Scientologist, and/or, if married, children of the marriage.

Breakdown of family members involved

Relationship to Scientologist	Number reporting	Percentage
Brother and/or sister	764	36.4
Parents (one or both)	446	21.3
Spouse	431	20.5
Children (one or more)	202	9.4
Relationship not specified	104	5.0
Whole family (immediate)	76	3.6
In-laws	74	3.5
Total reporting	2,097†	

†Those who answered gave more than one reply.

How individual members became interested in Scientology

Interest	Number reporting	Percentage
By own personal research	536	35.0
Through friends	269	17.6
Through other relatives	189	12.3
Through books on Scientology	168	11.0
Through word of mouth	248	16.1
Through public lectures	47	3.1
Through advertisements	23	1.5
Through personality tests	19	1.2
Unspecified	56	3.6
Total reporting	1,555†	

†More than one answer given to question in some cases.

Relations' attitudes towards Scientology

Attitude	Number reporting	Percentage
In agreement	2,139	70.6
Neutral — little interest either way	610	20.14
In disagreement	92	3.03
No answer	69	2.3
Unknown	118	3.9
Total reporting	3,028	

These answers were given by Scientologists — not by their families.

Social Habits of Scientologists

Alcoholic intake		
Classification	Number reporting	Percentage
Users	2,360	77.8
Non-users	659	21.7
No reply given	15	.5
Total reporting	3,028	

Percentage Distribution of frequency of drinking

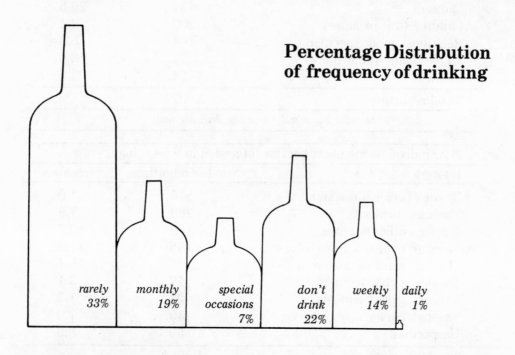

rarely 33%   monthly 19%   special occasions 7%   don't drink 22%   weekly 14%   daily 1%

Alcoholic intake pattern		
Frequency of intake	Number reporting	Percentage
Rarely — 1 to 6 times a year	1,001	33.05
Monthly	573	18.9
Not applicable as no intake	659	21.7
Weekly	422	13.9
Infrequently — special occasions	198	6.5
No answer	140	4.6
Daily	35	1.15
Total reporting	3,028	

Change of alcohol intake patterns since Scientology		
Degree of change	Number reporting	Percentage
Less	2,161	71.4
No answer — not applicable	440	14.5
Same	332	11.0
More	95	3.1
Total reporting	3,028	

Attitude toward alcohol		
Attitude	Number reporting	Percentage
Unnecessary	2,849	94.1
Needful	56	1.8
No answer — not applicable	81	2.7
Uncertain	42	1.4
Total reporting	3,028	

Pre-Scientology drug abuse pattern

Classification	Number reporting	Percentage
Priorly took drugs	1,886	62.3
Did not take drugs	1,101	36.4
No answer	41	1.3
Total reporting	3,028	

Does not include prescription drugs.

Current drug-taking pattern

Classification	Number reporting	Percentage
No drugs at all	3,003	98.2
Taking some drugs†	25	.8
Total reporting	3,028	

†23 answered they now take prescription drugs.

Percentage Distribution of drug takers prior to Scientology

Percentage Distribution of drug takers now

Percentage Distribution of current attitudes towards drugs

Overall drug-taking pattern while in Scientology

Classification	Number reporting	Percentage
None since entering	2,522	83.3
A few since entering but not currently	506	16.7
Total reporting	3,028	

Current attitude on drugs		
Attitude	Number reporting	Percentage
No need at all	2,918	96.3
Need them	. 5	.165
Need them for prescribed medical reasons	45	1.48
No answer	60	1.98
Total reporting	3,028	

Cigarette smoking patterns		
Classification	Number reporting	Percentage
Smokers	1,700	56.1
Non-smokers†	1,282	42.3
No answer	46	1.4
Total reporting	3,028	

†Includes 420 members who have given up smoking since Scientology participation.

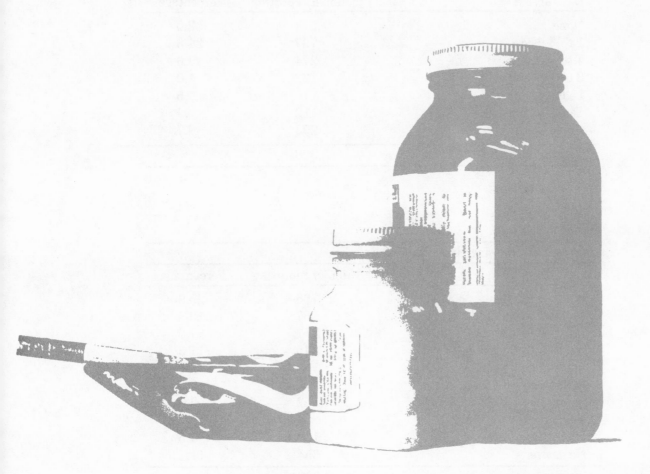

Illness Trends

Frequency of minor ailments

Frequency	Number reporting	Percentage
Never	405	13.4
Rarely *(at least one year between ailments)*	1,614	53.3
1 to 2 times a year	640	21.1
3 to 4 times a year	101	3.3
Every month	94	3.1
No answer	174	5.8
Total reporting	3,028	

Absenteeism from work due to illness (in last year)

Days absent	Number reporting	Percentage
None	1,574	52.0
1 to 3 days	737	24.3
4 to 7 days	274	9.0
8 to 14 days	122	4.0
15 days and over	16	.5
Can't remember	12	.4
No answer	293	9.7
Total reporting	3,028	

Length of time since last illness

When last ill	Number reporting	Percentage
In last 3 months	786	25.9
In last 4 to 6 months	557	18.5
In last 7 to 12 months	511	17.0
In last 1 to 3 years	345	11.3
In last 4 to 5 years	167	5.5
In last 6 to 10 years	70	2.3
In last 11 to 20 years	62	2.0
Years ago	37	1.2
Don't remember	139	4.5
No answer	354	11.7
Total reporting	3,028	

Percentage distribution of Absenteeism in last year due to illness

No Days	52.0%
No Answer	9.7%
Can't Recall	.4%
7 Days	4.5%
Over 8 days	4.5%
Under 7 Days	28.8%

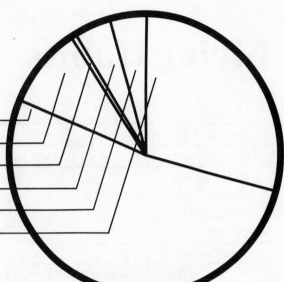

Illness trends

Average number of days absent from work in last year	1 day per person
Average frequency of illness	once every 2 years
Average length of time since last illness	20 months

Living Habits

Residential facilities		
Classification	Number reporting	Percentage
Rent	1,850	61.09
Home owners	623	20.57
No answer	400	13.21
Other†	155	5.11
Total reporting	3,028	

†Living at home with family or in limited staff housing facilities.

Percentage Distribution of Accomodations Patterns

Other	5.11%
No Answer	13.21%
Own	20.57%
Rent	61.08%

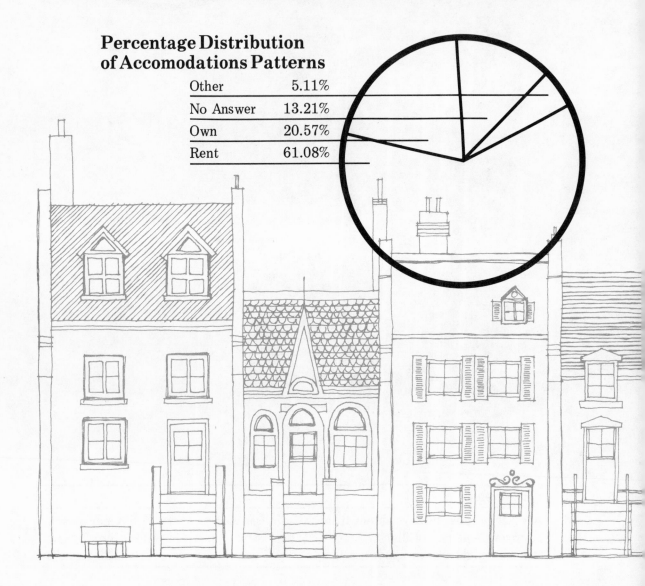

Distribution of welfare aid

Classification	Number reporting	Percentage
Not receiving welfare benefits	2,740	90.5
Receiving welfare benefits†	135	4.5
No answer	153	5.0
Total reporting	3,028	

†*Includes children's allowances, family allowances, pensions and other sundry benefits.*

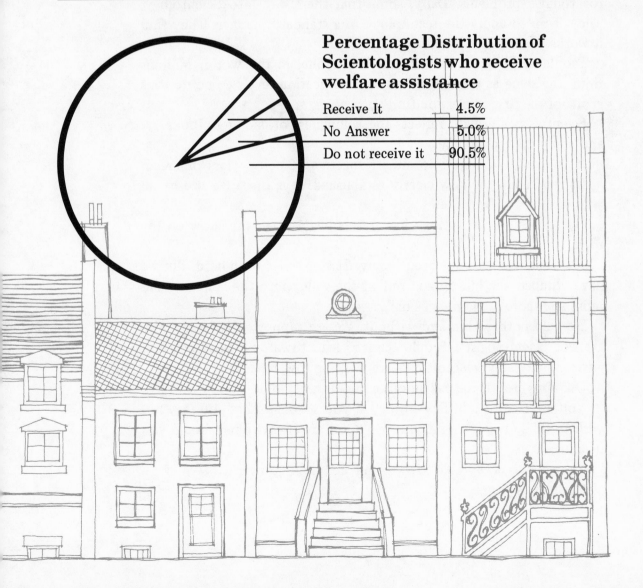

Percentage Distribution of Scientologists who receive welfare assistance

Receive It	4.5%
No Answer	5.0%
Do not receive it	90.5%

Conclusion:

It has long been said Scientology will go as far as it works.

As is set out here, many excellent results occur daily due to the workability of the subject.

There are many individuals in today's society seeking alternatives for today's problems. Daily, some find their way into Scientology. They learn to apply the technology in a standard manner. They find it works.

People are not actually isolated all alone, in the world. Millions think the same as you do. When communication levels come up, this is one of the first things you find out.

Scientology's growth reflects the willingness of people to look, try, and apply the technology.

It is readily available to all, irrespective of color, class or creed.

Its workability is now clearly established. It is there for use by all who wish.

Our policy in Scientology has always been to get the show on the road.

The road has at times been lonely. Has at times been hard. But we have climbed the hill up and out of the valley into the sunlight, and more and more are joining us daily.

We help both within and without. We are supported by many who are not Scientologists. People tend to lean towards a safe, peaceful environment, and Scientologists are working towards that end.

Our aims are simple, as laid out earlier in this book.

You are free to join Scientology if you so wish. That you may not wish to do so is your right. But our doors are always open should you need us.

Your help is acceptable to us — and we thank you for it.

Our help is yours.

17

List of Organizations

Following is a list of Scientology and Dianetics organizations and related groups. Due to ever increasing expansion of Scientology and Dianetics activities it must be noted that the addresses can change and the number of organizations increase rather rapidly so that not all may be listed even at the time of publication.

Key to Types of Organizations and Sequence of Listing

Organizations are listed in the following sequence:

1. Worldwide
2. International
3. Liaison Offices
4. Publications
5. Flag Land Base
6. Advanced & Saint Hill Organizations
7. Churches
8. Celebrity Centres
9. Missions
10. Groups
11. Social Reform Groups which use the technology of Scientology dealing with human rights, reform, public health and safety, mental retardation, old age, alcoholism, law enforcement and social justice, rehabilitation of criminals, etc.

Within these categories the general location sequence is as follows:

1. Western United States
2. Eastern United States
3. Central United States
4. Canada
5. Mexico
6. United Kingdom
7. Europe
8. Australia and New Zealand
9. Africa
10. others

Churches or Missions or Groups are then listed alphabetically by city.

Worldwide/International/ Liaison Organizations

Flag Land Base/Advanced/ Saint Hills/Publications Organizations

WESTERN UNITED STATES

Church of Scientology of California
LRH Communicator Network
International Headquarters
4833 Fountain Avenue
Los Angeles, California 90029

Church of Scientology of California
United States Guardian's Office
4833 Fountain Avenue
Los Angeles, California 90029

Church of Scientology of California
The Flag Bureaux
(Write care of your nearest FOLO
    addresses following) or
Post Office Box 23751
Tampa, Florida 33623

Church of Scientology of California
Flag Operations Liaison Office
    West U.S.
4833 Fountain Avenue, Main Annex
Los Angeles, California 90029

EASTERN UNITED STATES

Church of Scientology of California
Flag Operations Liaison Office
    East U.S.
30 West 74th Street
New York City, New York 10023

UNITED KINGDOM

Church of Scientology of California
Worldwide Guardian's Office
Saint Hill Manor
East Grinstead, Sussex, England
RH 19 4JY

Church of Scientology of California
    Worldwide
Saint Hill Manor
East Grinstead, Sussex, England
RH 19 4JY
Telephone: 0342-24571

Church of Scientology of California
Flag Operations Liaison Office
    United Kingdom
Saint Hill Manor
East Grinstead, Sussex, England
RH 19 4JY
Telephone: 0342-24571

EUROPE

Church of Scientology of California
Flag Operations Liaison Office
    Europe
Saxogade 78-82
1662 Copenhagen, Denmark

AUSTRALIA AND NEW ZEALAND

Church of Scientology of California
Flag Operations Liaison Office ANZO
    (Australia/New Zealand)
24 Dick Street
Henley, Sydney
New South Wales, Australia 2111

AFRICA

Church of Scientology of California
Flag Operations Liaison Office Africa
41 Olivia Road
Berea, Johannesburg, South Africa

UNITED STATES OF AMERICA

Church of Scientology of California
Flag Service Organization
210 South Fort Harrison Avenue
Clearwater, Florida 33516
Mailing Address: P. O. Box 23751
Tampa, Florida 33623
Telephone: 813-447-6258, 461-1282,
    461-1283

Church of Scientology of California
The Flag Land Base Estates
    Organization
The Fort Harrison
210 South Fort Harrison Avenue
Clearwater, Florida 33516
Mailing Address: P. O. Box 23751
Tampa, Florida 33623
Telephone: 813-447-6258

Church of Scientology of California
Universal Media Productions
Post Office Box 23751
Tampa, Florida 33623
Telephone: 813-447-6258

Church of Scientology of California
Advanced Organization Los Angeles
1306 North Berendo Street
Los Angeles, California 90027
Telephone: 213-665-5901

Church of Scientology of California
American Saint Hill Organization
1413 North Berendo Street
Los Angeles, California 90027
Telephone: 213-660-5553

Church of Scientology of California
American Saint Hill Foundation
1413 North Berendo Street
Los Angeles, California 90027
Telephone: 213-660-5553

Church of Scientology
Publications Organization United
    States
4833 Fountain Avenue, East Annex
Los Angeles, California 90029
Telephone: 213-389-8853

Church of Scientology of California
Pacific Area Estates
Hotel Organization for
    Scientologists
5930 Franklin Avenue
Hollywood, California 90028
Telephone: 213-464-5192

Church of Scientology of California
Pacific Area Estates Service
    Organization
4833 Fountain Avenue, Main Annex
Los Angeles, California 90029
Telephone: 213-665-7155

UNITED KINGDOM

Hubbard College of Scientology
Advanced Organization Saint Hill
Saint Hill Manor
East Grinstead, Sussex, England
RH 19 4JY
Telephone: 0342-24571

EUROPE

Church of Scientology
Advanced Organization Europe
Jernbanegade 6
1608 Copenhagen V, Denmark
Telephone: 01-11-11-69

Church of Scientology
Saint Hill Organization Europe
Jernbanegade 6
1608 Copenhagen V, Denmark
Telephone: 01-11-11-69

Church of Scientology
Publications Organization Denmark
Jernbanegade 6
1608 Copenhagen V, Denmark

Churches

WESTERN UNITED STATES

Church of Scientology Austin
2804 Rio Grande
Austin, Texas 78705
Telephone: 512-474-6631

Church of Scientology Austin
Foundation
2804 Rio Grande
Austin, Texas 78705
Telephone: 512-474-6631

Church of Scientology Denver
1640 Welton
Denver, Colorado 80202
Telephone: 303-778-1957

Church of Scientology Hawaii
143 Nenue Street
Honolulu, Hawaii 96821
Telephone: 808-373-2101

Church of Scientology Hawaii
Foundation
143 Nenue Street
Honolulu, Hawaii 96821
Telephone: 808-373-2101

Church of Scientology Las Vegas
2108 Industrial Road
Las Vegas, Nevada 89102
Telephone: 702-382-3561

Church of Scientology Las Vegas
Foundation
2108 Industrial Road
Las Vegas, Nevada 89102
Telephone: 702-382-3561

Church of Scientology Los Angeles
1415 North Berendo Street
Los Angeles, California 90027
Telephone: 213-385-2051

Church of Scientology Los Angeles
Foundation
1415 North Berendo Street
Los Angeles, California 90027
Telephone: 213-385-9051

Church of Scientology Portland
333 South West Park Avenue
Portland, Oregon 97205
Telephone: 503-227-0497

Church of Scientology Portland
Foundation
333 South West Park Avenue
Portland, Oregon 97205
Telephone: 503-227-0497

Church of Scientology Sacramento
819 19th Street
Sacramento, California 95814
Telephone: 916-446-0209

Church of Scientology Sacramento
Foundation
819 19th Street
Sacramento, California 95814
Telephone: 916-446-0209

Church of Scientology San Diego
926 "C" Street
San Diego, California 92101
Telephone: 714-239-8008

Church of Scientology San Diego
Foundation
926 "C" Street
San Diego, California 92101
Telephone: 714-239-8008

Church of Scientology San Francisco
414 Mason Street, Room 400
San Francisco, California 94102
Telephone: 415-391-3740

Church of Scientology San Francisco
Foundation
414 Mason Street, Room 400
San Francisco, California 94102
Telephone: 415-391-3740

Church of Scientology Seattle
1531 4th Avenue
Seattle, Washington 98101
Telephone: 206-622-8082

Church of Scientology Seattle
Foundation
1531 4th Avenue
Seattle, Washington 98101
Telephone: 206-622-8082

Church of Scientology St. Louis
3730 Lindell Boulevard
St. Louis, Missouri 63108
Telephone: 314-534-1060

Church of Scientology St. Louis
Foundation
3730 Lindell Boulevard
St. Louis, Missouri 63108
Telephone: 314-534-1060

Church of Scientology Twin Cities
730 Hennepin Avenue
Minneapolis, Minnesota 55403
Telephone: 612-338-0855

Church of Scientology Twin Cities
Foundation
730 Hennepin Avenue
Minneapolis, Minnesota 55403
Telephone: 612-338-0855

EASTERN UNITED STATES

Church of Scientology Boston
448 Beacon Street
Boston, Massachusetts 02215
Telephone: 617-266-9500

Church of Scientology Boston
Foundation
448 Beacon Street
Boston, Massachusetts 02215
Telephone: 617-266-9500

Church of Scientology Buffalo
1116 Elmwood Avenue
Buffalo, New York 14222
Telephone: 716-886-9633

Church of Scientology Buffalo
Foundation
1116 Elmwood Avenue
Buffalo, New York 14222
Telephone: 716-886-9633

Church of Scientology Chicago
1555 Maple Street
Evanston, Illinois 60201
Telephone: 312-866-8457

Church of Scientology Chicago
Foundation
1555 Maple Street
Evanston, Illinois 60201
Telephone: 312-866-8457

Church of Scientology Detroit
3905 Rochester Road
Royal Oak, Michigan 48073
Telephone: 313-585-8920

Church of Scientology Detroit
Foundation
3905 Rochester Road
Royal Oak, Michigan 48073
Telephone: 313-585-8920

Church of Scientology Miami
120 Giralda Street
Coral Gables, Florida 33134
Telephone: 305-443-2876

Church of Scientology Miami
Foundation
120 Giralda Street
Coral Gables, Florida 33134
Telephone: 305-443-2876

Church of Scientology New York
28-30 West 74th Street
New York, New York 10023
Telephone: 212-874-1701

Church of Scientology New York
Foundation
28-30 West 74th Street
New York, New York 10023
Telephone: 212-874-1701

Church of Scientology Philadelphia
8 West Lancaster Avenue
Ardmore, Pennsylvania 19003
Telephone: 215-649-7345

Church of Scientology Philadelphia
Foundation
8 West Lancaster Avenue
Ardmore, Pennsylvania 19003
Telephone: 215-649-7345

Founding Church of Scientology
of Washington, D.C.
2125 S Street, N.W.
Washington, D.C. 20008
Telephone: 202-797-3700

Church of Scientology
Washington, D.C. Foundation
2125 South Street, N.W.
Washington, D.C. 20008
Telephone: 202-797-3700

CANADA

Church of Scientology Montreal
15 Notre Dame Ouest
Montreal, Quebec, Canada H2Y 1B5
Telephone: 514-8445-5468

Church of Scientology Montreal
Foundation
15 Notre Dame Ouest
Montreal, Quebec, Canada HWY 1B5
Telephone: 514-844-5468

Church of Scientology Ottawa
292 Somerset Street West
Ottawa, Ontario, Canada D2P 9Z9
Telephone: 613-235-6445

Church of Scientology Ottawa
Foundation
292 Somerset Street West
Ottawa, Ontario, Canada D2P 9Z9
Telephone: 613-235-6445

Church of Scientology Toronto
385 Yonge Street
Toronto, Ontario, Canada M5B 151
Telephone: 416-967-1661

Church of Scientology Toronto
Foundation
385 Yonge Street
Toronto, Ontario, Canada M5B 151
Telephone: 416-967-1661

Church of Scientology Vancouver
4857 Main Street
Vancouver 10, British Columbia,
Canada
Telephone: 604-872-7033

Church of Scientology Vancouver
Foundation
4857 Main Street
Vancouver 10, British Columbia,
Canada
Telephone: 604-872-7033

UNITED KINGDOM

Hubbard College of Scientology
Saint Hill Foundation
Saint Hill Manor
East Grinstead, Sussex, England
RH 19 4JY
Telephone: 0342-24571

Hubbard Scientology Organization
London
68 Tottenham Court Road
London, W.1. England
Telephone: 01-580-3601

Hubbard Scientology Organization
London Foundation
68 Tottenham Court Road
London, W.1. England
Telephone: 01-580-3601

Hubbard Scientology Organization
Manchester
48A Faulkner Street
Manchester, England M1 4FH
Telephone: 061-236-5988

Hubbard Scientology Organization
Manchester Foundation
48A Faulkner Street
Manchester, England M1 4FH
Telephone: 061-236-5988

Hubbard Scientology Organization
Plymouth
39 Portland Square
Sherwell, Plymouth
Devonshire, England PL4 6DJ
Telephone: 0752-69575

Hubbard Scientology Organization
Plymouth Foundation
39 Portland Square
Sherwell, Plymouth
Devonshire, England PL4 6DJ
Telephone: 0752-69575

Hubbard Academy of Personal
Independence
Fleet House
20 South Bridge
Edinburgh, Scotland EH1 ILL
Telephone: 031-556-5074

Hubbard Academy of Personal
Independence Foundation
Fleet House
20 South Bridge
Edinburgh, Scotland EH1 1LL
Telephone: 031-556-5074

EUROPE

Church of Scientology Amsterdam
Singel 289
Amsterdam C, Netherlands
Telephone: 226-101

Church of Scientology
Amsterdam Foundation
Singel 289
Amsterdam C, Netherlands
Telephone: 226-101

Church of Scientology Copenhagen
Frederiksborgvej 5
2400 Copenhagen V, Denmark
Telephone: 01-342-233

Church of Scientology
Copenhagen Foundation
Frederiksborgvej 5
2400 Copenhagen V, Denmark
Telephone: 01-342-233

Church of Scientology Denmark
Hovedvagtsgade 6
1103 Copenhagen K, Denmark
Telephone: 01-128-008

Church of Scientology
Denmark Foundation
Hovedvagtsgade 6
1103 Copenhagen K, Denmark
Telephone: 01-128-008

Church of Scientology Goteborg
Magasinsgatan 12
S-411-18 Goteborg, Sweden
Telephone: 115-574

Church of Scientology
Goteborg Foundation
Magasinsgatan 12
S-411-18 Goteborg, Sweden
Telephone: 115-574

Church of Scientology Malmo
Skomakaregatan 12
S-211-34 Malmo, Sweden
Telephone: 115-524

Church of Scientology
Malmo Foundation
Skomakaregatan 12
S-211-34 Malmo, Sweden
Telephone: 115-524

Church of Scientology Munich
Lindwurmstrasse 29
8000 Munchen 2
Munich, West Germany
Telephone: 539-303

Church of Scientology Munich
Foundation
Lindwurmstrasse 29
8000 Munchen 2
Munich, West Germany
Telephone: 539-303

Church of Scientology Paris
12 Rue De La Montagne
Sainte Genevieve 75005
Paris, France
Telephone: 252-172

Church of Scientology Paris
Foundation
12 Rue De La Montagne
Sainte Genevieve 75005
Paris, France
Telephone: 252-172

Church of Scientology Stockholm
Kammakargatan 46
S-111-60 Stockholm, Sweden
Telephone: 117-415

Church of Scientology Stockholm
Foundation
Kammakargatan 46
S-111-60 Stockholm, Sweden
Telephone: 117-415

Church of Scientology Vienna
(Scientology-Osterreich)
Museumstrasse 5/18
1070 Vienna, Austria
Telephone: 930-469, 934-728

Church of Scientology Vienna
Foundation
(Scientology-Osterreich)
Museumstrasse 5/18
1070 Vienna, Austria
Telephone: 930-469, 934-728

AUSTRALIA
AND NEW ZEALAND

Church of Scientology Adelaide
Thorngate Building
57 Pulteney Street
Fullarton
Adelaide 5000, South Australia
Telephone: 223-6555

Church of Scientology Adelaide
Foundation
Thorngate Building
57 Pulteney Street
Fullarton
Adelaide 5000, South Australia
Telephone: 223-6555

Church of Scientology Melbourne
724 Inkerman Road
North Caulfield 3161
Melbourne, Victoria, Australia
Telephone: 509-8533

Church of Scientology Melbourne
Foundation
724 Inkerman Road
North Caulfield 3161
Melbourne, Victoria, Australia
Telephone: 509-8533

Church of Scientology Perth
Pastoral House
156 St. George's Terrace
Perth 6000, Western Australia
Telephone: 219-561

Church of Scientology Perth
Foundation
Pastoral House
156 St. George's Terrace
Perth 6000, Western Australia
Telephone: 219-561

Church of Scientology Sydney
1 Lee Street
Sydney 2000
New South Wales, Australia
Telephone: 212-1220, 212-5338

Church of Scientology Sydney
Foundation
1 Lee Street
Sydney 2000
New South Wales, Australia
Telephone: 212-1220, 212-5338

Church of Scientology Auckland
New Imperial Buildings
44 Queen Street
Auckland 1, New Zealand
Telephone: 362-973, 362-974

Church of Scientology Auckland
Foundation
New Imperial Buildings
44 Queen Street
Auckland 1, New Zealand
Telephone: 362-973, 362-974

AFRICA

Church of Scientology Bulawayo
508 Kirrie Bldgs.
Corner Abercorn & 9th Avenue
Bulawayo, Rhodesia
Telephone: 6-4311

Church of Scientology Bulawayo
Foundation
508 Kirrie Bldgs.
Corner Abercorn & 9th Avenue
Bulawayo, Rhodesia
Telephone: 6-4311

Church of Scientology Cape Town
3rd Floor Garmour House
127 Plein Street
Cape Town, South Africa 8001
Telephone: 45-1501

Church of Scientology Cape Town
Foundation
3rd Floor Garmour House
127 Plein Street
Cape Town, South Africa 8001
Telephone: 45-1501

Church of Scientology Durban
57 College Lane
Durban, South Africa 4001
Telephone: 31-9553

Church of Scientology Durban
Foundation
57 College Lane
Durban, South Africa 4001
Telephone: 31-9552, 31-9553

Church of Scientology Johannesburg
99 Polly Street
Johannesburg, South Africa 2001
Telephone: 234-981, 234-982

Church of Scientology Johannesburg
Foundation
99 Polly Street
Johannesburg, South Africa 2001
Telephone: 234-981, 234-982

Church of Scientology Port Elizabeth
2 St. Christopher's Place
27 Westborne Road
Port Elizabeth, South Africa 6001
Telephone: 33-4802

Church of Scientology Port Elizabeth
Foundation
2 St. Christopher's Place
27 Westborne Road
Port Elizabeth, South Africa 6001
Telephone: 33-4802

Church of Scientology Pretoria
224 Central House
Cor. Central & Pretorius Streets
Pretoria, South Africa 0002
Telephone: 3-7942, 2-5043

Church of Scientology Pretoria
Foundation
224 Central House
Cor. Central & Pretorius Streets
Pretoria, South Africa 0002
Telephone: 3-7942, 2-5043

Celebrity Centres

WESTERN UNITED STATES

Church of Scientology
Celebrity Centre Los Angeles
1551 N. La Brea
Hollywood, California 90028
Telephone: 213-851-7900

Church of Scientology
Celebrity Centre Las Vegas
2004 South Western Street
Las Vegas, Nevada 89102
Telephone: 702-385-1218

CANADA

Church of Scientology
Celebrity Centre Toronto
67 Pembroke Street
Toronto, Ontario, Canada
Telephone: 416-961-0085

EASTERN UNITED STATES

Church of Scientology
Celebrity Centre New York
65 East 82nd Street
New York, New York 10028
Telephone: 212-288-1526

Missions

Church of Scientology
U.S. Mission Office
1451 East Irvine Blvd.
Tustin, California 92680
Telephone: 714-838-1950

WESTERN UNITED STATES

Church of Scientology
Mission of Adams Avenue
6911 El Cajon Boulevard
San Diego, California 92115
Telephone: 714-464-2721

Church of Scientology
Mission of Albuquerque
2712 Carlisle Boulevard
Albuquerque, New Mexico 87110
Telephone: 505-265-9544

Church of Scientology
Mission of Amarillo
2046 South Hayden
Amarillo, Texas 79109
Telephone: 806-372-1713

Church of Scientology
Mission of Anchorage
1306 West 47th
Anchorage, Alaska 99503
Telephone: 907-279-1835

Church of Scientology
Mission of Bellevue
10575 North East 4th Street
Bellevue, Washington 98004
Telephone: 206-455-5225

Church of Scientology
Mission of Berkeley
1918 Bonita
Berkeley, California 94704
Telephone: 415-841-9622

Church of Scientology
Mission of Beverly Hills
6233 Wilshire Boulevard
Los Angeles, California 90048
Telephone: 213-931-1034

Church of Scientology
Mission of Boulder
2049 Broadway
Post Office Box 995
Boulder, Colorado 80302
Telephone: 303-449-6222

Church of Scientology
Mission of Burbank
124 North Golden Mall
Burbank, California 91502
Telephone: 213-846-7117, 213-849-7559

Church of Scientology
Mission of Castro Valley
20730 Lake Chabot Road
Castro Valley, California 94546
Telephone: 415-886-1399

Church of Scientology
Mission of Chico
133 Broadway
Chico, California 95926
Telephone: 916-895-8621

Church of Scientology
Mission of Chula Vista
192 Landis Avenue
Chula Vista, California 92010
Telephone: 714-426-3640

Church of Scientology
Mission of Colorado Springs
302 North Cascade
Colorado Springs, Colorado 80903
Telephone: 303-633-1961

Church of Scientology
Mission of Davis
1046 Olive Drive
Davis, California 95616
Telephone: 916-756-6993

Church of Scientology
Mission of Davis-Portland
709 Southwest Salmon Street
Portland, Oregon 97205
Telephone: 503-228-0116

Church of Scientology
Mission of Davis-Sacramento
1725 23rd Street
Sacramento, California 95816
Telephone: 916-446-6107

Church of Scientology
Mission of Davis-Sheridan
Route 2, Box 195
Sheridan, Oregon 97378
Telephone: 503-843-3500

Church of Scientology
Mission of Denver
1640 Welton
Denver, Colorado 80202
Telephone: 303-573-5764

Church of Scientology
Mission of East Bay
411 15th Street
Oakland, California 94612
Telephone: 415-452-3193

Church of Scientology
Mission of Edmond
Post Office Box 1246
Edmond, Oklahoma 73034
Telephone: 405-348-1299

Church of Scientology
Mission of El Paso
1912 East Yandell
El Paso, Texas 79903
Telephone: 915-544-2226

Church of Scientology
Mission of Fairbanks
402 7th Avenue
Fairbanks, Alaska 99701
Telephone: 907-452-6076

Church of Scientology
Mission of Fresno
1342 Van Ness Avenue
Fresno, California 93721
Telephone: 209-485-7670

Church of Scientology
Mission of Greeley
1600 8th Avenue
Greeley, Colorado 80631
Telephone: 303-353-0081

Church of Scientology
Mission of Hawaii
1282 Kapiolani Boulevard
Honolulu, Hawaii 96814
Telephone: 808-536-4374

Church of Scientology
Mission of Hollywood
7715 Sunset Blvd., Suite 230
Hollywood, California 90046
Telephone: 213-874-2733

Church of Scientology
Mission of Houston
4034 Westheimer
Houston, Texas 77027
Telephone: 713-965-0382

Church of Scientology
Mission of Marin
810 College Avenue
Kentfield, California 94904
Telephone: 415-459-0150

Church of Scientology
Mission of Lake Tahoe
Post Office Box 1540
South Lake Tahoe, California 95705
Telephone: 916-541-8150

Church of Scientology
Mission of Long Beach
1261 Long Beach Boulevard
Long Beach, California 90813
Telephone: 213-432-5466

Church of Scientology
Dianetics & Scientology Glendale/
  Los Feliz
312 1/2 North Brand Boulevard
Glendale, California 91203
Telephone: 213-247-5020, 213-247-5017

Church of Scientology
Mission of Los Gatos
10 Jackson Street, Suite 111
Los Gatos, California 95030
Telephone: 408-354-1201

Church of Scientology
Mission of Manhattan Beach
869 Manhattan Beach Boulevard
Manhattan Beach, California 90266
Telephone: 213-545-6240

Church of Scientology
Mission of the Meadows
4241 West Charleston Boulevard.
  No. H
Las Vegas, Nevada 89102

Church of Scientology
Mission of Monterey-Carmel
863 Lighthouse Avenue
Monterey, California 93940
Telephone: 408-649-5212

Church of Scientology
Mission of Mountain View
Middlefield Village
2483 Old Middlefield Way
Mountain View, California 94043
Telephone: 415-969-5262

Church of Scientology
Mission of Orange County
1451 East Irvine Boulevard, No. 30
Tustin, California 92680
Telephone: 714-544-5491

Church of Scientology
Mission of Palo Alto
600 Middlefield Road
Palo Alto, California 94301
Telephone: 415-328-8933

Church of Scientology
Mission of Pasadena
634 East Colorado Boulevard
Pasadena, California 91101
Telephone: 213-795-8118

Church of Scientology
Mission of Phoenix
121 West Camelback Road
Phoenix, Arizona 85013
Telephone: 602-264-2381

Church of Scientology
Mission of Phoenix
1722 East Indian School Road
Phoenix, Arizona 85016
Telephone: 602-264-0979

Church of Scientology
Mission of Canoga Park
22059 Sherman Way
Canoga Park, California 91303
Telephone: 213-340-5733, 340-5734

Church of Scientology
Mission of Richardson
725 South Central Expressway,
  Suite D-10
Richardson, Texas 75081
Telephone: 214-235-0579

Church of Scientology
Mission of Riverside
3485 University Street
Riverside, California 92501
Telephone: 714-683-4574

Church of Scientology
Mission of Sacramento
5136 Arden Way
Carmichael, California 95608
Telephone: 916-482-6721, 482-8092

Church of Scientology
Mission of Salt Lake City
253 East 2nd South
Salt Lake City, Utah 84111
Telephone: 801-534-1486

Church of Scientology
Mission of San Antonio
208 Primera
San Antonio, Texas 78212
Telephone: 512-824-4972

Church of Scientology
Mission of San Francisco
175 Taraval
San Francisco, California 94116
Telephone: 415-664-6654

Church of Scientology
Mission of San Luis Obispo
250 Grand Avenue
San Luis Obispo, California 93401
Telephone: 805-541-3067

Church of Scientology
Mission of Mid-Peninsula
4045 Picadilly Lane
San Mateo, California 94403
Telephone: 415-573-9433

Church of Scientology
Mission of Santa Barbara
20 West De La Guerra
Santa Barbara, California 93101
Telephone: 805-962-5037, 966-4322

Church of Scientology
Stevens Creek Mission
4340 Stevens Creek Boulevard,
  Suite 180
San Jose, California 95129
Telephone: 408-249-7050

Church of Scientology
Mission of Santa Rosa
721 Mendocino Avenue
Santa Rosa, California 95401
Telephone: 707-528-0174

Church of Scientology
Mission of Sausalito
300 Valley Street, Suite 203
Sausalito, California 94965

Church of Scientology
Mission of South Bay
607 South Pacific Coast Highway
Redondo Beach, California 90277
Telephone: 213-540-0066

Church of Scientology
Mission of the Southwest
Post Office Box 140459
Dallas, Texas 75204
Telephone: 214-827-5640

Church of Scientology
Mission of Steamboat Springs
Post Office Box 9057
Steamboat Springs, Colorado 80477
Telephone: 303-879-2664

Church of Scientology
Mission of Stockton
542 East Lindsay
Stockton, California 95202
Telephone: 209-465-5948

Church of Scientology
Mission of Tucson
4872 East Broadway
Tucson, Arizona 89711
Telephone: 602-327-3556

Church of Scientology
Mission of Tulsa
2139 East 21st Street
Tulsa, Oklahoma 74114
Telephone: 918-742-4556

Church of Scientology
Mission of the Valley
13561 Ventura Boulevard
Sherman Oaks, California 91403
Telephone: 213-990-1972, 872-1972

Church of Scientology
Mission of Vista
1027 East Vista Way
Vista, California 92083
Telephone: 714-758-3500

Church of Scientology
Mission of Walnut Creek
2363 Boulevard Circle, No. 5
Walnut Creek, California 94595
Telephone: 415-938-0614

Church of Scientology
Mission of Washoe Valley
924 Pyramid Way
Sparks, Nevada 89431
Telephone: 702-359-8231

Church of Scientology
Mission of Westwood-Wilshire
10930 Santa Monica Boulevard
Westwood, Los Angeles, California
  90025
Telephone: 213-477-7025

EASTERN UNITED STATES

Church of Scientology
Mission of Albany
141 Brunswick
Troy, New York 12180
Telephone: 518-272-5918

Church of Scientology
Mission of Arlington
3520 Lee Highway
Arlington, Virginia 22207
Telephone: 703-527-5306

Church of Scientology
Mission of Atlanta
375 Pharr Road
Atlanta, Georgia 30305
Telephone: 404-231-1320

Church of Scientology
Mission of Baton Rouge
1605 Main Street
Baton Rouge, Louisiana 70802
Telephone: 504-346-0506

Church of Scientology
Mission of Bayshore
7 Smith Avenue
Bayshore, New York 11706
Telephone: 516-666-7007

Church of Scientology
Mission of Cambridge
8 Essex Street
Cambridge, Massachusetts 02139
Telephone: 617-868-5565

Church of Scientology
Mission of Charlotte
1000 Dilworth Road
Charlotte, North Carolina 28203
Telephone: 704-377-2880

Church of Scientology
Mission of Cincinnati
3352 Jefferson Avenue
Cincinnati, Ohio 45220
Telephone: 513-961-8962

Church of Scientology
Mission of Cleveland
2055 Lee Road
Cleveland Heights, Ohio 44118
Telephone: 216-321-1353

Church of Scientology
Mission of Columbus
1074 East Broad Street
Columbus, Ohio 43205
Telephone: 614-253-7015

Church of Scientology
Mission of Coral Gables
4615 Ponce De Leon Boulevard
Coral Gables, Florida 33146
Telephone: 305-661-7689

Church of Scientology
Mission of Dayton
1954 North Main Street
Dayton, Ohio 45405
Telephone: 513-277-9359

Church of Scientology
Mission of Delaware Valley
31 West Main Street
Marlton, New Jersey 08053
Telephone: 609-983-5100

Church of Scientology
Mission of Elmira
111 North Main Street
Elmira, New York 14901
Telephone: 607-734-4977

Church of Scientology
Mission of Erie
3323 Liberty Street
Erie, Pennsylvania 16508
Telephone: 814-864-7129

Church of Scientology
Mission of Fifth Avenue
434 Avenue of the Americas
New York, New York 10011
Telephone: 212-228-8410

Church of Scientology
Mission of Flemington
27 Church Street
Flemington, New Jersey 08822
Telephone: 201-782-6303

Church of Scientology
Mission of Fort Lauderdale
423 North Andrews Avenue
Fort Lauderdale, Florida 33301
Telephone: 305-764-8445

Church of Scientology
Mission of Mt. Holly
403 Acorn Road, Rancocas Woods
Mt. Holly, New Jersey 08060
Telephone: 609-235-4843

Church of Scientology
Mission of New Britain
9 Russwin Road
New Britain, Connecticut 06053
Telephone: 203-225-6368

Church of Scientology
Mission of New Haven
356 Putnam Avenue
Hamden, Connecticut 06514
Telephone: 203-248-3356

Church of Scientology
Mission of New London
17 Fort Hill Road
Groton, Connecticut 06340
Telephone: 203-448-0749

Church of Scientology
Mission of New York
500 West End Avenue, Suite 2B
New York, New York 10024
Telephone: 212-877-4219, 799-6540

Church of Scientology
Park West Mission
51 West 81st Street
New York, New York 10024
Telephone: 212-724-1862

Church of Scientology
Mission of Orlando
210 Park Avenue North, Suite 7
Winter Park, Florida 32789
Telephone: 305-647-3070

Church of Scientology
Mission of Palm Beach
208 South Olive Avenue
West Palm Beach, Florida 33401
Telephone: 305-655-1355

Church of Scientology
Mission of Rochester
220 Broad Street East
Rochester, New York 14604
Telephone: 716-454-6860

Church of Scientology
Mission of Tampa
1220 South Dale Mabry, Suite B
Tampa, Florida 33060
Telephone: 813-254-4181

Church of Scientology
Mission of Toledo
3533 Monroe
Toledo, Ohio 43606
Telephone: 419-473-2818

Church of Scientology
Mission of Virginia Beach
2102 Mediterranean Avenue
Virginia Beach, Virginia 23451
Telephone: 804-428-5231

Church of Scientology
Mission of Washington, D.C.
3411 Massachusetts Avenue N.W.
Washington, D.C. 20007
Telephone: 202-333-9070

Church of Scientology
Mission of Waterbury
42 Bank Street
Waterbury, Connecticut 06702
Telephone: 203-753-6933

Church of Scientology
Mission of Westchester
Dunderberg Road
Putnam Valley, New York 10579
Telephone: 914-526-3540

Church of Scientology
Mission of Worcester
16 Front Street
Worcester, Massachusetts 01608
Telephone: 617-754-0868

CENTRAL UNITED STATES

Church of Scientology
Mission of Anderson
1111 Meridian Plaza
Post Office Box 664
Anderson, Indiana 46016
Telephone: 317-649-5673

Church of Scientology
Mission of Oakland County
16165 West 12 Mile Road
Southfield, Michigan 48076
Telephone: 313-559-5101

Church of Scientology
Mission of Carbondale
417 South Illinois Avenue
Carbondale, Illinois 62901
Telephone: 618-457-7464

Church of Scientology
Mission of Champaign-Urbana
1004 South 4th Street
Champaign, Illinois 61820
Telephone: 217-367-6025

Church of Scientology
Mission of Chicago
108 East Oak Street
Villa Park, Illinois 60181
Telephone: 312-833-9070

Church of Scientology
Mission of Flint
1154 North Ballenger Highway
Flint, Michigan 48504
Telephone: 313-234-2697

Church of Scientology
Mission of Fontenelle
2208 Hancock Street
Bellevue, Nebraska 68005
Telephone: 402-292-1688

Church of Scientology
Mission of Highland Park
508 Central, Office B
Highland Park, Illinois 60035
Telephone: 312-433-1100

Church of Scientology
Mission of Huron Valley
809 Henry Street
Ann Arbor, Michigan 48104
Telephone: 313-668-6113

Church of Scientology
Mission of Independence
206 North Main Street
Independence, Missouri 64050
Telephone: 816-461-7817

Church of Scientology
Mission of Indianapolis
3848 North Pennsylvania
Indianapolis, Indiana 46205
Telephone: 317-926-1271

Church of Scientology
Mission of Kansas City
4528 Main Street
Kansas City, Missouri 64111
Telephone: 816-531-7280

Church of Scientology
Mission of Lakeview
5858 South Kedzie
Chicago, Illinois 60629
Telephone: 312-833-9079

Church of Scientology
Mission of Milwaukee
3254 South 69th Street
Milwaukee, Wisconsin 53219
Telephone: 414-645-9490

Church of Scientology
Mission of New Hope
3040 Lyndale Avenue South
Minneapolis, Minnesota 55408
Telephone: 612-827-1751

Church of Scientology
Mission of Omaha
5016 California Street
Omaha, Nebraska 68132
Telephone: 402-556-6607

Church of Scientology
Mission of Peoria
625 West Main Street
Peoria, Illinois 61606
Telephone: 309-676-8739

Church of Scientology
Mission of Racine
1040 College Avenue
Racine, Wisconsin 53403
Telephone: 414-634-2058

Church of Scientology
Mission of St. Charles
138A North Main Street
St. Charles, Missouri 63301
Telephone: 314-946-4210

PUERTO RICO

Church of Scientology
Mission of Puerto Rico
1395 Americano Salas
San Turce, Puerto Rico 00909
Telephone: 809-724-7391

CANADA

Church of Scientology
Mission of Calgary
335 11th Avenue SW
Calgary, Alberta, Canada
T2R OC7

Church of Scientology
Mission of Edmonton
10023-103 Street
Edmonton, Alberta
Canada T5J 0X5
Mailing Address:
Post Office Box 1198
Edmonton, Alberta
T5J 2M4
Telephone: 403-420-1730

Church of Scientology
Mission of London
148 Dundas Street
London, Ontario, Canada N6A 191
Telephone: 519-432-7061

Church of Scientology
Mission of Ontario
22 College Street
Kitchener, Ontario, Canada N2H 4Z9
Telephone: 519-745-3521

Church of Scientology
Mission of Quebec
224 1/2 East Rue St. Joseph
Quebec City, Quebec, Canada G1K 3J6

Church of Scientology
Mission of Vancouver
1562 West 6th Avenue
Vancouver 3, British Columbia,
   Canada V6J 1R2
Telephone: 731-8241

Church of Scientology
Mission of Windsor
437 Ouellette Avenue
Windsor, Ontario, Canada N9A 4J2
Telephone: 519-252-2406

UNITED KINGDOM

Church of Scientology
Mission of Birmingham
3 St. Mary's Road
Moseley, Birmingham, 13 England
Telephone: 021-449-0946

Church of Scientology
Mission of Brightlingsea
5 Stanley Avenue
Brightlingsea, Colchester, Essex
   England

Church of Scientology
Mission of Bristol
6 Redland Green Road
Bristol 6, Avon, England
Telephone: 43350

Church of Scientology
Mission of Helensburgh
121 West King Street
Helensburgh, Dunbartonshire,
   Scotland G84 8DQ
Telephone: 0436-2459

Church of Scientology
Mission of Hove
56 Wilbury Road, Flat 1
Hove, Sussex, England
Telephone: 0273-739-862

Church of Scientology
Mission of Leeds
27 Manor Drive
Leeds, Yorkshire, England LS6 1DE
Telephone: 0532-759-644

Church of Scientology
Mission of Southampton
16 Rectory Court
Holmesland Garden Estate
Botley, Hants, England

Church of Scientology
Mission of Swansea
1 Highpool Close
Newton Mumbles, Glamorgan, Wales
Telephone: 69292

Church of Scientology
Mission of York
57 Huntingdon Road
York, England
Telephone: 30458

EUROPE

Church of Scientology
Mission of Angers
43 Rue Proust
49000 Angers, France
Telephone: 41-87-72-89, 88-36-46

Church of Scientology
Mission of Arhus
Frederiksgade 16B1
8000 Arhus C, Denmark

Church of Scientology
Mission of Basel
Gerbergasslein 25
4051 Basel, Switzerland
Telephone: 061-25-79-90

Centre De Scientology Du. Brabant
4 Rue De Pacifique
B-1180 Bruxelles, Belgium
Telephone: 02-3-45-63-21

Eglise De Scientology
Mission of Brussels
45A Rue De L'Ecuyer
B-1000 Bruxelles, Belgium
Telephone: 13-52-32

Church of Scientology
Mission of Franken
Fleinerstrasse 37
D-71 Heilbronn, West Germany
Telephone: 07131-68319

Church of Scientology
Mission of Frankfurt Am Main
Kennedy Allee 49
D-6000 Frankfurt
    Am Main, West Germany
Telephone: 0611-63-10-81

Church of Scientology
Mission of Frankfurt
Stegstrasse 42
D-6000 Frankfurt 70, West Germany
Telephone: 0611-62-54-42

Church of Scientology
Mission of Fribourg
1 Rue Des Pillettes
CH 1700 Fribourg, Switzerland
Telephone: 037-22-51-37

Church of Scientology
Mission of Gelsenkirchen
Klosterstrasse 7
465 Gelsenkirchen, West Germany

Church of Scientology
Mission of Geneva
24 Rue Des Usines
1227 Acacias, Geneva, Switzerland
Telephone: 43-04-68

Church of Scientology
Mission of Haldenstrasse
Haldenstrasse 37
6006 Lucerne, Switzerland
Telephone: 041-23-29-32

Scientology Center Hamburg
Gerhofstrasse 18
D-2 Hamburg 36, West Germany
Telephone: 040-34-35-77

Church of Scientology
Mission of Hässleholm
1:A Avenyen 13
28100 Hässleholm, Sweden

Church of Scientology
Mission of Helsingborg
Sodergatan 4
S-252/25 Helsingborg, Sweden
Telephone: 042-18-21-18

Church of Scientology
Mission of Horgen
Schmidweg 2
8810 Horgen, Switzerland

Church of Scientology
Mission of Klosterstrasse
465 Gelsenkirchen
Klosterstrasse 7, West Germany

Church of Scientology
Mission of Köln
An der Schanz
5000 Köln 160
Hansaring 149, West Germany

Church of Scientology
Mission of Le Bois D'Oingt
La Chapelle
69620 Le Bois D'Oingt, France

Church of Scientology
Mission of Lowenstrasse
Lowenstrasse 69
CH 8001 Zurich, Switzerland
Telephone: 01-27-26-92

Church of Scientology
Mission of Lucerne
Gutschstrasse 4
6003 Lucerne, Switzerland
Telephone: 041-23-48-78

Church of Scientology
Mission of Lyngby
Lyngby Hovedgade 49I
2800 Lyngby, Denmark
Telephone: 02-88-87-57

Church of Scientology
Mission of Lyon-Sarcey
La Chanta-Sarcey
69490 Pontcharra-Sur-Turdine,
    France
Telephone: 74-01-91-11

Church of Scientology
Mission of Munich
Kidlerstrasse 10
8 Munchen 70, West Germany
Telephone: 089-77-05-80

Church of Scientology
Mission of Neue Bruecke
Neue Bruecke 3
D-7000 Stuttgart IV, West Germany

Church of Scientology
Mission of Nyphenburg
Huberstustrasse 22
8000 Munchen 19, West Germany
Telephone: 17-67-77

Church of Scientology
Mission of Oslo
Korsvollbakken 15
Oslo 8, Norway

Church of Scientology
Mission of Salzburg
Franz-Jose-Strasse 20A
A-5020 Salzburg, Austria

Church of Scientology
Mission of Stuttgart
Hauptstaetterstrasse 126A
D-7000 Stuttgart, West Germany
Telephone: 0711-60-61-68

Church of Scientology
Mission of Uraniastrasse
Uraniastrasse 24/26
CH 8001 Zurich, Switzerland

Church of Scientology
Mission of Versailles
29 Bis Rue De Noailles
F-78000 Versailles, France

Church of Scientology
Mission of Vienna
Museumstrasse 5/18
A-1070 Vienna, Austria
Telephone: 52-22-43

Church of Scientology
Mission of Zurich
im Brutter 601
CH 8185 Wirkel, Switzerland
Telephone: 01-96-82-16

AUSTRALIA
AND NEW ZEALAND

Church of Scientology
Mission of Christchurch
35 Rapaki Road
Christchurch 2, New Zealand

Church of Scientology
Mission of Ellerslie
1 Ranier Street
Ellerslie, Auckland,
New Zealand

The New Faith Mission of Melville
15 Birdwood Road
Melville, West Australia 6156
Telephone: 30-5879

PACIFIC

Church of Scientology
Mission of Guam
Post Office Box 110
Agana, Guam 96910

AFRICA

Church of Scientology
Mission of Johannesburg
26 Roslin Street
Sydenham, Johannesburg,
South Africa 2192

Scientology and Dianetics Center
11 First Avenue
Highlands North
Johannesburg, South Africa 2192
Telephone: 40-6098

Groups

WESTERN
UNITED STATES

Scientology Group Anchorage
6811 East 12th Avenue
Anchorage, Alaska 99504

Scientology Group Austin
Post Office Box 7761
Austin, Texas 78712

Scientology Group Corona del Mar
615 Goldenrod Avenue
Corona del Mar, California 92625

Scientology Group Denver
3737 Tejon Street
Denver, Colorado 80211

Scientology Group Greeley
823 16th Street
Greeley, Colorado 80631

Scientology Group Harlington
1317 North Sunshine Strip
Harlington, Texas 78550

Ability Clinic Program
3336 Hamilton Way No. 4
Los Angeles, California 90026

Expansion Consultants
3866 West 6th Street
Los Angeles, California 90005

Scientology Group Los Angeles
201 North Rampart Street
Los Angeles, California 90026

Scientology Center Solana Beach
1722 North Ocadintiad No. 2
Los Angeles, California 90026

Scientology Group Verdugo Hills
3859 La Trobe
Verdugo Hills,
Los Angeles, California 90031

Scientology Group Shallowater
Post Office Box 483
Shallowater,
Lubbock, Texas 79363

Opus 8 Scientology Group
202 West Street
Salt Lake City, Utah 84103

Scientology Group San Antonio
200 Donaldson
San Antonio, Texas 78201

Scientology Viability Group
1430 Vallejo Street
San Francisco, California 94109

Scientology Group Santa Monica
2522 Kansas Avenue No. 9
Santa Monica, California 90404

Delphian Foundation
Route 2, Box 195
Sheridan, Oregon 97378

EASTERN
UNITED STATES

Scientology Group Brooklyn
1918 37th Street
Brooklyn, New York 11234

Scientology Group Harlem
310 Convent Avenue
Harlem, New York 10031

Scientology Group Hornesville
Post Office Box 27
Hornesville, New York 13361

Dianetic Counseling Group
1114 Ridge Road
Lewiston, New York 14092

Scientology Group Upper Manhattan
310 Convent Avenue No. 1F
Manhattan, New York 10031

Scientology Group Middletown
124 Oak Hill Drive
Middletown, Pennsylvania 17057

Scientology Group Oceanside
62 Harris Drive
Oceanside, New York 11572

Scientology Group New York City
1374 East 12th Street
New York, New York 10009

Scientology Group Virginia Beach
934 Maryland Avenue
Virginia Beach, Virginia 23451

Scientology Group Providence
264 Weybosset
Providence, Rhode Island 02903

Scientology Group Toledo
(Glenridge)
5456 Glenridge Drive
Toledo, Ohio 43614

Scientology Group Toledo
1941 Jerman Drive
Toledo, Ohio 43606

Agency for Individual Development
and Expansion
1726 19th Street Northwest, No. 2
Washington, D.C. 20009

Scientology Group Winter Park
210 Park Avenue North, Room 17
Winter Park, Florida 32789

Scientology Group Woodhaven
7620 Jamaica Avenue
Woodhaven, New York 11421

CENTRAL
UNITED STATES

Scientology Group Chicago Heights
90 East 12th Street
Chicago Heights, Illinois 60605

Scientology Group Cresmad
1134 Minoqua Street
Cresmad, Wisconsin 53705

Scientology Group Detroit
2040 Park Avenue
Detroit, Michigan 48226

Scientology Communication
Workshop
Fernhill Drive
Farmington, Michigan 48024

Scientology Group Flint
Post Office Box 3181
Flint, Michigan 48504

Scientology Group Kokomo
100 South Buckeye Street
Kokomo, Indiana 46901

PUERTO RICO

Scientology Group San Turce
Post Office Box 9302
San Turce, Puerto Rico 00908

MEXICO

Scientology Group Piedra Negras
Nuevo Leon 124 No. 4
Col. Gonzales
Piedra Negras, Coah., Mexico

Scientology Publications Mexico
Campos Eliseos 205
Mexico 5, Distrito Federal, Mexico

Associacion Cultural Dianetica, A.C.
2DA Cerrada De Frontera, No. 7
San Angel, Mexico D.F., Mexico

Instituto Tecnologico De Dianetica,
A.C.
Blvd. Manual Avila Camacho No. 179
Lomas De Chapultepec
Mexico 10, D.F., Mexico

Scientology Group Mexico, A.C.
Avenida Nuevo Leon 159, 10th Floor
Col. Condesa Mexico 11, D.F., Mexico

Academia De Dianetica
Avenedia Revolucion 591-B1
Mexico 18, D.F., Mexico

Associacion De Dianetica
Matamoros No. 5
A.P. 21875
Mexico 21, D.F., Mexico

Scientology Centre Empalme
A.P. 181 Guaymas
Empalme, Sonora, Mexico

Instituto De Dianetica en
Guadalajara, A.C.
Mexicaltzingo No. 1985
Sector Juarez, Guadalajara
Jalisco, Mexico
Telephone: 26-47-49

Instituto De Filosofia Aplicada
(Centro Cultural Latinoamericano
A.C.)
Haure 32, Col. Juarez
Mexico 6, D.F., Mexico

Organizacion De Dianetica, A.C.
Providencia No. 1000
Col. Del Valle
Mexico 12, D.F., Mexico

Centro De Dianetica, A.C.
Campos Eliseos 205
Mexico 5, D.F., Mexico

UNITED KINGDOM

Scientology Group Brighton
69 Hollingury Park Road
Brighton, England

Chorlton-cum-Hardy Scientology
Group
92 Sandy Lane
Chorlton-cum-Hardy
Manchester 22, England

Scientology Group Culerton
Nineria Cottage
Lower Moor Road
Culerton, England

Scientology OT Group
62 West Hill
East Grinstead,
Sussex, England

Scientology Gung-Ho Group East
Grinstead
Ship Street
East Grinstead,
Sussex, England

Scientology Group Central
East Grinstead
73 Cantelope Road
East Grinstead,
Sussex, England

Scientology Group Morningside
47 Morningside Drive
Edinburgh, Scotland

Dowan Hill Scientology Group
3 Huntley Gardens
Glasgow, Scotland

West Glasgow Scientology Group
605 Great Western Road, Top Flat
Glasgow, Scotland

Scientology Group Helensburgh
Ardewcaple Potteries
Helensburgh, Scotland

Scientology Field Staff Member
Group
Kilmer Ford
Oban, Scotland

Scientology Group Plymouth
10 St. Lawrence Road
North Hill
Plymouth, England

Reading Scientology Group
7 Green Road
Reading, England

Scientology Group Sholing
43 Butts Road
Sholing, Southampton, England

Scientology Southampton
22 Runny Mede, Westend
Southampton, England

Union Street Scientology Group
7 Union Street
Swindon, England

York Scientology Group
31 Parliament Street
York, England

EUROPE

Scientology Group Amsterdam
Mesdagstraat Post Bus. 11052
Amsterdam, Netherlands

Instituut Voor Dianetics
Ruys De Bereenbroucstraat 63
Amsterdam, Netherlands

Werkplatts Voor Toegepaste
Folosophie
(Institute of Applied Philosophy)
Mesdagstraate 32-34
Amsterdam, Netherlands

Arhus Scientology Center
Graven 83
8000 Arhus, Denmark

Scientology Group Breda
Taxiandialaand 5
Breda, Netherlands

Brugge Scientology Studie Centrum
Predikher Nstraat 40B
8000 Brugge, Belgium

Scientology O.T. Committee
H. Kong Georgsrej 112, 7th Floor
2000 Copenhagen, Denmark

Scientology Group Den Haag
197 Abrikozenstraat
Den Haag, Netherlands

Scientology Group Farum
Copenhagen Group
Nygeardterrasserne 271E
3520 Farum, Denmark

Dianetics College
Lachnerstrasse 6
Freechenheim 6
Frankfurt, West Germany

Centre de Scientology Fribourg
1 Rue des Pilettes, Bat Hotel
City Fribourg, Switzerland CH 1700

Scientology Group Gent
Eindrach Strass 83
Gent, Belgium

Scientology Group Koeln
53 Boon Tenusberg
Kiegern 26 BRD
Koeln, West Germany

College Fur Angewandte Philosophie
Widenmayer 28
8 Munchen 28, West Germany

Scientology Group Noville
116 Rue che Village, S/Mehaigne
Noville 5054, Belgium

Scientology Group Norway
Raderveien 79
Oslo, Norway

Scientology Group Oslo
Rodstuveien 4
Oslo, Norway

Strandvenjens Scientology Center
Skellebaekvej 2
3070 Snekkersten
Denmark

Scientology Group Vichy
Maison Lovis XI
Rue de Marche
Auble 03300 Cusset, France

AUSTRALIA AND
NEW ZEALAND

Australian Capital Territory
Scientology Group
26 Templeton Street
Cook, Australian Capital Territory
Australia 2614

Southern Dianetic Counseling Group
Road 5 Broadlands
Christchurch, New Zealand

Flyn Scientology Group
37 Campanion Crescent
Flyn, Australian Capital Territory
Australia

Scientology Group Lane Cove
2/130 Burns Bay Road
Lane Cove, New South Wales,
Australia

Hamilton Dianetic Counseling Group
Post Office Box 126
Hamilton, New Zealand

The Sydney Booksales Group
32 Grove Street
Lilyfield, New South Wales,
Australia

Wanganui Dianetic Counseling
Group
37 Wake Field Street
Wanganui East, New Zealand

Wellington Dianetic Counseling
Group
30 Wright Street
Wellington, New Zealand

INDIA

Scientology Group Punjab
Vill-P.O. Bajawa Kalan
District Jullundur
Punjab, India

ISRAEL

Scientology Institute of Negev
Post Office Box 698
Beer Sheva, Israel

Scientology Center of Tel Aviv
Post Office Box 39822
Ramat Aviv, Tel Aviv, Israel

ITALY

Instituto Italiano de Technologie
Applicate
Via F. Cavallotte 13
20122 Milano, Italy
Telephone: 02-799-917

JAPAN

Scientology Group Tokyo
Fukazawa 3 Chome 22-1
Tokyo 158, Japan

NIGERIA

Scientology Group Benin City
10 Esigie Street (2nd East Circle)
Benin City, Nigeria

Scientology Ebuto Metta
Zania Lodge, 40 Yaba Road
Yaba, Ebuto Metta, Nigeria

Scientology Group Lagos
No. 2 Bada Street
Idioro, Surulere
Lagos, Nigeria

Scientology Group Nigeria
16 William Street, 2nd Floor
Lagos, Nigeria

PHILIPPINES

Scientology Centre of the Philippines
Post Office Box 1182
Makati, Rizal, Philippines

SOUTH AMERICA

Madalena Meacham
Praia de Botafogo 472 (Apt. 913)
Rio de Janeiro
RJ Brazil

Fernando Gomez
P. O. Box 6591
Bogota, Colombia

EASTERN UNITED STATES

New England Elderly Demands
Society
c/o Church of Scientology
448 Beacon Street
Boston, Massachusetts 02215
Telephone: 617-262-0640

NEEDS (New England Elderly
Demands Society)
327 Tappan Street
Brookline, Massachusetts 02146
Telephone: 617-353-1542

Gerus Society
2125 S Street NW
Washington, D.C. 20028
Telephone: 202-797-3700

AUSTRALIA

Dignity for the Aged, Incorporated
57 Pulteney Street
Adelaide, 5000, Australia
Telephone: 223-4978

Aged Peoples Care Association
466 Guildford Road
Bayswater, Western Australia

Citizens Commission on Human Rights

WESTERN UNITED STATES

CCHR
P. O. Box 4620
Austin, Texas 78765
Telephone: 512-474-5603

CCHR
P. O. Box 18598
Denver, Colorado 80201
Telephone: 303-832-3916

CCHR
1600 N. LaBrea, No. 107
Los Angeles, California 90028
Telephone: 213-465-9996

CCHR
2015 J Street, Suite 31
Sacramento, California 95814

CCHR
321 20th Street
San Diego, California 94102
Telephone: 714-233-7872

CCHR
944 Market Street, Room 607
San Francisco, California 94102
Telephone: 415-397-2698

CCHR
417 Smith Tower
Seattle, Washington 98104
Telephone: 205-622-4563

EASTERN UNITED STATES

CCHR
327 Tappan Street
Brookline, Massachusetts 02146
Telephone: 617-353-1542

CCHR
101 W. 85th Street, Suite 1
New York, New York 10024
Telephone: 212-874-1740

CCHR
2125 S Street N.W.
Washington, D.C. 20028
Telephone: 202-797-1204

CENTRAL UNITED STATES

CCHR
19 Clifford, Rm. 505
Detroit, Michigan 48226

CCHR
925 Dempster Street
Evanston, Illinois 60201
Telephone: 312-864-6605

CCHR Twin Cities
2708 East Lake Street
Minneapolis, Minnesota 55406
Telephone: 612-721-6458

CANADA

CCHR Toronto
385 Yonge Street
Toronto, Ontario, Canada M5B 151

CCHR
335 11th Avenue SW
Calgary, Alberta, Canada T2R OC7

CCHR
15 Notre Dame Ouest
Montreal, Quebec H2Y 1B5

UNITED KINGDOM

CCHR Southampton
16 Rectory Court
Holmesland Garden Estate
Butley, Hants
Telephone: 048 926 126

CCHR
Saint Hill Manor
East Grinstead, Sussex, England
RH 19 4JY

CCHR Scotland
20 South Bridge
Edinburgh, Scotland EHJ, 1LL
Telephone: 031 556

CCHR
Tower Road
Hyde, Cheshire
Telephone: 061 368 1270

CCHR London
68 Tottenham Court Road
London W. I
Telephone: 01 5803601

Social Reform Groups

Alcoholism

UNITED STATES OF AMERICA

NAAPT (National Alliance on
Alcoholism Prevention and
Treatment)
327 Tappan Street
Brookline, Mass. 02146
Telephone: 617-353-1542

EUROPE

Alkoholikerbehandlingens
Humanisering (The Humanization
of the Treatment of Alcoholics)
Magevej 4, 2970 Horsholm, Denmark
Telephone: (02) 86 17 43, or (01)
123311

Care of the Aged

WESTERN UNITED STATES

Gerus Society
1811 North Tamarind, No. 327
Los Angeles, California 90028
Telephone: 213-469-4008

Gerus Society
745 N. Formosa
Los Angeles, California
Telephone: 213-936-1796

Gerus Society
2015 J Street, Suite 31
Sacramento, California 95814
Telephone: 916-443-5448

EUROPE

CCHR
Singel 289-293
Amsterdam C, Netherlands

CCHR
(Medborgernes Menneskerettigheds
Kommission)
Bagsvaerd H. Ovedgade 99, 12 J. 2880
Bagsvaerd, Denmark
Telephone: (02) 44 06 47

CCHR
Hovedvagtsgade 6
1103 Copenhagen K. Denmark

Kommitten for Manskliga Rattigheter
(The Committee for Human Rights)
Box 2338
403 15 Goteborg 2, Sweden
Telephone: 08-11-26-99

CCHR
Lindwurmstrasse 29
8000 Munchen 2
Munich, West Germany

CCHR
(Commission Des Citoyens Pour Les
Droits De L'Homme)
23 Rue Custine
75018 Paris, France

CCHR
12 Rue De La Montagne
Ste. Genevieve 75005
Paris, France

CCHR
Kammakaregatan 46
S-111 60 Stockholm, Sweden

AUSTRALIA

CCHR
57 Pulteney Street
Adelaide 5000, Australia
Telephone: 223-4978

CCHR
49 Mount Street
Coogee, NSW 2034, Australia
Telephone: Sydney 2125369

CCHR
Church of Scientology
724 Inkerman Road, Room 1
North Caulfield, Victoria 2161
Australia
Telephone: Melb. 5098533

CCHR
3/156 St. Georges Tc.
Perth, Western Australia
Telephone: 217840

CCHR
1 Lee Street
Sydney 2000, New South Wales,
Australia

Committee on Public Health and Safety

UNITED STATES OF AMERICA

COPHS
1640 Welton Street
Denver, Colorado 80202
Telephone: 303-534-7200

COPHS
143 Nenue Street
Honolulu, Hawaii 96821

COPHS
321 20th Street
San Diego, California 92102
Telephone: 714-233-7822

COPHS
2125 S Street NW
Washington, D.C. 20028
Telephone: 202-797-1204

NEW ZEALAND

COPHS
P. O. Box 6508
Wellesley Street
Auckland 1, New Zealand
Telephone: 362-974 ex. 86

Criminal Rehabilitation

UNITED STATES OF AMERICA

CREO (Committee to Re-involve
Ex-Offenders)
1415 North Berendo Street
Los Angeles, California 90027
Telephone: 213-385-9051

CREO
2015 J Street, Suite 31
Sacramento, California 95814
Telephone: 916-443-5448

CREO
321 20th Street
San Diego, California 92102
Telephone: 714-233-7872

CREO
417 Smith Tower
Seattle, Washington 98104
Telephone: 206-622-4563

UNITED KINGDOM

Criminon (A group seeking reform
of the prison system in the UK)
92 Sandy Lane
Chorlton, Manchester 16

Criminon
20 Pannell Close
East Grinstead, Sussex, England
Telephone: 26871

Criminon
14 Mannings Close
Pound Hill, Crawley
West Sussex, England
Telephone: 029-382-2331

EUROPE

RURI (Reform Group for Education
and Rehabilitation of Criminals)
Syriensvej 14, 2, th.
2300 Copenhagen S., Denmark
Telephone: (01) 151533

AUSTRALIA AND NEW ZEALAND

Criminal Rehabilitation and
Education
Advancement Movement
57 Pulteney Street
Adelaide, 5000, Australia
Telephone: 233-6555

Criminon for Re-education and
Rehabilitation of Criminals
P. O. Box 6508
Wellesley Street
Auckland 1, New Zealand

Criminal Rehabilitation and
Education Advancement
Movement
Pastoral House
156 St. Georges Terrace
Perth 6000, Western Australia
Telephone: 217-840

Criminal Rehabilitation and
Education Advancement
Movement
1 Lee Street
Sydney 2000,
New South Wales, Australia

Education

WESTERN UNITED STATES

Applied Scholastics Inc.
955 S. Western Avenue
Los Angeles, California
Telephone: 213-735-1333

Apple School Los Angeles
4155 Russell Avenue
Los Angeles, California 90027
Telephone: 213-664-7462

Apple School Westside (Los Angeles)
1941 Barrington Avenue
Los Angeles, California 90025
Telephone: 213-473-0314

Greenleaf School (An Apple affiliate)
1828 North 2nd Street
Flagstaff, Arizona 86001
Telephone: 602-779-1895

Golden Gate Apple School (San
Francisco area)
3755 13th Avenue
Oakland, California 94612
Telephone: 415-530-3355

Applied Scholastics Inc.
2015 J Street, Suite 32
Sacramento, California 98140
Telephone: 916-444-9276

Applied Scholastics Inc.
103 E. 41st
San Angelo, Texas 76903
Telephone: 915-658-1824

Apple School San Diego
5487 University
San Diego, California 92105
Telephone: 213-473-0314

Applied Scholastics Inc.
Smith Tower Building, Room 1101
Seattle, Washington 98101
Telephone: 206-622-4168

Childbirth Education Group
8340 Longdon
Sepulveda, California 91343
Telephone: 213-893-5515

EASTERN UNITED STATES

Applied Scholastics Inc.
2640 E. Wesley Terrace, No. 3
Atlanta, Georgia 30324

Applied Scholastics Inc.
6803 Fairfax Road
Bethesda, Maryland 20014
Telephone: 301-654-5947

Applied Scholastics Inc.
c/o SNAP
554 Columbus Avenue
Boston, Massachusetts 02118
Telephone: 617-267-7400

Education Improvement Centre
210 S. Fort Harrison Avenue
Clearwater, Florida 33516
Telephone: 813-461-1260

Apple-Ability School
210 West 91st Street
New York, New York 10024
Telephone: 212-595-8194

Applied Scholastics Inc.
128 Fort Washington, No. 48
New York, New York 10032
Telephone: 212-781-7304

CENTRAL UNITED STATES

Applied Scholastics Inc.
13 1/2 Ford No. 3
Highland Park, Michigan 48203
Telephone: 868-1555

St. Louis Apple School
1040 Dautel Lane
Creve Coeur, Missouri 63141
Telephone: 314-872-7124

CANADA

L.I.M. (Learning, Interest and
Motivation)
251-253 Spadina Road
Toronto, Ontario

MEXICO

Institute de Technologia Para La
Educacion
San Luis Potofe 45 A
Mexico 11, D.F.
Telephone: 905-564-6679

UNITED KINGDOM

EEA (Effective Education
Association)
43 Lewes Road
East Grinstead, Sussex, England
Telephone: 0342-24662

EEA Manchester
29, Cherwell Avenue
Heywood, Lanes
Manchester, England
Telephone: 0706-622881

EEA Brighton
141 St. Leonards Avenue
Hove, Sussex
Brighton, England
Telephone: 0273-413057

EUROPE

FEGU (Association of Effective
Basic Education)
Abel Christines Gade 7, Mezz
1654 Copenhagen V
Denmark
Telephone: (01)-246727

AUSTRALIA

Education Revision Movement
14 Thornton Avenue
Suarey Hills
Melbourne, Victoria, Australia

SOUTH AFRICA

Education Alive
Office — 23 Lenin Road
Race View, Alberton 1450
Johannesburg, South Africa
Telephone: 869-0409

Mentally Retarded

WESTERN UNITED STATES

Task Force on Mental Retardation
1413 North Berendo Street
Los Angeles, California 90027
Telephone: 213-487-2740

EASTERN UNITED STATES

Task Force on Mental Retardation
327 Tappan Street
Brookline, Massachusetts 02146
Telephone: 617-353-1542

AUSTRALIA

Mentally Retarded Association
25 Pola Street
Dianella, Western Australia
Telephone: 716671 Perth

SOUTH AFRICA

Self-Development Communities for
the Retarded
82 Hamilton Street
Goodwood, Capetown, South Africa
7460

Narconon

WESTERN UNITED STATES

Narconon Los Angeles
National Office
519 South Westmoreland
Los Angeles, California 90026
Telephone: 213-487-1088

Youth Training School Narconon
Program
Chino, California

Narconon Denver
2801 Colfax Avenue
Denver, Colorado 80206
Telephone: 303-333-0740

Lookout Mountain School for Boys
Narconon Program
Denver, Colorado

Narconon El Paso
1321 East Yandell
El Paso, Texas, 79902
Telephone: 915 533-1038

Narconon Hawaii
Hawaii State Prison
Honolulu, Hawaii
(mailing address: 738 Paoni Street,
Honolulu, Hawaii 96814)
Telephone: 808-841-8711

Narconon Berkeley
488 34th Street
Oakland, California 94604
Telephone: 415-653-9300

Narconon Palo Alto
532 Emerson Street
Palo Alto, California 94301
Telephone: 415-327-4250

Narconon Phoenix
11429 North 21st Drive
Phoenix, Arizona 85029
Telephone: 602-265-7550

Ventura Youth Training School for
Boys and Girls Narconon Program
Ventura, California

EASTERN UNITED STATES

Narconon Boston
120 London Street
East Boston, Massachusetts 02128
Telephone: 617-569-6780

Narconon Miami
189 South East 14th Lane
Miami, Florida 33131
Telephone: 305-374-2089

Narconon Connecticut
243 Captain's Walk
New London, Connecticut 06320
Telephone: 203-447-3041

Narconon New Orleans
1931 Palmyra
New Orleans, Louisiana 70112
Telephone: 504-568-1352

Orleans Parrish Prison Narconon
Program
New Orleans, Louisiana

Narconon New York
319 West 88th Street
New York, New York 10024
Telephone: 212-877-3115

Narconon Delaware
2227 North Market Street
Wilmington, Delaware 19802
Telephone: 302-658-7692

CENTRAL UNITED STATES

Ionia State Prison Narconon Program
Ionia, Michigan

Narconon Minnesota
3636 Grand Avenue
Minneapolis, Minnesota 55409
Telephone: 612-323-4434

St. Cloud State Reformatory for
Men Narconon Program
St. Cloud, Michigan

Narconon St. Louis
4231 Laclede
St. Louis, Missouri 63108
Telephone: 314-525-2153

CANADA

The Lower Mainland Regional
Correctional Centre Men's Unit
Narconon Program
5700 Royal Oak
Burnaby, British Columbia, Canada
Telephone: 604-732-5774

The Lower Mainland Regional
Correctional Centre Women's Unit
Narconon Program
5700 Royal Oak
Burnaby, British Columbia, Canada
Telephone: 604-732-5774

Narconon Incorporated, Toronto
Branch
157 Spadina Road
Toronto, Ontario, M5R, 2T9, Canada
Telephone: 416-967-6844

Narconon Society of British Columbia
1040 West 7th Avenue
Vancouver, British Columbia,
Canada
Telephone: 604-732-5774

MEXICO

Narconon Mexico Prison Program
Alencaster Number 220
Comas Virregas
Mexico 10, D.F.

UNITED KINGDOM

Narconon Bracknell
"The Close"
Broad Lane
Bracknell, Berkshire
Telephone: 0344-55816

EUROPE

Narconon Berlin
1 Berlin 33
5-7 Peter Lenne Strasse
West Germany

Narconon Sweden
Lissma Skola
Lannargen
142 00 Transgund
Sweden

NEW ZEALAND

Narconon New Zealand
77 Pukaki Road
Mangere
Auckland
Telephone: 55863

**National Commission
on Law Enforcement
and Social Justice**

WESTERN
UNITED STATES

NCLESJ
c/o Church of Scientology Austin
2804 Rio Grande
Austin, Texas 78705
Telephone: 512-474-5477

NCLESJ
c/o Church of Scientology Denver
1640 Welton
Denver, Colorado 80202
Telephone: 303-534-7200

NCLESJ
c/o Church of Scientology Celebrity
    Centre L.A.
1551 N. La Brea
Hollywood, California 90028
Telephone: 213-851-7922

NCLESJ
c/o Church of Scientology Portland
333 South West Park Avenue
Portland, Oregon 97205
Telephone: 503-227-0491

NCLESJ
c/o Church of Scientology Sacramento
819 19th Street
Sacramento, California
Telephone: 916-446-0209

NCLESJ
c/o Church of Scientology San Diego
926 "C" Street
San Diego, California 92101
Telephone: 714-239-1416

NCLESJ
c/o Church of Scientology San
    Francisco
414 Mason Street, Room 400
San Francisco, California 94102
Telephone: 415-391-2436

EASTERN
UNITED STATES

NCLESJ
c/o Church of Scientology Boston
448 Beacon Street
Boston, Massachusetts 02215
Telephone: 617-262-0640

NCLESJ
c/o Church of Scientology Miami
120 Giralda Street
Coral Gables, Florida 33134
Telephone: 305-373-5961

NCLESJ
c/o Church of Scientology New York
28-30 West 74th Street
New York, New York 10023
Telephone: 212-874-1061

NCLESJ
c/o Founding Church of Scientology
    Washington, D.C.
2125 "S" Street NW
Washington, D.C. 20008
Telephone: 202-797-3735

CENTRAL
UNITED STATES

NCLESJ
c/o Church of Scientology Twin Cities
2708 Lake Street
Minneapolis, Minnesota 55406
Telephone: 612-721-6458

NCLESJ
c/o Church of Scientology St. Louis
3730 Lindell Boulevard
St. Louis, Missouri 63108
Telephone: 314-535-3653

UNITED KINGDOM

National Society for Crime Reduction
    and Social Justice
St. Hill Manor
East Grinstead,
Sussex, England RH 19 4JY

National Society for Crime Reduction
    and Social Justice
20 Southbridge
Edinburgh, Scotland EH1, 1LL
Telephone: 031-557-0281

National Society for Crime Reduction
    and Social Justice
68 Tottenham Court Road
London W.1., England
Telephone: 01-323-2720

EUROPE

Kommission Zum Schutz Des Burgers
    Gegen
Datenmissbrauch E.V.
(Affiliated with National Commission
    on Law Enforcement and Social
    Justice, U.S.A.)
Oberlanderstrasse 24A/11
8 Munchen 70
Munich, West Germany
Telephone: 089-534-428

Gesellschaft Zur Wahrung Der
    Grunderechte
(Affiliated with National Society for
    Crime Reduction and Social
    Justice)
Drygalskiallee 118/15-29
8 Munchen 71
Munich, West Germany
Telephone: 089-791-861, 089-531-271

18

Future Prediction of Scientology

It has been both good fortune and problematic that since publication of *Dianetics: The Modern Science of Mental Health* in May 1950 that, like it or not, Scientologists have been placed in an increasingly influential and controversial position in relation to the societies in which they exist.

Nearly thirty years ago, the first early Dianeticists and Scientologists—applying the philosophy and technology of L. Ron Hubbard—posed the first serious challenge to an attempted domination by institutional psychiatry in its self-appointed role of judge, jury, executioner and high priest of public standards, values and heresies.

Across the years Scientologists have become more and more engaged in the community by involvement and delivery of the visible products of the philosophy of Scientology.

Such involvement has been divided into three main thrusts: firstly, social reform; secondly, rehabilitation, which is actually a logical sequence for any reformer; and thirdly, the provision of trained personnel—both executives and technically trained—to deliver the demand into the society at local community, national and international level.

For the Church of Scientology has advantages in terms of being able to see social problems in many lands—and do something about them. For whatever the country or location, Scientologists are not theorizing or waiting for handouts: they are involved at a down-to-earth level—without political or sectarian special interests.

A great deal can happen in thirty years: the release of the original Dianetic research marked a public end to the private beginning of study and application to discover a higher echelon of universal origin and destination.

L. Ron Hubbard forecast a better tomorrow: with Dia-

netics then in its youth—"a strong youth"—he was probably the only person with an architectonic view on the future and structure of his work. His premise, "the human mind is capable of resolving the problems of the human mind" holds as good today as then.

There have always been detractors, but friend or foe alike, there are two points all agree on. First, the Church of Scientology has a future, and second, L. Ron Hubbard's technology works. There has never been any question on its workability.

Asked in a recent interview if he had any idea of the impact of Dianetics and Scientology on the lives of so many people or what, indeed, he was "letting himself in for," L. Ron Hubbard replied:

"I had an exact idea of the scope, but to me at the time, 1950, as an explorer it was another exploration. I came upon some major breakthroughs in the field of the mind, and continued to research in this field. I knew the impact would be great but I didn't realize how much I would be forced into the area of public demand.

"The knocks have been nothing compared to the pleasure of really helping people. For violent attack makes the subject that is under attack KNOWN—so I don't worry about such things or take it too seriously."

Three decades later is a good time to look back and also forward to the future. What do others say, friend or foe? And what have they said, and how right or wrong were they?

In the United States, the American Medical Association (AMA) began a covert scrutiny of Dianetics from the moment it crossed the public threshold in 1950.

Few commentators predicted anything but a short term future. For example, Theodore Wiprud, of the Medical Society of the District of Columbia wrote in relation to Dianetics, "among the best psychiatrists this is nothing but the bunk."

Of course, today, Church membership includes doctors, nurses and other members of the medical profession. Scientologists work with non-Scientology allies in bringing reforms into the field of mental health.

Another, H. Houston Merritt actually considered Hubbard to be a ghost writer for a member of the American medical profession!

Dr. Austin Smith, then editor of the Journal of the American Medical Association suggested that the AMA ought to investigate Hubbard and Dianetics—"this is not for quoting until more facts are obtained." Dr. Smith also contacted the Director of the Federal Food and Drug Administration.

Dr. Nelson of the FDA replied "We don't seem to have any information on L. Ron Hubbard." But a Dr. M. Fishbein considered he had plenty, and writing for a captive audience in medical magazines Fishbein stated "Sooner or later, some official agency will have to give this method (Dianetics) a name." Implied, but not stated, was "a bad name."

The FDA then got busy attempting to name or label Scientology. A spy had been enrolled on Scientology courses in order to get data to show that diagnosis and treatment of disease was taking place. The AMA said this activity "is the only hope of achieving any interference with the activities of the Scientologists."

Thus from inception the motivation of the detractors is clear to see. But on the other side, a medical doctor wrote, having examined Dianetics for himself:

"In my opinion Dianetics is worthy of being called a New Idea, and is destined to take its place alongside of other milestones of progress."

The book, *Dianetics: The Modern Science of Mental Health* rose to the best seller lists. Twenty-seven years later, 1977, the paperback edition repeated the hardback original success on the West Coast of the United States.

During the 1960s, opinion and prediction ebbed and flowed. It was a period known as "middle-ground." The AMA-FDA detractors had been proved wrong, and even a raid by the FDA on the Founding Church in Washington had led them nowhere.

Controversy continued to be engendered. AMA men quoted other AMA men in the newspapers, and such articles were then clipped, filed, copied and circulated to be reported elsewhere. It looked authoritative: but Scientology, with the 1959 purchase of its new international central office at Saint Hill Manor in Sussex, England, was factually embarking on a period of vast expansion.

To quote a British press report of the period, "ebullient, jovial American millionaire, L. Ron Hubbard bounced into London and said, 'I'm here to stay.'"

"Scientology—the town's largest business," headlined one of East Grinstead's newspapers. Despite a small, temporary setback in Melbourne, Australia, the future looked bright. L. Ron Hubbard stated, in a policy letter, June 7,

1965, "Every movement amongst Man runs into the phenomena that when you try to help some people—or help them—they react like mad dogs. Trying to assist them is like trying to give a mad dog medicine. You are liable to be bitten.

"The more successful a movement is, the more evident this phenomena becomes."

There were bites, all right, in Melbourne. From 1957 onwards, attention on Scientology was being focused by a variety of people until in 1963 a one-man inquiry was set up to inquire into Scientology in Victoria.

Mr. Kevin Anderson, Q.C., stated in his report that "an attempt to suppress or prosecute Scientology and Scientologists specifically by name would probably be ineffective, and, in any event would be undesirable."

Seven years later, the Hon. H. M. Hamilton, a member of the Legislative Council stated in relation to Scientology in Victoria, "They are surviving pretty well."

A few months later, February 1973, the Federal Attorney General recognized the Church as a bona fide religious organization. Three years before, the Hon. J. W. Galbally had stated in relation to Victorian Scientologists, "I do not think they would have any sort of case."

In West Australia, Scientology was banned. Mr. Herbert Graham, Deputy Leader of the Opposition stated that when his party was elected "high on the list of priorities will be the repeal of this rotten piece of legislation."

It was: in 1973, the ban was repealed as promised—Mr. Graham led the repeal debate in the Parliament of West Australia.

In 1976, Mr. Graham attended the Church of Scientology's first International Conference on World Peace and Social Reform held at Anaheim, California.

Mr. Graham, speaking on religious freedom, told an enthusiastic audience:

"As my final words, I say to you sincerely and enthusiastically, congratulations to the Church of Scientology for the fortitude it displayed when being assailed in West Australia and other parts as well. I believe that as a consequence of that ordeal it is a better organization—it is a stronger organization. And because of the action that was taken by the government that I supported, I'm now able to stand up before you, tall and proud, to congratulate you upon the stand you took, the manner in which you faced adversity, the way you fought on.

"And I say therefore, Godspeed and best wishes for the accomplishment of the ideals which are set out for you by L. Ron Hubbard."

Herbert Graham is not the only public personage to comment upon the Church of Scientology, describe its future, sum up the past.

Many others have done so whether they have personal knowledge of the Church or not. In particular, this applies to the detractors.

Victoria, Australia, 1963. Mr. Walton, M.L.A., in reference to Scientology, "There is in our midst a Church of charlatans who are trying to take over the country. There can be no doubt that is their objective."

Mr. Galbally, Victoria: "Scientology is corrupting the

community, commencing at the very early age of six years."

Mr. Dickie, Minister of Health, Victoria: "The government will make sure that the banned cult of Scientology cannot reappear in Victoria under the veil of religion . . . Scientology has no chance of being recognized as a religion. Scientologists will take the consequences if they try to practice again."

And again: "There is no possibility whatsoever of allowing Scientology to operate here again. As far as the government is concerned — the matter is final."

On the seventh of February, 1973, Lionel Murphy, Attorney General of Australia, decided that the Church of Scientology should be declared as a bona fide religious organization in Australia.

The decision included the State of Victoria which in May 1977 officially licensed Scientology's first minister to officiate in that state, under the Chief Secretary, Mr. Dickie.

In the United Kingdom opinion has also been given. Trial by media has been a feature of this century's communication industry and it is fact that the Victorian inquiry was referred to 278 times in five months by the British media alone.

People get quoted, requoted; controversy is presented as the message is said for media reports so it is heard and duplicated. Thus those under attack have to develop an endurance factor, due to news having to be considered sensationalistic if it is to sell papers.

One man who held apparently conflicting viewpoints was the Minister of Health in the United Kingdom, a Mr. Kenneth Robinson. He stated, truthfully, in 1966, "I have not had evidence that Scientology has been directly and exclusively responsible for mental breakdown or physical deterioration in its adherents in this country."

In 1968, Robinson stated, "The government are satisfied, having received all the available evidence, that Scientology is socially harmful."

The evidence was never produced. Robinson quietly left the government a few months afterwards.

Overlooked by the British Government in its hasty, condemnatory rhetoric, was the capacity of Scientologists to endure and in Britain as elsewhere, they had plenty to persevere over.

As the *Sunday Times* stated in 1968, "The case against Scientology does not yet seem monumental enough to justify this kind of treatment."

The *Manchester Guardian* stated they were "watching with discomfort the witch hunt launched against the Scientologists." The article ended, "The future of more than Scientology is involved in them."

The *Daily Express* asked in relation to Robinson's about-turn, "Did he have a revelation, perhaps?" The *New Statesman* reported: "With two exceptions, all the press men have been quoting each other." It went on to say, "Once you start this sort of thing, everyone scrambles for stones."

The government had decided to restrict aliens from entering the United Kingdom to study Scientology. An inquiry was set up after the restrictions were announced to investigate the position under a Sir John Foster. His report saying the restrictions were improper was published just before Christmas 1971.

It provided Christmas cheer to many people, including Dr. D. H. Clark, a British psychiatrist, who wrote to a colleague in the mental health movement:

"I spent much of Christmas morning reading the Foster Report, and as I read it in detail I was filled with un-Christmas glee. I may be wrong, but I believe that Sir John Foster has dealt Scientology a subtle but grievous wound from which they will suffer for many years."

Future

In preparation for this chapter, Scientologists conducted a worldwide survey of both friends and detractors alike to see how they considered the future would be for the Church.

The answers are illuminating.

From Canada, known detractors of Scientology in response to the question, "Where do you think Scientology is going?" answered:

"I'd like to answer that, but our lawyers have told me not to say anything about Scientology. It's unfortunate, but I'm afraid that's the way it is."

Norm Perry, Commentator,
CTV

"I predict it will survive. I'm sure it will survive very comfortably."

Peter Worthington, Editor,
Toronto *Sun*

"That kind of question would take hours and hours of research to answer, and I'm not prepared to do that . . . I don't have an answer to that question and I'm not prepared to give one."

John Marshall, Reporter,
Globe and Mail, Toronto

"Historically, it should fade out. The odds are against Scientology historically, although there's no conclusive evidence that this will happen. The determining factor will be how effectively it meets needs and can demonstrate that it meets them. Often a thing looks good for a time and just then doesn't pass the test. This is really the acid test of the thing."

Sidney Katz, Journalist,
Toronto Star

"Despite these setbacks, (Australia) Scientology has continued to grow steadily everywhere."

From the Report of the
Ontario Committee
on the Healing Arts

Turning from the detractors, where apparently the race is to the swift and the battle to the strong, to professionals more kindly inclined all of whom are not members of the Church.

"You need intelligence to get into it. It appeals to people on the ball rather than general public, so I feel it will reach a peak, not be a large group, but be a group with solid members."

Peter Cozzi,
Canadian Lawyer

"I think it will prosper and grow."

Paul Champagne,
Canadian Lawyer

"Most of the things you are doing are coming about—Freedom of Information, human rights, handling psychiatric abuse, help for senior citizens.

"You are going to have to find more causes—you are going to run out.

"I think you can count on more harassment from the police.

"An awful lot of people do things for your organization for free. To me, this seems that it is a vital organization."

Bud Riley, News Director,
CVRT Radio, Toronto

"I've heard some good things and I deal with an awful lot of bad things but they seem to be stemming from one or few sources.

"It certainly has some worthwhile community projects, and is rattling a few sabres that need to be rattled—psychiatry and others. However some of these areas are pretty potent, and that might be detrimental.

"It's large enough to influence its longevity."

Robert Murray,
Canadian Lawyer

"Scientology has come a long way, and has grown in numbers.

"There are so many people of different types—and into different activities—art, human rights, rehabilitation and more.

"Obviously, it will last. It can be geared to individual interests, and even if the interests change, people can use the basic technology to adapt to new ones."

Loretta Needle, B.A.,
University of Toronto,
taking Master's Degree in
Theology, Princeton

"I certainly hope it will survive!

"I'm the lawyer on a number of cases—that's all I can say, really."

Frank Fellows, Q.C.,
Toronto

"I feel sure Scientology will continue to exist for the foreseeable future through to the 21st century. The reason is that it is so well organized. It is not just actual cash, it is very efficiently run.

"Its path could change. One route, Dianetics could well become the tail that wags the dog. The other route could have greater emphasis on religion."

Father A. Gibson,
Professor of Theology,
St. Michael's College,
University of Toronto

"The trend today is for people to go back to conservatism.

"As long as the Church of Scientology provides a visible alternative it's going to grow and expand.

"We are through the permissive age and people are questioning values. You will get larger if you continue to provide an active social side to the Church.

"If you continue to reassure people that it isn't all hopeless and the world isn't coming to an end you'll continue to do well."

Robert Carr, Journalist,
Ontario Parliament
Press Gallery

"I think it will develop according to the aims of the people in it and how successful they are."

Carolyn Wightman,
Professor of English,
York University, Toronto

"As long as Scientology is there in its pure state, it will get through."

Claudia O'Flynn,
Registered Nurse, Toronto

"I think it's going to expand more and more."

A Canadian Medical Doctor

"Scientology? There will be line-ups at the doors to the Churches and Missions."

Business Executive, Ontario

"You're apparently succeeding."

Bill Mathews,
Community Officer,
Toronto Metropolitan Police

From Australia

"It is inevitable that Scientology will expand because, from my experience, the types of people I have met are walking advertisements for it. I think more and more people are looking for a practical philosophy."

The Hon. Herbert Graham,
Perth, West Australia

"Scientology seems to be better organized and expanding than it used to be."

George Williams, Journalist
Perth *Daily News*

"Scientology has come a very long way. As far as I'm concerned it's going ahead."

Medical Doctor,
West Australia

And the opposing view:

"I have no interest in Scientology. 'No comment' on how far it has come, and I haven't the foggiest idea how it will develop."

Dr. Bell,
Director of Mental Health
Services, Perth

". . . Victoria has secured a notable success in stamping out Scientology. . . ."

Editorial, *Medical Journal
of Australia*, 1967

"The Chief Secretary, Mr. Dickie, last night confirmed that Mrs. Allen (a Scientologist), had been recognized as a minister of religion."

Melbourne Age, May 19,
1977, under the heading
'State says yes to
Scientology'

"It's come a long way since the witch hunts of the '60s."

Psychologist, Melbourne

"No idea where it's going, other than it seems to be concerned with social reform."

Gerald Lyons, Journalist,
Truth Newspaper

"Will probably spread its influence more. Tendency nowadays for people to seek the new religions."

Alan Stewart, Journalist,
Observer, Melbourne

From Europe

"Scientology will become a major religion in the western world before the end of the century."

Loek Hopstaken, Journalist,
Amsterdam

"I think it will expand only slowly."

Karl-Heinz Pfneudi
Publisher of
Extrablatt Magazine,
Austria

"It leads away from theoretical science to practical application."

Dr. Bartholner,
Austrian Lawyer

"No idea, but I hope not into bankruptcy. I know from reading the papers that a lot of prominent persons in Austria are enrolled. How it will develop I don't know — but I hope well. I will now read the book *Dianetics.*"

Professor Johann Muschik,
Austria

"Scientology is not without fault — but it will progress."

Dieter Stortz, Writer on
Psychiatric Topics

"It will grow further. I hope it will become bigger."

Dr. Ulrich Daum,
Bavarian Lawyer

"Scientology will develop. I'm not a prophet, but I think it will develop."

Dr. Karl Bach,
Financial Expert

"I cannot easily conceive that in this pluralistic world new religions can achieve more than old established ones can."

Professor Leo Scheffzyck,
Expert on Catholicism

"Scientology has made progress, but should do more."

Medical Doctor, Germany

"There are many people who work hard to do something. As it looks now, progress could tend to flatten out. But there are opportunities for the Church."

Herr Bachmaler,
Bailiff of Munich

"Observers of the Church seem to be predominantly of the opinion that as a phenomenon it will develop and become larger due to the symptoms shown by unsolved problems and conflicts in our technical-scientific world."

Rudolf Grimm, Reporter,
Berlin

"Special attention belongs to Scientology however. . . . It is the forerunner of coming religious and philosophical movements with absolutely separate ethics, no longer bound to western ethical ideas."

Pfarrer Haack, Evangelic
Expert, Germany

North to Sweden

"Politically, Scientology must be treated no differently than all other religions."

Allan Akerlind, M.P.

"Scientology will probably endure. There is no sign it will disappear, increase or diminish. It will be accepted more and more into normality as with other religious associations."

Svante Nycander, Writer

"Expansion seems to have gone slowly here: it's always more difficult in a welfare state."

Businessman, Sweden

"Since the 17th century, suspicion has been meted out to all new movements in their early beginnings. Right now Scientology is filling a big demand for people looking for something, and this will continue for another ten to twenty years—and develop."

Bjorn Sahlin, Swedish Historian of Religion

"I am open to all possibilities. It is good that people are waking up spiritually. How it will do depends on the people doing it."

Helga Henschen, Sweden

"The Church of Scientology would appear to be troublesome in the community. In what way it is going to be popular depends on how the public see the behavior of the teachers and church members. There seems to be a need for some teaching or method to relate to—so why not a technical methodology as is Scientology?"

Anders Gernandt, Retired M.P.

"It's a new religion, and it will meet many difficulties. But Scientology stands on fine ground, and all resistance will be broken down."

Harry Widemyr, Social Inspector

"I don't think Scientology will develop a great deal in Sweden. We Swedes—and I talk generally—are too materialistic and superficial. It will take a very long time before any new movement of any kind will go here—especially as many Swedes are conservative, even if they don't dare confess it."

Per Eric Nisser, M.P. Sweden

"I am not sure of the future of Scientology, but I hope that it will be good—providing you don't take our members from the Folk Church."

Ravn Olesen, Newspaper Editor

"It is four years since I have had anything to do with Scientology and then I attacked it.
"I think it will continue."

Elsa Gress, Writer

United Kingdom

"As a Church I don't believe Scientology will attract a large congregation in this country—it is perhaps too well organized, too 'commercial,' insufficiently 'comfortable' to attract the average man in the street.
"However, its campaigns will continue to attract campaigners who are not merely prepared to talk about social ills but wish to be active against them.
"I believe these campaigns and support for them will grow."

Reg Gale,
Former Chairman of the
Police Federation, UK

"Scientology is likely to be engaged more and more in public affairs. The main problem will be abuse and false information peddled by its opponents and those in public affairs who wish the public to be kept in ignorance. It is my view that the public generally who have little knowledge of the Church of Scientology will learn more—particularly through the media, who, I believe will be paying more positive attention to its activities."

Arthur Lewis, M.P.

South Africa

"It looks as if an attempt is being made to be more constructive than in the past. I can see major changes."

L. Vitus, Deputy Director,
South African National
Association for
Mental Health

"It has carried on despite harassment and intimidation: it is honest."

Michael Rantho, Voluntary
Social Workers Association

"They do good work—they have a good cause and do a good job."

Doctor J. H. Botha

"If statements made by the Church of Scientology about mental health conditions in South Africa could be proved false, the Church of Scientology would be out of business."

Senator B. R. Bamford

"This organization will probably always be at loggerheads in the treatment of mental patients. When they are proved wrong they will have to keep quiet."

Senator L. E. D. Winchester

"It is beginning to touch the fringes of society's awareness."

Max Fleisher, Journalist

"It may be being accepted overseas, but it will be a long time before it's accepted in South Africa."

Lambert Pringle, Journalist

"Perhaps I should say here that you people — the Church of Scientology — have a very important part to play in this dark world."

Lofty Adams, South African
Colored Representative
Council Member

United States of America

"Scientology now is highly profiled — recognized by bureaucrats. It has though reached a respectful syndrome — and you've done it on your own. I don't see you're going to win. You need to change the world first — and you can't change the world."

Johnny Ogden,
General Manager
KROY and KROI Radio
Stations, Sacramento

"Bright people."

Larry Camp, Anchorman,
KTXL Television News

"I see an uphill battle. Groups like this serve a need and there is a need for groups like yours."

Les Holcomb,
Executive Director,
Little Hoover Commission,
California

"It's far better known than it was a few years ago. People are more aware now. As society becomes more complex, people will want to associate with something to get a handle on life. I see this as a religious movement with all churches."

Michael Franchetti,
Deputy Attorney General
California

"It's the largest growing religious movement in the entire world. I see the future for Scientology just being bigger and bigger."

Richard Allatorre,
Assemblyman, California

"I think the Church has picked a cause célèbre in the care of mental patients. Stick to that — it will be an issue that will grow."

Tim Holt, Journalist,
California

"I see it growing and continuing. Any legal difficulties will help rather than hinder. It has helped so many people — otherwise it would not be such a popular movement."

Mrs. Stapleton,
Criminal Division,
Department of Justice,
Washington, D.C.

"Religion thrives on persecution, so the very people who feed the persecution by aiming to destroy actually help it grow. So Scientology will grow."

Doctor Rothkirch,
Editor, International
Media Service,
Washington, D.C.

"I don't know anything about it. I know it's a religious group but I've not looked into it. It's a small group — but strong."

Senator Ralph Marino

"It's very difficult to predict where it's going. I know it's going to be around, but personally have no hard facts on which to make a prediction. It seems to have a sounder base than it did before — and has developed new interests. Its appeal varies — doesn't narrow to a particular type. I have no reason to think it harms people — some show improvement."

Ken Briggs,
New York Times,
Religion Editor

"There will be more public interest and involvement — this is why it will grow."

Eunice Melbeck, Producer,
Channel 5, Seattle

"I feel that the Church has been a great help to many people. It has brought enlightenment — I hope you continue in your strides."

Lilyann Mitchell,
Argus Newspaper

"It's come further than it deserves."

Mathews Newspaper

"I guess the people who are in it will do it. I know it's around. Its message needs to get across to people."

James Hoffman,
State Representative

"I think the future is bright — it's progressing. I hear quite a bit about it now."

Major Moran,
Chief of Police

"No one knows about it."

John Doughterly,
Chief of Detectives

". . . from minor to major religion, on positive programs to fill human need."

Bob Hamilton, KSD Radio

"Oh, it'll continue. I guess it has the fastest growing membership. Sounds like a lot of people are joining and enrollment is going up."

Caroll Glenn, *Tampa Times*

"Knowing how slowly religious trends and thought changes, I think there will be many years of controversy along the way before any of the newer religions are accepted. I don't foresee any immediate acceptance for any of them, including Scientology."

Jean Pugh, Religion Writer,
St. Petersburg Times

"I feel that the future of any church that is trying to uplift the standards of the community such as your own, is good. I feel that society today is going morally bankrupt and that we need the services of all churches. You are an aware group and are trying to stem the tide of moral decay."

Ralph L. Baker,
Attorney-at-law

"Obviously there are some problems in the road for Scientology, but overall I think it's got a good future. There is a lot of controversy, but things like the FBI raid awaken people to the fact that the Church of Scientology is uncovering a lot of stuff people ought to know about."

Bill Shive, President,
Berkeley Interfaith Council

"I feel the future is good given the conditions in society today—and the need for people to find themselves. It's a good future, but a rough one, as long as organizations with strong religious prejudices exist and want to create problems for others. It's unfortunate, but inevitable."

Professor J. Stillson Judah,
The Graduate
Theological Union

"The Church of Scientology seems well-established, and well-established churches have a history of long life expectancy."

Richard D. Hongisto,
Sheriff, San Francisco

"I feel there have been great strides from your group. An educational program is needed as the next vital step."

Dave Nash, KANO Radio

"I don't know—would like to have you on a show."

David Leroy, KTCR Radio

"You'll do all right if you keep giving your detractors hell!"

Hank Verseleh, WTCN TV

In August 1976, the Church held its first International Conference for World Peace and Social Reform at Anaheim, California. Members of the Church attended from across the world—the United States, Mexico, Canada, Great Britain, Norway, Sweden, Denmark, Holland, Belgium, France, Spain, Germany, Austria, Switzerland, Italy, South Africa, Australia and New Zealand, plus Israel, India, the Caribbean, Middle and Far Eastern countries, and presented a wide selection of non-Scientology speakers from many different walks of life.

It is in the comments of the non-Scientology speakers that testimony to the dynamic thrust of Scientology's philosophy and technology is to be found. Because the speakers had had personal experience in seeing Scientologists in action, and being experts, they were able to make a professional comparison on the involvement of Scientologists in their field. All of the quotes that follow come from non-Scientologists:

"All this is spelled out in the book I have just finished. I urge you to read it, not because I wrote it, but because in researching for it I found out that the Church of Scientology, as in so many fields of social reform, was in fact the leading element, the first one to bring into a court of law the questions and issues that, in fact, go to the heart of the Interpol potential and the Interpol tyranny."

Omar V. Garrison, author of
*The Secret World of
Interpol*, speaking on
'Interpol and Violations of
Freedom and Privacy'

"My final suggestion is to do your thing, as Scientologists. . . . You've got to persist, and you've got to dig even deeper into case studies you already have. . . . Nothing happens if you don't stay with it."

A. Ernest Fitzgerald,
author of *The High Priests
of Waste*, speaking on
'Aspects of Government
Accountability'

"World peace and social reform. These are noble goals, and I'm very proud that the Scientologists have dedicated themselves to achieving them."

Victor Marchetti, co-author
of *The CIA and the Cult of
Intelligence*, formerly
Executive Assistant to the
Deputy Director of the CIA

"There is now a vigorous effort that is being undertaken by a new generation of the world that has decided that the old symbols, the old technology, have failed: that the time has come when we can no longer endure the luxury of very unhelpful symbols and very unhelpful techniques that leave the world wanting. This is where, as I understand it, the Church of Scientology is embarking upon new methods, but with the same objectives as those of the churches of the world. And I can tell you that that is endorsed by all the people of good faith of the entire world."

Daniel Sheehan, Attorney
for the Jesuit Office
of Social Ministries
in Washington, D.C.

"I've been exhilarated to have met so many people, and find something more of what work is being done here. . . . Who could argue with the words that are set out as the theme? In particular I like the 'evolution, not revolution' . . . for what you have shown me in Anaheim during the past few days, thank you very much."

The Hon. R. Davies,
Shadow Minister of Health,
West Australia

"Well, Interpol agents out in the audience . . . I'm here! You know, the Church of Scientology has made an impact, not only on American society, but Scientologists have made an impact on the minds of the legislature in California. From alcoholism to spies is quite a spectrum. . . . I urge you, before you leave California for those of you who are visiting, to tell our Governor to sign that bill, AB 1032†, which should be on his desk, eliminating electro-shock for all mental patients in the State of California."

Assemblyman Art Torres,
Member of the California
State Legislature

And what then of Scientologists? How do they themselves, be they new members or old, see their own future and that of the Church?

"I see lots and lots more reaches for Scientology, more programs using Scientology technology, a saner, safer place in which to live as a result."

Diane West

"A lot of hard work."

A New Student

"I would like to see Scientology very much involved in school in the education system."

Father Richard Frank,
a Catholic Priest

"More sophisticated public-image wise, and more involvement in the arts. There are no weak links."

Knox Martin, Artist

"More expansion into society—radio, TV programs, educational help on how to study."

Mike Garson, Jazz Musician

"It has all the data to solve any problem on the planet. It's not where it's going, it's already arrived!"

Madeline Broman, Waitress

"I use it every day, it's wild stuff."

Bill Scott, Retired Physician

"It will develop through books, dissemination, word-of-mouth, deeds and actions."

Robert Worley,
Attorney-at-Law

"It will develop through active participation of active Scientologists. It will demonstrate itself through the application of technology in many fields: the key word is integrity."

Gino Coco-Mir,
Staff Member

"More expansion and general acceptance. It has come a long way already."

Tom Broman, Student

"On a planetary level Scientology will become a great uniter of people."

Mike Just, Staff Member

"In the long range future, Scientology will be the vital leaven, so to speak, in the cycle of a new civilization."

Martin Choate, Berkeley
Interfaith Council

"I think that in a matter of months the presence of Scientology will be seen as a major dynamic philosophy and religion standing against materialism and Communism in defense of Western civilization."

Doctor Daniel Kuhn, M.D.
and Psychiatrist

"The interest we have shown in world affairs has made us less self-centered as a group. Scientology will increase for certain."

Marie Antoinette Benoit,
Actress

"Scientology will gain even more respect, will work more with governments, schools, and will help to clean up many areas in society."

Julia McGinness,
Opera Singer

"I think it will be just a few more years before Scientology becomes the thing everyone does."

David Gale,
Computer Company
President

"The more Scientologists, the less chance of nuclear war."

George Fine, Stockbroker

"It may well be the solution for the future, for a fine and just world. The data will better conditions. It will change many things."

Guy Contant, Teacher

"There's going to be a real rush on our Churches everywhere in the world."

Jean Francois Dodier,
Church Member

"Scientology will have a social impact. People will feel better. This will stimulate interest. There is no limit to expansion."

Jesus Lopez, Staff Member

†The bill was signed and is now law.

"There will be a lot more sanity in the world."

Gilles Lacour, Staff Member

"Scientology will expand by showing that its technology works. This will accelerate, though time is not important."

Lena Loof, Staff Member

"It will develop into a people's movement for ethics, integrity and honesty in all areas of life."

Christer Monten,
Staff Member

"It will increase enormously."

Hildegaard Kiene,
University Lecturer

"By good work it will become more and more known and will be totally accepted."

Klaus Dissler, Nurse

"An enormous amount of new people at present coming in. It is established and opposition voices are cracking."

Maike Braren,
Staff Member

"It can help all people—and will develop well."

Albin Lepuschitz,
Engine Driver

"We'll keep expanding, handling problem areas in society and in the environment."

Martin Jones, Staff Member

"I see a move towards involvement of professional artists, and promotion to such people is needed."

Diane Buxton,
Ballet Teacher

"I hope we will get groups of concerned Canadians going out and establishing themselves as people who care—making it all a safer, better place. Basically, involvement in the community."

Dini Petty,
Radio and TV Journalist

"It will grow. It is growing faster in the United States, but it will grow also in Australia."

Moshe Kroy,
Doctor of Philosophy

"The only hope for the world is that Scientology expands enough."

George Mapstone, Doctor
of Chemical Engineering

"I'd like to see more done in the field of education. I'm in that field—and boy, it's needed."

Kay Conley, New Student

"It should develop in such a way that it wins the race with the atom bomb."

Dr. Julius Boese, Lawyer

"It will develop the best features in individuals—and thus mankind."

Christa Anschutz, Student

"It will give more knowledge about oneself and life."

Charlotte Peche, Housewife

"It's amazing what Scientologists have done in the last decade. If there were no future for Scientology there certainly wouldn't be one for Man. The future of Scientology is the future of mankind, so it's a very, very good thing Scientology has a future!!"

Bert Schwitters,
Media Specialist

"In the future Scientology technology will be widely applied—in education, drug rehabilitation, social reform for the aged, the mentally retarded, and many other fields not yet thought of."

Ruth Tiedke,
University Graduate

"Scientology will be on everybody's lips within five years. The next five will be polishing what is on everybody's lips."

Loek Hopstaken, Journalist

"The future will be very flamboyant and exciting, dynamic."

Raymond van Helvert,
Church Member

"The demand will be huge. We're all with it."

Alicia Kantuzinski,
Model and Staff Member

"I think Scientology will turn around the world picture as it is today because it brings truth and helps the sanity of every individual."

Mari-Ann Lind,
Church Member

"We can handle so many situations. No one else is, so though it may be tough we are game to do so."

Peter Pinchot,
Dairy Farmer

"As we are honest and ethical, we will expand."

Finn Jensen,
Church Member

"Providing we offer the right remedies, and use them correctly we have a big future."

Knud Møller, Storeman

"Because Scientology creates a future we will survive with a steady, gradual expansion."

> Birthe Hauge,
> Staff Member

"It has no limits!"

> Ole Gerstrom,
> Ex-M.P.,
> Church Member

"There'll be some waves, but that's normal, and we'll handle and expand continually."

> Ole Hovmand, M.P.,
> Dentist and Church Member

"I am of the opinion that Scientology is the only movement that has any kind of practicality connected to a religious philosophy. It is still a very young religion—but it will become known to everyone and can be applied in daily life by all sane people."

> Per Schiottz,
> Naval Architect

"It has to have an enormous future because there is a need for it. It is like the plant that burst the rock."

> Anna Botha, Teacher,
> Church Member

"I don't know of anything else that has such a future."

> Naomi Kleyn, Social Worker

"A great future. It is still destined for much criticism, but I have no doubt it will become the most stabilizing influence on the future of mankind."

> Ralph Hancock,
> Businessman

"I see more acceptance in the community, and a growing awareness by Scientologists of their responsibilities."

> Caroline Charbonneau,
> Church Member

"It will become better known on a general public level, mainly through its community involvements."

> Nigel Oakes, Accountant

"Twenty-six years ago a dreamer of dreams put his wisdom and his goals into a framework and found agreement amongst people like ourselves who formed a true group.

"We will within the next decade number 1.5% or more of the population of the Western Hemisphere. We have a beginning through our social reform programs. Through our rehabilitation programs we have made a beginning. With legislation against psychiatric inhumanities in many lands, we have made a beginning.

"But we dare not compromise our certainty, if we are to take the tide upon the flood, and catch success for future generations.

"We have the means, the resources and the abilities to use our knowledge to improve the present, and the future. We are not revolutionary. It takes less courage to tear down than confront the existing structure with all its faults and improve it.

"Let us not omit to learn and use data which applies to our group and to mankind, for that is also part of the wisdom given to us, with which we may resolve the problems of our group and of the world."

> Jane Kember,
> The Guardian, Worldwide,
> Anaheim, August 1976

Predicting the future for Scientology has not simply been the attaining of a single statement, but rather, the collecting together of many statements and opinions from a variety of people, be they Scientologists or not. For future opinions must take into account both the favorable and the unfavorable. Time will prove who is right.

For in regarding the future for Scientology the key would seem to be in the issue of alternatives being offered by the Church and acceptance for those alternatives.

To date, part of the phenomena in the growth of Scientology lies in past acceptance for alternatives offered by the Church.

Thus the Church has successfully campaigned in many lands for rights for the mentally ill, for Freedom of Information laws, for the right of individuals to see and correct government files held upon them, for an end to government agency abuse.

The history of Scientology is full of the splendidness of the Church going places: legislation to end shock treatments, sane people being released from psychiatric institutions, police files being corrected on individuals resulting in no further harassment, and fresh viewpoints to old problems being presented; and uncommitted intelligent spectators are becoming more and more interested in the Scientology viewpoint.

Twenty-eight years is not a long time in the history of mankind. But for Scientology it has seen a growing awareness of the role of the individual, a rise in the quest to find the spiritual nature of Man, growing recognition of people as human beings, and a still growing awareness that materialism in itself is not the answer to Man's future.

Scientology's organizations have grown, its social reform programs have expanded enormously to now number several hundred across the world and, perhaps in some ways most important of all, there has been a growing secular use of the technology in areas outside of the Church itself.

Such secular use falls into two main areas, with a third coming up fast. Firstly drug rehabilitation and the success of the Narconon program now in use in many countries. In her book *Drugs and Drug Rehabilitation*, Kate Pitt wrote of Narconon, "Wherever its principles are standardly and thoroughly applied there is proof of Narconon's success as a viable solution to the problems of drug abuse, its prevention and ultimate elimination."

Narconon uses the communication technology developed by L. Ron Hubbard: proof of its workability lies in Narconon's expansion.

The second area is that of education. Children do not have basics in study: they all too often cannot use a dictionary, spell, or apply what the have learned in their lives. Thus they become confused and lose interest in study—some turn violent in the classroom, play truant or simply 'drop out' of society.

This is being rectified. The use of the study technology in schools is giving many willing children a second chance.

With parents who can also help their children at home through knowledge of study technology, many children are now developing new study skills, increasing their performance at school, and building a better and brighter future for themselves.

And thirdly there is growing use of Scientology organizational methods in business and personnel handling.

Scientology programs range across many areas—help for the aged, the mentally retarded, the alcoholic and the criminal. Reform of mental health acts, an adversary system in committing mental patients, thus gives fair play to the person suspected of being mentally ill and the acceptance of a Charter of Rights for Mental Patients.

A sporadic upsurge by the antireligious movement in North America and elsewhere was curtailed due to actions by Scientologists and their many allies. Protection of freedom of worship and belief has now taken over.

As Church membership grows, so does the file of individual success stories. The statements as to the future of Scientology contained here show no one expects the path to be easy. But hope for the future is always there, and the dynamic thrust forward is plain to all, be they supporter or detractor.

The theory that all men are basically good and that misdeeds, stupidities and wrongdoings stemmed from aberration has been an exciting and worthwhile challenge to millions. It has provided hope, expectancy, and results to many, for as a hypothesis it has been found valid and, even better, the means have been developed by which aberration can be eliminated.

This has meant redemption for many—the criminal, the alienated, the antisocial, the disruptive, the drug addict, the fearful, the puzzled, and above all, those who thought there was something wrong somewhere, but couldn't quite put their finger on it.

Thus today in this examination of predictions as to the future of Scientology, it is that broad hope of a newer and better way that shines as a beacon to an ever increasing number of people.

It shines for you, also.

19

The List of Dianetics and Scientology Publications, Films and Tapes

The materials of Dianetics and Scientology are vast. The following is a complete listing of publications and other releases from 1948 through present time.

Books

Books are listed giving title, author, publication date, original publisher and where first published.

E-Meters

There were many models of the E-Meter throughout the years of its development. In this listing the most important ones are noted as they appeared.

Films

A number of 16 mm films were made between 1958 and 1970. These are noted as they appeared.

In 1977 these films began to be released as 8 mm (Super 8) film cartridges.

A large number of new films are in progress and planned. These, as well as the older films, are being issued in the form of film cartridges. Where these appear in the listing they are noted as film cartridges.

Insignia

Each of the insignia of Dianetics and Scientology is shown and described as at the time of adoption.

Taped Lectures

These are an issue line of both administration and auditing technology.

Tapes are listed showing tape number, lecture code (where applicable) and title. The tape number is a code for the date as follows. The first two numbers give the year, the next two numbers the month, the C stands for copy, and the last two numbers give the day of the month. The lectures codes, used where the lecture is part of a particular series, are defined in the list of abbreviations.

L. Ron Hubbard has said, "There are about 25,000,000 words on tape in archives which provide the consecutive path of discovery.

"These tapes are not simply lectures. They are the ONLY existing record of all the advances which made possible the handling of the human mind."

A special unit has been set up at the Flag Land Base, to get all tape lectures transcribed and published as printed volumes. The project is currently underway and is known as the "Tapes to Books" project.

288

Tape Cassette

In 1977 the first taped lecture was made available in cassette form. Where these are listed they are noted as tape cassette.

Translations

Translations of many of these books and tapes have been made, a majority of which are available as tape recordings. These are noted throughout the listing.

Hundreds of Dianetics and Scientology courses have been evolved from this wealth of material and many of these have been translated onto tapes. A listing of translated course tapes appears at the end of this publications list.

1948

BOOKS

Dianetics: The Original Thesis, by L. Ron Hubbard. Originally entitled *Scientology: A New Science*, the title was changed to *Abnormal Dianetics* and in 1948 was first circulated in professional circles as a manuscript, then in 1951 was published as a book by the Hubbard Dianetic Research Foundation in Wichita, Kansas. *Translations:* Danish, Dutch, French, German, Swedish.

1950

BOOKS

Dianetics: The Evolution of a Science, by L. Ron Hubbard. Written in early 1950 was published first as a magazine article in May, 1950 and published as a book in September, 1955 by the Hubbard Dianetic Research Foundation, Phoenix, Arizona. *Translations:* Danish, Dutch, French, German, Greek, Spanish, Swedish.

Dianetics: The Modern Science of Mental Health, by L. Ron Hubbard. Written in early 1950 in Bay Head, New Jersey and published by Hermitage House, May 9, 1950. *Dianetics: The Modern Science of Mental Health* rose to the top of the *New York Times* best seller list and stayed there for months. Over fifty printings; hardback, paperback and

translations. Also available for the blind in braille, record and cassette editions. *Translations:* Danish, Dutch, French, German, Spanish, Swedish.

Notes on the Lectures of L. Ron Hubbard, was compiled and edited by the staff of the Hubbard Dianetic Research Foundation of Los Angeles, California from two lecture series given by L. Ron Hubbard in the Fall of 1950. The first edition was a limited mimeographed edition published in December, 1950. It was published in book form in January 1951. *Translations:* Danish, Dutch, French, German, Swedish.

The following are other books compiled by staff in 1950.

Group Dianetics, staff written from lectures of L. Ron Hubbard. Published by the Hubbard Dianetic Research Foundation, Elizabeth, New Jersey, 1950.

Essays on Groups, Business and Government by L. Ron Hubbard, An Advanced Study of Government, published by the Hubbard Dianetic Research Foundation, Elizabeth, New Jersey, 1950.

Organization of Dianetic Groups and Centers, published by the Hubbard Dianetic Research Foundation, Elizabeth, New Jersey, 1950.

Foundation Papers and Papers of Organization and Technological Interest, published by the Hubbard Dianetic Research Foundation, Elizabeth, New Jersey, 1950.

The Processing of Psychotics, staff written from L. Ron Hubbard lectures. (A synthesis of Institutional Dianetics.) Published by the Hubbard Dianetic Research Foundation, Elizabeth, New Jersey, 1950.

Professional Lecture Notes of Ten Auditor School Lectures Given by L. Ron Hubbard, published by the Hubbard Dianetic Research Foundation, Elizabeth, New Jersey, November, 1950.

1950

INSIGNIA

The Dianetics Symbol.

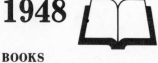

The Greek letter Delta is the basic form. Green for growth, yellow for life.

The four stripes represent the Four Dynamics of Dianetics: Survival as, I Self, II Sex and Family, III Group and IV Mankind.

This symbol was designed in 1950 and has been used since.

1950

TAPED LECTURES

At the end of May, 1950 the *First Professional Course* on Dianetics was announced. Lectures given by L. Ron Hubbard in June, July and early August at Elizabeth, New Jersey, are:

5006C17 Recognizing Contact of Engram—Use of Repeater

5006C20 Valences, Analytical Mind

5006C21 Engrams

5007C01 Address of Auditor to Pc

5007C08 How to Become an Auditor in One Easy Lesson

5007C10 Psychosomatics

5007C11 Standard Procedure

5007C12 Review of Standard Procedure

5007C13 Checking Data—Straightwire—Dramatizations

5007C14 Conception—Sperm Sequence

5007C15 Erasures

5007C19 Actuality—Parts of an Engram: Functions and interworkings of the analytical, reactive and somatic minds

5007C21 Somatic Strip: File Clerk, and getting a case started

5007C24 Diagnosis Data: Using the dramatization as a key to understanding and unlocking the preclear's engram bank

5008C02 Standard Procedure: The importance of getting engrams. Techniques on finding and erasing them (with a discussion of drugs and hypnosis under techniques)

5008C04 Affinity, Reality, Communication: What they are, how they relate to one another, how they apply to auditing and life, how they can be aberrative.

On 10 August 1950 L. Ron Hubbard made his first public appearance in Los Angeles, California, where he spoke to a jammed house of over 6000 enthusiastic people.

5008C10 Shrine Auditorium, Los Angeles

The following Monday professional level courses started under L. Ron Hubbard's personal direction at the Los Angeles Department of the Hubbard Dianetic Research Foundation.

5008C15 Anatomy of the Engram
5008C15 Analytical Mind
5008C16 Affinity, Reality, Communication: How breaks affect adversely, how cleaning up breaks effect increased ability, how ARC can be used in auditing
5008C17 Straightwire
5008C18 Demonstration and Talk on Denyers, Bouncers, Holders
5008C18 Engrams—Two Parts of the Mind
5008C21 SOP Step 1; Pc Inventory: Finding and making use of psychiatric treatment and its drawbacks, hypnosis dramatizations, valences, allies; using the inventory to establish affinity with pc
5008C22 SOP Step 2; Opening the Case—Engrams and Parts of the Mind: Anaten, prenatal bank, grief engrams, SOP, demonstration of getting a case moving on the track
5008C23 Engrams and Parts of the Mind: Boil-offs, file clerk, mind's filing systems, the somatic strip
5008C24 Engrams and Parts of the Mind: Action phrases walking engrams backwards, shape of engrams, migraines, importance of pleasure moments in therapy
5008C24 SOP Step 2; Running Engrams and Step 3, Demon Circuits and Valence Commands
5008C25 Step 3; Holders, Bouncers, Denyers, Taking Inventory, Psychotics
5008C25 Mechanical Arrangement of Engrams
5008C28 Engrams and Types of Cases (psychotic to Clear)
5008C29 Educational Dianetics
5008C30 Preventive Dianetics
5008C30 Educational Dianetics
5008C31 Engrams and Parts of the Mind
5008C31 Medical Dianetics
5009C01 Child Dianetics
5009C01 Drugs: Effects in Auditing
5009C04 Advertising Dianetics—propaganda—push-buttons
5009C05 Political Dianetics
5009C06 Aesthetics
5009C07 Language Adjustment—Definitions of words in a language
5009C08 The Complete Auditor (relations to other fields and to the public)

On 23 September 1950, L. Ron Hubbard gave a public lecture to ver 2,000 people at the Oakland Municipal Auditorium, Oakland, California.

009C23 OAK PLS-1 General Dianetics—Part 1 (Introduction to Dianetics) historical background, analytical and reactive mind, engrams, tone scale, time track

009C23 OAK PLS-2 General Dianetics—Part 2 What Dianetics can do

This was followed by a course covering four evenings at the Oakland Municipal Theatre. A lecture and demonstration was given each night. Part of the material presented during this lecture series is included in the book *Notes on the Lectures of L. Ron Hubbard.*

009C26 OAK PLS-3 The Auditor's Code—Standard Procedure

009C26 OAK PLS-4 Demonstration

009C27 OAK PLS-5 Different Types of Cases and Methods

009C27 OAK PLS-6 Demonstration

009C28 OAK PLS-7 Stalled Cases and How to Resolve with Standard Procedure

009C28 OAK PLS-8 Demonstration (Coitus Engram)

009C29 OAK PLS-9 Guk and Free Wheeling

009C29 OAK PLS-10 Demonstration (Running a Secondary)

The following lectures were given by L. Ron Hubbard during October and the first half of November, 1950.

5010C09 Standard Procedure

5011C__ Basic Course 1

5011C02 Standard Procedure Tools—Accessibility—Starting Case

5011C04 Affinity, Communication and Reality

5011C06&7 Twin Research

5011C07 STP Standard Procedure

5011C08 Twin Research

5011C07 STP Standard Procedure

5011C08 Child Dianetics

5011C08 Insulin Shock Demonstration

5011C09 Group Dianetics

5011C10 Handling Psychotics

5011C11 Educational Dianetics

5011C15 Demonstration Research

L. Ron Hubbard returned to Los Angeles where he gave a series of lectures to the Professional Auditor's Course students at the Hubbard Dianetic Research Foundation. Notes on most of these lectures are included in the book *Notes on the Lectures of L. Ron Hubbard.*

5011C20 STP-1 Thought, Life and the Material Universe

5011C21 STP-2A Spectrum of Logic—Tone Scale: The mind as a computer, the use of infinity valued logic, emotion, the ARC triangle, and what is humor.

5011C21 STP-2B Spectrum of Logic—The Tone Scale (cont'd)

5011C22 STP Auditor's Code and Beginnings of Standard Procedure

5011C22 STP Standard Procedure—Accessibility—ARC

5011C24 STP Case Entrance—Accessibility

5011C24 STP Case Entrance (cont'd)—Points of Entrance—Nonverbal Factors

5011C25 STP-5A ARC and the Four Dynamics—Accessibility Chart

5011C25 STP ARC and the Four Dynamics (cont'd)—Circuitry

5011C26 SOP "Access"

5011C27 STP-6A Standard Procedure—Chronic Somatics—Stuck on the Track

5011C27 STP Straight Memory—Affinity, Reality & Communication—Tone Scales

5011C28 STP Valences and Demon Circuits

5011C28 STP Title unknown

5011C29 STP Circuits, Valences, Accessibility, ARC

5011C29 STP-8B Straight Memory Techniques

5011C30 STP-9 Rudimentary Data on Groups: Lectures I, II, III

5011C30 STP-9B Completion of lecture on Groups and Questions and Answers: Lectures V, VI, VII

5011C30 STP-12 Standard Procedure Step 3

5012C01 STP Group Dianetics

Lectures given by L. Ron Hubbard in Los Angeles, California 7 to 19 December 1950.

5012C07 Affinity, Communication, Reality

5012C19 Chain Scanning

The following is a list of lectures by L. Ron Hubbard for which the specific date is not known.

___C__ Effort-Axioms-Thought-Emotion

___C__ Electropsychometer

___C__ How To Handle a Pc

___C__ Science Fiction

50__C__ Emergency Measures (when unfamiliar with the case)—Talk to Students

50__C__ Emotion—ARC—The Tone Scale

50__C__ Outline of Dianetic Standard Procedure

50__C__ Prenatal Engrams

50__C__ Standard Procedure Steps

50__C__ Tone Scale Emotion

50__C__ The Triangle Puzzle

1951

BOOKS

Dianetics Processing: A Brief Survey of Research Projects and Preliminary Results, staff written, published by the Hubbard Dianetic Research Foundation, Elizabeth, New Jersey, January, 1951.

Science of Survival: Simplified, Faster, Dianetic Techniques, by L. Ron Hubbard. Was released as a limited manuscript edition on the 28th of June, 1951, at the First Annual Conference of Hubbard Dianetic Auditors in Wichita, Kansas. The hardcover edition was published in August, 1951, by the Hubbard Dianetic Research Foundation. The title was later changed to *Science of Survival: Prediction of Human Behavior.* Included in each edition of *Science of Survival* is the Hubbard Chart of Human Evaluation. *Translations:* Dutch, French, German, Swedish.

Preventive Dianetics, taken from the lectures of L. Ron Hubbard, published by the Hubbard Dianetic Foundation, Wichita, Kansas, July, 1951.

Self Analysis, A Simple Self-Help Volume of Tests and Processes Based on the Discoveries Contained in Dianetics. This book was modified by L. Ron Hubbard in 1953 for creative processing and called *Self Analysis in Dianetics* in Britain and *Self Analysis in Scientology* in America. The original version is, however, the one used currently. Published by the International Library of Arts and Sciences, Wichita, Kansas, August, 1951. *Translations:* Danish, Dutch, French, German, Italian, Spanish, Swedish.

Education and the Auditor, taken from the lectures of L. Ron Hubbard, published by the Hubbard Dianetic Foundation, Wichita, Kansas, August, 1951.

A Synthesis of Processing Techniques: Function Processing, taken from the works of L. Ron Hubbard, published by the Dianetics Processing and Research Foundation, Chicago, Illinois, August, 1951.

Supplements to *Science of Survival,* contained articles written by various Dianeticists. Supplements No. 1 through No. 4 contained articles by L. Ron Hubbard which are preserved in *The Technical Bulletins of Dianetics and Scientology,* 1976. In all, six supplements were published by the Hubbard Dianetic Research Foundation, Wichita, Kansas.

Science of Survival Supplement No. 1, was published September, 1951.

Science of Survival Supplement No. 2, was published September, 1951.

Science of Survival Supplement No. 3, was published December, 1951.

Science of Survival Supplement No. 4, was published February, 1952.

Science of Survival Supplement No. 5, was published April, 1952.

Science of Survival Supplement No. 6, was published June, 1952.

The Dianetics Axioms, by L. Ron Hubbard, published by the Hubbard Dianetic Research Foundation, Wichita, Kansas, October, 1951. This book was issued during the October Midwest Conference and was the first release of the Axioms of Dianetics. (The Dianetic Axioms are available in the books *Advanced Procedure and Axioms, Axioms and Logics* and *Scientology 0-8.*)

Child Dianetics, Dianetic Processing for Children, was compiled from the research and lecture materials of L. Ron Hubbard by the staff of the Hubbard Dianetic Foundation of Los Angeles, California, and published at Wichita, Kansas, by the International Library of Arts and Sciences, October, 1951. L. Ron Hubbard wrote the introduction in August, 1951, about the same time as the book was actually typeset. *Translations:* Danish, French, Swedish.

Advanced Procedure and Axioms, by L. Ron Hubbard, first published by the Hubbard Dianetic Research Foundation in Wichita, Kansas, in late November, 1951. It was written as a companion book to *Handbook for Preclears* (which was published in December, 1951). *Translations:* Danish, Dutch, French, German, Spanish, Swedish.

Lectures on Effort Processing, taken from the works of L. Ron Hubbard, published by the Psychological Research Foundation, Phoenix, Arizona, November, 1951.

Handbook for Preclears, by L. Ron Hubbard, was the main theme of the Second Annual Conference of Hubbard Dianetic Auditors at which it was introduced. *Handbook for Preclears* is intended as a companion volume to *Advanced Procedure and Axioms.* It contains the Hubbard Chart of Attitudes. Originally published in December 1951 at Wichita, Kansas, it was later republished by Scientific Press in Phoenix, Arizona, under the title *Scientology: Handbook for Preclears. Translations:* Danish, Dutch, French, German, Spanish, Swedish.

New Developments from the Foundation, published by the Hubbard Dianetic Research Foundation, Wichita, Kansas, December, 1951. This book was compiled by the staff.

Conference Report, compiled by staff, was published by the Dianetics Processing and Research Foundation, Chicago, Illinois, late 1951.

1951

E-METER

Volney Mathison presented L. Ron Hubbard with the first E-Meter, the Model-B. It was used for research throughout 1951. Also in 1951 the first projection meter was built, the Model-A Meter. This meter was useful in auditing demonstrations in that the meter dial could be projected so the students could see it.

1951

TAPED LECTURES

Lectures given by L. Ron Hubbard in California in January, 1951:

5101C09 An Essay on Management

5101C18 Accessibility

5101C18 Accessibility (cont'd) — Hurdy-Gurdy Straightwire & Haywire

Beginning in December, 1950, L. Ron Hubbard gave a series of fifteen-minute lectures over 126 radio stations. On the West Coast of America they were broadcast daily, Monday through Friday, at 10:15 a.m. Seven of these lectures are listed below.

5102C07 R/BRCST Group Dianetics — How to straighten out a group — The group and the individual

5102C08 R/BRCST Dianetics — its ability to handle community's individual's and nation's problems

5102C09 R/BRCST Valence — Straight Memory

5102C12 R/BRCST Valence — Grief and Valence

5102C13 R/BRCST Husbands and Wives (etc.) Auditing each other

5102C14 R/BRCST Communication Breaks: Seeing, hearing, speaking, etc.

5102C15 R/BRCST Tone Scale of Individuals and Nations

In the Spring of 1951, the Hubbard Dianetic Research Foundation moved from Elizabeth, New Jersey, to Wichita, Kansas. On the evening of 21 May 1951, L. Ron Hubbard spoke to a filled lecture hall at the Wichita Foundation. This was his first major lecture in several months, as he had been engaged in completing *Science of Survival*, and he presented technological improvements and expansions and clarifications of theory.

5104C09 Time

5104C09 Motion

5105C21 Introduction to Science of Survival

5106C__ Validation Processing

5106C04 All Possible Aberration — 1

5106C04 All Possible Aberration — 2

5106C12 Demonstration

5106C12 Theory Behind Theta and MEST

The First Annual Conference of Hubbard Dianetic Auditors was held by the Hubbard Dianetic Foundation at Wichita, Kansas, June 25-30, 1951. L. Ron Hubbard lectured to the conferees every day of the conference.

5106C25 Introduction to Conference and New Book

5106C25 Techniques — Tone Scale

5106C25 Theta — MEST (Survive and Succumb)

5106C26 HEV-1 Chart of Human Evaluation

5106C27 VP-1 Validation Processing — Intro to Self-Auditing-Guk

5106C27 VP-2 Chronic Somatics

5106C27 VP-3 Demonstration (Validation Processing)

5106C28 CAC The Completed Auditor, Part I — Auditing techniques — the dynamics — interior and exterior — standard procedure — auditing — lock scanning — ARC straightwire

5106C28 CAC The Completed Auditor, Part II — Intro, extroversion — past deaths and lives — conclusion of conference

5106C29 HDA-1 HDA Conference No. 1

5106C30 HDA-2,3 MEST, Theta, ARC — Part 1

5106C30 HDA-4,5 Final Lecture at Conference (Questions & Answers)

The Wichita Monday Lectures. L. Ron Hubbard gave the following Monday lectures to Foundation students at Wichita, Kansas, in July and August, 1951.

5107C09 VMP-1 Validation Processing

5107C09 VMP-2 MEST Processing

5107C09 VMP-3 Addenda — MEST Processing

5107C16 VMP-4 Some Educational Material

5107C16 VMP-5 More on MEST Processing

5107C16 Advice to the Auditor

5107C21 Validation Processing

5107C23 Time Track

5107C23 Basic Processing

5107C30 Basic Reason, Part I

5107C30 Basic Reason, Part II

5108C06 Survival Processing, Part

5108C06 Survival Processing, Part

The Human Evaluation Cours Lectures. During the week of Augus 13, L. Ron Hubbard gave a series o lectures launching the Special Cours in Human Evaluation, as another im portant branch of Dianetics. Amon those attending were representative of the major industries in Wichita Kansas.

5108C13 HEV What is Dianetics

5108C13 HEV-2 The Value of th Chart of Human Evaluation and it Application

5108C13 HEV What Dianetics Ca Do

5108C13 HEV-3 The Dynamics o Existence — Derivation and Uses o the Chart of Human Evaluation

5108C14 HEV-4 Life Force Endow ment, Personality and Tone Scale R action to the Universe (Conquest o the physical universe)

5108C14 HEV-5 Behavior and Pun ishment — Evolution on Theta an GE Lines (Parts of the mind)

5108C15 HEV-6 Tone Scale, Part — How to Talk About the Tone Scal to the Non-Dianeticist

5108C15 HEV-7 Tone Scale, Part — Chronic Position on the Tone Scal

5108C16 HEV-8 Motion and Emo tion and Its Relationship to Man an the Tone Scale

5108C16 HEV-9 Motion and Emo tion (cont'd) — Physiology

5108C17 HEV-10 Motion and Emo tion (cont'd) — Physiological Aspects

5108C17 HEV-11 Review of Motio and Emotion — ARC Triangle

Lectures given by L. Ron Hubbar at the Foundation in Wichita, Kansa from 20 August to 20 Septembe 1951.

5108C20 Motion

5108C21 Standard Procedure

5108C27 Motion and Emotion — Lin Charge, Parts 1-5

5108C28 Psychotics

5108C28 Analytical Mind

5109C04 PLS-12 Time and Motio (Geriatrics)

5109C04 Illusion

5109C10 PLS-13 Mimicry

5109C10 PLS-14 Arithmetic

5109C10 The Cellular Postulate

5109C14 Effort Processing

5109C17 Black Dianetics

5109C17 The Cellular Postulate

5109C20 Introduction to Survival

5109C20 Effort Processing

51__C__ Resolution of Effort an Counter-Effort

Lectures given by L. Ron Hubbar

Wichita, Kansas, from 23 September through 1 October, 1951.

09C23 A Lecture on Dianetics

09C24 OCTSER-0A Effort Processing—Description of effort and e energy as it pertains to effort ocessing

09C24 OCTSER-0B Effort Processing (cont'd)—Behavior bands on ne scale explained and motion tolance

10C01 OCTSER-OC Self-Determinism—Effort Processing (cont'd)

10C01 OCTSER-OC Self-Determinism—Effort Processing

The October Midwest Conference ctures. October 8th 1951 found e Foundation (Wichita, Kansas) st to a number of interested Diaticists coming together from all er the country to gather information on latest developments in Diatics.

10C08 OCTSER-1A Axioms and fort Processing—Demo of Effort ocessing

10C08 OCTSER-1B Axioms and fort Processing (cont'd)

10C09 OCTSER-2A Effort Processing—Statics and Motions—Difrence between belief with and witht understanding

10C09 OCTSER-2B Dianetic xioms, 1-14

10C10 OCTSER-3A Dianetic xioms, 14-32

10C10 OCTSER-3B Theory of icenters—1

10C11 OCTSER-4A Dianetic xioms, 33-51

10C11 OCTSER-4B Theory of icenters—2—Self-Determinism

10C12 OCTSER-5A Dianetic xioms—Randomness and Motion, rt 1

10C12 OCTSER-5B Dianetic xioms concluded—What to look for an effort engram

The Wichita Foundation Auditor's urse. L. Ron Hubbard gave the lowing lectures to the Hubbard anetic Auditor Course students at e Foundation in Wichita, Kansas, October, 1951.

10C15 FAC-1A Postulate Procssing, Part 1—ARC Effort Processg

10C15 FAC-1B,2,2B Postulate ocessing, Part 2—ARC Postulate ocessing, Part 3 (Effort processing, stulate processing, and postulate ocessing's relationship to self-derminism, epicenters and the tone ale) Postulate Processing, Part 4

10C22 The Human Mind Versus e Electronic Computer

10C22 The Human Mind Versus e Electronic Computer (cont'd)

10C23 FAC-3A Foundation Audir's Course, Part 1—Three Methods Processing

10C23 FAC-3B Foundation Audir's Course, Part 2—Three Methods Processing (cont'd)—On the Eighth ynamic

5110C24 FAC-4 Foundation Auditor's Lecture, Part 1—Overall Processing: Conclusion Processing and Effort Processing

5110C24 FAC-5 Foundation Auditor's Lecture, Part 2—The Dynamics, Self-Determinism and S.C.S.

5110C25 FAC-6A&B Chronic Somatics and the Service Facsimilie

5110C26 FAC-7 Evolution of Man According to the Facsimile, Part 1

5110C26 FAC-8 Evolution of Man According to the Facsimile, Part 2

5110C26 FAC Evolution of Man, Part 3

These are two lectures given by L. Ron Hubbard in Wichita, Kansas, on 29 October 1951.

5110C29 The Theta Facsimile, Part 1

5110C29 The Theta Facsimile, Part 2

The following are lectures given by L. Ron Hubbard in Wichita, Kansas, from 4 November to 21 December 1951.

5111C__ Search for Incidents on the Track

5111C04 A C & R

5111C05 Notes on Postulates

5111C12 Basic Postulates

5111C12 Prime Thought

5111C19 Cause and Effect, Part I

5111C19 Cause and Effect, Part II

5111C26 An Analysis of Memory, Parts 1 & 2

5111C26 An Analysis of Memory, Parts 3 & 4

5112C03 Discussion of Advanced Procedure, Part 2

5112C03 Advanced Procedures and Cause & Effect

5112C10 PLS-7 Dead Man's Goals (E-Meter use in Dianetics)

5112C10 PLS-8 Resolution of Cases (conclusion of PLS-7)

5112C17 Regret and Seriousness—Counter Efforts

5112C18 Counter-Effort, Counter-Emotion, Counter-Thought

5112C21 Regret and Seriousness, Part 1

5112C21 Regret and Seriousness, Part 2

5112C21 On *Handbook for Preclears* —Service Fac 1

The Second Annual Conference of Hubbard Dianetic Auditors was held in Wichita, Kansas, from the 27th to the 30th of December, 1951. Lectures, demonstrations and seminars evolved around L. Ron Hubbard's latest book, *Handbook for Preclears*, introduced at this meeting, and *Advanced Procedure and Axioms*.

5112C27 DCL-1A&1B 1st December Conference Lecture, Part I & II

5112C27 DCL-1A The Handbook for Preclears

5112C27 DCL-1B Definition of Terms, Scientology and Milestone 1 Defined

5112C28 The Handbook for Preclears

5112C28 DEMO Don Purcell auditing LRH

5112C28 DCL-2A Chart of Attitudes

5112C28 DCL-2B Chart of Attitudes, Part 2—Life Continuum Theory

5112C29 DCL-3A The Goal of Processing (The Ideal State of Man), Part I

5112C29 DCL-3B The Goal of Processing (The Ideal State of Man), Part II

5112C29 Resolution of the Life Continuum Problem

5112C29 DCL-4A Cause and Effect and Remarks on Second Dynamic

5112C29 DCL-4B Use of *Handbook for Preclears* and *Self Analysis*

5112C30 DCL-5A Effort Processing—Notes on Children's Illnesses

5112C30 DCL-5B Effort Processing—Yes, No, Maybe Remarks

On the Monday following the December conference a group of Dianeticists met at Ron's home for an informal discussion on auditing techniques. The following recordings were made 31 December 1951.

5112C31 Counter-Efforts

5112C31 Discussion at Ron's Home

5112C31 Discussion at Ron's Home (cont'd)

1952

BOOKS

Scientology and Dianetics Advanced Procedures, notes and transcripts on lectures by L. Ron Hubbard and others in Wichita, Kansas, January through March 1952, compiled and published by the Central Pennsylvania Dianetics Group, Middletown, Pennsylvania.

Address by L. Ron Hubbard— Arcadia Theatre, Wichita, Kansas, published by Scientific Press, Phoenix, Arizona, February, 1952.

The Auditor's Manual, staff written and edited. Published by the Hubbard Dianetic Foundation, Inc., Wichita, Kansas, 1952.

Prologue to Survival, Part I, II and III, (3 books), published by the Psychological Research Foundation, Inc., Phoenix, Arizona, March, 1952. Based on the works of L. Ron Hubbard.

Text of Summary Course Lectures, published by the Scientific Press, Phoenix, Arizona, March, 1952. These were the first 27 books of what was later in 1952 issued as the *Professional Course Booklets.* (See the *Professional Course Booklets* for a full listing of titles.)

Electropsychometric Auditing-Operators Manual, by L. Ron Hubbard. Published by the Office of L. Ron Hubbard, Phoenix, Arizona,

June, 1952. (The text of this book is printed in full in *The Technical Bulletins of Dianetics and Scientology,* 1976.)

A Key to the Unconscious—Symbological Processing, by L. Ron Hubbard. Published by Scientific Press, Phoenix, Arizona, June, 1952. (The text of this book is printed in full in *The Technical Bulletins of Dianetics and Scientology,* 1976.)

Individual Track Map, by L. Ron Hubbard. Published by the Office of L. Ron Hubbard, Phoenix, Arizona, June, 1952. (The text of this book is printed in full in *The Technical Bulletins of Dianetics and Scientology,* 1976.)

Health and Happiness, published by the Psychological Research Foundation, Inc., Phoenix, Arizona, 1952. Based on the works of L. Ron Hubbard.

What to Audit, by L. Ron Hubbard, was published in Phoenix, Arizona, by the Scientific Press, July, 1952. The same text was issued as *History of Man* in London in July, 1952.

History of Man, by L. Ron Hubbard. Published by the Hubbard Association of Scientologists Incorporated, London, July, 1952. It was the same text as *What to Audit.* A later edition was entitled *Scientology: A History of Man,* which is its current title. *Translations:* Danish, Swedish.

The Professional Course Lecture Summary, also known as the *Professional Course Booklets,* were 50 course booklets compiled and rewritten from transcripts of lectures given by L. Ron Hubbard during the Spring and Summer of 1952.

The first 27 booklets were originally entitled the *Summary Course Booklets,* published by the Scientific Press, Phoenix, Arizona, March, 1952. Their titles follow.

1. *Introduction to Scientology, 1—Second Echelon of Knowledge*
2. *Introduction to Scientology, Part 2—Second Echelon of Knowledge*
3. *Properties of Theta*
4. *Motion on the Tone Scale*
5. *Thought*
6. *Emotion: The Handling of Motion*
7. *Effort and Counter-Effort, Responsibility; ARC*
8. *The Attack on the Preclear*
9. *How to Handle Facsimiles*
10. *Indoctrination of the Preclear*
11. *Resolution of Effort and Counter-Effort; Overt Acts*
12. *The Electropsychometer*
13. *Thought, Emotion, Effort, Maybes*
14. *Effort Processing: Demonstration*
15. *Training Auditors: Demonstration*
16. *Anatomy of Fac One: Demonstration*
17. *Theta Bodies*
18. *Entities*

19. *Remarks about Knowledge, and A History of the Theta Line*
20. *Theta Line, MEST Body Line*
21. *Theta-Body Anatomy*
22. *How to Audit a Theta Line*
23. *Theta Bodies*
24. *Electro-Psychometric Auditing: Demonstration*
25. *Analysis of Memory and Aberration (Part 1)*
26. *Analysis of Memory and Aberration (Part 2)*
27. *Search for Incidents on the Track*

In May, 1952, *Professional Course Booklets* 28 through 31 were published by the Scientific Press, Phoenix, Arizona. Their titles follow.

28. *Theta's Goal of Being, Technique 80*
29. *Dynamics and the Tone Scale, Technique 80*
30. *Cause and Effect, Technique 80*
31. *The Importance of a Body, Technique 80*

The Balance of the *Professional Course Booklets* were issued throughout June, July and August, 1952, published by the Hubbard Association of Scientologists, Incorporated, Phoenix, Arizona. Their titles follow.

32. *The Degeneration of Illusion, Technique 88*
33. *The Solidness of Apathy, Technique 88*
34. *Handling of Motion, Technique 88*
35. *Tone Scale of Indecision, Technique 88*
36. *Hollow Spots and Ridges, Technique 88*
37. *Attention Unit Running, Technique 88*
38. *The Behavior of Auditors, Technique 88*
39. *DEDs and DEDEXes, Technique 88*
40. *Religion and Scientology, Technique 88*
41. *Evolution of Techniques, Technique 88*
42. *Invasions and Reality, Technique 88*
43. *Sex Practices of Thetans, Technique 88*
44. *What to Tell Preclears, Technique 88*
45. *Blanketing and Imprisoned Thetans, Technique 88*
46. *Facsimiles—Real or Borrowed, Technique 88*
47. *Energy Flows and Ridges, Technique 88*
48. *Running Flows in Balance, Technique 88*
49. *"88" Straightwire, Technique 88*
50. *Whole Track Incidents—Black-and-White, Technique 88*

Scientology: 88, by L. Ron Hubbard, was a unique limited edition, handwritten by L. Ron Hubbard and printed on special lithographic plates. Distributed by the Hubbard Association of Scientologists, Phoenix, Arizona, September, 1952. The

technology from *Scientology: 88* can be found in *Scientology: 8-80.*

Electropsychometry, published by Volney Mathison, Los Angeles, California, 1952, was based on the works of L. Ron Hubbard and contained the text of *Electropsychometric Auditing* by L. Ron Hubbard, published earlier in 1952.

Self Analysis in Dianetics—A Handbook of Dianetic Therapy, by L. Ron Hubbard, published in London, England, by Derricke Ridgeway Ltd, October, 1952. The original *Self Analysis* is the one now in use and it has replaced this Creative Processing version which is now out of print.

Scientology 8-80, by L. Ron Hubbard, published by the Hubbard Association of Scientologists, Phoenix, Arizona, November, 1952. This technique is a considerable extension beyond the data given in the Summer Session Course (Phoenix, June, 1952), but has that course as its basic. *Translations:* Danish, French, Greek, German, Swedish.

Scientology 8-8008, by L. Ron Hubbard, published by the Hubbard Association of Scientologists, London, England, December, 1952. *Scientology 8-8008* was written by L. Ron Hubbard in England in October-November 1952. He had the first copy with him when he flew to the United States and presented it at the opening of the Philadelphia Doctorate Course on December 1st, in Philadelphia, Pennsylvania. *Translations:* Danish, French, German, Spanish, Swedish.

1952

E-METER

The Model H-52-IR E-Meter became available in 1952 and was in use through 1954.

1952

INSIGNIA

The Scientology Symbol
There are two triangles, over which the S is imposed.

The S stands for Scientology which is derived from "SCIO" (Knowing in the fullest sense).

The lower triangle is the A-R-C triangle—its points being Affinity—Reality—and Communication. These are the three elements which combined give Understanding.

The upper triangle is the K-R-C triangle. The points are K for Knowledge, R for Responsibility and C for Control.

The KRC triangle acts like the ARC triangle. When one corner is increased the other two also rise.

The Scientology symbol ("S" and double triangle) first appeared in 1952.

The Scientology symbol as well as appearing in auditors' blazer badges, Release pins and Clear bracelets, is worn as lapel pins, tie tacks, rings of various designs, earrings, key rings, money clips, cigarette lighters, brooches, necklaces, and otherwise displayed in car badges, decals, flags, etc.

1952

TAPED LECTURES

The Wichita Foundation Lectures were given to the students at the Wichita Foundation from January 1 to February 8, 1952.

5201C01 A Service Facsimile
5201C07 Survival
5201C07 Question and Answer Period
5201C11 The Service Facsimile
5201C14 The Emotional Curve
5201C14 Some Aspects of Dianetics on Society: The time element required for body to repair after Dianetics
5201C14 Aspects of Dianetics on Society (cont'd)
5201C21 The Anatomy of the "Overt Act", Part I
5201C21 The Anatomy of the "Overt Act", Part II
5201C28 The Anatomy of "Service Facsimile", Part I
5201C28 The Anatomy of "Service Facsimile", Part II
5201C29 HDFL Anatomy of Service Facsimiles
5202C02 Psychogalvanometer, Mysticism Groups
5202C08 Summary of Service Fac Chain
5202C08 Motive of SLP 8
5202C08 Application of Games to Processing

On February 6, 1952, L. Ron Hubbard addressed the general public, including many members of the faculty and student bodies of the Wichita and Friends Universities at the Arcadia Theatre in Wichita, Kansas.

5202C06 Dianetics, The Modern Miracle

The Hubbard College Lectures. On February 12th 1952 L. Ron Hubbard founded the Hubbard College in Wichita, Kansas. During February he delivered the following lectures to professional auditing course students.

5202C18 Code of Honor
5202C18 Care of the Body (and the cycle of birth, growth, decay and death)
5202C25 HPC-1 Review of Progress of Dianetics and Dianetics Business

5202C25 HPC-2/3/4 Summary Aberrative Incidents (before t begins, Fac 1, helper, 300-400 ba motivator for violence, basic overt acts, world closed in incide how early track eases up, overt incidents—resumé of how these i dents run)

The Summary Course Lectu During March 1952 L. Ron Hubb gave the following lectures to fessional course students at Hubbard College.

5203C03 HCL-1 Introduction Scientology: Milestone One
5203C03 HCL-2 Introduction Scientology: Outline of Therapy
5203C03 HCL-2A Demonstrat by Ron of E-Meter, Running Entit
5203C04 HCL-3 Axioms and H They Apply to Auditing
5203C04 HCL-4 Thought, Emot and Effort, and the Tone Scale
5203C04 HCL-Spec Description of Facsimile One
5203C05 HCL-5 Thought and Preclears
5203C05 HCL-6 Emotion
5203C05 HCL-6A Question and Answer Period
5203C05 HCL-Spec Demonstration of Auditing
5203C06 HCL-7 Effort and Counter-Effort
5203C06 HCL-8 Attack on the P clear
5203C07 HCL-9 How to Han Facsimiles
5203C07 HCL-10 Indoctrination the Preclear
5203C08 HCL-11 Resolution of fort and Counter-Effort, Overt Ac
5203C08 HCL-12 Indoctrination Use of E-Meter, Parts 1 & 2
5203C08 HCL-12A Indoctrinat in Use of E-Meter, Part 3
5203C09 HCL-13 Thought, E tion and Effort, and Counter-Effor
5203C09 HCL-14 Demonstrati Effort, Counter-Effort (Straightwi
5203C10 HCL-15 Training A tors: The Anatomy of Facsimile O
5203C10 HCL-16 The Anatomy Facsimile One—Demo (cont'd)
5203C10 HCL-17 Three Dem strations—Running Effort a Counter-Effort
5203C10 HCL-18 Entities (Dem stration cont'd)
5203C10 HCL-19 History of M Series I: Organization of Dat Series II: Main theta line & s theta line (description of the phil phies and religions as routes to derstanding)
5203C10 HCL-20 History of M Series III: The theta and gene lines of earth—Series IV: Princi incidents of the theta line
5203C__ HCL-21 Anatomy of Theta Body
5203C__ HCL-22 How to Audi Theta Line
5203C22 HCL-23 Theta Bodies
5203C22 HCL-23A The Impulse the Thetan

5203C__ HCL-24 Demonstration: Electropsychometric Scouting

5203C__ HCL-24A Theta Bodies

5203C25 HCL-25 An Analysis of Memory and Human Aberration and Psychosomatic Illness, Part I

5203C25 HCL-26 An Analysis of Memory, Part II

5203C__ HCL-27 How to Search for Incidents on the Track—I

5203C__ HCL-27A How to Search for Incidents on the Track—II

5204C__ HCL-Spec Electropsychometric Scouting—Battle of the Universes (MSH audits Ron)

On 30 March 1952 L. Ron Hubbard opened a new office in Phoenix, Arizona. These lectures were the first given in Phoenix.

5204C15 Phoenix Talk about Wichita and Purcell

5204C15 Theta Body Lecture

5204C15 Demonstration and Brief Explanation (whole track and bodies in pawn)

5204C16 Anatomy of the Theta Body

5204C16 "Theta-Psychometer": Theta body demonstration

5204C20 The Goals and Purposes of Theta and MEST

5205C06 Anatomy of Thought

The Technique 80 Lectures. Transcripts of L. Ron Hubbard's Technique 80 lectures were rewritten as *Professional Course Books* 28 through 31. These lectures follow.

5205C19 T80-1A ARC Triangle in Relation to Infinity, Beingness Along the Dynamics

5205C19 T80-1B Definition of Technique 80, Emotional Wavelengths

5205C19 T80-1C Tone and Ability

5205C19 T80-1D Wavelength and Tone Scale

5205C20 T80-2A Decision: Maybes, Time, postulates, cause and effect in relation to dynamics

5205C20 580-2B. Early Methods of Dealing with People, Entities

5205C21 T80-3A Therapy Section of 80: Clearing up overt acts, dependencies

5205C21 T80-3B Therapy Section of 80 (cont'd)

The Summer Session—Technique 88 Lectures. Nearly a hundred auditors attended the Summer Session in Phoenix, Arizona, June 23rd through June 28. Those attending the session were given twenty-two hours of lecture by L. Ron Hubbard on the developments of Scientology in the field of processing.

5206C23 T88-1A Technique 88: Course outline, disentangling body from the thetan, wide open and occluded case, what are entities, thetan body, anatomy of maybe, the time scale, decision to be

5206C23 T88-1B Technique 88: Matter, solid thought, home universe, theory of origin of MEST, erasing law on time scale, incidents, space and time, restimulation, for-

getting, emotional curve, identity, auditing

5206C23 T88-1C Technique 88: Mechanics of aberration, tone scale and maybe, axioms, effort, nowness and thenness, axioms of knowingness, pervasion, Q & A

5206C24 T88-2A Technique 88: Motion and maybes, attention unit flows, flares, hypnosis, control, shock

5206C24 T88-2B Technique 88: Tone scale of attention unit behavior, formation of ridges, around hollow spots, attention unit running, motionless areas, apathy incident

5206C24 T88-2C Technique 88: Concept running, DEDs, aloneness, obsession and motion

5206C24 T88-3A Validation and Invalidation

5206C24 T88-3B Overt Acts, Motivators and DEDs

5206C24 T88-3C Overt Acts, Motivators and DEDs (cont'd)

5206C25 T88-4A Invalidation, simplicity of data, counter-effort, aberrated thought, overt acts, motivators, DEDs

5206C25 T88-4B Technique 88 and the Whole Track

5206C25 T88-4C Technique 88 and the Whole Track (cont'd)

5206C26 T88-5A The Anatomy of Dramatization, the Actions of Energy

5206C26 T88-5B Acquisition of Bodies

5206C26 T88-5C Theta and Genetic Lines

5206C27 T88-6A Confusion, Action of Track as Result of Energy Behavior

5206C27 T88-6B Symbological Processing

5206C28 T88-7A Individualism

5206C28 T88-7B Q & A Period

The Technique 88 Supplementary Lectures, 8 July through 4 September 1952. L. Ron Hubbard gave the following additional lectures on Technique 88 to students at Hubbard College in Phoenix, Arizona.

5207C08 T88 Supp-1A Standard Process of 88, Black and White, Part A

5207C08 T88 Supp-1B Standard Process of 88, Black and White, Part B

5207C08 T88 Supp-1C Standard Process of 88, Black and White, Part C

5207C08 T88 Supp-1D Standard Process of 88, Black and White, Part D

5207C24 T88 Supp-2A Behavior of Energy as it Applies to Thought Flows

5207C24 T88 Supp-2B E-Meter Behavior Versus Flow Lines and Patterns

5208C07 T88 Supp-3A Straightwire 88

5208C07 T88 Supp-3B Standard Process of 88

5208C07 T88 Supp-3C A Straightwire Process

5208C07 T88 Supp-3D A Straightwire Process

5208C08 Title unknown

5208C28 Talk for Associates about Fellowships

5209C04 T88 Supp Where We Are At

5209C04 T88 Supp Creation and Use of Energy (remedy for over and under abundance)

5209C___ T88 Supp Black and White Processing

Technique 88 Supplementary Lectures. Lectures given by L. Ron Hubbard in London, England, to the London Professional Course Students.

5209C21 T88 Supp Basics of Scientology and Dianetics

5209C21 T88 Supp Basics of Scientology—Nature of Flows (elasticity of flows)

5209C21 T88 Supp Basics of Scientology—Stuck Flows

5209C22 T88 Supp Scientology—Tone Scale Characteristics

5209C22 T88 Supp Scientology—Flows, Tone Scale

5209C23 T88 Supp The Resolution of the Second Dynamic—Case Level V

5209C23 T88 Supp Blanketing—Exteriorization

5209C24 T88 Supp Scientology—The Three Types of Energy Flows

5209C24 T88 Supp Activity of the Auditor (in Theta Clearing)

The Standard Operating Procedure for Theta Clearing Lectures. The material in these lectures given by L. Ron Hubbard to the professional course in London, England, in October, 1952, was incorporated into the professional auditor's courses then being given in Philadelphia, Pennsylvania, and Phoenix, Arizona.

5210C__ SOP-1 Title unknown

5210C__ SOP-2 Title unknown

5210C__ SOP-3 Title unknown

5210C__ SOP-4A "Summary of Technique 8-80", Thetans, G.E. Line

5210C__ SOP-4B Present Time Use of Energy Manifestations

5210C__ SOP-5A Theory of Flows—Counter-Elasticity

5210C__ SOP-5B Flows

5210C__ SOP-5C Basics of Scientology—Black and White Processing, Discharging Flows

5210C__ SOP-6A Basic Summary on SOP of Technique 8-80

5210C__ SOP-6B Phenomena of the Thetan

5210C__ SOP-7A Service Facsimile Chain (Section E, Act 5. SOP, Scientology 8-80 Making a Theta Clear)

5210C30 SOP-8A The Role of Earth (incidents from the fourth and fifth invader forces—their brief role on earth as a prison)

5210C30 SOP-8B Illusion Processing and Therapy

L. Ron Hubbard gave several lectures in London, England, from the 1st to the 16th of November 1952.

5211C01 Resolution of Effort and Counter-Effort

5211C06 LS-1 Methods of Research, the Thetan as an Energy Unit

5211C06 LS-2 Creating Different Space and Time—Responsibility—Code of Honor

5211C07 LS-3 Have as *Homo sapiens* and as Thetans, Clearing by Communication "Have"

5211C14 LS-4 Be, Have, Do (time, space, energy, in relation to do)

5211C16 LS-5 MEST-Self-MEST Universe in Connection with Creative Processing

The Logics and Axioms Lectures. These lectures were given by L. Ron Hubbard in London, England, from the 10th to the 12th of November 1952.

5211C10 L&A-1&2 Introduction—The Q List and Beginning of Logics *Translations:* Danish, Swedish.

5211C10 L&A-3&4 Logics 1-7 *Translations:* Danish, Swedish.

5211C12 L&A-5&6 Precision Knowledge—Necessity to Know Terminology and Law

5211C12 L&A-7&8 Logics 7-9 and 10-23 *Translations:* Danish, Swedish.

The London Professional Course Lectures (Standard Operating Procedure, Issue 2) were given by L. Ron Hubbard to the students on the London Professional Course at London, England.

5211C10 LPC-1 Introduction to the Course—Definitions of Dianetics and Scientology, other philosophies, Scientology 8-8008

5211C12 LPC-2 8-8008 Continued, Time and Space

5211C14 LPC-3 Time, Create, Destroy, Have

5211C14 LPC-4&5 Standard Operating Procedure, Issue 2, Steps 7, 6 & 5

5211C14 LPC-6&7 SOP Issue 2, Step 5 (cont'd) and Creative Processing Assessment

5211C17 LPC-8 ARC

5211C17 LPC-8A ARC (cont'd)

5211C17 LPC-9 ARC, Motion, Emotion, Tone Scale, Flows, Ridges

5211C17 LPC-10 Creative Processing—the basic anatomy of creative processing, MEST universe, MEST, self universe, hypnotism, Part I

5211C17 LPC-11 Ridges

5211C17 LPC-11 Ridges, Self-Determinism—Tone Scales

5211C19 LPC-12 Attention, Part I

5211C19 LPC-13 Attention, Part II

5211C19 LPC-14 The Control of the Individual by an Unknown

5211C19 LPC-14A What is Cause

5211C19 LPC-15 Responsibility

5211C19 LPC-15 Responsibility (cont'd), Tone Scale of Responsibility

5211C20 LPC-16 Creative Processing, Lecture 1, Validation of MEST, Have and Agree

5211C20 LPC-17 Creative Processing, Lecture 2, Validation of MEST, Have and Agree (cont'd)

5211C20 LPC-18 Creative Processing Directed Toward Breaking Pc's

Agreement with Natural Laws of the MEST Universe, Lecture 3

5211C20 LPC-18A Creative Processing (cont'd)

5211C20 LPC-19 Creative Processing (cont'd), Lecture 4

5211C20 LPC-19A Creative Processing (cont'd)

5211C21 LPC-20 Assessment of Pc —The Dynamics: Be, Have, Do

5211C21 LPC-21 Creative Processing—How Different Levels of the Tone Scale React in Regard to Handling Illusions

5211C21 LPC-21A Structure and Function as Regards Mechanisms of Processing—Clearing by Communication, "Have"

The Philadelphia Doctorate Lectures were given in Philadelphia, Pennsylvania, from Monday, 1 December, through Friday, 19 December 1952. The material covered included a wide analysis of human behavior, the handling and control of *Homo sapiens*, the highest level of atomic and molecular phenomena, a complete coverage of Standard Operating Procedure, Issue Five, and a full expansion of the new professional course textbook, *Scientology 8-8008*.

5212C01 PDC-1 Scientology: How to Understand and Study It

5212C01 PDC-2 E-Meter: Description, Demonstration

5212C01 PCD-3 Creative Processing, Demonstration of E-Meter Auditing

5212C02 PDC-4 Locks, Secondaries, Engrams, How to Handle

5212C02 PDC-5 Gradient Scales of Handling Space, Energy and Objects

5212C02 PDC-6 The "Q": Highest Level of Knowledge, Axioms, Energy Phenomena of Thought and Facsimiles, Differentiation *Translations:* Danish, Swedish.

5212C02 PDC-7 A Thetan Creates (MEST) by Postulates—Q2

5212C03 PDC-8 The Track of Thetan/G.E., Space/Time

5212C03 PDC-9 Anatomy of Processing—Energy Phenomena/Sensation

5212C03 PDC-10 Specific Parts of Self-Determinism, Spacation

5212C04 PDC-11 Spacation: Energy Particles and Time

5212C04 PDC-12 Spacation: Locating, Space, Time

5212C04 PDC-13 Spacation: Anchor Points, Origin

5212C04 PDC-14 The Logics: Methods of Thinking

5212C04 PDC-15 The Logics: Infinity-valued Logic

5212C05 PDC-16 Cycles of Action

5212C05 PDC-17 The Tone Scale: Moving the Preclear up the Scale

5212C05 PDC-18 Conditions of Space/Time/Energy

5212C06 PDC-19 Axioms and Logics—Further Data

5212C06 PDC-20 Formative State of Scientology: Definition of Logic

5212C08 PDC-21 ARC/Cycles: Theory and Automaticity

5212C08 PDC-22 More on Automaticity

5212C08 PDC-23 ARC, Force, Be/Do/Have

5212C09 PDC-24 What's Wrong With This Universe: A Working Package for Auditor

5212C09 PDC-25 Flows: Reverse Vector of Physical Universe

5212C09 PDC-26 Flows: Characteristics of

5212C09 PDC-27 Flows: The Part Force Bears in Clearing

5212C09 PDC-28 Flows: The Part Force Bears in Clearing

5212C09 Plus and Minus

5212C10 PDC-29 Flows: Pattern of Interaction

5212C10 PDC-30 Flows: Rate of Change, Relative Size, Anchor Points

5212C10 PDC-31 Flows: Basic Agreement and Prove It!

5212C10 PDC-32 Flows: Dispersals and Ridges

5212C10 PDC-33 Anatomy of the Genetic Entity

5212C11 Single Data and Its Evaluation

5212C11 PDC-34 8-8008: Understanding the Phenomena

5212C11 PDC-35 The D.E.I. Scale

5212C11 PDC-36 Structure/Function: Selective Variations of

5212C11 PDC-37 Chart of Attitudes: Rising Scale Processing

5212C11 PDC-38 Rising Scale Processing

5212C12 PDC-39 Game Processing

5212C12 PDC-40 Games/Goals

5212C12 PDC-41 SOP Issue 3: Postulate, Creative Process

5212C13 PDC-42 Standard Operating Procedure (SOP)

5212C13 PDC-43 On Auditing—How to Succeed/Fail, Assess

5212C13 PDC-44 SOP: Assessment (cont'd)

5212C13 PDC-45 Development of Scientology: Characteristics of Living Science

5212C13 PDC-46 Goal: Rehabilitation of Thetan, Case Step 1

5212C15 PDC-47 SOP Issue 5

5212C15 PDC-48 SOP Spacation

5212C15 PDC-49 SOP Spacation (cont'd)

5212C16 PDC-50 SOP Spacation Step 3, Flow Processing

5212C16 PDC-51 SOP Issue 5

5212C16 PDC-52 Memory (Not Human Memory)

5212C16 PDC-53 Memory and Automaticity

5212C17 PDC-54 Summary to Date: Handling Step 1 and Demonstration

5212C17 PDC-55 Demonstration on Step 1 (cont'd)

5212C17 PDC-56 Discussion of Demonstration: Above Agreement With Flows

5212C17 PDC-57 Continued Demonstration Step 4

5212C18 PDC-58 About the "Press" Tone Level: Psychometry

5212C18 PDC-59 Chart of Havingness

5212C18 PDC-60 How to Talk About Scientology *Translation:* German.

5212C18 PDC-61 How to Talk to Friends About Scientology *Translations:* German, Swedish.

5212C18 PDC-62 Your Own Case: To You the Student

The following are lectures given by L. Ron Hubbard in 1952 for which there are no specific dates.

52_C_ Activity of an Auditor

52_C_ Attention Units, Tone Scale of

52_C_ Confusion—Mest Bodies

52_C_ Entities

52_C_ Phenomena of the Thetan

52_C_ Service Facsimile

1953

BOOKS

The December Lecture Charts of L. Ron Hubbard, published by the Hubbard Foundation, Philadelphia, Pennsylvania, 1953. Some 70 charts were drawn by L. Ron Hubbard in the course of the *Philadelphia Doctorate Course Lectures* and these were made into a book to be used by students studying the course in the future.

Self Analysis in Scientology—A Handbook of Self Processing in Scientology, by L. Ron Hubbard, published by the Hubbard Association of Scientologists, Philadelphia, Pennsylvania, April, 1953. This was the original *Self Analysis* adapted to Creative Processing. This edition of *Self Analysis* is out of print and the original *Self Analysis* is in use.

How To Live Though An Executive: The Hubbard Manual of Communications, by L. Ron Hubbard, published by the Hubbard Association of Scientologists, Phoenix, Arizona, April, 1953. *Translations:* Danish, Dutch, Spanish, Swedish.

L. Ron Hubbard—London Lecture Notes—March-April, 1953, compiled from the lectures of L. Ron Hub-bard, published by the Phoenix Sc entology Institute, Phoenix, Arizona 1953.

This is Scientology: The Scienc of Certainty, by L. Ron Hubbar published by the Hubbard Associa tion of Scientologists, Philadelphi Pennsylvania, June, 1953. This boo was later combined with the *Scien tology: Auditor's Handbook* an other material to make the book *Th Creation of Human Ability*.

Introduction to Scientology, take from the works of L. Ron Hubbar published by the Scientology Counci Los Angeles, California, June, 1953.

The Hubbard Foundation Note book, taken from the works of L Ron Hubbard, published by the Hub bard Foundation, Philadelphia, Penn sylvania, late 1953. This notebook was awarded to all the students wh successfully completed the course a the Foundation during the span o its existence; March 1952 throug October 1953.

On Auditing, taken from the work of L. Ron Hubbard, published in An Arbor, Michigan, late 1953.

Look Don't Think, L. Ron Hubbar Lectures, Philadelphia Congress— 1953, September 30th through Octo ber 4th 1953, published by Scientolc gy Northern California, 1953.

1953

E-METERS

Since the range of earlier meter was insufficient to register all pre clears the Model H-53-DS (Double Scale) was designed with an expand ed range and made available in 1953 The Model HM-4 was also intro duced in 1953. HM-4 stands for Hub bard Meter No. 4—the first mete being Model 1, the H-52-IR bein Model 2, the H-53-DS being Mode 3 and the HM-4 being Model 4. A four meters looked much the same The Model E-54 was presented at th First International Congress of Dia neticists and Scientologists, Septem ber 1953, in Philadelphia, Pennsy vania, but it was overly complex an was never much used in auditing.

1953

TAPED LECTURES

The London Group Auditor's Course Lectures. L. Ron Hubbard gave these lectures in early 1953, in London, England.

53_C_ LGC-1 Educational System, How to Group Process

53_C_ LGC-2 History of the Organization, Self Analysis

53_C_ LGC-3 Mechanics of the Mind, Source of Data, Group Auditing and the Tone Scale *Translations: Danish, Dutch, Spanish, Swedish.*

53_C_ LGC-4 Gradient Scales, Admiration Particle

5301C13 LGC-5 Creative Processing

5301C14 LGC-6 Group Processing and Individual Processing

5301C15 LGC-6 Mock-ups, Certainty, Group Processing

The Philadelphia Doctorate Course Supplementary Lectures were given by L. Ron Hubbard in London, England, in January, 1953.

5301C12 PDC Supp-A Agree and Disagree — Have, Not Have

5301C12 PDC Supp-B Anchor Points — Driving Them In and Out

5301C14 PDC Supp-1 SOP 5 Long Form Step I: Quality of Mock-ups at Different Levels of the Tone Scale

5301C14 PDC Supp-2 Processing of Step I: Cyclic Aspect of Scientology Research

5301C16 PDC Supp-3 SOP 5 Long Form Step II: Stage Fright, Commanding People

5301C16 PDC Supp-4 Demonstration

5301C19 PDC Supp-5 SOP Long Form Step III: Differentiation on Theta Clearing

5301C19 PDC Supp-6 SOP Long Form Step III (cont'd): Spacation

5301C21 PDC Supp-7 SOP Long Form Step IV: Gita, Space, Case Conditions

5301C21 PDC Supp-8 SOP Long Form Step IV (cont'd)

5301C23 PDC Supp-9 SOP 5 Long Form Step V

5301C23 PDC Supp-10 SOP 5 Long Form Step VI

5301C23 PDC Supp-11 Concluding Long Form of Step V — Admiration Processing

L. Ron Hubbard gave these lectures in March, 1953, in London, England.

5303C_ GR/PROC
Group Processing

5303C_ Notes on 18 Hours

The London Spring Lectures. L. Ron Hubbard gave the following series of lectures in March and April, 1953, to students in London, England.

5303C23 SPRL-1 Review of Dianetics, Scientology and Para-Dianetics/Scientology

5303C23 SPRL-2 What's Wrong With the Pc

5303C24 SPRL-3 SOP Issue 5: Steps 1 to 7

5303C24 SPRL-4 SOP Issue 5: (cont'd)

5303C25 SPRL-5 The Elements With Stress on How to Run Matched Terminals

5303C25 SPRL-6 The Elements With Stress on How to Run Matched Terminals (cont'd)

5303C26 SPRL-7 How and When to Audit

5303C26 SPRL-8 Present Time

5303C27 SPRL-9 SOP Utility

5303C27 SPRL-10 SOP Utility (cont'd)

5303C27 SPRL-11 Beingness, Agreement, Hidden Influence, Processes

5303C27 SPRL-12 Types of Processes (cont'd)

5304C07 SPRL-13 Data on Case Level 5, Step for Case 5

5304C07 SPRL-14 Data on Case Level 5 (cont'd)

5304C07 SPRL-15 Exteriorization — Demonstration and Explanation

5304C07 SPRL-16 Demonstration (cont'd)

5304C08 SPRL-17 Case Level 6 & 7

5304C08 SPRL-18 Case Level 6 & 7, Psychotic (cont'd)

On 24 April 1953, one day after he wrote The Factors, L. Ron Hubbard gave these lectures in London, England:

5304C24 SPRL-19 The Factors

5304C24 SPRL-20 SOP 8

The Birmingham Lectures. Lectures given by L. Ron Hubbard in Birmingham, England, 21 May 1953.

5305C21 BL-1 Three Universes

5305C21 BL-2 Three Universes (cont'd)

5305C21 BL-3 Tone Scale — ARC, Present Time

5305C21 BL-4 Tone Scale (cont'd)

These two lectures were given by L. Ron Hubbard in London, England, upon his return from a three month stay in Spain.

5309C03 Training Auditors

5309C23 G.E. Track, Exteriorization

The First International Congress of Dianeticists and Scientologists Lectures, given September 30 through October 4, 1953 to nearly 300 delegates attending, at the Broadwood Hotel in Philadelphia, Pennsylvania.

5309C30 ICDS-1 History and Development of Dianetics

5309C30 ICDS-2 The Problem to Be Solved/The Elements of a Problem

5310C01 ICDS-3 Processing and Its Goals

5310C01 ICDS-4 The Most Favorable Processes

5310C01 ICDS-5 SOP-8

5310C01 ICDS-5A Demonstration — The Use of Q & A

5310C01 ICDS-6 SOP-8

5310C02 ICDS-7 SOP-8, Additional Material

5310C02 ICDS-8 SOP-8, Step 1, 2, 3

5310C02 ICDS-9 SOP-8

5310C03 ICDS-10 Six Steps to Better Beingness

5310C03 ICDS-11 Uses and Future of Scientology

5310C03 ICDS-12 Processes for Rough Cases

5310C04 ICDS-13 Wasting

5310C04 ICDS-14 Effort

The First American Advanced Clinical Indoctrination Course Lectures, given in Camden, New Jersey, 5 October to 14 November 1953, proved so popular that a 2nd Advanced Clinical Course had to be scheduled for the 16th of November.

5310C06 AICL-1A Looking, Definition of Static

5310C07 AICL-1B Q & A, Step V

5310C07 AICL-2A Exteriorization

5310C08 AICL-2B Thetan Control, Handling Occlusion, Parts I & II

5310C08 AICL-3A Occlusion, Resolve of

5310C09 AICL-3B Psychotics, Classification of Cases

5310C09 AICL-4A Occluded Case

5310C12 AICL-4B Exteriorization, Difficult Cases

5310C12 AICL-5A SOP: Step II

5310C12 AICL-5B SOP: Step II (cont'd)

5310C13 AICL-6A Anesthesia in Bodies, Parts I & II

5310C13 AICL-6B Anesthesia in Bodies, Part III

5310C14 AICL-7A Randomity, Control and Prediction, Part I

5310C14 AICL-7B Randomity, Control and Prediction, Part II

5310C14 AICL-8A Inverted Dynamics

5310C15 AICL-8B Thinking Action, Machines

5310C16 AICL-9A Subjective Processes

5310C16 AICL-9B Subjective Processes (cont'd)

5310C16 AICL-10A Subjective Processes (cont'd)

5310C17 AICL-10B Thinking Processes

5310C17 AICL-11A Forget and Remember, Good and Evil

5310C19 AICL-11B Forget and Remember, Good and Evil (cont'd)

5310C19 AICL-12A Change Processes, Action

5310C19 AICL—12B Change Processes (cont'd)

5310C20 AICL-13A Certainty of Anchor Points Processing

5310C21 AICL-13B Liabilities of Being Processed

5310C21 AICL-14A Processing to Step I

5310C21 AICL-14B Speed Up-Wasting

5310C22 AICL-15A Wasting Effects, etc.

5310C22 AICL-15B Wasting Effects (cont'd), Looking

5310C23 AICL-16A Looking

5310C23 AICL-16B Change Processing

5310C26 AICL-17A Restimulation of Engrams, Experiences

5310C26 AICL-17B An Assumption, Lines, Chords, Havingness

5310C26 AICL-18A Time, Assumption, Facsimiles, Overt Acts, DEDs

5310C27 AICL-18B Fixed Attention, Duplication, How to Audit Children

5310C27 AICL-19A Assessment, Memories, Ridges; Demonstration: Acceptance Level Processing

5310C27 AICL-19B Acceptance Level Processing (cont'd)

5310C28 AICL-20A Case Reports, SOP-8C, SOP-8L

5310C28 AICL-20B SOP-8L (cont'd)

5310C28 AICL-21A Anchor Points, Space, Games, Indicated Drills of Processes

5310C29 AICL-21B Spacation, Anchor Points and Attention

5310C29 AICL-22A Study of the Particle

5310C29 AICL-22B Study of the Particle (cont'd)

5310C30 AICL-23A The Particle With Regard to Time (cont'd)

5310C30 AICL-23B Consideration, Extent of Viewpoint, Step III Commands

5310C30 AICL-24A Part 1 — How to Run Change Processing

5310C30 AICL-24AA Part 2 — Considerations and the MEST Universe

5311C02 AICL-24B "Cause and Effect, Automaticity, Ridges" Processing

5311C02 AICL-25A Occluded Case Reports — Black Spot Processing, Certainty

5311C03 AICL-25B The Logics — Their Relation to Aberration and Space

5311C03 AICL-26A Anchor Points and Space (cont'd)

5311C03 AICL-26B The Logics, Part 2

5311C04 AICL-27A Randomity and Automaticity, Process to Resolve

5311C04 AICL-27B Process to Resolve Randomity and Automaticity (cont'd)

5311C04 AICL-28A Process to Resolve Randomity and Automaticity (cont'd)

5311C05 AICL-28B Certainty

5311C05 AICL-29A Communication — ARC — Demonstration

5311C05 AICL-29B Communication — ARC — Demonstration — Space (cont'd)

5311C06 AICL-30A Inverted Dynamics, Inflow-Outflow, Material, Time

5311C06 AICL-30AA Inverted Dynamics (cont'd)

5311C06 AICL-30B Space

5311C06 AICL-30BB Demonstration: Havingness, Energy, etc.

5311C09 **AICL-31A** Randomly, Anchor Points, etc.

5311C09 **AICL-31B** Randomly, Anchor Points (cont'd)

5311C09 **AICL-31BB** Exteriorization by Feeling

5311C09 **AICL-32A** Exteriorization by Feeling (cont'd)

5311C10 **AICL-32B** Types of Processes, Space, Create-Destroy

5311C10 **AICL-33A** SOP-8C Steps

5311C10 **AICL-33B** SOP-8C Steps (cont'd)

5311C11 **AICL-34A** Group Processing

5311C11 **AICL-34B** Future Processing

5311C11 **AICL-35A** Questions: SOP-8C, 3 Universes, SOP-8, Significances, Exteriorization

5311C12 **AICL-35B** Process to Use on Cases, Gradient Scales

5311C12 **AICL-36A** Process to Run by Gradient Scale on Specific Cases

5311C12 **AICL-36AA** Self-Determinism in Relation to a Thetan

5311C12 **AICL-36B** Gradient Scale Straightwire (cont'd)

5311C12 **AICL-37A** Gradient Scale Straightwire Demonstration

5311C12 **AICL-37B** Gradient Scale Straightwire Demonstration (cont'd)

5311C13 **AICL-38A** Final Talk on First Course

5311C13 **AICL-38B** Last Lecture of Advanced Course, Camden 1953, Reviewing Student's Ability to Process

5311C13 **AICL-38C** Group Processing After Afternoon Lecture

The 2nd American Advanced Clinical Course Lectures. L. Ron Hubbard gave the following lectures to the students on the 2nd American Advanced Clinical Course in Camden, New Jersey, between 17 November and 22 December 1953.

5311C17 **2ACC-1A** Opening Lecture: Emotional Tone Scale

5311C17 **2ACC-1B** SOP-8C First Lecture

5311C17 **2ACC-2A** Getting Up Speed—Part I

5311C17 **2ACC-2B** Getting Up Speed—Part II

5311C18 **2ACC-3A** Step I of 8-C, Beingness

5311C18 **2ACC-3B** Black Mock-ups, Persistence, MEST

5311C18 **2ACC-4A** Step II, Automaticities

5311C18 **2ACC-4B** Waste a Machine

5311C19 **2ACC-5A** Effects, Reaching End of Cycle

5311C19 **2ACC-5B** More on Machines

5311C20 **2ACC-6A** Resistance to Effect

5311C20 **2ACC-6B** Plan of Auditing

5311C23 **2ACC-7A** Formula "Phi," Creation of MEST

5311C23 **2ACC-7B** Summary of Steps I, II, III of SOP-8C

5311C24 **2ACC-8A** Anchor Points, Knowingness of Location

5311C24 **2ACC-8B** Steps 5, 6, 7; Duplication, Unconsciousness (also known as The Death Wish)

5311C24 **2ACC-8BX** Additional Remarks

5311C25 **2ACC-91** Steps 5, 6, 7; Time

5311C25 **2ACC-9B** SOP-8C, Summary of

5311C25 **2ACC-9** Machines, Attention

5311C26 **2ACC-10A** Electronic Theory, Anchor Points

5311C26 **2ACC-10B** Exteriorization

5311C26 **2ACC-10BX** Additional Remarks

5311C27 **2ACC-11A** Anchor Points, Justice

5311C27 **2ACC-11B** Symbols

5311C28 **2ACC-12A** Wasting Machines

5311C28 **2ACC-12B** Machine Duplication

5311C28 **2ACC-12** Demonstration: Group Processing

5311C28 **2ACC-12** Special Session —Experimental Process

5311C28 **2ACC-12** 2nd Demonstration: Group Processing

5311C30 **2ACC-12BX** Additional Remarks—Experimental Session

5311C30 **2ACC-13AA** Space, Perception, Knowingness

5311C30 **2ACC-13A** MEST Universe Agreements—Time a Single Terminal—Barriers—Problems

5312C01 **2ACC-13B** Space, Lack of, Resistance

5312C02 **2ACC-14A** Ron Junior Remarks on 2ACC-13 A&B

5312C02 **2ACC-14B** Blackness

5312C03 **2ACC-15A** Time as a Barrier

5312C03 **2ACC-15B** Time, Cause and Effect

5312C03 **2ACC-15BX** Additional Remarks

5312C04 **2ACC-16A** Plan of SOP-8C

5312C04 **2ACC-16B** LRH Questions the Class on Exteriorization

5312C07 **2ACC-17A** Barriers, Occlusion

5312C07 **2ACC-17B** Outline of SOP-8C

5312C08 **2ACC-18A** Essence of SOP-8C

5312C08 **2ACC-18B** Problems of Auditing

5312C09 **2ACC-19A** Summary: The Dynamics

5312C09 **2ACC-19B** Bodies

5312C10 **2ACC-20A** Knowingness

5312C10 **2ACC-20B** SOP-8C: General Discussion

5312C11 **2ACC-21A** SOP-8C: Patter

5312C13 **2ACC-21B** Force—Part I

5312C13 **2ACC-22A** Force—Part II

5312C14 **2ACC-22B** SOP-8C: Step 8, Definitions

5312C14 **2ACC-23A** Cause and Effect, Assignment of Cause, G.E.

5312C15 **2ACC-23B** SOP-8C: Step 5

5312C15 **2ACC-24A** Energy Problems

5312C16 **2ACC-24B** Techniques Which Do or Do Not Assign Cause/Technique To Assign Cause

5312C16 **2ACC-25A** Comm Line: Overt Act-Motivator Sequence

5312C17 **2ACC-25B** SOP-8C: Formulas

5312C17 **2ACC-26A** Space Opera

5312C18 **2ACC-26B** The Only One

5312C18 **2ACC-27A** Beingness

5312C18 **2ACC-27B** SOP-8C: General

5312C18 Philadelphia 1953 last hour

5312C19 **2ACC-28A** Mass

5312C__ Mocking Up Mass, Putting It on Head

5312C20 **2ACC-28B** Communicating

5312C20 **2ACC-29A** Auditing by SOP-8C, Formula H

5312C20 **2ACC-29B** Reach/Withdraw

5312C21 **2ACC-30A** Ability to Accept Direction

5312C21 **2ACC-30B** Knowingness and Certainty

5312C21 **2ACC-30C** State of Man Today

5312C21 **2ACC-30D** Group Processing

5312C22 **2ACC-31A** Remedy of Havingness

5312C22 **2ACC-31B** Postulates

5312C22 Organization of Man

5312C22 Group Processing

5312C23 Problem of Auditing Handled

Lectures given by L. Ron Hubbard in December, 1953.

5312C__ Chart of Attitudes

5312C__ Exteriorizing—Group Auditing

5312C__ Group Auditing—Tone Scale

The International Congress of Dianeticists and Scientologists Lectures. L. Ron Hubbard presented over forty lectures during 28 through 31 December 1953, to the delegates of the International Congress in Phoenix, Arizona. Of these many were group auditing sessions using techniques recently perfected in the Camden Advanced Clinical Courses.

5312C28 Cycle of Action

5312C28 **PHC-1** Goals of Scientology

5312C28 **PHC-2** Goals of Scientology (cont'd)

5312C28 **PHC-2A** Mock-ups, Energy

5312C28 **PHC-3** Basic Theory of Definitions

5312C28 **PHC-4** Basic Theory of Definitions (cont'd), Group Processing

5312C28 **PHC-5** Group Processing

5312C28 **PHC-6** Group Processing

5312C28 **PHC-7** How to Be a Group Auditor

5312C28 **PHC-8** How to Be a Group Auditor

5312C28 **PHC-9** Group Processing

5312C28 **PHC-10** Group Processing (cont'd)

5312C29 **PHC-11** Create, Survive, Destroy Curve

5312C29 **PHC-12** Duplication

5312C29 **PHC-13** Use of SOP-8C

5312C29 **PHC-14** Use of SOP-8C

5312C29 **PHC-15** Role of the Auditor

5312C29 **PHC-16** Demonstration (Group Process)

5312C29 **PHC-17** Group Processing —Short Lecture

5312C29 **PHC-18** Group Processing

5312C29 **PHC-19** Design of SOP-8C: Processes for Groups, Percentages of Successes and Failures

5312C29 **PHC-20** SOP-8C (cont'd)

5312C29 **PHC-21** Group Process

5312C29 **PHC-22** Group Process

5312C29 Havingness

5312C30 **PHC-23** Talk on E-Meter

5312C30 **PHC-24** Talk on E-Meter (cont'd)

5312C30 **PHC-25** Automaticity

5312C30 **PHC-26** Beingness

5312C30 **PHC-27** Title not Available

5312C30 **PHC-28** Title not Available

5312C30 **PHC-29** Title not Available

5312C30 **PHC-30** Title not Available

5312C30 **PHC-31** Group Processing

5312C30 **PHC-32** Group Processing

5312C31 **PHC-33** Step 5, SOP-8C (Group Processing)

5312C31 **PHC-34** Emotions in MEST (Group Processing)

5312C31 **PHC-35** Group Processing, Short Lecture

5312C31 **PHC-36** Group Processing

5312C31 **PHC-37** Group Processing Step I, SOP-8C

5312C31 **PHC-38** Through Barrier to Nothingness

5312C31 **PHC-39** Group Process for HAS Associate Group

5312C__ **PHC** Group Processing— Reach and Withdraw Across the Dynamics

5312C31 Group Process for HAS Associate Groups

The following lectures were given by L. Ron Hubbard during the year 1953. The specific dates are unknown.

53_:C__ Exteriorization-Interiorization

53__C__ Group Processing

53__C__ Power of Choice

53__C__ Raising Abilities

1954

BOOKS

Group Auditor's Handbook, by L. Ron Hubbard, published by the Hubbard Association of Scientologists International, Phoenix, Arizona, June, 1954. The *Group Auditor's Handbook, Volume One,* was released at the Universe Processes Congress given in Phoenix, where it was made available to delegates and used by seminar leaders.

Scientology: Auditor's Handbook —Including Intensive Procedure, by L. Ron Hubbard, published by the Hubbard Association of Scientologists International, Phoenix, Arizona, August, 1954. (This book combined with other material was published as *The Creation of Human Ability*, 1955.)

Group Auditor's Handbook, Volume Two, by L. Ron Hubbard, published by the Hubbard Association of Scientologists International, Phoenix, Arizona, September, 1954.

Dianetics 55!, by L. Ron Hubbard, was published in April, 1955. A limited manuscript edition was available at the Unification Congress in Phoenix, Arizona, December, 1954. *Dianetics 55!* was published by the Hubbard Dianetics Research Foundation, Phoenix, Arizona. *Translations:* Danish, Dutch, French, German, Spanish, Swedish.

Scientology Workbook, taken from the works of L. Ron Hubbard, published by the Hubbard Association of Scientologists International, Phoenix, Arizona, June, 1954.

1954

E-METERS

Though more a curiosity than an auditing tool, the "Beep" meter was first available in 1954. It would give off a sound—a beep—when a probe was connected to a painful area of the body. Lecture No. 34 of the 3rd American ACC was entitled "Audio

(Beep) Meter Demo" in which L. Ron Hubbard demonstrated and discussed this meter. The beep meters available in 1954 were the AR (Audio Registration)-4 SPECIAL, the AR-5 and later in the year the E-AR-400. Fancier and more complex meters were also made available during 1954—few were ever used in auditing. These were the E-400-A and E-400-B models. These were the last of the Mathison meters. In the years 1955 through 1957 E-Meters were not generally in use.

1954

INSIGNIA

The Hubbard Association of Scientologists International was formed in the Spring of 1954. Its purpose is to disseminate Scientology, to advance and protect its membership, to hold the lines and data of Scientology clean and clear, to educate and process people toward the goal of a civilized age on Earth second to none, to survive on all dynamics.

The Minister's Medallion and Pin

The minister's ceremonial medallion and ribbon was first introduced in 1953 or 1954.

It is a gold cross on a white field, 2 1/2 inches in diameter, 3/8" thick. The ribbon is black.

The minister's lapel pin is the same design as the minister's medallion, but lapel pin size.

These insignia are worn by ordained ministers of the Church of Scientology.

1954

TAPED LECTURES

The 3rd American Advanced Clinical Course Lectures. L. Ron Hubbard gave the following lectures to the students attending the 3rd American Advanced Clinical Course in Phoenix, Arizona, 4 January through 12 February 1954.

5401C04 3ACC-1 Introduction to 3rd ACC

5401C04 3ACC-2 Perception and Ownership

5401C05 3ACC-3 Communication and Not Over-instructing the Pc

5401C05 3ACC-4 Boredom, Pace of Living, Truth

5401C05 3ACC-5 Symbols and a Group Processing Demonstration

5401C06 3ACC-6A Symbols and a Group Processing Demonstration (cont'd)

5401C06 3ACC-6B Symbols and a Group Processing Demonstration (cont'd)

5401C06 3ACC-7 Processing Demonstration: Randomity & Automaticity

5401C07 3ACC-8 Communication

5401C07 3ACC-9 Anchor Points, Flows

5401C08 3ACC-10 Exteriorization from Masses

5401C11 3ACC-11 How to Know What Pc is Doing, Opening Procedure & Variations (also issued as—Exteriorization from Masses—cont'd)

5401C11 3ACC-12 Exteriorization, Theory & Demonstration

5401C11 3ACC-13 Exteriorization Demonstration (cont'd)

5401C11 3ACC-13B Agreement, Motion & Perception

5401C12 3ACC-14 Exteriorization and Motion—Acceptance & Rejection of Ideas

5401C12 3ACC-15 Exteriorization, Lecture & Demonstration

5401C12 3ACC-16 Exteriorization, Demonstration on Groups

5401C12 3ACC-17 Machines, Demonstration

5401C12 3ACC-17 SPL Special Message from L. Ron Hubbard to London Congress of Dianeticists and Scientologists

5401C13 3ACC-18 Competence of Prediction, Demonstration

5401C13 3ACC-19 Competence of Prediction, Demonstration (cont'd)

5401C13 3ACC-20 Exteriorization: Step I, Procedure

5401C14 3ACC-21 Labels: In Society and Preclears

5401C14 3ACC-22 Labels: Beingness and Justice

5401C14 3ACC-23 Labels: Beingness and Justice (cont'd)

5401C15 3ACC-24 Present Time, Self Analysis

5401C15 3ACC-25 Present Time (cont'd)

5401C15 3ACC-26 Present Time (cont'd) & Demonstration

5401C18 3ACC-27 Time: Barrier

5401C18 3ACC-28 Time: Basic Process on

5401C18 3ACC-29 Time: Sense, Particles, Survival Place

5401C18 3ACC-29-1 Processing Time on a Group

5401C19 3ACC-30 Summary of Course to Date

5401C19 3ACC-31 Exteriorization: Demonstration

5401C19 3ACC-32 Comm by Emotion: Flows, Ridges

5401C19 3ACC-32-1 Group Processing

5401C20 3ACC-33 E-Meter, Use of

5401C20 3ACC-34 Audio (Beep) Meter Demonstration

5401C20 3ACC-35 Exteriorization, Communication in Theta & MEST

5401C21 3ACC-36 Livingness Processing Series

5401C21 3ACC-37 Livingness Processing Series (Dyingness)

5401C22 3ACC-38 Livingness Processing Series (Machinery)

5401C22 3ACC-39 Livingness Processing Series (Demonstration)

5401C22 New York Congress Introduction—L. Ron Hubbard

5401C25 3ACC-40 Goals of 8-0 (O.T.), Abilities

5401C25 3ACC-41 Basic Data on 8-0 (O.T.)

5401C26 3ACC-42 Exteriorization, Knowingness, Reality

5401C26 3ACC-42A Instruction, Simplicity—Static & Zero, Science, Reason Why

5401C27 3ACC-43 O.T., Inversion: Courage and Mobility

5401C28 3ACC-44 Exteriorization: Courage and Serenity

5401C28 3ACC-45 Courage Processing

5401C29 3ACC-46 Parked Personality: Exteriorization, Stuck Flows

5401C29 3ACC-47 Evaluating Cases

5402C01 3ACC-48 Exteriorization, Taking Direction

5402C01 3ACC-49 Processing Havingness Lecture

5402C02 3ACC-50 Havingness Series (cont'd): Acceptance and Rejection of Havingness

5402C02 3ACC-51 Havingness Series (cont'd): Comm Lines

5402C03 3ACC-52 Havingness Series (cont'd): Ownership

5402C03 3ACC-53 Repairing a Case & Demonstration

5402C04 3ACC-54 Review on Havingness & Demonstration

5402C04 3ACC-55 Certainty: Maybes, Problems, Entrance

5402C05 3ACC-56 Endowment of Livingness: Extroverting Attention

5402C05 3ACC-57 Group Processing on Certainty, 8 Dynamics

5402C08 3ACC-58 Summary of Course Data & Machinery

5402C08 3ACC-59 Group Processing, Automaticities

5402C09 3ACC-60 Auditing Groups

5402C09 3ACC-61 Group Processing on Class: Barriers

5402C09 3ACC-62 Short Discussion & Group Processing Demonstration

5402C10 3ACC-63 Group Processing on Class: Being MEST

5402C10 3ACC-64 Group Processing on Class: Black/White

5402C10 3ACC-65 Group Processing on Class: Being MEST

5402C11 3ACC-66 Group Processing on Class: Things to Be

5402C11 3ACC-67 Group Processing on Class: Resist Effect

5402C11 3ACC-68 Group Processing: Exterior

5402C11 3ACC-69 Group Processing on Class: Sound

5402C12 3ACC-70 Group Processing on Class: Balance

5402C12 3ACC-71 Group Processing on Class: Time

The 4th American Advanced Clinical Course Lectures. In this course L. Ron Hubbard gave the students several weeks of Group Processing before he had them audit each other. The course went from 15 February through 29 March 1954, in Phoenix, Arizona.

5402C15 4ACC-1 Introduction to 4th American ACC

5402C16 4ACC-2 Group Processing: Ownership

5402C17 4ACC-3 Group Processing: Not Suppressing Time

5402C17 4ACC-4 Exteriorization Demonstration Process

5402C17 4ACC-5 Demonstration Process

5402C18 4ACC-6A Group Processing: Spotting Things

5402C18 4ACC-6B Group Processing: Spotting Things

5402C18 4ACC-7A Demonstration

5402C18 4ACC-7B Group Processing: Things Telling Where Things Were (Are?)

5402C19 4ACC-8 Group Processing: Demonstration

5402C19 4ACC-9 Group Processing: 2nd Dynamic

5402C19 4ACC-10 Group Processing: Imagination

5402C22 4ACC-11 Group Processing: Straightwire, Energy

5402C22 4ACC-12 Group Processing: Consideration

5402C23 4ACC-13 Group Processing: Certainty

5402C23 4ACC-14 Group Processing: Ownership

5402C24 4ACC-15 Group Processing: Time

5402C24 4ACC-16 Group Processing: Stabilization Process

5402C25 4ACC-17 Group Processing: Goals, Duplicating

5402C25 4ACC-18 Group Processing: Being and Giving

5402C26 4ACC-19 Group Processing: Havingness

5402C26 4ACC-20 Group Processing: Changing Ideas

5403C01 4ACC-21 Group Processing Series A: Be, Do, Have

5403C01 4ACC-22 Group Processing Series A: Time

5403C01 4ACC-23 Group Processing Series A: Certainties

5403C02 4ACC-24 Group Processing Series A: Exteriorization

5403C02 4ACC-25 Group Processing Series A: Courage

5403C02 4ACC-26 Group Processing Series A: Location

5403C03 4ACC-27 Group Processing Series B: Sound

5403C03 4ACC-28 Group Processing Series B: Light/Sound

5403C03 4ACC-29 Group Processing Series B: 3rd Hour

5403C04 4ACC-30 Group Processing Series B: Spaces

5403C04 4ACC-31 Group Processing Series B: Attention

5403C04 4ACC-32 Group Processing Series B: Work

5403C05 4ACC-33 Group Processing Series C: Putting Things

5403C05 4ACC-34 Group Processing Series C: Putting Things (cont'd)

5403C05 4ACC-35 Group Processing Series C: Putting Things (cont'd)

5403C08 4ACC-36 Group Processing Series C: Beingness

5403C09 4ACC-37 Group Processing Series C: Basic Process

5403C09 4ACC-37B Beingness

5403C11 4ACC-38 Group Processing Series C: Beingness

5403C11 4ACC-39 Group Processing Series C: (Title unknown)

5403C12 4ACC-40 Group Processing Series C: SOP-8C

5403C12 4ACC-41 Group Processing Series C: Similarities and Definitions

5403C15 4ACC-42 Group Processing Series D: 1st Hour

5403C15 4ACC-43 Group Processing Series D: Talk/Beingness

5403C15 4ACC-44 Group Processing Series D: Talk/Beingness

5403C16 4ACC-45 Group Processing Series D: 2nd Hour

5403C16 4ACC-46 Group Processing Series D: Talk/Beingness

5403C16 4ACC-47 Group Processing Series D: Outline of Processes

5403C17 4ACC-48 Group Processing Series D: 3rd Hour

5403C17 4ACC-49 Group Processing Series D: Evaluation

5403C17 4ACC-50 Group Processing Series D: Invalidation

5403C18 4ACC-51 Group Processing Series D: 4th Hour

5403C18 4ACC-52 Group Processing Series D: Duplication

5403C18 4ACC-53 Group Processing Series D: Following Orders (Orders and Duplication)

5403C19 4ACC-54 Group Processing Series D: 5th Hour

5403C19 4ACC-55 Group Processing Series D: Senior Processes

5403C19 4ACC-56 Group Processing Series D: Processes Talk

5403C22 4ACC-57 Group Processing Series D: 6th Hour

5403C22 4ACC-58 Group Processing Series D: Lecture/Pc What Your Pc is Trying to Do

5403C22 4ACC-59 Group Processing Series D: Lecture/Pc

5403C23 4ACC-60 Universe Series: All Cases

5403C23 4ACC-61 Universe Series: Beingness

5403C23 4ACC-62 Universe Series: Beingness

5403C24 4ACC-63 Universe Series: Group Processing

5403C24 4ACC-64 Universe Series: Beingness and Protection

5403C24 4ACC-65 Universe Series: Prediction

5403C25 4ACC-66 Universe Series: Communication

5403C25 4ACC-67 Universe Series: Outline of Processes

5403C25 4ACC-68 Universe Series: More on Processes

5403C26 4ACC-69 Universe Series: Group Processing

5403C26 4ACC-70 Universe Series: Morals, Laws, Codes

5403C26 4ACC-71 Universe Series: How Not To Get Results

5403C29 4ACC-72 Universe Series: Self Analysis

54__C__ 4ACC Axioms

54__C__ 4ACC Smooth in Comm Bridge in Auditing

The 5th American Advanced Clinical Course Lectures. The 5th American Advanced Clinical Course convened in Phoenix, Arizona, on Monday, 29 March 1954, and ran through Friday, May 7th. L. Ron Hubbard delivered the following lectures and group processing sessions.

5403C30 5ACC-1 Universes

5403C31 5ACC-2 Simple Processes

5404C01 5ACC-3 Basic Simple Procedures

5404C02 5ACC-4 Presence of an Auditor

5404C05 5ACC-5 Group Processing: Safe Place for Things

5404C06 5ACC-6 Lecture: Universes

5404C07 5ACC-7 Universe: Basic Definitions

5404C08 5ACC-8 Universe: Processes, Experience

5404C09 5ACC-9 Universe: Conditions of the Mind

5404C12 5ACC-10 Universe: Change and Rehabilitation

5404C13 5ACC-11 Universe: Manifestation

5404C14 5ACC-12 SOP-8D (also issued as —Universe: Manifestation)

5404C15 5ACC-13 SOP-8D: Exteriorization and Stabilization

5404C15 5ACC-13B Untitled

5404C16 5ACC-14 SOP-8D: Lecture

5404C19 5ACC-15 SOP-8D: Process Universe Assessment

5404C19 5ACC-15B Untitled

5404C20 5ACC-16 SOP-8D: Process Remedying Havingness

5404C21 5ACC-17 SOP-8D: Elements of Auditing

5404C22 5ACC-18 SOP-8D

5404C23 5ACC-19 SOP-8D

5404C26 5ACC-20 SOP-8D: General Handling of Pc

5404C28 5ACC-21 SOP-8D: Anchor Points and Space

5404C28 5ACC-22 SOP-8D: Space and Havingness

5404C29 5ACC-23 SOP-8D: Space

5404C30 5ACC-24 SOP-8D

5405C03 5ACC-25 SOP-8D: Viewpoint Straightwire—How to do Viewpoint; also issued as PRO-22

5405C04 5ACC-26 SOP-8D: Be, Do, Have Straightwire

5405C06 5ACC-27 Anatomy of Universes

5405C07 5ACC-28 Energy—Exteriorization

Special Group Processing Sessions. On 21 April 1954, L. Ron Hubbard gave the following special Group Processing Sessions in Phoenix, Arizona.

5404C21 GPSpec-1 Exteriorization and Stabilization

5404C21 GPSpec-2 Exteriorization and Stabilization (cont'd)

5404C21 GPSpec-3 Remedy of Havingness

5404C21 GPSpec-4 Remedy of Havingness (cont'd)

5404C21 GPSpec-5 Certainty Assessment on All Dynamics

5404C21 GPSpec-6 Processing on Certainty

5404C21 GPSpec-7 Universes: Assessment

5404C21 GPSpec-8 Universes: Assessment (cont'd)

Public Lecture Series. L. Ron Hubbard gave the following Public Lectures in Phoenix, Arizona, in May and June, 1954.

5405C05 PLS-1 Efficacy of Processes

5405C05 PLS-1 Remedying Reasons Why

5405C05 PLS-2 Rundown of Processes

5406C05 PLS-3 Human Evaluation

Special Radio Broadcast. L. Ron Hubbard recorded these tapes in April and May 1954, in Phoenix, Arizona.

5404C28 BC-1 Sample Recording— Proposed Radio Talk Introduction

5405C20 BC-2 Special Radio Broadcast: Introductory Talk for the Scientology Road Show

The 6th American Advanced Clinical Course Lectures. L. Ron Hubbard gave the following lectures and group processes to the 6th ACC, between 10 May and 18 June 1954, in Phoenix, Arizona.

5405C10 6ACC-1 Introduction, Materials and Publications

5405C11 6ACC-2 Affinity, Reality, Communication

5405C11 6ACC-3 Significance, Symbols, Orientation

5405C11 6ACC Goals of Scientology in Processing

5405C12 6ACC-4 Goal of the Auditor

5405C12 6ACC-4B Practical Applications of the Definitions of Scientology

5405C12 6ACC-5 Basic Definitions

5405C13 6ACC-6 Definition: Cycle of Action and Time

5405C13 6ACC-7 SOP-8C by Definitions

5405C14 6ACC-8 Randomness, Surprise & Prediction, Automaticity, Beingness

5405C14 6ACC-9 Remedy of Havingness

5405C14 6ACC-9A Command Postulates

5405C14 6ACC-9B Opening Procedure of 8-C

5405C17 6ACC-10 Simple Processes, Specifics

5405C17 6ACC-11 Simple Processes Summary

5405C18 6ACC-12 Barriers

5405C18 6ACC-13 Barriers, Processing of; PTP, Help

5405C19 6ACC-14 Third Dynamics

5405C19 6ACC-14A Communication and the Dynamics *Translations:* Dutch, French, Swedish.

5405C19 6ACC-15 Imagination, Viewpoint Processes

5405C20 6ACC-16 How to Put Procedure Together

5405C20 6ACC-17 Definitions: A-R-C

5405C20 6ACC-17A First Dynamic

5405C21 6ACC-18 Consideration and Intention

5405C21 6ACC-19 Seminar

5405C22 Be, Do, Have, Scientology

5405C24 6ACC-20 Conduct of the Auditor, Communication Lag

5405C25 6ACC-21 Conduct of the Auditor, Older Therapies

5405C25 6ACC-21A Connecting Point Between Older Therapies and Auditing

5405C25 6ACC-22A Valences

5405C25 6ACC-22B Beingness Processing

5405C26 6ACC-23A Third Dynamic ARC

5405C26 6ACC-23B Command Process

5405C26 6ACC-24 Practical Aspects of Auditing

5405C27 6ACC-25 How to Do Viewpoint Straightwire

5405C27 6ACC—26 Demonstration Session

5405C28 6ACC-27 Demonstration Session

5405C28 6ACC-28 SOP-8D With Wheel, Know to Sex Scale

5405C28 6ACC-28A Know to Sex Scale

5405C31 6ACC-29 Processing of Problems: Theta-MEST Theory

5405C31 6ACC-29A Processing Attention, Beingness

5405C31 6ACC-30 Procedure 30 Series: Granting Beingness

5405C31 6ACC-30A Procedure 30 Series: Issue I

5406C01 6ACC-31 Procedure 30 Series: Op Pro by Dup

5406C01 6ACC-31A Problems

5406C01 6ACC-32 Procedure 30 Series: Granting Beingness: also issued as PRO-21—Granting Beingness

5406C01 6ACC-32A Granting Beingness (cont'd)

5406C02 6ACC-33 When to Use Procedure 30

5406C02 6ACC-33A Procedure 30 Series: How to Process a Case

5406C02 6ACC-34 Procedure 30 Series: Granting Beingness

5406C02 6ACC-34A Granting Beingness

5406C03 6ACC-35 Study of Man: Demonstration of Procedure

5406C03 6ACC-36 Consideration: Time, Beginning and End

5406C04 6ACC-37 Know to Sex Scale: The Mind and the Tone Scale

5406C04 6ACC-38 Imagination and Abilities

5406C09 6ACC-39 Energy: Distractions of

5406C10 6ACC-40 Basic Elements of Scientology

5406C11 6ACC-41 Procedure 30: Handling of Cases

5406C11 6ACC-41A Processing Solutions: Procedure 30, Issue III

5406C11 6ACC-42 Basic Impulses

5406C11 6ACC-42A Basic Impulses (cont'd)

5406C11 Ron's Life

5406C14 6ACC-43 General Lecture: Anchor Points, Viewpoints

5406C14 6ACC-44 Energy Machines, Survival

5406C15 6ACC-45 Functional Processes

5406C15 6ACC-45A Types and Forms of Commands

5406C15 6ACC-46 Dependency

5406C16 6ACC-47 Capabilities of Thetan

5406C16 6ACC-48 Contact with the Public. *Translation:* German.

5406C17 6ACC-49 Betrayal, Ridicule, the Game Cycle

5406C17 6ACC-49A Betrayal, Ridicule (cont'd)

5406C17 6ACC-50 Lecture: On Group Processing

5406C17 6ACC-50 Training of Auditors

5406C17 6ACC-50A Assists—Part 1

5406C17 6ACC-50B Assists—Part 2

5406C18 6ACC-51 Summary: Training Processing

5406C18 6ACC-51A Summary: Processing Demonstrations

5406C18 6ACC-52 Certificates and Degrees

The Universe Process Congress Lectures. The Universe Process Congress (also called the *Fourth International Congress of Dianeticists and Scientologists*) was held in Phoenix, Arizona, June 5 through 8, 1954. The delegates received fourteen hours of lectures and group processing from L. Ron Hubbard.

5406C05 UPC-1 Opening Lecture— History of Dianetics and Scientology

5406C05 UPC-2 Procedure 30— Duplication

5406C05 UPC-3 Theta-MEST Theory—Tone Scale, Freedom, Space, etc.

5406C06 UPC-4 Group Processes: Procedure 30, Step 1—Opening Procedure by Duplication; also issued as PRO-19

5406C06 UPC-5 Lecture and Processing

5406C06 UPC-6 Group Processing (Look at that Object)

5406C07 UPC-7 Scientology Workbook—Journal of Scientology 31-G

5406C07 UPC-8 Processing Procedure 30, Step 3 (Granting of Beingness) Session I

5406C07 UPC-9 Processing (Granting of Beingness) Session II

5406C07 UPC-10 Group Processing (What Do—Didn't Have)

5406C07 UPC-11 Theta-MEST Theory—Being a Problem Aspect

5406C08 UPC-12 Group Processing (Solution to Something)

5406C08 UPC-13 Processes of Exteriorization

5406C08 UPC-14 Group Processing (Straight Exteriorization Process)

The 7th American Advanced Clinical Course Lectures. The 7th American Advanced Clinical Course convened in Phoenix, Arizona, on June 21, 1954 and continued until July 30, 1954. This was the last of a series of seven ACCs taught by L. Ron Hubbard, one after another, with no pause between them.

5406C23 7ACC-1A Opening Procedure 8C

5406C23 7ACC-1B Further Uses of Opening Procedure 8C

5406C24 7ACC-2 Summary of Plan of Course

5406C25 7ACC-3 Review of Procedure: PTP, ARC Straightwire, Two-way Comm

5406C25 7ACC-3A Review of Procedure: Starting a Session, Two-Way Comm

5406C25 7ACC-4A Opening Procedure of 8D: Demonstration

5406C25 7ACC-4B Opening Procedure of 8D: Demonstration (cont'd)

5406C28 7ACC-5A Exteriorization

5406C28 7ACC-5B Exteriorization (cont'd)

5406C29 7 ACC-6A&B General Lecture: Straightwire, Communication

5406C30 7ACC-7 Rundown of Essentials

5406C30 7ACC-7A Group Processing

5406C30 7ACC-8 Group Processing and Lecture, Something, Nothing

5407C01 7ACC-9 Group Processing: Communication, Duplication, Spotting Spots

5407C01 7ACC-9A Communication, Duplication and Spotting Spots

5407C01 7ACC-10 Exteriorization by Distance, Cause

5407C01 7ACC-10A Exteriorization, Distance and Time

5407C01 7ACC-11 Things in Time and Space

5407C05 7ACC-11A A Bright Resistive Case

5407C05 7ACC-12 The Role of Laughter in Processing—Dangerousness

5407C06 7ACC-13 Remedy of Havingness and Spotting Spots; also issued as—PRO-23

5407C06 7ACC-14 ARC, Time, Life and Universe

5407C07 7ACC-15 Intensive Procedure: Lecture 1

300

WHAT IS SCIENTOLOGY

5407C07 7ACC-15A Intensive Procedure: Lecture 2

5407C07 7ACC-16 Intensive Procedure: Lecture 3

5407C07 7ACC-16A Intensive Procedure: Lecture 4, Basic Processes Patter

5407C09 7ACC-17 The Nature and Effect of Communication in Games

5407C09 7ACC-17A Communication and Barriers in Society and the PC

5407C12 7ACC-18 Two Types of Cases

5407C12 7ACC-18A Time: Havingness

5407C12 7ACC-19 Intensive Procedure: Nothing-Something

5407C13 7ACC-19A Auditor's Code in Practice

5407C14 7ACC-20 Power of Life and Death

5407C14 7ACC-20A Application of Theory to Cases, Life and Death, Only One

5407C15 7ACC-21 The Difference Between a Good and a Bad Auditor, Part I

5407C15 7ACC-21A SOP-8D: Its Application

5407C15 7ACC-22 SOP-8D: Orientation Points (also issued as — The Difference Between a Good and a Bad Auditor, Part II)

5407C16 7ACC-22A Training of Auditors

5407C16 7ACC-23 Teaching Formula: Duplication

5407C19 7ACC-24 Duplication: Religious Aspects of Scientology (also titled: Scientology: Its General Background [Part II as PRO-2])

5407C19 7ACC-25A&B Scientology and Civilization (also titled: Scientology: Its General Background [Part I and Part III as PRO-1 and PRO-3]) *Translations:* Dutch, Swedish.

5407C20 7ACC-26 Bridge Between Scientology and Civilization *Translation:* Swedish

5407C20 7ACC-27A What a Student Should Know (also issued as — PRO-4 — Consideration, Mechanics and the Theory Behind Instruction)

5407C20 7ACC-27B What a Student Should Know (cont'd) (also issued as — PRO-5 — Consideration and Isness)

5407C23 7ACC-28A The Four Conditions of Existence (also issued as — PRO-6 Isness)

5407C23 7ACC-28B The Four Conditions of Existence (cont'd) (also issued as — PRO-7)

5407C23 7ACC-29A The Most Elementary Processes — The Four Conditions of Existence (cont'd) (also issued as — PRO-8)

5407C23 7ACC-29B The Most Elementary Processes — The Four Conditions of Existence (cont'd) (also issued as — PRO-9)

5407C23 7ACC-30 The Four Conditions of Existence (cont'd) (also issued as — PRO-10 and PRO-11)

5407C27 7ACC-31A&B Two-way Comm and the Present Time Problem (also issued as — PRO-17, Opening Procedure of 8C and PRO-18) *Translations:* Dutch, French, Swedish.

5407C27 7ACC-32 Afternoon Lecture remarks especially on Telepathy and ESP

5407C__ 7ACC-33 Title unknown

5407C__ 7ACC-34 Title unknown

5407C28 7ACC-35A Description Processing (also issued as — PRO-24)

5407C28 7ACC-35B Group Processing (also issued as — PRO-2)

5407C__ 7ACC-36 Title unknown

5407C__ 7ACC-37 Time (also issued as — PRO-12)

5407C__ 7ACC-37B Types of Processes (also issued as — PRO-18)

5407C__ 7ACC-38 Title unknown

5407C__ 7ACC-39 Scientology and Living (also issued as — PRO-26)

5407C30 Certificates of Dianetics and Scientology

The Axioms Lectures. L. Ron Hubbard gave the following lectures in Phoenix, Arizona, on the 20th of August 1954.

5408C20 AX-1 Axioms, Part I (also issued as — PRO-13)

5408C20 AX-2 Axioms, Part II (also issued as — PRO-14)

5408C20 AX-3 Axioms, Part III (also issued as — PRO-15)

5408C20 AX-4 Axioms, Part IV (also issued as — PRO-16)

These lectures were given by L. Ron Hubbard in Phoenix, Arizona, in August and September, 1954.

5408C28 PLS-2 The Auditor's Public

5409C14 Dianetic Group Processing

5409C15 Church of Scientology Training Program and Lecture on Group Processing

The 8th American Advanced Clinical Course Lectures. L. Ron Hubbard conducted the 8th American Advanced Clinical Course in Phoenix, Arizona, from October 4th through November 12th 1954. During the time period of the 8th ACC he also gave the Route One Lectures and most of a series of Public Lectures and Group Processing Sessions.

5410C04 8ACC-1A&B Introduction: Organization of Scientology *Translations:* Dutch, Swedish.

5410C05 8ACC-2 Two-way Comm, Straightwire, 8-C

5410C05 8ACC-3 Basic Elements of Processing

5410C06 8ACC-4 Two-way Communication *Translations:* Danish, Dutch, French, German, Spanish, Swedish.

5410C07 8ACC-5A Elementary Straightwire

5410C07 8ACC-5B Intensive Processing

5410C08 8ACC-6 Opening Procedure of 8-C

5410C11 8ACC-7 Opening Procedure by Duplication

5410C12 8ACC-8 Remedy of Havingness

5410C13 8ACC-8 Step II SOP-8

5410C13 8ACC-9 Spotting Spots

5410C13 Retraining Unit B & C

5410C13 8ACC-9 Demonstration of SOP Step II

5410C14 8ACC-10 Creation of Human Ability, Route II

5410C14 8ACC-10A Group Processing (Creation of Human Ability)

5410C15 8ACC-11 Creation of Human Ability, Route I

5410C18 8ACC-12 Creation of Human Ability, Route I

5410C19 8ACC-13 Axioms of Dianetics

5410C20 8ACC-14 The Parts of Man, Overt Acts and Motivators

5410C21 8ACC-15 Route 2: Overt-Motivator Sequence

5410C21 8ACC-16 Route 2-61, Good and Evil — Spotting Spots; Route 2-62, Overt-Motivator, Remedy of Havingness

5410C22 8ACC-17 Two-way Communication

5410C25 8ACC-18 Communication and Straightwire

5410C26 8ACC-19 Survive

5410C27 8ACC-20 Hypnotism

5410C28 8ACC-21 Process: What Would You Do If . . . ?

5410C29 8ACC-22 The Factors *Translations:* Danish, Dutch, French, Swedish.

5411C01 8ACC-23 Two-way Communication *Translations:* Danish, Dutch, French, German, Spanish, Swedish.

5411C02 8ACC-24 Homo sapiens

5411C03 8ACC-25 Shame, Blame and Regret

5411C04 8ACC-26 Title unknown

5411C05 8ACC-27 Factors Present in Good and Bad Auditing

5411C08 8ACC-28 Nonverbal Communication

5411C09 8ACC-29 Application of Axioms to Auditing

5411C10 8ACC-30 Definitions: Axioms

5411C11 8ACC-31 Scope of Dianetics and Scientology

5411C12 8ACC-32 Question-and-Answer Period, Dissemination

The Route One Lectures. The Route One Lectures are twelve 15-minute lectures given by L. Ron Hubbard in October, 1954, at Phoenix, Arizona.

5410C08 PIP-1 Route 1, Step 4

5410C08 PIP-2 Route 1, Step 5

5410C10 PIP-3 Route 1, Step 6

5410C10 PIP-4 Route 1, Step 7

5410C10 PIP-5 Route 1, Step 8

5410C10 PIP-6 Route 1, Step 9

5410C10 PIP-7 Route 1, Step 10

5410C10 PIP-8 Route 1, Step 11

5410C18 PIP-9 Route 1, Step 12

5410C18 PIP-10 Route 1, Step 13

5410C18 PIP-11 Route 1, Step 14

5410C18 PIP-12 Route 1, Step 15

The Public Lecture and Group Processing Series. L. Ron Hubbard gave the following public lectures and group processing sessions in Phoenix, Arizona, in October, November and December 1954.

5410C20 PLS On Comprehending the Incomprehensible

5410C20 PPS-1 "Rising Scale" on the Tone Scale and "Find Something Incomprehensible"

5410C20 PPS-1A Group Processing

5410C27 PLS Life of Dynamics

5410C27 PLS Principal Difference Between Scientology and Dianetics

5410C27 PPS-2 "Electing Cause" — "Something You Can't Control"

5411C03 PLS Organization of Scientology

5411C17 PPS-3 "Accept" and "Reject" (Group Processing)

5411C17 PLS The Wrong Thing to Do Is Nothing

5411C24 PLS Creation of Human Ability (also issued as — Accent on Ability)

5411C24 PPS-4 Group Process — "Find Shortest Comm Line" — "Create a Memory"

5412C01 PLS Awareness of Awareness

5412C01 PPS-5 "Decide to Be Silent" — "Find Some Secrets"

5412C03 PLS Title unknown

5412C08 PPS-6 "Waiting," "Something You Can Associate With"

5412C08 PPS Group Processing

5412C15 PLS Acceptance Level

The Phoenix Certification Course Lectures. The Phoenix Certification Course Lectures deal with the fundamental data of Scientology and the exact and precise use of techniques and processes. L. Ron Hubbard gave these lectures 15 November through 4 December 1954, in Phoenix, Arizona.

5411C16 HCAP-1 Elementary Straightwire

5411C17 HCAP-2 Background of Six Basic Steps

5411C18 HCAP-3 Elementary Straightwire

5411C19 HCAP-4 Remedy of Havingness

5411C22 HCAP-5 Levels of Case Ability

5411C23 HCAP-6 Addressing Groups and Starting Sessions

5411C24 HCAP-7 Following Orders

5411C24 HCAP-8 Two-way Communication

5411C30 HCAP-9 Solving Cases

5412C01 HCAP-10 Opening Procedure of 8-C

5412C03 HCAP-11 Op Pro by Dup with Two-way Comm (also issued as — PRO-20)

5412C04 HCAP-12 Last Lecture

The Unification Congress of Dianeticists and Scientologists Lectures. The Unification Congress of Dianeticists and Scientologists, given under the joint sponsorship of the Hubbard Dianetics Research Foundation and the Hubbard Association of Scientologists International, in Phoenix, Arizona, was held from the 28th through the 31st of December 1954. It was during this congress that the book *Dianetics 55!* was first released.

5412C28 UC-1 Introduction

5412C28 UC-2 Group Processing (incomplete)

412C28 UC-3 History of Dianetics Abilities vs Disabilities)

412C28 UC-4 Dianetics '55 (What a Clear)

412C28 UC-5 Communication and ARC

412C29 UC-6 Games

412C29 UC-7 Title unknown

412C29 UC-8 Title unknown

412C29 UC-9 Terminals and Communication

412C29 UC-10 Errors in Communication (also titled: "Aims and Goals of Dianetics and Scientology")

412C30 UC-11 Communication and Problems

412C30 UC-12 Group Processing (Sub-Zero Scale Relation to Scale of Awareness)

412C30 UC-13 Title unknown

412C30 UC-14 Problems and Games

412C30 UC-15 Title unknown

412C30 UC-16 Pan-Determinism

412C31 UC-17 Title unknown

412C31 UC-18 Title unknown

412C31 UC-19 Title unknown

412C31 UC-20 Title unknown

4__C__ UC Unification Congress: Communication—Dianetics '55

4__C28 UC Unification Congress: Goals

The 9th and 10th American Advanced Clinical Course Lectures. L. Ron Hubbard began the 9th American Advanced Clinical Course in Phoenix, Arizona, December 6th 1954. It was announced that Hubbard Certified Auditors could enroll in the ACC every three weeks. ACCs customarily ran for 6 weeks, so the 9th and 10th ACCs overlapped.

412C06 9ACC-1 Introduction to 9th ACC, Havingness

412C07 9ACC-2 Essence of Auditing, Know to Mystery Scale

412C08 9ACC-3 Rundown on Six Basics

412C09 9ACC-4 Communication Formula

412C10 9ACC-5 Practice of Dianetics and Scientology

412C13 9ACC-6 Conduct of the Auditor

412C14 9ACC-7 Mechanics of Communication

412C15 9ACC-8 Havingness

412C16 9ACC-9 Pan-Determinism and One-way Flows

412C17 9ACC-9A History and Development of Processes—Games and the Limitations in Games (also issued as—History of Processes)

412C17 9ACC-9B Q & A Period

412C20 9ACC-10 Games (Fighting)

412C21 9ACC-11 Anatomy of Games, Part A

412C21 9ACC-11A Anatomy of Games, Part B

412C22 9ACC-12 One-way Flows (in Processing)

412C22 9ACC-12A Q & A Period

412C22 9ACC-13 Q & A Period

412C23 9ACC-13 Havingness and Communication Formulas

5412C23 9ACC-13A After-Lecture Comments

5412C24 9ACC-14 Pan-Determinism

5412C24 9ACC-14A Q & A Period

5412C27 9ACC-15 Training New People

5412C27 9ACC-15A Curiosa From Dianetics '55&Q&A

The following lectures were given by L. Ron Hubbard during the year 1954. No specific dates are known for them.

54__C__ Lecture 2, Valences

54__C__ Remedy of Havingness

54__C__ Lecture 6, Facsimiles—Solids

54__C__ Exteriorization Stabilization

54__C__ Lecture 18, Chronic Somatics

54__C__ The Dynamics, OT/ARC, As-isness

54__C__ Illusion Processing

54__C__ GR/PROC Group Session—Reaching and Withdrawing

54__C__ Reach and Withdraw

54__C__ Resistive Level 5's

54__C__ Space and the Pc and Self-Determinism

1955

BOOKS

Notes on the Lectures given by L. Ron Hubbard at Phoenix, 1954, taken from the lectures of L. Ron Hubbard, published by the Hubbard Association of Scientologists International, Johannesburg, South Africa, early 1955.

Key to Tomorrow, (also entitled *Scientology: Its Contribution to Knowledge*), taken from the works of L. Ron Hubbard, published by the Hubbard Communications Office, Phoenix, Arizona, May, 1955.

The Scientologist—A Manual on the Dissemination of Material, by L. Ron Hubbard, published by the Hubbard Association of Scientologists International, Phoenix, Arizona, March, 1955. (The text of this manual has been reprinted in full in *The Technical Bulletins of Dianetics and Scientology,* 1976.)

The Elementary Scientology Series, taken from the works of L. Ron Hubbard, published by the Scientology Council, Los Angeles, California, early 1955.

The Creation of Human Ability, by L. Ron Hubbard, published by Scientology Publications in London, England, in April, 1955 and in the United States a few weeks later. *Translations:* Danish, French, German, Spanish, Swedish.

Straightwire: A Manual of Operation, by L. Ron Hubbard, published by the Hubbard Communications Office, Washington, D.C., July, 1955. (The text of this manual has been reprinted in its entirety in *The Technical Bulletins of Dianetics and Scientology,* 1976.)

L. Ron Hubbard's Professional Auditor's Bulletins Book 1, by L. Ron Hubbard, published by the Hubbard Communications Office, Washington, D.C., 1955, was a reissue of Ron's Professional Auditor's Bulletins, numbers 1 through 15. (The Professional Auditor's Bulletins have been reprinted in *The Technical Bulletins of Dianetics and Scientology,* 1976.)

The Co-Auditor's Manual—The Basic Theory and Practice of Scientology as developed by L. Ron Hubbard—presented for use in Co-Auditing, based on the works of L. Ron Hubbard, published by the Hubbard Communications Office, Washington, D.C., December, 1955.

Brainwashing—Published as a Public Service, published by the Hubbard Communications Office, Washington, D.C., December, 1955. (A manuscript received anonymously turned out to be based on a German language book entitled *Psychopolitics,* available from the Library of Congress. *Brainwashing* was published to inform those who might run into its effects in auditing preclears.)

1955

INSIGNIA

The Hubbard Communications Office Insignia

This is a shield with the S and double triangle and the initials HCO placed vertically, to the right.

Below the shield on a banner is the motto of HCO: "Bring Order."

HCO is basically a communications office. Formed in the 1950s, HCO builds, holds, maintains, mans and controls the organization and it is the orders issue section.

The Scientology Cross

The Scientology Sunburst Cross, the basic design of which was found by L. Ron Hubbard in an ancient Spanish Mission in Arizona, is the exact official insignia for Scientology ministers.

The cross is three inches high and two inches wide, made of sterling silver and worn as a neckpiece by men and women alike. The cross is suspended on a fine silver chain.

The cross is at once simple and ornate, and has eight points. It is available nowhere outside the Church of Scientology. It is a true eight dynamic Scientology cross.

The Scientology cross is displayed in larger and smaller sizes. Large crosses of wood and other materials are not uncommon as wall hangings.

Very small versions are also **worn** as pins.

1955

TAPED LECTURES

5501C03 9ACC-16 Auditing Requirements, Differences

5501C03 10ACC-1 Pan-Determinism of Auditors—Auditing Requirements

5501C04 10ACC-2 Pan-Determinism of Auditors—Time

5501C04 9ACC-16A Time

5501C04 9ACC-16AA Q & A Period

5501C05 10ACC-3 Exteriorization by Gradient Scale, Remedy of Havingness—Adjusting Anchor Points

5501C05 10ACC-4 Title unknown

5501C05 9ACC-17 Auditing at Optimum

5501C06 9ACC-18 Exteriorization

5501C06 10ACC-5 Route 1—Exteriorization (same as 9ACC-18)

5501C06 10ACC-6 Condensation of Know to Mystery Scale (same as 9ACC-19)

5501C07 9ACC-19 Elementary Material: Know to Mystery Scale

5501C10 9ACC-20 Education: Goals in Society—Adult Education

5501C11 9ACC-21 Fundamentals of Auditing

5501C11 9ACC-21A Auditor's Conference

5501C12 9ACC-22 Definition: Aberration, Vias, G.E.

5501C13 9ACC-23 Definitions: Glossary of Terms

5501C14 9ACC-24 Definitions: Perfect Duplication, Life Continuum

5501C17 9ACC-25 Auditing Demonstration: Six Basics in Action

5501C17 9ACC-25A Auditors' Conference

5501C18 9ACC-26 Auditing Demonstration: Spotting Spots

5501C18 9ACC-26A Auditors' Conference

5501C19 9ACC-27 Auditing Demonstration: Exteriorization

5501C20 9ACC-28
Background Music to Living

5501C21 9ACC-29 Axioms: Laws of Consideration, What an Axiom Is

The Third International Congress of Scientologists Lectures. During the 9th ACC given in Phoenix, Arizona, L. Ron Hubbard made a tape especially for congress delegates to the Third International Congress of Scientologists held in London, England. The delegates also listened to the latest Phoenix Congress tapes.

5501C16 3ICGB-1 Address to Congress Delegates by L. Ron Hubbard

The Public Lectures and Group Processing Series. These are public lectures and group processing sessions given by L. Ron Hubbard January through May, 1955, in Phoenix, Arizona.

5501C01 Public Processing

5501C01 Special Group Processing

5501C05 PLS-1 The Society at Large

5501C05 PPS Group Processing

5501C12 Processing Session

5501C12 PLS-2 Games

5501C12 PLS ARC Triangle

5501C19 PLS-3 Communication and ARC Triangle *Translation:* Swedish.

5501C19 PPS Group Processing

5501C26 PLS Goals of HDA (Dianetics) and Scientology

5501C26 PLS-4 Scientology and Auditors (also Auditing)

5501C26 PPS Alcoholism (Group Processing)

5502C02 PLS-5 Alcoholism

5502C02 PPS Group Processing

5502C02 PLS Variations on Six Basic Processes

5502C09 PLS-6 Miracles

5502C09 PPS Session: Control of Body, Think a Thought

5502C23 PLPS-1 Scientology and Ability

5502C23 PPS Group Processing

5502C23 PLPS-2 Session: "Find a Mystery"

5503C02 PLPS-3 Efficiency, Thought, Emotion and Effort

5503C09 PLPS-4 Health and Certainty

5503C09 PLPS-5 Session: Only One, Things Real and Unreal

5503C09 PPS Group Processing

5503C16 PLPS-6
What We Are Doing

5503C23 PLPS-7&8 Scientology: A Technical Subject — Communication Lag, Principal Kinds Found in a Pc

5503C30 PLPS-9 Conquered Territory (a summary of the achievements and directions of Scientology)

5503C30 PPS Group Processing — Conquered Territory

5503C30 PLPS-10 Session: "Making Things Real and Unreal"

5504C02 PLPS
The Second Dynamic

5504C06 PLPS-11 On The Second Dynamic

5504C06 PLS Cause & Effect

5504C06 PLS
Cause & Effect — Session

5504C06 PLPS-12 Session: "What Could You Say To . . .?"

5504C13 PLPS-14
The Eight Dynamics

5504C13 PLPS-15 Session: Find Present Time

5504C20 PLPS-16 Para-Scientology — or Things That Go Boomp in the Night

5504C20 PLPS-17 Session: Change and No-Change

5504C27 PLPS-18 The Direction of Modern Scientology

5504C27 PLPS-19 Grey Dianetics

5504C27 PLPS-20 Session: "Something You Could Say To..." and "Ownership"

5505C04 PLPS-21 Cause and Effect and Its Use in Processing

5505C04 PLPS-22 Session: Cause and Effect

5505C11 PLPS-23 Operation Manual for the Mind

5505C11 PLPS-24
Session: "Enchantment" Processing

5505C11 PLPS-25 Lookingness and Cause

The Hubbard Professional College Lectures. In March and May, 1955, L. Ron Hubbard gave ten one-hour lectures to the students attending Hubbard Professional College in Phoenix, Arizona.

5503C14 HPC-1 Death Wish — The Only One (The mechanics and solution of the occluded case)

5503C26 HPC-2 Axiom 51

5504C02 HPC-3 Axiom 51 in Action (The creation and uncreation of energy and masses by postulate; Knowingness; and Communication)

5504C09 HPC-4 Consequences and a New Understanding of the Six Basic Processes (How to discover with precision and raise the reality level of the preclear)

5504C16 HPC-5 Service Facsimiles (Its handling by modern auditing)

5504C23 HPC-6 Thinkingness

5504C30 HPC-7 Ownership Processing

5505C07 HPC-8 Meaningness (The basic formula for happiness — a new process), Part I

5505C07 HPC-9 Meaningness, Part II, Auditing Tips

5505C14 HPC-10 The Tone Scales (An important new understanding of the tone scale)

5505C17 HPC Meaningfulness

5505C__ HPC Ron's Reports — Police Conference with Ron in Phoenix, Parts A&B

L. Ron Hubbard Auditing Demonstrations. These demonstrations by L. Ron Hubbard were presented live on television to ACC students in Phoenix, Arizona, in March and April, 1955.

Also included in this list are *Auditor's Conferences* which took place January through May, 1955, and lectures that are not part of any other series.

5501C10 Auditors' Conference

5501C10 Auditors' Conference-Lecture: Exteriorization Process

5502C12 Auditors' Conference

5502C23 Staff Auditors' Conference

5502C23 Basic Reason

5502C23 Auditors' Conference

5503C08 History of Research and Investigation

5503C08 Auditing Demonstration

5503C14 L. Ron Hubbard Auditing Demonstration

5503C14 L. Ron Hubbard Auditing Demonstration

5503C14 Auditors' Conference

5503C15 How to Audit Paying Pcs

5503C15 Auditing Demonstration

5503C15 L. Ron Hubbard Auditing Demonstration

5503C16
Demonstration — L. Ron Hubbard

5503C16 Auditing Demonstration — L. Ron Hubbard

5503C17 Auditing Demonstration — L. Ron Hubbard

5503C17 Auditing Demonstration — L. Ron Hubbard

5503C18 Auditing Demonstration — L. Ron Hubbard

5503C18 Auditing Demonstration — L. Ron Hubbard

5503C21 Auditing Demonstration — L. Ron Hubbard

5503C21 Auditing Demonstration — L. Ron Hubbard

5503C22 Auditing Demonstration — L. Ron Hubbard

5503C22 Auditing Demonstration — L. Ron Hubbard

5503C23 Communication Lag

5503C23 Auditing Demonstration — L. Ron Hubbard

5503C23 Auditing Demonstration — L. Ron Hubbard

5503C23 Auditing Demonstration — L. Ron Hubbard

5503C24 Auditing Demonstration — L. Ron Hubbard

5503C24 Auditing Demonstration — L. Ron Hubbard

5503C25 Auditing Demonstration — L. Ron Hubbard

5503C25 Auditing Demonstration — L. Ron Hubbard

5503C28 Auditing Demonstration — L. Ron Hubbard

5503C28 Auditing Demonstration — L. Ron Hubbard

5503C29 Afternoon Auditing Demonstration

5504C01 L. Ron Hubbard Auditing Demonstration — & Staff Auditors' Conference

5504C01 Auditing Demonstration — L. Ron Hubbard

5504C01 SAC-1 1st Hour Staff Auditors' Conference Series

5504C04 SAC-2 Scale of Awareness

5504C04 Auditing Demonstration — L. Ron Hubbard

5504C07 Auditing Demonstration — L. Ron Hubbard

5504C08 Staff Auditor Conference — Peggy's Report and Ron's Comment

5504C18 Dianetics and Scientology (Phoenix Congress)

5504C18 Auditor's Conference

5504C19 Auditor's Conference

5504C19 Auditing Demonstration — L. Ron Hubbard

5504C20 Auditing Demonstration — L. Ron Hubbard

5504C21 Auditing Session — Demonstration Rud Session by L. Ron Hubbard

5504C21 Auditors' Conference

5504C25 Auditing Session — L. Ron Hubbard — Truth and Ownership

5504C26 Discussion & Education of the Pc

5504C26 Demonstration Auditing Session — What Can You Get In and Out of Control

5504C27 Education on Problems — Who Doesn't Think You're Insane

5504C27 L. Ron Hubbard Auditing and Discussion

5504C28 Demonstration Auditing — More Education on Ownership Process

5504C28 Demonstration Auditing — Ownership Part IV

5504C29 L. Ron Hubbard Discussion and Auditing of Ownership and Control

5504C29 L. Ron Hubbard Discussion and Auditing of Ownership and Control Part VI

5504C29 SAC 6th Hour Conference

5505C02 ALS-Spec Talk on "Think a Thought" in Connection with Ownership

5505C02 SAC Staff Auditors' Conference Part A & Part B

5505C07 Auditing Session

5505C08 Auditing Session

5505C09 Auditing Session

5505C10 Auditing Session

5505C13 Auditing Demonstration Part A & B

5505C__ Auditing Session

The Anatomy of the Spirit of Man Congress Lectures. The Anatomy of the Spirit of Man Congress was held in Washington, D.C., the 3rd through the 6th of June 1955. L. Ron Hubbard gave lectures to over 250 delegates attending.

5506C03 ASMC-1 Address of Welcome — The Hope of Man *Translations:* Danish, Dutch, French, Swedish

5506C03 ASMC-2 Practicalities of a Practical Religion

5506C03 ASMC-3 History of Research and Investigation

5506C04 ASMC-4 Direction of Truth in Processing

5506C04 ASMC-5 The Tone Scale — Three Primary Buttons of Exteriorization

506C04 ASMC-6 Group Processng—Meaningness

506C04 ASMC-7 Composition of eingness—Postulates, Exterioriza-on, Beingness

506C04 ASMC-7A After Lecture s & As

506C04 ASMC-8 Group Processing

506C05 ASMC-9 The Descent of Man

506C05 ASMC-10 How to Chart he Preclear, Knowingness and Un-nowingness

506C06 ASMC-11 Six Basic Steps -Some Fundamentals of Auditing

506C06 ASMC-12 The Mechanisms f Ownership in Living (the owner-hip of information)

506C06 ASMC-13 Group Process-ng—Additional Processing on Mean-gness

506C06 ASMC-14 The Game Called Man

506C06 ASMC-15 What Scientol-gy is Doing—Organizations, The ontrol & Division of Man

The Academy Lecture Series. L. on Hubbard gave the following lec-ures as part of the auditor training ourse in the Academy of Religious rts and Sciences at the Church of cientology, Washington, D.C. These ectures were given between 11 July nd 21 September 1955. (The last ecture was given in London. Eng-and.)

507C11 HCA Seven Basic Steps n this tape Ron describes the cur-iculum of the HCA Course and the art the six steps play in the train-ng of an auditor.)

508C23 ALS-1 he Auditor's Public

508C23 ALS-2 Axiom 53: The xiom of the Stable Datum

508C30 ALS-3 ugged Individualism

508C30 ALS-4 nion Station—R-46

509C14 ALS-5 The Unknown Da-um—a MEST-Shaking Lecture

509C21 ALS-6 Postulates 1,2,3,4 n Processing—A New Understand-ng of Axiom 36

The 4th London Advanced Clinical Course Lectures. The first Advanced Clinical Course given in England by .. Ron Hubbard personally, com-nenced on 3 October 1955, in Lon-on.

510C03 4LACC-1 Fundamentals of cientology and Rudiments of Audit-ng

510C03 4LACC-2 Fundamentals of cientology and Rudiments of Audit-ng

510C04 4LACC-3 1st and 2nd Pos-ulates in Living

510C04 4LACC-4 1st to 4th Pos-ulates in Living

510C05 4LACC-5 Smoothness of uditing

510C05 4LACC-6 Smoothness of uditing (cont'd)

510C06 4LACC-7 Communication nd "I Don't Know" (Confusion)

5510C06 4LACC-8 Stable Datum and Confusion

5510C07 4LACC-9 Relations to Time Continuance

5510C07 4LACC-10 Base Time and Time Continuum

5510C10 4LACC-11 Establishing of the Auditor

5510C10 4LACC-12 Communication and the Subject of Communication

5510C11 4LACC-13 Data of Com-parable Magnitude

5510C11 4LACC-13A Data of Com-parable Magnitude (cont'd)

5510C11 4LACC-14 Comm Bridge, Confusion, Time Factor

5510C12 4LACC-15 Communication and Intentions, Deteriorization of

5510C12 4LACC-16 The Communication Bridge

5510C13 4LACC-17 The Antiquity of Auditing

5510C13 4LACC-18 Affinity, Real-ity and Communication

5510C14 4LACC-19 Exteriorization and Interiorization

5510C14 4LACC-20 Further Aspects of Exteriorization

5510C17 4LACC-21 Tolerance of Havingness

5510C17 4LACC-22 Establishing a Session

5510C18 4LACC-23 Beginning and Continuing a Session

5510C18 4LACC-24 Processing: Level One

5510C19 4LACC-25 The Senior De-sire of a Thetan

5510C19 4LACC-26 Third Level of a Process

5510C20 4LACC-27 The Pc's Pre-sent Time Problem—the Body

5510C20 4LACC-28 An Under-standing of Creative Processing

5510C21 4LACC-29 Native State and Postulates 1,2,3,4

5510C21 4LACC-30 Native State and Communication (also titled: Na-tive State and Confusion)

5510C24 4LACC-31 Resumé of Cre-ative Processes

5510C24 4LACC-32 Lack of Ter-minals

5510C25 4LACC-33 Engrams—Dis-semination of Material

5510C25 4LACC-34 The Handling of Confusion in Any Pc or on Any Dynamic

5510C26 4LACC-35 Stable Datum and the Study of Science

5510C26 4LACC-36 Solving En-grams with Stable Datum, Communi-cation Terminals

5510C27 4LACC-37 The Role of a Scientologist

5510C28 4LACC-38 The Anatomy of Terminals

5510C28 4LACC-39 Six Basic Levels

5510C28 4LACC-40 Intolerance

5510C31 4LACC-41 How to Audit

5510C31 4LACC-42 Training of an Auditor

5511C01 4LACC-43 The Preclear's Reality

5511C01 4LACC-44 Improvement in Technology

5511C02 4LACC-45 Trying and Communication

5511C02 4LACC-46 Randomity and Automaticities

5511C03 4LACC-47 A Review of the 4th London ACC

5511C03 4LACC-48 Attitude and Conduct of Scientologists

5511C16 4LACC-49 New Under-standing of Universes

5511C17 4LACC-50 End of Course Lecture

The London Public Lecture Ser-ies. These lectures were given to the public in London, England. All but one were given on four consecutive Saturdays in October, 1955. The lec-ture hall was so crowded that despite standing room being occupied, speakers had to be run elsewhere so that no one had to be turned away.

5510C08 LPLS-1 Goals of Dianetics and Scientology

5510C08 LPLS-2 Individual to Na-tional Levels of Intention, Confusion and Communication

5510C11 LPLS History of Dianetics and Scientology

5510C15 LPLS-3 How Good You Can Get

5510C15 LPLS-4 The Dynamics *Translations:* Danish, Dutch, French, Swedish.

5510C15 LPLS-4A The Eight Dynamics

5510C22 LPLS-5 The Goodness of Man

5510C22 LPLS-6 The Soul—Good and Evil

5510C29 LPLS-7 Automaticity—Cause and Effect

5510C29 LPLS-8 Power of Choice and Self-Determinism

The Hubbard Professional Course Lectures. L. Ron Hubbard gave the following lectures to the Hubbard Professional Course in London, Eng-land, during November, 1955.

5511C08 HPC N5-1 Six Levels of Processing, Issue 5, Level 1

5511C08 HPC N5-2 Six Levels of Processing, Issue 5, Level 2

5511C09 HPC N5-3 Six Levels of Processing, Issue 5, Level 3

5511C09 HPC N5-4 Six Levels of Processing, Issue 5, Level 4

5511C10 HPC N5-5 Six Levels of Processing, Issue 5, Level 5

5511C10 HPC N5-6 Six Levels of Processing, Issue 5, Level 6

Taped recordings, date not specifi-cally known, made during 1954-1955.

54__C__ The Dynamics—OT/ARC—As-isness

55__C__ Interview—Phoenix Press —L. Ron Hubbard

55__C__ Elementary Straightwire

55__C__ L. Ron Hubbard Auditing —"What Wouldn't You Mind Fight-ing"

55__C__ Two-way Comm

1956

BOOKS

Creative Learning—A Scientolo-gical Experiment in Schools, based on the works of L. Ron Hubbard, was published by the Hubbard Com-munications Office, London, England, in early 1956.

Scientology: The Fundamentals of Thought, The Basic Book of the Theory and Practice of Scientology for Beginners, by L. Ron Hubbard, was first published as a series of Professional Auditor's Bulletins starting June, 1956. *Fundamentals of Thought* was published in book form by the Hubbard Association of Scientologists International, Wash-ington, D.C., in September, 1956. *Translations:* Danish, Dutch, French, German, Greek, Spanish, Swedish.

L. Ron Hubbard's Professional Au-ditor's Bulletins Book 1 (Professional Auditor's Bulletins 1-15) by L. Ron Hubbard, published by the Hubbard Communications Office, Washington, D.C., 1955.

L. Ron Hubbard's Professional Au-ditor's Bulletins Book 2 (Professional Auditor's Bulletins 16-30) by L. Ron Hubbard, published by the Hubbard Communications Office, Washington, D.C., 1956.

L. Ron Hubbard's Professional Au-ditor's Bulletins Book 3 (Professional Auditor's Bulletins 31-46) by L. Ron Hubbard, published by the Hubbard Communications Office, Washington, D.C., 1956.

L. Ron Hubbard's Professional Au-ditor's Bulletins Book 4 (Professional Auditor's Bulletins 47-69) by L. Ron Hubbard, published by the Hubbard Communications Office, Washington, D.C., 1956.

(Note: the text of the Professional Auditor's Bulletins appears in *The Technical Bulletins of Dianetics and Scientology,* 1976.)

The Problems of Work, by L. Ron Hubbard, first published by Scientol-ogy Consultants to Industrial Effi-ciency, Washington, D.C., December, 1956. *Translations:* Danish, Dutch, French, German, Hebrew, Italian, Spanish, Swedish.

1956

TAPED LECTURES

The London Auditors' Meeting Lectures. L. Ron Hubbard gave the following lectures at the London Auditor's Meetings, beginning 1 De-cember 1955.

5512C01 LAM-1 The Lowest Level Case

5512C01 LAM-2 The Fundamentals of Auditing Style

5611C08 OS-9 Definition and Construction of Organization, Part I *Translations:* Dutch, Swedish.

5611C15 OS-10 Definition and Construction of Organization, Part II *Translations:* Dutch, Swedish.

5611C16 HCO Communications

5611C22 OS-11 The Consequence of Organization

5611C22 OS-12 The Deteriorization of Liberty

5611C29 OS-13 Hope

5611C29 OS-14 How to Present Scientology in a Mad World

5611C29 OS-14A The Scale of Havingness

5612C06 OS-15 Money

5612C06 OS-16 A Postulate Out of a Golden Age

5612C13 OS-17 Confusion and the Stable Datum

5612C13 OS-18 Randomity

5612C16 Promotion for Registrar

The Anti-Radiation Congress Lectures. L. Ron Hubbard gave 14 hours of lectures and group processing at the Anti-Radiation Congress held in Washington, D.C., December 29 through 31, 1956.

5612C29 ARC-1 Opening Lecture

5612C29 ARC-2 Scientology View on Radiation

5612C29 ARC-3 Proofing Up a Body

5612C29 ARC-4 Group Process—"Put it There"

5612C29 ARC-5 Group Process—Confrontingness

5612C30 ARC-6 Solution to Psychosis

5612C30 ARC-7 Project Third Dynamic

5612C30 ARC-8 Insanity—Scarcity of Importances

5612C30 ARC-9 Group Process—Mocking Up Bodies

5612C30 ARC-10 Group Process—Making Problems and Confusions With ____

5612C31 ARC-11 Background on Scales of Havingness

5612C31 ARC-12 Sub-Zero Scales—Relation to Scale of Awareness

5612C31 ARC-13 Confrontingness

5612C31 ARC-14 Confrontingness (cont'd)

1957

BOOKS

Scientology Training Course Manual: Field Validation and Hubbard Apprentice Scientologists, (also known as the *HAS Training Manual*) taken from the works of L. Ron Hubbard, published by the Hubbard Association of Scientologists International, Washington, D.C., 1957.

All About Radiation, by L. Ron Hubbard, published by the Hubbard Communications Office, London, England, May, 1957. *Translation:* Swedish.

Advanced Clinical Course (ACC) Preparatory Manual—for Advanced Students in Scientology, taken from the works of L. Ron Hubbard, published by the Hubbard Communications Office, Washington, D.C., summer of 1957.

Hubbard Certified Auditor Student Manual, taken from the works of L. Ron Hubbard, published by the Hubbard Communications Office, Washington, D.C., November, 1957.

Scientology: Clear Procedure, Issue I, by L. Ron Hubbard, published by the Hubbard Communications Office, London, England, December, 1957. *Translations:* Danish, Dutch, French, German, Spanish, Swedish.

Control and the Mechanics of S.C.S., by L. Ron Hubbard, published by the Hubbard Communications Office, Washington, D.C., December, 1957. *Translations:* Danish, Dutch, French, German, Spanish, Swedish.

Fortress In The Sky, by L. Ron Hubbard. Copyright 1957, 1967. Published by Hubbard College of Scientology, a nonprofit corporation in U.S.A., registered in England.

1957

TAPED LECTURES

The 16th American Advanced Clinical Course Lectures. L. Ron Hubbard gave the following lectures to students attending the 16th American ACC in Washington, D.C., 2 January through 11 February 1957.

5701C02 16ACC-1 Course Outline

5701C03 16ACC-2 Reality Scale in Action

5701C05 16ACC-3 Havingness: Particles, Solids, Spaces

5701C07 16ACC-4 Learning Process: No-Game Condition

5701C08 16ACC-5 Agreements and Postulates of the 8 Dynamics

5701C09 16ACC-6 Obnosis

5701C10 16ACC-7 The Postulate of Game

5701C11 16ACC-8 Postulates of Action-Reaction

5701C14 16ACC-9 Control

5701C15 16ACC-10 Evil

5701C16 16ACC-11 Havingness

5701C17 16ACC-12 Communication, Randomities of

5701C18 16ACC-13 Auditing Techniques: Self-Denial, Responsibility

5701C22 16ACC-14 Auditing Techniques: Order of Processes

5701C23 16ACC-15 Auditing Techniques: Scale of Processes

5701C24 16ACC-16 Auditing Techniques: Altering Cases

5701C25 16ACC-17 Auditing Techniques: Specifics

5701C28 16ACC-18 Auditing Techniques: Stimulus-response

5701C29 16ACC-19 Auditing Techniques: Action, Reaction

5701C30 16ACC-20 Auditing Techniques: Workable and Unworkable

5701C31 16ACC-21 Auditing Techniques: Solids

5702C01 16ACC-22 Auditing Techniques: Games Conditions

5702C04 16ACC-23 Auditing Techniques: Procedure CCH

5702C05 16ACC-24 Auditing Techniques: How Far South?

5702C06 16ACC-25 Demonstration

5702C07 16ACC-26 Summation

5702C08 16ACC-27 General Use of Procedure

5702C11 16ACC-28 Question and Answer Period

5702C11 16ACC-29 Final Lecture—Question and Answers

The 17th American Advanced Clinical Course Lectures. L. Ron Hubbard gave the following lectures to students attending the 17th American ACC in Washington, D.C., 18 February through 31 March 1957.

5702C25 17ACC-1 Opening Lecture, CCHs, the Future of Scientology

5702C26 17ACC-2 ARC Triangle and Associated Scales

5702C27 17ACC-3 Communication and Isness

5702C27 17ACC Inflow/Outflow

5702C28 17ACC-4 The Parts of Man *Translations:* Dutch, Spanish, Swedish.

5703C01 17ACC-5 Problems: Their Handling and Running

5703C01 17ACC-5A Q & A Period about Problems & Responsibility

5703C04 17ACC-6 Control

5703C05 17ACC-7 The Scale of Techniques

5703C06 17ACC-8 Reaching the Lowest Possible Level

5703C06 17ACC-8A Q & A on Control

5703C06 17ACC-8B Lecture on G.E. Anchor Points (Demonstration)

5703C07 17ACC-9 "Ought to Be"

5703C07 17ACC-9A Q & A Period on "Ought to Be"

5703C10 17ACC-10 Valences

5703C10 17ACC-10A Q & A Period after Lectures

5703C11 17ACC-11 Summary of Techniques

5703C11 17ACC-11A Comments and Question and Answer Period

5703C12 17ACC-12 Survival

5703C12 17ACC-12A Question and Answer Session on Lecture

5703C13 17ACC-13 Techniques in Practice

5703C14 17ACC-14 A Summary of an Intensive

5703C15 17ACC-15 Exact Control

5703C15 17ACC Q & A—Three Goals of Processing

5703C19 17ACC-16 Outline of Modern Intensive

5703C19 17ACC Control of *Homo sapiens*

5703C20 17ACC-17 Games Conditions

5703C21 17ACC-18 The Assist

5703C22 17ACC-19 Effect: Axiom 10

5703C23 Science Survey: Atomic Radiation

5703C25 17ACC-20 The Uses of Control

5703C25 17ACC-21 Rest Points and Confusions

5703C26 Processing on Rest Points and Confusions

5703C27 17ACC-22 Extroversion-Introversion, Its Relationship to Havingness and Communication

5703C28 17ACC-23 Valences and Control

5703C29 17ACC-24 The Professional Scientologist

5703C31 17ACC-25 Techniques in Practice

The London Congress on Nuclear Radiation and Health Lectures. L. Ron Hubbard gave the following lectures in London, England, from 12 April through 15 April 1957.

5704C12 LCNRH-1 Control, Communication and Havingness—I

5704C12 LCNRH-2 Control, Communication and Havingness—II

5704C12 LCNRH-3 Control Processes

5704C12 LCNRH-4 Demonstration "Dr. Ash"

5704C12 LCNRH-4A Havingness

5704C12 LCNRH-4B Flying Saucers

5704C13 LCNRH-5 Radiation and the Scientologist

5704C13 LCNRH-6 Radiation in Peace

5704C13 LCNRH-7 Radiation in War

5704C13 LCNRH-8 Group Processing: Emphasis on Control

5704C13 LCNRH-9 Group Processing: Emphasis on Control (cont'd)

5704C14 LCNRH-10 The Reality Scale and the Effect Scale

5704C14 LCNRH-11 The Reality Scale and the Effect Scale (cont'd)

5704C14 LCNRH-12 Scientology and Children

5704C14 LCNRH-15 Group Processing—"Sit in your chair, Wear a Head, Have two feet, etc."

5704C14 LCNRH-16 On Auditing

5704C15 LCNRH-17 The Control of Hysteria

5704C15 LCNRH-18 Effective Dissemination

The Hubbard Certified Auditor Course Lectures. L. Ron Hubbard gave the following lectures to the Hubbard Certified Auditor Course in Washington, D.C., in May, 1957.

5705C15 HCA-1 Comm Course, TRs 1, 2, 3, 4

5705C15 HCA-2 Comm Course, TR 5

5705C16 HCA-3 Procedure CCH: Background

5705C16 HCA-4 Procedure CCH: CCH Steps

5705C30 HCA-5 Outline of a Course and Its Purpose

L. Ron Hubbard made the following recordings in Washington, D.C., in April and June, 1957.

5704C18 Auditor's Training Evening, CCHs

5706C28 Lecture

5706C28 Question and Answer Period

The Freedom Congress Lectures. L. Ron Hubbard gave lectures and group processing from 4 to 7 July, 1957, at the Freedom Congress in Washington, D.C.

5707C04 FC-1 Opening Lecture—How We Have Addressed the Problem of the Mind

5707C04 FC-2 Man's Search and Scientology's Answer

5707C04 FC-3 Definition of Control

5707C05 FC-4 Basic Theory of CCHs

5707C05 FC-5 Group Processing—Acceptable Pressures

5707C05 FC-6 Group Processing—"Hold floor to earth"

5707C05 FC-7 Purpose and Need of Training Drills

5707C05 FC-8 Training Drills Demonstrated

5707C06 FC-9 Third Dynamic and Communication—Demonstration of High School Indoc

5707C06 FC-10 Training Demonstration of High School Indoctrination

5707C06 FC-11 Explanation & Demonstration of "Tone 40" on an Object

5707C06 FC-12 Levels of Skill

5707C06 FC-13 Explanation & Demonstration of "Tone 40" on a Person

5707C07 FC-14 Child Scientology (including Naming Ceremony) *Translations:* Danish, Dutch, French, Swedish.

5707C07 FC-15 CCH Steps 1 through 4: Demonstration

5707C07 FC-16 CCH Steps 5 through 7: plus Solids

The 18th American Advanced Clinical Course Lectures. L. Ron Hubbard gave the following lectures to the students on the 18th American ACC starting on July 15th, in Washington, D.C.

5707C15 18ACC-1 What is Scientology?

5707C16 18ACC-2 CCH Related to ARC

5707C17 18ACC-3 Theory and Definition of Auditing

5707C18 18ACC-4 What Scientology is Addressed to

5707C19 18ACC-5 The Five Categories

5707C22 18ACC-6 Control

5707C23 18ACC-7 The Stability of Scientology

5707C24 18ACC-8 Auditing Styles

5707C25 18ACC-9 Scales (Effect Scale)

5707C25 18ACC History of Clearing

5707C25 18ACC Q & A Period

5707C26 18ACC-10 The Mind: Its Structure in Relation to Thetan and MEST

5707C26 18ACC Anatomy of Problems—Coaching Athletics

5707C29 18ACC-11 Optimum 25-Hour Session

5707C30 18ACC-12 Death *Translations:* Danish, Dutch, French, Swedish.

5707C31 18ACC-13 Surprise—The Anatomy of Sleep

5708C01 18ACC-14 Thinnies

5708C02 18ACC-15 Ability—Laughter—The Scale of Withhold

5708C05 18ACC-16 The Handling of I.Q. (Factors Behind)

5708C06 18ACC-17 The Scale of Withhold

5708C07 18ACC-18 CCH—Havingness, Endurance, Progress

5708C08 18ACC-19 Confronting, Necessity Level

5708C09 18ACC-20 Instructing a Course

5708C16 18ACC-21 The Future of Scientology

5708C16 18ACC Awards

The following lectures and ceremonies were done by L. Ron Hubbard in Washington, D.C., in 1957.

5703C09 Wedding Ceremony, Naming Ceremony

5707C23 Wedding Ceremony

5711C26 Lecture to J. Fudge and Staff

5711C26 Lecture to Staff (cont'd)

The Ability Congress Lectures. L. Ron Hubbard gave nine lectures to the delegates to the Ability Congress in Washington, D.C., from 29 through 31 December 1957.

5712C29 AC-1 Experience—Randomity and Change of Pace

5712C29 AC-2 The Clear—Defined

5712C29 AC-3 Clear Procedure

5712C30 AC-4 Cause and Effect—Education, Unknowing and Unwilling Effect

5712C30 AC-5 Creating a Third Dynamic / United Survival Action Clubs

5712C30 AC-6 Upper Route to Operating Thetan/Not Know & Know—Perception & Telepathy

5712C31 AC-7 Responsibility (How to Create a Third Dynamic)

5712C31 AC-8 The NAAP (The National Academy of American Psychology)

5712C31 AC-9 Creative Processing Steps

1958

BOOKS

Academy of Scientology—Instructions & Information for Students in HCA, Validation or Special Communication Courses, based on the works of L. Ron Hubbard, published by the Hubbard Association of Scientologists International, Washington, D.C., 1958.

Axioms and Logics, by L. Ron Hubbard, published by the Hubbard

Communications Office, Washington, D.C., August, 1958. This is a compilation of materials originally published between the years 1951 and 1955. *Translations:* Danish, Dutch, French, German, Spanish, Swedish.

ACC Clear Procedure (20th American ACC), by L. Ron Hubbard, published by the Hubbard Communications Office, Washington, D.C., October, 1958. (The text of this book appears in full in *The Technical Bulletins of Dianetics and Scientology,* 1976.)

L. Ron Hubbard's Professional Auditor's Bulletins Book 5 (Professional Auditor's Bulletins 70-80) by L. Ron Hubbard, published by the Hubbard Communications Office, Washington, D.C., October, 1958. (The text of the Professional Auditor's Bulletins is printed in *The Technical Bulletins of Dianetics and Scientology,* 1976.)

1958

E-METERS

The new "Blue" American transistorized E-Meter was ready in time for the 19th American ACC in January, 1958. A meter was also developed around this time that projected and displayed the meter dial and the tone arm. It was used for classroom auditing demonstrations.

The use of the earlier Mathison meters was cancelled at this time.

In Great Britain the "Green and Gold" meter was built. At the time of the 5th London ACC L. Ron Hubbard had a number of these modified so that they would read standardly. The "Green and Gold" meter was used in this ACC.

but have now been made available as Super 8 mm film cartridges.

5807C04 CC-1 The Fact of Clearing

5807C04 CC-2 The Factors of Clearing (Four Elements)

5807C05 CC-3 The Freedoms of Clear

5807C05 CC-4 Evaluation of Importance, Things to Know in Clearing, Prerequisites to Auditing

5807C05 CC-5 Clear Procedure, Part I: CCH-0, Help

5807C05 CC-6 Clear Procedure, Part II: Creativeness

1958

TAPED LECTURES

The 19th American Advanced Clinical Course Lectures. L. Ron Hubbard gave the 19th American ACC in Washington, D.C., in January and February 1958.

5801C20 19ACC-1 The Four Universes

5801C20 19ACC-1A The E-Meter

5801C21 19ACC-2 Intensive Procedures

5801C21 19ACC-2A Question and Answer Period

5801C22 19ACC-3 The Bank Out of Control and Its Stabilization

5801C23 19ACC-4 Clearing Fields

5801C23 19ACC-4A Question and Answer Period plus Comments

5801C24 19ACC-5 E-Meter Identification and Association

5801C24 19ACC-5A Question and Answer Period: Step 6, Clearing Children

5801C27 19ACC-6 Clear Procedure I: What It Is You Clear, Something and Nothing

5801C27 19ACC-6A Q & A Period

5801C28 19ACC-7 Clear Procedure II: Man the Animal and Man the God *Translations:* Danish, Dutch, French, Swedish.

5801C28 19ACC-7A Clear Procedure II: Q & A, Handling the PT Problem

5801C29 19ACC-8 Clear Procedure

1958

FILMS

The Clearing Congress Lectures. L. Ron Hubbard had the first six lectures of the Clearing Congress in Washington, D.C. (4 and 5 July 1958) filmed in color. These films were originally available as 16 mm reels,

III: One Clear Procedure, Q & A Period

5801C30 19ACC-9 Clear Procedure IV: Test for Clears

5801C30 19ACC-9A Clear Procedure IV: Q & A, Space

5801C31 19ACC-10 Clear Procedure V: Importance of Theory Behind Clearing Procedure

5801C31 19ACC-10A Clear Procedure V: Q & A Period

5802C03 19ACC-11 Clear Procedure VI

5802C03 19ACC-11A Q & A Period

5802C04 19ACC-12 How to Find a Preclear, Responsibility and Help, Clear Procedure VII

5802C04 19ACC-12A Q & A Period

5802C05 19ACC-13 Clear Procedure VIII: The Basic Approach to Clearing, Finding the Auditor

5802C05 19ACC-13A Clear Procedure VIII: Q & A Period

5802C06 19ACC-14 CCH-0, S.C.S., Connectedness

5802C06 19ACC-14A Q & A

5802C07 19ACC-15 Help — How to Get Started

5802C07 19ACC-15A Q & A Period and Group Processing

5802C10 19ACC-16 Conduct of Clear

5802C10 19ACC-16A Q & A Period: Help, Clearing a Command

5802C10 19ACC-17 The Key Processes of Clearing

5802C11 19ACC-17A Q & A Period

5802C12 19ACC-18 Havingness, Anaten, Flows — in Relation to Clearing

5802C12 19ACC-18A Q & A Period: Postulates, Flows, Valences

5802C13 19ACC-19 Other Processes — the Help Button

5802C13 19ACC-19A Q & A Period

5802C14 19ACC-20 Responsibility for Mock-ups

5802C14 19ACC-20A Q & A Period: Present Time Problem

5802C14 19ACC-20B Q & A Period: Present Time Problem (cont'd)

The Clearing Congress Lectures. L. Ron Hubbard gave ten lectures during the Clearing Congress in Washington, D.C. between the 4th and 6th of July 1958. The first six lectures were filmed and are available as films.

5807C04 CC-1 The Fact of Clearing

5807C04 CC-2 The Factors of Clearing (Four Elements)

5807C04 CC-3 The Freedoms of Clear

5807C05 CC-4 Evaluation of Importance, Things to Know in Clearing, Prerequisites to Auditing

5807C05 CC-5 Clear Procedure, Part I: CCH-0, Help

5807C05 CC-6 Clear Procedure, Part II: Creativeness

5807C06 CC-7 The Magic Button

5807C06 CC-8 The Goal of Auditing

5807C06 CC-9 Violence

5807C06 CC-10 Juvenile

The 20th American Advanced Clinical Course Lectures. L. Ron Hub-

bard conducted the 20th American ACC from 7 July through 15 August 1958, in Washington, D.C.

5807C14 20ACC-1 Opening Lecture

5807C15 20ACC-2 ACC Procedure Outlined, E-Meter TRs

5807C15 20ACC-2A ACC Procedure Outlined, E-Meter TRs

5807C15 20ACC-2B Question and Answer Period

5807C16 20ACC-3 Course Procedure Outlined: How to Clear a Command, Simplicity, CCH-0

5807C16 20ACC-3A Question and Answer Period

5807C17 20ACC-4 Beginning and Ending Session — Gaining Pc's Contribution to the Session

5807C17 20ACC-4A Question and Answer Period

5807C18 20ACC-5 ACC Training Procedure: CCH-0, Problems and Goals

5807C18 20ACC-5A Question and Answer Period

5807C21 20ACC-6 The Key Words (Buttons) of Scientology Clearing

5807C21 20ACC-6A Question and Answer Period

5807C22 20ACC-7 The Rock

5807C22 20ACC-7A The Rock (cont'd), Question and Answer Period

5807C23 20ACC-8 Special Effects Cases — Anatomy

5807C23 20ACC-8A Question and Answer Period

5807C24 20ACC-9 Anatomy of Needles — Diagnostic Procedure

5807C24 20ACC-9A Question and Answer Period

5807C25 20ACC-10 The Rock

5807C25 20ACC-10A Question and Answer Period: Clearing the Command

5807C28 20ACC-11 ACC Command Sheet, Goals of Auditing

5807C29 20ACC-12 ACC Command Sheet (cont'd)

5807C30 20ACC-13 ACC Command Sheet (cont'd)

5807C31 20ACC-14 Running the Case and the Rock

5808C01 20ACC-15 Case Analysis — Rock Hunting

5808C01 20ACC-15A Case Analysis — Rock Hunting (cont'd)

5808C04 20ACC-16 Case Analysis (cont'd)

5808C04 20ACC-16A Q & A Period

5808C05 20ACC-17 ARC

5808C06 20ACC-18 The Rock, Its Anatomy

5808C07 20ACC-19 The Most Basic Rock of All Rocks

5808C07 20ACC-19A Question and Answer Period

5808C08 20ACC-19B Question and Answer Period (cont'd)

5808C08 20ACC-20 Auditor Interest

5808C08 20ACC-20A Requisites and Fundamentals of a Session

5808C15 20ACC-21 Summary of 20th ACC

The London Clearing Congress

Lectures. L. Ron Hubbard gave seven lectures at the London Clearing Congress in London, England, from 18 October through 20 October 1958.

5810C18 LCC-1 Story of Dianetics and Scientology

5810C18 LCC-2 The Skills of Clearing

5810C18 LCC-3 Confronting

5810C20 LCC-4 The Rock

5810C20 LCC-5 Confusion and Order

5810C20 LCC-6 The Clearing Technique of 1947

5810C20 LCC-7 The Future of Scientology and the Western Civilization

The 5th London Advanced Clinical Course Lectures. L. Ron Hubbard gave the following lectures to the 5th London ACC in the period 27 October through 18 November 1958, in London, England.

5810C27 5LACC-1 Clearing and What It Generally Means to Man

5810C28 5LACC-2 Compartmentation of 4 Universes

5810C28 5LACC-2A Question Time

5810C29 5LACC-3 Types of Pictures

5810C29 5LACC-3A Q & A

5810C30 5LACC-4 Mental Image Pictures, Engrams

5810C31 5LACC-5 Engrams

5811C03 5LACC-6 The Detection of Engrams

5811C04 5LACC-7 The Detection of Engrams with an E-Meter

5811C05 5LACC-8 Detection of Engrams III, "Finding Truth with an Electronic Gimmick"

5811C06 5LACC-9 Difficulties Encountered in Search for Engrams

5811C07 5LACC-10 Detection of Circuits and Machinery

5811C10 5LACC-11 Auditing: Its Skills

5811C11 5LACC-12 The Skill of an Auditor, Part I

5811C12 5LACC-13 The Skill of an Auditor, Part II

5811C13 5LACC-14 The Attitude of an Auditor

5811C14 5LACC-15 What an Auditor is Supposed to Do with an Engram

5811C17 5LACC-16 The Effect of the Environment on an Engram

5811C17 5LACC-17 How to Audit an Engram, Use of an E-Meter

5811C19 5LACC-18 How to Start and Run a Session

5811C20 5LACC-19 Attitude and Approach to Auditing

5811C28 5LACC-20 Summary, "Seeing the Monster"

5811C__ 5LACC-21 Final Lecture

Lectures and Conferences by L. Ron Hubbard during the year 1958 that are part of no other series.

5801C09 How to Run PTPs — Why Pc's Are Taking so Long to Clear

58__C__ SLP-8 Level 1

5803C27 Comments on Auditing

5806C27 Processing and Clearing

5808C24 Dictation to J. Fudge

5809C01 How to Run Present Time Problems

5809C27 HGC Auditor Conference at 1812 19th St. on Clear Procedure & Clearing People

5810C17 Talk to Staff on Arrival in England

5812C10 Flows & Ridges

5812C16 WST-1 PR&R-1: Promotion and Registration *Translation:* Swedish.

5812C29 HCO Area Sec Hat *Translations:* Dutch, Swedish.

1959

BOOKS

Hubbard Communications Office Manual of Justice, by L. Ron Hubbard, published by the Hubbard Communications Office, London, England, 1959.

The Hubbard Electrometer, based on research and development by L. Ron Hubbard, published by the Hubbard Communications Office, Washington, D.C., 1959.

Ceremonies of the Founding Church of Scientology, by L. Ron Hubbard, published by the Hubbard Communications Office, Washington, D.C., 1959. (This book has been replaced by *The Background and Ceremonies of The Church of Scientology,* 1970, which contains its text in full.)

1959

E-METERS

In the years 1959 through 1960 the British Mark I, Mark II and Mark III E-Meters were used in the United Kingdom. These meters were designed under the direct supervision of L. Ron Hubbard.

1959

TAPED LECTURES

The 1950 Success Congress Lectures. L. Ron Hubbard gave six lectures to the delegates to the 1950 Success Congress in Washington, D.C., on the 3rd and 4th of January 1959.

5901C03 SC-1 The Future of Scientology

5901C03 SC-2 Engrams and Clearing

5901C03 SC-3 Preliminary to Engram Running

5901C04 SC-4 Engram Running

5901C04 SC-5 Overt Act-Motivator Sequence

5901C04 SC-6 Leadership

5901C05 Summary of Techniques and Processes in Use

The 21st American Advanced Clinical Course Lectures. L. Ron Hubbard gave the lectures of the 21st ACC in Washington, D.C., 5 January through 13 February 1959.

5901C05 21ACC The Basics of Scientology

5901C06 21ACC Compartmentization of Universes

5901C07 21ACC Types of Pictures

5901C08 21ACC Engrams

5901C09 21ACC Engrams; The Rock Engram

5901C12 21ACC The Detection of Engrams

5901C13 21ACC Detection of Engrams with an E-Meter

5901C14 21ACC Detection of Engrams (3rd Part); Finding Truth with an E-Meter

5901C15 21ACC More on Detection of Engrams

5901C16 21ACC Detection of Circuits and Machinery, and the Observation of Special Types of Engrams

5901C19 21ACC Auditing Skills

5901C20 21ACC Skill of an Auditor

5901C21 21ACC Skills of an Auditor

5901C22 21ACC Attitude of an Auditor

5901C23 21ACC What an Auditor is Supposed to Do with an Engram

5901C26 21ACC The Effect of the Environment on an Engram

5901C26 21ACC-S1 How a Process Works

5901C27 21ACC How to Audit an Engram

5901C27 21ACC-S2 What Doesn't Make an Auditor

5901C28 21ACC How to Start and Run the Session

5901C28 21ACC-S3 The Establishment of "R"

5901C29 21ACC Attitude and Approach of the Auditor

5901C29 21ACC-S4 Muzzled Auditing

5901C30 21ACC Plan of Clearing

5901C30 21ACC-S5 The Grouper

5902C02 21ACC-S6 Axiom 10

5902C04 21ACC-S7 Diagnosis of an Uncracked Case

5902C05 21ACC Scout on Dynamics

5902C06 21ACC-S8 Setting Up Co-Auditing Groups, Processes Used in 21st ACC

5902C13 21ACC-S9 Summary of Data, Part I

5902C13 21ACC-S10 Summary of Data, Part II

Other lectures given by L. Ron Hubbard in February 1959, in Washington, D.C.

5902C02 WST-2 PR&R-2: "R" Factor Talk to Registrar

5902C16 Auditors' Conference

The Special Hubbard Professional Auditor's Course Lectures. L. Ron Hubbard gave the following lectures to the Special Hubbard Professional Auditor's Course in London, England, 6 April through 1 May 1959.

5904C06 SHPA-1 Beingness and Communication

5904C07 SHPA-2 Universes

5904C07 SHPA-3 The Dynamics

5904C08 SHPA-4 Scales

5904C08 SHPA-5 States of Being

5904C09 SHPA-6 Anatomy

5904C09 SHPA-7 What Can Be Done with The Mind (Reality Scale)

5904C14 SHPA-8 Mechanisms of the Mind *Translations:* Danish, Dutch, Spanish, Swedish.

5904C14 SHPA-9 Overt Act-Motivator Sequence

5904C15 SHPA-10 Codes

5904C15 SHPA-11 The Code of a Scientologist

5904C16 SHPA-12 The Logics and Axioms of Dianetics and Scientology

5904C16 SHPA-13 Axioms: Second Lecture

5904C21 SHPA-14 Types of Auditing

5904C21 SHPA-15 Modern Auditing Types

5904C22 SHPA-16 Types of Cases

5904C22 SHPA-17 Assessment

5904C23 SHPA-18 Present Time

5904C23 SHPA-19 Uses of the E-Meter in Locating Engrams

5904C28 SHPA-20 Theory of Processes

5904C28 SHPA-21 Processes

5904C29 SHPA-22 Specialized Auditing

5904C29 SHPA-23 Processing of Children

5904C30 SHPA-24 HAS Co-Audit

5904C30 SHPA-25 Electronic Phenomena of the Mind

5905C01 SHPA-26 End of Course Lecture

The 6th London Advanced Clinical Course Lectures. L. Ron Hubbard conducted the 6th London ACC at the Academy of Scientology in London, England, from 4 May through 13 June 1959.

5905C12 6LACC-1 Clearing

5905C13 6LACC-2 Second Lecture on Clearing Methodology

5905C14 6LACC-3 Clearing Technology

5905C18 6LACC-3A Title unknown

5905C19 6LACC-4 The Theory of Clearing

5905C20 6LACC-5 Clearing: Practice of

5905C21 6LACC-6 Clearing: Process—Special Cases

5905C26 6LACC-7 Clearing: Theta Clear Procedure

5905C27 6LACC-8 Clearing: General Processes (Lecture 2)

5905C28 6LACC-9 Clearing: General Cases—Communication Processes

5906C02 6LACC-10 Clearing: Fixed Ideas

5906C03 6LACC-11 Clearing: By Communication Processes, Specific

5906C04 6LACC-12 Clearing: By Communication, Special Problems

5906C09 6LACC-13 Clearing: Possibilities of

5906C10 6LACC-14 Clearing: Case Entrance Points

5906C11 6LACC-15 Clearing: General Results

The Theta Clear Congress Lectures. L. Ron Hubbard lectured to the Theta Clear Congress in Washington, D.C., July 4 and 5, 1959.

5907C04 TCC-1 HCO WW and Research

5907C04 TCC-2 Clearing

5907C04 TCC-3 HAS Co-audit

5907C05 TCC-4 Survive and Succumb ("Black Grampus")

5907C05 TCC-5 Communication Processes

5907C05 TCC-6 How to Conduct a HAS Co-audit and Why

5907C06 TCC How to Co-audit

5907C18 Communication and Hope

L. Ron Hubbard gave the following lecture at Saint Hill Manor, East Grinstead, Sussex, England, on the 12th of October 1959.

5910C12 Talk to HGCs

The Melbourne Congress Lectures. L. Ron Hubbard gave the following lectures to the Melbourne Congress in Melbourne, Australia, on November 7 and 8, 1959.

5911C07 MC-1 Welcome Address

5911C07 MC-2 Recent Developments on O.T.

5911C07 MC-3 The Route Through Step Six

5911C08 MC-4 Importances

5911C08 MC-5 Valences

5911C08 MC-6 Final Lecture

The 1st Melbourne Advanced Clinical Course Lectures. L. Ron Hubbard gave the following lectures to the students of the 1st Melbourne ACC in Melbourne, Australia, between November 9th and 30th in 1959.

5911C09 1MACC-1 The Know-how of Auditing

5911C09 1MACC-2 Demonstration of an Assist

5911C10 1MACC-3 Valence Splitting—Entering a Mind Process

5911C10 1MACC-4 Demonstration of Knocking Down a Tone Arm

5911C11 1MACC-5 Cycle of Action, Create, Destroy, Relative Importances

5911C11 1MACC-6 Demonstration: Force Process—Discreditable Creation

5911C12 1MACC-7 The Rule of the Weak Valence

5911C12 1MACC-8 Demonstration: Dynamic Straightwire Assessment

5911C12 1MACC-9 The Rehabilitation of Judgment

5911C13 1MACC-10 How to Have a Game Instead of a Case

5911C16 1MACC-11 The Collapsed Cycle of Action

5911C16 1MACC-12 Getting the Pc into Session

5911C17 1MACC-13 Case Assessment

5911C17 1MACC-14 Demonstration: Case Assessment

5911C18 1MACC-15 Alter-isness, Keynote of all Destruction

5911C18 1MACC-16 Demonstration: Minus Randomity Areas

5911C19 1MACC-17 Minus Randomity, Clue to Case Assessment

5911C19 1MACC-18 Intricacies of Create—Create Series

5911C20 1MACC-19 Rationale of Create Series

5911C20 1MACC-20 Responsibility of Creation

5911C23 1MACC-21 Responsibility for Zones of Creation

5911C23 1MACC-22 Demonstration: Responsibility for Destruction

5911C24 1MACC-23 The Universe of a Thetan

5911C24 1MACC-24 Demonstration: Turning on Pictures

5911C25 1MACC-25 Counter-create

5911C25 1MACC-26 Individuation *Translations:* Dutch, Swedish.

5911C26 1MACC-27 The Constancy of Fundamentals of Dianetics and Scientology

5911C26 1MACC-28 The Handling of Cases—Greatest Overt

5911C27 1MACC-29 Clearing Up the Whole Track

5911C27 1MACC-30 Principal Incidents on the Track

5911C30 1MACC-31 The Anatomy of Havingness

5911C30 1MACC-32 Processes

L. Ron Hubbard gave the following demonstration on his arrival at Saint Hill back in England, from Melbourne, Australia—10 December 1959.

5912C10 Demonstration of New HGC Process by L. Ron Hubbard

1960

BOOKS

Have You Lived Before This Life? A Scientific Survey, by L. Ron Hubbard, published by the Hubbard Communications Office, Saint Hill Manor, East Grinstead, Sussex, England, March, 1960.

1960

TAPED LECTURES

The State of Man Congress Lectures. L. Ron Hubbard gave the following lectures to the State of Man

Congress in Washington, D.C., the 1st through the 3rd of January 1960.

6001C01 SMC-1 Opening Lecture

6001C01 SMC-2 Responsibility *Translations:* Danish, Dutch, French, German, Spanish, Swedish.

6001C01 SMC-3 Overts and Withholds

6001C02 SMC-4 A Third Dynamic in Scientology—Why People Don't Like You

6001C02 SMC-5 Marriage *Translations:* Danish, Dutch, French, Swedish.

6001C02 SMC-6 Group Processing

6001C03 SMC-7 Zones of Control and Responsibility of Governments *Translation:* Dutch.

6001C03 SMC-8 Create and Confront

6001C03 SMC-9 Your Case

The Hubbard Clearing Scientologist Course Lectures. L. Ron Hubbard addressed the students of the Hubbard Clearing Scientologist Course Unit which began on 4 January 1960, in Washington, D.C.

6001C04 HCS-1 E-Meter Phenomena

6001C04 HCS-2 E-Meter and Time Track Structure

6001C05 HCS-3 Processing Against an E-Meter

6001C05 HCS-4 Operating an E-Meter in Processing—Fields & Location in Time

6001C06 HCS-5 Auditing

6001C06 HCS-6 Identity

6001C07 HCS-7 Inability to Withhold

6001C07 HCS-8 Case Level and Needle State

60__C__ HCS Supplementary Lecture 8: Specialized Problems

6001C08 HCS-9 Sessioning and Withholds

The London Open Evening Lectures. L. Ron Hubbard gave the following lectures in London, England, between 23 June and 7 July 1960.

6006C23 LOE-1 Differences Between Scientology and Other Studies

6006C23 LOE-2 Title unknown

6006C30 LOE-3 Some Aspects of Help

6007C07 LOE-4 Help

The London Congress on Dissemination and Help Lectures. L. Ron Hubbard gave the following lectures to the attendees of the Dissemination and Help Congress on the 7th of August 1960, in London, England.

6008C07 LCDH-1 Clearing and Presessioning

6008C07 LCDH-2 Pre-sessioning

6008C07 LCDH-3 Plant Research—Sickness—Will to Live—Adjustment of the Cycle of Action in Pre-sessioning (alternative title: Victim & Succumb)

These two lectures were given by L. Ron Hubbard to be played to congress attendees.

6002C__ Opening Speech to Jr. Congress Delegates

6007C04 Tenth Anniversary Congress

The 1st Saint Hill Advanced Clinical Course Lectures. L. Ron Hubbard gave the following lectures to the students on the 1st Saint Hill ACC at Saint Hill Manor, East Grinstead, Sussex, England, from 8 August to 16 September 1960.

6008C08 1SHACC-1 Introduction to Course

6008C10 1SHACC-2 Regimen 1

6008C12 1SHACC-3 Skill in Auditing

6008C15 1SHACC-4 Auditor Requirements

6008C16 1SHACC-5 Fundamentals with Regard to Cases

6008C17 1SHACC-6 Elements of Pre-sessioning

6008C18 1SHACC-7 Organization Programs

6008C19 1SHACC-8 Auditor Weakness

6008C22 1SHACC-9 Why Auditing Works

6008C23 1SHACC-10 Handling of Insanity

6008C24 1SHACC-11 Basic Relationship of Auditing

6008C25 1SHACC-12 Development of Scientology Data

6008C26 1SHACC-13 Fundamentals and Cases

6008C29 1SHACC-14 The Importance of an E-Meter

6008C30 1SHACC-15 Circuits and Havingness

6008C31 1SHACC-16 Theory 67

6009C01 1SHACC-17 Theory 67

6009C02 1SHACC-18 Case Improvements

6009C05 1SHACC-19 Successful Processes for Handling MEST

6009C06 1SHACC-20 Correct Use of E-Meter

6009C12 1SHACC-21 In-Sessionness

6009C13 1SHACC-22 How Havingness Relates to Circuits

6009C14 1SHACC-23 Formula of Havingness

6009C15 1SHACC-24 In-Sessionness and Havingness

6009C16 1SHACC-25 Final Lecture—6th and 7th Dynamics

The Anatomy of the Human Mind Congress Lectures. L. Ron Hubbard gave the following lectures to the attendees of the Anatomy of the Human Mind Congress in Washington, D.C., 31 December and 1 January 1961.

6012C31 AHMC-1 The Genus of Dianetics and Scientology

6012C31 AHMC-2 The Things of Scientology *Translations:* Danish, Dutch, German.

6012C31 AHMC-3 A Talk on South Africa

1961

BOOKS

E-Meter Essentials 1961, by L. Ron Hubbard, published by the Hubbard Communications Office, Saint Hill Manor, East Grinstead, Sussex, England, May 1961. *Translations:* Danish, Dutch, French, German, Spanish, Swedish.

Man Free From Man, taken from the works of L. Ron Hubbard, published by the Hubbard Communications Office, Saint Hill Manor, East Grinstead, Sussex, England, 1961.

1961

E-METERS

The British Mark IV E-Meter was introduced in early 1961. There were two versions of the Mark IV available in 1961. As of June the only Meter allowed in Academies of Scientology was the British Mark IV.

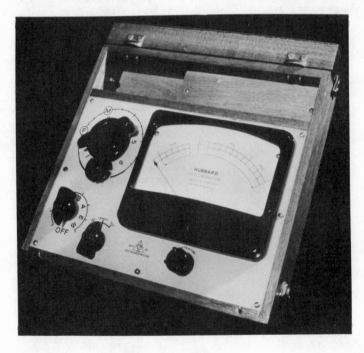

1961

TAPED LECTURES

6101C01 AHMC-4 Dianetics 1961 and the Whole Answer to the Problems of the Mind

6101C01 AHMC-5 The Field of Scientology

6101C01 AHMC-6 Scientology Org-

anizations *Translations:* Dutch, Swedish.

The 22nd American Advanced Clinical Course Lectures. L. Ron Hubbard gave the following lectures to the students of the 22nd American ACC in Washington, D.C., 2 January through 10 February 1961.

6101C02 22ACC-1 Present Time Problems—Why Cases Don't Move

6101C02 22ACC-2 Present Time Problems and Withholds

6101C03 22ACC-3 E-Meter

6101C03 22ACC-4 Withholds

6101C04 22ACC-5 What a Reactive Bank Is—The Mechanics of the Reactive Bank

6101C04 22ACC-6 Clearing Procedure

6101C05 22ACC-7 Dianetics and Present Time Problems

6101C05 22ACC-8 Methods of Clearing Technology—Finding of Havingness and Confront Processes—Pre-session 37

6101C06 22ACC-9 Dianetic Assist and Pre-session 38

6101C06 22ACC-10 Clearing Routine

The South African Anatomy Congress Lectures. L. Ron Hubbard gave the following lectures to the congress attendees in Johannesburg, South Africa, 21 and 22 January 1961.

6101C21 ACSA-1 Opening Lecture

6101C21 ACSA-2 The Parts of the Mind *Translations:* Danish, Dutch, German.

6101C21 ACSA-3 Aberration and the Handling of

6101C22 ACSA-4 Evolution of Early Research—Prehav Scale

6101C22 ACSA-5 Cycle of Action,

Time Track, Terminals, Stable Datum, Reactive Thought *Translations:* Danish, Dutch, German.

6101C22 ACSA-6 Johannesburg Staff Intros, Lecture: Clearing Certs for Clears

The 3rd South African Advanced Clinical Course Lectures. L. Ron Hubbard gave the following lectures to the students on the 3rd South African ACC in Johannesburg, South Africa, from 23 January to 17 February 1961.

6101C23 3SA ACC-1 HAS Co-audit Processes and E-Meter

6101C24 3SA ACC-2 Pre-session 38

6101C25 3SA ACC-3 Model Session Revised

6101C26 3SA ACC-4 Difference Between Dianetics and Scientology —Pre-session 38

6101C27 3SA ACC-5 Creative Ability

6102C02 3SA ACC-6 Auditor Failures

6102C03 3SA ACC-7 Regimen and Prehavingness—Advances

6102C06 3SA ACC-8 Making Formulas Out of the Prehav Scale

6102C07 3SA ACC-9 What Are You Auditing?

6102C08 3SA ACC-10 Case Behavior Under Processing

6102C09 3SA ACC-11 Mental Healing: Sanity and Insanity

6102C10 3SA ACC-12 Organization Lines

6102C13 3SA ACC-13 The Three Therapies of Earth

6102C14 3SA ACC-14 Fundamentals of Auditing

6102C15 3SA ACC-15 Havingness and Confront Scales

6102C16 3SA ACC-16 Machines and Havingness

6102C17 3SA ACC-17 Case Conditions

The Saint Hill Special Briefing Course Lectures. From 7 May 1961 to 13 December 1966, L. Ron Hubbard gave regular lectures to the students on the Saint Hill Special Briefing Course at Saint Hill Manor, East Grinstead, Sussex, England.

6105C07 SHSBC-1 E-Meter Talk and Demonstration

6105C12 SHSBC-2 Assessment

6105C19 SHSBC-3 E-Meter

6105C26 SHSBC-4 On Auditing

6106C01 SHSBC-5 Flattening Process and E-Meter

6106C02 SHSBC-6 Flows, Prehav Scale, Primary Scale

6106C05 SHSBC-7 Routine One, Two and Three

6106C06 SHSBC-8 Routine One, Two and Three

6106C07 SHSBC-9 Points in Assessing

6106C08 SHSBC-10 Q & A Period and Ending an Intensive

6106C09 SHSBC-11 Reading E-Meter Reactions

6106C12 SHSBC-12 E-Meter Actions, Errors in Auditing

6106C13 SHSBC-13 Seminar—Q & A Period

6106C14 SHSBC-14 Seminar—Withholds

6106C15 SHSBC-15X Not Know

6106C16 SHSBC-16X Confront and Havingness—Routine 1, 2, & 3

6106C19 SHSBC-15 Q & A Period —Auditing Slowdowns

6106C20 SHSBC-16 Sec Check Questions—Mutual Rudiments

6106C21 SHSBC-17 Seminar at Saint Hill (Auditing Speed)

6106C22 SHSBC-18 Running CCHs *Translations:* Danish, Dutch, French, German, Spanish, Swedish.

6106C23 SHSBC-19 Q & A Period —CCHs—Auditing

6106C26 SHSBC-20 Dealing With Attacks on Scientology

6106C27 SHSBC-21 CCHs—Circuits

6106C28 SHSBC-22 Raw Meat—Trouble Shooting Cases

6106C29 SHSBC-23 Wrong Target —Sec Check

6106C30 SHSBC-24 Training on TRs—Talk on Auditing *Translation:* Dutch.

6107C03 SHSBC-26X Routine 1A —Problems

6107C04 SHSBC-27X Routine 1A —Problems and Solutions

6107C05 SHSBC-25 Q & A Period Procedure in Auditing

6107C06 SHSBC-26 Routine 1A—Problems

6107C11 SHSBC-27 Routine 1A—Problems and Solutions

6107C12 SHSBC-28 Q & A Period

6107C14 SHSBC-29 Checking Ruds and Withholds

6107C18 SHSBC-30 Can't Have—Create—Fundamentals of all Problems

6107C19 SHSBC-31 Q & A Period: Auditor Effect on Meter

6107C20 SHSBC-32 Games Conditions

6107C22 LAC-1 Ron's Opening Talk and Slides—Los Angeles Congress

6108C03 SHSBC-33 Creation and Goals

6108C04 SHSBC-34 Methodology of Auditing—Not Doingness and Occlusion

6108C08 SHSBC-35 Forgettingness

6108C09 SHSBC-36 Q & A—Goals Search

6108C10 SHSBC-37 Q & A—Goals Assessment, Behavior of Pc

6108C11 SHSBC-38 Basics of Auditing—Matter of Factness

6108C15 SHSBC-39 Q & A—Anatomy and Assessment of Goals

6108C16 SHSBC-40 Unknown—Cyclic Aspect of Goals

6108C17 SHSBC-41 Rudiments—Valences

6108C18 SHSBC-42 Control of Attention

6108C22 SHSBC-43 PTPs—Unknownesses *Translation:* Dutch.

6108C23 SHSBC-44 Basics of Auditing

6108C24 SHSBC-45 Rudiments

6108C29 SHSBC-46 Basics of Auditing

6108C30 SHSBC-47 Auditing Quality

6108C31 SHSBC-48 What is Auditing?

6109C06 SHSBC-49 Principles of Auditing

6109C06 SHSBC-50 Subjective Reality

6109C07 SHSBC-51 Reality in Auditing

6109C12 SHSBC-52 Clearing Breakthrough

6109C13 SHSBC-53 Sec Check and Withholds

6109C14 SHSBC-54 Goals and Terminals Assessment

6109C19 SHSBC-55 Q & A Period —Prehav, Sec Checks, ARC Break Process, Sec Check and Withholds

6109C20 SHSBC-56 Seminar at SH Q & A Period—What is Knowable to Pc (when an E-Meter will react), Attention, Motion, Still Pictures

6109C21 SHSBC-57 Smoothness of Auditing

6109C26 SHSBC-58 Teaching the Field—Sec Checks

6109C27 SHSBC-59 Q & A Period; States of Beingness

6109C28 SHSBC-60 Grades of Auditors

6110C03 SHSBC-61 The Prior Confusion *Translations:* Danish, Dutch, French, German, Spanish, Swedish.

6110C04 SHSBC-62 Moral Codes: What is a Withhold? *Translations:* Danish, Dutch, French, German.

6110C05 SHSBC-63 Sec Checking —Types of Withholds *Translations:* Danish, Dutch, French, German, Spanish, Swedish.

6110C10 SHSBC-64 Problems Intensive *Translations:* Danish, Dutch, French, German, Spanish, Swedish.

6110C11 SHSBC-65 Problems Intensive Assessment *Translations:* Danish, French, German, Spanish, Swedish.

6110C12 SHSBC-66 Problems

6110C17 SHSBC-67 Problems Intensive Procedures

6110C18 SHSBC-68 Valences—Circuits

6110C19 SHSBC-69 Q & A Period —Flows

6110C24 SHSBC-70 Clearing

6110C25 SHSBC-71 Importance of Goals Terminals

6110C26 SHSBC-72 Security Checking Auditing Errors

6110C31 SHSBC-73 Rudiments

6111C01 SHSBC-74 Formation of Commands

6111C02 SHSBC-75 How to Security Check

6111C07 SHSBC-76 Routine 3A

6111C08 SHSBC-77 Checking Case Reports

6111C09 SHSBC-78 Effective Auditing

6111C14 SHSBC-79 Routine 3D

6111C15 SHSBC-80 Routine 3D Continued

6111C16 SHSBC-81 Points in Assessing

6111C21 SHSBC-82 Running 3D

6111C22 SHSBC-83 Reading the E-Meter

6111C23 SHSBC-84 Auxiliary Pre-Have: 3D Scale

6111C28 SHSBC-85 Havingness

6111C29 SHSBC-86 E-Meter Tips

6111C30 SHSBC-87 Parts of 3D

6112C05 SHSBC-88 Assessing 3D

6112C06 SHSBC-89 Sec Checks Necessary

6112C07 SHSBC-90 Expectancy of 3D

6112C12 SHSBC-91 Sec Checks in Processing

6112C13 SHSBC-92 Assessing 3D

6112C14 SHSBC-93 Anatomy of Problems

6112C19 SHSBC-94 Parts of 3D

6112C20 SHSBC-95 Upgrading of Auditors

6112C21 SHSBC-96 Probabilities of 3D

The Clean Hands Congress Lectures. L. Ron Hubbard gave nine lectures to the attendees of the Clean Hands Congress in Washington, D.C., 30 December 1961 through 1 January 1962.

6112C30 CHC-1 Scientology, Where We Are Going

6112C30 CHC-2 Auditing Perfection and Classes of Auditors

6112C30 CHC-3 Parts of the 3D Package

6112C31 CHC-4 The Goals Problems Mass

6112C31 CHC-5 The E-Meter and Its Use—Demonstration

6112C31 CHC-6 Havingness, Quality of Reach

6201C01 CHC-7 The Valence, How It Works

6201C01 CHC-8 Goals Package Balance of Valences and Identification

6201C01 CHC-9 Effectiveness and Your Effectiveness Now

1962

E-METERS

The first British Mark V E-Meter became available in 1962. Its sensitivity range was greatly increased over all previous meters. An even more sensitive Mark V became available in 1963.

1962

TAPED LECTURES

The Saint Hill Special Briefing Course Lectures continued throughout 1962 and 1963.

6201C09 SHSBC-97 Twenty-Ten— 3DXX

6201C10 SHSBC-98 Sec Checks— Withholds

6201C11 SHSBC-99 How to Audit

6201C16 SHSBC-100 Nature of Withholds *Translations:* Danish, Dutch, French, German, Spanish, Swedish.

6201C17 SHSBC-101 Anatomy of 3D GPM

6201C18 SHSBC-102 3D Criss Cross—GPM

6201C23 SHSBC-103 Basics of Auditing

6201C24 SHSBC-104 Training— Duplicaton *Translations:* Danish, Dutch, French, German, Spanish, Swedish.

6201C25 SHSBC-105 Whole Track

6201C30 SHSBC-106 In-sessionness

6201C31 SHSBC-107 Usages of 3DXX

6202C01 SHSBC-108 Flows

6202C06 SHSBC-111 Withholds

6202C07 SHSBC-112 Missed Withholds

6202C08 SHSBC-109 3DXX Assessment

6202C13 SHSBC-110 Prep Clearing

6202C14 SHSBC-117 Directing Attention

6202C15 SHSBC-118 Prepchecking

6202C20 SHSBC-113 What is a Withhold? *Translations:* Danish, Dutch, French, German, Spanish, Swedish.

6202C21 SHSBC-114 Use of Prepchecking

6202C22 SHSBC-119 Prepclearing and Rudiments

6202C27 SHSBC-115 Prepchecking

6202C27 SHSBC-116 Auditor's Code

6203C01 SHSBC-120 Model Session I

6103C01 SHSBC-121 Model Session II

6203C19 SHSBC-122 The Bad "Auditor"

6203C19 SHSBC-123 Mechanics of Suppression *Translations:* Dutch, Swedish.

6203C20 SH TVD-1 3DXX Assessment

6203C20 SH TVD-2 3DXX Assessment (cont'd)

6203C21 SHSBC-124 Prepchecking

6203C21 SHSBC-125 Prepchecking

6203C27 SHSBC-130 Prepchecking Data

6203C29 SHSBC-126 CCHs

6203C29 SHSBC-127 Q and A Period

6204C03 SHSBC-131 The Overt-Motivator Sequence *Translations:* Danish, Dutch, French, German, Spanish, Swedish.

6204C05 SHSBC-128 Sacredness of Cases—Self-Determinism, Other-Determinism and Pan-Determinism

6204C05 SHSBC-129 As-isness, People Who Can and Can't As-is

6204C17 SHSBC-132 Auditing

6204C17 SHSBC-133 How and Why Auditing Works

6204C19 SHSBC-134 Gross Auditing Errors

6204C19 SHSBC-135 Determining What to Run

6204C24 SHSBC-136 Rundown on 3DXX, Part I

6204C24 SHSBC-137 Rundown on 3DXX, Part II

6204C25 SH TVD-3 Checking Line Plots

6204C26 SHSBC-138 Rundown on Prepchecking (Professional Attitude)

6204C26 SHSBC-139 Rundown on Routine 3: Routine 3DXX

6205C01 SHSBC-140 Missed Withholds

6205C01 SHSBC-141 Routine 3G, Experimental Preview of a Clearing Process

6205C02 SH TVD-4A Prepchecking, Part I

6205C02 SH TVD-4B Prepchecking, Part II

6205C03 SHSBC-142 Craftmanship—Fundamentals

6205C03 SHSBC-143 Prepchecking

6205C15 SHSBC-144 New Training Sections

6205C15 SHSBC-145 New TRs

6205C16 SH TVD-5A Patching Up 3DXX Cases, Part I

6205C16 SH TVD-5B Patching Up 3DXX Cases, Part II (L. Ron Hubbard Audits 5 different Pcs)

6205C17 SHSBC-146 Auditing Errors

6205C17 SHSBC-147 Prepchecking

6205C22 SHSBC-150 Administration of Courses

6205C22 SHSBC-151 Missed Withholds *Translations:* Danish, Dutch, French, German, Spanish, Swedish.

6205C23 SH TVD-6 Check on "What" Questions and Havingness Probe

6205C23 SH TVD-7 Fish and Fumble—Checking Dirty Needles

6205C24 SHSBC-148 E-Meter Data—Instant Reads, Part I

6205C24 SHSBC-149 E-Meter Data—Instant Reads, Part II

6205C25 SHSBC-152 Question and Answer Period

6205C29 SHSBC-153 Security Check Prepchecking

6205C30 SH TVD-8A Getting Rudiments In (L. Ron Hubbard auditing demonstration), Part I

6205C30 SH TVD-8B Getting Rudiments In, Part II

6205C31 SHSBC-154 Value of Rudiments

6205C31 SHSBC-155 Middle Rudiments

6206C12 SHSBC-160 How to Do Goals Assessment

6206C12 SHSBC-161 Middle Rudiments

6206C13 SH TVD-9 Checking Out a Goal, Part I

6206C13 SH TVD-10 Checking Out a Goal—Fish and Fumble—Part II

6206C14 SHSBC-156 Future Technology

6206C14 SHSBC-157 Listing *Translations:* Danish, French, German, Spanish, Swedish.

6206C19 SHSBC-158 Do's and Don'ts of R3GA

6206C19 SHSBC-159 Question and Answer Period

6206C20 SH TVD-10 Special New Model Session

6206C21 SHSBC-162 Model Session Revised

6206C21 SHSBC-163 Question and Answer Period

6206C26 SHSBC-164 E-Meter Quality

6206C26 SHSBC-165 Prepchecking

6206C28 SHSBC-166 Rudiments

6206C28 SHSBC-167 Question and Answer Period

6207C10 SHSBC-168 Repetitive Rudiments and Repetitive Prepchecking, Part I

6207C10 SHSBC-169 Repetitive Rudiments and Repetitive Prepchecking, Part II

6207C12 SHSBC-174 Meter Reading

6207C12 SHSBC-175 Meter Training

6207C17 SHSBC-170 E-Meter Reads and ARC Breaks

6207C17 SHSBC-171 Anatomy of ARC Breaks *Translation:* Dutch.

6207C19 SHSBC-172 The E-Meter

6207C19 SHSBC-173 Question and Answer Period

6207C24 SHSBC-176 Routine 3GA, Part I

6207C24 SHSBC-177 Routine 3GA, Part II

6207C26 SHSBC-178 Routine 3GA

6207C26 SHSBC-179 Prepchecking

6208C07 SHSBC-180 Routine 3GA Data on Goals, Part I

6208C07 SHSBC-181 Routine 3GA Data on Goals, Part II

6208C08 SH TVD-11 Routine 3GA Nulling Goals Demonstration

6208C09 SHSBC-182 Clearing

6208C09 SHSBC-183 Goals Listing

6208C14 SHSBC-184 Rock Slams and Dirty Needles

6208C14 SHSBC-185 World Clearing

6208C15 SH TVD-12A 3GA Dynamic Assessment—Listing Items for Dynamics, I

6208C15 SH TVD-12B 3GA Dynamic Assessment—Listing Items for Dynamics, II

6208C16 SHSBC-186 3GA Dynamic Assessment

6208C21 SHSBC-187 Finding Goals by Dynamic Assessment

6208C21 SHSBC-188 Basics of Auditing *Translations:* Danish, Dutch, French, German, Spanish, Swedish.

6208C22 SH TVD-13A Dynamic Assessment and Item Assessment, Part I

6208C22 SH TVD-13B Dynamic Assessment and Item Assessment, Part II

The Clearing Success Congress Lectures. L. Ron Hubbard gave nine lectures to the Clearing Success Congress delegates in Washington, D.C., 1 to 3 September 1962.

6209C01 CSC-1 Presentation of the GPM

6209C01 CSC-2 The Point Where the Pc Begins to Get Clear

6209C01 CSC-3 Basic Purpose

6209C02 CSC-4 The Healing Effect of Preparatory Auditing (Suppress Button)

6209C02 CSC-5 Staff Introduction—Demonstration

6209C02 CSC-6 The Problems Intensive, Mechanics and Buttons

6209C03 CSC-7 World Clearing and You

6209C03 CSC-8 Slide Show

6209C03 CSC-9 Your Scientology Orgs and What They Do for You *Translations:* Dutch, Swedish.

Saint Hill Special Briefing Course Lectures continued—

6209C18 SHSBC-189 Directing Pc's Attention

6209C18 SHSBC-190 3GA Dynamic Assessment by Rock Slam

6209C19 SH TVD-14A Tiger Drill, Part 1

6209C19 SH TVD-14B Tiger Drill, Part 2

6209C20 SHSBC-191 Listing Lines *Translation:* Dutch.

6209C20 SHSBC-192 Geriatrics

6209C25 SHSBC-193 Current Trends

6209C25 SHSBC-194 3GA Assessment

6209C26 SH TVD Nulling Goals Session

6209C27 SHSBC-195 3GA Listing

6209C27 SHSBC-195A 3GA Listing Lines by Tiger Buttons

6210C02 SHSBC-196 3GA Listing Lines by Tiger Buttons

6210C02 SHSBC-197 3GA Listing Session—Listing Lines by Tiger Buttons—2nd Lecture

6210C03 SH TVD-15A Prechecking a Goal, Part I

6210C03 SH TVD-15B Prechecking a Goal, Part II

6210C04 SHSBC-198 Modern Security Checking

6210C04 SHSBC-199 Making a Goal Fire

6210C09 SHSBC-200 Future Org Trends *Translations:* Dutch, Swedish.

6210C09 SHSBC-201 Instructors' Bugbear

6210C11 SHSBC-202 3GA Goals Finding

6210C11 SHSBC-203 3GA Goals Finding

6210C23 SHSBC-202X 3GA Criss Cross

6210C23 SHSBC-203X 3GAXX Following the Rock Slam

6210C25 SHSBC-208 3GAXX

6210C25 SHSBC-209 3GAXX Secondary Pre-Hav Scale

6210C30 SHSBC-204 Pre-Hav Scales and Lists

6210C30 SHSBC-205 Listing Goals

6211C01 SHSBC-206 The Missed Missed Withhold *Translations:* Danish, Dutch, French, German, Spanish, Swedish.

6211C01 SHSBC-207 The Road to Truth *Translations:* Danish, Dutch, French, German, Spanish, Swedish.

6211C13 SHSBC-210 The Difficult Case

6211C13 SHSBC-211 Entrance to Cases

6211C15 SHSBC-212 Terminals

6211C15 SHSBC-213 Clearing Technology

6211C20 SHSBC-214 The GPM

6211C20 SHSBC-215 Fundamentals of Auditing

6211C22 SHSBC-216 Q & A Period, Part 1

6211C22 SHSBC-217 Q & A Period, Part 2

6211C27 SHSBC-218 Routine 2-12

6211C27 SHSBC-219 Routine 2-12

6211C29 SHSBC-220 R2-12 Theory and Practice, Part I

6211C29 SHSBC-221 R2-12 Theory and Practice, Part II

6212C11 SHSBC-222 R2-12 Data

6212C11 SHSBC-223 Phantom R/S

6212C13 SHSBC-224 R2-12 Data—Needle Behavior

6212C13 SHSBC-225 Repair of R2-12—Clean Needle

1963

E-METERS

A new British Mark V E-Meter became available in 1963 with double

the sensitivity of the first Mark V. The Mark IV and the Mark V were both in use throughout 1965. The Mark IV was discontinued in December 1965.

1963

FILMS

An Afternoon at Saint Hill With Ron. This film was made at Saint Hill Manor, East Grinstead, Sussex, England in 1963.

1963

TAPED LECTURES

The Saint Hill Special Briefing Course continued throughout 1963.

6301C08 SHSBC-226 R2-10 and R2-12

6301C08 SHSBC-227 Case Repair

6301C10 SHSBC-228 R2-12

6301C10 SHSBC-229 How to Audit

6301C10 Saint Hill Press Interview, L. Ron Hubbard with Australian Press at Saint Hill

6301C15 SHSBC-230 R2-12 Dead Horses

6301C15 SHSBC-231 R2-12 Nerves

6301C16 SHSBC-232 TVD-16 TR 0 Demonstration *Translation:* Swedish.

6301C16 SHSBC-233 TR 0 Lecture

6302C06 Instructors Conference

6302C07 SHSBC-234 R-3 MX, Part I

6302C07 SHSBC-235 R-3 MX, Part II

6302C12 SHSBC-236 Routine 3M

6302C13 SHSBC-237 TVD-16 Mid Rud. and Hav.

6302C13 SHSBC-238 Discussion by L. Ron Hubbard of TVD

6302C14 SHSBC-239 Routine 3M

6302C19 SHSBC-240 Rundown on Processes

6302C20 SHSBC-241 Talk on TV Demonstration—Finding RRs

6302C21 SHSBC-242 R-2 and R-3 Current Auditing Rundown

6302C26 SHSBC-243 R-3M Current Rundown by Steps

6302C27 SHSBC-246 TVD-17 Case Repair (Auditor: L. Ron Hubbard)

6302C27 SHSBC-246A TVD-17A Case Repair (Auditor: L. Ron Hubbard)

6302C28 SHSBC-244 Goals Problems Mass

6303C05 SHSBC-245 R-2 and R-3 Urgent Data

6303C07 SHSBC-247 When Faced with the Unusual, Do the Usual

6303C13 SHSBC Auditing and Assessment

6303C19 SHSBC-250 R-3M How to Find Goals

6303C19 SHSBC Flattening a Process

6303C20 SH TVD-18 Rudiments and Havingness Session and Short Lecture (Auditor: L. Ron Hubbard)

6303C21 SHSBC-251 R-2G Series

6303C26 SHSBC-252 Case Repair

6303C27 SHSBC-254 TVD-19 Sec Checking, Talk by L. Ron Hubbard

6303C28 SHSBC-253 The GPM

6304C02 SHSBC-256 Line Plot, Items

6304C04 SHSBC-255 Anatomy of the GPM

6304C16 SHSBC-257 Top of GPM

6304C18 SHSBC-258 Directive Listing

6304C20 PAC-1 Clearing

6304C20 PAC-2 Clearing

6304C23 SHSBC-259 Goals Problems Mass

6304C25 SHSBC-260 Finding Goals

6304C30 SHSBC-261 Directive Listing

6305C02 SHSBC-262 Running the GPM

6305C14 SHSBC-263 Implant GPMs

6305C15 SHSBC-264 TVD-20 Blocking Out and Dating Items and Incidents Prior to Implants

6305C16 SHSBC-265 The Time Track

6305C21 SHSBC-266 The Helatrobus Implants

6305C22 SHSBC-267 TVD-21 Engram Running—Helatrobus Implant (Auditor: L. Ron Hubbard)

6305C23 SHSBC-268 State of O.T.

6305C28 SHSBC-269 Handling ARC Breaks *Translations:* Danish, Dutch, French, German, Spanish, Swedish.

6305C29 SHSBC-270 Programming Cases, Part 1

6305C30 SHSBC-271 Programming Cases, Part 2

6306C11 SHSBC-272 Engram Chain Running

6306C12 SHSBC-273 ARC Straightwire

6306C13 SHSBC-274 Levels of Case

6306C18 SHSBC-275 Beingness

6306C19 SHSBC-276 Summary of Modern Auditing

6306C20 SHSBC-277 History of Psychotherapy

6306C25 SHSBC-278 Routine 2H

6306C26 SHSBC-279 TVD-22 Listing Assessment for Engram Running, 1

6306C27 SHSBC-280 TVD-23 Listing Assessment for Engram Running, 2

6307C09 SHSBC-281 The Free Being

6307C10 SHSBC-282 Auditing Skills for R-3R

6307C10 SHSBC-284A Preliminary Steps of R-3R, Part 1

6307C10 SHSBC-284B Preliminary Steps of R-3R, Part 2

6307C11 SHSBC-283 ARC Breaks

6307C16 SHSBC-285 Tips on Running R-3R

6307C17 SHSBC-286 Dating

6307C18 SHSBC-287 Errors in Time

6307C23 SHSBC-288 Between Lives Implants

6307C24 SHSBC-289 ARC Breaks and the Comm Cycle—The Revised Model Session *Translations:* Danish, Dutch, French, German, Spanish, Swedish.

6307C25 SHSBC-290 Comm Cycles in Auditing *Translations:* Danish, Dutch, French, German, Spanish, Swedish.

6308C06 SHSBC-291 Auditing Comm Cycles—Definition of an Auditor *Translations:* Danish, Dutch, French, German, Spanish, Swedish.

6308C07 SHSBC-292 R-2H Fundamentals *Translations:* Danish, Dutch, French, German, Spanish, Swedish.

6308C08 SHSBC-293 R-2H Assessment

6308C14 SHSBC-294 Auditing tips

6308C15 SHSBC-295 The Tone Arm *Translation:* French.

6308C20 SHSBC-296 The Itsa Line *Translations:* Danish, Dutch, French, German, Spanish, Swedish.

6308C21 SHSBC-297 The Itsa Line (cont'd) *Translations:* Danish, Dutch, French, German, Spanish, Swedish.

6308C22 SHSBC-298 Project 80

6308C27 SHSBC-299 Rightness and Wrongness *Translations:* Danish, Dutch, French, German, Spanish, Swedish.

6308C28 SHSBC-300 The TA and the Service Facsimile

6308C29 SHSBC-301 The Service Facsimile (cont'd)

6309C03 SHSBC-302A R3SC

6309C04 SHSBC-302 How to Find a Service Facsimile *Translations:* Dutch, French, German, Spanish, Swedish.

6309C05 SHSBC-303 Service Fac Assessment

6309C10 SHSBC-304 Destimulation of a Case

6309C11 SHSBC-306 Service Facs and GPMs

6309C12 SHSBC-305 Service Facs

6309C17 SHSBC-307 What You Are Auditing

6309C18 SHSBC-308 Saint Hill Service Fac Handling

6309C19 SHSBC-309 Routine 4M TA (HCOB 2 Oct 63 cancels R4M TA)

6309C24 Summary I (Cancelled by HCOB 12 Oct 63)

6309C25 SHSBC-310 Summary II Scientology 0 *Translation:* French.

6309C26 SHSBC-311 Summary III About Level IV Auditing

6310C15 SHSBC-312 Essentials of Auditing

6310C16 SHSBC-313 The Itsa Maker Line

6310C17 SHSBC-314 Levels of Auditing

6310C21 SHSBC-315 Attack and GPMs

6310C22 SHSBC-316 The Integration of Auditing

6310C23 SHSBC-317 Auditing the GPM

6310C29 SHSBC-318 Routine 4

6310C30 SHSBC-319 R4 Case Assembly

6310C31 SHSBC-320 R4M2 Programming

6311C05 SHSBC-321 Three Zones of Auditing

6311C07 SHSBC-322 Relationship of Training to O.T.

6311C16 Interview with the Saturday Evening Post

6311C17 Interview with the Saturday Evening Post

6311C26 SHSBC-323 R4 Auditing

6311C27 SHSBC-330 TVD-25 Auditing Demonstration and Comments by L. Ron Hubbard

6311C28 SHSBC-324 Seven Classifications

6311C28 Auditing Demonstration

6311C28 Auditing Demonstration

6311C29 Auditing Demonstration

6312C02 Auditing Demonstration: L. Ron Hubbard

6312C03 SHSBC-325 Certifications and Classifications

6312C03 L. Ron Hubbard Auditing Demonstration

6312C04 SHSBC-326 TVD-24 Basic Auditing

6312C04 O.T. Processes (L. Ron Hubbard Auditing Demonstration)

6312C05 SHSBC-327 Basic Auditing

6312C10 SHSBC-328 Scientology 0 *Translation:* French.

6312C10 SHSBC-327E The Dangerous Environment

6312C11 Goals to Do and Think (Auditing Demonstration)

6312C12 SHSBC-329 Summary of O.T. Processes

6312C13 Auditing Demonstration: L. Ron Hubbard

6312C15 Auditing Demonstration: L. Ron Hubbard

6312C20 Auditing Demonstration: L. Ron Hubbard

6312C22 Auditing Demonstration: L. Ron Hubbard

6312C23 Auditing Demonstration: L. Ron Hubbard

6312C31 Auditing Demonstration: L. Ron Hubbard

6312C30 SH SC-1A Summary of R6, Part 1

6312C30 SH SC-1B Summary of R6, Part 2

6312C31 SH SC-2&3 Objects of the Mind

1964

BOOKS

The Book of Case Remedies—A Manual Covering Preclear Difficulties and Their Remedies, by L. Ron Hubbard, published by the Department of Publications, Worldwide, Saint Hill Manor, East Grinstead, Sussex, England, November 1964. *Translations:* Danish, Dutch, French, German, Spanish, Swedish.

What Everyone Should Know about Scientology, by L. Ron Hubbard, published by the Hubbard Communications Office, Worldwide, Saint Hill Manor, East Grinstead, Sussex, England, 1964.

Three Routes to Freedom, by L. Ron Hubbard, published by Scientology Publications, Ltd, Saint Hill Manor, East Grinstead, Sussex, England, 1964.

A Plan for World Peace, by L. Ron Hubbard, published by Scientology Publications, Ltd, Saint Hill Manor, East Grinstead, Sussex, England, 1964.

1964

E-METERS

The Azimuth Alignment Meter became available in 1964. It was a "see-through" meter—the dial being glass both front and back. This enabled an auditor to look through the dial while writing to ensure that no movement of the needle be missed. It is a Mark V meter in function.

1964

FILMS

The Pattern of The Bank, Part 1 and Part 2, is a three-hour filmed lecture by L. Ron Hubbard at Saint Hill Manor on 5 February 1964.

Track Analysis, a filmed lecture by L. Ron Hubbard at Saint Hill Manor given to the students on the Saint Hill Special Briefing Course, 12 March 1964.

Running GPMs, a filmed lecture given to the students on the Saint Hill Special Briefing Course, by L. Ron Hubbard, on the 12th of March 1964.

Mastery of the GPMs, a filmed lecture by L. Ron Hubbard given to the students on the Saint Hill Special Briefing Course on the 22nd of December 1964.

Pattern of the Bank, a filmed lecture by L. Ron Hubbard to the students on the Saint Hill Special Briefing Course on the 30th of December 1964.

1964

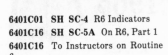

TAPED LECTURES

The Saint Hill Staff Course Lectures. Given by L. Ron Hubbard at Saint Hill Manor, East Grinstead, Sussex, England, from 1 January 1964 through 1 June 1964.

6401C01 SH SC-4 R6 Indicators

6401C16 SH SC-5A On R6, Part 1

6401C16 To Instructors on Routine 6

6401C16 SH SC-5B On R6, Part 2

6401C20 SH SC-6A R6 Line Plots and Admin, Part 1

6401C20 SH SC-6B R6 Line Plots and Admin, Part 2

6401C21 SH SC-7A R6 Case Analysis, Part 1

6401C21 SH SC-7B R6 Case Analysis, Part 2

6402C05 SH SC-8A The Pattern of the Bank (film), Part 1

6402C05 SH SC-8B The Pattern of the Bank (film), Part 2

6402C06 SH SC-9 R6 on Items and Goals

6402C11 SH SC-10 Bad Indicators

6402C13 SH SC-11A Goals, Part 1

6402C13 SH SC-11B Goals, Part 2

6402C17 SH SC-12A Goals Listing and Plotting, Part 1

6402C17 SH SC-12B Goals Listing and Plotting, Part 2

6402C18 SH SC-13A Technical Rules and Bad Indicators, Part 1

6402C18 SH SC-13B Technical Rules and Bad Indicators, Part 2

6402C19 SH SC-14A GPM Series and Examination Review, Part 1

6402C19 SH SC-14B GPM Series and Examination Review, Part 2

6402C20 SH SC-15 Goals Finding and Plotting

6402C24 SH SC-16 Q & A on R6

6402C25 SH SC-17A The Goals Pattern, Part 1

6402C25 SH SC-17B The Goals Pattern, Part 2

6406C01 SH SC-18 The Line Plot—Goals Plot—Series Plot

The *Saint Hill Special Briefing Course* continued throughout 1964 with a new series starting from December 31st 1963.

6312C31 SHSBC-1 Indicators

6401C01 L. Ron Hubbard Auditing Demonstration—R6

6401C07 SHSBC-2 Good Indicators (Lower Levels)

6401C09 SHSBC-3 Bad Indicators

6402C04 SHSBC-4 Auditor Self-Criticism

6402C06 SHSBC-5 Comm Cycle in Auditing *Translations:* Danish, Dutch, French, German, Spanish, Swedish.

6402C09 Auditing Session—Demonstration

6402C09 L. Ron Hubbard Auditing Demonstration—"First Recorded Session on Bringing About Commands"

6402C25 SHSBC-6 What Auditing Is and What It Isn't

6403C03 SHSBC-7 Auditing and Assessment *Translation:* Dutch.

6403C05 SHSBC-8 Case Analysis—Healing

6403C10 SHSBC-9 Summary of Lower Levels—Clearing at Level Four

6403C12 SHSBC-10A Track Analysis (film)

6403C12 SHSBC-10B Running GPMs (film)

6403C17 SHSBC-11 The Road to Perfection

6403C18 SH TVD TV Demonstration—Comments by L. Ron Hubbard (Auditing Demonstration on Goals Plotting R-6 Model Session, Handling an ARC Break)

6403C19 SHSBC-12 Flattening a Process *Translation:* French.

6403C24 SHSBC-13 International City

6404C10 SHSBC-14 How to Manage a Course

6404C14 SHSBC-15 The Classification-Gradation Program

6404C16 SHSBC-16 Auditing by Lists *Translation:* Dutch.

6404C21 SHSBC-17 Problems and Solutions *Translations:* Danish, Dutch, French, German, Spanish, Swedish.

6404C28 SHSBC-18 Wisdom as an Auditor *Translation:* Dutch.

6404C30 SHSBC-19 Effectiveness of Processing

6405C19 SHSBC-20 The Preclear and Getting Auditing to Work

6405C19 SHSBC-20A R6 Remarks One Goal End Word Running

6406C04 SHSBC-21 R6 Auditing Skills

6406C09 SHSBC-22 The Cycle of Action—Its Interpretation on the E-Meter

6406C16 SHSBC-23 "Communication" Overts and Responsibility *Translation:* Dutch.

6406C18 SHSBC-24 Studying, Introduction *Translations:* Danish, Dutch, French, German, Hebrew, Spanish, Swedish.

6406C30 SHSBC-25 Cause Level, OT and the Public *Translation:* Dutch.

6407C02 SHSBC-26 O/W Modernized and Reviewed *Translation:* Dutch.

6407C07 SHSBC-27 Dissemination

6407C09 SHSBC-28 Studying—Data Assimilation *Translations:* Danish, Dutch, French, German, Hebrew, Spanish, Swedish.

6407C14 SHSBC-29 Track and Bank Anatomy

6407C15 SHSBC-30 Organizational Operation *Translations:* Dutch, Swedish.

6407C27 Address to HASI Ltd Share Holders

6407C28 SHSBC-31 Campaign to Handle Psychosomatic Ills *Translation:* Danish.

6407C30 SHSBC-32 Psychosomatic—Its Meaning in Scientology *Translation:* Danish.

6408C04 SHSBC-33 A Summary of Study *Translations:* Danish, Dutch, French, German, Hebrew, Spanish, Swedish.

6408C06 SHSBC-34 Study—Gradients and Nomenclature *Translations:* Danish, Dutch, French, German, Hebrew, Spanish, Swedish.

6408C11 SHSBC-35 Evaluation of Information *Translations:* Danish, Dutch, French, German, Hebrew, Spanish, Swedish.

6408C13 SHSBC-36 Study and Education *Translations:* Danish, Dutch, French, German, Hebrew, Spanish, Swedish.

6409C01 SHSBC-37 The PE Course

6409C03 SHSBC-38 Clearing—What It Is

6409C15 SHSBC-39 Scientology and Tradition

6409C22 SHSBC-40 A Review of

Study *Translations:* Danish, Dutch, French, German, Hebrew, Spanish, Swedish.

6409C29 SHSBC-41 Gradients *Translations:* Danish, Dutch, Swedish.

6410C13 SHSBC-42 Cycles of Action *Translations:* Danish, Dutch, French, German, Spanish, Swedish.

6410C20 SHSBC-43 Levels—The Reason for Them

6410C27 SHSBC-44 The Failed Case

6411C03 SHSBC-45 Programs

6411C04 SHSBC-48 Comments on Clay Table TVD by L. Ron Hubbard

6411C10 SHSBC-46 PTPs, Overts and ARC Breaks *Translation:* Swedish.

6411C17 Interview with Mr. Phelon

6411C17 SHSBC-47 Styles of Auditing

6412C15 SHSBC-49 Communication—A Gradient on Duplication *Translation:* Dutch.

6412C22 SHSBC-50 Mastery of the GPMs (film)

6412C30 SHSBC-51 Pattern of the Bank (film)

1965

BOOKS

The Book of E-Meter Drills, by L. Ron Hubbard, published by the Department of Publications Worldwide, Saint Hill Manor, East Grinstead, Sussex, England, February, 1965. *Translations:* Danish, Dutch, French, German, Spanish, Swedish.

Scientology Abridged Dictionary, based on the works of L. Ron Hubbard, was published by the Hubbard College of Scientology, Saint Hill Manor, East Grinstead, Sussex, England, 1965. *Translations:* Danish, Dutch, French, German, Spanish, Swedish.

Scientology: A New Slant on Life, by L. Ron Hubbard, was published by the Hubbard Communications Office, Worldwide, Saint Hill Manor, East Grinstead, Sussex, England, December, 1965. *Translations:* Danish, Dutch, French, German, Spanish, Swedish.

Sanity for the Layman—A New Understanding of Life and Human Behavior, taken from the works of L. Ron Hubbard, published by the Scientology Center, San Diego, California, 1965.

1965

E-METERS

As of December 1965 the only meters permitted for use in the Academies of Scientology were the

British Mark V and the Azimuth Alignment Meter. These were the only allowed meters until 1970 when the American Mark V was also authorized.

1965

FILMS

Material of the R6 Bank, a filmed lecture by L. Ron Hubbard to the students on the first Clearing Course. This lecture was given 3 September 1965 at Saint Hill Manor, East Grinstead, Sussex, England.

Classification and Gradation, a filmed lecture given to the students on the Saint Hill Special Briefing Course by L. Ron Hubbard on the 9th of September 1965.

1965

INSIGNIA

The Scientology Pin (or Membership Pin)

Worn by members of the Hubbard Association of Scientologists International, it is a gold lapel size pin of the Scientology symbol.

Following the release of the Classification Gradation and Awareness Chart of Levels and Certificates in **1965**, a series of insignia became

available that could be worn to show an individual's training level and grade of release.

Auditor Blazer Badge for Class IV Auditor

A shield with two horizontal stripes across the top.

The top stripe is yellow with the Roman numerals "O-IV" in red.

The second stripe is black with the word "auditor" in gold.

The bottom of the shield is green with a gold Scientology symbol.

Below the shield is a gold banner with the words "Standard Tech" in red.

Auditor Blazer Badge for Class VI Auditor

A shield with two horizontal stripes across the top.

The top stripe is yellow with the Roman numeral "VI" in red.

The second stripe is black with the word "auditor" in gold.

The bottom of the shield is blue with a gold Scientology symbol.

Below the shield is a gold banner with the words "Standard Tech" in red.

The Release Pin

A small lapel size pin. It is the Scientology symbol in gold with a red "R" (for Release) mounted on it. It signifies a release, Grades 0 through IV.

The Power Release Pin

When a preclear has attained Grades V, VA or VI, the release pin is the S and double triangle (Scientology symbol) with the red "R" plus a gold wreath encircling.

6503C16 SHSBC-55 The Progress and Future of Scientology

6503C30 SHSBC-56 ARC Breaks and Generalities

6504C06 SHSBC-57 Org Board and Livingness *Translations:* Danish, Dutch, French, German, Spanish, Swedish.

6504C13 SHSBC-58 The Lowest Levels

6504C27 SHSBC-59 Awareness Levels

6505C11 SHSBC-60 ARC Breaks and PTPs, the Differentiation

6505C18 SHSBC-61 Organization and Ethics *Translations:* Dutch, Swedish.

6505C25 SHSBC-62 The Five Conditions *Translations:* Dutch, French, German, Swedish.

6506C08 SHSBC-63 Handling the PTS

6506C29 SHSBC-64 The Well-Rounded Auditor

6507C27 SHSBC-65 Stages of Release

6509C03 CC-1 Material of the R6 Bank (film)

6509C09 SHSBC-66 Classification and Gradation (film)

6509C21 SHSBC-67 Out Tech

6510C09 Three Main Points Watched for in Review

6510C14 SHSBC-68 Briefing to Review Auditors

6512C01 Conference

6512C20 Conference on Speed Up of Waiting Lists

1966

BOOKS

The Book Introducing the E-Meter, by L. Ron Hubbard, published by the Hubbard College of Scientology, Saint Hill Manor, East Grinstead, Sussex, England, September, 1966. *Translations:* Danish, French, German, Spanish, Swedish.

A New Understanding of Life, taken from the works of L. Ron Hubbard, published by the Hubbard College of Scientology, Saint Hill Manor, East Grinstead, Sussex, England, 1966.

What Are People For?—An Introduction to Scientology, taken from the works of L. Ron Hubbard, published by the Hubbard College of Scientology, Saint Hill Manor, East Grinstead, Sussex, England, 1966. *Translation:* Danish.

1966

FILM

Introduction to Scientology, a one-hour filmed interview with L. Ron Hubbard answering questions commonly asked about Scientology. Filmed at Saint Hill Manor, East Grinstead, Sussex, England, in December, 1966.

1966

TAPED LECTURES

The Saint Hill Special Briefing Course continued until the end of 1966.

6607C19 SHSBC-69 About Rhodesia

6607C21 SHSBC-70 Dianetic Auditing *Translations:* Danish, Dutch, French, German, Spanish, Swedish.

6607C26 SHSBC-71 The Classification Chart and Auditing *Translations:* Danish, Dutch, French, German, Spanish, Swedish.

6607C28 SHSBC-72 Dianetic Auditing and the Mind *Translations:* Danish, Dutch, French, German, Spanish, Swedish.

6608C02 SHSBC-73 Suppressives and GAEs *Translations:* Danish, Dutch, Swedish.

6608C04 SHSBC-74 Dianetics, Scientology and Society

6608C16 SHSBC-75 Releases and Clears

6608C18 SHSBC-76 Study and Intention (also known as Round-up of Study Materials) *Translations:* Danish, Dutch, French, German, Hebrew, Spanish, Swedish.

6608C23 SHSBC-77 Organization *Translations:* Dutch, Swedish.

6608C25 SHSBC-78 The Anti-Social Personality *Translations:* Dutch, Swedish.

6609C01 SHSBC-79 Gradients and ARC

6609C08 SHSBC-80 States of Identity

6611C01 SHSBC-81 Government and Organization *Translations:* Dutch, Swedish.

6611C29 SHSBC-82 Scientology Definitions I—OT and Clear Defined

6612C06 SHSBC-83 Scientology Definitions II

6612C13 SHSBC-84 Scientology Definitions III

The following are lectures given by L. Ron Hubbard in 1966.

6601C25 Conference with Compilations

6602C12 Internes Conference, Part 1

6602C12 Internes Conference, Part 2

6605C06 Ron's Talk to Saint Hill and Worldwide Staff

6606C27 Solo Session Demonstration by L. Ron Hubbard

The Clear Bracelet

Grade VII Clear is signified by a silver identification bracelet with the S and double triangle on it. The bracelet is sterling silver. The underside bears the words "Scientology Clear", L. Ron Hubbard's initials, the engraved name of the person and the date they were declared Clear and their Clear number.

The O.T. (Operating Thetan) Bracelet

Operating Thetan is signified by a gold identification bracelet with the S and double triangle on it.

1965

TAPED LECTURES

The Saint Hill Special Briefing Course continued throughout 1965.

6502C23 SHSBC-52 Level VII

6503C02 SHSBC-53 Technology and Hidden Standards

6503C09 SHSBC-54 The New Organization Structure *Translations:* Dutch, German, Swedish.

1967

BOOKS

Information for Releases, taken from the works of L. Ron Hubbard, published by the Hubbard College of Scientology, Saint Hill Manor, East Grinstead, Sussex, England, 1967.

Scientology and the Bible, compiled by staff from the works of L. Ron Hubbard, published by the Department of Publications, Worldwide, Saint Hill Manor, East Grinstead, Sussex, England, 1967. *Translation:* Dutch.

Kangaroo Court, staff written, concerning the inquiry into Scientology in Victoria, Australia, published by the Hubbard College of Scientology, Saint Hill Manor, East Grinstead, Sussex, England, 1967.

1967

FILM

Affinity. Based on the works of L. Ron Hubbard was filmed at Saint Hill Manor, East Grinstead, Sussex, England, in the Autumn of 1967. 20 Minutes.

1967

INSIGNIA

The Operating Thetan Symbol

The symbol used for OT activities is an oval "O" with a horizontal bar and a vertical bar down from its center to the bottom of the "O". A person attaining Section V OT may have a wreath completely around the out-

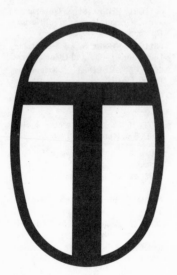

side of the "O." The OT symbol is worn on necklaces and rings.

The Sea Organization Symbol

The laurel wreath represents victory. Used throughout history to crown poets, artists and champions. It not only represents the physical victory, but the series of inner victories achieved by the individual. It is associated with the head—the traditional abode of the spirit.

The star is the symbol of the spirit. The five-pointed star signifies "rising up towards the point of origin".

The laurel wreath and star in combination signify the victory of the spirit. Its proper color is always gold. The star is not trapped in its victory, but is in the open field towards the top of the wreath, allowing free exit beyond its victory. The symbol is in a field of blue symbolizing Truth.

The Sea Organization, founded August 12, 1967, is a fraternal organization existing within the formalized structure of the Churches of Scientology.

The Sea Organization symbol is worn as cloth badges, brooches and rings.

1967

TAPED LECTURES

These lectures were given by L. Ron Hubbard during 1967.

6701C12 OT & Clear Graduation aboard *Royal Scotman*

6702C25 The Big Auditing Problem

6709C20 Ron's Journal 1967

6711C16 SO Watch Quarter and Station Bill (WQSB)

6711C18 SO A Talk to Saint Hill and Worldwide Ethics Officers *Translations:* Dutch, German, Swedish.

6711C30 SO Crew Training

6712C10 SO Form and Manner of Keeping Watches *Translations:* Danish, Dutch.

1968

BOOKS

The Findings on the U.S. Food and Drug Agency, staff written, published by the Department of Publications, Worldwide, Saint Hill Manor, East Grinstead, Sussex, England, 1968.

The Character of Scientology, staff written, published by the Department of Publications, Worldwide, Saint Hill Manor, East Grinstead, Sussex, England, 1968.

Successes of Scientology, staff written, published by Publications Organization, Worldwide, Saint Hill Manor, East Grinstead, Sussex, England, 1968.

A Test of Whole Track Recall, by L. Ron Hubbard, limited first edition published by the Publications Organization, Worldwide, Saint Hill Manor, East Grinstead, Sussex, England, 1968. *A Test of Whole Track Recall*, was later expanded and republished as *Mission Into Time*, by Publications Organization, U.S., Los Angeles, California, 1973.

Miracles for Breakfast—A startling new approach to raising children, based on the works of L. Ron Hubbard, published by Scientology Ann Arbor, Ann Arbor, Michigan, April, 1968. *Translations:* Danish, French, Spanish.

Magazine Articles on Level 0 Checksheet, a compilation of magazine articles by L. Ron Hubbard that are part of Level 0 auditor training, published by the Hubbard College of Scientology, Saint Hill, East Grinstead, Sussex, England, 1968.

Magazine Articles on Level II Checksheet, a compilation of magazine articles by L. Ron Hubbard that are part of Level II auditor training, published by the Publications Organization, Worldwide, Saint Hill, England, 1968.

Introduction to Scientology Ethics, by L. Ron Hubbard, published by the Publications Organization, Worldwide, Saint Hill Manor, East Grinstead, Sussex, England, 1968. *Translations:* Danish, Dutch, French, German, Spanish, Swedish.

The Phoenix Lectures, by L. Ron Hubbard, published by the Publications Organization, Worldwide, Saint Hill Manor, East Grinstead, Sussex, England, 1968. *Translations:* Dutch, French, German, Swedish.

The Field Staff Member Magazine, staff compiled, published by the Publications Organization, Worldwide, Saint Hill Manor, East Grinstead, Sussex, England, 1968.

Hubbard Dianetics Auditor's Course Textbook, compiled from the works of L. Ron Hubbard, published by the Publications Organization, Worldwide, Edinburgh, Scotland, 1968. (The material in this textbook appears in *The Technical Bulletins of Dianetics and Scientology*, 1976.)

Scientology Basic Staff Hat Book, Number 1, by L. Ron Hubbard, published by the Publications Organization, Worldwide, Saint Hill Manor, East Grinstead, Sussex, England, 1968. (The material in this book is printed in full in *The Organization Executive Course*, 1974.)

Level 0 PABs—for the Saint Hill Special Briefing Course, by L. Ron Hubbard, published by the Publications Organization, Worldwide, Edinburgh, Scotland, 1968. *Translations:* Danish, Swedish.

1968

INSIGNIA

The Class VIII Badge

The Class VIII Badge is a shield with two horizontal stripes across the top with the word "auditor" and the Roman numeral VIII. The bottom of the shield contains the Scientology symbol and the banner below it, the words "Standard Tech."

The Class VIII Badge is all red with gold lettering and numbering. It is given to permanent Class VIII auditors only.

The Distribution Division Six Badge

The purpose of the 6th Division of the Church of Scientology is to make Scientology grow. This is the Distribution Division. Its symbol and the symbol worn by its personnel is the Affinity-Reality-Communication (ARC) triangle interwoven with the symbol for infinity.

1968

TAPED LECTURES

The following lectures were given by L. Ron Hubbard during 1968.

6801C05 AO-1 Fast Flow and Inspection Before the Fact

6801C12 AO-2 Those Who Will Put Things Right

6801C17 SO Weather

6801C26 A0-4 Ron's Talk at 4th Graduation on *Royal Scotman* (renamed *Apollo*)

6803C09 Validity of Track Recall

6808C22 Technology

6809C16 On Case Supervision

6809C18 On The Class VIII Course

The following lectures were given to the First Class VIII Course in September and October 1968.

6809C24 SO Class VIII—1 Welcome to the Class VIII Course—An Introduction to Standard Tech

6809C25 SO Class VIII—2 What Standard Tech Does

6809C26 SO Class VIII—3 The Laws of Case Supervision

6809C27 SO Class VIII—4 Standard Tech Defined

6809C28 SO Class VIII—5 The Standard Green Form and Rudiments

6809C29 SO Class VIII—6 Mechanics of Techniques and Study Matter

6809C30 SO Class VIII—7 Case Supervisor Do's and Don'ts—The Total Rationale and Background of Auditing

6810C01 SO Class VIII—8 Certainty of Standard Tech

6810C02 SO Class VIII—9 Laws of Listing and Nulling

6810C03 SO Class VIII—10 Assists

6810C07 SO Class VIII—11 Assessments and Listing Basics

6810C08 SO Class VIII—12 More on Basics

6810C09 SO Class VIII—13 Ethics and Case Supervision

6810C10 SO Class VIII—14 Auditor Attitude and the Bank

6810C11 SO Class VIII—15 Auditor Additives, Lists and Case Supervising

6810C12 SO Class VIII—16 Standard Tech

6810C13 SO Class VIII—17 The Basics and Simplicities of Standard Tech

6810C14 SO Class VIII—18 The New Auditor's Code

6810C15 SO Class VIII—19 An Evaluation of Examination—Answers and Data on Standard Tech

1969

BOOKS

A Summary on Scientology for Scientists, by L. Ron Hubbard, published by the Church of Scientology of California (Worldwide) Saint Hill Manor, East Grinstead, Sussex, England, 1969.

Level I PABs—for the Saint Hill Special Briefing Course, by L. Ron Hubbard, published by the Publications Organization, Worldwide, Edinburgh, Scotland, 1969.

Triple Grades and Review Dictionary, based on the works of L. Ron Hubbard, Kansas City, Missouri, 1969.

How to Save Your Marriage, taken from the works of L. Ron Hubbard, published by Scientology Publications Organization, Copenhagen, Denmark, 1969.

Scientology for the Millions, by Walter Braddeson, published by the Sherbourne Press, Los Angeles, California, 1969.

What Every Preclear Should Know, based on the works of L. Ron Hubbard, published by Scientology Ann Arbor, Ann Arbor, Michigan, 1969.

When in Doubt, Communicate . . . Quotations from the Works of L. Ron Hubbard, published by Scientology Ann Arbor, Ann Arbor Michigan, 1969., *Translation:* Spanish.

Congress Drill Book, based on the works of L. Ron Hubbard, published by Scientology Publications Organization, Copenhagen, Denmark, 1969.

The Best of The Auditor, a collection of articles by L. Ron Hubbard from *The Auditor* Magazine, published by the American Saint Hill Organization, Los Angeles, California, 1969.

Dianetic Case Histories Book, staff compiled, published by the Sea Organization, Division V, Flag, late 1969.

1969

FILM

Reality. Based on the works of L. Ron Hubbard, was produced in Copenhagen, Denmark, in 1969. 20 minutes.

1969

TAPED LECTURES

The following lectures were given by L. Ron Hubbard in 1969.

6904C03 & 04 Dianetics Program

6905C29 First Standard Dianetics Graduation—The Dianetic Program *Translations:* Danish, Dutch, French, German, Spanish, Swedish.

6910C27 Confusion and Stable Datum

6910C27 Confusion—Find Out What It Is

L. Ron Hubbard gave the Welcome To The Sea Organization Lectures in October 1969.

6910C15 WSO-1 Welcome to the Sea Organization—Quality of the Sea Organization—What is a Seaman *Translations:* Danish, Dutch, French, German.

6910C16 WSO-2 Welcome to the Sea Organization: Drills. *Translations:* Danish, Dutch, French, German.

6910C17 WSO-3 Welcome to the Sea Organization: Why the Sea Org is Successful. *Translations:* Danish, Dutch, French, German.

6910C20 WSO-4 Welcome to the Sea Organization: Third Dynamic Activity and Making Things Go Right

6910C21 WSO-5 Welcome to the Sea Organization: It's a PRO World *Translations:* Danish, Dutch, French, German.

1970

BOOKS

The Background and Ceremonies of the Church of Scientology of California, Worldwide, based on the works of L. Ron Hubbard, published by the Church of Scientology, Worldwide, Saint Hill Manor, East Grinstead, Sussex, England, 1970. *Translation:* Dutch.

What is Understanding?, based on the works of L. Ron Hubbard, published by Children's Scientology Publications, New York, New York, 1970.

Who Are You?, based on the works of L. Ron Hubbard, published by Children's Scientology Publications, New York, New York, 1970.

Scientology and Dianetics, based on the works of L. Ron Hubbard, published by the Church of Scientology of California, Los Angeles, California, 1970.

Scientology 0-8, The Book of Basics, by L. Ron Hubbard, published by the Publications Organization, Copenhagen, Denmark, 1970. *Translations:* German. Soon to be available: French.

1970

E-METERS

In 1970 the American Mark V E-Meter became available. It along with the British Mark V and Azimuth Alignment Meter became the standard meters and have continued until present time.

1970

FILM

Freedom. Based on the works of L. Ron Hubbard, was filmed in Los Angeles, California, in 1970. 20 minutes.

1970

TAPED LECTURES

L. Ron Hubbard gave the following lectures in 1970.

7001C30 A Succinct View of Public Relations

7005C09 The 20th Anniversary of *Dianetics: The Modern Science of Mental Health*

7006C11 Drills, Watches, Signals, Radar, QM Log

7006C21 Ron's Address to The Grand National Convention in Los Angeles

1971 📖

BOOKS

You Can Have a New Understanding of Life Through Scientology, based on the works of L. Ron Hubbard, published by Publications Organization, U.S., Los Angeles, California, 1971.

Is Confusion a Friend of Yours?, based on the works of L. Ron Hubbard, published by Children's Scientology Publications, Honolulu, Hawaii, 1971.

Expanded Grades Dictionary, published in Irving, Texas, 1971.

Assault on a Church, based on the works of L. Ron Hubbard, published by the Church of Scientology Information Service, Los Angeles, California, 1971.

Scientometric Testing, published by Scientology Orange County, Tustin, California, 1971.

How to Have Money, based on the works of L. Ron Hubbard, published in Santa Fe Springs, California, 1971.

Dianetics Information Group, Series One, published in East Grinstead, Sussex, England, 1971.

The Basic Scientology Picture Book, taken from the works of L. Ron Hubbard, published by Publications Organization, U.S., Los Angeles, California, September, 1971. *Translations:* Danish, French, German, Spanish, Swedish.

The Standard Dianetics Picture Book, a visual aid for a quicker understanding and dissemination of standard Dianetics and Dianetic pastoral counseling, taken from the works of L. Ron Hubbard, published by the American Saint Hill Organization, Publications Department, Los Angeles, California, December, 1971.

1971 🎞️

TAPED LECTURES

In January and February 1971, L. Ron Hubbard lectured to the students on the Flag Executive Briefing Course.

7011C17 SO FEBC-1 Welcome to the FEBC

7101C18 SO FEBC-2 PR Becomes a Subject. *Translation:* Swedish.

7101C18 SO FEBC-3 The Org Officer/Product Officer System, Part I

7101C18 SO FEBC-4 The Org Officer/Product Officer System, Part II

7101C23 SO FEBC-5 How to Post An Org

7101C23 SO FEBC-6 The Org Officer and His Resources, Part I

7101C23 SO FEBC-7 The Org Officer and His Resources, Part II

7101C24 SO FEBC-8 Viability and the Role of the HAS

7101C24 SO FEBC-9 Production and Resources of the HAS

7101C24 SO FEBC-10 The HAS and the "Coins" of the Organization

7102C03 SO FEBC-11 As You Return to Your Org

7102C03 SO FEBC-12 The FEBC Org Board and Its VFPs

The following lectures were given by L. Ron Hubbard in 1971.

7105C09 SO Training People to Train. *Translations:* Danish, Swedish.

7106C12 Welcome to the Interneship

7109C05 SO A Talk on a Basic Qual, Part I

7109C05 SO A Talk on a Basic Qual, Part II

1972 📖

BOOKS

The Management Series, 1970-1972, by L. Ron Hubbard, published by Scientology Publications Organization, Copenhagen, Denmark, 1972.

Child Scientology, an aid to family and marriage guidance, based on the works of L. Ron Hubbard, published in Auckland, New Zealand, 1972.

Fundamentals of Success, based on the works of L. Ron Hubbard, published in Phoenix, Arizona, 1972.

Tell It Like It Is—A Course in Scientology Dissemination, published in Phoenix, Arizona, 1972.

The Basic Dianetics Picture Book, a visual aid to a better understanding of Man and the mind, taken from the works of L. Ron Hubbard, published by the Publications Organization, U.S., Los Angeles, California, September, 1972. *Translation:* German.

How to Choose Your People, based on the works of L. Ron Hubbard, published by Scientology Ann Arbor, Ann Arbor, Michigan, 1972. *Translation:* French.

Scientology: Twentieth Century Religion, based on the works of L. Ron Hubbard, published by the Church of Scientology, Worldwide, Saint Hill, England, December, 1972. *Translations:* Danish, Swedish.

Basic Study Manual, compiled from the works of L. Ron Hubbard, published by Applied Scholastics, Inc., Los Angeles, California, 1972. *Translations:* Danish, Dutch, French, German, Spanish, Swedish.

The TR Series, thirteen books about Scientology training drills and related material, compiled from the works of L. Ron Hubbard, published by the Sea Organization, Public Relations and Consumption Bureau, 1972. *Translations:* Dutch, French, German, Swedish.

The following are the individual titles of each of the TR Series:

TR Series Volume 0—Intro to the TR Series

TR Series Volume 1—OT TR 0

TR Series Volume 2—TR 0

TR Series Volume 3—TR I

TR Series Volume 4—TR II

TR Series Volume 5—TR III

TR Series Volume 6—TR IV

TR Series Volume 7—Upper Indoc TRs

TR Series Volume 8—TR Repair and Rehab

TR Series Volume 9—Coaching

TR Series Volume 10—Auditing Comm Cycle

TR Series Volume 11—Obnosis

TR Series Volume 12—TR Course
Translations: Dutch, French, German, Swedish.

1972

TAPED LECTURES

The following lectures were reissued by L. Ron Hubbard in February, 1972.

7202C26 LRH/MTS-1 CCH: Steps 1-4 Demonstration (Reissue of 5707C07 FC-15) *Translations:* French, German.

7202C26 LRH/MTS-2 Demonstration of an Assist (Reissue of 5911C09 1MACC-2) *Translations:* French, German.

7202C26 LRH/MTS-3 Patching up Two 3DXX Cases (Reissue of 6205C16 SH TVD-5 A&B) *Translations:* French, German.

7202C26 LRH/MTS-4 Check on "What" Questions and Havingness Probe (Reissue of 6205C23 SH TVD-6) *Translations:* French, German.

7202C26 LRH/MTS-5 Fish and Fumble—Checking Dirty Needles (Reissue of 6205C23 SH TVD-7) *Translations:* French, German.

7202C27 A Turn for the Better

7202C29 Personnel and Establishment Actions

L. Ron Hubbard gave the following lectures in March 1972 for the training of Establishment Officers.

7203C01 ESTO-1 Estos Instant Hat, Part I

7203C01 ESTO-2 Estos Instant Hat, Part II

7203C02 ESTO-3 Evaluation and Handling of Personnel, Part I

7203C02 ESTO-4 Evaluation and Handling of Personnel, Part II

7203C03 ESTO-5 Handling Personnel, Part I

7203C03 ESTO-6 Handling Personnel, Part II

7203C04 ESTO-7 Hold the Form of the Org, Part I

7203C04 ESTO-8 Hold the Form of the Org, Part II

7203C05 ESTO-9 Revision of the Product/Org System, Part I

7203C05 ESTO-10 Revision of the Product/Org System, Part II

7203C06 ESTO-11 F/Ning Staff Members, Part I

7203C06 ESTO-12 F/Ning Staff Members, Part II

L. Ron Hubbard gave the following lectures to the students on the first Expanded Dianetics Course.

7203C30 SO XDN-1 Expanded Dianetics. *Translations:* French, German.

7204C07 SO XDN-2 Expanded Dianetics and Word Clearing. *Translations:* French, German.

7204C07 SO XDN-3 Auditor Administration. *Translations:* French, German.

7204C07 SO XDN-4 Illness Breakthrough. *Translations:* French, German.

L. Ron Hubbard gave the following lectures in 1972.

7203C08 SO General Evaluation

7203C12 SO New Names and Promotion

7203C12 SO Surveys and Advance Magazine

7203C22 SO A "Why"

7203C23 SO Course Supervision

7203C27 SO Supervision—Study

7203C28 SO Training Program

7203C28 SO Study and Student Hat

7203C29 SO Study "Why"

7204C06 SO The Primary Rundown

7204C11 SO Justice Policy Letter —February 7, 1970

7204C17 SO Preclear Folder

7204C18 SO Talk to an Establishment Officer

7204C20 SO How to Write Mission Orders

7204C24 SO Public Relations Function

7205C12 SO PTS

7205C25 SO Talk on Filmscripts

7205C26 SO 2nd Talk on Filmscripts

7205C27 SO 3rd Talk on Film-scripts

7206C14 SO Superliteracy

7206C27 SO Photographs

7206C27 SO Public Relations Officer Functions

7206C28 SO Evaluations

7207C01 SO Registration Line

7207C02 SO How to Load a Bassamatic

7207C18 SO Printing and Colors

7207C21 SO Slides

7207C22 SO Posters—Re: Kodak Film

7207C28 SO Photography

7211C13 SO A Talk to Preparations Unit Staff

1973

TAPED LECTURES

L. Ron Hubbard gave the following lectures during 1973.

7309C23 SO Children

7309C24 SO Making a Better World

7309C25 SO Policy and Evaluation Correction

7309C26 SO Nature of Research

7310C21 SO A Pc Folder and Case Supervisors

7310C31 SO Public Relations Tech

1973

BOOKS

Freedom Reports on the IRS, published by Freedom—The Independent Journal of the Church of Scientology, Los Angeles, California, 1973.

Viewpoints, published by the Church Information Service, Los Angeles, California, 1973.

Primary Rundown Glossary, compiled by the Sea Organization, Public Relations and Consumption Bureau, published by the American Saint Hill Organization, Los Angeles, California, 1973.

How to Write Invoices—A Flag Mini Hat Booklet, compiled and published by the Sea Organization, Public Relations and Consumption Bureau, 1973.

The Language of Salesmanship—A Glossary and Index, published by the Public Relations and Consumption Bureau of the Sea Organization, 1973. *Translation:* Dutch.

How to Clear Your Community—An Illustrated Guide for Churches, Missions, and Field Staff Members, taken from the works of L. Ron Hubbard, published by the Public Relations and Consumption Bureau, The Church of Scientology of California, September, 1973.

Dissemination Division Picture Book, published by the Public Relations and Consumption Bureau, The Church of Scientology of California, 1973.

Perhaps Happiness . . . , based on the works of L. Ron Hubbard, published by the Publications Organization, U.S., Los Angeles, California, 1973.

Mission Into Time, by L. Ron Hubbard, published by the Publications Organization, Los Angeles, California, September, 1973.

L. Ron Hubbard's PABs Books, Volumes 1-6 (PABs 1-160), by L. Ron Hubbard, published by Publications Organization, Copenhagen, Denmark, 1973.

1974

BOOKS

Scientology: A World Religion Emerges in the Space Age, based on the works of L. Ron Hubbard, published by the Church of Scientology Information Service, Los Angeles, California, 1974.

Scientometric Testing Manual, taken from the works of L. Ron Hubbard, published by the Southern California Institute Press, Tustin, California, 1974.

Marriage Hats, by Mary Sue Hubbard, published by the Publications Organization, U.S., Los Angeles, California, 1974.

The Management Series, 1970-1974, by L. Ron Hubbard, published by the American Saint Hill Organization, Los Angeles, California, 1974. *Translations:* French, Swedish.

Look It Up—How to Use the Dictionary to Understand Any Subject, based on the works of L. Ron Hubbard, published in Los Angeles, California, 1974.

Hymn of Asia—An Eastern Poem, by L. Ron Hubbard, published by the Publications Organization, Los Angeles, California, December, 1974.

The Organization Executive Course—An Encyclopedia of Scientology Policy, Volumes 0-7, by L. Ron Hubbard, published by Scientology Publications Organization, Copenhagen, Denmark, between 1970 and 1974.

Volume 0—Basic Staff Volume. *Translations:* Danish, Dutch, French, German, Swedish.

Volume 1—HCO Division. *Translations:* Danish, Dutch, French, German, Swedish.

Volume 2—HCO Dissemination Division. *Translations:* Danish, Dutch, German, Swedish.

Volume 3—Treasury Division. *Translations:* Danish, Dutch, Swedish.

Volume 4—Technical Division. *Translations:* Dutch, Swedish.

Volume 5—Qualifications Division. *Translations:* Dutch, Swedish.

Volume 6—Distribution Division. *Translations:* Danish, German, Swedish.

Volume 7—Executive Division—The Executive's Handbook. Translations: Dutch, Swedish.

What Is Scientology? based on the works of L. Ron Hubbard, published by Scientology Ann Arbor, Ann Arbor, Michigan. *Translation:* French.

Towards Peace on Earth, published by the Church of Scientology, Worldwide, Saint Hill, England.

Worldwide—Church of Scientology—Social Reform, Human Rights and Rehabilitation Activities, published by the Church of Scientology, Worldwide, Saint Hill Manor, East Grinstead, Sussex, England.

1974

TAPED LECTURES

L. Ron Hubbard gave the following lectures in 1974.

7403C06 & 07 SO Ron's Talk to the Marineros (Music Group)

7403C07 SO Ron's Talk to the Apollo Stars' Choreographer

7403C14 SO Instructions to Apollo Stars Musicians

7403C20 SO Talk to a Photographer

7403C21 SO Talk to a Choreographer

7404C08 SO Ron's Talk to the Apollo Stars

7405C20 SO Ron's Talk with Musicians

7405C20 SO Songs

7408C31 SO Accenting Melodies

1975

BOOKS

Dianetics Today, by L. Ron Hubbard, published by the Publications Organization, Los Angeles, California, March, 1975. *Translations:* French, Swedish.

Executive Survival Kit, based on the works of L. Ron Hubbard, published by Freedom Magazine—The Independent Journal published by the Church of Scientology, Los Angeles, California, 1975.

Dianetics and Scientology Technical Dictionary, by L. Ron Hubbard, published by the Publications Organization, U.S., Los Angeles, California, July, 1975.

Interpol Dossier, published by Freedom Magazine—The Independent Journal published by the Church of Scientology, Los Angeles, California, 1975.

1975

TAPED LECTURES

The following lectures were given by L. Ron Hubbard in 1975.

7510C29 SO First Lecture—Special Rundown

7510C30 SO Second Lecture—Special Rundown Pilot

7510C31 SO Third Lecture—Special Rundown Pilot

7511C01 SO Fourth Lecture—Special Rundown pilot

7511C02 SO Fifth Lecture—Special Rundown Pilot

7511C03 SO Sixth Lecture—Special Rundown Pilot

7511C04 SO Seventh Lecture—Special Rundown Pilot

7511C05 SO Eighth Lecture—Special Rundown Pilot

7511C06 SO Ninth Lecture—Special Rundown Pilot

7511C07 SO Tenth Lecture—Special Rundown Pilot

7511C08 SO Eleventh Lecture—Special Rundown Pilot

7511C10 SO Twelfth Lecture—Special Rundown Pilot

7511C11 SO Thirteenth Lecture—Special Rundown Pilot

7511C12 SO Fourteenth Lecture—Special Rundown Pilot

7511C13 SO Fifteenth Lecture—Special Rundown Pilot

7511C14 SO Sixteenth Lecture—Special Rundown Pilot

7511C17 SO Seventeenth Lecture—Special Rundown Pilot

7511C18 SO Eighteenth Lecture—Special Rundown Pilot

7511C19 SO Nineteenth Lecture—Special Rundown Pilot

7511C20 SO Twentieth Lecture—Special Rundown Pilot

7511C21 SO Twenty-first Lecture—Special Rundown Pilot

7511C24 SO Twenty-second Lecture—Special Rundown Pilot

7512C08 SO Ron's Talk

1976

BOOKS

About Art, taken from the works of L. Ron Hubbard, published by the Church of Scientology—Celebrity Centre, Los Angeles, California, 1976.

Evidence on the Religious Bona Fides and Status of the Church, published by the Church of Scientology Information Service, Los Angeles, California, April, 1976.

Hubbard Communications Office Policy Letter Subject Index, published by Publications Organization, U.S., Los Angeles, California, March, 1976. (also known as the *HCOPL Subject Index*)

The Indispensability of Scientology, Press Volume I, Issues I-VI (6 volumes), published by the Church of Scientology Information Service, Los Angeles, California, 1976.

How to Use The Freedom of Information Act, compiled and published by the Council of Scientology Ministers, Los Angeles, California, July, 1976.

Introducing Scientology, based on the works of L. Ron Hubbard, published by the Publications Organization, U.S., Los Angeles, California, 1976. (also known as the *Field Staff Member Magazine*)

Church of Scientology—Religious Nature and Community Activities, published by the Church of Scientology Information Service, Los Angeles, California, 1976.

Success With Scientology, based on the works of L. Ron Hubbard, published by the Church of Scientology, Information Service, Los Angeles, California, 1976.

New Viewpoints, published by the Information Service of the U.S. Churches of Scientology, Los Angeles, California, 1976.

Efficiency, based on the works of L. Ron Hubbard, published by Scientology Ann Arbor, Ann Arbor, Michigan, 1976.

Ups and Downs, based on the works of L. Ron Hubbard, published by Scientology Ann Arbor, Ann Arbor, Michigan, 1976.

All The Happiness, based on the works of L. Ron Hubbard, published by Scientology Ann Arbor, Ann Arbor, Michigan, 1976.

The Technical Bulletins of Dianetics and Scientology, 10 volumes, by L. Ron Hubbard, published by Scientology Publications Organization, Copenhagen and Publications Organization U.S., Los Angeles, California, August, 1976.

Technical Bulletins Volume I 1950-1953

Technical Bulletins Volume II 1954-1956

Technical Bulletins Volume III 1957-1959

Technical Bulletins Volume IV 1960-1961

Technical Bulletins Volume V 1962-1964

Technical Bulletins Volume VI 1965-1969

Technical Bulletins Volume VII 1970-1971

Technical Bulletins Volume VIII 1972-1975

Auditing Series Volume IX 1965-1975

C/S Series Volume X 1970-1975

The Volunteer Minister's Handbook, by L. Ron Hubbard, published by Publications Organization, U.S., Los Angeles, California, December, 1976.

Modern Management Technology Defined—Hubbard Dictionary of Administration and Management, by L. Ron Hubbard, published by Pub-

lications Organization U.S., Los Angeles, California, 1976.

1976

TAPE CASSETTES

L. Ron Hubbard tape recorded a message for each individual Church of Scientology in December 1976.

7612C__ Ron's Journal No. 28

1977

BOOKS

Proceedings of The International Conference for World Peace and Social Reform and Human Rights Prayer Day, published by the Church of Scientology Information Service, Los Angeles, California, 1977.

Can We Ever Be Friends?, published by the Church of Scientology of California, Worldwide, Saint Hill, England, 1977.

The American Inquisition, U.S. Government Agency Harassment, Religious Persecution and Abuse of Power, published by the U.S. Ministerial Conference of Scientology Ministers, Los Angeles, California, 1977.

The Membership, Interpol Dossier, Part Two, published by the editors of Freedom news journal, Saint Hill Manor, East Grinstead, Sussex, England, 1977.

Press View, the FBI Raid, published by the Church of Scientology of California, Los Angeles, 1977.

Church of Scientology—Press, Volume I, Issue VII, published by the Church of Scientology Information Service, Los Angeles, California, 1977.

The Volunteer Minister Booklets, 1 to 9, by L. Ron Hubbard, published by Publications Organization, Los Angeles, California, 1977.

Communication

Understanding Others—Affinity, Reality, Communication

Do You Make Many Mistakes?

The Eight Dynamics

Assists

The Conditions of Existence

The Parts of Man

The Aims of Scientology

The Third Party Law

1977

TAPE CASSETTES

7707C__ Can We Ever Be Friends? *Translations:* French, German, Swedish, Dutch, Danish.

The Story of Dianetics & Scientology, (originally given as the first lecture of the London Clearing Congress—18 October 1958), reissued 1977.

1977

FILM CARTRIDGES

The Clearing Congress Lectures. The first six lectures of the Clearing Congress given in Washington, D.C. in July 1958, were recorded on film. These same lectures have been re-released as convenient 8mm film cartridges. Re-released 1977.

5807C04 CC-1 The Fact of Clearing, Part 1 and 2

5807C04 CC-2 The Factors of Clearing (Four Elements), Part 1, 2 and 3

5807C04 CC-3 The Freedoms of Clear, Part 1, 2 and 3

5807C05 CC-4 Prerequisites to Auditing (Evaluation of Importance, Things to Know in Auditing), Part 1, 2 and 3

5807C05 CC-5 Clear Procedure, Part I: CCH-0, Help, Part 1, 2 and 3

5807C05 CC-6 Clear Procedure, Part II: Creativeness, Part 1, 2 and 3

The Secret of Flag Results, written by L. Ron Hubbard, produced by Universal Media Productions, released 9 December 1977.

1978

BOOKS

Have You Lived Before This Life?, (a new expanded edition) by L. Ron Hubbard. Published by Publications Organization, Los Angeles, California, March 1978.

From the preceding panorama of material hundreds of Dianetics and Scientology courses—both technical and administrative have been created.

The following is a list of just those course materials which have been translated. These translations are all recorded on magnetic recording tape and are available from the Scientology Publications Organization in Copenhagen, Denmark. This list of translations grows almost daily, so write for a list of translations currently available.

STUDY TECHNOLOGY COURSES

Method One Co-Auditing Course *Translations:* Danish, Dutch, French, German, Swedish.

Mini Word Clearing Course *Translations:* Danish, German, Swedish.

Professional Word Clearer's Course *Translations:* Dutch, French, German, Swedish.

Student Hat *Translations:* Danish, Dutch, French, German, Hebrew, Spanish, Swedish.

Word Clearing Co-Auditing Course *Translations:* French, German.

Word Clearing Series *Translation:* Swedish.

INTRODUCTORY AND TECHNICAL COURSES

Academy Level 0 *Translations:* Danish, Dutch, French, German, Spanish, Swedish.

Academy Level I *Translations:* Danish, Dutch, French, German, Spanish, Swedish.

Academy Level II *Translations:* Danish, Dutch, French, German, Spanish, Swedish.

Academy Level III *Translations:* Danish, Dutch, French, German, Spanish, Swedish.

Academy Level IV *Translations:* Danish, Dutch, French, German, Spanish, Swedish.

Basic Assist Course *Translations:* Dutch, French, Swedish.

Class Four Case Supervisor Course *Translations:* Dutch, French, Spanish, Swedish.

Confessional Course/Hubbard Integrity Processing Course *Translations:* Dutch, Danish, French, German, Spanish, Swedish.

European Special Relief Rundown *Translation:* Swedish.

Expanded Dianetics Course *Translations:* French, German.

Hubbard Apprentice Scientologist Course *Translations:* Danish, Dutch, Finnish, French, German, Greek, Spanish, Swedish.

Hubbard Causative Leadership Course *Translations:* German, Swedish.

Hubbard Dianetic Graduate Course *Translation:* Danish.

Hubbard Mini Course Supervisor Course *Translations:* Danish, Dutch, French, German, Hebrew, Spanish, Swedish.

Hubbard Professional Course Supervisors Course *Translations:* Danish, Dutch, French, German, Spanish, Swedish.

Hubbard Qualified Scientologist Course *Translations:* Danish, Dutch, French, German, Spanish, Swedish.

Hubbard Standard Dianetics Course *Translations:* Danish, Dutch, French, German, Spanish, Swedish.

Hubbard Standard Dianetics Course Case Supervisor's Course *Translations:* Danish, Dutch, French, Spanish, Swedish.

Interiorization Rundown Course *Translation:* Swedish.

Mini Checksheet for Scientology Auditors *Translation:* Swedish.

Minister's Course *Translations:* Dutch, French, Swedish.

New Life Without Drugs Course *Translation:* Swedish.

PTS/SP Detection and Handling Course *Translations:* Danish, Dutch, French, German, Swedish.

PTS/SP Study Pack *Translations:* Dutch, French, German, Swedish.

TRs and Objectives Course *Translations:* Dutch, French, German, Swedish.

Two-Way Communication Checksheet *Translations:* Dutch, French, German, Swedish.

INTERNESHIP MATERIALS

Class IV Interneship/Class IV OK to Audit *Translations:* Dutch, French, German, Swedish.

Class IV OK to Case Supervise *Translations:* French, Spanish.

Dianetics Internship/Qual OK to Audit Dianetics *Translations:* Danish, Dutch, French, German, Spanish, Swedish.

Dianetics OK to Case Supervise *Translations:* French, Swedish.

Hubbard Mini Course Supervisor Course OK to Supervise Interneship *Translations:* French, German, Swedish.

Hubbard Professional Course Supervisor Course OK to Supervise Interneship *Translations:* French, German.

Interne Hat Pack *Translations:* Danish, Dutch, French, German, Spanish, Swedish.

Qual OK to Assess Prepared Lists *Translations:* Danish, Dutch, French, German, Spanish, Swedish.

Qual OK to Audit the Drug Rundown *Translation:* Dutch.

Qual OK to Audit Listing and Nulling *Translations:* Dutch, French, German, Spanish, Swedish.

Qual OK to Audit Objectives *Translations:* French, German, Swedish.

Qual OK to Audit Word Clearing *Translations:* French, German, Swedish.

Qual OK to Correct Listing and Nulling *Translations:* Dutch, French, German, Spanish.

Qual OK to FES (Folder Error Summary) *Translation:* Spanish.

Qual OK to Operate an E-Meter *Translations:* Danish, Dutch, French, German, Spanish, Swedish.

TECHNICAL SERIES

Basic Auditing Series *Translations:* French, German, Swedish.

Case Supervisor Series *Translations:* Dutch, German, Swedish.

Cramming Series *Translation:* Swedish.

ADMINISTRATIVE AND STAFF COURSES (HATS)

Basic FBO (Flag Banking Officer) Hat *Translation:* Swedish.

Ethics Officer Mini Hat *Translation:* German.

European Finance Course *Translations:* Danish, Dutch, French, German, Swedish.

FESer Hat (Folder Error Summary) *Translation:* French.

Get More Starts Hat *Translation:* Dutch.

Hats Officer Mini Hat *Translation:* Spanish.

Hubbard Apprentice Scientologist Course Staff Briefing *Translation:* Danish.

Hubbard Communications Office Area Secretary Mini Hat *Translations:* German, Spanish.

Hubbard Guidance Center Auditor Mini Hat *Translation:* French.

Professional Salesmanship Course *Translations:* Danish, Dutch, French, German, Swedish.

Qualifications Secretary Mini Hat *Translations:* German, Spanish.

Sea Organization—Product 0—Introduction to Scientology Ethics Course *Translations:* Danish, Dutch, French, German.

Sea Organization—Product 0—Introduction to Scientology Study Technology *Translations:* Danish, Dutch, French, German.

Sea Organization—Product 0—Introduction to the Sea Organization *Translations:* Danish, Dutch, French, German.

Stable Terminal Checksheet *Translation:* German.

Staff Book Hat *Translations:* Dutch, French.

Staff Book Hat Reference Materials *Translations:* Danish, German, Swedish.

Staff Status 0 *Translations:* Danish, Dutch, French, Swedish.

Staff Status I *Translations:* Danish, Dutch, French, German, Spanish, Swedish.

Staff Status II *Translations:* Danish, Dutch, French, German, Swedish.

Your Division 6 Program *Translations:* Danish, Dutch, French, German, Swedish.

ADMINISTRATIVE SERIES

Account Audits Series *Translation:* Swedish.

Administrative Know-How Series *Translation:* Swedish.

Data Series *Translations:* Dutch, French, German, Spanish, Swedish.

Establishment Officer (Esto) Series *Translations:* French, Swedish.

Executive Series *Translations:* Dutch, French, Swedish.

Finance Series *Translations:* Danish, French, Swedish.

Organizing Series *Translations:* French, Swedish.

Personnel Programming Series *Translation:* Swedish.

Personnel Series *Translation:* Swedish.

Public Relations Series *Translations:* Dutch, German, Spanish, Swedish.

Qual Lines Series *Translation:* Swedish.

Target Series *Translation:* Swedish.

For prices and availability of these publications, write to your nearest Scientology Publications Organization:

The Church of Scientology of California
Publications Organization U.S.
4833 Fountain Avenue
East Annex
Los Angeles, California 90029

Scientology Publications Organization Denmark
Jernbanegade 6
1608 Copenhagen V
Denmark

About the Founder

L. Ron Hubbard was born in Tilden, Nebraska, on 13th March, 1911. His father was Commander Harry Ross Hubbard of the United States Navy. His mother was Dora May Hubbard (nee Waterbury de Wolfe, a thoroughly educated woman, a rarity in her time!).

Ron spent many of his childhood years on a large cattle ranch in Montana. It was on this ranch that he had learned to read and write by the time he was 3½ years old.

L. Ron Hubbard found the life of a young rancher very enjoyable. Long days were spent riding, breaking broncos, hunting coyote and taking his first steps as an explorer.

For it was in Montana that he had his first encounter with another culture — the Blackfoot (Pikuni) Indians. He became a blood brother of the Pikuni and was later to write about them in his first published novel, *Buckskin Brigades*.

Before Ron was 10 years old, he had become very thoroughly educated both in schools as well as by his mother.

So it was that by the time he was 12 years old, L. Ron Hubbard had already read a large number of the world's greatest classics — and his interest in philosophy and religion was born.

Not that the explorer in him had been stilled. Far from it. A Montana newspaper of the period reported thusly on one of Helena's newest high school students:

"Ronald Hubbard has the distinction of being the only boy in the country to secure an Eagle Scout badge at the age of 12 years. He was a Boy Scout in Washington, D.C., before coming to Helena."

In Washington, D.C., he had also become a close friend of President Coolidge's son, Calvin Jr., whose early death accelerated L. Ron Hubbard's interest in the mind and spirit of Man.

The following years, from 1925 to 1929, saw the young Mr. Hubbard, between the ages of 14 and 18, as a budding and enthusiastic world traveller and adventurer. His father was sent to the Far East and having the financial support of his wealthy grandfather, L. Ron Hubbard spent these years journeying throughout Asia.

He explored many out-of-the-way places and saw many strange-seeming peoples and customs. But it was in Northern China and India, while studying with holy men, that he became vitally engrossed in the subject of the spiritual destiny of mankind.

With the death of his grandfather, the Hubbard family returned to the United States, and, after intense study at Swavely Preparatory School in Manassas, Virginia and at Woodward Preparatory School in Washington, D.C., he enrolled at the George Washington University Engineering School in the fall of 1930.

At George Washington, L. Ron Hubbard became associate editor of the University newspaper, *The Hatchet*, and was a member of many of the University's clubs and societies including the Twentieth Marine Corps Reserve, the George Washington College Company.

It was while at George Washington University that he learned to fly and discovered a particular aptitude as a glider pilot.

Here, also, he was enrolled in one of the first nuclear physics courses ever taught in an American university.

As a student, barely 20 years old, he supported himself by writing and within a very few years had established himself as a professional photographer and technical article writer in aviation and sports magazines.

He made the time during these same busy college years to act as a director with the Caribbean Motion Picture Expedition of 1931.

In 1932, L. Ron Hubbard, age 21, achieved an ambitious 'first.' Conducting the West Indies Minerals Survey, he made the first complete mineralogical survey of Puerto Rico. This was pioneer exploration in the great tradition, opening up a predictable, accurate body of data for the benefit of others. Later, in other less materialistic fields, this was to be his way many, many times over.

In the '30s, he became an established writer and published his work in over 90 periodicals and magazines.

His aviation articles in *The Sportsman Pilot* dealing, among other things, with aerial navigation of the Indies, date from this period.

By 1936, at the age of 25, Hubbard was in Hollywood, ready for adventures of a different sort. Working as a scriptwriter on several films, he made his reputation there, appropriately enough, with the highly profitable Columbia production titled "The Secret of Treasure Island."

Hollywood has always been a good place to study "what makes men tick," and the late '30s were no exception. In fact, L. Ron Hubbard dates his own statement of the discovery of the primary law of life, summarily expressed by the command "Survive!" at 1938. He says, "A work was written at that time which embraced Man and his activities." This was the still-unpublished "Excalibur," a sensational volume which was a summation of life based on his analysis of the state of mankind. The part played in this by his explorations, journeys and experiences in the four corners of the earth, amongst all kinds of men, was crucial.

As a logical consequence of his achievements in the field, L. Ron Hubbard on December 12th, 1939, not yet 30 years old, was proposed as a member of the Explorers Club of New York. He was duly elected a member on February 19th, 1940. Now the honors were coming.

In May of the same year, 1940, he was awarded his first Explorers Club flag for conducting the Alaskan Radio Experimental Expedition. Carrying the Club's flag on an expedition is one of the highest honors granted.

He found time to take his sailing ship (a ketch) *Magician* which he called "Maggie," along the coasts of Alaska adding to the existing knowledge of unfrequented navigational passages and islands in America's northwest ocean waters.

Also in 1940, on 17th December, he earned his "License to Master of Steam and Motor Vessels" from the U.S. Department of Commerce. Within 4½ months he had further obtained a second certificate attesting to his marine skill: "License to Master of Sail Vessels" ("Any Ocean"), for the U.S. Navy Hydrographic Office.

In 1941, he was ordered to the Philippines (which he had known as a youngster) at the outbreak of World War II.

He survived the early war in the South Pacific. He saw enough of war at firsthand to be sickened by it. In 1944, crippled and blinded he found himself in Oak Knoll Naval Hospital. From Commander Thompson of the Medical Corps of the U.S. Navy, a friend of his father and a personal student of Sigmund Freud, he had received while still young an extensive education in the field of the human mind. He developed techniques that would help him overcome his injuries and regain his abilities.

Altogether, he spent nearly a year at Oak Knoll, during which time he synthesized what he had learned of Eastern philosophy, his understanding of nuclear physics and his experiences among men. He says, "I set out to find from nuclear physics and a knowledge of the physical universe, things entirely lacking in Asian philosophy."

He concluded that the results he was obtaining could help others toward greater ability and happiness, and it was during this period that some of the basic tenets of Dianetics and Scientology were first formulated.

By 1947 he recovered fully.

In 1948 he wrote *Dianetics: The Original Thesis*, his first formal report of his discoveries about the mind and life. The manuscript was copied out extensively and quickly passed from hand to hand in many countries.

A grass roots interest in Dianetics spread. Letters began to pour in asking for clarifications and advice. Answering them was becoming a full-time occupation.

What was needed was a complete popular text on the subject which would answer all questions. A publisher, Hermitage House, was anxious to print such a book. There was one condition: the manuscript had to be delivered in six weeks.

The book was written in six weeks.

This was the anatomy of the mind, and a technology called auditing. 180,000 words of breakthrough, *Dianetics: The Modern Science of Mental Health* exploded onto the booklists of May, 1950, like a roman candle of life and hope. Providing, as it did, for a truly workable school of the mind which would predictably improve the human condition, it leapt to the top of the *New York Times* best seller list and just stayed there.

Almost immediately, thousands of readers began to·

apply the data from the book and Dianetic groups sprang up across the country, with and without sanction.

Realizing already at this stage that the mind in itself, no matter how liberated, was limiting and that there was something 'animating' the mind, he permitted the founding in 1950 of the Hubbard Dianetic Research Foundation to facilitate investigation into the realm of the spirit. Thus was Scientology born.

The United States Government at this time attempted to monopolize all his researches and force him to work on a project "to make man more suggestible" and when he was unwilling, tried to blackmail him by ordering him back to active duty to perform this function. Having many friends he was able to instantly resign from the Navy and escape this trap. The government never forgave him for this and soon began vicious, covert international attacks upon his work, all of which were proven false and baseless, which were to last 28 years and finally culminated in the government being sued for 750 million dollars for conspiracy.

The pace of research and writing quickened. To an already crammed schedule, lectures were added. These lectures, usually arranged in a series spread across one or two weeks of intensive meetings, were later to become famous, and many are preserved on tape and in book form.

The Oakland Lecture Series in September of 1950 and the Los Angeles Lecture Series in late November of that same year are preserved in book form in *Notes on the Lectures*.

1951 saw the publication of *Self Analysis*, a very practical self-help volume giving a way to improve memory, reaction time and general ability.

Also in 1951, *Science of Survival* was published, a 506-page volume outlining and describing in detail the relationship of Man to the physical universe and an exact pattern for the prediction of human behavior.

In 1952, a new series of lectures was delivered in Philadelphia, in course format: The Philadelphia Doctorate Course. These lectures, all of which were preserved on tape and are available today, went into great detail about the behavioral patterns of the spirit—a breathtaking delineation of the spiritual landscape he was now surveying.

Many awards and honors were offered and conferred on L. Ron Hubbard. He did accept an honorary Doctor of Philosophy given in recognition of his outstanding work on Dianetics and "as an inspiration to the many people ... who had been inspired by him to take up advanced studies in this field. ..."

An historic milestone in the history of Dianetics and Scientology was passed in February, 1954, with the founding of the first Church of Scientology. This was in keeping with the religious nature of the tenets dating from the earliest days of research. It was obvious that he had been exploring religious territory right along. And whatever the name given to the technique or study and whatever way it had been interpreted by skeptics or sensation-mongers, it was apparent to those with a sense of history and Man's ages-old spiritual quest that this was indeed the realm of the soul and its havens.

And Dianetics and Scientology were snowballing across the United States and reaching other shores—England first of all. *Dianetics: The Modern Science of Mental Health* was everywhere. As early as 1951, the publisher Casini had brought out the first Italian edition in Rome.

In 1954, there was another lecture series, in Phoenix, Arizona. These were startling talks on the qualities and fundamental nature of all life. Today they can be studied in book form: *The Phoenix Lectures*. It was in this series that he described the Axioms of Scientology, those self-evident truths which provide the philosophical foundation for the entire religion.

And in 1955, the U.S. District Court for the District of Columbia certified that he was a Minister of the Church.

On November 13th, 1957, the International Oceanographic Foundation, with headquarters in Miami, Florida, made him a Fellow of the Society, "by virtue of contributions to the advancement and extension of knowledge and discovery in oceanography and the marine sciences."

At the end of the fifties, L. Ron Hubbard moved his home to Saint Hill Manor, a vast and beautiful Georgian residence in the green hills of Sussex, in England. Increasingly effective techniques had been developed for the further liberation of the spirit and the exploration he now conducted was leading inevitably to spiritual freedom, the ages-long quest of Man's greatest religious leaders.

On a literally 'down-to-earth' level, though, L. Ron Hubbard was moving in a direction new even for him. 1959 and 1960 saw him, now firmly established at Saint Hill, conducting a series of revolutionary experiments on plants in a fully-equipped greenhouse laboratory on the Manor grounds. On September 25, 1959, a local paper was able to record that "L. Ron Hubbard ... whose researches in plant life at the Manor look like revolutionizing horticulture, has carried out an experiment which points to the fact that plants react in much the same way to certain situations as do human beings."

His discoveries on the nature of life in plants were described by one journal as "25 years in advance of today's methods and ideas." This proved prophetic for 13 years subsequent to L. Ron Hubbard's findings; experiments on plant life reaction in Swiss, German, Russian, American, British and Canadian scientific institutions have validated his findings in rigorous test conditions.

In 1961 he set up an educational visit to teach the now standard methods of Dianetics and Scientology, to ensure uniform quality of application. Students came from all over the world, and over the next few years returned to their local academies to use study methods which revolutionized the philosophy of education.

Student failures could be recovered. Study barriers by 1965 had been overcome.

For more than two millenia Man had dreamed of a spiritual state where, free of his own mental aberrations, he would be truly himself. L. Ron Hubbard called this state "Clear." And, at Saint Hill, in August of 1965, he announced the attainment of Clear.

The dream of Buddha, attained by the few, was a reality —Man could be Clear.

And the reality which was and is Clear was to be available to all who followed the exact route he had laid out. This route he called The Bridge. For it was as a span across the abyss of misery and degradation and sorrow to a higher plateau of ability and happiness.

In 1966, having paved the way to Clear so that it was safe and sure for others to walk, the Founder resigned from any official administrative capacity in Scientology.

He discovered and developed the astonishing materials above Clear now known as the Advanced Courses. These are the eight OT Sections, enabling one who has attained Clear to regain abilities never before accurately credited to the human spirit, as an Operating Thetan, a spiritual being operating independently of the laws of the physical universe.

In July of 1966, OT I and OT II were released and, during the last months of 1967, came the breakthrough of OT III.

A research accomplishment of immense magnitude, OT III has been called "The Wall of Fire." Here are contained the secrets of a disaster which resulted in the decay of life as we know it in this sector of the galaxy. The end result of OT III is truly the stuff of which dreams are spun: the return of full self-determinism and complete freedom from overwhelm.

The formation of a new Scientology group dates from this same period. Hearing of L. Ron Hubbard's plans for further exploration and research into, among other things, past civilizations, many Scientologists wanted to join him and help. They adopted the name "Sea Organization."

January, 1968, saw the release of OT Sections IV, V and VI as a sequence of spiritual abilities to be reached. And, in September of 1970 came OT VII. The release of OT VIII was announced on September 19, 1978.

These OT Sections and the abilities and awarenesses they restore to the individual are the greatest gifts to Man of an honest man who has retained 'his common touch' and humility.

People all over the world consider that they have no truer friend.

Abbreviations

Numerical abbreviations are listed at the end of the alphabetical abbreviations.

AC, Ability Congress Lectures.

ACC, Advanced Clinical Course.

A C & R, affinity, communication and reality.

ACSA, South African Anatomy Congress Lectures.

AD, or A.D., after Dianetics (1950) e.g. 1965 = AD 15.

ADMIN, 1. administration. 2. administrative.

AESPs, Attitudes, Emotions, Sensations, Pains.

AFRA, Association for the Rehabilitation of Alcoholics.

AHMC, Anatomy of the Human Mind Congress Lectures.

AICL, First American Advanced Clinical Indoctrination Course Lectures.

ALS, Academy Lecture Series.

AMA, American Medical Association.

ANZO, Australia New Zealand Oceania.

AO, Advanced Organization.

AOLA, Advanced Organization Los Angeles.

AO/SH, Advanced Organization/ Saint Hill.

AR, audio registration.

ARC, 1. affinity, reality, communication. 2. Anti-Radiation Congress Lectures.

ASIO, Australian Security Intelligence Organization.

ASMC, Anatomy of the Spirit of Man Congress Lectures.

ASR, Association of Scientologists for Reform.

AX, Axioms Lectures.

BC, Special Radio Broadcast.

BL, Birmingham Lectures.

BRUN, Befolkningens Ret Til Uforfalsket Nyhedsformidling (Danish press reform group).

C & A, Certifications and Awards.

CAC, Completed Auditors Course.

CC, Clearing Congress Lectures.

CCH, communication, control and havingness.

CCHR, Citizens Commission on Human Rights.

CERT, certificate.

CHC, Clean Hands Congress Lectures.

CIC, Control Information Center.

CLO, Continental Liaison Office.

CO-AUDITING, cooperative auditing.

COMM, communication.

CONF, conference.

COPHS, Committee on Public Health and Safety.

CRA, communication, reality, affinity.

CREAM, Criminal Rehabilitation and Education Advancement Movement.

CREO, Committee to Re-Involve Ex-Offenders.

C/S, 1. Case Supervisor. 2. a Case Supervisor direction of what to audit on a pc.

CS, Commodore's Staff.

CS-1, Commodore's Staff for Division 1 (HCO Division).

CS-2, Commodore's Staff for Division 2 (Dissemination Division).

CS-3, Commodore's Staff for Division 3 (Treasury Division).

CS-4, Commodore's Staff for Division 4 (Technical Division).

CS-5, Commodore's Staff for Division 5 (Qualifications Division).

CS-6, Commodore's Staff for Division 6 (Public Division).

CSC, Clearing Success Congress Lectures.

CS-G, Commodore's Staff Guardian.

DAS, Demonstration Auditing Session.

DCL, First December Conference Lectures.

DEI SCALE, Desire-Enforcement-Inhibit Scale.

DEMO, demonstration.

DEPT, department.

DHEW, Department of Health, Education and Welfare.

DIV, division.

DK, Denmark.

D,M&A, Drugs, Medicines and Alcohol.

DN, Dianetics.

D.P.M., Diploma in Psychological Medicine.

DSEC, Data Series Evaluators Course.

ECEU, Executive Council Europe.

ECT, electroconvulsive therapy.

EEA, Effective Education Association.

EEC, European Economic Community.

E-METER, 1. electropsychometer. 2. Hubbard Electrometer.

EP, end phenomena.

ESTO, Establishment Officer.

EULO, European Liaison Office.

EUS, Eastern United States.

EXAMS, Examinations (Department of Examinations).

EX DN, Expanded Dianetics.

EXEC, executive.

EXEC SEC, executive secretary.

FAC, 1. facsimile. 2. Foundation Auditor's Course.

FAC 1, facsimile one.

FBDL, Flag Bureaux Data Letter.

FBI, Federal Bureau of Investigation (US).

FBO, Flag Banking Officer.

FC, Freedom Congress Lectures.

FDA, Food and Drug Administration (US).

FEBC, Flag Executive Briefing Course.

FEGU, Association of Effective Basic Education (started in Denmark).

FES, folder error summary.

FLAF, Flag Operations Liaison Office Africa.

FLANZO, Flag Operations Liaison Office ANZO.

FLEU, Flag Operations Liaison Office Europe.

F/N, floating needle or free needle.

FOI ACT, Freedom of Information Act.

FOLO, Flag Operations Liaison Office.

FOLO EUS, Flag Operations Liaison Office Eastern United States.

FOLO WUS, Flag Operations Liaison Office Western United States.

FORMULA H, Formula Hope.

FSM, Field Staff Member.

GAE, gross auditing error.

GC, Games Congress Lectures.

GE, genetic entity.

G.O., Guardian Office.

GPM, goals problem mass.

GPSPEC, Special Group Processing Sessions.

GR/PROC, group processing.

HAA, Hubbard Advanced Auditor.

HACS, Hubbard Advanced Courses Specialist.

HAS, 1. Hubbard Association of Scientologists. 2. Hubbard Apprentice Scientologist. 3. Hubbard Communications Office Area Secretary.

HASI, Hubbard Association of Scientologists International.

HATS, Hubbard Advanced Technical Specialist.

HAV, havingness.

HBA, Hubbard Book Auditor.

HCA, Hubbard Certified Auditor.

HCAP, Hubbard Certified Auditor's Course Phoenix.

HCL, Hubbard College Lectures.

HCO, Hubbard Communications Office.

HCOB, Hubbard Communications Office Bulletin.

HCO EXEC SEC, Hubbard Communications Office Executive Secretary.

HCOPL, Hubbard Communications Office Policy Letter.

HCO WW, Hubbard Communications Office Worldwide.

HCS, Hubbard Clearing Scientologist Course Lectures.

HDA, Hubbard Dianetic Auditor.

HDC, Hubbard Dianetic Counselor.

HDFL, Hubbard Dianetic Foundation Lectures.

HDG, Hubbard Dianetic Graduate.

HEV, Human Evaluation Course.

HGA, Hubbard Graduate Auditor.

HGC, Hubbard Guidance Center.

HGDS, Hubbard Graduate Dianetic Specialist.

HMCSC, Hubbard Mini Course Supervisor Course.

HNEDA, Hubbard New Era Dianetics Auditor.

HNEDG, Hubbard New Era Dianetics Graduate.

HPA, Hubbard Professional Auditor.

HPC, 1. Hubbard Professional Course Lectures. 2. Hubbard Professional College Lectures.

HPC A, Hubbard Professional Course August 1956.

HPC F, Hubbard Professional Course, February 1956.

HPC N5, Hubbard Professional Course November 1955.

HPCSC, Hubbard Professional Course Supervisor Course.

HQS, Hubbard Qualified Scientologist.

HRS, Hubbard Recognized Scientologist.

HSCSC, Hubbard Senior Course Supervisor Course.

HSDC, Hubbard Standard Dianetics Course.

HSS, Hubbard Senior Scientologist.

HSST, Hubbard Specialist of Standard Tech.

HSTS, Hubbard Standard Technical Specialist.

HTS, Hubbard Trained Scientologist.

HVA, Hubbard Validated Auditor.

ICDS, First International Congress of Dianeticists and Scientologist Lectures.

INDOC, indoctrination.

INT RD, Interiorization Rundown.

IRS, Internal Revenue Service (US).

ISBN, International Standard Book Number.

JOBURG, Johannesburg.

KRC, knowledge, responsibility, control.

L, abbreviation for list. Example: L-10 is a list of questions that make up a particular Scientology process.

L&A, Logics and Axioms Lectures.

LAC, Los Angeles Congress.

LACC, London Advanced Clinical Course.

LAM, London Auditor's Meeting Lectures.

LCC, London Clearing Congress Lectures.

LCDH, London Congress on Dissemination and Help Lectures.

LCHP, London Congress on Human Problems Lectures.

LCNRH, London Congress on Nuclear Radiation and Health Lectures.

LGC, London Group Auditor's Course Lectures.

L.I.M., Learning, Interest and Motivation.

LOE, London Open Evening Lectures.

LPC, London Professional Course Lectures.

LPLS, London Public Lecture Series.

LRCP, Licentiate of the Royal College of Physicians.

LRH, L. Ron Hubbard.

LRH/MTS, L. Ron Hubbard Model Tape Session.

LS, Lecture Series.

MACC, Melbourne Advanced Clinical Course.

MB, *Medicinae Baccalaureus* (Latin—Bachelor of Medicine).

MC, Melbourne Congress Lectures.

MEST, the symbol for the physical universe is MEST, from the first letters of the words matter, energy, space and time or the Greek letter phi (φ).

METER, E-Meter.

MHMR PROGRAM, Mental Health and Mental Retardation Program.

MID RUD, middle rudiment.

MLC, Member of the Legislative Council.

MRCS, Member of the Royal College of Surgeons.

MSH, Mary Sue Hubbard.

MTS, model tape session.

NAAP, National Academy of American Psychology.

NAAPT, National Alliance on Alcoholism Prevention and Treatment.

NAMH, National Association for Mental Health.

NCLE, National Commission on Law Enforcement and Social Reform.

NCLESJ, National Commission on Law Enforcement and Social Justice.

N.E.D., New Era Dianetics.

NEEDS, New England Elderly Demands Society.

NIAAA, National Institute of Alcohol Abuse and Alcoholism.

OAK PLS, Oakland Public Lecture Series.

OCA, Oxford Capacity Analysis.

OCTSER, October Series.

OEC, Organization Executive Course.

OP PRO BY DUP, Opening Procedure by Duplication (a process).

ORG, 1. organization. 2. organizing.

ORG BOARD, organizing board.

ORG EXEC COURSE, Organization Executive Course.

ORG EXEC SEC, Organization Executive Secretary.

ORG OFFICER, Organizing Officer.

OS, Organizational Series Lectures.

O.S.C., Oblates of Saint Charles.

OT, operating thetan.

OTL, 1. Operation and Transport Liaison Offices. 2. OT (Operating Thetan) Liaison Office.

O/W, overt/withhold.

PABS, Professional Auditor's Bulletins.

PAC, Professional Auditor's Congress.

PC, preclear.

PDC, Philadelphia Doctorate Course Lectures.

PDC SUPP, Philadelphia Doctorate Course Supplementary Lectures.

PE, 1. personal efficiency. 2. Personal Efficiency Course.

PE COURSE, Personal Efficiency Course.

PHC, First Phoenix Congress Lectures.

PIP, Printed Intensive Procedure Lectures.

PLPS, Phoenix Public Lecture and Processing Series.

PLS, Public Lecture Series.

PPS, Public Processing Series.

PR, public relations.

PR&R, promotion and registration.

PRE HAV, prehavingness.

PREHAV SCALE, prehavingness scale.

PRO, 1. Public Relations Officer. 2. Professional Course.

PROV, provisional.

PT, present time.

PTP, present time problem.

PTS, potential trouble source.

Q, came from *quod* in Q.E.D. or "therefore" in geometry. "It follows."

Q & A, 1. questioning the pc's answer. 2. question and answer.

QM, quartermaster.

QUAL, 1. qualifications. 2. Qualifications Division.

R, 1. routine. 2. reality. 3. release.

R-2, Routine Two.

R-2G, Routine Two-G.

R-2H, Routine Two-H.

R2-10, Routine Two-Ten.

R2-12, Routine Two-Twelve.

R-3, Routine Three.

R3GA, Routine Three GA.

R-3M, Routine Three M.

R3-MX, Routine Three-M experimental.

R-3R, Routine Three Revised.

R3SC, Routine Three Service Facsimile Clear.

R4, Routine Four.

R4M, Routine Four-M.

R4M2, Routine Four-M Two.

R-46, Routine Forty-six.

R6, Routine Six.

R/BRCST, radio broadcast.

RD, rundown.

REHAB, 1. rehabilitate. 2. rehabilitation.

R.P. and C., rest points and confusions.

RR, rocket read.

R/S, rock slam.

R/SERS, rock slammers.

RURI, Reform Group for Education and Rehabilitation of Criminals (group started in Denmark).

SAC, Staff Auditor's Conference Series.

SC, Success Congress Lectures.

SCN, Scientology.

SCS, start, change, stop.

SEC CHECK, security check.

SERVICE FAC, service facsimile.

SH, Saint Hill.

SHPA, Special Hubbard Professional Auditor's Course Lectures.

SHSBC, Saint Hill Special Briefing Course.

SH SC, Saint Hill Staff Course.

SH TVD, Saint Hill television demonstration.

SLP, Six Levels of Processing.

SLP-8, Six Levels of Processing—Issue 8.

SMC, State of Man Congress.

SO, Sea Organization.

SO FEBC, Sea Organization, Flag Executive Briefing Course.

SOP, 1. Standard Operating Procedure. 2. Standard Operating Procedure for Theta Clearing Lectures.

SOP-8, Standard Operating Procedure 8.

SOP-8-C, Standard Operating Procedure 8-C.

SOP-8-D, Standard Operating Procedure 8-D.

SO XDN, Sea Organization, Expanded Dianetics.

SP, suppressive person.

SPEC, special.

SPL, special.

SPRL, London Spring Lectures.

SS, staff status.

SSS, Special Services Staff—of the Internal Revenue Service, (US).

STAT, statistic.

STP, Standard Procedure Lectures.

SUPP, supplementary lecture.

T, technique.

TA, 1. tone arm. 2. tone arm action.

TCC, Theta Clear Congress Lectures.

TECH, 1. technology. 2. technical.

TFA, Task Force on Alcoholism.

TFMR, Task Force on Mental Retardation.

T80, Technique 80 Lectures.

T88, Technique 88 Lectures.

T88 SUPP, Technique 88 Supplementary Lectures.

TR, training regimen (training drill).

TVD, television demonstration.

UC, Unification Congress of Dianeticists and Scientologists Lectures.

UKLO, United Kingdom Liaison Office.

UPC, Universe Process Congress Lectures.

UPPER INDOC TR, Upper Indoctrination TR.

USLO, United States Liaison Office.

VFP, valuable final product.

VMP, Validation Mest Processing.

VP, Validation Processing.

WFMH, World Federation for Mental Health.

WSO, Welcome to the Sea Organization Lectures.

WST, Washington Staff Talk.

WUS, Western United States.

WW, worldwide.

XDN, Expanded Dianetics.

YA, Youth Authority.

YTS, Youth Training School.

Numerical Abbreviations

1MACC, First Melbourne Advanced Clinical Course Lectures.

1SHACC, First Saint Hill Advanced Clinical Course Lectures.

2ACC, Second American Advanced Clinical Course Lectures.

3ACC, Third American Advanced Clinical Course Lectures.

3D, Routine Three D.

3DXX, Routine Three D Criss Cross.

3GA, Routine Three GA.

3GAXX, Routine Three GA Criss Cross.

3ICGB, Third International Congress of Scientologists Lectures.

3SA ACC, Third South African Advanced Clinical Course Lectures.

4ACC, Fourth American Advanced Clinical Course Lectures.

4LACC, Fourth London Advanced Clinical Course Lectures.

5ACC, Fifth American Advanced Clinical Course Lectures.

5LACC, Fifth London Advanced Clinical Course Lectures.

6ACC, Sixth American Advanced Clinical Course Lectures.

6LACC, Sixth London Advanced Clinical Course Lectures.

7ACC, Seventh American Advanced Clinical Course Lectures.

8ACC, Eighth American Advanced Clinical Course Lectures.

8-C, 1. Standard Operating Procedure 8-C. 2. Routine 8-Control. 3. control.

8D, Standard Operating Procedure 8D.

8-80, see TECHNIQUE 8-80 in Glossary.

8-8008, see SCIENTOLOGY 8-8008 in Glossary.

80, Technique 80.

88, Technique 88.

9ACC, Ninth American Advanced Clinical Course Lectures.

10ACC, Tenth American Advanced Clinical Course Lectures.

15ACC, Fifteenth American Advanced Clinical Course Lectures.

16ACC, Sixteenth American Advanced Clinical Course Lectures.

17ACC, Seventeenth American Advanced Clinical Course Lectures.

18ACC, Eighteenth American Advanced Clinical Course Lectures.

19ACC, Nineteenth American Advanced Clinical Course Lectures.

20ACC, Twentieth American Advanced Clinical Course Lectures.

21ACC, Twenty-first American Advanced Clinical Course Lectures.

22ACC, Twenty-second American Advanced Clinical Course Lectures.

Glossary

Aberration, a departure from rational thought or behavior. From the Latin, *aberrare*, to wander from; Latin, *ab*, away, *errare*, to wander. It means basically to err, to make mistakes, or more specifically to have fixed ideas which are not true. The word is also used in its scientific sense. It means departure from a straight line. If a line should go from A to B, then if it is "aberrated" it would go from A to some other point, to some other point, to some other point, to some other point and finally arrive at B. Taken in its scientific sense, it would also mean the lack of straightness or to see crookedly as, in example, a man sees a horse but thinks he sees an elephant. Aberrated conduct' would be wrong conduct, or conduct not supported by reason. When a person has engrams, these tend to deflect what would be his normal ability to perceive truth and bring about an aberrated view of situations which then would cause an aberrated reaction to them. Aberration is opposed to sanity, which would be its opposite.

Abridged Style Auditing, (Level III style), by abridged is meant "abbreviated," shorn of extras. Any not actually needful auditing command is deleted. In this style we have shifted from pure rote to a sensible use or omission as needful. We still use repetitive commands expertly, but we don't use rote that is unnecessary to the situation.

Academy, in Scientology the Academy is that department of the technical division in which courses and training are delivered; Department 11, Division 4.

Acceptance Level, the degree of a person's actual willingness to accept people or things, monitored and determined by his consideration of the state or condition that those people or things must be in for him to be able to do so.

Administrative TRs (Admin TRs), the purpose of these TRs is to train the student to get compliance with and complete a cycle of action on administrative actions and orders, in spite of the randomities, confusions, justifications, excuses, traps and insanities of the third and sixth dynamics, and to confront such comfortably while doing so.

Admin Scale, a scale for use which gives a sequence (and relative seniority) of subjects relating to organization. The full scale and how to use

it for organizational success, is contained in *The Volunteer Minister's Handbook*.

ADVANCE! Magazine, the magazine of the Advanced Organization. Its purpose is to promote advanced courses, solo training, books, tapes and meters, and monitor the line of information and reality to those following the route to OT.

Advanced Clinical Course, basically a theory and research course which gives a much further insight into the phenomena of the mind and the rationale of research and investigation.

Advanced Organization, organization whose function is to run the Clearing and OT Courses.

Affinity, the feeling of love or liking for something or someone. Affinity is a phenomena of space in that it expresses the willingness to occupy the same place as the thing which is loved or liked. The reverse of it would be antipathy, "dislike" or rejection which would be the unwillingness to occupy the same space as or the unwillingness to approach something or someone. It came from the French, *affinite*, affinity, kindred, alliance, nearness and also from the Latin, *affinis*, meaning near, bordering upon.

Alter-Is, a composite word meaning the action of altering or changing the reality of something. Is-ness means the way it is. When someone sees it differently he is doing an alter-is; in other words, is altering the way it is. This is taken from the *Axioms*.

Alter-Isness, see As-Isness.

American Personality Analysis, see Oxford Capacity Analysis.

Amytal® Sodium (amobarbital sodium), a drug used for the control of convulsive seizures. It is used for the management of catatonic and manic reactions or seizures resembling epilepsy.

Anadin®, a brand name for a tablet similar to an aspirin for relieving headaches.

Analytical Mind, that mind which combines perceptions of the immediate environment, of the past (via pictures) and estimations of the future into conclusions which are based upon the realities of situations. The analytical mind combines the potential knowingness of the thetan with the conditions of his surroundings and brings him to independent conclusions. This mind could be said to consist of visual pictures either of the

past or the physical universe, monitored by, and presided over, by the knowingness of a thetan. The keynote of the analytical mind is awareness, one knows what one is concluding and knows what he is doing.

Antisocial Personality, see Suppressive Person.

ARC, a word from the initial letters of Affinity, Reality, Communication which together equate to Understanding. It is pronounced by stating its letters, A-R-C. To Scientologists it has come to mean good feeling, love or friendliness, such as "He was in ARC with his friend." One does not however, fall out of ARC, he has an ARC break.

ARC Break, a sudden drop or cutting of one's affinity, reality, or communication with someone or something. Upsets with people or things come about because of a lessening or sundering of affinity, reality, or communication or understanding. It's called an ARC break instead of an upset, because if one discovers which of the three points of understanding have been cut, one can bring about a rapid recovery in the person's state of mind. It is pronounced by its letters A-R-C break. When an ARC break is permitted to continue over too long a period of time and remains in restimulation, a person goes into a "sad effect" which is to say they become sad and mournful, usually without knowing what is causing it. This condition is handled by finding the earliest ARC break on the chain, finding whether it was a break in affinity, reality, communication or understanding and indicating it to the person, always, of course, in session.

ARC Straightwire, purpose—to make a person able to run secondaries and engrams. ARC Straightwire was fantastically effective in moving a person from "neurotic" to "normal." (See also Straightwire)

ARC Triangle, it is called a triangle because it has three related points: affinity, reality and the most important, communication. Without affinity there is no reality or communication. Without reality or some agreement, affinity and communication are absent. Without communication, there can be no affinity or reality. It is only necessary to improve one corner of this very valuable triangle in Scientology in order to improve the remaining two corners. The easiest corner to improve is communication: improving one's ability to communicate

raises at the same time his affinity for others and life, as well as expands the scope of his agreements.

Artane® (trihexyphenidyl hydrochloride), used as an antispasmodic drug which exerts a direct inhibitory effect upon the parasympathetic nervous system. It has a relaxing effect on certain muscles.

As-Is, to view anything exactly as it is without any distortions or lies, at which moment it will vanish and cease to exist.

As-Isness, the considerations resulting in conditions of existence are four-fold: (a) as-isness is the condition of immediate creation without persistence, and is the condition of existence which exists at the moment of creation and the moment of destruction, and is different from other considerations in that it does not contain survival.

(b) **alter-isness** is the consideration which introduces change, and therefore time and persistence into an **as-isness** to obtain persistency.

(c) **is-ness** is an apparency of existence brought about by the continuous alteration of an **as-isness**. This is called, when agreed upon, Reality.

(d) **not-isness** is the effort to handle **is-ness** by reducing its condition through the use of force. It is an apparency and cannot entirely vanquish an **is-ness**.

Assessment, assessment isn't auditing, it is simply trying to locate something to audit.

Assist, 1. an action undertaken by a minister to assist the spirit to confront physical difficulties which can then be cared for with medical methodology by a medical doctor as needful. 2. simple, easily done processes that can be applied to anyone to help them recover more rapidly from accidents, mild illness or upsets.

Attest, see Declare.

Auditing, 1. the application of Scientology processes and procedures to someone by a trained auditor. 2. the action of asking a preclear a question (which he can understand and answer), getting an answer to that question and acknowledging him for that answer. Auditing gets rid of unwanted barriers that inhibit, stop or blunt a person's natural abilities as well as gradiently increasing the abilities a person has so that he becomes more able and his survival, happiness and intelligence increase enormously.

3. Scientology processing is called auditing by which the auditor (practitioner) listens, computes, and commands.

Auditing by Lists, a technique using prepared lists of questions. These isolate the trouble the pc is having with auditing. Such lists also cover and handle anything that could happen to a student or staff member.

Auditing Command, a certain exact command which the preclear can follow and perform.

Auditor, 1. one who listens and computes; a Scientology practitioner. 2. Scientology processing is done on the principle of making an individual look at his own existence, and improve his ability to confront what he is and where he is. An auditor is the person trained in the technology and whose job it is to ask the person to look, and get him to do so. The word auditor is used because it means one who listens, and a Scientology auditor does listen.

Auditor's Code, a collection of rules (do's and don'ts) that an auditor follows while auditing someone, which ensures that the preclear will get the greatest possible gain out of the processing that he is having.

Auditor, The, 1. the Journal of Scientology. Journal means: a daily newspaper; a periodical dealing especially with matters of current interest. 2. a magazine issued at Saint Hill called *The Auditor.*

Aversion Therapy, aversion therapy is a form of *psychological* treatment in which such an unpleasant response is induced to his psychological aberration that the patient decides to give it up. Thus the victim of alcoholism is given a drug that makes the subsequent drinking of alcoholic liquors so unpleasant by inducing nausea and vomiting that he decides to give up drinking. Another commonly used method of inducing aversion is an electric shock. (Note: This is a psychology practice, not a Scientology one.)

Awareness Characteristics, see Awareness Scale.

Awareness Scale, there are fifty-two levels of awareness from Unexistence up to the state of Clear. By "level of awareness" is meant that of which a being is aware. A being who is at a level of this scale is aware only of that level and the others below it.

Axioms, the Axioms are agreed-upon considerations. They are the central considerations which have been agreed upon. They are considerations. A self-evident truth is the dictionary definition of an axiom. No definition could be further from the truth. In the first place, a truth cannot be self-evident because it is a static. So, therefore, there is no self-evidency in any truth. There is not a self-evident truth, never has been, never will be. However, there are self-evident agreements and that is what an axiom is.

Bank, see Reactive Mind.

Beingness, the assumption or choosing of a category of identity. Being-

ness is assumed by oneself or given to oneself, or is attained. Examples of beingness would be one's own name, one's profession, one's physical characteristics, one's role in a game —each and all of these things could be called one's beingness.

Belladonna (atropine), the poisonous drug atropine obtained from belladonna and similar plants. Used to dilate the pupils of the eyes and to relieve pain or spasms.

Black Propaganda, (black = bad or derogatory, propaganda = pushing out statements or ideas), the term used to destroy reputation or public belief in persons, companies or nations. It is a common tool of agencies who are seeking to destroy real or fancied enemies or seek dominance in some field.

Blew, see Blow.

Blow, 1. *slang,* unauthorized departure from an area, usually caused by misunderstood data or overts. 2. the sudden dissipation of mass in the mind with an accompanying feeling of relief.

Board of Investigation, the purpose of a Board of Investigation is to discover the cause in any conflict, poor performance or down statistic. A Board of Investigation is composed of not less than three and not more than five members. A majority of the members must be senior to the persons being investigated except when this is impossible. The board may investigate by calling in a body on the persons concerned or by sitting and summoning witnesses or principals. A Board of Investigation is a much less serious affair than a Committee of Evidence. Persons appearing before it are not under duress or punishment. The whole purpose is to get at the facts. A board may recommend a Committee of Evidence.

Bridge, The, see Classification Gradation and Awareness Chart.

Briefing Course, see Saint Hill Special Briefing Course.

Bulletin, see Hubbard Communications Office Bulletin.

Bureau, in a Scientology management organization, managing other Scientology orgs, each division is called a bureau instead, i.e. Management Bureau.

Button(s), items, words, phrases, subjects or areas that cause response or reaction in an individual by the words or actions of other people, and which cause him discomfort, embarrassment, or upset, or make him laugh uncontrollably.

Bypassed Charge, mental energy or mass that has been restimulated in some way in an individual and that is either partially or wholly unknown to that individual and so is capable of affecting him adversely.

Camphor Convulsive Treatments, the use of camphor to produce convulsions in the patient. Since camphor is poisonous its use has been largely discontinued and replaced with Metrazol® to accomplish the same purpose. (Note: This is a psychiatric practice, not a Scientology one.)

Case, the way a person responds to the world around him by reason of his aberrations.

Case Gain, the improvements and resurgences a person experiences from auditing.

Case Supervisor, that person in a Scientology Church who gives instructions regarding, and supervises the auditing of preclears. The abbreviation C/S can refer to the Case Supervisor or to the written instructions of a Case Supervisor depending on context.

Cause, cause could be defined as emanation. It could be defined also, for purposes of communication, as source-point.

CCHs, several associated processes which bring a person into better control of his body and surroundings, put him into better communication with his surroundings and other people, and increase his ability to have things for himself. They bring him into the present, away from his past problems.

Celebrity Centre, it is responsible for ensuring that celebrities expand in their area of power. This organization is also responsible for a celebrity's basic training in Scientology.

Certifications and Awards, the department in a Scientology organization that issues certificates and awards to students who have completed courses or preclears who have completed auditing actions.

Chain, a series of recordings of similar experiences. A chain has engrams, secondaries and locks.

Chaplain's Court, the chaplain (or the permanent or part-time assisting arbiter) presides over all court hearings and renders judgment. Only civil matters may be heard or judged. The purpose of the Chaplain's Court Unit is to resolve matters of dispute between individuals. Staff personnel, pcs, students and Scientologists may utilize this court unit to resolve their own disputes or legal affairs.

Charge, harmful energy or force accumulated and stored within the reactive mind, resulting from the conflicts and unpleasant experiences that a person has had. Auditing discharges this charge so that it is no longer there to affect the individual.

Checkout, the action of verifying a student's knowledge of an item given on a checksheet.

Checksheet(s), a list of materials, often divided into sections, that give the theory and practical steps which, when completed, give one a study completion. The items are selected to add up to the required knowledge of the subject. They are arranged in the sequence necessary to a gradient of increasing knowledge on the subject. After each item there is a place for the initial of the student or the person checking the student out. When the checksheet is fully initialed, it is complete, meaning the student may now take an exam and be granted the award for completion. Some checksheets are required to be gone through twice before completion is granted.

Chloral, a colorless oily liquid with a pungent odor, made from chlorine

and alcohol, and used in making chloral hydrate and DDT (a very powerful insecticide). Chloral hydrate is used as an hypnotic to quiet nervousness and produce sleep.

Chloral Hydrate, see Chloral.

Church of the New Faith, incorporated, Adelaide, South Australia, 18 August 1969. There is no significant difference between the Church of the New Faith and the Church of Scientology. A decision of the Court of Petty Sessions held at Perth, Western Australia, decided on 2nd December 1970 *inter alia* "The Church of the New Faith is a religion."

Circuit, 1. a part of an individual's bank that behaves as though it were someone or something separate from him and that either talks to him or goes into action of its own accord, and may even, if severe enough, take control of him while it operates. A tune that keeps going around in someone's head is an example of a circuit. 2. divisions of your own mind that seem to make up other personalities and these other personalities affect you and argue with you and so forth.

Circuits, United States Federal Circuit Courts.

Class, 1. refers to the level of classification of an auditor. 2. a technical certificate in Scientology goes by classes on the gradation chart.

Classification, Gradation and Awareness Chart, the route to Clear, the Bridge. On the right side of the chart there are various steps called the states of release. The left-hand side of the chart describes the very important steps of training on which one gains the knowledge and abilities necessary to deliver the grades of release to another. It is a guide for the individual from the point where he first becomes dimly aware of a Scientologist or Scientology and shows him how and where he should move up in order to make it. Scientology contains the entire map for getting the individual through all the various points on this gradation scale and for getting him across the Bridge to a higher state of existence.

Clay Demo, abbreviation for clay demonstration. A Scientology study technique whereby the student demonstrates definitions, principles, etc. in clay to obtain greater understanding by translating significance into actual mass.

Clear, 1. a thetan who can be at cause knowingly and at will over mental matter, energy, space and time as regards the first dynamic (survival for self). The state of Clear is above the release grades (all of which are requisite to clearing) and is attained by completion of the Clearing Course at an Advanced Organization. 2. the name of a button on an adding machine. When you push it, all the hidden answers in the machine clear and the machine can be used for a proper computation. So long as the button is not pressed the machine adds all old answers to all new efforts to compute and wrong answers result. Really, that's all a Clear is. Clears are beings who have been cleared of wrong answers or useless answers which keep them from living or thinking. 3. a thetan cleared of enforced and unwanted behavior patterns and discomforts.

Coach(ing), to train intensively by instruction, demonstration and practice. In training drills, one twin is made the coach and the other the student. The coach in his coaching actions, coaches the student to achieve the purpose of the drill. He coaches with reality and intention following exactly the materials pertaining to the drill to get the student through it. When this is achieved the roles are then reversed—the student becoming the coach and the coach becoming the student.

Co-Auditing, is an abbreviation for cooperative auditing. It means a team of any two people who are helping each other reach a better life with Scientology processing.

Co-Auditor, one who audits another co-auditor under supervision and after training at a given level.

Cognitions, something a pc suddenly understands or feels. "Well, what do you know about that?"

Command Intention, a word arising out of the Sea Organization. The orders and policies written by L. Ron Hubbard for the Sea Organization constitute command intention.

Committee of Evidence, 1. a fact-finding body composed of impartial persons properly convened by a convening authority which hears evidence from persons it calls before it, arrives at a finding and makes a full report and recommendation to its convening authority for his or her action. 2. a fact-finding group appointed and empowered to impartially investigate and recommend upon Scientology matters of a fairly severe ethical nature.

Committee of Evidence for Review, (any Committee of Evidence) findings and convening authority endorsement may be subject to review by any upper level committee. Review must be applied for by anyone named as an interested party but no other, and only if a penalty was recommended (whether endorsed or not). A Committee of Evidence for Review is convened and handled in exactly the same way as an ordinary Committee of Evidence but it cannot call new or even old witnesses or the interested parties. All it can do is listen to the tapes of the hearings, examine the evidence given in the original hearings and recommend to its own convening authority one of two things: (1) that a new committee be convened on the site by the upper convening authority to examine points thought to be in question, (2) that the penalty be changed. A Committee of Evidence for Review can recommend to increase or decrease the penalty.

Communication, the consideration and action of impelling an impulse or particle from source-point across a distance to receipt-point, with the intention of bringing into being at the receipt-point a duplication and understanding of that which emanated from the source-point. The formula of communication is: cause, distance, effect, with intention, attention and duplication with understanding.

Communication Course (Comm Course),

a basic Scientology course consisting mainly of the TRs; also called the H.A.S. (Hubbard Apprentice Scientologist Course).

Communication Cycle, a cycle of communication and two-way communication are actually two different things. A cycle of communication is not a two-way communication in its entirety. In a cycle of communication we have Joe as the originator of a communication addressed to Bill. We find Bill receiving it and then Bill originating an answer or acknowledgment back to Joe and thus ends the cycle.

Communication Formula, see Communication.

Communication Lag, the length of time, whether verbal or silent, intervening between the auditor's asking of a specific question and the specific and precise answer of that question by the preclear. It would not matter then whether the preclear continued to talk about something else than the question, or simply remained silent, this would still be communication lag.

Condition(s), the state or condition of any person, group or activity can be plotted on this scale of conditions which shows the degree of success or survival of that person, group or activity at any time. Data on the application of these conditions is contained in *The Volunteer Minister's Handbook*.

Conditions Formulas, each of the conditions in Scientology has a precise formula which if applied will raise a person or activity to a higher condition, i.e., correctly applying the condition formula for the Condition of Emergency results in the Condition of Normal Operation which is the next condition above Emergency.

Confessional, an auditing procedure directed toward relieving a preclear of the pressure of his overt acts (transgressions).

Confront(ing), 1. an action of being able to face. 2. the ability to be there comfortably and perceive.

Control Circuit Phrases, see Circuit.

Convening Authority, that duly appointed official of Scientology who appoints and convenes a Committee of Evidence to assist him in carrying out and justly exercising his or her authority, and who approves, mitigates or disapproves the findings and recommendations of the Committee of Evidence he or she appoints.

Counseling, see Pastoral Counseling.

Counseling Group, see Dianetic Counseling Group.

Counter-Intention, a determination to follow a goal which is in direct conflict with those known to be the goals of the group.

Course Supervisor, basically, someone who in addition to his other duties can refer the person to the exact bulletin to get his information and never tells him another thing.

Court of Ethics, an ethics action which is less severe than a Committee of Evidence. It is convened on a person or persons when evidence of a misdemeanor or crime exists. A Court of Ethics may not demote,

transfer or dismiss a staff member. It may suspend a staff member from post for a reasonable length of time.

Cramming, a section in the Qualifications Division where a student is given high pressure instruction at his own cost after being found slow in study or when failing his exams.

Criminon, Criminon has the purpose to ensure that reforms in criminal laws and prison systems come about. Criminon is dedicated to the successful rehabilitation of prisoners to make them useful members of society. Criminon is completely reversing the 80% recidivism of criminals with fantastic success.

C/Sing, abbreviation for case supervising, the action of a Case Supervisor writing down in the pc folder the directions the auditor must follow in auditing a particular pc. The Case Supervisor C/Ses the pc folder before each session the auditor has with the pc.

Cycles of Action, the sequence that an action goes through, wherein the action is started, is continued for as long as is required and then is completed as planned.

Dagga, standard South African name for *cannabis indica* (hashish, marijuana).

Data Series, the Data Series is a series of policy letters written by L. Ron Hubbard which deal with logic, illogic, proper evaluation of data and how to detect and handle the causes of good and bad situations in any organization to the result of increased prosperity.

De-aberrate, to remove aberration from the preclear's case. The use of Dianetics and Scientology processing de-aberrates a person.

Declare, an action done in Qual after a pc has completed a cycle of action or attained a state. The pc or pre-OT who knows he made it must be sent to Exams and Certs and Awards to attest. A declare completes his cycle of action and is a vital part of the action.

Demo Kit, demonstration kit. Consists of various small objects such as corks, caps, paper clips, pen tops, batteries—whatever will do. These are kept in a box or container. Each student should have one. The pieces are used while studying to represent the things in the material one is demonstrating. It helps hold concepts and ideas in place. A demo kit adds mass, reality and doingness to the significance and so helps the student to study.

Department, there are five sections plus the department's director in a department; three departments and the secretary, a deputy and a communicator in a division.

Department of Public Servicing, (Department 17, Division 6, Public Division) contains demonstrations/indoctrination, film and tape plays, introductory lectures and events, books and memberships selling. There is a Public Registration Section and the valuable final product is people interested enough to buy something and do.

Department 17, Department of Public Servicing.

Destimulate, to take away the restimulation. Destimulate does not mean the erasure of the original incident, it means simply the knockout of the point of restimulation.

Determinism, see Self-Determinism.

Dianetic Counseling Group, delivers New Era Dianetics auditing and the New Era Dianetics Course, using a certified New Era Dianetics Course Supervisor from a Scientology Church as supervisor for the course. Running the NED Course is optional, but if conducted, it must be taught by a supervisor certified by the Church of Scientology to do so. The New Era Dianetics Course Supervisor may not undertake to train or graduate other NED Course Supervisors. Only Churches may do this.

Dianetics, 1. *dia* (Greek) through, *nous* (Greek) soul, deals with a system of mental image pictures in relation to psychic (spiritual) trauma. The mental image pictures are believed on the basis of personal revelation to be comprising mental activity created and formed by the spirit, and not by the body or brain. 2. Dianetics addresses the body. Thus Dianetics is used to knock out and erase illnesses, unwanted sensations, misemotion, somatics, pain, etc. Dianetics came before Scientology. It disposed of body illness and the difficulties a thetan was having with his body.

Director, see Department.

Director of Processing, the HGC is headed by the Director of Processing, under whom come all individual cases, (public and staff).

Direct Style Auditing (Level IV style), by direct we mean straight, concentrated, intense, applied in a direct manner. By direct, we don't mean frank or choppy. On the contrary, we put the pc's attention on his bank and anything we do is calculated only to make that attention more direct.

Division, there are seven divisions in a Scientology org. Each division is headed by a secretary, i.e. the Treasury Division is headed by the Treasury Secretary. Each division has three departments. A director is the head of a department, i.e. the Department of Income in the Treasury Division is headed by the Director of Income.

Doingness, what one ought to be doing in order to get creation or do creation.

Dramatization, to repeat in action what has happened to one in experience. That's a basic definition of it, but much more important, it's a replay now of something that happened then. It's being replayed out of its time and period.

Drills, actions the student has to become familiar with before doing processes. The actual process is never used as a drill. A drill takes the action the auditor will use when doing a process and gets him familiar with it.

Drug(s), drugs essentially are poisons. The degree they are taken determines the effect. A small amount gives a stimulant. A greater amount acts as a sedative. A larger amount acts as a poison and can kill one dead. This is true of any drug.

Drug Rundown, a series of auditing actions designed to free a person of the attitudes, emotions, sensations and pains that caused or accompanied his use of drugs.

Duplication, cause, distance, effect, with the same thing at effect as is at cause.

Dynamics, there could be said to be eight urges (drives, impulses) in life. These we call dynamics. These are motives or motivations. We call them the eight dynamics. The first dynamic—is the urge toward existence as one's self. Here we have individuality expressed fully. This can be called the self dynamic. The second dynamic—is the urge toward existence as a sexual or bisexual activity. This dynamic actually has two divisions. Second dynamic (a) is the sexual act itself and the second dynamic (b) is the family unit, including the rearing of children. This can be called the sex dynamic. The third dynamic—is the urge toward existence in groups of individuals. Any group or part of an entire class could be considered to be a part of the third dynamic. The school, the society, the town, the nation are each part of the third dynamic, and each one is a third dynamic. This can be called the group dynamic. The fourth dynamic—is the urge toward existence as mankind. Whereas the white race would be considered a third dynamic, all the races would be considered the fourth dynamic. This can be called the mankind dynamic. The fifth dynamic—is the urge toward existence of the animal kingdom. This includes all living things whether vegetable or animal. The fish in the sea, the beasts of the field or of the forest, grass, trees, flowers, or anything directly and intimately motivated by life. This could be called the animal dynamic. The sixth dynamic—is the urge toward existence as the physical universe. The physical universe is composed of matter, energy, space and time. In Scientology we take the first letter of each of these words and coin a word, MEST. This can be called the universe dynamic. The seventh dynamic—is the urge toward existence as or of spirits. Anything spiritual, with or without identity, would come under the heading of the seventh dynamic. This can be called the spiritual dynamic. The eighth dynamic—is the urge toward existence as infinity. This is also identified as the Supreme Being. It is carefully observed here that the science of Scientology does not intrude into the dynamic of the Supreme Being. This is called the eighth dynamic because the symbol of infinity ∞ stood upright makes the numeral "8." This can be called the infinity or God dynamic.

Effect, receipt point and what is received at the receipt point.

Eight(8), the symbol of infinity ∞ stood upright makes the numeral "8."

8-C, name of a process. Also used to mean good control.

Elavil® (amitriptyline hydrochloride), an antidepressant with an anxiety reducing, sedative component to its action. Its mechanism of action in Man is not known. It is used for the relief of symptoms of depression.

Electrometer, see E-Meter.

Electropsychometer, see E-Meter.

E-Meter, Hubbard Electrometer. An electronic instrument for measuring mental state and change of state in individuals, as an aid to precision and speed in auditing. The E-Meter is not intended or effective for the diagnosis, treatment or prevention of any disease.

End Phenomena, "those indicators in the pc and meter which show that a chain or process is ended." It shows in Dianetics that basic on that chain and flow has been erased, and in Scientology that the pc has been released on that process being run.

Engram(s), a mental image picture which is a recording of a time of physical pain and unconsciousness. It must by definition have impact or injury as part of its content.

Engram Chain(s), a basic engram and a series of similar incidents.

Entheta, means enturbulated theta (thought or life); especially refers to communications, which based on lies and confusions, are slanderous, choppy or destructive in an attempt to overwhelm or suppress a person or group.

Erased, the words "vanished" or "erased," when applied to an engram which has been treated mean that the engram has disappeared from the engram bank. It cannot be found afterwards except by search of the standard memory.

Erasure, the act of erasing, rubbing out, locks, secondaries or engrams.

Establishment Officer, the purpose of Establishment Officers is to establish and maintain the establishment of the org and each division therein. The term Esto is used for abbreviation.

Establishment Officer Series, a series of policy letters written by L. Ron Hubbard which isolate the procedures necessary to establish an organization or activity and train or handle personnel to obtain production.

Ethics, 1. ethics actually consist, as we can define them now in Dianetics, of rationality toward the highest level of survival for the individual, the future race, the group and mankind, and the other dynamics taken collectively. Ethics are reason. The highest ethic level would be long-term survival concepts with minimal destruction, along any of the dynamics. 2. ethics is a personal thing. By definition the word means "the study of the general nature of morals and the specific moral choices to be made by the individual in his relationship with others." When one is ethical or "has his ethics in" it is by his own determination and is done by himself.

Ethics Hearing, an Ethics Hearing may be convened by an Ethics Officer to obtain data for further action or inaction. An Ethics Hearing has

no power to discipline but may advise on consequences.

Ethics Officer, when ethics isn't in, it's put in. Ethics Officers put ethics in. An Ethics Officer removes counter-intention from the environment.

Ethics Presence, ethics presence is an "X" quality made up partly of symbology, partly of force, some "now we're supposed to's" and endurance. As an executive you get compliance because you have ethics presence.

Evil Intention (Evil Purpose), a definite obsessive desire to destroy.

Examinations (Department of Examinations), that department which examines students and preclears to ensure that they have actually completed courses or levels of auditing and that the high technical standards of Scientology are being properly delivered.

Examiner, that person in a Scientology church assigned to the duties of noting pc's statements and indicators after session, or when pc wishes to volunteer information.

Executive Court of Ethics, a Court of Ethics may not summons a director, a secretary or an executive secretary. An Executive Court of Ethics only may be convened on a director, secretary or executive secretary. See also Court of Ethics.

Executive Director, 1. the org is commanded by the Commanding Officer (Sea Org orgs) or the Executive Director (non Sea Org orgs). 2. the Commanding Officer or Executive Director of an org is responsible for managing the org and keeping it going.

Executive Ethics Hearing, no one of the rank of director or above may be summoned for an Ethics Hearing, but only an Executive Ethics Hearing, presided over by a person superior in rank. See also Ethics Hearing.

Executive Secretary, in a Scientology org a secretary is in charge of a division. An executive secretary is in charge of three divisions. There are two executive secretaries in an org, the HCO Executive Secretary (HCO Exec Sec) and the Organization Executive Secretary (Org Exec Sec).

Expanded Dianetics, is not the same as Standard Dianetics as it requires special training and advanced skills. The main difference between these two branches is that Standard Dianetics is very general in application. Expanded Dianetics is very specifically adjusted to the pc. Some preclears, particularly heavy drug cases, or who have been given injurious psychiatric treatment or who are physically disabled or who are chronically ill or who have had trouble running engrams (to name a few) require a specially adapted technology. [Note: Standard Dianetics was released in 1969. In 1978, L. Ron Hubbard did further extensive research on Dianetics and released New Era Dianetics which now contains the most modern developments and techniques on the subject of Dianetics.]

Expanded Grades, the lower grades harmonic into the OT levels. They

can be run again with full 1950-1960 to 1970 processes as given on the Saint Hill courses all through the 1960s. These are now regrouped and sorted out and are called Expanded Lower Grades.

Exteriorization, the state of the thetan, the individual himself, being outside his body. When this is done, the person achieves a certainty that he is himself and not his body.

Facsimile, see Mental Image Picture.

Field Staff Members, they are missionaries who disseminate Scientology, sell books, courses, and counseling services, and introduce people to the Church. They often support themselves in the field by receiving ten per cent payment from their local Scientology organization on the donations paid by those they select for Scientology services.

First Dynamic, see Dynamics.

Flag, the Church of Scientology of California once operated a marine mission aboard a chartered vessel. This marine mission was commonly referred to as Flag. It was operated under the aegis (protection, support) of the Church of Scientology of California. Although no Sea Organization vessels are in operation today, the term Flag is still used in the Sea Org.

Flag Bureaux, the international management body of the Sea Organization with additional advisor and management activities.

Flag Executive Briefing Course, the curriculum consists of the technology of upper level executive management, using existing materials with a very high concentration on practical drills. The exact intention of the Flag Executive Briefing Course is to bring executive action up to the high level of precision now only attained in auditing.

Flag Land Base, Flag has established a new land base. It is called the Flag Land Base, as it delivers services which formerly were only available on the Flagship of the Sea Organization.

Flag Operations Liaison Office, FOLOs have been set up to maintain one single command channel from Flag to orgs. They are Flag's link to the orgs and are vital to Flag management and expansion of orgs. They consist of Flag staff members working in the field on making Flag planning become an actuality.

Flag Representative, the Flag Rep has the primary duty of safeguarding that those actions necessary to the delivery of Scientology by an area or org are implemented and continued and to prevent the destruction of the org by omissions, alter-is or counter-intention and to keep Flag abreast of the existing scene so that efficient operation can be directed.

Flagship, see Flag.

Flat, meaning that the incident when "flat" has been discharged of all bad consequences to the preclear.

Flattening, 1. to continue a process as long as it produces change and no longer. 2. flattening something means to do it until it no longer produces a reaction. See also End Phenomena.

Floating Needle, a floating needle is a rhythmic sweep of the dial at a slow, even pace of the needle.

Flows, an impulse or direction of energy particles or thought or masses between terminals.

Flow 0,1,2,3,
  F-1, flow one, something happening to self.
  F-2, flow two, doing something to another.
  F-3, flow three, others doing things to others.
  F-0, flow zero, self doing something to self.

Folder, see PC Folder.

Foundation, an evening, part-time organization. The purpose of the evening organization is to operate as a bridge from the public to the daytime org and to make money in its own right. The evening organization and the weekend is called: The Scientology Foundation.

Fourth Dynamic, see Dynamics.

Fourth Dynamic Engram, the humanitarian objective is to make a safe environment in which the fourth dynamic engram can be audited out. By engram we mean the mental block that prevents peace and tolerance. By fourth dynamic we mean that impulse to survive as mankind instead of just individuals.

Freedom, *Freedom* is Scientology's international newspaper. It is published by Churches of Scientology around the world and appears in many languages.

Freedom of Information Act (United States), the Freedom of Information Act is a law passed by Congress in 1966, which totally reverses long-standing government policies and customs on divulging information to the public. There are two basic categories of materials that one can seek under the Act: 1. files regarding oneself or one's group. 2. files regarding an agency's work.

Frontoparietal Regions, of or pertaining to the frontal and the parietal bones of the skull which are underneath the forehead and temple regions.

Gain, see Case Gain.

Gains, see Case Gain.

Game, a game consists of freedom, barriers and purposes. It also consists of control and uncontrol. An opponent in a game must be an uncontrolled factor. Otherwise one would know exactly where the game was going and how it would end and it would not be a game at all.

Genetic Line, protoplasm line. Its cycle is preconception, conception, birth, procreation, preconception and so on. That unending string of protoplasm goes through earth time.

Good Indicators, 1. what you are treating is getting better, by which we mean, less present; betterness to us is less present, his bad ankle is getting better. We mean the badness of the ankle is less present so that's a good indicator. How much less present is the degree of the goodness of the indicator. 2. those

indicators of a person (or group) indicating that the person is doing well, e.g. fast progress, high production statistics, person happy, winning, cogniting, are said to be good indicators.

Gradation Chart, see Classification Gradation and Awareness Chart.

Grade(s), 1. the word used to describe the attainment of level achieved by a preclear. Grade is the personal points of progress on the Bridge. A preclear is Grade 0, I, II, III, IV, V, VA or VI depending on the technology successfully applied. 2. a series of processes culminating in an exact ability attained, examined and attested to by the pc. 3. grade and level are the same but when one has a grade one is a pc and when one has a level one is studying its data.

Grade Chart, see Classification Gradation and Awareness Chart.

Gradient, a gradual approach to something, taken step by step, level by level, each step or level being, of itself, easily surmountable—so that, finally, quite complicated and difficult activities or high states of being can be achieved with relative ease. This principle is applied to both Scientology processing and training.

Grant Beingness, 1. the ability to assume or grant (give, allow) beingness is probably the highest of human virtues. It is even more important to be able to permit (allow) other people to have beingness than to be able oneself to assume it. 2. the willingness to have somebody else be something.

Group(s), another type of organization is the group. Official groups and official congregations of the various churches exist in very large numbers in the United States and Great Britain and elsewhere throughout the world.

Group Engram, each time instantaneous action is demanded of the group by compressed time situations, and commands are given by the selected individual or individuals to cope with those moments of emergency, it can be observed that an engram has been implanted in the group. The instantaneous orders and commands are indicators of an engram. The engram actually was received during a moment of shock when the ideals, ethics, rationale and general thought and energy of the group collided forcefully with MEST.

Group Processing, techniques, usually already codified, administered to groups of children or adults. The group (preclears) is usually assembled and seated in a quiet room where they will not be disturbed by sudden noises or entrances. The group auditor then takes his position in the front of the group and talks to them briefly about what he is going to do and what he expects them to do. The auditor then begins with his first command.

Guardian, the most senior executive of Scientology. The character of the post is best understood legally as "trustee" or even "proprietor sole" and exercises the powers and carries out duties similar to that of a high

church officer entrusted with the funds or survival of his group.

Guardian Office, the Guardian Office is the administrative bureau for the Church. It handles public relations, finances, legal and social matters and is active in defending and seeing to the viability of the Church. Guardian Office personnel are executives of Scientology.

Guiding Style Auditing (Level Two style), the essentials of Guiding Style Auditing consist of two-way comm that steers the pc into revealing a difficulty followed by a repetitive process to handle what has been revealed.

HAS Co-Audit, using precise processes developed for this section only, the HAS Co-audit (do-it-yourself processing) seeks to improve cases and further interest people in Scientology so that they will take individual HGC processing and individual training.

HAS Course (Hubbard Apprentice Scientologist Course), this level teaches about elementary communication and control. Processes taught are training drills on communication and to put the student at cause over the environment (TRs 0-4). End result is improved ability in the origination and handling of communication and in handling oneself in life situations and predicting and handling others.

Hat, the duties of a post. It comes from the fact that jobs are often distinguished by a type of hat as fireman, policeman, conductor, etc. Hence the term hat. A hat is really a folder containing the write-ups of past incumbents on a post plus a checksheet of all data relating to the post plus a pack of materials that cover the post.

Have, see Having.

Having, to be able to touch or permeate or to direct the disposition of.

Havingness, 1. the feeling that one owns or possesses. 2. the concept of being able to reach or not being prevented from reaching.

HCO Bulletins, see Hubbard Communications Office Bulletins.

Help Processing, there are probably thousands of ways help could be run. But the one general process on help that would rank high would be "What have you helped?" "What have you not helped?" alternated. This is the best way I know of to run the sense of what help one has given plus what help one has withheld. This lets the pc as-is his failures to help as well as his denials of help.

Hidden Standard, a hidden standard is a problem a person thinks must be resolved before auditing can be seen to have worked. It's a standard by which to judge Scientology or auditing or the auditor. This hidden standard is always an old problem of long duration. It is a postulate-counter-postulate situation. The source of the counter-postulate was suppressive to the pc.

HQS Course (Hubbard Qualified

Scientologist Course), this course is a basic course in the fundamentals of Scientology technology and gives a gradient of application of a few vital principles. This course, particularly its TRs, can be used to get a person off drugs or to help a person who has been on drugs dry out.

Hubbard Advanced Auditor, a Class IV auditor. This level teaches about service facsimiles and ability.

Hubbard Advanced Technical Specialist, a Class IX auditor. This level teaches advanced procedures and developments since Class VIII. It is available at Saint Hill organizations.

Hubbard Apprentice Scientologist Course, see HAS Course.

Hubbard Certified Auditor, a Class II auditor. This level teaches about overt acts and withholds.

Hubbard Communications Office (HCO), it's in charge of the org boards, in charge of the personnel, it's in charge of hatting, it's in charge of the communication, which gives it communication lines, because an organization consists of the lines. It's in charge of inspection and it's in charge of ethics. HCO builds, holds, maintains, mans and controls the organization and it's the orders issue section.

Hubbard Communications Office Bulletins, written by L. Ron Hubbard only. These are the technical issue line. They are valid from first issue unless specifically cancelled. All data for auditing and courses is contained in HCOBs. These outline the product of the org. They are distributed as indicated, usually to technical staff. They are red ink on white paper, consecutive by date.

Hubbard Communications Office Policy Letter (HCO PL), orders or directions in Scientology for policy: green ink on white paper, signed by L. Ron Hubbard.

Hubbard Dianetic Graduate, one who is trained to teach the Dianetic Course after graduating from the HSDC. [Note: The Hubbard Standard Dianetics Course (HSDC) was replaced by the Hubbard New Era Dianetics Course in July 1978.]

Hubbard Dianetic Research Foundation, the first organization of Dianetics in the United States.

Hubbard Graduate Auditor, a Class VII auditor. Only available to Sea Org or five year contracted Church staff. This level teaches the Power Processes and review auditing. It is not a prerequisite to Class VIII, however. It is delivered in Church of Scientology Saint Hill Organizations.

Hubbard Graduate Dianetic Specialist, Expanded Dianetics auditor. This level teaches about Expanded Dianetics.

Hubbard Guidance Center, that department of the technical division of a Scientology Church which delivers auditing. Department 12, Division 4.

Hubbard Professional Auditor, a Class III auditor. This level deals with ARC and ARC breaks.

Hubbard Qualified Scientologist Course, see HQS Course.

Hubbard Recognized Scientologist,

a Class 0 auditor. This level teaches about communication.

Hubbard Senior Scientologist, a Class VI auditor. An HSS is a graduate of the Saint Hill Special Briefing Course. This course consists of the full practical application of Scientology grades, repair, setups, assists and special cases tech up to Class VI.

Hubbard Specialist of Standard Tech, Class VIII case supervisor.

Hubbard Standard Technical Specialist, a Class VIII auditor. The Class VIII Course teaches exact handling of all cases up to 100 per cent results, as well as Class VIII procedures, all case setup actions, all processes and corrective actions, as well as *flubless* Class VIII auditing.

Hubbard Trained Scientologist, a Class I auditor. This level teaches about problems.

Hubbard Validated Auditor, a Class V auditor. This level is taught at Church of Scientology Saint Hill Organizations and contains materials about the chronological development of Scientology with full theory and application.

In, 1. things which should be there and are or things that should be done and are, are said to be in, i.e. "We got scheduling in." 2. it is said that its (an organization's) ethics, tech and admin must be in, which means they must be properly done, orderly and effective.

In-Ethics, see Ethics.

In Session, the definition of in session is interested in own case and willing to talk to the auditor. When this definition describes the session in progress, then of course the pc will be able to as-is and will cognite.

Intensive, an intensive is defined as any one single period of 12 1/2 hours or 25 hours of auditing delivered all within one single week or weekends on a set schedule.

Interested Party, a person, plaintiff or defendant, called before a Committee of Evidence for whom penalties may be recommended or decisions awarded by the committee. An interested party may not be called before another committee or a later convened committee for the same offense or complaint after having been summoned and heard for that offense, or his complaint at one or more meetings of the current committee.

Interiorization, interiorization means going into it too fixedly, and becoming part of it too fixedly. It doesn't mean just going into your head.

Interiorization Rundown, the Interiorization Rundown is a remedy designed to permit the pc to be further audited after he has gone exterior. The Int Rundown is not meant to be sold or passed off as a method of exteriorizing a pc.

Intern(e)ship(s), serving a period as an interne, or an activity offered by a Church of Scientology by which experience can be gained. The apprenticeship of an auditor is done as a Scientology Church interne. A course graduate becomes an auditor by auditing. That means lots of auditing.

Is-ness, see As-isness.

Judiciary Dianetics, covers the field of adjudication within the society and amongst the societies of Man. Of necessity it embraces jurisprudence and its codes and establishes precision definitions and equations for the establishment of equity. It is the science of judgment.

Justice, 1. moral rightness; equity. 2. honor, fairness. 3. good reason. 4. fair handling: due reward or treatment. 5. the administration and procedure of the law.

Key-in, a moment when the environment around the awake but fatigued or distressed individual is itself similar to the dormant engram. At that moment the engram becomes active. It is keyed-in and can thereafter be dramatized.

Key-out, release or separation from one's reactive mind or some portion of it.

Knowingness, knowingness would be self-determined knowledge.

KRC Triangle, the upper triangle in the Scientology symbol. The points are K for knowledge, R for responsibility, and C for control. It is difficult to be responsible for something or control something unless you have knowledge of it. It is folly to try to control something or even know something without responsibility. It is hard to fully know something or be responsible for something over which you have no control, otherwise the result can be an overwhelm. Little by little one can make anything go right by: increasing knowledge on all dynamics, increasing responsibility on all dynamics, increasing control on all dynamics.

Largactil® (chlorpromazine), the same drug as Thorazine®. It is a strong tranquilizer (anti-psychotic) used to restore emotional calm and for relief of severe anxiety, agitation, and psychotic behavior.

Leucotomy (lobotomy), the operation of cutting the white nerve fibres in the frontal lobes of the brain. This operation severs the connections of the frontal cortex with other parts of the nervous system, especially the thalamus and the hypothalamus. The operation is done in psychotic patients who suffer from severe depression or tense obsessional states.

Level(s), 1. grade and level are the same thing but when one has a grade one is a pc and when one has a level one is studying its data. 2. level means "that body of Scientology data for that point of progress of the individual."

Liaison Office, see Flag Operations Liaison Office.

Librium® (chlordiazepoxide hydrochloride), a tranquilizer used to relieve anxiety and tension. Often used on patients suffering from withdrawal symptoms connected with alcoholism and to relieve preoperative anxiety or apprehension.

Life, when we say "life" we mean understanding, and when we say "understanding" we mean affinity, reality and communication. To understand all would be to live at the highest level of potential action and ability. Because life is understanding it attempts to understand. When it faces the incomprehensible it feels balked and baffled.

Lines, the communication lines of an organization or individual.

List, (noun) 1. a list of items given by a pc in response to an auditing question. 2. a list of questions made up by the auditor or Case Supervisor to ask the pc. 3. a prepared list. (verb) the action of the pc giving items to the auditor in response to an auditing question. See also Listing.

Listen Style Auditing, at Level 0 the style is Listen Style auditing. Here the auditor is expected to listen to the pc. The only skill necessary is listening to another. Listen Style should not be complicated by expecting more of the auditor than just this: Listen to the pc without evaluating, invalidating or interrupting.

Listing, a special procedure used in some processes where the auditor writes down items said by the preclear in response to a question by the auditor in the exact sequence that they are given to him by the preclear.

Listing and Nulling, the action of listing and then nulling the list.

Lithium (lithium carbonate), a drug used to control manic episodes in manic-depressive psychosis. It has a toxicity level which can occur at doses close to therapeutic levels.

Livingness, is going along a certain course impelled by a purpose and with some place to arrive. It consists mostly of removing the barriers in the channel, holding the edges firm, ignoring the distractions and reinforcing and reimpelling one's progress along the channel. That's life.

Livingness Repair Rundown, addresses the individual's handling of livingness, with the appropriate processes then done, to bring about the awareness of ability to change conditions.

Lobotomy, see Leucotomy.

Locational Assist, see Locational Processing.

Locational Processing (locationals), the object of Locational Processing is to establish the adequacy of communication terminals in the environment of the preclear. It can be run in busy thoroughfares, parks, confused traffic or anywhere that there is or is not motion of objects and people. Example command: "Notice that *(person)*."

Locks, 1. an analytical moment in which the perceptics of the engram are approximated, thus restimulating the engram or bringing it into action, the present time perceptics being erroneously interpreted by the reactive mind to mean that the same condition which produced physical pain once before is now again at hand. Locks contain mainly perceptics; no physical pain and very little misemotion. 2. conscious level experiences which sort of stick and the individual doesn't quite know why.

LRH, L. Ron Hubbard, Founder and Source of Dianetics and Scientology.

LRH Communicator, the title of that person in a Scientology church who is responsible for the communication and handling of LRH matters with regard to that Church.

Management Series Volume, a volume composed of several series of policy letters by L. Ron Hubbard dealing with the areas of data evaluation, public relations, personnel, organizing, finance, executives and establishment.

Mandrax® (Methaqualone), a drug used as an hypnotic (sleep inducer). With low dosage it is used to relieve mild to moderate anxiety or tension (sedative effect). With higher dosage it is used to relieve insomnia (hypnotic effect).

Mass, a composition of matter and energy existing in the physical universe. Mental mass is contained in mental image pictures.

Master at Arms, this is a naval term used in the Sea Org and is equivalent (but senior) to the Ethics Officer in a Scientology Church.

Medical Liaison Officer, see Qualifications Medical Liaison Officer.

Mellaril® (thioridazine), a drug used in the management of manifestations of psychotic disorders and especially to reduce excitement, abnormal or excessive movement or abnormal initiative in patients.

Mental Image Pictures, in Scientology we call a mental image picture a facsimile when it is a "photograph" of the physical universe sometime in the past. We call a mental image picture a mock-up when it is created by the thetan or for the thetan and does not consist of a photograph of the physical universe. We call a mental image picture an hallucination or more properly an automaticity (something uncontrolled) when it is created by another and seen by self.

Mest Universe, see Physical Universe.

Method One Word Clearing, the action taken to clean up all misunderstoods in every subject one has studied. It is done by a word clearing auditor. The result of a properly done Method One Word Clearing is the recovery of one's education.

Metrazol® (pentylenetetrazol), it is a central nervous system stimulant often used to enhance mental and physical activity of elderly patients. It is used as an antidote in respiratory depression or failure due to poisoning with barbiturates, alcohol, or certain central nervous system depressants.

Miceology, the idea of commanding the environment is opposed to the coined word Miceology which represents the school of thought which teaches one to conform to the environment.

Mind, a network of communications and pictures, energies and masses, which are brought into being by the activities of the thetan versus the physical universe or other thetans. The mind is a communication and control system between the thetan and his environment.

Misemotion, anything that is unpleasant emotion such as antagonism, anger, fear, grief, apathy or a death feeling.

Misemotional, 1. such a word would indicate that a person did not display the emotion called for by the actual circumstances of the situation. 2. being misemotional is synonymous with being irrational.

Missed Withholds, 1. an undisclosed contra-survival act which has been restimulated by another but not disclosed. 2. a missed withhold is a should have known. The pc feels you should have found out about something and you didn't.

Mission, a group granted the privilege of delivering elementary Scientology and Dianetic services. Does not have Church status or rights.

Mock-Up, see Mental Image Pictures.

Mogadon® (nitrazepam), drug used as a hypnotic and sedative.

Motivators, an aggressive or destructive act received by the person or one of the dynamics. It is called a motivator because it tends to prompt that one pays it back — it "motivates" a new overt.

Muzzled Style Auditing, in muzzled auditing, the auditor says only two things. He gives the command and acknowledges the answer to that command. If the pc says anything that is not an answer to that command, the auditor nods his head and awaits an answer before giving acknowledgment.

Narconon, meaning non-narcosis, is a drug rehabilitation program for the redemption of druggies in or out of prisons. It was organized in Arizona State Prison by an inmate who himself was a hard-core addict of thirteen years. He put to use the basic principles of the mind contained in L. Ron Hubbard's book *Scientology: The Fundamentals of Thought,* and by doing so completely cured himself and helped twenty other inmates do the same. Through Narconon no drugs whatever are used for withdrawal and on this program the usual withdrawal effects such as "cold turkey" are most often completely bypassed.

New Era Dianetics, a new and much more workable version of Dianetics. It is called New Era Dianetics. Dianetics in its early days produced quite a few miracles and many, many well and happy pcs. As time went on it underwent many refinements and changes and also, unfortunately, suffered the loss of a lot of its tech. So recently L. Ron Hubbard overhauled it extensively. New Era Dianetics is more precise. It achieves, in skilled hands, anything older Dianetics ever sought to achieve.

Not-Isness, see As-isness.

Nulling, the auditor's action in saying items from a list to a preclear and noting the reaction of the preclear's bank by the use of an E-Meter.

Objective Processes (Objectives), 1. Objective Processes deal with body motions and observing and touching objects in the auditing room. 2. look around or physical contact processes are "objective." Pcs who have been on drugs obviously have to be run on Objective not Subjective Processes. Anyone can be brought more into present time with Objective Processes.

Objectives Course, a course that teaches one how to run Objective Processes.

Obnosis, this is a coined (invented) word meaning observing the obvious. There is no English or any other language precise equivalent for it.

Only One, if an individual can discover that he is only playing on the first dynamic and that he belongs to no other team it is certain that this individual will lose for he has before him seven remaining dynamics. And the first dynamic is seldom capable of besting by itself all the remaining dynamics. In Scientology we call this condition the "only one." Here is self-determinism in the guise of selfish-determinism and here is an individual who will most certainly be overwhelmed. To enjoy life one must be some part of life.

Opening Procedure by Duplication, its goal is the separating of time, moment from moment. This is done by getting a preclear to duplicate the same action over and over again with two dissimilar objects.

Operating Thetan, 1. a Clear who has been refamiliarized with his capabilities. 2. a being at cause over matter, energy, space, time, form and life. Operating comes from "able to operate without dependency on things" and thetan is the Greek letter theta (Θ), which the Greeks used to represent "thought" or perhaps "spirit" to which an "n" is added to make a new noun in the modern style used to create words in engineering. 3. this state of being is attained by drills and familiarity after the state of Clear has been obtained. A real OT has no reactive bank, is cause over matter, energy, space, time and thought and is completely free.

Optimum Solution, the solution which brings the greatest benefit to the greatest number of dynamics.

Organizing Board, the actual diagrammatic pattern of the organization showing the divisions, departments, their personnel, functions and lines of communication. This pattern fully drawn out is known as the org (organizing) board.

Organizing Series, a series of policy letters by L. Ron Hubbard which tell how to organize an area in order to get production.

Other-Determined, see Other-Determinism.

Other-Determinism, simply something else giving you orders or directions.

Out, things which should be there and aren't or should be done and aren't are said to be "out," i.e. "Enrollment books are out."

Out-Ethics, an action or situation in which an individual is involved contrary to the ideals and best interests of his group. An act or situation or relationship contrary to the ethics standards, codes or ideals of the group or other members of the group. An act of omission or commission by an individual that could or has reduced the general effectiveness of a group or its other members. An individual act of omission or commision which impedes the general well-being of a group or impedes it in achieving its goals.

Out-Tech, means that Scientology is not being applied or is not being correctly applied.

Overrun(s), 1. gone on too long or happened too often. 2. continuing a process past the optimum point.

Overt, see Overt Act.

Overt Act, 1. an overt act is not just injuring someone or something; an overt act is an act of omission or commission which does the least good for the least number of dynamics or the most harm to the greatest number of dynamics. 2. an intentionally committed harmful act committed in an effort to resolve a problem. 3. that thing which you do which you aren't willing to have happen to you.

Oxford Capacity Analysis (OCA), the OCA is the English version of the American Personality Analysis (APA). Either may be used. Their administration, scoring and evaluation are handled in the same way. The OCA (or APA) consists of 200 questions. These 200 questions are divided up into series of 20 questions, each of which measures a single personality trait. Thus ten traits are measured in all.

Pack, a pack is a collection of written materials which match a checksheet. It is variously constituted — such as loose-leaf or a cardboard folder or bulletins in a cover stapled together. A pack does not necessarily include a booklet or hardcover book that may be called for as part of a checksheet.

Pan-Determinism, defined as determining the activities of two or more sides in a game simultaneously.

Past Lives, times lived before this life. Past lives are not "reincarnation." That is a complex theory compared to simply living time after time, getting a new body, eventually losing it and getting a new one.

Pastoral Counseling, Dianetics is practiced in the Church of Scientology as pastoral counseling, addressing the spirit in relation to his own body and intended to increase well-being and peace of mind. Auditing is a pastoral counseling procedure by which an individual is helped, in stages, to recover his self-determinism, ability and awareness of self, restoring respect for self and others.

PC Folders, a folded sheet of cardboard which encloses all the session reports and other items. The folder is foolscap size, light card, usually blue or green in color.

Permanent Certificate, in the case of an auditor, an internship or formal auditing experience is required. When actual honest evidence is presented to C&A that he can demonstrated that he can produce flubless results his certificate is validated with a gold seal and is a permanent certificate. With other courses the person must demonstrate that he can apply the materials studied by producing an actual, honest statistic in the materials studied. He presents this evidence to C&A and receives a validation gold seal on his certificate.

Personal Efficiency Course, what is the goal of a PE Course? Internationally the goal is to bring about a superior civilization in which peace can exist on earth. The modus operandi by which this is done is education in the actual, simple facts of existence, the data of which is contained in *Scientology: The Fundamentals of Thought.*

Personnel Series, a series of policy letters by L. Ron Hubbard which gives the basics of how to recruit, train and post personnel in an organization.

Phenobarbital, a white powder used as an hypnotic, anticonvulsant or sedative. It is a barbiturate.

Phenobarbitone, see Phenobarbital.

Physical Universe, the universe of matter, energy, space and time. It would be the universe of the planets, their rocks, rivers, and oceans, the universe of stars and galaxies, the universe of burning suns and time. In this universe we would not include theta as an integral portion, although theta obviously impinges upon it as life.

Planicop Machine, automatic printing plate maker.

Point of View, 'point from which he is looking,' rather than 'his opinions.'

Policy Letter, see Hubbard Communications Office Policy Letter.

Postulate, (noun) a self-created truth would be simply the consideration generated by self. Well, we just borrow the word which is in seldom use in the English language, we call that postulate. And we mean by postulate, self-created truth. He posts something. He puts something up and that's what a postulate is. (verb) In Scientology the word postulate means to cause a thinkingness or consideration. It is a specially applied word and is defined as causative thinkingness.

Potential Trouble Source, PTS means potential trouble source which itself means a person connected to a suppressive person. All sick persons are PTS. All pcs who roller-coaster (regularly lose gains) are PTS. Suppressive persons are themselves PTS to themselves.

Power Processes (Power), the processes audited only by Class VII auditors which make Grade V Power Releases.

Preclear, 1. a spiritual being who is now on the road to becoming Clear, hence preclear. 2. one who is discovering things about himself and who is becoming clearer.

Prefrontal Leucotomy (prefrontal lobotomy), a brain operation in which the·nerves between the hypothalamic region and cerebral cortex are cut to relieve the symptoms of mental illness.

Pre-OT, a thetan beyond the state of Clear who, through the Advanced Courses, is advancing to the full state of operating thetan.

Prepared List, is one which is issued in an HCOB and is used to correct cases.

Prepchecking, the target of a prepcheck question is a chain of withholds. The purpose of prepchecking is to set up a pc's rudiments so they will stay in during further clearing of the bank. The reason this is called prepchecking and the reason it isn't called withhold system and it isn't called anything else but prepchecking is it's preparatory to clearing.

Present Time, when we say that somebody should be in present time we mean he should be in communication with his environment. We mean, further, that he should be in communication with his environment as it exists, not as it existed.

Present Time Problem, see Problem.

Primary Rundown, the Primary Rundown consists of word clearing and study tech. It makes a student Super-Literate.

Problem, a problem is the conflict arising from two opposing intentions. A present time problem is one that exists in present time, in a real universe.

Process(ed), (verb) drilled in Scientology with Scientology exercises.

Process(es), (noun) a set of questions asked by an auditor to help a person find out things about himself or life. More fully, a process is a patterned action, done by the auditor and preclear under the auditor's direction, which is invariable and unchanging, composed of certain steps or actions calculated to release or free a thetan. There are many processes and these are aligned with the levels taught to students and with grades as applied to preclears, all of which lead the student or the preclear gradiently to higher understanding and awareness.

Processing, see Auditing.

Professional Auditor's Bulletin, a series of technical booklet issues.

Pro-Survival, (adj.) assisting survival.

Provisional Certificate, the student graduate is given a provisional certificate. This looks like any other certificate but is not gold-sealed and has "provisional" plainly on it. Provisional certificates expire after one year if not validated. (See also Permanent Certificate).

Psyche, 1. a thetan, the spirit, the being himself. 2. a Greek word meaning spirit.

Psychos, psychotics.

Psychosis, we know what psychosis is these days. It is simply an evil purpose; it means a definite obsessive desire to destroy.

Psychosomatic, "psycho" of course refers to mind and "somatic" refers to body; the term psychosomatic means the mind making the body ill or illnesses which have been created physically within the body by derangement of the mind.

Psychosomatic Illness, this we call physical illness caused by the mind. In brief, such illness is caused by perceptions received in the reactive mind during moments of pain and unconsciousness.

Psychotic, a person who is physically or mentally harmful to those about him out of proportion to the amount of use he is to them.

Psychotic Break, a neurotic person has not given up the strain of keeping some of his attention in present time, and will not do so until forced by chronic, constant restimulation to do so. When this happens the neurotic suddenly becomes psychotic. A psychotic break has occurred.

PTS Rundown, a series of auditing steps undertaken to relieve a preclear of the effects and upsets of being or having been connected to a suppressive person or persons.

Public Division, that division of a Scientology church which handles communication to and contact with the broad public to bring the religion of Scientology to them.

Q and A, means "Question and Answer." When the term Q and A is used it means one did not get an answer to his question. It also means not getting compliance with an order but accepting something else. Example: Auditor, "Do birds fly?" Pc, "I don't like birds." Auditor, "What don't you like about birds?" Flunk. It's a Q and A. The right reply would be an answer to the question asked and the right action would be to get the original question answered.

Qual, the Qualifications Division (Division 5 of a Church) where the student is examined and where he may receive cramming or special assistance and where his awarded completions and certificates and where his qualifications as attained on courses or in auditing are made a permanent record.

Qualifications Medical Liaison Officer, a Medical Liaison Officer in Department 14 of any land based organization is a Liaison Officer. He is a terminal in an org to whom a C/S may send public or staff in order to arrange for the necessary medical tests or treatment by a properly registered medical doctor. A Medical Liaison Officer is not permitted to give any medical treatment other than first aid or to arrange for a suitable doctor who can administer needed treatment.

Quickie(d), in the dictionary you will find "quickie also quicky: something done or made in a hurry. Also: a hurriedly planned and executed program (as of studies)." Anything that does not fully satisfy all requirements is quickie. So "quickie" really means "omitting actions for whatever reason that would satisfy all

demands or requirements and doing something less than could be achieved." In short a quickie is not doing all the steps and actions that could be done to make a perfect whole.

Randomity, the amount of predicted and unpredicted motion a person has, in ratio.

Reactive Mind, the reactive mind is a stimulus-response mechanism, ruggedly built and operable in trying circumstances. The reactive mind never stops operating. Pictures of the environment, of a very low order, are taken by this mind even in some states of unconsciousness. The reactive mind acts below the level of consciousness. It is the literal stimulus-response mind. Given a certain stimulus it gives a certain response.

Reality, 1. is, here on earth, agreement as to what is. This does not prevent barriers or time from being formidably real. It does not mean either that space, energy or time are illusions. It is as one knows it is. 2. is not what the individual thinks reality is. Reality is what the majority agrees it is.

"Reasonable," a staff member or executive can be "reasonable" and accept reasons why something cannot be done, accept incomplete cycles as complete, and fail to follow through and get completions. All of which results in further traffic.

Recall Process, processes which deal with the pc remembering things that happened in his past.

Rehabilitation (Rehabilitation of former release), when the person was originally released he had become aware of something that caused the reactive mind to de-stimulate at that point or become weak. And so he released. You have to find that point of sudden awareness again.

Release (noun), 1. one who knows he or she has had worthwhile gains from Scientology processing and who knows he or she will not now get worse. 2. a release purely and simply is a person who has obtained results in processing and has a reality on the fact that he has attained those results. That severely is the definition of release.

Religious Philosophy, implies study of spiritual manifestations; research on the nature of the spirit and study on the relationship of the spirit to the body; exercises devoted to the rehabilitation of abilities in a spirit.

Repair, repair is undertaken to eradicate errors made in auditing or the environment which impede the use of major processes.

Repetitive Process, is simply a process that is run over and over with the same question of the pc. The pc answers the thing and the auditor gives him an acknowledgement.

Restimulation, 1. where the environment reactivates a facsimile, which then acts back against the body or awareness of awareness unit of the person. This is a very simple system

of stimulus-response. 2. where the perceptics of the engram are approximated by those of the present time environment.

Review, the Department of Review is in the Qualifications Division. The entire purpose of the Department of Review is repair and correction of auditing and training difficulties.

Ritalin® (Methylphenidate hydrochloride), a drug used as a stimulant in the treatment of mental illness and certain depressive states. Often used on children exhibiting short attention span, distractibility or hyperactivity while they are undergoing other remedial measures (psychological, educational, social).

Rock Slam, the crazy, irregular, *left-right* slashing motion of the needle on the E-meter dial. R/Ses repeat left and right slashes unevenly and savagely, faster than the eye easily follows. The needle is frantic. The width of an R/S depends largely on sensitivity setting. It goes from one-fourth inch to whole dial. And it slams *back and forth.* A rock slam (R/S) means a hidden evil intention on the subject or question under auditing or discussion.

Roller Coaster, a case that betters and worsens. A roller coaster is always connected to a suppressive person and will not get steady gains until the suppressive is found on the case or the *basic* suppressive person earlier. Because the case doesn't get well he or she is a potential trouble source to us, to others and to himself.

Routine, a standard process, designed for the best steady gain of the pc at that level.

Routing Form, when particles arrive at the org space proper they must be routed and must continue to be routed from the moment they enter until they leave the org space. Thus there must be a reception for bodies, for mail, for phone, for telexes and for messages in general. There must also be an exit point for all these things and someone to send them on their way out of the org space. Once the particle (body, dispatch, raw materials, whatever) is at the door Reception must establish the routing. This is done usually with each step signed off the Routing Form that gives the full road map of the particle.

R6EW, Routine 6 End Words. This is the process run by a solo auditor which results in a Grade VI Release, the grade attained just before Clear.

Rudiments, 1. a series of auditing questions usually used at the beginning of a session which clear up any ARC breaks, present time problems or missed withholds the pc may have his attention on. 2. the reason you use rudiments is to get the pc in session so you can have the pc (1) in communication with the auditor and (2) interested in own case. The purpose of rudiments is to set up a case to run, not to run a case.

Run, undergo processing.

Rundown, a series of steps which are auditing actions and processes designed to handle a specific aspect of a case and which have a known end phenomena.

Saint Hill (SH), the name of L. Ron Hubbard's home in East Grinstead, Sussex, England, and location of the worldwide headquarters of Scientology, and the UK Advanced Organization and SH (AOSH UK). L. Ron Hubbard taught the original Saint Hill Special Briefing Course at Saint Hill from 1961 to 1965. The term SH now applies to any organization authorized to deliver those upper level Scientology services, hence we also have the "American Saint Hill Organization" (ASHO) and the "Advanced Organization and Saint Hill in Denmark" (AOSH EU) and "Saint Hill Europe" (SH EU).

Saint Hill Hubbard College of Scientology, the College of Scientology was formed in 1965 with its headquarters being at Saint Hill, England. Saint Hill Organizations (of which there are three at this time; Saint Hill Organization, England, Saint Hill Organization, Los Angeles, California and Saint Hill Organization, Copenhagen, Denmark) have Hubbard Colleges of Scientology and the Churches of Scientology have Academies of Scientology.

Saint Hill Special Briefing Course (SHSBC), the Saint Hill Special Briefing Course has certain distinct purposes. The course was begun to do two things. (1) to study and resolve training and education. (2) to assist people who wanted to perfect their Scientology. The Scientologists studying here are supposed to concentrate on only three things: (a) the acquisition of the ability to achieve a rapid and accurate understanding of data given to them for study and to put that material into effect; (b) to achieve auditing results; (c) to get a reality on the achieving of auditing results by exact duplication of current methodology and not by additives or extraordinary solutions.

Sanity, the ability to recognize differences, similarities and identities.

Scale of Awareness, see Awareness Scale.

Scientologist, one who understands life. His technical skill is devoted to the resolution of the problems of life.

Scientology, it is formed from the Latin word *scio*, which means *know* or *distinguish*, being related to the word *scindo*, which means *cleave*. (Thus the idea of differentiation is strongly implied.) It is formed from the Greek word *logos*, which means THE WORD, or OUTWARD FORM BY WHICH THE INWARD THOUGHT IS EXPRESSED AND MADE KNOWN; also THE INWARD THOUGHT OR REASON ITSELF. Thus, SCIENTOLOGY means KNOWING ABOUT KNOWING, or SCIENCE OF KNOWLEDGE.

Scientology 8-8008, was a formula. It said: the attainment of infinity, that is the first eight, is achieved by the reduction of the physical universe from infinity, that is the second eight, to zero, which is the first zero and the building of one's own universe from zero to an infinity of one's own universe and by that one achieves the attainment of infinity.

Sea Organization (Sea Org) (SO), a fraternal organization existing within the formalized structure of the Churches of Scientology. It consists of highly dedicated members of the Church. These members take vows of eternal service. The Sea Organization life-style of community living is traditional to religious orders.

Seconal® (secobarbital), a white barbiturate used as a sedative for nervousness and sleeplessness.

Secondary, a mental image picture of a moment of severe and shocking loss or threat of loss which contains unpleasant emotion such as anger, fear, grief, apathy or "deathfulness." It is a mental image recording of a time of severe mental stress. A secondary is called a secondary because it itself depends upon an earlier engram with similar data but real pain.

Second Dynamic, see Dynamics.

Secretary, see Division.

Section, 1. a Scientology org has seven divisions. Each division has three departments and each department has five sections. 2. a City Office has sections where higher orgs have departments and divisions.

Security, security itself is an understanding. Men who know are secure. Insecurity exists in the absence of knowledge. All security derives from knowledge.

Selective Service System, the responsible body for drafting persons into the U.S. Armed Services.

Self Analysis Lists, the lists of questions by which the individual can explore his past and improve his reactions toward life. These lists can be found in L. Ron Hubbard's book, *Self Analysis*.

Self Audit(ing), the manifestation of going around running concepts or processes on one's self out of session. It is detrimental to the preclear and is advised against. Self auditing is not solo auditing since solo auditing is done in session with a meter only after the preclear has reached a high level and has been trained in how to solo audit.

Self-Determinism, 1. self-determinism is that state of being wherein the individual can or cannot be controlled by his environment according to his own choice. In that state the individual has self-confidence in his control of the material universe and the organisms within it along every dynamic. He is confident about any and all abilities or talents he may possess. He is confident in his interpersonal relationships. He reasons but does not need to react. 2. means the ability to direct himself.

Serax® (oxazepam), a drug used for anxiety associated with depression. It is often used in the management of anxiety, tension, agitation and irritability in older patients. It is also used on alcoholics with anxiety associated with alcohol withdrawal and other symptoms in alcoholics.

Service Facsimile, these are called "service facsimiles." "Service" because they serve him. "Facsimiles" because they are in mental image picture form. They explain his disabilities as well. The facsimile part is actually a self-installed disability that "explains" how he is not responsible for not being able to cope. So he is not wrong for not coping. Part of the "package" is to be right by making wrong. The service facsimile is therefore a picture containing an explanation of self condition and also a fixed method of making others wrong.

Session, a period in which an auditor and preclear are in a quiet place where they will not be disturbed. The auditor gives the preclear certain and exact commands which the preclear can follow.

Setups, a series of auditing actions or processes that prepare a person to run a grade or major auditing action.

Sixth Dynamic, see Dynamics.

Social Personality, the social personality naturally operates on the basis of the greatest good. He is not haunted by imagined enemies but he does recognize real enemies when they exist. The social personality wants to survive and wants others to survive. Basically, the social personality wants others to be happy and do well.

Sodium Amytal, see Amytal Sodium.

Solo (Solo auditing), on Grade VI through the OT levels the preclear solo audits. Here the preclear is also the auditor and solo auditing is done in session using an E-Meter only after being trained in the procedure. It is not the same as self auditing.

Somatic(s), this is a general word for uncomfortable physical perceptions coming from the reactive mind. Its genus is early Dianetics and it is a general, common package word used by Scientologists to denote "pain" or "sensation" with no difference made between them. To the Scientologist anything is a somatic if it emanates from the various parts of the reactive mind and produces an awareness of reactivity.

Source, the magazine of the Flag Land Base located in Clearwater, Florida.

Special Drug Rundown, the Special Drug Rundown was issued to handle persons currently on drugs. Such persons have to be weaned off drugs in order to be audited. This is done by having the person do TRs and is further assisted by vitamins.

Spirit, see Thetan.

Stable Datum, any body of knowledge is built from one datum. That is its stable datum. Invalidate it and the entire body of knowledge falls apart. A stable datum does not have to be the correct one. It is simply the one that keeps things from being in a confusion and on which others are aligned.

Staff Status 0-II, three different courses (Staff Status 0, Staff Status I and Staff Status II). They are basic training courses for Scientology staff members which show how a Scientology organization functions and give some basic principles of administration. A person's staff status depends on how many of these courses have been completed.

Standard Tech, a standardization of processes so that they apply to 100 per cent of the cases to which they are addressed.

States of Conditions, see Conditions.

Static, a static is something without mass, without wavelength, without time, and actually without position. That's a static and that is the definition of zero.

Stelazine® (trifluoperazine), a strong tranquilizer (anti-psychotic) used to restore emotional calm, relieve severe anxiety, agitation and psychotic behavior. How this drug works has not been completely established.

Stemetil® (prochlorperazine), a strong tranquilizer used to relieve severe nausea and vomiting, restore emotional calm, relieve severe anxiety, agitation and/or psychotic behavior.

Stimulus-Response, mechanism whereby the individual is restimulated or upset or stimulated by the environment.

Straightwire, any recall in which the preclear stays in present time, and remembers what people have said or done to him throughout his lifetime, is called Straightwire.

Student, a student is one who studies. He is an attentive and systematic observer. A student is one who reads in detail in order to learn and then apply. As a student studies he knows that his purpose is to understand the materials he is studying by reading, observing, and demonstrating so as to apply them to a specific result. He connects what he is studying to what he will be doing.

Study, the absorption of knowledge for the purpose of application.

Success Officer, one of the key public line posts in Division 6. He is the last tech police point in the org. The Success Officer's purpose is: to help Ron get volume high communication success stories into the hands or notice of the org's publics, enhancing and increasing desire for the org's services. His immediate day to day function would be to man the Success Officer desk on the public flow line, and interview each org completion, to get the person to write up his success story in duplicate and to finally read and acknowledge the person for his success and congratulate him/her upon this achievement.

Success Story, means an originated written statement by the pc. The statement of benefit or gains or wins by a student or a preclear or pre-OT to the Success Officer or someone holding that post in an org.

Super-Literate, super-superiority in size, quality, number or degree. Literacy—the ability to read and write. What is really needed is the ability to comfortably and quickly take data from a page and be able at once to apply it. Anyone who could do that would be Super-Literate. Super-Literacy is the end product of a Primary Rundown.

Supervisor, see Case Supervisor; Course Supervisor.

Suppressive Person(s), 1. those who are destructively antisocial. 2. a person with certain behavior characteristics and who suppresses other people in his vicinity and those other people when he suppresses them become PTS or potential trouble sources. 3. is one that actively seeks to suppress or damage Scientology or a Scientologist by suppressive acts.

Technique 8-80, a specialized form of Scientology. It is, specifically the electronics of human thought and beingness. The "8-8" stands for "Infinity-Infinity" upright, the 0 represents the static, theta.

Technology, by tech is meant technology, referring of course to the application of the precise scientific drills and processes of Scientology.

Theta, energy peculiar to life or a thetan which acts upon the material in the physical universe and animates it, mobilizes it and changes it; natural creative energy of a thetan which he has free to direct toward survival goals, especially when it manifests itself as high-tone, constructive communications.

Thetan, 1. (spirit) is described in Scientology as having no mass, no wavelength, no energy and no time or location in space except by consideration or postulate. The spirit is not a thing. It is the creator of things. 2. the personality and beingness which actually is the individual and is aware of being aware and is ordinarily and normally the "person" and who the individual thinks he is. The thetan is immortal and is possessed of capabilities well in excess of those hitherto predicted for Man.

Thinkingness, the potential of considering.

Third Dynamic, see Dynamics.

Third Party, one who by false reports creates trouble between two people, a person and a group or a group and another group.

Third Party Law, the law would seem to be: a third party must be present and unknown in every quarrel for a conflict to exist. Or, for a quarrel to occur, an unknown third party must be active in producing it between two potential opponents. Or, while it is commonly believed to take two to make a fight, a third party must exist and must develop it for actual conflict to occur.

Thorazine® (chlorpromazine), a strong

tranquilizer (anti-psychotic) used to restore emotional calm and for relief of severe anxiety, agitation and psychotic behavior. Also used to prevent and stop nausea and vomiting.

Time Track, the consecutive record of mental image pictures which accumulates through the preclear's life or lives. It is very exactly dated.

Tone, see Tone Level.

Tone 40, giving a command and just knowing that it will be executed despite any contrary appearances.

Tone Level (tone), any one of the various emotional tones on the Tone Scale, such as enthusiasm, boredom or anger.

Tone Scale, the main gradient scale of Scientology. One of the most important observations which led to the formulation of this scale was the change in emotional manifestation exhibited by a person who was being processed. Under affinity we have the various emotional tones ranged from the highest to the lowest and these are, in part, serenity (the highest level), enthusiasm (as we proceeded downward towards the baser affinities), conservatism, boredom, antagonism, anger, covert hostility, fear, grief, apathy. This in Scientology is called the tone scale.

Top Triangle, see KRC Triangle.

Touch Assist(s), an assist which brings the patient's attention to injured or affected body areas.

TR (training regimen or drill), often referred to as a training drill. TRs are a precise training action putting a student through laid out practical steps gradient by gradient, to teach a student to apply with certainty what he has learned. Training drills on Scientology courses which train students to communicate and audit.

Track, see Time Track.

Training, a formal activity imparting the philosophy or technology of Dianetics and Scientology to an individual or group and culminates in the award of a grade or certificate.

Truxal® (chlorprothixene), drug used as a tranquilizer and anti-psychotic agent.

Tryptizol® (amitriptyline hydrochloride), the same drug as Elavil®. An anti-depressive and sedative drug used in depressed patients, in whom anxiety and tension are predominant symptoms, in manic-depressives and anxiety hysteria.

Tuinal® (secobarbital sodium and amobarbital sodium), a drug combining equal parts of Seconal® Sodium and Amytal® Sodium which results in a moderately long-acting, rapidly effective hypnotic. Used whenever prompt and moderately sustained hypnotic effect is required.

Twin, the study partner with whom one is paired. Two students studying the same subject who are paired to check out or help each other are said to be "twinned."

Two-Way Communication, 1. the precise technology of a process used to clarify data with another for the other. It is not chatter. It is governed by the rules of auditing. It is used by supervisors to clear up blocks to a person's progress in study, on post, in life or in auditing. It is governed by the communication cycle as discovered in Scientology. 2. a two-way cycle of communication would work as follows: Joe, having originated a communication, and having completed it, may then wait for Bill to originate a communication to Joe, thus completing the remainder of the two-way cycle of communication. Thus we get the normal cycle of a communication between two terminals.

Upper Indoc TRs (upper indoctrination TRs), the drills that teach the CCHs. The CCHs are then run on pcs.

Valence(s), 1. the combined package of a personality which one assumes as does an actor on a stage except in life one doesn't usually assume them knowingly. 2. a valence is a synthetic beingness, at best, or it is a beingness which the pc is not, but is pretending to be or thinks he is.

Valium® (diazepam), used in the relief of tension and anxiety states re-

sulting from stressful circumstances or whenever somatic complaints accompany emotional factors. Valium is used for relief of anxiety and tension in patients who are to undergo surgical procedures and for the relief of a number of symptoms accompanying alcohol withdrawal.

Verbal Data (verbal tech), about the most ghastly thing to have around is verbal tech which means tech without reference to an HCOB and direct handling out of the actual material.

Viewpoint, a point of awareness from which one can perceive.

Volunteer Minister, a person who helps his fellow man on a volunteer basis by restoring purpose, truth and spiritual values to the lives of others.

Whole Track, see Time Track.

Why, 1. that basic outness found which will lead to a recovery of statistics. 2. the real reason found by the investigation.

Why Finding, the procedure of how to find a Why.

Win(s), if a pc is getting wins then the pc gets more able, earns more or finds more wherewithal, and accomplishes more in a given period of time, leaving more time to use for auditing.

Withhold, a withhold is an unspoken, unannounced transgression against a moral code by which the person was bound.

Word Clearer, one who is qualified in and uses the technology of word clearing.

Word Clearing, a technique for locating and handling (clearing) misunderstood words. There are nine methods of word clearing.

Worldwide (WW), the name given to a division of the Mother Church caring for the correct applications of the religious philosophy and offering administrative advice to Scientology churches.

Wrong Why, the incorrectly identified outness which when applied does not lead to recovery.

Subject Index

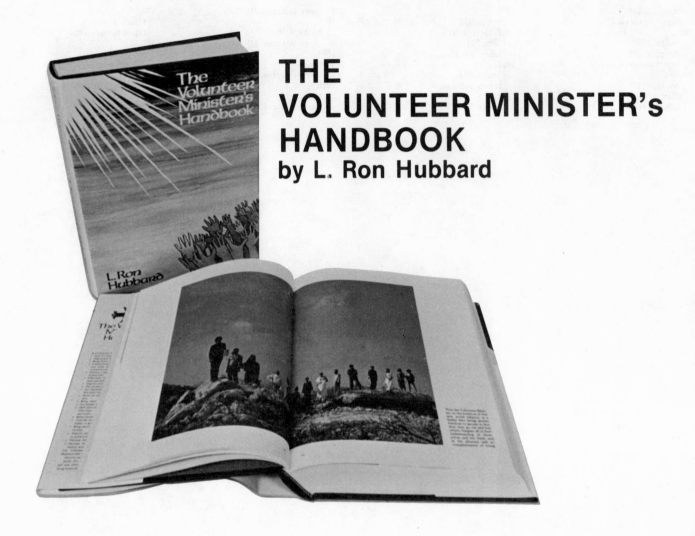

THE VOLUNTEER MINISTER's HANDBOOK
by L. Ron Hubbard

HOME STUDY COURSE

The Volunteer Minister's Handbook is a complete home study course on the improvement of human relationships and conditions.

The handbook is specifically arranged in such a way that each section is a small specialized course, arranged in easy to do steps which, when done in order, bring about a continuously expanding understanding of the materials. There are twenty-one sections covering such things as the Basics of Study Technology (How to Study), Marriage and Children, Communications and Public Relations.

It belongs next to the family cookbook and first aid kit. It is a complete handbook on what to do in a family crisis, what the individual can do to handle drug or alcohol abuse, how to make your family happier and healthier, how to get projects accomplished and much more.

Crime vs. Religion

One of the most important factors in a society is, and has always been, its religion. It is unfortunate that to some the word *religion* has negative connotations. Yet in its purest form, religion simply means: the expression of Man's belief in a power or force which is separate from and above the condition of *human being.* Religion is that which gives direction to Man's ethical behavior, gives him his sense of community, morals and ethics.

L. Ron Hubbard discovered that the occurrence of a rising crime rate was concurrent with a decline in church attendance.

He found that people were not attending their traditional churches. They no longer sought the minister, or priest, or rabbi to give solace and guidance and minister to the solutions of life's problems.

Man's need in this area was obvious enough. Alcoholism, suicide, drug abuse, divorce, crime, were all soaring. But he knew of no sanctuary from it all, nor did he know of a place to go for the answers. He didn't know of anyone with understanding and with a workable means with which to handle these problems.

Hardback, 748 pages, 48 in full color. Big, easy to read type.

To get your copy send $28.00 to your closest Scientology Church or Mission (See the List of Organizations chapter of this book) or order direct from the publisher:

In North and South America:
Publications Organization
4833 Fountain Avenue, East Annex
Los Angeles, California 90029 U.S.A.

What You Can Do

The individual using this volume can successfully help his friends over the rough spots in life. It is not really so difficult. One begins by obtaining a copy of the Volunteer Minister's Handbook. He studies it at his own rate of speed and develops knowledge from the handbook of how to assist himself and his fellow man.

Although the handbook is intended for home study, one is always welcome at a Church of Scientology for assistance with any difficulties, whether in the study of the materials or in the actual application of the principles contained in the book.

In Europe, the Commonwealth
Countries and Asia:
Publications Organization
Jernbanegade 6,
1608 Copenhagen V,
Denmark

**Apply for Your Free Six-Month
Scientology Membership Today!**

As an International Member of Scientology you receive
a 10 per cent discount on all books priced over $1.25, tape
recorded L. Ron Hubbard lectures and other items. You
also receive free magazines with vital data, world Scientology news and modern technical information. New
members are eligible for all International Membership
privileges (including 10 per cent discount) as of date of
application.

Apply to:
Membership Officer, your nearest Church of Scientology.